THE SHORT OXFORD HISTORY
OF THE MODERN WORLD

General Editor: J. M. ROBERTS

THE SHORT OXFORD HISTORY OF THE MODERN WORLD
General Editor: J. M. ROBERTS

Already published in this series

THE CRISIS OF PARLIAMENTS: ENGLISH HISTORY 1509–1660
Conrad Russell

'this is a remarkable, and an extremely accomplished piece of writing. Happy the student – be he sixth-former or undergraduate – whose mentor is Mr. Russell; while *The Crisis of Parliaments* may be strongly recommended as a sustaining *vade mecum* alike to the serious general reader and to the professional teacher of history.' *Times Literary Supplement*

THE OLD EUROPEAN ORDER 1660–1800
William Doyle

'extremely stimulating . . . students for years to come will benefit from the wide-ranging intelligence with which he has attacked his very demanding subject.' *History*

ENDURANCE AND ENDEAVOUR: RUSSIAN HISTORY 1812–1980
Second Edition
J. N. Westwood

'Each volume added to the "Short Oxford History of the Modern World" is a delight. . . . This history of Russia should become the standard work on the period.' *The Assistant Masters Association*

THE LIMITS OF LIBERTY: AMERICAN HISTORY 1607–1980
Maldwyn A. Jones

'Above all, it offers the great virtues of clear, simple, elegant prose. . . . It is beautifully organized, mobilizing a vast amount of information covering all aspects of American development. . . . Its judgments are sound, its facts reliable, and the generalizations illuminated by skilful use of pertinent detail.' *Times Higher Education Supplement*

THE BRITISH EMPIRE 1558–1983
T. O. Lloyd

'it must be said at once, and with considerable respect, that this is by far the best one-volume history of the empire so far written.' *Times Literary Supplement*

MODERN INDIA: THE ORIGINS OF AN ASIAN DEMOCRACY
Judith M. Brown

EMPIRE TO WELFARE STATE

———

ENGLISH HISTORY
1906—1985

———

T. O. LLOYD

Professor of History
University of Toronto

THIRD EDITION

OXFORD UNIVERSITY PRESS
1986

Oxford University Press, Walton Street, Oxford OX2 6DP

Oxford New York Toronto
Delhi Bombay Calcutta Madras Karachi
Petaling Jaya Singapore Hong Kong Tokyo
Nairobi Dar es Salaam Cape Town
Melbourne Auckland
and associated companies in
Beirut Berlin Ibadan Nicosia

Oxford is a trade mark of Oxford University Press

Published in the United States
by Oxford University Press, New York

© Oxford University Press 1970, 1979, 1986
First edition 1970
Second edition 1979
Third edition 1986

ISBN 822135 5 (hb)
ISBN 822134 7 (pb)

Printed in Great Britain
at the University Printing House, Oxford
by David Stanford
Printer to the University

GENERAL EDITOR'S PREFACE

ONE way in which changes in historical taste and outlook are reflected—though sometimes slowly—is in the forbidding demands of examiners and makers of syllabuses. This series is meant to be of practical value to the students and teachers who have to meet them. But such demands themselves are only reflections of deeper and more important changes in historical thinking. And that thinking must be reflected directly, as well as indirectly, in new historical books. *The Short Oxford History of the Modern World* is consciously designed to take account of the most important recent historical work. It seems worth while, therefore, to say what the developments are which have been thought important and how the principles of design of this series are related to them.

One obvious change in recent historical activity has been a geographical widening of the history we study. Parts of the world hitherto neglected, or comparatively neglected, by historians bred in the western tradition of scientific history are now for the first time attracting interest and attention. In part this is a reflection of our humanitarian and political concerns: we are coming to realize that we live in one world, and believe we ought therefore to know more about the parts of it with which we are unfamiliar. In part, too, it reflects changes in what is available as source-material. Whatever the source, the impulse is beginning to make its mark in schools and colleges. They now need books about Latin America, Africa, or Asia on the scale and at the level of those which in the past introduced them to European or English history.

This series will include such books, but also others on more familiar and traditional areas of study. There is, after all, a great need for the achievements of up-to-date scholarship to be given wide currency in English and European history. Consequently, this series is tripartite. It consists of a series of four volumes on modern European history, in which the British Isles are treated as a part of European society as a whole. The second group of four volumes is more specialized, being confined to English history. The third group will be larger and will contain introductory volumes, covering fairly long periods, on those areas and countries which are only now beginning to be studied widely. Some of these are conceived as of continental scope, the projected volume on Latin America, for example. Those on the United States and Russia, on the other hand, limit themselves to a single political entity. In each case, the books in this stream are distinguished by being about a big and important topic for which good introductory manuals are not yet easily available.

The unity which binds these books together, although they will have different levels of detail and scope, is that they all deal with the 'modern world' referred to in the title of the series. This phrase, however, is to be read in a special sense and it is this which makes the series a whole. The subject-matter of *The Short Oxford History of the Modern World* is limited in time, but the chronological limitation is not the same for each book. Conventionally, series of books on the Modern History of different countries line up all their runners at approximately the same starting-gate and get them off together, whether in 1400, 1500, 1600, or any other dramatic, convenient, or merely 'significant' moment. In this series we follow a different scheme. The latest era of world history is here defined thematically, not chronologically. It is the era in which the fundamental institutions of modern European society first take shape and then spread round the world.

Some of these institutions are so widespread that we too readily take them for granted—the national sovereign state, for example. Yet this is even in Europe only a recent innovation and in many parts of the world it did not appear until after 1945. Formally representative political systems (whether real or fictitious) are another of Europe's institutional exports to the world, and there are economic ones, too, such as capitalism, or ideological ones such as Marxist communism or Christianity. In all these instances (and many others could be cited), we have examples of a process by which European gradually became World civilization. Sometimes this has produced new examples of developed 'Western' societies; sometimes it has led to more striking disruptions of tradition and eventually to altogether new institutions and cultural forms. The process, however it ends, defines an era by the break it provides with the past. This era begins at different times in different countries: in roughly 1500 in west European history, in about 1800 in the case of Russia, and at an even later date in the history of China, for example. These are the epochs in the history of different countries and regions in which can be discerned the processes which eventually tie them into the single world in which we live.

Besides moving to different rhythms, it is another consequence of this that not all the books in *The Short Oxford History of the Modern World* will have the same pattern. Differences in presentation are needed to bring out differences of national and regional life. But they will form a coherent series in a methodological sense too. They will have in common a deliberate effort to incorporate recent research and recent thinking which has begun to change the conventional shape of historical writing. This affects both their organization and the proportions of their subject-matter. The core of a good history must be the provision of the essential basic information which is necessary to the exercise of historical imagination and judgement. But lately ideas about what basic information is needed have been changing, for example by a new emphasis on society and its structure at the expense of the traditional political narrative. Historians and their public—which includes even examiners—have begun to think that it may be more revealing to study, say, the growth of cities in nine-teenth-century England and its repercussions, than, say, the party struggle. This is only one example of the recent rapid popularizing of the old idea that history is more than past politics. This series attempts to take account of this. Many of its authors are young scholars who, because of their own research interests, are familiar with what is going on at the frontier of current historical work. They and their colleagues will seek to absorb into their accounts the flood of social, cultural, demographic, and many other sorts of monograph which has poured out since 1945 to confuse and muddle the ordinary historical student and the general reader.

The purpose of general books has, of course, always been to reduce to manageable thinking the detailed scholarship of the specialists. But another recent historical tendency has made it all the more important that this should be done. This is the problem, facing teachers of history at all levels, of the crumbling of boundaries which delimited and land-marks which directed their studies. The conventional separation of English and European history is now often an encumbrance to under-standing the many processes in which this country was as much involved as any continental state: industrialization is an example. Another would be our changing views of the importance of certain dates. 1917, for example, or 1941, can be defended as much more significant breaks in the continuity of European history than 1914 or 1939. In some places, old guidelines seem almost to have disappeared altogether.

In part these changes arise because much new evidence is becoming available; in part it is because research has addressed itself to old evidence in a new way; in part it is a matter of changing perspective. More fundamentally, it reflects a basic truism about history: that it is theoretically boundless, a continuing debate, and that historians in each generation re-map and re-divide its subject-matter in accordance with their interests and the demands of society.

This series tries to provide a new map. It is bound to be provisional; that is of the nature of general history. But general history can be scholarly in its standards and imaginative in its presentation. Only by combining both qualities can it provide the authoritative guidance which each generation of readers needs if it is to pick its way through the flood of specialized studies now pouring from what has become one of our major cultural industries.

J. M. R.

September 1969

AUTHOR'S PREFACE

'The age of chivalry is gone. That of sophists, economists and calculators has succeeded, and the glory of [England] is extinguished forever.' Thus Burke, with only one word changed, might have described the history of England in the twentieth century. In 1900 England stood as the envy of 'less happy breeds', and Englishmen were very conscious of this; history could be told as the history of great men, whether of leading politicians like Gladstone or empire-builders like Cecil Rhodes who, when asked by Queen Victoria what he had been doing since she last saw him, could reply quite truthfully: 'I have added 12,000 miles of territories to your dominions.'

Individual heroes can no longer achieve such feats. In the First World War Lloyd George may have been 'the man who won the war', but in the Second World War Churchill was the man who saved England from losing the war after a crippling defeat—the best that the individual hero can do is to hold back the forces of history and stop their onward march until better times. And those forces more and more take material form: millions of tons of steel, billions of pounds in the balance of payments, hundreds of thousands of soldiers.

But these changes, which rob history of the colour and glamour of kings and queens and heroic charges in battle, are only the reverse of the growth of democracy and of a greater concern for ordinary people—perhaps it should be added that it is the result of a greater capacity to make concern for ordinary people into an effective political force. Building an empire was much easier in the past, when new subjects could be acquired without much resistance. Lord Rosebery once said that if all the Indians in India spat at us, we should drown; and in a way this was what happened. The British Empire was dissolved in a fairly amiable way, without any disastrous wars to try to preserve it, which showed that Englishmen realized that the weight of numbers made it impossible to continue with the old system.

And the same sort of change has taken place inside the country. The dominance of the statesman as an example of Carlyle's hero, which was the way that people saw the late nineteenth-century struggles between

Gladstone and Disraeli, has been replaced by the idea that politicians are the servants of the people, required to give the people what they want. And what do the people want? The simple answer is 'More'. There are signs that this may not be enough, but even in the simple terms of maximizing the gross national product the politicians of today are asked to take on a rather harder job than Gladstone or Disraeli had to face. How can we tell when politicians have done their job? We can try measuring it, and in the age of economists and calculators the evidence is available to do so. Statistics can be misleading and tables of figures (including those at the end of this book) give an appearance of accuracy and certainty that is never completely justified, but they do provide new sources of information.

In fact there are great masses of evidence for almost everything. Perhaps it is a little harder to find out about the people at the very top; in the past they used to negotiate with each other by writing notes to each other, but now that they can talk on the telephone, the historian finds the evidence is gone. Fortunately the intrigues of politicians seem a little less important than in the past—they still matter, and they still deserve attention, if only because the actions of the government have so great an effect on the lives of its subjects. As late as 1900 the voters could treat politics as a form of drama in which the politicians put on a variety of plays which were watched and admired or condemned. By 1906 things were already a little different; politicians were trying to send up the price of food (for good and reasonable purposes). And throughout the century the government has been ready to take on new roles, fighting wars on a larger scale than ever before, providing more education, looking after people's health, trying to disentangle the problems of industry.

All these activities of government are documented. And private activity is documented as well. Newspapers tell more than they used to; television tells things that were never told before. The Inland Revenue and the Companies Act find out more about the rich than in the past; sociologists and market researchers find out more by sample surveys about the poor. The brilliant descriptive phrase or the moment of insight can be as important as ever, but in the past historians had to rely on such evidence because there was nothing else. It is still pleasanter (for the writer and for the reader) if the evidence comes in this attractive form, but if the worst comes to the worst the historian can always sit down with his adding-machine and work out how much the country imported, or how many people vote Conservative because they think the upper class should rule the country.

This does not mean that the historian writing about the twentieth century has a harder job than anyone writing about an earlier period, but it does mean that he has a different job. Historians writing about earlier periods have to search for evidence, and they usually have to work at piecing together an imperfect record to make up a coherent story. The historian of the twentieth century has to make sure that he has found the right materials, but he never finds himself short of things to read; telling a coherent story is just as hard as it is for any other century, because the twentieth-century material comes in large enough quantities to support two or three different and contradictory stories.

The economist and calculators could not flourish in the past; there was no material to support them. And chivalry is an ideal that was always confined to a few people, who could afford to have ideals that were denied to the great mass of the population. It would be silly to pretend that the twentieth century is in every way better than those which have gone before, but anyone who has too many regrets for the world we have lost should remember Tom Paine's comment that Burke had pitied the plumage and forgotten the dying bird. The statesman as hero has less freedom of action, both at home and abroad, than he had at the beginning of the century; ordinary people in Britain have distinctly more freedom, political and economic, than they had eighty years ago.

* * *

I should like to acknowledge the help of the University of Toronto, who gave me a year's leave of absence in which much of the work for this book was completed. I should like to thank Sheila Hill and Nicholas Faith for their help with the first edition, and to thank Nicholas Faith and my brother Ifan for their comments on Chapter 15, and Dr. Hartwell, who kindly allowed me to use in my Tables statistical material he had compiled for another book. I should also like to thank John Roberts, the editor of this series, who read the later drafts and carried out the work of editing with tolerance and imagination.

And lastly I should like to dedicate this book to my parents, from whom I have learnt a good deal of what I know about this century.

CONTENTS

MAPS, CHARTS, AND TABLES

(at end)

1. Time of hope   1906–1911

The Liberals come to power

SIR HENRY CAMPBELL-BANNERMAN, the leader of the Liberal party, sat waiting at home in his long frock coat and black trousers. Unexpectedly a journalist came in, to try and smooth relations between Campbell-Bannerman and Lord Rosebery, the last Liberal leader-but-one. Sir Henry listened with a curious and characteristic twinkle in his eye, and brushed it aside. 'Within two hours from now I expect to have accepted the King's commission to form a government.'[1]

The royal summons of 4 December 1905 was the end of twenty years of frustration for the Liberal party, even though the invitation came only because the government was collapsing from internal disagreements. A twenty-year period in which the country was willing to accept political change had been ended decisively when Gladstone's attempt to pacify Ireland by giving her 'Home Rule'—some control over her own affairs—had been defeated in 1886. Some Liberals had joined the Conservatives and the combined Unionist forces had held a majority in the Commons for seventeen of the next twenty years; in the general election of 1900 they had a majority of about 130 and though they had lost some by-elections they still had about a hundred seats more than the Liberals and their Irish allies in 1905. Campbell-Bannerman's tenure of office might be short-lived, and he would obviously have to hold a general election if he was to win effective power.

He might reasonably have accepted the Premiership in the spirit of Lord Melbourne, who was encouraged to take the post seventy years earlier by a friend who said 'such a position was never held by any Greek or Roman and if it lasts only three months it will be worth while to have been Prime Minister of England'.[2] The Prime Minister had a position

---

[1] J. A. Spender, *Life, Literature and Politics* (1927), i. 127.
[2] Lord David Cecil, *Lord M* (1954), 111.

worthy of an Emperor, for England was the country that other nations wanted to imitate.

They picked out many different aspects for imitation: American plutocrats imitated London Society; American reformers wanted their political systems to move towards the English pattern; autocratic rulers in Russia and Turkey found it impossible to avoid giving their subjects some form of parliamentary institutions; team-games like football were spreading all over the world from England; Anglo-German relations were made more complicated by Kaiser William II's mixed feelings of love and annoyance about England. The diffusion of English influence throughout the world was due partly to the fact that England had been the first country to become industrialized so that she had more experience of modern conditions, partly to her position of economic and political power all through the nineteenth century, and partly to the stability of her society, which had been free from revolutions and invasions for well over a century.

The British government held the gorgeous east in fee; hundreds of millions of people in India were ruled by a handful of British soldiers and civil servants. The far-flung colonies settled by immigrants from England had control over their internal affairs, but were not seriously considered in the formation of the foreign policy of the British Empire. In the last twenty years of the nineteenth century there had been a sudden expansion of British territory in Africa, placing almost another 100,000,000 subjects under British rule. The latest acquisition, the two Afrikaner Republics in South Africa, had been made only after a war which lasted too long and cost too much, but there was no sign that the Boer War (1899–1902) was to be the last time England fought to gain more territory.

England was the world's major financial power; the international short-term money market depended on a steady flow of credit based on the pound sterling, and most long-term loans for development in countries outside Europe and the United States were made in London. But she was not the commanding commercial power that she had been fifty years earlier; the United States was already the world's leading industrial power, and in some respects Germany was ahead of England. The rate of growth of the economy had slackened, and industrialists had not been as ready as the Americans and Germans to take an interest in the new developments in steel, chemicals, and electricity.[1] Early in the nineteenth century

[1]

1900:	U.S.	Britain	Germany
Million tons steel	13·5	6	8
Million tons pig-iron	16	8	6

ed. A. J. P. Taylor and J. M. Roberts, *History of the 20th Century* (1968–), 5, 35.

almost half the world's trade was with England; by 1913 the figure had fallen to one-sixth (by the 1970s it had fallen to about 7 per cent). The Royal Navy dominated the seas, but the German army held an equally commanding position on land. Even in the 1890s some English politicians were worried by the possibility that the country would soon be over-shadowed by Russia and the U.S.A.

At first some of them thought the danger could be met by developing the Empire, though imperial enthusiasm in England was frothy rather than deep-seated—Oscar Wilde could make his joke about the spend-thrift having to choose between this world, the next world, and Australia at a time when imperial sentiment was at its highest pitch.[1] One very attractive feature about Empire-building was that it cost so little; when the Boer War began to cost substantial sums, enthusiasm declined; and the tactics used in the later stages of the war, which led to discomfort and death for many women and children—Campbell-Bannerman called these tactics 'methods of barbarism'—also made imperial expansion less attractive.

Lord Salisbury who had been Prime Minister ever since 1885, with two Liberal interludes, was fading from the scene, and on 11 July 1902 he resigned and was succeeded by his nephew Arthur Balfour. New ideas were bubbling to the surface and endangering the unity of the Conserva-tive party: in three years the new forces destroyed the government and led to Campbell-Bannerman's summons to office. Balfour's own first step was in the field of education. A legal decision had declared that School Boards were not entitled to run the technical and 'advanced' departments which they had opened to give something more than the elementary teaching intended by the 1870 Act; Balfour introduced legislation in 1902 which dissolved the School Boards, handed their powers to the County Councils and gave the Councils the responsibility of organizing a system of secondary schools.

This may not have been the best way to deal with the educational situation: the secondary schools established by the Councils closely resembled the private grammar schools, in particular by charging rela-tively high fees and laying heavy emphasis on Latin and Greek, and rejecting the interest in technical and scientific subjects shown by the 'advanced' departments of the School Boards. The Education Act also dealt with the position of Voluntary Schools, which were run by the Churches. The County Councils were required to levy an education rate, part of which went to Church of England and Roman Catholic Schools.

---

[1] Cecily Cardew in Act II of *The Importance of Being Earnest*, first performed in 1895.

This division of funds enraged the Nonconformists, and some of them refused to pay their rates as a result. This passive resistance, which was particularly strong in Wales, showed that something more than ordinary political feelings had been aroused.

Joseph Chamberlain, a Unitarian who had left the Liberals over Home Rule in 1886, was unhappy about the Education Act. However, as Colonial Secretary he was more concerned about the Empire. The Prime Ministers of the self-governing colonies had insisted at the imperial conferences of 1897 and 1902 that they wanted a system of Imperial Preference; England had got rid of practically all protective tariffs in the 1840s and was devoted to Free Trade, but Chamberlain was not a man to be restrained by established custom. If Imperial Preference would bring the Empire closer together, and perhaps encourage the self-governing colonies to make military contributions to an imperial foreign policy, he would take up Preference.

In September 1903 he resigned from the Cabinet to campaign for 'Tariff Reform', as the Imperial Preference scheme became known. At the same time Balfour squeezed some of the more determined Free Traders out of the Cabinet and committed his party to using tariffs when they would help push foreign countries into giving trading concessions to England. Chamberlain's programme aroused a good deal of enthusiasm among convinced Protectionists and believers in the Empire, but did not win new support; Balfour's programme was not easy to understand, and did not hold the party together. The response to the two schemes reflected the personality of the two leaders. Balfour was an aristocrat of immense charm; it was said that everybody who talked to him came away feeling that on this occasion he had talked with unusual brilliance. And underneath this Balfour was very resolute, and unshakeable once he had decided on his policy. The trouble was that he had no capacity for arousing enthusiasm, so that his well-balanced policies did not attract followers. Chamberlain was equally resolute, but in his other qualities very different. He could awaken great loyalty, but he could not negotiate with people inclined to be hostile to him and win them to his side—he could only lead his own followers out to the fight.

Chamberlain was trying to deal with genuine problems. Unemployment was nothing new, but it was just beginning to be regarded as an important issue, so the campaign stressed that 'Tariff Reform means Work for All'. Industries were not reorganizing to face new developments, apparently as a result of inefficiency and lack of enterprise among the industrialists. The government had very few ways of helping the economy and perhaps a tariff was the best method at its disposal. The

Tariff Reformers said that the country's balance of payments was in a disastrous condition because visible exports amounted to little more than two-thirds the value of visible imports; in 1906, which was a typical year, there was a deficit of £147m. on merchandise. But this gap was more than covered by what were coming to be known as 'invisible' exports: fees and commissions from shipping, banking, and insurance gave a surplus of £130m., and dividends from foreign investments made in the past provided a further £134m. So there was a surplus of £117m. available for business men to lend overseas.[1] Some of them made long-term investments, notably in building railways all over the world; others made short-term loans, which meant that if interest rates went up in London they could bring their money back to help borrowers there. The dependence on 'invisible' exports was an unusual way to run an economy, and might be vulnerable in wartime; the habit of foreign investment might encourage manufacturers to stick to traditional products because they could find export markets; and London bankers tended to assume that there would always be a surplus for foreign investment, even when this was no longer the case.

Tariff Reform was an attempt to deal with problems that troubled England for a long time to come, but it was not immediately attractive. The free flow of invisible exports could run most easily if there were no restrictions on trade. Almost every British industry depended on importing raw materials, working them up, and selling the finished product. Chamberlain said that raw material would come in free of charge under Tariff Reform, but he never managed to define a raw material: sugar was raw material for the jam manufacturer but foreign refined sugar was a dangerous competitor for British refiners, and steel plates from overseas were a threat to the steel masters but a valuable raw material for shipbuilders. There were supporters of Tariff Reform in some sections of these trades; there were practically none in the cotton textile trade. This industry exported more than any other, and it still held the mid-nineteenth-century position of world dominance that other trades were losing. It depended on cheap imports of cotton, and cheap food to make sure that wage rates were not driven up too far. Most of Lancashire depended for its prosperity on the cotton trade and although Lancashire was Conservative from Church of England and anti-Irish feeling, it was most unlikely to support a Protectionist Conservative party.

Another factor, and one that weakened the Tariff Reformers all over the country, was that the self-governing colonies were exporters of food

---

[1] A. H. Imlah, *Economic Elements in the Pax Britannica* (Cambridge, Mass., 1958), 75.

and could be given worthwhile preferences in the English market only if imports of food from other countries were taxed. This aroused memories of the Corn Laws; the Liberals issued posters showing the 'big loaf', or standard loaf of the time, and the 'little loaf' which they claimed would be the result of imposing duties on foreign wheat to help the self-governing colonies. Several Conservatives were disturbed by these arguments; Winston Churchill, a Conservative M.P. since 1900, left his party and joined the Liberals. The less impulsive Conservatives organized for action inside the party.

The Liberals amused themselves by putting down resolutions in favour of Free Trade for debate in the Commons. Balfour avoided the issue with great, almost perverse skill, even leading his entire party out of the House to avoid one vote which would have shown how strong the Unionist Free Traders were. He was determined to hold on to office, partly because he hoped the split might heal, but also because some important issues had to be faced and he did not want to leave them to another government. To reduce the problems of drunkenness he had a Licensing Act passed which gave some compensation to the owners of pubs which were closed down; without compensation, he claimed, no magistrates would be so heartless as to deprive an owner of his livelihood, even if his pub was clearly a centre of disturbance and rowdiness. But the idea of compensation for a licence annoyed the Temperance interest, who thought forfeiture should be imposed as a penalty and did not like the prospect of having to pay compensation for all licences if they were able to establish Prohibition.

The Conservative government brought to an end the twenty years of strained relations with France that began in 1882 when England became the dominant power in Egypt and had almost boiled over into war when the imperial ambitions of the two countries clashed at Fashoda on the Nile in 1898. In the 1890s the British attitude to Europe had been described as 'splendid isolation'; the first signs of emergence came with the Anglo-Japanese agreement of 1902, which was designed to protect British interests in the Far East. As war between Japan and Russia was likely, there was a risk that the new alliance might lead to a war with Russia's ally, France. To avoid this, England and France patched up their relations: France accepted the established position in Egypt, in return for British recognition of special claims in Morocco. Apart from this change of policy, the Conservatives wanted to do something to improve the army which had emerged badly from the Boer War. In this they were not successful, though Balfour did establish the Committee of Imperial Defence to work out the principles of British grand strategy.

A new political force opposed to the government had been growing in strength since 1900. In 1893 a small group of socialists under the leadership of Keir Hardie, a Scottish miner who had been elected in 1892 as an independent labour M.P., set up the Independent Labour Party (I.L.P.). Hardie was a good leader for a small missionary group, energetic, always ready to address meetings and tirelessly devoted to the cause. He was not a good organizer, and fresh talent would be needed for the I.L.P. to grow into a national force. The new party spent much of its energy in trying to persuade the trade union movement to take an interest in its political aspirations. Several union leaders were socialists, but many others were enthusiastic Liberals and a few were Conservatives. The Trades Union Congress would probably not have gone into politics to support a socialist programme, but because the Liberal constituency organization very rarely, except in miners' areas, selected working-class men as candidates, many trade unionists thought they should arrange to get their point of view heard in Parliament rather better. The Labour Representation Committee (L.R.C.) was set up in 1900 with no commitment more ideological than to secure an increased number of Labour representatives, though the composition of the 12-man executive (7 trade unionists, 5 representatives of socialist groups like the I.L.P., the Social Democratic Federation, and the Fabian Society) showed that it would have a strong inclination to the left. The I.L.P. continued to act as a pressure-group, trying to pull the L.R.C. to a more distinctly socialist position.

At first the trade unions took little interest in the body they had helped to launch. But in 1902 the House of Lords gave a legal decision on appeal (the 'Taff Vale' case) which, especially when taken with other recent verdicts, suggested that a trade union could be obliged to pay out of its funds for all the financial loss caused by a strike. Previously it had been fairly generally believed that union funds were not liable in this sort of case. The unions were determined to restore the previously accepted view and as a result a large number of new unions enrolled in the L.R.C.

Herbert Gladstone, the Liberal Chief Whip, was alarmed at the thought of a flood of L.R.C. candidates who might draw off working-class votes which would otherwise go to the Liberals. He discussed the question with Ramsay MacDonald, the secretary of the L.R.C., and they were able to reach agreement; because the Conservatives had done so well in 1900, it was more a matter of sharing out the seats the allies hoped to gain than of giving up Liberal seats to working-class representatives. Only about two-thirds of the adult male population had the vote, so that the manual workers were not a dominant section of the electorate and the L.R.C. could not expect many seats. It did not hope to form a government, and in this way was rather like the Home Rule party, which returned about 80 Members from Ireland to press for greater autonomy.

Taff Vale and the L.R.C. provided a political organization for the working-class, but 'Chinese slavery' was at least as damaging an issue for the government among ordinary workers who were not very interested in politics. Milner, the talented but politically insensitive High Commissioner in South Africa, believed that the quickest way to get the gold mines of the Witwatersrand running again after the Boer War was to bring in Chinese workers on long-term contracts. The contracts were not slavery, but the Chinamen were pitied by benevolent Liberals and were disliked by the working class, who thought the Chinese workers were the early stages of a flood of cheap and non-unionized labour.[1] When Jews fled from pogroms in Eastern Europe to England at the beginning of the century, working-class pressure forced the government to pass an Aliens Act reducing the previous freedom of access to the country. The Tariff Reformers claimed that protecting labour by limiting immigration was just the same as protecting industry with a tariff; on the whole the working class was against immigration and was also against tariffs. Some Liberals entered into the spirit of the working-class objections; Lloyd George, who had gained a reputation by his oratory in opposition to the Boer War, asked if they were to have slavery on the hills of Wales. J. A. Hobson in his wide-ranging and influential book *Imperialism* (1902) suggested that English capitalists would intensify their foreign investments in China in order to obtain more cheap labour, which would weaken the economy and increase the risk of imperialist wars.

None of these developments improved the prospects for the Conservatives, and the quarrels inside the party were getting worse. Balfour thought he saw signs that the Liberals were about to quarrel among themselves over Home Rule, and gave his resignation to the King. And so Sir Henry Campbell-Bannerman found himself awaiting his summons to the Palace. Because an election would have to be held immediately, the Liberals were under heavy pressure to present a united front; Asquith, Grey, and Haldane, three active Liberal imperialists, had intended to refuse to serve under Campbell-Bannerman unless he went to the Lords and made Asquith leader in the Commons, but they could not abandon the cause of Liberalism and Free Trade on the eve of an election.

Campbell-Bannerman's Cabinet has become legendary for its talent. Its social composition was unusual: English cabinets had previously consisted almost entirely of landowners; since 1906 they have normally con-

---

[1] Graham Wallas, *Human Nature in Politics* (1908), has a comment on Chinese Slavery on pp. 107–8.

sisted of men of private means (whether hereditary or acquired in a successful business career), trade unionists, and professional politicians. The 1906 Cabinet contained a large number of professional men, almost all drawn either from the law (Asquith, Haldane, Lloyd George, and later Simon and Isaacs) or the higher journalism (Morley, Birrell, Bryce, and later Churchill and, for a few months, Masterman). It contained Whig aristocrats like Grey and Lord Crewe, and its most striking innovation was that it included a man from the working class, John Burns. The ministers who dominated the government for the next ten years had highly trained intellects; the jobs they held before joining the government had given them relatively little practice in administration, but they showed great administrative capacity in office.

This government carried out great changes, but it owed its initial strength to its willingness to preserve the mid-Victorian settlement of a number of issues. Campbell-Bannerman personified the solid willingness to undertake slow improvement that flourished around the beginning of Gladstone's first ministry in 1868 and provided the basic principles of the government of 1906. The position of the unmoving, unyielding Liberals who had stood by the cause in the defeats of 1895 and 1900 was put by Bernard Shaw in his play *John Bull's Other Island*.

BROADBENT: Of course there are some questions which touch the very foundations of morals; and on these I grant you even the closest relationship cannot excuse any compromise or laxity. For example—

DOYLE: (impatiently) For instance, Home Rule, South Africa, Free Trade and putting the Church schools on the Education Rate.[1]

Campbell-Bannerman was a sound party man on the last three issues; he believed in the Liberal position and was ready to press for it to be applied at once. Home Rule, he made it clear, would come on a step-by-step basis, which meant it would not come in the lifetime of the Parliament about to be elected. This reassured Liberal Unionists that they could vote Liberal against Protection without any immediate fear of Home Rule.

The Liberal majority was overwhelming

	Votes	Seats	% of all votes cast
Conservative	2,451,454	157	43·6
Liberal	2,757,883	400	49
Labour	329,748	30	5·9
Irish nationalist	35,031	83	0·6[2]

[1] Act I of *John Bull's Other Island*, first performed in 1904.

[2] These figures, and the figures for subsequent general elections, are from D. E. Butler and J. Freeman, *British Political Facts 1900–67* (1968), 141–4. Irish nationalists were usually returned unopposed.

The government had to decide what to do with its success. The Liberals in 1906 had not asked for a clear statement of public support for a single proposal like Gladstone's Disestablishment of the Irish Church in 1868.

External problems

In foreign policy the government had begun to take up a position before the election. The German government had been bullying the French over Moroccan issues in the Algeciras conference; the settlement of colonial issues between England and France had developed into a revival of the *entente cordiale* of the 1850s, but if this was to guide policy in future, England would be to some extent committed to France's side against Germany. Grey, who had just been appointed Foreign Secretary, promised support to France and by initiating military talks he brought the two countries closer than before. He told Campbell-Bannerman, Asquith, and Haldane about this, but did not tell the rest of the Cabinet when it reassembled after the election. According to Lloyd George foreign policy was not discussed in the Cabinet and when questions of foreign policy were raised, Grey and Asquith waved them aside as though they were too delicate for so large a body.[1] The picture of Lloyd George, soon joined in the Cabinet by Churchill, being silenced in this way is pleasant, but not convincing. Members of the Cabinet knew about the technical details of war preparation, but may have forgotten them simply because they were technical. A full-dress discussion of the topic might have been uncomfortable, because ministers would be to some extent committed by it; if they left the subject alone, they might never have to face it.

The enemies of secret diplomacy were not entirely justified in saying, after 1918, that Grey had deceived the Cabinet or deliberately left it in ignorance of his intentions. Haldane, the Secretary of State for War, had reorganized the army in a way that showed quite clearly the direction in which British foreign policy was moving. His predecessors had tried to reform the army without knowing what sort of war it would be required to take part in. All that they knew was that Cardwell's army, which had proved satisfactory in small-scale colonial wars, had not met the needs of the Boer War. Haldane was certain that the country needed an army that could cross the Channel and take part in a European war. Granted this assumption, all the rest followed—there were to be six divisions ready to go overseas and a second line of defence, the Territorials, to defend England against any troops that might be put on shore by an enemy that had managed to evade the Navy. Haldane's objective was clear cut:

[1] D. Lloyd George, *War Memoirs* (1938), i. 28.

We should have an expeditionary force sufficient in size and also in rapidity of mobilising power to be able to go to the assistance of the French Army in the event of an attack on the Northern or North-Eastern parts of France,[1]

his army was designed accordingly, and it implied a whole attitude to foreign affairs. It is not clear why the Cabinet never examined his assumptions.

The other serious overseas problem facing the government was South Africa. The Treaty of Vereeniging which brought the Boer War to an end in June 1902 had laid down that the Dutch republics would become self-governing colonies in due course, and that the native population would not be enfranchised before self-government. The British found it hard to defeat the Boers and were in no position to insist on the franchise, and as only 65 per cent of adult males had the vote in England the South African system that enfranchised only 25 per cent did not look so bad; no doubt the British expected that twentieth-century South Africa would see the same gradual extension of the franchise that had taken place in nineteenth-century England. The Conservatives had put forward a constitution which granted representative institutions but left control of the executive in the hands of the Colonial Office—the system that had existed in Canada in 1839 when Lord Durham wrote his Report pointing out its disadvantages; Campbell-Bannerman saw no advantage in delay, because self-government was going to be granted and no great changes would take place before it came. He had probably decided to act before he saw Smuts, the representative of the Transvaal Afrikaners, but in any case it was after their interview that he announced that the ex-Republics would become self-governing as soon as could be arranged. This seems, in terms of the next thirty or forty years, to have been a very wise step: the Afrikaners were a majority of the white, politically effective population of South Africa and they remained a majority despite the efforts of men like Milner to bring out British settlers, but the policy of Kitchener at Vereeniging and Campbell-Bannerman in 1907 attached a section of the Afrikaners, led by Botha and Smuts, to British interests long enough to commit South Africa to Britain's side in the two world wars.[2]

In 1907 the Liberals faced a conference in London of the Prime Ministers of the self-governing colonies—Canada, Australia, New Zealand, Newfoundland and the four provinces that were soon to be

[1] R. B. Haldane, *An Autobiography* (1929), 187.

[2] Left-wing Liberals and members of the Labour party protested at the flimsy guarantees for African rights contained in the South African Act of Union of 1910 but, unless it was willing to fight another war in which British and Afrikaner settlers would have fought together against British intervention, there was nothing the government could have done.

united in the Union of South Africa. In his enthusiasm for imperial union Chamberlain had wanted to find out what sort of connection would be acceptable to everybody; when he advocated Imperial Preference he was accepting the colonies' idea of the way the Empire should be linked together. The English voters had shown in 1906 what they thought of the idea, but the Liberals still had to explain their attitude to the colonial Premiers, who were unanimous for Imperial Preference. The self-governing colonies were in future to be called Dominions, but no steps were taken along the lines suggested by Deakin of Australia to set up institutions that might lead in the direction of a federation.

British interest in imperial expansion had been replaced by a feeling of uneasiness about German policy. In 1898 the German government had begun to build a navy which, while not as large as the British, nevertheless looked like being big enough to be embarrassing. The essential diplomatic point was put, in an undiplomatic way, by Churchill some years later: a fleet was for Germany something of a luxury and for England was a necessity.[1] Germany would suffer no immediate harm without a powerful navy, but England depended on imports so much that her whole international position would change if she ceased to be dominant at sea. German shipbuilding made England build as well, and made Englishmen worry about Germany. Haldane's estimate that it might be just as well to prepare the army for a German invasion of France was no more than an unemotional calculation, but the civil servants at the Admiralty under Fisher and at the Foreign Office, such as Eyre Crowe, came much closer to emotional anti-Germanism. The sentiment was quite understandable, and it did not show itself in so obvious and vulgar a form as German anti-English feeling, but in the years before 1914 Englishmen did come to feel, not that war was inevitable, but that if war came it would be a war against Germany.

Liberal legislation and the people's budget

Many of the newly elected Liberal Members were less interested in the naval race than in poverty and unemployment. The reports on the conditions of the poor drawn up by Booth and Rowntree had awakened interest, and in books like *The Heart of the Empire*[2] young Liberals had argued that people should worry about social conditions in England as well as the problems of Empire. There was no social legislation ready for discussion, but the Labour party (as the L.R.C. chose to be called after

---

[1] The word 'luxury' (translated *luxus*, which has a pejorative meaning) was taken as an insult in Germany. W. S. Churchill, *The World Crisis* (1923), i. 101.

[2] G. P. Gooch, G. M. Trevelyan, and others, *The Heart of the Empire* (1901).

the election) had its proposals for reversing the Taff Vale decision by freeing trade unions from practically all risk of legal prosecution. The Liberals wanted to reverse the Taff Vale decision by making some complicated changes in the law of agency which would protect trade unions less completely but Campbell-Bannerman decided to accept the more sweeping Labour proposals in order to keep the Labour party closely linked to the Liberal party. Balfour thought it unwise to oppose the Trade Disputes Bill, and the House of Lords was much more concerned with questions about land and the Church than industrial matters, so it passed easily.

If Labour deserved its reward, so did the Nonconformists. The 1906 Education Bill was exclusively concerned with the religious organization of schools: all schools that received any help from the rates were put under the County Councils, who were to provide facilities for religious education and, in order to make sure that teachers were appointed on the basis of their teaching ability rather than their religious affiliations, no full-time teachers were to give religious education. In the Lords the Bill was amended out of recognition, and was then laid aside, so Balfour could claim some success for his assertion that 'the great Unionist party should still control, whether in power or opposition, the destinies of this great Empire'.[1] The Liberals seemed to have no idea what to do next; in 1907 no substantial legislation was put forward and, for the last time but one, there was no autumn session of the Commons. The great Liberal majority had been elected for better things than this, and Campbell-Bannerman spoke of coming to a conflict with the Lords. Before this could happen he retired, on 5 April 1908, and died a fortnight later. He had held his party together at a very difficult time during the Boer War; his two immediate successors in the Liberal leadership, Asquith and Lloyd George, were abler and certainly more brilliant men, but after a quarter-century of their leadership the party was shattered beyond repair.

Asquith's emergence as Prime Minister in 1908 was inevitable. He was a fine if rather formal speaker, and while he was a quick-witted debater he also had the ability to sort out the long-term implications of a policy. He was not perhaps very original in his thinking, and in fact he seems not to have enjoyed thinking about politics any more than was strictly necessary, but this was no problem as long as he could find ministers with original minds for his Cabinet. And in this he was well provided for; to prevent the ministry leaning towards the Liberal imperialist side he brought forward two radical Little Englanders, making Lloyd George Chancellor of the Exchequer and putting Churchill in the Cabinet as

[1] Randolph Churchill, *Winston S. Churchill* (1967), ii. 316.

President of the Board of Trade. Both of them were young and active, and were looking for ways to distinguish themselves; the government soon began to find in social reform the positive reason for existence which had almost been lacking. The Liberals still had to pay off their obligations to their Nonconformist supporters and an Education Bill and a Bill revising Balfour's 1904 Licensing Act were brought forward in 1908. Both Bills were killed in the Lords.

Clearly these defeats were serious. The by-election losses suffered by the government in 1908 were attributed to a defeatist mood among Liberals who saw themselves helpless before the Lords. The voters were probably affected by the depression of trade and a recovery of trade might have restored the government's position, but at the time the morale of its supporters was low. There had, however, been some hints of the social legislation which was to establish the fame of the government, even before the period of intense activity that began with the budget of 1909.

In 1907 Asquith had begun to use the budget as an instrument of social change. At that time income-tax, levied on incomes above £160 a year, was paid by the most prosperous 10 per cent of the population. The budget made a distinction for the first time between earned and un-earned incomes, and reduced the level of tax from 5p to 3·75p on earned incomes below £2,000 a year. The vast majority of income-taxpayers would benefit from the remission; and probably the very rich and the receivers of unearned income were Conservatives while relatively prosperous people working for a living were Liberals.

Although he had just become Prime Minister, Asquith introduced the 1908 budget himself, as it contained the proposals for Old Age Pensions that he had been working out. Pensions of 25p a week, starting at 70, were given as a right to old people, who were freed by this from the fear of having to go into the workhouse.[1] Lloyd George took charge of the budget, after it had been introduced, and administered the pension scheme. It was popular, and some of its popularity rubbed off on him. '"God bless that Lord George (for [the pensioners] could not believe that one so powerful and munificent could be a plain 'Mr.') and God bless *you*, miss!" and there were flowers from their gardens and apples from their trees for the girl who merely handed them the money.'[2]

Another, smaller but still significant piece of legislation in 1908 estab-lished an 8-hour working-day for miners. This was the first time Parlia-

---

[1] The 1834 Poor Law required all people who needed government assistance to go into a workhouse to receive it, and required workhouse conditions to be 'less eligible' (i.e. more unpleasant) than an unskilled labourer's standard of living.

[2] Flora Thompson, *Lark Rise* (1939), 100, quoted in E. H. Phelps Brown, *The Growth of British Industrial Relations* (1959), 305.

ment had taken upon itself the specific task of limiting the working-hours of adult males. In theory the nineteenth-century factory Acts had been passed to limit the working-day for women and children, on the grounds that they were weak and needed more protection than men, though of course in practice the Acts limited men's working-hours as well. Because the 1842 Act had kept women and children out of the mines, working-hours had been unregulated. If the government entered the field of legislation for adult men, where would it stop? When Churchill was asked why the government had confined itself to legislating for the mines, he said he saw no reason for not going further. The tide of social reform was beginning to flow.

The rising interest in social reform had been encouraged by the Boer War, which had convinced people that an unhealthy and poverty-afflicted nation was a weak nation. In the slowing-down of trade that helped launch the Tariff Reform movement there was more concern about the unemployed than in previous recessions: the Protectionist slogan 'Tariff Reform means Work for All' showed that some politicians had gone beyond the idea of the classical economists that the unemployed were idle fellows who could find a job if they set their minds to it, and had realized that men out of work were suffering from the effects of the 'free play of the market'.

On his last day of office Balfour set up a Royal Commission on the Poor Law, under the chairmanship of Lord George Hamilton, with Beatrice Webb as one of the members. The Poor Law was in theory still the legislation of 1834, designed to be unpleasant enough to stop anybody asking for help who was not on the verge of starvation, and the privately run Charity Organization Society—which appears to have taken 'cold as charity' as its motto—was still run on 1834 principles. The Local Government Board, the government department which tried to co-ordinate the policy of the municipal authorities, was more merciful; for instance, in 1900 it issued instructions that people who wanted help simply because they were too old to work should not be forced to come into workhouses and should be given grants on which they could live at home. The more humane municipalities already took this approach, and the Board was only extending the practice to the whole country.

The Old Age Pensions of 1908 were a great change even from this; because they granted as a right, rather than as something for which the elderly poor had to make a special request, many more people applied for them than had asked for poor relief previously. The reputation of the Poor Law had kept people away and stopped them asking for help. John Burns, the President of the Local Government Board from 1906 to 1914, is often said to have missed a great chance to take the lead in social reform. Undoubtedly his attitude was surprisingly conservative for a man who had been a radical trade union leader in the nineties, and the officials of his department did nothing to make him more active, but the Local Government Board was not a good place from which to launch great changes in the twentieth century. From the first very rudimentary social legislation of the sixteenth century onwards, responsibility had always lain with local authorities: parishes, Poor Law Unions, municipalities. However, changes had always been in the direction of great centralization, and almost all the twentieth-century social legislation has involved transferring services to the central government.

The establishment in 1908 of labour exchanges, where men out of work and employers looking for men could register their requirements and hope to get in touch with each other, was almost inevitably a matter for the central government. This step towards a better-informed labour force could not have upset the most *laissez-faire* of Liberals; in fact the leading negotiator in labour disputes of the day, G. R. Askwith, later complained that the exchanges made it too easy for employers to return to the nineteenth-century notion of a reserve army of unemployed. At the time, however, they were accepted as a useful innovation. Trade Boards, set up the next year as official bodies to investigate the 'sweated industries' and lay down minimum wages, were more of a departure from *laissez-faire*; apart from the simple humanitarian arguments, it was pointed out that in these industries the workers were so downtrodden that they could not form trade unions to defend themselves, and employers who wanted to pay a decent wage needed the Boards to make sure that they were not undercut.

The Commission on the Poor Law presented a Majority and a Minority Report in 1909. Both Reports said that the system of Boards of Guardians to run the Poor Law should end; the majority wanted the duties of the Guardians handed to the municipal and county councils but the minority wanted 'the break-up of the Poor Law' by which they meant that the different categories of people asking for help—old, ill, unemployed, widowed, orphaned—would be assisted by separate and specialized agencies. Over the next fifty years authority was transferred by stages to municipal and county councils on what turned out to be a temporary basis: the central government took over one section of the welfare services after another, usually in schemes financed to some extent by insurance payments, and in this way enacted bit by bit the programme suggested by the Minority Report. By the time of her death in 1944 Beatrice Webb, who had done a great deal of the work on the Minority

Report, had triumphed over the principles of 1834 and of the Majority Report.

Asquith's budgets had depended to some extent on economies at the War Office and the Admiralty. By 1908 the period of easy budgeting was coming to an end. The trade depression reduced revenue, and early in 1909 the Admiralty claimed that it needed another six battleships to be sure of retaining command of the sea. The Lloyd George-Churchill wing of the Cabinet said the Exchequer could only provide four, and eventually the Cabinet reached an apparently acceptable compromise, by agreeing to build four at once, with a commitment to build another four in the immediate future. However, the Admiralty was equal to the situation; Fisher, the First Sea Lord, provided the Conservative journalist Garvin with all the information needed to launch a strong campaign in favour of eight ships at once—hence the slogan 'We want eight and we won't wait'. Garvin's success was fatal to his party; he had pressed for higher naval expenditure in the belief that it could not be paid for except by tariffs, and he gained such prestige in the naval agitation that he was allowed to lead the party into extreme courses that did it no good. His success on the naval issue pushed the Liberals into producing a bold budget in 1909 that revived the fortunes of the government; the Conservative reaction to this budget was so ill judged that it forfeited the powers of the House of Lords in 1911, and in their attempt to save the House of Lords the Opposition announced that they would not introduce tariffs until they had been approved by a referendum, which was a polite way of saying 'Never'.

Lloyd George's budget was intended to increase the government's revenue by about 8 per cent—from £148m. to £160m.—and to provide the basis for future increases. The income-tax, which had previously been graduated only by remissions for incomes between £160 and £700, was now graduated at the top by means of a super-tax, so that incomes above £2,000 paid more. The tobacco duties were increased. So were the alcohol duties, which gratified the temperance Liberals who had been frustrated by the Lords' rejection of the Licensing Bill, but annoyed the Irish who voted against the budget as a result. Motor vehicles were taxed, and the receipts were reserved for a Road Fund. In addition there were taxes on landlords, and this had the tactical advantage that an attack on land-lords was the best way to hold together an alliance of employers and employees, as Joseph Chamberlain had shown in 1885. The main tax on land was a form of capital gains tax, levied on resale at 20 per cent and on new leases at 10 per cent. Like any other capital gains tax it was expected to take some years to become fully productive. There was also a tax on land that was lying idle and not being used for farming or building or mining. The form-filling caused by this tax was an extra irritant to landlords.

The budget itself was sweeping and even provocative, though there is no evidence that it was intended to sting the Lords into rejection. Lloyd George's budget speech was long and uncharacteristically dull, and in the months of parliamentary debate that followed, running from the end of April until early November with only a week or two of recess, he was polite and business-like. In the Commons his job was to get the budget through; in public speeches he had to rouse the Liberals by showing that their cause was righteous and would prevail. He did both jobs well, and if his speeches annoyed the House of Lords, that was an additional tactical advantage. His speech at Limehouse on 30 July was regarded as very fierce, though in fact it was all in the normal language of party speeches from the platform. Most of it was concerned with the sharp increases in land prices; the section that was considered most inflammatory dealt with the terms on which the Duke of Westminster renewed the lease granted to Gorringe's Stores, which was built on his land. Lloyd George said of the terms, which included a £50,000 fine on renewal and gave the Duke a veto on any building put up on the land leased, 'it is not business, it is blackmail'. This was not polite, and Lloyd George did not really understand the leasehold system, but the Lords responded far too violently for their own good. If they were going to attack the budget they were committed to public activity and would have been prudent to keep cool. But they were not accustomed to being attacked, much less to be laughed at. So the Duke of Beaufort said he wanted to see Lloyd George and Churchill in the middle of twenty couple of foxhounds and the Duke of Buccleuch announced he was going to save a guinea by giving up his subscription to the local football club. The Dukes seemed eager to prove Lloyd George was right in calling them 'a class that declined to do the duty that it was called on to perform'.

The budget passed the Commons at the beginning of November. The Lords could not amend the budget but in theory they could reject it. Experts of the constitution could not agree whether theory could legitimately be translated into practice,[1] but the Lords had tasted blood; ignoring the fact that rejections of previous legislation had been successful only because they had picked out unpopular Bills, or perhaps assuming —entirely incorrectly—that the budget was unpopular, they prepared to reject it. Lord Milner told them to reject the budget and damn the consequences; they followed him all too enthusiastically. Lloyd George,

---

[1] Erskine May (cont. F. Holland), *Constitutional History of England* (1912), iii. 358 on the constitutional experts.

Churchill, and their closest allies hoped for rejection, but did not do anything to provoke rejection by teasing Balfour or taunting the Lords with
their helplessness, perhaps because they knew how little their Cabinet
colleagues would like such a step.

By November the official Conservative leaders, Balfour and Lord
Lansdown, would have had great difficulty restraining their followers
even if they had tried. The budget was thrown out in the Lords. Lloyd
George, as if aware that the time had come for a more solemn approach,
withdrew to devise new measures of social welfare and left the work of
constitutional rebuke to Asquith. On 2 December the Prime Minister
moved a resolution which declared that the Lords had no right to touch
a Bill concerned with taxation and announced that there would be a
general election.

The two elections of 1910 and the House of Lords

The resolution had of course no legal effect. It was part of the Liberal
election programme, along with the controversial budget itself. The
Lords had forced the government to dissolve Parliament, if only because
no taxes had been voted, and if the government simply won a majority
for the budget it would be conceding the Lords' claim to force an election
any time they chose. By the time of the first election Asquith knew he
would have to have a second general election before he could expect the
royal support, in the form of a promise to create peers, that might be
necessary to make the Lords accept his solution. Asquith was a very
far-sighted political tactician, and acted very skilfully between late 1909
and the summer of 1911; he had probably seen just how far he would
have to go, and could devote himself to keeping the game to the lines he
had chosen.

He had first to win his election in January 1910.

	Votes	Seats	% of all votes cast
Conservative	3,127,887	273	46·9
Liberal	2,880,581	275	43·2
Labour	511,392	40	7·7
Irish nationalist	124,586	82	1·9

The Conservatives said the result simply meant that the budget had been
approved. The Liberal and Labour parties said it also meant that the
Lords should lose their power to reject legislation. The Irish said it meant
the Lords should lose their powers and a Home Rule Bill should be
passed. Asquith knew his Labour allies would stand by him, though the

decision in the Osborne case, in December 1909, that trade unions were not entitled to spend their funds on political activity, made it necessary to amend trade union law again.

The Irish had voted against the budget, because they disliked the taxes on spirits. They could not vote against it in the new Parliament, though they could abstain. Their hope of Parliamentary success depended on finding an occasion when the two large parties were equally balanced; it was partly because they had not been equally balanced since 1895, that Home Rule had dropped almost out of sight. Now it revived, and its prospects seemed better than before because the Liberals were about to destroy the Lords' power to reject a Home Rule Bill.

Redmond, the Irish leader, was so eager to break the Lords' veto that he wanted Asquith to amend their powers before reintroducing and passing the 1909 budget; Asquith was determined to pass the budget first, and was afraid he would have to resign if Redmond insisted on the point. Further inquiry showed that Redmond would be satisfied if he felt sure that Asquith was in earnest about attacking the Lords. Asquith had no doubts on the issue; some people played about with schemes to change the membership of the Upper House but he defined his position sharply in his three Resolutions of 21 March:

The Lords were not allowed to touch a Bill if the Speaker said it was a Money Bill.

A Bill passed by the Commons in three successive Sessions would pass into law whether the Lords consented or not.

The length of a Parliament should be shortened from seven years to five.

During the course of debates on these Resolutions the Irish became convinced that Asquith was in earnest, and after this the Liberal majority was safe. The 1909 budget was then put quickly through the Commons, and was accepted by the Lords. It remained to be seen whether the Parliament Bill, enacting the three Resolutions, would go through with anything like the same ease.

The Lords, who had been sure they could judge which legislation should be returned to the electorate, showed signs of self-doubt and debated possible reforms of their membership. The party leaders began to be afraid that things were slipping out of control and when Edward VII died unexpectedly on 6 May 1910 they decided to try to reach a peaceful compromise. For six months the whole issue was taken out of sight and discussed by a committee of four Liberal and four Conservative leaders. Home Rule was the real point of division; the Liberals seem to have conceded that the first time the Lords rejected it there should be a general election, but they wanted the Commons to be able to pass it eventually.

The Conservatives wanted the Lords to have the power to force legisla- tion concerning the Constitution, which would include Home Rule, to be submitted to a referendum. It was also suggested that a joint sitting of the Commons and a section of a modified House of Lords should decide on disputed legislation, which probably meant that a Liberal government would not be able to pass its Bills if its majority in the Commons was under fifty.

Lloyd George, who was always happiest when he could make agree- ments and get something done, suggested a coalition government that could reach a compromise on Ireland and on other issues as well. On Ireland the compromise was bound to move towards the Liberal policy, but on issues like tariffs or compulsory military training any compromise involved a change in the direction favoured by the Conservatives. Several of the party leaders in the committee and outside were interested in the proposals, but when Conservative back-bench opinion was consulted it was distinctly hostile. The parties returned to the open battlefield.

When the Constitutional Conference broke down, Asquith asked the King to promise that if the government gained an adequate majority in the election that was clearly imminent, peers would be created. The King understandably disliked being asked to commit himself in advance and, less reasonably, thought it unfair that this pledge was to be kept secret. He gave his word, though it seems he might have been rash enough to refuse if he had known that Balfour, contemplating just such a situation, had said he would form a government to save the King from having to give an assurance in advance. By this time the Conservatives' attitude to the constitution was becoming a little cavalier. Balfour's apparent willing- ness to replace Asquith suggests either that he thought the King had the right to dismiss a Prime Minister who held a majority in the Commons or that he believed the King's natural personal reluctance to create peers had some constitutional validity.[1] When the Parliament Bill reached the Lords the Conservatives advocated great constitutional changes: they again asked for legislation of fundamental importance to be subject to a referendum.

The Conservative view that each individual item of legislation should be acceptable to the public meant that a government elected to carry out a popular programme which depended on some unpopular measures might find the whole programme destroyed. In the circumstances of 1910 it meant that the government might be re-elected with every intention of

---

[1] F. W. Maitland, *Constitutional History of England* (Cambridge, 1908), 397: 'The king is bound to act on the advice of his ministers; he must choose his ministers, or rather his first minister, in accordance with the will of the House of Commons.'

carrying Home Rule for Ireland and then find that it could not pass the measure in a referendum.

When the second 1910 election was held, in December, the Conservatives pressed for the referendum and warned the voters that if the Liberals won they would bring in Home Rule as well as passing the Parliament Bill. Balfour was generally considered to have scored a great point for his party when he said that Tariff Reform would also be submitted to a referendum, which was expected to bring the Unionist Free Traders back to the party. If it did, it left very little trace on the results; the number of contests dropped, the number of votes cast dropped even further, a fairly large number of seats changed hands, but at the end of it all the parties were exactly where they had been at the beginning of the campaign, with the one difference that nobody could contemplate a third general election and so the issue had to be settled in a way that would satisfy Asquith and his parliamentary majority.

	Votes	Seats	% of all votes cast
Conservative	2,424,566	272	46·3
Liberal	2,293,868	272	43·8
Labour	376,581	42	7·2
Irish nationalist	131,721	84	2·5

The Conservatives did not admit defeat. As the Parliament Bill passed through the Commons the Lords prepared schemes for altering the composition of their House. Asquith made it clear that the limitations on the Lords' right of rejection would apply to any Upper House, no matter what its membership. Despite this sign of firmness, a strange idea spread among the Conservative peers that the government was only bluffing. The more unrealistic of them decided to throw out the Parliament Bill and see if Asquith would then dare to create peers to override their decision. As it became clearer and clearer that he would, the resistance grew increasingly frantic. When he announced at the end of July that he had in November obtained the King's promise to create peers, he was shouted down in the Commons by the Conservatives. This did nothing to take the knife from the Lords' throat; the Liberal ministers were not men to be hurried into a false step. On 9 and 10 August the Lords debated the Bill. The Ditchers (i.e. the peers who were ready to die in the last ditch by rejecting the Bill and bringing about an immense creation of new peers) outnumbered the tiny Liberal group in the Lords; by this time the only way to avoid a creation of peers was to find enough Conservatives to vote for the Bill, and against their own inclinations. The reality of the choice was made clear; Lord Morley read a message that the King would assent 'to a creation of peers sufficient in number to guard against any possible combination of the different Parties in Opposition by which the Parliament Bill might again be exposed a second time to defeat',[1] or, in numerical terms, 500 Liberal peers would be created to pass the Bill, a Home Rule Bill, and any other proposals that the government might put forward. Enough Conservative moderates were found for the Parliament Bill to pass, 131 to 114.

Social and class structure

The list of proposed peers found among Asquith's papers, containing names like Bertrand Russell, Thomas Hardy, and Ian Hamilton, suggests that a large addition would have added to the personal distinction of the House of Lords.[2] But it would not have altered the fact that a heavy blow was dealt to the old British upper class. The struggle over the Lords, and perhaps the death of Edward VII the previous year, mark a distinct step in the crumbling of its position. The First World War did not change the way things were moving, though it may have accelerated the process.

Lansdowne picked out the central feature of the upper class when he said that he hoped the members of a revised House selected from among the existing peers would be 'familiar with country life, familiar with landed property'.[3] The upper class consisted of men whose ownership of land and influence over their tenants gave them some political power, if only at the local level. The ownership of land was ceasing to give this sort of power, and it was becoming impossible for people to reach positions of political importance without earning them by a record of achievement.

Lloyd George said in 1911 that paying income-tax was the dividing-line between gentility and subsistence; 1,150,000 paid income-tax, and most of them belonged to the middle class. Above them was the richest 1 per cent of the population, which owned about 66 per cent of all property. When Marx studied the English social structure in the 1860s the country could be divided into property-owners, who had land or business interests, and the rest. The professional class was small and the salaried professional class almost non-existent. By 1910 the salaried professional class had become an important part of the middle class, and because it managed a good deal of industrial and financial property the ownership

[1] R. Jenkins, *Mr. Balfour's Poodle* (1954), 179.
[2] J. A. Spender and C. Asquith, *Life of Asquith* (1932), 329–31, give a list of 249 potential peers Asquith had picked out.
[3] R. Jenkins, op. cit. 126.

of property did not have the same decisive effect as it had fifty years earlier.

Most of the middle class was dominated by the desire for respectability, and the ideal of a sober, thrifty, church-going family life was accepted by a large part of the population. It was of the essence of respectability that everybody had someone a very little below him, on whom he could look down, and so respectable society was intersected by twenty or thirty million graduations which between them contrived that a member of respectable society (like God) never saw his equal. Though the ideal first took root in the middle class, it spread upwards and downwards. Members of the upper class who wanted effective political power had to behave, at least in public, in a middle-class way.

Naturally there were members of the upper class who behaved in a more traditional manner; as Edward VII was one of them, the jolly and slightly vulgar way of life of the members of the upper class who did not think it was their business to go round setting a good example became known as Edwardian. Upper-class life, strict or relaxed, of the Edwardian period has since then become the subject of laments for the splendour that has been lost. The general level of prosperity increased greatly in the next sixty years, but the richest salaried people and professional men in the 1970s are less well off than people in equivalent positions before 1914. It is not clear whether property-owners have lost ground to the same extent, because the desire to reduce their tax burdens has led rich men to hold their property in increasingly complicated ways during the century.[1] Rich men clearly continue to exist, but they are less noticeable than at the beginning of the century, partly because they no longer feel confident that their wealth commands respect, and partly because it is harder to spend money in a way that produces so much outward show. The number of servants has conspicuously declined in the last fifty years and, less conspicuously, the increase in real wages has led to a sharp increase in the price of things made by individual labour unassisted by machinery.

The shooting-parties of Edwardian days, in which enormous flights of carefully reared birds were driven by armies of beaters over a line of men armed with splendidly designed hand-made guns, were practicable only when servants and craftsmen got low wages; as wages went up, strictly

[1] Guy Routh, *Occupation and Pay in Great Britain 1906–60* (1965), 55, shows that the real post-tax income of employees rose on the average by 80 per cent between 1906 and 1960, but the income of the top millile fell by 22 per cent. Pp. 62–5 show that the highest paid professional people lost even more ground. R. M. Titmuss, *Income Distribution and Social Change* (1962) shows how hard it is to draw firm conclusions from statistics on the ownership of property.

upper-class entertainment became harder and harder to afford. About 800,000 families, which would include almost all of the middle and upper classes, employed servants in 1911; 60 per cent of them had only one, 20 per cent had two, and the remaining 20 per cent had more than two.[1] The style of life based on battalions of servants has disappeared, perhaps mainly because of the increase in wages, but also partly because a good deal of the work they used to do, such as carrying hot water to bedrooms and lighting fires, is now performed more efficiently and for a much larger proportion of the population by hot water systems and central heating.

The middle-class ideal of respectability spread downwards into the working class. The dividing-lines of occupation and of income did not correspond precisely; people who worked with their hands were probably considered members of the working class and people below the income-tax line were probably not well enough off to be established members of the middle class, but there were undoubtedly exceptions to be found on both sides of any line chosen. Just as the dividing-line between the middle class and the working class was real but hard to draw, there was a dividing-line within the working class, between the poor and the relatively comfortable, that was equally real but hard to draw. The relatively comfortable would in most cases have a vote (if male), would often be union members or skilled craftsmen working on their own account, and could aspire to some aspects of respectability if they chose to. About 30 per cent of the population were poor; they were below the poverty line indicated in Charles Booth's survey of London and Seebohm Rowntree's survey of York; they rarely had the vote, they had difficulty becoming unionized, and only with a great effort could they live respectably. The municipal and central governments were just beginning to consider doing something about the housing conditions of the poor, though the problem turned out to be very intractable. One reason was that wages made up a large part of the total cost of housing and so, unlike almost everything else except upper-class luxury goods, the cost of housing went up about as fast as real wages for most of the century.

The ideas of the Edwardians

This emphasis on the gradations of society and on respectability may seem peculiarly Victorian. Perhaps it was more marked during the Queen's reign than in the dozen years before 1914, and certainly the literary climate of the years before the war was more relaxed than in the nineteenth century. This relaxation must not be overstated, even

[1] D. Lloyd George, 16 Nov. 1911, *Commons Debates*, xxxi. 541.

though the pattern of life indicated by writers in the 1900s spread and became accepted as the normal way of life for the middle class: the Lord Chamberlain intervened to forbid performance of plays such as Bernard Shaw's *Mrs. Warren's Profession*. The social material of novels remained unchanged; authors wrote about tension between society and the individual, with problems of love and sex taken as the issues that most often brought them into conflict. To a considerable extent readers were shocked by bold new literary departures, whether novels or plays or poetry, simply because they were concerned about the solidarity of society; in the course of the century readers grew less worried about the possibility that society might collapse as the result of some novel or play.

The writers and thinkers who dominated intellectual circles in the 1900s wanted to be reasonable, wanted to be modern, and felt a fairly strong tendency to puritanism, which expressed itself in disapproval of the upper classes. Bernard Shaw illustrated this very well. A good deal of his best work had been done before 1906, and even in the years before 1914 there was a slight falling-off in the flow of his writing. In the 1890s and the early years of the new century he wrote about a play a year, including some of his best work, such as *Candida*, *The Doctor's Dilemma*, and *Man and Superman*. By 1912 he had written another half-dozen substantial plays and had progressed from being a playwright of considerable prestige to being a commercial success. Years previously he had said that managers who cared about being up to date made a point of putting on plays by newcomers who became fashionable fifteen years later; Shaw's allotted fifteen years had elapsed and he had arrived. There were still a few important plays, such as *Heartbreak House* and *St. Joan*, to come but the bulk of his work was done by the time Edward VII died. Shaw and the other writers of the pre-First War years shaped an audience for themselves, and in some ways they came into their own after the war. Of course, they could not change society by themselves; they flourished at a time when the old dominance of the upper class was crumbling under blows like the Parliament Act and the much heavier impact of the First World War. The post-war world was not completely satisfactory to pre-war writers like Wells and Shaw and Forster but it was a world that had moved in the direction that they had pointed in the years before the war.

The literary climate of the Edwardian years did not have much in common with the Modern movement. Sometime around 1908, when Ezra Pound arrived in England, or 1911, when the Diaghilev Ballet first came to London, a new spirit appeared that was quite different from the measured rational approach of the liberal reforming writers. When Roger

Fry organized an exhibition of Post-Impressionist painting in 1910, it was very clear that there was an even wider gulf in popular understanding: people who had learned to accept the liberal reformist writers rushed forward in denunciation, like Sargent the fashionable portrait painter, who said: 'I am absolutely sceptical as to their having any claim whatsoever to being works of art.'[1] Painting in England tended to follow the style fashionable in Paris, but at an interval of several years. English painting was digesting impressionism, but it was still assumed that the subject in the picture should be recognizable without much effort to accept the particular point of view of the artist and, as acceptance of the point of view of the artist became increasingly important for comprehension, the opportunities for misunderstanding and incomprehension grew larger and larger. The success of the Diaghilev Ballet at first owed something to the support of aristocratic society, which felt that it was an upper-class form of entertainment. This opened the gates a little to the modern artists who designed the stage settings, and to modern composers like Stravinsky. English music of the period was by general European standards not very distinguished and Elgar, the leading composer, was at least on the surface rather too inclined to accept some of the complacencies of Edwardianism.

The writers of the 1900s had a good deal in common with the philosophers of the time. English philosophy had become an amalgam of Hegel and nineteenth-century Liberal thought, in which Hegel's admiration for the state and for the gradual combination of disparate parts into a whole was found in surprising but apparently harmonious combination with the Utilitarian concern for the maximization of the happiness of the free individual. Karl Marx represented one version of this combination, but much the most fashionable version was that of T. H. Green who, as a tutor at Balliol and a writer on political philosophy, had been a strong influence on several members of the Cabinet. Bosanquet and F. H. Bradley continued the tradition of Hegelian thought at the universities; in the Cabinet, Haldane was something of a Hegelian scholar.

Two distinct but related lines of attack on modified Hegelianism were appearing at Cambridge in the last years of the nineteenth century. The mathematical philosophers Russell and Whitehead set out to show that a basis for mathematics could be found in logical propositions. Their *Principia Mathematica* (1910) reduced and harmonized the assumptions to be made; its approach was so elegant and attractive that the same principles were applied, by them and by later writers, to philosophy in

[1] *The Annual Register of World Events for 1910*, pt. 2, p. 100. He made a partial exception for Gauguin.

general, with results that were disastrous to Hegelianism, at least in England. Their mathematical work had cut the ground from under the feet of philosophers who had tried to show, by devising paradoxes, that mathematics was not logical and that therefore the visible world was illogical and not real. Whitehead later tried to reintroduce quasi-Platonic Ideals into the world that he and Russell had been stripping of such things, but the main stream of English philosophy followed the line of Russell's axiom that all meaningful statements are either assertions about sense-data, which could in some circumstances be tested, or else are tautologies that extract logical conclusions from assumptions, in the same way as mathematical equations. Most of the successors of Russell and Whitehead lacked the mathematical technique of their leaders, and in any case the logical problems concerned with mathematics seemed to have been finally resolved. English philosophers turned their attention to problems of language and tried to resolve its problems in the same way. This line of approach, expressed most briskly in Ayer's *Language, Truth and Logic* (1937), had a considerable impact in the English-speaking world, and very little outside it; although one of the most respected of the linguistic philosophers was the Austrian Wittgenstein, who settled at Cambridge, the interest in European philosophy which had been noticeable in the nineteenth century diminished. In a way the withdrawal from ambitious problems about the nature of things to smaller—though equally intractable—problems about the nature of statements about things was a return to the relatively unambitious approach of the English empirical philosophers, with a strong addition of the scepticism of David Hume thrown in. Reasoning of this sort was not likely to produce a philosophy of the old sort which gave people advice on how they ought to act and could be adopted as a 'philosophy of life'.

A philosophy of life could be found in the work of G. E. Moore, a Cambridge philosopher who wrote a few years earlier than Russell and Whitehead. His ethical system began from fairly austere foundations about men's duty to do what was good but it developed into an assertion that the really important things in life are personal relationships and artistic experiences, and that other things are valuable only as means to these ends.[1] Moore enjoyed a great reputation for the rigour of his logic, and his friends remembered long afterwards the incisiveness with which he asked 'Now exactly what do you mean by that?', a question that was later a great favourite among the linguistic philosophers. It may not be wholly

---

[1] G. E. Moore, *Principia Ethica* (Cambridge, 1903), 25. His statement on p. 188 about 'the most valuable things which we know or can imagine' puts his view concisely though in language that is now out of date.

unjust to the admirers of Moore to suggest that part of the reason for the popularity of his philosophy of life was that it provided a blend of puritanism and hedonism which was what they were looking for, and was what suited a larger and larger number of people in the new century.

One of the most important ways in which Moore's philosophy found its way to a wider audience was through the attitudes of the people who came to be known as 'Bloomsbury'; they were not professional philosophers, but they were strongly affected by Moore's teaching. Bloomsbury, as a gathering of writers, artists, and art critics, was less concerned with the rights and wrongs of society than were Galsworthy or Arnold Bennett, or D. H. Lawrence; people like Fry and Duncan Grant and Clive Bell were not particularly worried about the general state of the world, and the novelist Virginia Woolf was clearly not very interested in the problems of society. Lytton Strachey was concerned with these problems in the rather special sense that he devoted a fair amount of his writing, and owed a great deal of his reputation, to his attack on the constrictions of Victorian respectability: his *Eminent Victorians* (1918) and even his *Queen Victoria* (1921), though not intended as an unqualified attack on the dead Queen, were among the weapons with which people of the 1920s developed their attack on the conventions of society. But two other distinguished members of Bloomsbury, Leonard Woolf and Maynard Keynes, deeply influenced by the hedonistic aspects of Moore, also reflected the other side of his principles and were ready to take part in politics to help other people. Woolf in the Labour party and Keynes in the Liberal party were close enough together to show why, even after 1918, some people could think of the Labour party and the Liberal party as two parties of the Left, with much more in common with each other than either had with the Conservative party. E. M. Forster at moments seemed almost ready to say in books like *A Passage to India* (1924) that all political problems are a matter of proper personal relationships, but he could not quite bring himself to say that this approach would solve the problems of economics or of war.

In *Howard's End* (1911) Forster looked at the question

Does [England] belong to those who have moulded her and made her feared by other lands, or to those who have added nothing to her power, but have somehow seen her, seen the whole island at once, lying as a jewel in a silver sea, sailing as a ship of souls, with all the brave world's fleet accompanying her towards eternity?[1]

The book, as might be expected from this passage, comes down on the side of the seers.

[1] E. M. Forster, *Howard's End* (1911), 172.

In his attractive account of the beginnings of Bloomsbury, Leonard Woolf explained how he came back in 1911 from seven years in Ceylon and found that in the circle of his friends, who were advanced and liberal in thought, some of the stiffness and formality of life had eased while he was overseas. He also wrote that anyone who doubted his account of the stiffness of life had no idea what Victorianism was all about.

Clearly that revolt which Shaw and his generation began and my generation helped to extend was so effective that our successors are not even aware how and why, while we were born in chains, they are comparatively free.[1]

Some of these chains were undoubtedly the special manacles of the middle class, forged by a concern about respectability. In what sounds like an autobiographical passage of *Eyeless in Gaza* Aldous Huxley records the thoughts of a young intellectual at Oxford in 1912 watching the freedom from inhibition of the upper-class undergraduates.

By the mere force of social and economic circumstances these ignorant barbarians found themselves quite naturally behaving as he did not dare to behave even after reading all Nietzsche had said about the Superman, or Casanova about women.[2]

Oxford and Bloomsbury had little immediate impact on ordinary members of the middle class. One great liberating influence for many of them was H. G. Wells. In the first few years of the century he was turning from the science-fiction in which he had first earned his reputation and was becoming a novelist of the conventional type. At this time science was entering a period of development which made it harder for the amateur to understand it; Lord Salisbury could take an active amateur interest in science when he first became Prime Minister in 1885 but this would have been much harder by the end of his tenure of office. The Michelson–Morley experiments on the speed of light had shown that the universe was not built in quite the way common sense had suggested and had led (just before Campbell-Bannerman became Prime Minister) to Einstein's Special Theory of Relativity. Radioactive elements had been purified and Rutherford was beginning his study of the particles they threw off and the possible disintegration of matter. Two other Cambridge scientists, Soddy and J. J. Thomson, were demonstrating that while all the atoms in an element were chemically identical they might have different atomic weights and different radioactive properties. Developments like this were making physics into the dominant science of the new century, but they were also making it much less intelligible to anyone with

[1] L. Woolf, *Beginning Again* (1964), 34.
[2] A. Huxley, *Eyeless in Gaza* (Paris, 1938), 91.

no specialist training in the subject. Wells had received a scientific education and had a good journalistic understanding of what was going on—he
referred to an 'atomic bomb' in 1913—and might have become a very
good guide to these developments if he had not turned to writing novels
of the traditional type.

In the years before 1914 it was probably on the subject of women and
women's rights that he wrote most and had most influence. One of his
first non-science-fiction novels, *The Wheels of Chance* (1896), was based
on the enthusiasm for bicycling in the last years of the nineteenth century
and the emancipating effect it had on young men and women. *The New
Machiavelli* (1911), if it is mentioned at all today, is remembered because
it satirizes the work-habits, the meagre hospitality, and the relentless
string-pulling of those determined social reformers Sidney and Beatrice
Webb. But when it was written Wells was disagreeing with the Webbs on
a serious issue of social policy: they thought the next step in social reform
should be to destroy the old Poor Law of 1834, as they had indicated in
the Minority Report on the Poor Law, and he thought the next step
should be to pay all mothers a living wage to enable them to bring up
their children in decent conditions. Wells's proposal would have struck a
blow at all the many aspects of poverty related to large families and it
would also have meant that, as a mother could bring up her family without being financially dependent on the father, the institution of marriage
would be considerably altered. *Ann Veronica* (1909) was more 'daring',
(and somewhat autobiographical) because the heroine went to live with a
married man but, like *The New Machiavelli*, argued that women were
unable to make free choices in work or marriage and need to be liberated
from the forces of convention which restrict them. The social planners
took note of this as one of the factors to be considered when extending
welfare services; the women themselves responded by going into revolt.

Wells was not as good a writer as Shaw; he lacked the clarity of
argument which, while not essential for writing novels, is a great help for
writing novels with a social purpose, and he had none of Shaw's wit or
readiness to explore the impossible side of a paradox. But he was always
up to date with the problems that everybody was interested in, and he had
a considerable stock of material to work on: his own early life in the
lower middle class, working behind a shop-counter, was useful, in *Kipps*
(1907), when shopworkers' hours were being discussed in Parliament. He
took it for granted that his readers did not have religious beliefs and had
problems as a result. He did not offer solutions to the problem of loss of
belief; he simply accepted that the difficulty did exist, which showed that
he understood his audience better than either the writers who thought the

problem of belief could be solved by a determined effort to believe or the writers who took loss of faith for granted.

Loss of religious faith was not the dominant intellectual problem that it had been a little earlier. On the whole the philosophies of Mill or of Moore, sometimes diluted with an attitude of respect to the Deity, satisfied the highly educated, and during the course of the twentieth century a blend of puritanism and hedonism spread more and more widely, sometimes in a theistical form but more usually in an unaggressively non-theistic form. In the middle of the nineteenth century it had been estimated that half the adult population went to church. By the end of the century the figure was probably rather lower. One reason for the change was that the Protestant churches were never successful at getting in touch with the urban poor; the Roman Catholic church did hold its own among the poor, helped by the fact that almost all Catholics were Irish immigrants who were subject to the pressures of anti-Irish feeling. But once poor people from elsewhere in the United Kingdom had reached a big city, they were very likely to lose touch with any Christian church. The Salvation Army had been started in the 1880s to deal with just this problem, and it had had some success. The attitude of derision, and sometimes of active hostility, that other Christian organizations took to its efforts shows the way that church-going and respectability were linked, and suggests that the unrespectable were not welcome inside the church.

Respectable people went to church about as regularly under Edward as in the later years of Victoria; some people thought there was a slight falling-off, but everybody agrees that it was nothing to the drop in church attendance of the two decades after the First World War. But enthusiasm about religion was distinctly less in the years before the war than it had been a decade or two earlier; Anglo-Catholicism provided opportunities for a few would-be martyrs and a few would-be heresy-hunters, and some clergymen took part in the growing concentration of attention on social reform, but religion was no longer a central issue. From the 1840s to the 1880s the conflict between the assertions of religion and the theories of science had occupied the attention of many of the cleverest men in the country—Gladstone took this to an extreme when he published an article on the theological problems of the Gadarene swine just before forming his Home Rule government in 1886, but there were many other laymen who felt deeply concerned about these religious arguments. In the next great struggle in the church, over Modernism and the extent to which the church ought to adapt to a changing world, laymen showed much less interest. The churches were to follow the view of the majority during the First World War with a lack of restraint or reservation that probably did them no good in the long run, but the slight decline in their position meant that following the majority became more attractive; the English churches had not stood up against men in authority for many years and 1914 did not seem to be the time to begin. And it was among men of authority that the churches were losing ground; apart from the drift among the highly educated, there was a shift of opinion among politicians, even though their followers had not yet noticed the change. The Nonconformists followed Lloyd George in the years before the war, just as they had followed Gladstone a generation earlier; but Lloyd George's attitude to life and to politics was not permeated by religious feeling in the way that Gladstone's had been. Victorianism appeared to stand relatively unshaken; in fact its foundations were crumbling.

2. *Heedless of their fate* 1911–1914

WHEN Lloyd George emerged from the inconspicuous position he had adopted during the struggle over the Parliament Bill, it was to present his National Insurance Bill in which he offered, as he put it, ninepence for fourpence (i.e. 3·75p of weekly benefits for 1·66p of insurance payments). Part I of the Bill, the section which caused all the fuss, covered most people who worked for a living against ill health: people whose earnings fell below the income-tax limit paid 1·66p a week, their employers paid 1·25p, and the State 0·83p, which made up the 3·75p; people earning less than 12½p a day were excused from payment. An insured worker received 50p a week in sick pay (falling to 25p in cases of prolonged sickness) and was entitled to call on the services of the doctors who had enrolled on the insurance panels. Arguments went on for some months over the question of the 'approved societies' and for even longer on the claims of the doctors. Any organization, trade union, insurance company, or Friendly Society which had been insuring people previously could be an 'approved society' and continue to act as an insuring agent. This increased the number of trade unionists, increased the profits of the insurance companies, and saved a number of Friendly Societies, which had been too optimistic in their rates of benefit, from bankruptcy.

The doctors were less easy to conciliate. Some of their claims were simple requests for more money: Lloyd George, always ready to oblige, increased the capitation fee paid to a doctor for each patient on his list. Other claims, such as the demand that coverage should be given only to people with under £2 a week, thus excluding the more prosperous members of the working class, came closer to destroying the principle of the Act. The British Medical Association, an organization that has always been bellicose in defending the interests of its members, threatened not to take part in the scheme, but found by 1912 that too few of its members would support it for resistance to be practicable. The scheme was never-theless not immediately popular; employers and employees disliked the cost of the insurance stamps, which was the only direct tax paid by the employees, and probably a lot of contributors felt that the whole thing was a nuisance. The opponents of the scheme made themselves a little ridiculous by holding a mass-meeting of servants and their mistresses who all said that they would never lick the stamps needed for insurance, but the Liberals' losses in a number of by-elections about this time were attributed to the unpopularity of the Insurance Act. On the other hand, when Law, the new Conservative leader, suggested that he would repeal the Insurance Act, this was taken to be a blunder. Not many people were very enthusiastic for the Act, and a number of people were determinedly opposed to it, but a solid majority accepted the Act and wanted to keep it.

Part II of the Act, which aroused much less controversy, provided insurance against unemployment for workmen in the building and engineering trades, in which the demand for labour fluctuated particu-larly sharply. Part II, enlarged in 1920, became grimly relevant in the inter-war years, but until then attracted little attention. It had been pushed forward by Churchill as a natural part of the labour exchange scheme; a man went to the exchange seeking work, but if he could not obtain it he had proved his good intentions and should receive benefit.

The entire Act was a considerable departure in British social legisla-tion, though so much of Part I was borrowed from German experience that it had no great claims to originality. Lloyd George showed his gift for getting things done in the establishment of the scheme. Most Chan-cellors of the Exchequer found their time absorbed by departmental routine, including the struggle to keep down the defence estimates; Lloyd George did not neglect this traditional duty of his office, and at the same time was able to set up an administrative system that might have been a full-time job for a normal departmental minister.

About the only thing that united the two parts of the Act, which were going to be run by two different ministries, was the principle of insurance, based on a flat-rate *per capita* charge and yielding a flat rate of benefit. The more consciously socialist members of the parliamentary Labour party objected to the flat-rate charge and said the whole cost should be paid from general taxation, as in the case of Old Age Pensions. Labour party members who were more conscious of being trade unionists were ready to accept the charges, on the grounds that they strengthened work-men's claims to receive benefit as a matter of right.

Lloyd George's 1911 budget gave M.P.s a salary of £400 a year. This led to complaints that it opened the doors to professional politicians and adventurers, which was a way of saying that poor men might go into politics for the sake of the salary. A member of the working classes, who would probably have been making at best £150 a year, could go into the Commons and, despite increased living expenses, would emerge no worse off. A salaried member of the middle class, on the other hand, suffered a considerable drop in his standard of living, and in any case would probably find that he had to pay a great deal to keep up his constituency organization. The result of the change was that unionized members of the working class could join the landowners, large-scale industrialists, rentiers, lawyers, and financiers who made up almost the whole of the Commons; and dominance of the middle and lower-middle class in the electorate was not reflected in the House.

Payment of Members was almost the last Liberal measure of any importance that actually passed into law, but as will be seen there was no slacking of legislative enthusiasm; the difficulty was that the Lords were determined to exercise the power of delay allowed by the Parliament Act at the expense of the three large-scale pieces of legislation which the government brought forward in the hope of eventual success. The Home Rule Bill was the most important but the Lords also rejected the Welsh Disestablishment Bill and the Plural Voters Bill. The Bills were put forward again in 1913 and 1914; but none of them had passed into law under the Parliament Act when war broke out.

Conservative opposition to the Liberal programme became more dogged and tenacious, though perhaps less skilful, after Balfour retired on grounds of ill health in November 1911. It was obvious that Balfour's ill health had been aggravated, or possibly caused, by his followers' annoyance that they had done so badly during the eight years of his leadership. Two men had obvious claims to lead the Conservatives in the Commons: Austen Chamberlain, who had the support of the Liberal Unionists, most of the Tariff Reformers, and most of the urban Conservatives including the growing business interest; and Walter Long, who was supported by the landed interest and the people who wanted a Conservative of the traditional sort. Their forces were evenly balanced and in a curious mood of self-denial both of them withdrew in favour of Bonar Law, a Glasgow business man who originally came from Canada. Law's initial support came from a small section of the more extreme Tariff Reformers, but he represented the mood of the whole party very well; he was a bitter and determined debater who believed, correctly, that he was not Asquith's equal in parliamentary warfare. Ulster and Tariff

Reform were the two political issues that interested him, though the latter broke in his hand. He argued that the offer to submit Tariff Reform to a referendum no longer applied, apparently without realizing that the offer of a referendum was what held the party together in Scotland and the North of England. Under pressure from the north Law was forced to say that a Conservative government would not impose taxes on imports of food until after a general election on the issue. Foodstuffs made up so large a part of the exports of the Dominions that this pledge destroyed most of the proposals for Imperial Preference. For the next ten years the Conservatives' policy on tariffs could never really be pinned down, though they continued to recommend Protection as a solution to problems.

The Opposition tried to reunite itself by opposing every measure put forward. For thirty years Wales had been as strongly committed to the Liberal party as Ireland was to the Home Rule party. The great symbolic issue for Welsh Liberals was Disestablishment of the Church of England in Wales: while they could accept the Church of England as one Pro-testant church among many, they disliked its privileged position, and its connection with the English landowning class. The government proposed that, as had happened when the Church of England in Ireland was dis-established, part of the Anglican endowment would be taken over for education and other national purposes in Wales, and understandably there was heated argument about the scale of disendowment. The Con-servatives took an unconciliatory attitude to the Welsh, as can be seen from Law's statement in one debate

If it be true that [the Church of England] can make no appeal to the Welsh temperament, I think that it is a condemnation not of the Church but of the Welsh temperament.[1]

The Plural Voting Bill was resisted in much the same spirit. The Bill was designed to establish 'one elector, one vote' which would undoubtedly have helped the Liberals because men with several votes from widely distributed property, sometimes reinforced with an extra vote for a university seat, were usually Conservative. The Opposition claimed that this should be accompanied by a redistribution of constituencies, but redistribution would have been hard to carry out at the point the Irish question had then reached. Ireland was conspicuously over-represented because the number of seats had been fixed by the Act of Union before the population was reduced by the Famine and subsequent emigration of the 1840s. Irish representation would be reduced by the Home Rule Bill

[1] 21 Apr. 1914, *Commons Debates*, lxi. 868.

that was about to be introduced, and until the fate of the Bill was known it was hard to work out redistribution for the United Kingdom.

Historians have argued about the condition of the country in the two or three years before the outbreak of war in 1914. Some people see the years just before the war as a period of golden tranquillity. Other writers dismiss this picture as the fantasy of classes whose financial and social position suffered during the war. The sober and responsible Halévy speaks of boredom and anarchy; the less scrupulous Dangerfield foresees revolution in every direction. The decade before 1914 was certainly not as calm and peaceful as reminiscences about the Oxford of Raymond Asquith and the Cambridge of Rupert Brooke suggest. The established upper-middle class led a very pleasant and untroubled existence in these years, and it was untypical of what was going on in the country at large. Apart from the large problem of Ireland, people were worried by the activities of the trade unions and by the agitation carried on by women who wanted to vote. Trade unions were undoubtedly more active just before the war than they had been for at least two decades, but this militancy had mainly economic causes, and was not a sign that anarchy and revolution were at hand.

Threats to stability: unions and suffragettes

From the early 1870s to the middle of the 1890s, trade in England had been dull: interest rates were falling but this did not attract much new investment, unemployment rates were higher than had been normal in the nineteenth century, prices fell, and so did money wages, but because they fell more slowly the level of real wages rose. It may be misleading to call this a period of depression, but it was not a period in which great fortunes were made or in which people were conscious of new opportunities opening up. New development was hindered by the way that English industrialists turned their backs on the new areas of enterprise and stuck to well-tried old favourites, such as railways and textiles, at a time when Germans and Americans were taking more interest in steel, chemicals, and the uses of electricity.[1]

The twenty years before 1914 present rather a different picture. The level of foreign investment, which had in fact been dropping for some years before Hobson published his denunciation of it in *Imperialism* in 1902, rose steadily for the next twelve years; from 1906 to 1913 it was always higher than investment in England and by 1913 it had reached 9 per cent of the national income. Most of this foreign investment involved a certain amount of export credit and so helped British trade. There was a smaller, but perceptible, increase in government spending on armaments,

[1] See note on statistical evidence at the end of this chapter.

which helped the coal and steel trades and, in particular, shipbuilding. Trade was also stimulated by the increase in the world gold supply as more and more was discovered in South Africa. The economy became more active, unemployment diminished and prices went up. Wages went up more slowly; real wages did not rise above the 1900 level and sometimes dropped below it.[1] It used to be thought that the share of national income going to profits was increasing quite sharply during this period, but apparently *per capita* income for the whole country was stationary. The population was increasing, and infant mortality was declining, so that the national income was larger, but individuals were not in general better off. This is not what the people of the years before the war imagined was happening, and they would have found it hard to reconcile with all the visible signs of expansion. Even the writers who argue that economic growth in these years was small do add that there was a high level of conspicuous consumption. In these circumstances disturbed labour relations were only to be expected. The slight recessions of 1904, which helped the Tariff Reform movement win its initial successes, and of 1908, which temporarily weakened the position of the Liberal government, were only minor incidents in a period of steady full employment.

With their position strengthened by the ready availability of jobs, the unions set out to restore real wages to at least the 1900 level. Dangerfield's *Strange Death of Liberal England*, one of the most excitingly written of the books arguing that England stood on the verge of social catastrophe in 1914, relies (to an even greater extent than is apparent from the footnotes) upon G. R. Askwith's memoirs of the period, and it is particularly relevant to look at Askwith's own approach. He performed prodigies in bringing together employers and employees in the negotiations of the period, and saw more disputes from closer quarters than anyone else at the time. He wrote (in a passage not quoted by Dangerfield): 'What is to be said about these disputes? My own strong opinion is that they were economic. . . . Prices had been rising, but no sufficient increase of wages, and certainly no general increase, had followed the rise.' Later he added that a desire for recognition of the union, a claim whose value he thought employees overestimated, caused some strikes and, very much in third place, he mentioned the existence of what he called 'irritation' strikes.[2] This account seems to explain most of what happened in disputes between 1910 and 1914; a lot of working days were lost in strikes but this did not mean that the fabric of society was crumbling or even that English industrial relations were collapsing.

[1] A. L. Bowley, *Wages and Income in the United Kingdom since 1880* (1937), 94.
[2] G. R. Askwith, *Industrial Problems and Disputes* (1920), 175, 350, and 353.

One slightly unsettling influence was that ministers liked being seen dealing with strikes. They had done so at times in the past twenty years, and a Liberal government was especially likely to intervene because its own electoral position depended on an alliance of employers and employees. At first it seemed that the alliance could stand a considerable amount of strain and that the government worried too much about the effect of strikes on it. The great nine-month strike in the South Wales coalfields (October 1910 to June 1911) was well under way by the time of the second 1910 election but did not affect the position of the Liberals. In the summer of 1911 there was a wave of strikes, of which the one that affected people most immediately was a dockers' strike first at Hull and Manchester and then at London. Part of the obstinacy of the two sides was attributed to the great heat of the summer, which also weakened the bargaining position of the employers by making perishable goods rot faster. Within a week the economy was affected by an even more disruptive strike by the railway workers; Lloyd George did a lot to end this by appealing to the two sides to remember that the international situation was uneasy and that the government needed industrial peace for the sake of its diplomacy. During these strikes there was some fear of danger to law and order, and the Home Secretary had to see that there were enough police to keep the peace and to provide troops in support of the police if necessary. Troops were provided in the South Wales coal strike, and during the railway strike preparations were made to run the railway lines on a military basis if the European situation deteriorated. Soldiers were also used to protect trains running the limited service that the companies provided; near Llanelly soldiers opened fire and killed two men. The working-class memory of the story was that Churchill, as Home Secretary, was the minister responsible for two miners being killed at Tonypandy. The confusion with the miners' strike of the previous winter was inaccurate, but the general impression was not unjust: introducing soldiers with loaded rifles into an industrial dispute was asking for trouble. It must be remembered that the Cabinet, except for John Burns, had no idea what a strike was like, and they were at once too easily frightened and too ready to assume that things could be controlled by a display of force.

The situation seemed all the more alarming because some strikers adopted syndicalist slogans. As a political theory syndicalism, in the English version, meant that workers should take over and run the industries in which they worked. This gave workers a principle with which to oppose their leaders' insistence that trade unions should stick to negotiating about wages and conditions and should strike only when the leaders thought it appropriate; the leaders had learnt their business in the difficult days of dull trade in the eighties and nineties, and may easily have been too cautious for the times. Syndicalism also provided a basis for opposition to the Labour alliance with the Liberal government, and if hostility to the government rested more on dislike for the Insurance Act than on admiration for the theories of G. D. H. Cole and of Orage, the editor of the *New Age* magazine, its effects were still serious. In its strictly theoretical form syndicalism was one of the few attempts to apply an anarchist version of socialism in England, though even when it seemed most successful the fruits of its success came in the more conventional form of extending the activity of the government.

This became apparent in the coal strike of 1912. The government did its best to bring together coalminers and coalowners, and found it had chosen a remarkably difficult problem. In most strikes both sides and the people outside the dispute expected a fairly quick decision; the effect of a rail strike or a dock strike was felt too quickly to be allowed to last long. In the coal strikes from the 1870s to 1926 a struggle of months was regarded as nothing abnormal. When the government intervened in 1912, it did not understand how slowly things would move, and once it had become involved it felt it had to settle the dispute quickly. The government introduced a Minimum Wage Act, which set up Boards to grant minimum wages, on a district basis, to miners who were handicapped by the difficulty of the seam in which they were working. The miners would have liked daily rates set by law, 25p for a man and 10p for a boy, and they would have preferred national rates to district rates, but although they did not get their own way on these details they had induced the government to take a long step away from *laissez-faire*: workers in the 'sweated industries' might need state help because they could not set up unions of their own, but the miners had a very effective union and they used it to obtain more state intervention.

Membership of the T.U.C. increased fairly sharply during the years before 1914, rising from 1,648,000 in 1910 to 2,232,000 by 1913. The increase may be attributed partly to successful strikes, because a strike was often itself an occasion for recruiting new members in a partially unionized labour force. The Insurance Act of 1911 also helped increase membership; trade unions were among the 'approved societies' with which people could insure, and Charles Masterman, the Financial Secretary to the Treasury, said in 1913 that this was the real reason for the increase in membership.[1] He did not refer to the industrial disputes of these years, so his explanation was incomplete, but the Insurance Act had certainly

[1] Lucy Masterman, *Charles Masterman* (1939), appendix 3, especially p. 387.

done a great deal for union membership. Probably he ignored the disputes because he regarded them as a normal part of negotiation at a time of full employment; the decade from 1910 to 1920 was the only long period of full employment in the British economy between 1874 and 1939, and nobody had acquired much practice in dealing with this unusual phenomenon. In Dublin James Larkin, a union leader more skilled in oratory than in negotiation, did say alarming things, but Ireland was not urbanized enough for industrial workers to become a dominant factor in the economy. In England the foundations were being laid for the Triple Alliance of mineworkers, railway workers, and transport workers.

Trade union activity shows little sign of an imminent breakdown of law and order, but the conduct of the women's agitation for the vote does suggest that the more militant defenders of the Union with Ireland were not isolated in their disregard for the law. The number of women in jobs had increased sharply between 1891 and 1911, and many of the new working women were in responsible jobs, teaching, nursing, or office-work. The House of Commons in two Parliaments before 1906 had voted for the principle of women's suffrage, but there had been no time for further discussion. The first signs that women intended to attract attention to their cause by demonstrations came just before the 1906 election; Ann Kenney and Christabel Pankhurst were fined (and went to prison rather than pay) for disorderly conduct at a meeting at which Churchill and Sir Edward Grey were speaking. It was a curious foretaste of future suffragette tactics that they chose to interrupt two supporters of women's suffrage.

The 1906 House of Commons contained a large majority in favour of women's suffrage, but the government still saw no need to provide time for a Bill and the Liberal supporters of an extension of the franchise saw no reason for immediate action: an extension of the franchise was usually followed fairly quickly by a general election, and in addition the Liberals were waiting for a Bill giving the vote to the remaining one-third of the adult male population which was not enfranchised after 1884. But from 1906 onwards there was a steady succession of incidents in which militant supporters of the right to vote broke the law and were arrested. At first they tried to force their way into the House of Commons, refused to move when asked by the police to leave and used the normal means of civil disobedience. The question of civil disobedience divided the women who were struggling for the vote; the law-abiding National Union of Women's Suffrage Societies (suffragists) and the Women's Social and Political Union (suffragettes), which was dominated by Christabel Pankhurst and her mother Emmeline, could not agree about the means to their common goal. The process of demonstration followed by imprisonment went on into 1909, when women prisoners went on hunger-strike and the authorities retaliated by feeding them forcibly.

By this stage two distinct struggles were developing. The suffragists would have been satisfied if they could get a Bill through Parliament, and they realized that considerations of party tactics made this harder than it looked. The suffragettes were beginning to see the issue as a contest between men and women in which women would not be treated fairly unless the eventual solution accepted women's right to vote as a paramount principle. They ceased to be interested in any compromise plan, or in any scheme to combine a measure of women's enfranchisement with the extension of male suffrage. As this mood developed it became more and more a matter of asserting that women had to be taken seriously, and less a question of politics. Most of the legal restrictions on women's activities—admission to universities, right to own property, right to enter the professions—had been removed in the late nineteenth century, and this had not altered the fact that women were not treated equally. The vote seemed to be the last formal issue on which there could be a struggle and the suffragettes wanted to use it as a battleground on which to assert the general principle of equality or, it sometimes seemed in the more passionate outpourings of the Pankhursts, the principle that in everything except brute strength women were men's superiors.[1] The women's struggle for the vote became, in its more extreme manifestations, an unpolitical movement. The cause attracted supporters who were rebelling against the trammels of family life or against inequalities imposed on women that had nothing to do with the law. In all previous agitations for the extension of the franchise, the lead had been taken by politicians who were already enfranchised and thought that other people should be brought into the electorate. In the struggle for votes for women, the great bulk of the work of agitation was carried on by women, though a few men were useful auxiliaries: Pethick-Lawrence was perhaps the most helpful and George Lansbury, who resigned his seat in Parliament and fought unsuccessfully in the subsequent by-election as a Women's Suffrage candidate was the most quixotic.

In 1910 a Conciliation Bill was introduced; it was designed to enfranchise a small enough number of women to convince the opponents of women's suffrage that there was nothing dangerous about it. Slightly over a million women who possessed in their own right property which would have allowed them to vote if they had been men were to be enfranchised. This formula would have given the vote to a relatively wealthy

[1] See C. Pankhurst, *The Great Scourge* (1913).

and relatively elderly section of the female population, and so it would have benefited the Conservative party. Churchill spoke for those Liberals who wanted women to have the vote, but did not like the idea that these particular women should have the vote. The Bill was killed by being sent to a committee of the whole House, but it continued to attract the suffragettes because it was a measure for women only.

A less pro-Conservative version of the Conciliation Bill got a second reading, but was again killed, in 1911. In the intervening election the government had committed itself to giving all men the right to vote and had declared that opportunities for women's suffrage amendments would be provided. It repeated these pledges after the 1911 derailment of the Conciliation Bill. The suffragettes regarded this as intolerable, because it meant that women's suffrage was to be tacked on to men's suffrage. Civil disobedience had been going on, with occasional truces, since 1906 and had helped establish the question in the public eye: meetings had been interrupted and speakers had been attacked. The suffragettes had already accepted the principle of using violence to advocate their cause. However, from the beginning of 1912 violence became more organized and deliberate: Mrs. Pankhurst advised her followers to break windows, and they broke windows. They broke them all the more enthusiastically when the Speaker ruled on 27 January 1913 that it would not be possible to turn a Bill based on manhood suffrage into one based on adult suffrage as the amendments would be altogether too drastic, and the government dropped the Bill altogether. The constitutional supporters of women's suffrage were left with nothing to do but bring forward another Bill moved by Dickinson, a Liberal back-bencher. The suffragettes moved on to arson and other violent methods; Emily Davison threw herself in front of the horses at the Derby and was trampled to death.

Extreme militancy does not seem to have helped the cause of women's suffrage. In the House of Commons opinion moved against giving women the vote. In 1911 the House had accepted the principle by giving a Second Reading to the Conciliation Bill; in 1913 a private member's Bill was defeated. In the same year the government felt strong enough to arm itself against hunger strikers by passing an Act allowing it to release hunger strikers and then rearrest them as soon as they were well enough to serve their sentences. The Act, nicknamed the 'Cat and Mouse' Act, probably helped the women's cause; the public seems to have accepted that civil disobedience was a reasonable method by which women could show that they were in earnest though 'militancy'—the use of violence and the destruction of property—was not accepted in the same way. Perhaps because of militancy, or a calculation that women's suffrage would help the Conservatives, or irritation at the way the W.S.P.U. treated as its main enemy the Liberal and Labour parties, most of whom supported women's suffrage, the political struggle seemed less hopeful in late 1913 than for some years. The defeat of the private member's Bill meant that the government no longer felt it had to provide time for another Bill, so the cause was blocked indefinitely unless the Prime Minister took a hand. And as Asquith had all along been the most eminent of the opponents of women's suffrage, it seemed unlikely that he would do anything.

He left the door slightly ajar. On 20 June 1914 he received a delegation of working-class women, from the East End of London, organized by Sylvia Pankhurst. At the meeting he seems to have been convinced that working-class women did want the vote; these women he saw were so poor that nothing short of an adult suffrage Act would enfranchise them, and he accepted the need for such an Act. The suffragettes responded with a new and more violent outburst of destruction; the Act was not going to be a measure for women only, and in any case Mrs. Pankhurst and her pretty daughter Christabel had moved a long way from the family's original socialism to which Sylvia Pankhurst was still loyal.

Threats to stability: Ireland

While the suffragettes caused alarm and confusion for some years, they could not overthrow the government or bring about a collapse of law and order. Things were different in Ireland; by the time Asquith had given way on the suffrage question he was keenly aware that there were two private armies formed in Ireland, and that his government was about to pass into law legislation that might launch the armies at one another's throats.

The Home Rule Bill set up a parliament for the whole island of Ireland and gave it roughly the powers enjoyed by the parliament of Northern Ireland until 1972, though the financial provisions were less generous than the eventual settlement for Northern Ireland because they assumed that Ireland would someday cease receiving money from the English taxpayer. The landlords were being bought out by a government-financed scheme, set up by the Conservatives in 1903, so they were no longer worried by the prospect of Home Rule. The Protestants of Ulster did object, and their objections were encouraged by the English Conservatives. Opponents of the Bill produced a number of unsubstantial grounds for saying that it was not constitutional. They said that, because the Parliament Act declared in its preamble that the membership of the Lords ought to be revised, the Lords ought to retain their veto until the revision took place. They said that on this subject Irish votes ought not to count. There was some logic in a Conservative Home Ruler like W. S. Blunt saying 'though with a majority of 126, Asquith is really in an English minority of fourteen', but when other Conservatives said similar things it amounted to saying that Irishmen were not to be allowed a parliament of their own and their votes at Westminster were not to be counted.[1]

The Parliament Act imposed such long delays that opponents of the Bill had time to prepare to resist it by force. Before it was even introduced into the House of Commons the Ulster Protestants had begun to hold large demonstrations, had entrusted Carson with the leadership of their movement and had spoken of setting up a provisional government if a Home Rule Bill were passed. The Bill was introduced for the first time in April 1912, and Ulster preparations became a little more organized. Orangemen drilled, which they were legally entitled to do once they had obtained the permission of two magistrates; Law declared that he 'could imagine no length of resistance to which [Protestant Ulstermen] might go in which they would not be supported by the overwhelming majority of the British people'.[2] It would be hard to go much further in the direction of incitement to rebellion without giving direct orders to break the law.

At the end of September the Ulstermen produced their Covenant, on the lines of the Covenant which the Scots had signed before resisting the government of Charles I. Hundreds of thousands of people came forward to commit themselves to standing together against any government that tried to impose Home Rule. Some of them signed in blood; all of them were clearly moving in the direction of rebellion; equally steadily the government took the Home Rule Bill through the House of Commons in 1912, resisting suggestions of a special status for Ulster, and did the same thing in 1913. During 1913 the Cabinet certainly considered proposing a special status for the Protestants of Ulster, but they knew that their parliamentary majority, depending as it did on the Home Rulers, would not survive a precipitate move towards compromise. Meanwhile the Conservatives protested that the whole thing was a corrupt bargain, that Asquith had only pressed on with Home Rule because he had promised to do so in order to get the Irish to vote for the budget and the Parliament Bill, and that Home Rule had never been before the electorate. Why it should be corrupt for Asquith to promise to do something which had been part of the Liberal programme for twenty-five years was not explained, and Home Rule had been before the people in the election of

---

[1] W. S. Blunt, *My Diaries* (1920), ii. 347.
[2] Robert Blake, *The Unknown Prime Minister* (1953), 130.

December 1910, for the Conservatives had referred to it frequently. The Lords had not dominated the contest to the exclusion of all other issues; Home Rule Free Traders and Protectionist Unionists had put their arguments forward, and the electorate outside Ireland voted against Protection and the Lords without showing much interest in Ireland.

The Conservative party in Great Britain in this period behaved as though it was above the constitution. It was entirely reasonable for the Ulster Protestants to hold demonstrations to show fully their earnest hatred of the idea of being ruled from Dublin. It may have been defensible for them to make plans to set up a provisional government. It was not reasonable for them to say that, because the Protestant section of Ulster wanted to remain part of the United Kingdom and at the same time was opposed to partition, there should be no Home Rule for Ireland. For Redmond to oppose partition was to deny the rights of a minority in Ireland; for Carson to oppose partition was to deny the rights of a majority in Ireland. But if Carson's attitude was indefensible, that of the English Unionists who took up a secret collection to finance a rebellion was worse, and that of Sir Henry Wilson who used his position at the War Office to undermine the government's control of the army was even more disreputable.

By the beginning of 1914 the government admitted that the Ulster Protestants were entitled to some sort of special treatment. They devised an Amending Bill which would go forward when the Home Rule Bill set off on its third and final trip round the parliamentary course. The counties of Ulster would be allowed to hold plebiscites, which would allow the four indisputably Protestant counties of Antrim, Armagh, Derry, and Down, and perhaps the two evenly divided counties of Fermanagh and Tyrone, to opt out of the new Ireland ruled from Dublin: it was taken for granted that the three Catholic counties in Ulster would all opt in. The Bill provided that after the four or the six counties had opted out, they would be handed over to Dublin at the end of six years. This curious arrangement meant that, if the Conservatives won either of the two general elections that would be held in these six years, they could amend the Home Rule Act and allow the counties to opt out for ever. Redmond accepted this; many of his followers preferred to go off and join the Nationalist Volunteers who were drilling and preparing like the Ulstermen.

The government had abstained from any action so far; in March it prepared to send troops into Ulster to secure points of strategic value, but when it moved forward for this purpose it found itself confronted with what has been called, rather misleadingly, the Mutiny at the Curragh.

Haldane's successor at the War Office, Colonel Seely, had been asked by Keir Hardie in 1912 if it would be possible for recruits to make a declaration in advance whether they were willing to take part in action against strikers or not, and Seely had said the idea was fantastic. There was a good reason for his answer: if a soldier simply obeys legal orders he can do his duty without approving the policy implied by the orders but if he has to choose whether to obey certain orders, he has to commit himself to approving of the policy. Seely saw the disadvantage of asking soldiers whether they were willing to shoot strikers or not, but he failed to make it clear that this applied to Ireland as well. When the movement forward to secure the strategic points was being planned, General Paget, who was in command at the Curragh camp to the west of Dublin, called on Seely and asked that some consideration should be shown for officers from Ulster; Seely said that officers from Ulster could 'disappear' for the duration of the operation. When Paget met his officers and told them of the plans, they formed the impression that resistance to the advance into Ulster was expected, and that officers from Ulster were given an option of 'disappearing' and returning later, while other officers were being asked to resign their commissions if they did not choose to go forward against Ulster. Almost all the officers at the Curragh resigned; they had been asked to commit themselves to the policy of Home Rule and to agree to shoot civilians if that was necessary to carry the policy out. Seely tried to repair the damage by issuing a statement of policy drawn up by the Cabinet, but he only made matters worse when he added extra paragraphs promising that the army would not be used to impose Home Rule on Ulster. This was too much and Seely's resignation was accepted. The episode left the Opposition confident that the government had disarmed itself and that it was now impossible to impose Home Rule.

Carson's provisional government became bolder; it allowed people to know that arms had been imported and that Ulster was beginning to feel a strong attachment to Germany. As the rest of Ireland drilled to prevent Ulster's secession the situation grew more tense. Redmond became afraid that he had been too concerned with parliamentary affairs, and forced the Nationalist Volunteers to accept him as their leader. Their organization was two years behind that of Ulster, and they did not have Mr. Astor, the Duke of Bedford, and other rich men to finance purchases of arms but of course there was in both these para-military organizations a good deal of parading to show weight of numbers and opinion rather than actually to fight.[1] Even so, it would have been very hard to set up Home Rule in Ireland without dealing with the question of Ulster, because the

[1] A. M. Gollin, *Proconsul in Politics* (1964), 188.

establishment of Home Rule would have been followed by the proclamation of a provisional government in Belfast which would have had
the support of Protestant Ulster. The Unionists in England who were
ready for civil war did not command widespread support for their violent
approach even within their own party. The Conservatives had been saying, ever since the introduction of the Home Rule Bill, that there ought
to be a general election on the issue; however, when the die-hard Unionists
suggested privately that the House of Lords should use its remaining
powers and reject the annual Army Act in order to force an election, the
moderates refused to hear of such a thing, partly because they did not
think it would be very sensible to disband the army and partly because
they thought an election on the issue of the Army Act would be a Liberal
landslide.

The Amending Bill to the Home Rule Bill was introduced into the
Lords and was altered out of recognition. As a result the government
could foresee a situation in which the Home Rule Bill would have passed
the Commons the requisite three times and there would be no Amending
Act to hand. George V apparently would have had doubts—which the
Conservatives were anxiously fanning—whether he should sign the Home
Rule Bill if it came to him unaccompanied by an Amending Bill. He was
afraid that he would be denounced by half his subjects whether he signed
or did not sign; he seems not to have noticed that this apparent dilemma
could arise on any controversial legislation as soon as he departed from
the safe course of accepting his Prime Minister's advice as binding. But
this line of argument made him all the more eager to bring together the
leaders of the Liberal and Conservative parties and of Ulster and the
Home Rule organization to work out an agreed settlement. A conference
was held at his suggestion; it started on 21 July, but as it could not agree
on the boundaries of Protestant Ulster, which ran somewhere through the
counties of Fermanagh and Tyrone, it broke up on the 24th. The next
day brought another reminder of the seriousness of the position; the
Irish Volunteers had arranged to bring in 1,500 rifles at Howth, which
might be thought to be only a fair exchange for the 30,000 that the
Orangemen had brought ashore at Larne in April. But there was a
difference; after Larne it had been established that importing arms was
illegal, which was not clear previously. The Dublin authorities sent troops
to intercept the rifles, but were unsuccessful; the Dublin mob threw
stones at the soldiers as they marched back to barracks, and in Bachelor's
Walk the soldiers' discipline broke down; they opened fire without
orders and killed three people. The Nationalist Volunteers became more
bellicose than before.

The calm of the government in the face of these events was alarming, but not incomprehensible. General Macready, in command in Northern Ireland, must have reported to Asquith along the lines indicated in his autobiography:

I have often been asked what would have happened in Ulster if the [First World] war had not intervened. I do not know. When going about the country outside Belfast during the summer of 1914 it would seem from the reports of the police and soldiers that the state of feeling between Catholics and Protestants was improving. . . . In the North, Belfast was the centre of all trouble, and in travelling through the country one noticed the change of feeling directly that city was out of sight . . . the troops looked on with amused indifference at the warlike preparations of the Ulstermen, and I had no more fear that the soldiers would be the aggressors in any conflict than that they would not carry out their duty if called upon. . . . The policy I did advocate was 'Govern or get out,' and that is exactly what in 1914 Mr. Asquith would not do.[1]

Asquith might reasonably have replied to the last comment that he was trying to get out (of Ireland) as fast as the Lords would let him. He could not do much while he was waiting for the Bill. Carson had probably committed sedition or even treason, but a state trial would only have inflamed the situation and neither conviction nor acquittal would have carried much weight because it was almost impossible to find a politically unbiased jury. In the negotiations, the Ulstermen would not even agree that they would accept the result if another general election were held specifically on Home Rule: the government was left to conclude that any concessions on Ulster would only have encouraged pressure for further concessions on other points. The government decided to wait and see what the final Ulster position was, and meanwhile relied on Macready's troops and the fact that the general public, if things came to civil war, would tend to be against the people who fired the first shots.

Future prospects: tension in politics and art

From the government's point of view Ireland was only one of a cluster of problems that surrounded the future of the Liberal party, its allies in the House of Commons, and the next stage in the development of its policy. The Home Rulers would stick by the government, despite their uneasiness about the Cabinet's evident willingness to compromise over Ulster, as long as a substantial measure of Home Rule went through. Finding something for the Liberal and Labour supporters in Great Britain was a little harder. One energetic social reformer, Churchill, had left the field; on moving to the Admiralty in October 1911 he had thrown

---

[1] C. F. N. Macready, *Annals of an Active Life* (1924), i. 196–8.

himself into his new work, become exigent in his demands for more money for bigger ships and correspondingly less enthusiastic about spending money on domestic welfare. Lloyd George was led by the success of his 1909 budget, with its attack on the landed interest, to believe that there was a ready audience for a programme that would, by changing the structure of land ownership, open the way to a great many other reforms. The first and most fully developed part of his programme would have broken up the great estates and created a Ministry of Land to finance development by tenant-farmers, encourage smallholdings and enforce a minimum wage for farm labourers. It seems unlikely that this programme would have been electorally very attractive or that it could have had much effect on the land. The flow of population from country to town was very hard to stop, let alone reverse, which was what Lloyd George's plan called for. Farmers may have been slightly underfinanced, but they were competing with North American farmers who, even when less well financed, could undersell them because of the scale of operations on the open prairies. Nothing short of tariffs or subsidies, neither of them acceptable to the party of Free Trade, could have enabled English farmers to compete with the 'last, best West' in Canada which was at this time being heavily settled for the first time. The immense British capital exports of the time, a large part of which went to build the Canadian Northern Railway, showed that English financial opinion thought Canadian wheat was unlikely to be displaced by Lloyd George's programme.

The urban part of the programme probably held out better prospects for the Liberal party. Urban landlords have never held the positions of honour and respect attained by the best rural landlords, and have often been very unpopular. The urban programme linked the ownership of land with the removal of slums and the improvement of housing; governments had been hovering on the edge of taking some responsibility for housing for three decades, and the Liberals would have gained a great advantage if Lloyd George could have convinced the electorate that they would really do something.

The land programme would probably have been launched a little earlier if Lloyd George's career had not suffered a sharp temporary check in 1913. Early in 1912 the government had given the English Marconi Company a contract to build wireless stations for communications round the Empire. Shortly after, rumours were heard that ministers had been making money for themselves by buying Marconi shares at a time when they knew the company was going to benefit from this contract. The rumour was started by the anti-semitic Chestertons, who

thought the Postmaster-General, Herbert Samuel, had given the contract
to Godfrey Isaacs, managing director of Marconi and brother of Rufus
Isaacs, the Attorney-General, as part of a Jewish conspiracy. The award of
the contract was entirely justified; however, Isaacs had suggested to his
brother Rufus that he should take up shares in the American Marconi
Company, and Rufus Isaacs had not only taken up the shares but had
passed some on to Lloyd George and also to the Liberal Chief Whip.
Perhaps this was a natural thing to happen inside a family and in any case
the contract to English Marconi brought no benefit to American Marconi.
But when the issue came up in Parliament in October Rufus Isaacs and
Lloyd George showed that they knew their behaviour would be hard to
justify; they denied buying English Marconi shares and they avoided
mentioning American Marconi at all. A Select Committee of the House of
Commons was set up to investigate the rumours; inevitably the purchases
of American Marconi shares came out and equally inevitably the failure to
mention them in October made the whole transaction look even worse
than it was. In June 1913 the Committee presented two reports. The
Liberal majority said the purchasers had no stain on their honour,
though the Liberal chairman had wanted to say the purchase was ill
advised. The Conservative minority said the purchase was a grave indiscretion. The reports were debated, and the House divided on the normal
party lines. There is no sign that Lloyd George felt any lasting gratitude
to Asquith for keeping him in the government when dismissing him
would have been a way of reducing tension, or felt any lasting resentment
against the Conservatives who had wanted to crush him. In 1914 he
showed all his old ability to take on two jobs at once; apart from running
the land campaign he produced another complicated budget which increased taxes, though it did not impose any new ones, and provided much
larger grants from the central government to local authorities to cover the
higher level of spending on social welfare. The budget turned out to be
too time-consuming for a parliamentary timetable cluttered with Irish
business, so the grants had to wait till the next year, but the proposal did
show that the government had not run short of new schemes for the
future.

The Opposition was happily placed; for purposes of criticism they
could simultaneously ask for increased spending and denounce the high
level of the existing taxes, and justify this by saying that Tariff Reform
would provide the extra money needed. On the whole they wasted their
opportunity by concentrating on asking for more expenditure on armaments, a request that probably gained few votes. The government had its
problems, but was not directly troubled by the strength of the Opposition

in 1914. In the days before opinion polls people relied on by-election results to measure the government's standing; the government's share of the vote went down at elections between 1910 and 1914, but this is quite usual at by-elections. The pattern of seats lost was more significant. Apart from Lansbury's seat lost on Women's Suffrage, the government and their Labour allies lost fifteen seats in this period: in three of the eight seats lost before the end of 1912 Liberal and Labour candidates opposed one another but between them polled a majority of the votes cast, and this also happened in five of the seven seats lost in the next nineteen months. If this pattern of results had continued, the fate of the next election would have depended on the course of relations between the Liberal and Labour parties. MacDonald and his supporters in the Labour party were quite willing to continue to operate the division of seats originally arranged for the 1906 election, and if they had been able to make sure that three-cornered contests were confined to by-elections, the Liberal and Labour parties would have been in a fairly good position. They would have benefited from the Plural Voting Bill, which was due to pass into law in 1914, and if an Adult Suffrage Bill had been passed that would also have helped them. Despite Ireland, the government was well placed politically on the eve of war.

One obstacle to a renewal of good relations between Liberal and Labour parties was the creation of the Triple Alliance, an agreement to co-operate reached by the railway workers, coalminers, and transport workers, who were mainly dockers and carters in the days before commercial motor transport. There were relatively few labour disputes in the early months of 1914, but it was generally accepted that this was only the lull before the storm; a combined strike by the Triple Alliance was thought to be very likely, and their command over transport would have made it into something very like a general strike. In economic terms probably the situation would have produced nothing worse than the 'strenuous time' which Askwith anticipated for the autumn,[1] but in political terms a general strike would have made the immediate prospect for the Liberal-Labour alliance rather poor. The slight slackening of trade noticed in 1914 would have made a strike less likely, but it would have damaged the government's political prospects in other ways.

While England in 1914 was not on the verge of plunging into disorder and chaos, people were uneasy and uncertain about what was happening. Something of this state of tension can be seen in the division to be found among poets at the time. While the writers who flourished during the reign of Edward VII had very little in common with the modern

[1] G. R. Askwith, op. cit. 356.

movement, writers were emerging in the years before the war who had relatively little in common with the rational prophets of progress who had dominated the literary scene. This development is clearer in retrospect than it was at the time: in the first years of the reign of George V the most obvious change in the literary scene was the appearance of a new group of poets who were published in *Georgian Poetry*. They may today be dismissed as the last thin squeezings from the great flow of romantic poetry that had begun with Wordsworth, but at the time they were seen as something altogether more lively, and at times Georgian poets like Rupert Brooke even upset the critics by the frankness with which they wrote about such things as seasickness.

There is not much sign that the Georgians knew about any poetic tradition except the Wordsworthian; Kipling could have told them that there had been quite a number of new ideas about poetry in France since the death of Wordsworth. The approach to poetry of the Symbolists was coming to England during these years before the war, but this poetic wave of the future received relatively little attention. Because he was seen as a war poet of the early, optimistic part of the struggle and because of his death at the Dardanelles in 1915, Brooke gained much more attention than, poetically speaking, he deserved; later on he was picked out as one of the pre-war writers to be attacked by supporters of the modern school. His contemporary, T. S. Eliot (born in 1888, a year after Brooke) came to England just after the war had begun, and in a few years had set English poetry down its new path. But it is not possible to look backwards and pass judgement on what would have happened if the war had not come: the methods of the Symbolists were, under the guidance of men like Pound and Lewis, being accepted in England before Eliot arrived, but on the other hand the war encouraged among thoughtful and artistic people a pessimistic feeling that welcomed *The Waste Land* and the general attitude of Eliot. Just as nobody can say whether the Georgian poets would have developed, in a happier world, into a dominant and effective school of writers, on the wider stage nobody can say whether the peaceful and tranquil England that they represented would have survived the problems that confronted it in mid-1914 if the war had not come.

The outbreak of war

In July 1914 war was certainly not one of the things that worried the government: the suffragettes, Ireland, the possibility of widespread strikes in the autumn and perhaps the question of relations with the Labour party had to be faced but, so far as can be seen, not even Grey had realized that the murder of the Archduke Franz Ferdinand at Sarajevo on 28 June could lead to disaster. This was a curious oversight on Grey's part, for he had played a considerable part the previous year in damping down conflict in the Balkans and making sure that it did not spread so far that it would involve the Great Powers. The international situation seemed better in 1914 than for some time; in 1911 there had been some tense weeks when the German government had sent a warship, the *Panther*, to Agadir to demonstrate the seriousness of German claims to a position of influence in Morocco, and for a few years after 1908 Germany had been building battleships at a rate which seemed to be threatening Britain's maritime supremacy. But by 1914 the race was virtually over; after a moment of anxiety in 1909 Britain had settled down to building two battleships a year more than Germany, and the British preparations for additional ships were further advanced. Relations between France and Germany had also grown less strained. Englishmen were not unprepared for war with Germany over naval or colonial issues, and probably many of them were willing to fight to preserve the Balance of Power if Germany attacked France, but the idea that England might be involved in a war over a country in the Balkans had occurred to very few of them. Grey's own leisurely approach is easy to understand: during the three weeks between the assassination and his proposal of a conference, very little seemed to be happening. The Austrian government was screwing up its courage to make use of the imprudently wide-ranging promise of support given to it by the German government, but its ultimatum of 24 July, which gave the Serbian government forty-eight hours to accept terms which left little of the sovereignty of Serbia intact, was unexpected and was out of keeping with the pace of development up to that time. It was delivered on the day of the breakdown of the King's conference on Ireland, when English politicians were understandably preoccupied; Churchill wrote that 'a strange light began immediately, but by perceptible gradations, to fall and grow upon the map of Europe',[1] and some of his colleagues did not see the first of these gradations of light. Churchill himself agreed with the First Sea Lord's decision that the naval squadrons, which had been concentrated at Portsmouth for exercises, should not be dispersed, and Grey again attempted to arrange a conference. Austria-Hungary refused to be placed on the same footing as Serbia, for the whole object of her diplomacy was to demonstrate that she was superior; accordingly, on the 28th she declared war on Serbia, who had accepted most of the ultimatum of the 24th but had appealed to her ally Russia to defend her from the more humiliating terms.

[1] W. S. Churchill, *The World Crisis* (1923), i. 193.

This had presumably been foreseen in Germany; one effect of the ultimatum was to test Russia's ability to protect Serbia. If she did not protect her ally she would be humiliated as she had been in 1908 in the dispute over the Austrian annexation of Bosnia and Hercegovina, and the value of the Russian alliance would look more doubtful to the French. The British government by now understood what might happen: the fleet was moved to its battle station at Scapa Flow and Grey advised the German ambassador that if the war spread Britain might not remain neutral. Some Austrian troops marched into Serbia on the 29th; when Russia ordered mobilization on the 31st, the Germans told the Russians to stop mobilizing and told the French not to start.

Russia might have allowed Serbia to be bullied without intervening on her behalf but Russia and France could hardly let Germany dictate about their mobilization. On the other hand a fully mobilized Russia would be a threat to Germany. A war on the Continent was probably inevitable by this stage. The French Ambassador, Cambon, asked Grey on 31 July if England would enter the war; Grey gave a non-committal reply, pointing out perfectly accurately that England had no commitments to France and that they would have to wait. Grey might have been able, at this point, to ensure that England did not have to enter the war immediately, though probably she would have been drawn in to preserve the balance of power when it was seen that France was losing. Instead he asked France and Germany for promises that they would not invade Belgium. France gave the required promise, but Germany declined. Next day, the German ambassador asked if this promise would by itself be enough to keep England out of the war, but Grey declined to answer. Grey had probably decided that, if there was a major war, he would try to bring the country in to support France as soon as he could, but he did not want to make this clear to the French because it might encourage them to fight if they knew they could reckon on British help. Later writers have suggested that Grey should have said unequivocally that England would fight and thus deter Germany as much as possible, but a statement of this sort might easily have made France more bellicose. In any case his diplomacy was almost paralysed because he was not certain that he could speak for a united government. If he had taken ministers into his confidence earlier he might have been able to intervene more effectively. Lloyd George seemed ready to place himself at the head of the peace party on 31 July, and this would have meant that England would not enter the war united. Lloyd George was ready to fight on 1 August; on the second he was at the head of three other opponents of British entry in the Cabinet. The discussion went on;

two of the opponents resigned, but two, of whom Lloyd George was one, remained.

In the Cabinet the decisive question seems to have been German command of the Channel: in the course of the non-binding military conversations between French and English, the English had encouraged the French fleet to move to the Mediterranean, and the Cabinet was not prepared to let the Germans dominate the Channel as a result of this decision. However, the German government announced on 3 August that it was willing to treat the Channel as a neutral zone if England stayed neutral. By this time it was too late; in the evening of the 2nd, after the Cabinet had dispersed, the German government sent an ultimatum to Belgium demanding to be allowed to send troops through Belgium to attack France.

What is now known of the rigid plans of the German High Command makes it hard to see why war had been delayed even this long. Germany had prepared for a war against France; arrangements for mobilization were laid down in the Schlieffen Plan, which took it for granted that in any war Germany would have to fight France and Russia simultaneously. The plan provided for a holding operation against Russia in the east while the bulk of the German army marched, not against the difficult terrain of the Franco-German frontier, but round the north through Belgium, outflanking the French army and eventually surrounding it as it had been surrounded at Sedan. The German High Command seems to have had no alternative plan prepared; this was why they insisted on forcing France into the war, by the ultimatum of the 31st, and their plan faced with complete unconcern the possibility that the invasion of Belgium would lead England to enter the war. No doubt the High Command would have preferred her not to join in, and Kaiser William was undoubtedly very disturbed to hear that she might do so. But the High Command certainly did not think that the risk of British entry should deter them from marching through Belgium, and the Kaiser did not think the risk of British entry should lead him to oppose the policy of the High Command. Because there were no other plans, it would have been very hard for Germany to go on with the war at all without invading Belgium; the British response was not thought important enough to affect the issue, and even if the German ambassador had reported on the 1st that England would remain neutral if Belgium were not invaded, devising a new plan would have been very difficult.

In the years after 1914, Grey's diplomacy was often criticized. Some of the attacks came from German apologists, who in essence said that if they had known that England took the neutrality of Belgium seriously they would have respected it. This is not convincing: it was hard to negotiate with the German leaders about Belgium because they had already made an undertaking in a Treaty that they would respect it, and if they were ready to break the Treaty, they might also break any subsequent engagements that they made. Grey was also criticized by the British Left. They wanted the country's policy to be peace-loving and upright, and they were determined to make their government live up to these ideals. But they had two distinct objectives which were hard to reconcile; they wanted Belgium to be protected, and they did not want England to go to war. They overestimated England's place in the world: it was not at all certain that an English threat of war would have saved Belgium from invasion, and in any case Grey could deliver such a threat in a convincing way only by taking a bellicose attitude that the Left would have found very objectionable. There is an irritating philosophic calm about Grey's remark that 'the lights are going out all over Europe', but probably there was nothing that he could have done about it.

The invasion of Belgium made it relatively easy for him to rally the House of Commons behind the government on the 3rd. The Conservatives had already made it clear that they were ready for war; Grey's task was to win over his own backbenchers and the opinion of the neutral world. He was greatly helped in both tasks when Redmond said that the violent agitation for Home Rule would be called off and the Volunteers would place themselves at the disposal of the government. But the voice of the Gladstonian approach to foreign policy was not completely silent; one speaker did say that this was not a war for Belgium but a war that would upset the whole balance of Europe. It was not a good omen for the Liberal party that the speaker was the leader of the Labour party, Ramsay MacDonald.

Next day, 4 August, the government called on Germany to pledge itself to respect Belgian neutrality. German troops had already crossed the frontier; at 11.00 p.m. England entered the war.

A note on statistical evidence

Very few figures are as definite and conclusive as they look. For instance, the occupational background of M.P.s has been analysed in two different ways: J. A. Thomas in *The House of Commons 1832–1901* (Cardiff, 1939) and *The House of Commons 1906–11* (Cardiff, 1958) records each major economic activity of the M.P.s he is studying, and on the average each M.P. turns up twice in his lists. J. F. S. Ross in *Parliamentary Representation* (1943) and *Elections and Electors* (1955) assigns each M.P. to one fixed category or another. Which is better? Both approaches have their advantages, which means that neither of them gives a conclusive answer.

Economic statistics are sometimes even less definite than political. The movement of real wages provides an example: an index of money wages can be a reasonably accurate approximation, an index of the cost of living is only a rather rough approximation, and an index of real wages obtained by dividing one into the other is even rougher. Anyone who compares A. L. Bowley, *Wages and Incomes in the United Kingdom since 1880* (1937), 94–5 with W. Ashworth, *An Economic History of England, 1870–1939* (1960), which speaks of national income rising and real wages remaining unchanged, or with S. Pollard, *Development of the British Economy* (1962), 24, which speaks of a slow rise in national income per head, a fall in real wages and a distinct fall in the proportion of national income paid in wages, will see that economic figures are very slippery. The figures for the balance of payments mentioned in the previous chapter (p. 5) are also not conclusive; even in the 1950s (see below, p. 323) the British government was not able to establish accurate balance-of-payments figures for its own use.

The components of a cost-of-living index change so much with the passage of time that they are always hard to compare, and it is particularly difficult in periods when prices change rapidly: letters cost twenty times what they did in 1906, but many more people have telephones and almost everyone has television as a distraction from letter-writing. The consumer price index, which is designed to measure the working-class standard of living, somewhat more than doubled from 1914 to 1920, from 1939 to 1951, and from 1970 to 1976, and rose more gradually in the 1950s and 1960s, so that the prices of the components of this index have risen twelvefold or sixteenfold. Average wages rose slightly faster in all subdivisions of the period, so there were no declines in real wages for more than a year or two at a time. Relative living standards changed a great deal, and those outside the class whose condition is most directly measured by these two indicators suffered a number of considerable shocks to their position.

Studying change is made a little harder by changes in the currency. British coinage had for centuries been based on the pound of silver divided into twenty shillings which were subdivided into twelve pence (in Latin, *libra, solidi,* and *denarii,* hence £.S.D.). In 1971 the final step was taken to a decimal coinage, keeping the pound at its existing value and subdividing it into one hundred pennies. This came in the early stages of a great increase in prices; it has been suggested that the change increased the inflation by making people ignore the value of money, but the physical details of the change were handled well enough.

Another almost simultaneous change makes income-tax figures harder to follow. The broad indicator always used for income-tax is the 'standard rate', which is the marginal rate for a large majority of those who pay the tax. It has always been expressed in pennies (or shillings) in the pound; until 1914 it moved up or down 1*d*. (0·42p) in a budget, for most of the century it moved 3*d*. (1·25p) or 6*d*. (2½p) at a time, and since 1971 it has moved by 1p (2·4*d*.) at a time. Taxpayers used to pay on only a major fraction of earned income that did not come from interest, rent, or dividends. By 1973 they paid on only $\frac{7}{9}$ of their income. In 1973 this changed so that an investment surcharge was paid on interest, rent, and dividends, and the declared standard rate was the full marginal rate paid by most taxpayers. After all of this, 30p is the same standard rate as 7*s*. 9*d*., and 35p is the same as 9*s*. in the pound had been in the 1950s and 1960s.

3. 'Blow out, you bugles, over the rich dead'[1]　　1914–1918

Grand strategy

HALDANE once said he wanted a Hegelian army; and certainly the 1914–18 war was a Hegelian war, drawing more of the nation's resources into the hands of government, giving more power to the State and making the national survival more dependent on wise decisions by its rulers than ever before in British history. All this was even more true in the Second World War, but the difference between the First World War and the Second was a matter of degree. The First World War was different in kind from any previous war in which Britain had fought.

A sketch of the grand strategy of the war will set the activities of the British people and its government in context. In August and September 1914 the German army, following the Schlieffen Plan, swept through Belgium and forced its way almost to Paris. It was checked by a counter-attack on the Marne and forced to fall back, but it continued to occupy almost all of Belgium and a large slice of north-east France. To some extent German attention was distracted by an attack on its eastern frontier by the Russian army, which proved more mobile than Schlieffen had expected. The Russian attack was defeated; the German High Command reversed the strategy of the Schlieffen Plan, stayed on the defensive in the west (with one big exception) until 1918, and devoted their offensive efforts to the east. In 1915 the French and, to a lesser extent, the English attacked the German defensive lines. English interest, though not the bulk of English resources, concentrated on the attempt to force a way through the Dardanelles, hold the Bosporus, and open a line of communication to Russia where most of the materials needed for modern war were already running short. In 1916 the Germans made their only serious

[1] This is the first line of Rupert Brooke's third war sonnet, 'The Dead'.

offensive in the west between 1914 and 1918, in an unsuccessful attempt to capture Verdun and later in 1916 the newly-recruited British armies made their first full-scale attack on the German defensive position. This was also unsuccessful, and although the British command of the sea, on which her tightly constricting blockade of Germany depended, was not broken at the battle of Jutland, a German counter-blockade by submarine became a more serious threat. In the east Rumania entered the war against Germany and Austria-Hungary and was quickly crushed by them, and the Russian military and political structure began to disintegrate. Early in 1917 the United States entered the war as an 'associate' of England and France, and a revolution swept away the Tsarist government of Russia. The submarine blockade became increasingly dangerous until the adoption of convoy tactics defeated the threat to British supplies. The German defensive line was attacked by the French in the first half of 1917 and by the English in the second half of the year. The Germans held their position almost unchanged and completed the work of destroying Russia as an effective force; by the end of the year a Bolshevik government was in power with little choice but to make peace immediately, and the German High Command could bring their troops back to the west. By 1918 the Germans had to take the initiative; the blockade was slowing down their whole economy, and England and France could afford to wait until American support reached them. From March to July the Germans launched five great offensives upon the English and French, forcing their enemies back in almost every case without ever gaining a decisive victory. By the end of July their forces were overstrained and their reserves used up. The western powers had held on successfully; in the summer and autumn of 1918 they once more attacked the German line and this time broke it. Weighing the factors that caused the sudden collapse is difficult; however, within four months of the last German offensive the generalissimo of the western powers granted an armistice to the leaders of the German army and saw the old constitution founded on the hegemony of Prussia and the rule of the house of Hohenzollern swept away.

The volunteers' war

In August 1914 the War Book which listed all the instructions to be sent out to British forces when war began was in good order. The Fleet was in position. The British Expeditionary Force crossed the Channel, and moved forward into Belgium. It got as far forward as Mons, and here came into contact with the weight of the German advance. The retreat from Mons that inevitably followed was conducted quite skilfully, but it was already clear that the French and English High Commands had not worked out how to co-ordinate their operations. The German armies, which might conceivably have fulfilled Schlieffen's ambitious plan if they had marched south-west from Belgium towards Paris, slipped into marching due south. As a result they lost their chance of outflanking the French and English armies, and opened their own left wing to an attack by the troops of the garrison of Paris; half of one division was hurried to the front by taxicab. The German army, which had reached the river Marne, fell back in late September to the river Aisne, about forty miles north. At this stage there were no forces worth mentioning north or west of the exposed German left wing but both sides quickly extended their lines. The Germans hoped to capture the Channel ports and impede England's communications with France; the French and English were correspondingly determined to save the ports. The German assault was held up for a few days by a makeshift force put together and sent to Antwerp by Churchill, who offered to leave the Cabinet to become an army commander. But the days for imaginative expedients were coming to an end, though Churchill had two other ideas to offer later. The German outflanking attempts were checked at the first battle of Ypres, where the pounding tactics which dominated most of the war were already to be seen. By the end of November the Channel ports were safe, and the line ran north from the German position on the Aisne to the sea. The armies dug their trenches deeper and deeper, and prepared for the next season's campaign.

By the end of the year the Navy had swept the oceans clear of the German ships which had been at sea when war began; most of them had been sunk but two German ships, the *Goeben* and the *Breslau*, had slipped through the Mediterranean at the very beginning of the war, and helped to persuade Turkey to enter the war on the German side. The destruction of a German squadron at the Falkland Islands, after its initial success at Coronel, meant that British trade was safe from attack until the submarine offensive began. The blockade of Germany was already effective, though it could have been made even more complete if the Foreign Office had not been obliged, by constant American protests, to remind the Admiralty that the United States was a neutral power and that her shipping had to be treated with some respect. Throughout the first three years of the war the governments at war had to show some respect for 'neutral' opinion, which really meant the opinion of the United States. The British and French understood the importance of the United States, though sometimes they assumed that the anglophiles and francophiles of the east coast, led by ex-President Theodore Roosevelt, were typical of all American opinion. This was not true; although American opinion always leaned in the direction of England and France, so that there was no likelihood that she would enter the war against them, which would have led almost immediately to their defeat, most Americans hoped to remain at peace. Immensely exaggerated accounts of German atrocities in Belgium encouraged anti-German feeling in the United States, as well as building up enthusiasm for the war in England and France, but the Germans were quite wrong to think that the United States was committed against them, or to imagine that its views were of no importance. Wilson was re-elected President in 1916 as the man who kept the United States out of the war; if he had not been provoked by the remarkably foolish and (by the standards of the day) barbarous policy of submarine warfare, he would probably have continued to keep her out.

The German forces in German East Africa (later Tanganyika) avoided capture until the end of the war, but Samoa was captured in 1914, German South West Africa in 1915, and the Cameroons early in 1916. All the Dominions took it for granted in 1914 that when England was at war, they were at war; they raised volunteer armies in a mood of imperial enthusiasm and unity. Before the campaign in South West Africa the South African government of Botha and Smuts, which was completely committed to support of the British Empire, dispersed some rebels who wanted to take the opportunity to reverse the verdict of the Boer War.

In England a mood of 'business as usual' went on into the winter of 1914. Lloyd George's first war-time budget contained only small increases in taxation and set the pattern of paying for the war by loans; this was maintained to the end and only in 1918 did income-tax reach 30p in the pound. In the first instance the rich and the middle classes paid for the war, but as a good deal of their contribution came in loans at high rates of interest, those who had spare money to invest were repaid later. Price levels went up sharply during the period of 'business as usual' and wage rates lagged behind; many rich people responded to war by cutting down spending, companies found themselves unable to carry on their old lines of trade and so unemployment rose initially. The slogan 'business as usual' was partly intended to help people put out of work during the first few months of the war. Although wage rates did not catch up with prices while the war was on, few workers suffered a decline in real wages, because employment was much more continuous once the first dislocation was over, and a great many people changed jobs and moved to better paid work.

Thinking about the war in a more imaginative way than most people, the First Lord of the Admiralty produced two suggestions during the winter. Several other people around the same time thought of building an armoured vehicle running on caterpillar tracks which could crawl over a line of trenches, an idea which had effects for decades to come. It was not immediately made effective but his other suggestion, that the British should force the Dardanelles, knock Turkey out of the war, and open a line of communication with Russia, dominated the British government's approach to the war for most of 1915. At first he thought the older battleships not needed for watching the German High Sea fleet could do the job. As most authorities then and later (though not Lord Fisher, once more First Sea Lord) agreed, his plan must have had some substance to it, even though taking forts with ships is a difficult operation. The naval attack took place on 25 March, and was held up by uncharted mines; the Admiralty began to have doubts about the operation when three battleships were sunk by them. Although persistence would have brought success, the naval attack was not likely to be resumed. However, the government had decided just after the naval attack to allot a division to the operation; on 25 April troops landed at Gallipoli and established themselves on the shore but could not press forward.

In France the Germans stood on the defensive most of the time; the French attacked fiercely and with no noticeable success. The English regular army was too small to absorb losses of the size suffered by all armies in 1914, and if they had been free to choose the British government and its generals might have spent the year in building up a strong army in France from Kitchener's volunteers. The demands of the alliance made this passive role impossible. The second battle of Ypres was the most important British battle in France in 1915. It began with an ill-organized German attack, preceded by the first use of poison gas, at just about the same time as the British landing at Gallipoli. The struggle at Ypres was kept going by a series of British counter-attacks to pin down German troops while the French prepared their offensive. As the battle went on, it became clear that British forces were paralysed by a shortage of shells for their guns because the pre-war supply department of the War Office had not foreseen the large-scale bombardments which now proved necessary.

In mid-May the Liberal government found itself obliged to take the Conservatives into a coalition. M.P.s knew about the shell shortage and blamed the government; suddenly they heard that Fisher had resigned from the Admiralty because he disapproved of the Gallipoli operations. The Conservatives were ready to oppose the policy of the government openly: Asquith hurriedly put together a coalition to prevent this, partly to avoid revealing any weaknesses at just the moment Grey was persuading Italy to enter the war on the British side, but mainly because the political position of the Liberals was not strong enough for them to resist.

The old ministers dominated the Cabinet of the First Coalition; Asquith and Grey remained unchanged, Kitchener gave up the War Office supply responsibilities to Lloyd George who became Minister of Munitions, McKenna replaced Lloyd George at the Exchequer, and the only Conservative who gained a position of central importance was Balfour who replaced Churchill at the Admiralty. Although Haldane was dropped and Churchill relegated to the Chancellorship of the Duchy of Lancaster the allocation of jobs suggests that the Liberals still controlled the situation. This may have encouraged the Conservatives not to feel any great loyalty to Asquith's coalition.

Reinforcements were sent to Gallipoli in August. Another opportunity to press forward was presented, and again it was not taken. After this the Turks and Germans brought up large reinforcements, and the Cabinet slowly realized that the position was too exposed for winter operations. By January 1916 the force had been withdrawn tidily and bloodlessly. Gallipoli remains one of the great question-marks over the war. We now know, from German and Turkish sources, that on two or three occasions a little extra speed or resolution would have carried the English forward to the European side of the Bosporus. Supporters of the expedition said, and say to this day, that such an advance would have led to Turkey's collapse. Supplies would have reached Russia, the 1917 revolutions could have been averted, and Germany would have been crushed between two well-armed opponents. The British High Command believed that the only essential area was the western front; they, and their later supporters, argued that even if Turkey had been defeated there was no real surplus of arms to give to Russia and that conducting a campaign in the Balkans was too difficult. The second point was illustrated a little later: Britain and France set up a large army at Salonika in Northern Greece, but while this force ensured that Greece did not follow the pro-German inclinations of her King, it was not able to march north into the Balkans.

While the preparations for evacuation were being made at Gallipoli, the British army in France was launching another attack on the German defensive line. Sir John French, the British commander in France, mismanaged the battle of Loos and was soon replaced by Haig, but it seems unlikely that more skilful handling would have led to a breakthrough.

This failure added force to the pressure for conscription in England. When the war began people in England spoke of it being 'all over by Christmas'; their ideas of war were clearly drawn from the wars in Europe in 1866 and 1870, which ended quickly, rather than from the long-drawn-out American Civil War of 1861–5, in which the power of the defence and the importance of industrial preparation were made clear.

The government believed in 1914 that the main British contribution would be naval, financial, and industrial; the small, highly trained professional army would be sent to France as planned, and England would supply materials for France and Russia. Kitchener had been made Secretary of State for War when the war began. The job was enormous. It involved raising troops, equipping them, and supervising the formation of strategy. Kitchener was an immense figure, a hero from the wars of colonial expansion in the 1880s and 1890s with a commanding presence that few people would argue with. In one of his moments of deep insight he saw that it would be a long war—he estimated three years. This justified raising and training a large army; if the war was to be over by Christmas the volunteers who had rushed forward at the outbreak of war could not have played any effective part in the fighting. Whether Kitchener saw the other consequences of a long war will not be known; he said too little about his policy, and forfeited his chances of winning support for it.

Voluntary recruiting was easy at first. Men came forward in the spirit of Rupert Brooke's poem that began 'Now God be thanked who has matched us with His hour,' and while this may not have been great poetry, it was not rashly ignorant of danger. All five of Brooke's very popular war poems are permeated with the thought of the 'best enemy and friend', death. People were ready not only to accept but to welcome war; the idea that war meant that 'nobility had returned to the earth' would not have found a welcome in England at any time after 1914. Grey was, by the standards of the diplomats of his time, rather unwilling to consider war as a normal instrument of policy, but most of the people of England were as willing to accept it as people elsewhere.

If this had simply meant that armies could have been filled by voluntary methods, the administrative inconvenience might have been justified by the moral benefits. But volunteering was not a simple matter of individual choice; enthusiasm had to be stimulated and social pressure applied to possible recruits. Demagogues like Horatio Bottomley took to the platform to stir young men to come forward, and they found it helped if they encouraged the wild anti-German feeling that had broken out. Because Germany was at war with England people broke the windows of shopkeepers with German names, denounced dachshund-owners as unpatriotic, and suggested that the music of Beethoven and Bach was worthless. The sharp decline from Brooke the romantic poet to Bottomley, a company promoter with the distinction of being expelled from the House of Commons for financial misconduct on two occasions, who was paid fees for his recruiting speeches, showed the strain imposed by the need to keep up the flow of volunteers.

This hysteria did not help the war effort. Battenberg, the First Sea Lord, who had taken the initial decision to mobilize the fleet and was married to a granddaughter of Queen Victoria, was obliged to give up his post because of his name (which he changed to Mountbatten, at about the same time as the royal family declared its name to be Windsor). Women took to giving white feathers to men they thought should be in uniform; when they picked on soldiers on leave this was merely offensive, but when they picked on skilled munitions workers they were—to use their own language—doing the Kaiser's work. Voluntary recruitment made good sense when a small army had to double in size, but the government ought to have looked at the implications before deciding to raise a large army for a long war. Instead it behaved as though war was a matter of running a budget and getting troops over to France, without thinking about prices and about the rational use of manpower.

Asquith's last year

When the Asquith coalition had been formed, Lloyd George found a great deal to be done in his new Ministry of Munitions, despite the War Office's attempts to reorganize its supply department. He turned his energies to everything: he set up state factories despite the traditional view, backed by *laissez-faire* Liberal theory, that these things were done best by private firms; he brought businessmen in to help run his Department; he recognized the need to negotiate with trade unions, and he persuaded the engineering unions to break down the barriers of job demarcation and allow unskilled workers to do work that had previously been reserved for skilled craftsmen. At the same time he became convinced of the strength of the case for conscription and began to press for it in Cabinet. His views came closer to those of the Conservatives, who also wanted conscription, though acquaintance with the Liberal ministers renewed Conservative suspicions of Lloyd George's methods and made them more ready to see the virtues of McKenna, the leading exponent of the case against conscription.

The reasons for supporting conscription were varied: the Army Council wanted it in order to get more troops, the Conservatives shared this view and thought in addition that it would be easier to control the working classes if 'industrial conscription' could be imposed so that everybody had to work where he was told, and Lloyd George found it very hard to manufacture munitions when many skilled men had already volunteered and more were doing so. He set about getting skilled men back from the front and making sure that no others went. The attitude of the military men was the least reasonable: they spoke, throughout the war, as though they could have an unlimited supply of men and at the same time have an unlimited supply of munitions. The Conservative attitude had a harsh logic about it when taken to an extreme, as it was by F. S. Oliver, who was in favour of 'beating that dog [organized labour] to a jelly'.[1] If this could have been done without breaking civilian morale, it would no doubt have provided a flexible labour force; without such a preliminary process, 'industrial conscription' was bound to lead to an even more bitter struggle than military conscription. The difference, which supporters of 'industrial conscription' seemed unable to see, was that it was one thing to conscript men to go and fight—this was unpopular with the trade unions but would be accepted—and quite another thing to conscript men to go and work for somebody else's profit. If employers knew the government would supply employees who could not defend themselves by strike action, their handling of labour relations was likely to become more insensitive. Lloyd George's approach to conscription was more moderate; he wanted to keep skilled workers out of the trenches, and to do this he had to provide other people to go and fight.

Kitchener had been ready, and even flattered, to serve as recruiting-sergeant to the Empire, and as long as he accepted this role and declared that the voluntary system was adequate it was hard for anyone to stand against him and say that conscription was necessary, but by late 1915 his authority was beginning to weaken. Asquith held back the pressure for a few more months by getting Lord Derby to lead a last great campaign of voluntary recruiting, in which all men of service age were asked to say that they would serve when called upon, on the understanding that unmarried men would be called upon first. It was relatively easy, after this recruiting campaign clearly had not brought men forward in the quantities required, for Asquith to bring in the first Conscription Bill in January 1916. It called up unmarried men, on the grounds that it would be unfair to make married men go to the front, as a result of their pledge under the Derby scheme, while unmarried men remained in England. Asquith's Bill passed with little opposition: the libertarian Liberals, the trade unions, and the economists who did not believe that Britain's resources could stand conscription were able to muster only 31 votes in the Commons. The main upholders of the economic argument in the Cabinet were Runciman and McKenna, and Asquith, Balfour, and Kitchener were impressed by what they said. However, Lloyd George, the newspapers of Lord Northcliffe, the majority of the Conservative party, and the national feeling that everybody ought to do his share of the work were on the side of conscription. The Act of January 1916 was

[1] A. M. Gollin, *Proconsul in Politics* (1964), 540.

not enough; another Act, covering all men of military age, was passed in April.

Conscription kept the British armies in France at a steady level of about a million men; two and a half million troops were raised on a volunteer basis by early 1916, and almost as many were raised by conscription during the rest of the war. Sir Auckland Geddes, the Minister of National Service, later wrote: 'With perhaps more knowledge than most of the working of conscription in this country . . . I hold the fully matured opinion that, on balance, the imposition of military conscription added little if anything to the effectiveness of our war effort.'[1] Conscription enabled the government to regulate the flow of men; if it had been accompanied by a sensible classification of jobs, and taxation at a level that convinced factory workers that the owners were not profiting immoderately from the war, it could have been used to co-ordinate the various sections of the war effort. The simplest way for the government to control the economy was by regulating something vital that was in short supply. Manpower was the first thing that could have been used for the purpose. The opportunity was missed, mainly because Asquith had been in office too long; his urge to intervene and get things done, never very strong, had been worn away. Co-ordination of effort had to wait until the shortage of shipping early in 1917.

The supporters of all-out warfare, most of whom believed that all Britain's efforts should be concentrated in France, gained another success in December 1915. Kitchener had been in effect, though not in name, Chief of the Imperial General Staff as well as Secretary for War, initiating strategy as well as directing his Department. The results had not been satisfactory, and he was pressed to appoint an effective C.I.G.S. The choice fell on Sir William Robertson, who laid down detailed rules for his position which excluded the Secretary for War, and as a result the Cabinet, from the formation of strategy. Though no outstanding leaders emerged during the war, Allenby, Haig, Plumer, and Wilson were not completely lacking in imagination, but Robertson behaved at times as though having ideas was a symptom of pro-German tendencies. The new commander in France, Douglas Haig, had a more open mind; like Robertson he was committed to the policy of unremitting concentration on the western front, but it was his job to win in France, while it was Robertson's duty as C.I.G.S. to think about the war as a whole. Haig was quite ready to look at new suggestions like the tank and to consider rearrangement of forces in the west, and to accept civilian experts like Sir Eric Geddes, who was made a major-general so that he could

[1] Geddes's views are discussed in B. H. Liddell Hart, *Memoirs* (1965), ii. 532.

organize transport more effectively. Although Haig was not enthusiastic about unity of command (which, given the larger numerical contribution made by the French, naturally meant a French commander-in-chief), he was distinctly less opposed to it than Robertson.

The triumph of the conscriptionists, and the changes in command, came at a time when the war was beginning to have a distinct effect on British society. During the first year of the war the position of women did not change very much; during the next twelve months the shortage of men led to the appearance of women in all sorts of work that had been done by men. Girls making munitions, land girls working on farms, and bus-conductresses seem to have been the most obvious signs of a changed world. The decline in the number of domestic servants is some-times overestimated. Their numbers fell by only 25 per cent during the war. Many of the new women workers had not previously had jobs—they came from the classes in which women who worked were not thought respectable. Women munition-workers would probably have worked in mills or factories before the war; it was women from higher up the social scale whose position had been changed by the war.

Trade unionists were not happy with their position early in the war. They were ready to accept women workers under the rules for 'dilution' —allowing unskilled workers to do work that had previously been reserved for skilled men. On the other hand they wanted to make sure that wages kept pace with the rapidly rising cost of living, and they had no intention of losing the rights they had built up in negotiations before the war. The fiercer conscriptionists said that the soldiers in the trenches had no use for trade unionists quarrelling over who should do what. But soldiers sometimes wrote back from the trenches to tell their brother unionists not to give up the Rule Book; they were fighting to preserve liberty, and for them the Rule Book was a substantial part of liberty. In forming his 1915 coalition Asquith brought in Henderson, the leader of the Labour party. Asquith disliked creating new ministries, so at first Henderson was nominally President of the Board of Education, but it was understood that he would act as Minister of Labour.

The government preferred to do business with people who employed union labour, partly to show that the government was treating labour fairly and partly because it had been realized that union labour would strike less often and could be negotiated with more easily than non-union labour. The Ministry of Munitions was particularly insistent that its contractors should employ union labour, because this meant that troubles could be dealt with before they led to a strike. Lloyd George was not himself a very good negotiator in labour disputes, except in the sense that he was prepared to be rather generous with the employers' money for the sake of harmony,[1] but the conduct of his ministry did change the pattern of labour relations for most of the country. Union membership rose steadily throughout the war, and trade union leaders were accepted as men who could make a serious and statesmanlike contribution to the war effort.

The war led to enormous profits for manufacturers in any way connected with the war effort. The comfortable classes sneered at these profits and suggested that there was something immoral about becoming rich during a war, but if the government was not going to control the economy and was going to rely on private manufacturers, the manufacturers were bound to make profits. They also made enemies, as can be seen from the complaints about *nouveaux riches* heard so often for a dozen years after 1914. The response of the unions was more straight forward. They had no special status that was menaced by the success of the munition-millionaires, but they wanted some of the money. When the traditional union leaders were too committed to the war effort, new leaders emerged. The shop stewards, unpaid organizers in factories, took over some of the functions of the paid union officials for wage negotiating. Their position was particularly strong on the Clydeside, where discontent was increased by the housing conditions, bad enough at the best of times and made much worse by the influx of new workers.

In Britain, the government interfered with personal liberty much less than in other countries in the war. However, the Defence of the Realm Act entitled it to do a great many things by Order in Council, including imprisoning people for hindering the war effort. Relatively few people were worried by this and probably more people were annoyed by the government's persistent policy of diluting beer than by infringements of the more textbook forms of liberty. Ordinary members of the working class felt that, what with light beer and steps towards industrial conscription, the war was not really being fought for them at all, and some Liberal and Socialist intellectuals supported them in this view. The government deported a few shop stewards to other parts of the country; it also imprisoned conscientious objectors. Neither group of 'prison graduates' rose as high in politics as their Irish contemporaries, but they were not to be without influence after the war; their influence was likely to be opposed to any idea that the Labour party could treat the Liberal party of Asquith and Lloyd George (the two Prime Ministers who had interfered with their liberty) as a party of the Left.

[1] G. R. Askwith, *Industrial Problems and Disputes* (1920), 394–5, on his settlement of the South Wales coal strike in 1915.

Pacifists were not a legal problem until after conscription. Some people had been opposed to British foreign policy, such as MacDonald and the left-wing fringe of the Liberal party who formed the Union for Democratic Control (that is, control of foreign policy). Some people thought it wrong to fight in the war, because they thought shedding blood was wrong or because they thought the war was wicked. When conscription came, the government set up tribunals to investigate the sincerity of the 'conscientious objectors'. The tribunals tended to be more sympathetic to an objection based on long-standing religious principles than to any other, and they had relatively little difficulty in finding non-combatant duties for anyone who was simply concerned to avoid killing his fellow men. Agricultural work could be accepted as work of national importance, and many conscientious objectors spent the war digging. The position of the most rigorous objectors, who believed the entire war to be wicked, was harder. If they were lucky they were sentenced to two years' imprisonment, with the prospect of further imprisonment if they declined to join the army on release. If they were less lucky they were put into the army, which inevitably led to a series of field punishments for refusing to obey orders, and a number of objectors did not survive this process.

Once conscription had been enacted, the generals could plan to attack in France. The initiative was not entirely in their hands. The only important German attack in France between 1914 and 1918 was the 1916 onslaught on the fortress of Verdun. It was chosen for attack because the French could not afford to lose it, but on the other hand were in so unfavourable a position, with artillery massed on three sides of the town, that they were likely to suffer more than the attackers. Verdun held out, but the French army was cruelly punished and its commanders became more and more insistent that the British should attack elsewhere to relieve the pressure.

The government had problems closer to home. The willingness of the Home Rule party to support the war had alienated the more determined nationalists, and a few of them prepared to fight for independence under the leadership of Paidrig Pearse and James Connolly. At Easter a rebellion broke out in Dublin, and Pearse was proclaimed President of the Irish Republic. The rising was suppressed after a few days of bitter fighting. Most of the surviving rebel leaders were tried by court martial and shot, which inflamed hostility to England in the United States, where Irish opinion was of some importance—Eamonn de Valera, one of the leaders of the rising, was saved from execution because he was an American citizen. After the rebellion Lloyd George brought the Ulstermen and the Home Rulers together, and succeeded in getting them to agree on a scheme for granting Home Rule, but the landed interest in the Cabinet, led by Lansdowne and Long, declined to accept the scheme, and what proved to be the last chance to settle the Irish question peacefully was lost. Yeats wrote that in Easter 1916 a terrible beauty was born; there was also born an Irish determination to settle the question without bothering about parliamentary methods.

At the end of May the German High Seas Fleet steamed out into the North Sea. On 31 May it met the British Grand Fleet in a confused action, the battle of Jutland. The fast, easily manœuvrable battle-cruisers of the two fleets were the first to meet; the German battle-cruisers drew the British on until they were almost in contact with the entire German fleet. The German fleet pursued the battle-cruisers until, early in the evening, the German fleet found itself immediately to the south of the British fleet. The British had not planned this, and had suffered losses in reaching this position; nevertheless the immense and unquestioned power of the British battle-line meant that the German fleet was on the brink of destruction. It turned away, on a course that took it to the west so that it was cut off from its base; when it tried to steam east, its move had been anticipated and the British line-of-battle was waiting for it. The Germans turned away to the west again, and by this time it was too dark for the British to be sure of keeping in touch. Because of this, and because some intercepted German wireless messages were not sent on to the British commander, the German fleet was able to slip past the British in the night. In terms of ships sunk Jutland was a German success; however, the battle demonstrated that the German fleet could not stand and fight, and so British command of the sea was secure. A decisive British victory would have had effects on the morale of both countries, but it could not have affected the strategy of the war very much.

A few days later British morale was affected more sharply than by the failure to win decisively at Jutland. Kitchener, the Secretary for War, was shipwrecked and drowned on his way to Russia. His reputation among his colleagues was by this time low, but he was still greatly admired outside the circle of the men at the top. After a short tussle his place was taken by Lloyd George. Asquith had wanted to take the War Office himself, which would have solved the problems of keeping the government in touch with the military administration. The Conservative leaders objected, and in view of Asquith's lack of driving force, they were probably right. But Lloyd George's emergence as Secretary for War, with Tory support, led Mrs. Asquith to fear that her family's days in Downing Street were numbered.

Once installed at the War Office, Lloyd George tried to remain some of the control over strategy that Kitchener had surrendered to Robertson. Before he could make any progress in this direction the battle of the Somme had begun, and for the rest of the year the British army was committed to the struggle. The desire to relieve the strain on Verdun, the feeling that it was time for the new armies raised since the beginning of the war to do something, and the belief that the war could be won only by a direct attack on the Germans all combined to make the battle a natural part of British policy. There was a less satisfactory reason for joining battle: in 1915 the idea had grown up, initially at Joffre's headquarters, that as the population of England and France exceeded that of Germany, victory could be won by a process of attrition which would leave a surplus on the Anglo-French side; this surplus would emerge even if the Anglo-French losses were up to 25 per cent higher than those of the Germans. The Somme began disastrously. After an enormous and remarkably ineffective bombardment, vast, well-disciplined masses of troops marched forward in rigid lines, and in rigid lines they fell before the German machine-guns. Nearly 60,000 men (about 1 per cent of the entire male population of military age) were killed or wounded on 1 July 1916, the first day of the battle. The battle lasted for four-and-a-half months, and though the casualties were not at the same high rate they remained damaging enough. The British losses were over 400,000, the French perhaps 200,000. Argument about the German losses still goes on; though the Official History places them at 680,000 it seems unlikely that the defenders would lose more men than the attackers, who neither broke nor outflanked their lines, and later criticism suggests that the official estimate was 30 per cent too high. Certainly the battle on the Somme did not tie down German military strength; while it was going on, the German armies in the east were forcing Rumania to make peace.

At this moment, as Lord Beaverbrook (then Sir Max Aitken) put it,

a strange figure sprang into the arena to do battle.
It was clad in a jewelled breastplate set in a vesture of rags and tatters. It faltered in its walk and yet sprang with a wonderful swiftness. The sword looked as fragile as a rapier and yet smote with the impact of a battleaxe.[1]

Lloyd George was indeed a most improbable war leader. Like Churchill in the Second World War he had been a partisan and controversial figure in pre-war politics; unlike Churchill his physical courage was not beyond question. And, again unlike Churchill, he had not spent time before the war arousing interest in rearmament; his main concern had been with

---

[1] Lord Beaverbrook, *Men and Power* (1956), 344.

social reform, and his chief supporters had been men of a pacific inclination in politics. He was a great orator, but not an orator whose phrases will be remembered—whether dealing with one man or with a crowd he could gauge exactly what his listeners were thinking, and could adapt what he had to say so that their interests and his interests always seemed to be the same. When he roused people to enthusiasm it was more by the way that he seemed to express their own best instincts than by an eloquent statement of new ideals.

The Somme convinced him that the generals had no idea how to handle the Western front. He had three ideas for strategy: unity of command, switching troops to Italy, switching troops to the east end of the Mediterranean. To make any one of them effective, he had to regain control over strategy. In the struggle to change the system of government in 1916 his determination to fight an all-out war gained him allies who agreed neither with his views on strategy nor with his ideas about the relationship between generals and politicians.

President Wilson hinted at a negotiated settlement; Lloyd George stepped forward and, entirely ignoring the existence of the Foreign Secretary, said in a press interview on 29 September that England and France would end the war by a 'knock-out' blow. He had accepted the logic of conscription to the full: under the voluntary system England could think in terms of an almost infinitely protracted war, but once she was committed to maintaining a large army there was a definite limit to the length of time she could fight. The enormous industrial effort brought this limit all the closer; at the Somme the English superiority over the Germans in the supply of munitions was one of the things that had depressed the German generals. But fighting in this immensely expensive way could not go on for ever; apart from the strain on industry, there was the strain on foreign exchange and foreign credit imposed by the need to import material from the United States. Credit was by no means exhausted at the end of 1916, but it would not last for ever.

Lloyd George's talk of a 'knock-out blow' upset his Liberal colleagues, and it encouraged the section of the Conservative party which thought that the country should make an unlimited effort. On 8 November the Commons debated a sale of property in Nigeria that was supposed to symbolize the desire to get on with the war. So many Conservatives voted against the government that Law felt it was necessary to come to terms with Carson, the leader of the rebels. Carson, Law, and Lloyd George were brought together by a Conservative backbencher, Sir Max Aitken, and at the end of November they proposed to Asquith that he should appoint the three of them as an executive committee for running the war.

Asquith accepted the scheme, in a modified and weakened form; Lloyd George sent Asquith's proposal on to Law, with a brief note 'The life of the country depends on resolute action by you now.'[1] In an interview with Law, Asquith gained the impression that the Conservative leaders would resign if the scheme was not accepted in its original form, and he agreed to set up the committee on condition he could attend its meetings whenever he chose. Then he discovered that, except for Law, the Conservative leaders were not committed to the scheme; on the whole they were hostile to Lloyd George but what they really wanted was a settlement of the conflict one way or the other. Heartened by this, Asquith withdrew his acceptance of the scheme. Lloyd George then resigned, and it became clear that Asquith could not reconstruct his government and replace his War Minister. Accordingly he in turn resigned.

Asquith's motives and hopes at the time of resignation have been a matter of controversy. Some historians have suggested, apparently following an account written by Lord Beaverbrook, that Asquith intended his resignation as a tactical move to show that he was the only man who could form a government. However, Beaverbrook made it quite clear that by the end Asquith had to resign.[2] His hopes of returning were quite well founded because he knew almost all his Liberal colleagues would not serve under anyone else, and four of the more important Conservative Cabinet ministers had also pledged their support. Asquith declined to serve under anyone; Lloyd George first gained the support of Balfour, Milner, the majority of the Labour party, and about half the Liberal party (126, of whom almost all were backbenchers and none were in the Cabinet) before he could break down the resistance of the Conservative ministers who had been on Asquith's side. But when they joined him, any hopes Asquith may have had that he would return to office as the indispensable Prime Minister were dashed.

Lloyd George's first year

Asquith had tried to run the war by allocating responsibility for new problems to ministerial committees, of which the War Committee was the most important, and he relied on the Cabinet to co-ordinate their decisions. But the committees could not meet often enough and the Cabinet turned out to be too slow-moving to be an effective co-ordinating body. Lloyd George set up a number of new ministries, and he established his executive committee as a War Cabinet of five—Law, who was to be Leader of the Commons, a post previously held by the Prime

---

[1] Lord Beaverbrook, *Politicians and the War* (1960), 406.
[2] Ibid. 452.

Minister unless he sat in the Lords, Curzon and Milner, who as imperial pro-consuls in India and South Africa respectively were accustomed to taking decisions, Henderson as the representative of labour, and himself. The Cabinet in its previous form disappeared; the new Cabinet was the direct descendant of the War Committee of Asquith's Cabinet, freed from the need to refer things back to any larger authority. The War Cabinet continued and extended the War Committee's practice of calling experts, civil servants, and ministers who were not members; the C.I.G.S. and the First Sea Lord had been at many meetings of the War Committee and continued to attend the new War Cabinet. The War Cabinet, like the War Committee, kept minutes and it inherited the Committee's invaluable Secretary, Hankey, who had done much to make Lloyd George think the War Committee was the model to follow. As the new Cabinet ministers, except for Law, had no departmental duties, they could meet every day, which the War Committee had not been able to do.

On the whole the new ministries were successful, though Lord Devonport, the first Minister of Food, was a conspicuous exception. This threatened the whole British war effort, because food was beginning to be short by the beginning of 1917. The Minister of Agriculture encouraged farmers to plough up grazing land by giving guaranteed prices, in order to increase grain production. But Devonport was convinced that rationing was undesirable and concentrated on issuing statements of the amount that people ought to eat. His suggestions were ignored. He had to be replaced by Lord Rhondda, a man of considerable political experience, who began by imposing fixed prices and, when this left demand understandably unchecked, moved towards rationing. Early in 1918 cards were issued which entitled the holder to a fixed amount of meat, and as the year went on the scheme was extended. In July books were issued that contained coupons to buy a fixed quantity of meat, sugar, butter, margarine, and cooking fat. Prudently, additional cards were included in the booklet, so that if any other food had to be sold in limited quantities the machinery would be available.

In other new ministries Sir Joseph Maclay was very successful in organizing Shipping, and Lord Beaverbrook was equally successful in organizing propaganda at the Ministry of Information. Despite his later doubts about its worth, Geddes ran the National Service system efficiently, Northcliffe had a triumphant period in the United States co-ordinating the British and American war efforts, and Lord Cowdray did reasonably well at the Air Board. By bringing these business men into the new departments Lloyd George made them feel part of the political community; before the war it had been hard for anyone who had not retired from all connection with business to be considered for a political position, but in 1916 the business men provided a new supply of talent, with experience of running larger concerns than civil servants had handled. The long-term results cannot have pleased Lloyd George, for the business men became convinced that once they were established in politics no more reforms were needed; before the war 'a business men's government' would have been a radical cry, but after the war it was a reactionary slogan.

While most of the new posts went to business men, the Ministry of Labour and the Ministry of Pensions went to Labour M.P.s. Once the Liberal party was divided, the Labour party could not simply follow the Liberals and had to devise a policy for itself. The appointment to office of Labour M.P.s reminded people that Labour was an important part of the economy and had to be treated seriously.

The year 1917 was the one in which prices ran furthest ahead of wage rates, and the effect of a once-for-all shift into better jobs was wearing off for most workers. As the government was not sufficiently in control of the economy to stabilize prices, it had to allow wages to go up, with all the dislocation that wage negotiations involve. This economic discontent began to make trade unionists think that perhaps the war was not as unquestionably justified as they had previously believed. Until 1917 the objections to the war of the Liberal and Socialist intellectuals had gained very little support; Galsworthy had suggested, with memories of the Boer War, in *The Mob* (produced in March 1914) that an anti-war speaker might get lynched, and although this never happened meetings were broken up and opponents of the war were beaten up. MacDonald had to resign the leadership of the Labour party in 1914 because he opposed British entry to the war; whatever his views of Grey's diplomacy, he did not say that the war was wicked, but he insisted so strenuously that Britain should take any chance to secure a negotiated peace that he was regarded as an ally of the people who said the war was wicked.

Henderson became leader of the party in the House of Commons but insisted that there was to be no proscription of MacDonald, who remained Treasurer of the party, or of the pacifists. Henderson's restraint may seem natural and obvious, but at the time it was not at all an easy matter. In all the countries at war, parties of the Left were invited to co-operate with the government. In France, Germany, and Italy they not only co-operated with the government, but also purged their ranks of their anti-war colleagues. When war-weariness swept over the working class in 1917, the old parties of the Left could do very little about it. Their expelled colleagues could appeal to the example of Russia, which in

February had overthrown the Tsar; the pacific Left in Europe was pro-Russian before Lenin and the Bolsheviks seized power on a platform of 'peace, bread, and land' in the November Revolution, and it became all the more pro-Russian when it saw that Lenin was actually doing something to stop the war.

The English working class did not need to look to Russia in this way. Because there had been no splits and expulsions, MacDonald and the pacifists could put their case at party conferences, and by 1917 they were getting some response. Henderson was well aware of the growing desire for a negotiated peace, and had a good deal of sympathy with it. A proposed meeting at Stockholm of socialist leaders from all belligerent countries led to a crisis in the government: Henderson wanted to go; Lloyd George wanted him not to go, and also wanted him to stay in the Cabinet. If Lloyd George had accepted Henderson's resignation when it was first offered, they might have parted company in a dignified way instead of quarrelling in the House of Commons about where Henderson had had to wait while the Cabinet tried to decide whether to accept his resignation, but the principle was clear: Henderson and a large proportion of the Labour party wanted a negotiated peace, and were quite ready to act separately from either section of the Liberal party. George Barnes took Henderson's place in the War Cabinet, but he sat as an ambassador from labour, not as the leader of the Labour party.

Lloyd George had no desire for a negotiated peace and was not free to ask for one. He had been placed in power by people who thought Asquith was not getting on with the war; his policy had to be (as Clemenceau put it) '*Je fais la guerre*'. Lloyd George's energy and determination, and his readiness to sweep away any obstacle to making war were invaluable, and no one else in the country could make everybody feel that things were moving, that the government knew what it was doing and that effort would not go wasted and unappreciated. A great leader has to be a fountain of ideas and of inspiration: Lloyd George always had new ideas, was always ready to listen to other people's ideas, and was always able to inspire almost everyone with the belief that things were going well and could go even better.

His colleagues in the War Cabinet were also open to new ideas; his followers in the Commons, including his ministers, were much more ready to accept the dominance of the experts, just as Asquith had done. The most obvious example, and the one most nearly fatal to England's chances in the war, was Carson, who had become First Lord of the Admiralty in the new government. He had complete, and unjustified, faith in his Sea Lords; in normal times this might have done no harm, but the Admiralty was about to be faced with a crisis. At about the same time as Lloyd George was overthrowing Asquith the German government was also going through an upheaval in which the men determined to wage all-out war were successful. The significant difference in Germany was that these men were unable to resist the military High Command. Submarine warfare was the vital issue: naval calculations suggested that if submarines waged unrestricted warfare, torpedoing without warning any ships they saw, then England would be cut off from imports and unable to carry on after August. The Germans realized this policy had the disadvantage that it would probably bring the United States into the war. However, they knew the United States could not do anything before August.

Unrestricted submarine warfare began; American ships were sunk and American lives were lost (the British blockade was distasteful to the United States, but nobody had been killed). On 6 April 1917 the United States entered the war. Britain and France were now bound to win if they could hold out until the U.S. could take an effective role in the war. If there had been no submarine warfare, and no American entry to the war, British financial credit might easily have broken down, and the British and French might have found themselves with neither equipment nor men to resist the German attacks of early 1918. But so many ships were sunk that the German calculations seemed justified. The rate of losses rose from 1·1m. tons in 1915 and 1·5m. tons in 1916 to about 2·5m. tons in the first half of 1917. Despite efforts to economize on shipping and a few steps towards the rationing of food, it was estimated that England would have to ask for peace. The Admiralty wrung its hands and said everything possible was being done but that, with 2,500 ships a week coming into English ports, it was impossible to protect them all. And Carson remained immobile in his support of his naval subordinates who seemed unable to do anything.

Lloyd George made his inquiries, consulting junior officers secretly and in defiance of custom. He learnt that, out of the 2,500 ships, 2,400 were in the coasting trade; only 100 ships a week had to be protected against attacks on the high seas. The Admiralty had insisted that merchant seamen were incapable of the precise navigation needed for sailing in convoy; Lloyd George showed that they were already sailing the Channel in convoy. At the end of April the War Cabinet made it known that the convoy system was going to be imposed on the Admiralty; on 30 April Lloyd George and Curzon took the Admiralty over for the day, saw that convoys would be organized, and arranged for the creation of a naval general staff. It is not formally correct to say that Lloyd George changed naval policy during his visit, because the admirals had been given two or three days' notice that they would have to submit, but this was one of the decisive interventions of the war. And it was one that made Lloyd George even less respectful about expert opinion than before. Convoys did not solve the problem immediately; about 0·5m. tons of shipping was sunk while travelling in convoy. Nevertheless the crisis was over.

Lloyd George had schemes for winning the war on land as well as for saving it at sea. His proposal that troops should be sent to Italy was unsound in principle; it was perfectly true, as the staffs told him, that if British or French troops were moved to the Italian front, the Germans could move troops to meet them and, because they had better rail communications, would be able to do it faster. There was much more to be said for his next proposal, that there should be a unified command in France, but instead of winning support for it by argument in the War Cabinet and presenting it to Robertson as official policy, he slipped it through the Cabinet and brought it forward without preparation at a conference with the French about transport. Nivelle, the French commander, was accepted by the British generals as commander for the duration of the coming offensive, but they did not feel any more inclined to trust Lloyd George after this, and the abrupt manner of command which Nivelle revealed on one or two occasions made matters worse. There were several weak points in the German front at the beginning of 1917; as Hindenburg and Ludendorff, who had been given control of the entire German army in August 1916 and had gone on to assert their control over the politicians as well, were still intent on operations in the east, they withdrew in the west to the well-prepared defences of the Hindenburg line, and Nivelle was left aiming a blow into empty space. He hastily reorganized his attack and in April threw his army against the German line of the Chemin des Dames. His attack was more successful than that of Joffre in 1915 or that of Haig in 1916, but his army had expected a decisive victory. The French soldiers suffered heavy losses and they refused to go forward again, though they defended their own lines; while Pétain coaxed them back to some semblance of fighting spirit by the end of the year, any further full-scale attack in 1917 would have to be by the English.

Haig's offensive east from Ypres is one of the hardest things to explain in the whole war.[1] It is fairly certain that he did not make it to take pressure off the French; it appears that he did not know the extent

[1] J. A. Terraine, *Haig* (1963), 298; Royal United Services Institution *Journal* (published in London), Nov. 1959, B. H. Liddell Hart, 'Basic Truths of Passchendaele'.

to which the French were paralysed by the mutinies. In part he was driven on by the incorrect belief of Jellicoe, the First Sea Lord, that the submarines mainly operated from Belgian ports and could be overcome only by the actual capture of the ports. In part he was led on by a belief that the morale of the German army was breaking down; this was also incorrect. He attacked in what had become the traditional manner: an enormously heavy artillery barrage, followed by an infantry attack. The weakness of this method was that it rested on a great overestimate of the effectiveness of shells; only a very small proportion of shells fired ever killed or even wounded anyone.[1] Staff calculations spoke of a barrage 'which no man could live through'; in pursuit of this elusive goal they put a larger and larger quantity of high explosive into the area they wanted to occupy. This was, apart from being a fairly clear guide to the German command where to put its reserves, a rash gamble with the weather. August, when Haig began his attack from Ypres, was wetter than usual; the barrage broke up the drainage system and condemned the troops to advance into a morass. September was a month of drought, with a rainfall under a quarter of the normal amount.[2] The policy of artillery bombardment was more successful and a series of three neat and small advances were made with its help. October was again wet; the British army forced its way through the last few thousand yards of mud to the village of Passchendaele in November.

Liddell Hart tells the story of the staff officer who was driven up towards the front line. When he entered the great bog he said: 'Good God, did we send men to fight in that?' 'It gets worse further on' was the answer, and around the battle-line the mud was so deep that a man who left the well-defined paths—which were under shell-fire—could sink in it and, encumbered by his service equipment, drown.[3] Passchendaele was one of the extreme horrors of the war, but anyone who considers the general conditions under which men fought in France and Belgium will be astonished that so few people broke down under the strain of the constant presence of death, the absence of any chance of a swift and heroic offensive, and the natural discomforts of mud, lice, cold, and isolation. Soldiers in other wars have had the consolations of inspired leadership, or the hope of loot, or the thought that it would soon be over. In the First

[1] In the first five months of fighting at Verdun 37 million shells were fired, and there were about 500,000 casualties, of whom a great number were killed or wounded by bullets, bayonets, gas, hand-grenades, shovels, and bare hands. A. Horne, *The Price of Glory: Verdun 1916* (1962), 300.

[2] D. Lloyd George, *War Memoirs* (1938—this edition contains letters from people who fought at Passchendaele), 1306.

[3] B. H. Liddell Hart, *The Real War* (1930), 367.

World War the generals were not in the front line, the war was fought in a narrow strip of devastated and desolated land which became more and more like the craters of the moon, and there was no sign that the remorseless grinding process would come to an end as long as there were men alive on both sides. The men who did break down under the strain met little mercy. Soldiers who would in later wars have been treated for shell-shock were court-martialled and shot.

The sacrifices of Passchendaele brought very little strategic advantage. The Germans were able to hold their line in the west and at the same time complete the destruction of Russia as an effective military force. Later in November a tank attack at Cambrai, where the land was unbroken by shellfire, gained in a couple of days about as much ground as the long slaughter of Passchendaele. The British commanders were convinced the German army was almost broken by the fighting for Passchendaele, and did little to prepare for a counter-attack on this newly gained territory which came at the end of the month and recaptured almost all the ground won by the tanks.

1918

Lloyd George had to put up with the generals because his own political position depended on Conservative votes and was never strong enough to allow him freedom of action. By the end of 1917 his colleagues in the War Cabinet agreed with his low opinion of English generalship and its constant passion for the offensive. But the House of Commons was another thing again, and Lloyd George did not feel confident of his position there. He thought it might be possible to control the generals either by returning to the policy of unity of command, or by restricting the number of men supplied to them. Unity of command became involved all too closely with the attempt to circumvent the power of Robertson as C.I.G.S. In February 1918 an Executive War Board was set up by the American, British, French, and Italian governments to control the military reserves; Lloyd George nominated Sir Henry Wilson as British representative, and made it clear that the C.I.G.S. would not have any authority over him. Robertson resigned rather than accept this division of power, and after failing to persuade Plumer to take his place, the War Cabinet gave it to Wilson who worked better with the politicians as C.I.G.S., though he was no more prepared than Robertson to share power with a general at Versailles.

The idea of unity of command seemed to have been dealt the final blow when Haig declined to contribute any troops to the proposed central reserve; he preferred to rely on an arrangement for exchanging reserves that he had worked out with Pétain. Wilson warned him that he might find Pétain's charity very cold. The British government did not press the point, because it did not want to have to provide any fresh troops; by this time its faith in Haig's estimates of future needs was very low because of his 'constant depreciation of the Germans when he wanted to attack'.[1] There were many other demands on any available manpower: ships and munitions had to be provided, people were sent back to the land to grow more food and the Navy and the Royal Flying Corps (changed to Royal Air Force in April) had to be expanded.

On 21 March the German armies attacked the British line just south of Arras, broke it and in a couple of weeks' fighting came very close to capturing Amiens and paralysing railway communication between the British and French. The attack showed that the trench line could be broken, and suggested that surprise, rather than the siege methods used previously, was the best way to do the job. A short bombardment to destroy communications rather than kill the defenders, an early morning attack to make use of any fog there might be, and small groups who pressed forward rather than neatly aligned waves of troops seemed to be the answer. Using these new tactics—or, rather, applying traditional tactics to a new situation—Ludendorff seemed able to break the English or French line at will. Five attacks between March and July met with varying degrees of success, but all of them gained more ground than the British advances on Cambrai the previous November over which there had been so much exultation. Under this pressure a Supreme Commander was at last appointed; Foch was accepted as generalissimo over the British, French, and American armies, though his powers were never as great as they sounded. His staff was small and the reserve at his disposal was never intact because of the calls made on the troops which might have been allotted to it before the 1918 battles began. His tactics were fairly simple; he encouraged the generals under his command to attack as soon as they could, and he tried to build up a strategic reserve to make this possible. But the German attacks went on, and the English and French were visibly not doing much more than holding on until American troops or German exhaustion saved them.

In London Lloyd George had passed through a period of difficulty. When Lord Lansdowne in November 1917 argued that the government should try to get a negotiated peace, an Asquith–Lansdowne ministry was thought possible. The desire to know what peace terms would be given to Germany was a sign that people were growing tired of the war, though not that they were ready to end it. Anti-German feeling was no

[1] M. P. A. Hankey, *The Supreme Command 1914–1918* (1961), ii. 803.

longer enough to keep up morale, and in early 1918 President Wilson made his War Aims explicit in his Fourteen Points. Lloyd George put roughly the same policy, though with a little less emphasis on self-determination, to the T.U.C., which was accepted as the leading respectable body supporting a negotiated peace. The aims of Wilson, Lloyd George, and the people who listened to them approvingly were not a real basis for a negotiated peace; no German government would accept the Fourteen Points except after military defeat. The statement of war aims was more an exercise in domestic public relations than in diplomacy, but it did show that the government had to take popular feeling seriously even in foreign policy. The Soviet publication of some of the secret treaties reduced people's willingness to let their governments carry on diplomacy in secret.

Lloyd George's government realized that it needed to show people what the country was fighting for. A Ministry of Reconstruction had been set up in 1917. A large measure of electoral reform was passed in 1918: it trebled the electorate by giving the vote to all men over 21, instead of confining it to householders, and also to women over 30—the age difference was introduced to make sure that men should remain a majority in the electorate. Plural voting was reduced to one extra vote for a university degree or for business premises. What attracted people's attention was the granting of votes to women, but this change did not have an immediately visible political effect. To some extent women had wanted the vote to assert their right to greater equality, and other changes were doing something to bring this about. It is impossible to say whether votes for women changed the basis of political struggle; new issues, such as housing and the non-religious aspects of education, became important after the war, and they may have been emphasized because women were likely to be interested. The vote may also have had defensive uses: in the years of high unemployment after the war there might have been attempts to stop women working if they had not been enfranchised; even so, the number of women in the labour force had fallen back to the 1911 level by 1921.

The effect of giving the vote to the one-third of adult males who had not previously been enfranchised was more far-reaching. If enfranchisement had come before the war the Liberal party would probably have got the largest share of these new votes because it had the organization to do the work and had a wider appeal among the poor than the Conservatives. But in 1918 the Liberal party was divided, and it had a rival for the votes of the poor. Two or three times as many people were organized in trade unions at the end of the war as at the beginning and so could be organized for the Labour party as well. Because it had had to think about foreign policy, and because it could no longer trust the Liberal party to follow a Gladstonian policy, the Labour party had to consider becoming a party of government in order to carry out its own foreign policy. While Henderson was in the Cabinet this tendency was held in check but after he had left the Cabinet on a foreign policy issue he was all the more willing to undertake the work of changing the party. As a negotiated peace was becoming more acceptable, the prestige of MacDonald in the party was rising and as the obvious domestic effect of the war had been an increase in measures of collectivist legislation, the great expert on collectivism, Sidney Webb, was drawn into the inner circles of the party.

By 1918 Lloyd George had demonstrated that the state could take over most of the economy and run it effectively enough to maintain 5 million men under arms and keep most of the population no worse off than they had been before the war. The old I.L.P. point seemed proved; if people were to be treated reasonably in the economic sphere, the first step was to nationalize industry. Clause IV of the new constitution adopted by the Labour party in 1918 included a commitment to nationalization; the founders of the I.L.P. had achieved their objective of setting up a party based on organized labour which would accept the policy of nationalization. The Labour party now had branches in constituencies, where they served as parallel organizations to the old I.L.P. branches. This was intended to make the party more attractive by enabling people to join it without having to join a socialist group like the I.L.P. though, as the Labour party itself was now socialist, the distinction was hard to see. The main effect of setting up Labour party branches on a separate basis was to leave the old I.L.P. branches in a position where they were bound to see themselves as the conscience of the party, and it might have led to a quieter life for everybody if they had been allowed to continue as the basis of the constituency organization of the Labour party.

The German offensive of March 1918 had political effects in England. It helped the Labour party by making reunion harder for the Liberals. In February Asquith had supported Robertson in his efforts to remain as C.I.G.S. with unrestricted authority; this made life no easier for Lloyd George, who came close to resigning on the issue. When the March offensive broke the English front, swift action had to be taken to repair the damage; a more skilful deployment of troops might have made the line harder to break, but once the attack had come it was too late to worry about such things. The government sent troops to France from

England and once again diverted people from making munitions into the ranks of the army—Hankey commented that 'the withdrawal of a few thousand engineers to the Army . . . caused the tank programme to fall by half', which illustrated why it was not possible both to keep the army at the strength the generals wanted and provide the weapons they wanted.[1]

When he explained the situation to the House of Commons Lloyd George said British troops in France in 1918 were at their 1917 level. The Director of Military Operations, General Maurice, published a letter in *The Times* on 7 May saying that the Prime Minister was not telling the truth. For the only time in the war Asquith made an attack on the Prime Minister which he carried to the extent of voting against the government; he was careful not to say that Maurice's figures were correct but he insisted that there should be a committee of inquiry. During the debate Asquith's case was destroyed; Lloyd George gave figures which, he stated, had been sent by General Maurice's own office. Apparently the original figures Lloyd George had used included British troops in Italy. Maurice had corrected them, and his figures in *The Times* were accurate though it is not clear Lloyd George knew this. In any case Maurice's letter was bound to look like an attempt to use confidential information to embarrass Lloyd George and benefit Asquith and the generals. The debate on Maurice's charges and the division, which the government won 293–106, relieved Lloyd George from the fear that he might lose control of the House of Commons. Two secretaries say that Maurice's corrected figures were later found in an unopened dispatch box, but that Lloyd George never saw this second version.[2]

By July the German army had committed almost all its reserves to the battle and, although it had broken the trench-line in several places and created very large salients, it had not been able to use these advantages to turn the flank of either the English or the French armies. The German attacks lost momentum and when the counter-attack began, at the end of July, the German position was very ill placed for resisting it. The salients created by the great offensive meant that the line was longer than it would otherwise have been, and because the reserves had been used up in attacks the German generals had lost almost all power to decide how they should defend themselves. The arrival of tanks in adequate numbers made their position worse; on 8 August a very successful British tank attack destroyed the last German chances of concentrating troops for a counter-

[1] M. P. A. Hankey, op. cit. ii. 829.
[2] Lord Beaverbrook, *Men and Power*, 262–3; John Gooch 'The Maurice Debate', *Journal of Contemporary History*, iii. 4.

attack.[1] On 29 September Ludendorff's self-control broke down and he declared that peace must be made at once; it is possible that the German diplomats could have made better terms for an armistice if they had not been hustled into the preliminary negotiations in this way. But by October it was quite clear that no effective resistance could be offered by the Germans on French soil. Their best hope was to carry out a very considerable retreat and then try to defend the Rhineland, but it was doubtful that the authority of the German High Command would have survived such a step.

Lloyd George's domestic position was accordingly eased, and he could look to the future. By mid-1918 people in England were showing signs of exhaustion, though not of any loss of determination. An influenza epidemic whose victims were comparable in number to the entire war-casualty list, struck Europe in the later months of 1918. The anti-German hysteria of the early stages of the war reappeared and this led to an Act against naturalized enemy aliens—that is to say, Germans who had come to England, taken out British citizenship, and settled down. The earlier attack on people of German origin could be rationalized by saying that after all they might be spies; by 1918 it was altogether more obvious that they were being persecuted because of their former nationality. Lloyd George summed up the feeling very well in a speech on 10 December when he said that he stood for 'Britain for the British'.

By that time he was involved in a general election. Probably an election would have been held late in 1918 whether the war was over or not. Lloyd George had to prepare for it; in September he invited Asquith to join the government as Lord Chancellor and take part in drawing up the Peace Treaties. Asquith said he would help with the Peace Treaties but did not intend to join the government. Lloyd George did not want Asquith (or Lord Northcliffe) at the peace conference untrammelled by ministerial responsibility. If Asquith would not join it, the Coalition would have to go on unchanged, and in October the Whips of the Conservatives and the pro-Lloyd George Liberals drew up an agreement by which the Conservatives would leave 150 seats uncontested, which would give Lloyd George as many Liberal followers after an election as he had in the existing House.

By November the war had drawn towards an end. The events of the last weeks did not provide decisive evidence to show what grand strategy should have been adopted in the war. The pressure was kept up in the

---

[1] 'Ludendorff in the most frequently quoted passage of his *Memoirs* described 8 August as "the black day of the German army"', C. R. M. Cruttwell, *A History of the Great War* (1934), 550.

west and the German army was driven back, but on the other hand
Germany's three allies, Turkey, Bulgaria, and Austria-Hungary all
collapsed shortly before she was forced to ask for an armistice. Italy had
ceased to be much of a danger to Austria after the battle of Caporetto in
October 1917. Turkey had first been driven out of Arabia and then
defeated in Palestine and Syria, but while the campaigns of Allenby and
the guerrilla warfare of T. E. Lawrence had been interesting and
imaginative, they were never a danger to vital German interests. On the
other hand, Germany had been obliged to divert resources to help her
allies. The fiercely committed Lloyd George, supported by the somewhat
more impartial Hankey, argued that the collapse of her allies left
Germany helpless; the supporters of the claims of the western front
pointed out that all through the war the number of men fighting in
France was much larger than in any of the areas that distracted Lloyd
George's attention, so that if the Germans had won in France they could
have mopped up all the other theatres of war at their leisure; and the
supporters of the blockade stressed the industrial and domestic weakness which was depriving Germany of the means to continue the war.

One historian of the war, unable to determine what was decisive, concluded: 'The simple truth is that Germany ended the war because she
had come to the end of her endurance, and it is doubtful whether any
other country would have endured so long.' The tribute to what Liddell
Hart called 'an epic of military and human achievement' is not un-
deserved; because of the blockade, and because the generals took too
many people from the farms for the army, the Germans were at an
immense disadvantage, and the German and Austrian urban populations suffered much worse than anybody else, except the inhabitants of
the areas that were overrun by the armies.[1] At all levels but the highest,
German strategy would have been hard to improve; in the realm where
strategy joins hands with diplomacy it was disastrous, because it made
Britain's entry certain when she might have stayed out, and it provoked
the United States' entry quite unnecessarily. But, apart perhaps from the
shifting of the weight of force away from the original pattern of the
Schlieffen Plan, it is very hard to see any way in which the German
generals could have handled better the problem of being outnumbered
and forced to fight on two fronts that they had created for themselves.

However deserved the tributes to the Germans, the countries opposed
to them showed no less capacity for endurance. An American who had
seen the last stages wrote: 'This western front business couldn't be
done again, not for a long time. The young men think they could do it

---

[1] Cruttwell, op. cit. 597; B. H. Liddell Hart, op. cit. 508.

but they couldn't. . . . This took religion and years of plenty and tremendous sureties and the exact relation that existed between the classes. . . . You had to have a whole-souled sentimental equipment going back further than you could remember.'[1] The English writers who had begun the war in a mood of nobility untouched by reality became silent. It was impossible to describe what was going on in the trenches, except in words that showed that no long-term benefits promised by politicians could justify the suffering. The most immediate impact was that of Sassoon, whose *Counter-Attack* (1918) was published while the war was on, though the posthumous anti-war poems of Owen (1920) and Rosenberg (1922) have influenced subsequent writing rather more. When the war came to an end at 11 a.m. on 11 November 1918 the feeling of triumph and the desire for vengeance was uppermost in almost every-body's mind. This mood did not last, and one reason why it came to an end was that people began to realize—as they had never allowed them-selves to do while the war was on—just what it had been like to spend months and years in the trenches.

[1] F. Scott Fitzgerald, *Tender is the Night* (1934), 75.

4. *Rooted in nothing*[1]   1918–1922

The peace settlement of 1919

THE day after the Armistice was announced, Lloyd George told a gathering of about 150 of his Liberal followers that he was going to have an election. The Asquithian Liberals complained loudly, and the complaints have gone on ever since. But Lloyd George's decision to have an election was quite natural. Parliament had been sitting for eight years and had just trebled the electorate. The Asquithians never explained what else Lloyd George could have done: Asquith would not join the government, Lloyd George was not likely to step down from the Premiership and ask to be accepted as second-in-command of the Asquith party, and it was really not possible to tell the electorate to do without an election until the two Liberal leaders had sorted out their relationship.

On the other hand, if the government could unite the 'Lloyd George vote' and the Conservative vote (and the rather small vote of the pro-Coalition Liberals), it could look forward to an enormous majority. If the Liberals had been united, and had had the prestige of Lloyd George on their side, they would very possibly still have lost the election, but they would probably have emerged as an Opposition of a respectable size, in no danger of being overtaken by the Labour party. But if Lloyd George and the Conservatives were on the same side, there was very little hope for any Liberal candidate unless he had a guarantee of respectability from Lloyd George and Bonar Law. The guarantee of respectability— the letter, signed by Lloyd George and Law, saying that a candidate was a good and loyal servant of the Coalition—was the point that the Liberals

---

[1] 'Mr. Lloyd George is rooted in nothing', J. M. Keynes, *Essays in Biography* (1933), 37. The phrase was originally in his *Economic Consequences of the Peace* but was omitted in a not wholly successful attempt to make the book mild and conciliatory.

fastened on; Asquith called it 'the coupon' (i.e. a ration coupon), and 'the coupon election' it has remained. But, if Lloyd George's influence was going to be thrown against his old party, the 'coupon' was the only way that a Liberal remnant could be preserved.

While the distribution of the 'coupons' under the agreement made in October was natural enough, the course of the election ran steadily downhill. Lloyd George had told his Liberal followers on 12 November that he would take a line that Liberals would have no difficulty in following. During the campaign he never fully committed himself to the policy of hanging the Kaiser and making Germany pay which was supported by the ordinary run of pro-Government candidates, but his reservations were not very explicit: they might have been understood in the House of Commons, but were out of place in an election. The ordinary voter was interested in hearing that Germany was going to have to pay for the war; quite apart from any thoughts of revenge, it meant that the social benefits summed up in the phrase 'a fit country for heroes' would be provided without any extra taxation. Lloyd George did not use his position and prestige to warn the electorate that things might not be so easy—of course, he may really have thought that making Germany pay was a matter of making a German Minister of Finance sign a large cheque, but if he understood the situation he should have warned the electorate. An election is a great opportunity for political education, and a party which is likely to win a big victory has a particular responsibility to warn public opinion and avoid being swept along by uninformed popular feeling.

Any educating of the public in 1918 would have had to begin among the Coalition's own candidates, who clearly shared the feelings of the electorate. Neither the Asquithian Liberals nor the Labour party were immune from anti-German feeling and a belief in making Germany pay, though in both parties there were groups who urged restraint. Polling day came, with all constituencies voting on the same day for the first time, and the Coalition won an enormous majority.

	Votes	Seats	% of all votes cast
Coalition parties	5,121,259	478	47·6
Other Conservatives	663,097	48	6·1
Liberal	1,298,808	28	12·1
Labour	2,385,472	63	22·2
Sinn Fein[1]	486,867	73	4·9

The results were in one way even more devastating for the parties in opposition than the figures show. Not a single Liberal ex-minister was

[1] Sinn Fein ran only 102 candidates, of whom 25 were returned unopposed.

re-elected, and the most talented Labour leaders, MacDonald, Snowden, and Henderson, were also defeated; Adamson, the Scottish miner who had been made chairman of the parliamentary Labour party, was leader of the largest party sitting in opposition. The Labour party had put forward many more candidates than before the war, and had laid the foundations for a nation-wide effort, but the Labour Members elected in 1918 were trade unionists of the pre-war type. In the previous Parliament 25 of them had served as solid backbenchers; they had done no harm then, but their presence in the new Parliament showed that the opposition was weak in talent as well as in numbers. There were practically no Home Rulers in the new House. The Irish electorate had lost patience with the delays of the English parliamentary system and returned Sinn Fein Members who declared themselves to be the parliament of Ireland and did not come to Westminster.

These years immediately after 1918 are immensely crowded, and crowded with events that have little connection with one another. In the first half of 1919 Lloyd George was watching over demobilization, restraining his War Minister Churchill from sending the army to Russia to overthrow Lenin and the Bolshevik revolution, facing a series of strikes most of which were simple economic disputes but a few of which—like that of the miners with their demand for nationalization—had political implications that could not be neglected. And at the same time he was negotiating the Treaty of Versailles. He was accused of taking too much on himself. This may have been so, but his experiences with Churchill did not encourage him to delegate power very widely, and in any case Wilson and Clemenceau were at the Versailles negotiations so he had to be there.

Germany had asked for an armistice that would lead to a Peace Treaty which embodied Wilson's Fourteen Points. Roughly, very roughly, the Treaty did embody the Points but it fell away from them on a number of issues, always in the direction contrary to German interests. Lloyd George had to consider the situation at three distinct levels: because of the climate of opinion in England which had at the very least not been discouraged at the General Election, he could not assent to a Treaty that could be denounced for being too soft to the Germans; at the diplomatic level there were a great number of relatively secondary points on which England wanted her own way; and he was aware that it would not really be to her advantage in the long run to destroy Germany completely. It was particularly easy for England to be moderate in discussions about frontiers in Europe, because this was not what concerned her. The integrity of Belgium was taken for granted; after this, England was concerned with naval strength, colonies, and reparations. The German navy was in British hands as a result of the armistice and, just before the Treaty was signed, obligingly cleared the stage by scuttling itself. Colonies were out of fashion, but the British Empire spread wider yet, by taking over new territories as 'mandates', a term devised by General Smuts. Germany forfeited her colonies, which were in Africa and the Pacific; small slices in Africa went to France and Belgium, but the bulk of them went to England and the Dominions—Tanganyika was entrusted to England, South West Africa to South Africa, New Guinea to Australia, and Samoa to New Zealand. These transactions did have their symbolic importance for the Empire or, as it now began to be called, the Commonwealth. The Dominions had undertaken one of the functions of sovereign states by organizing their own war efforts, and they now undertook another, almost anachronistic function by acquiring new territory by right of conquest; President Wilson found the Australians a little too outspoken about this for his taste. Undoubtedly the position of the Dominions had altered, though the direction in which the Commonwealth was moving was not yet decided. Botha of South Africa, Borden of Canada, and Hughes of Australia, the major Dominion Prime Ministers of the war years, were good nationalists, and at the same time were strongly in favour of the British connection. All three were self-confident men; they had no fear that close association with England would necessarily mean that their countries would become subordinate to her. In 1917 Lloyd George had held an imperial Conference which was more detailed in its discussions and more willing to take decisions than previous Conferences had been, and it was referred to as the Imperial War Cabinet; it had a common policy, that of beating Germany, and needed only to agree on ways of carrying out that policy. The Prime Ministers hoped that after the war they could continue on the same basis, with a common policy worked out in discussion and applied by a united Empire. In the past the countries in the Empire had been committed by British policy, in the sense that if England was at war all the Dominions were legally in a state of war, but they had not been obliged to do anything about it. The British government could put pressure on them to help, as Chamberlain had pressed the governments of the self-governing colonies to help in the Boer War. But in the Empire that Lloyd George envisaged the Dominions would be politically committed to help, because they would have helped to form policy. Whether this was practicable remained to be seen, but at Versailles the Commonwealth acted as a unit though the autonomy of its members was recognized when they signed the Treaty as individual countries; at first it had been suggested that the Dominions were only pawns in the hands of the British government, but this went down very badly with the Dominion representatives who pointed out that they had done as much in the war as any of the countries at Versailles except England and France.

While the treatment of the German colonies prompted questions about imperial relations, the division of Turkey-in-Asia was mainly an Anglo-French problem. The negotiators accepted the Sykes–Picot agreement of 1916 which meant that most of these territories were to be partitioned between England and France; they also accepted that the British government had special commitments because of the Balfour Declaration of 1917 which said that a National Home for the Jewish people would be set up in Palestine. It was clear that any promises to the Arabs, made in the course of persuading them to rebel against Turkish rule, would be ignored if they did not fit in with the Sykes–Picot and Balfour policies. The French were given a mandate for Syria (which contained what is now the Lebanon), England got mandates for Palestine, Iraq, and Transjordan, and the Arabs were left with Arabia and an understandable sense of grievance. When the Arab leader Faisal was eventually turned out of Damascus to make way for the French, he was compensated by being made ruler of Iraq, where the British had a form of mandate that would run for only a short time. Palestine, into which dedicated and industrious Jewish immigrants began to flow, was obviously going to be a harder problem; the Arabs who lived there lacked the skill and capital to compete with the newcomers, and regarded them with fear and resentment.

Reparations came closer to the heart of the Treaty. Lloyd George's first concern was to make sure that England got some share of whatever the Germans were made to pay. On a plain reading of the Fourteen Points and the accompanying correspondence, the Germans had promised at the time of the armistice to pay for the restoration of all civilian property destroyed in the war. Apart from merchant ships torpedoed, very little English civilian property had been damaged, and if the straightforward reading of the terms had been accepted, Lloyd George's boasts about making Germany pay would have looked very silly. The British government argued successfully that all war pensions should be included in the total bill to be paid, and it was really as a result of this decision that Reparations took the form so brilliantly and effectively attacked by Keynes in *The Economic Consequences of the Peace* (1919). Keynes's argument was that civilian damage would amount to £2 billion, and that this was just about the amount that Germany could pay; pensions would raise the cost to £7 or 8 billion, a completely impossible debt which would never be repaid and would cripple Germany. The implication of his book was that France had agreed to expand the debt to impossible dimensions in the hope of destroying all possibility of German economic recovery, and that this policy (which he called the 'Carthaginian Peace') was contrary to the interests of everybody involved. His argument was applauded at the time, and was soon accepted by the conflicting countries: the Versailles conference did not feel able to agree on the level of reparations, and referred the issue to a committee which fixed a nominal total of £6,600m. to be paid, but fairly clearly did not really hope to obtain much more than £2,500m.; this reduced figure was formally accepted in the Dawes Plan for payment worked out in 1924. The introduction of war pensions at Versailles had merely transferred to Britain a share in the payments, without having much effect on the total. Germany proved more or less able to keep up the payments until the international system broke down at the end of the twenties. Historians have argued whether Keynes's calculations were correct or not, often without noticing that the Dawes Plan accepted them.

Keynes's book made it intellectually respectable to condemn the Treaty, and people may have been too ready to follow the fashion. Even if there had been no argument over reparations, Germany was unlikely to obey the Treaty willingly. She had been disarmed but the other nations showed relatively little desire to adopt corresponding programmes of disarmament. Self-determination was supposed to be the guiding principle of the Treaty, but while there were good economic reasons for giving Danzig to Poland, good strategic and economic reasons for giving the Sudetenland to Czechoslovakia and good balance-of-power reasons for not allowing Austria to join Germany, each of these decisions ignored the principle of self-determination. French politicians justified the Treaty by arguing that Germany was a dangerous country and all Europe should devote its energies to holding her down for an indefinite time to come, but when they pressed for harsher terms, they might have asked themselves what chance they had of getting support for this policy; it was easy for them to feel sure that their country would remain hostile to Germany, but it was unwise of them to commit France to a policy which depended on perpetual support from England. A 'Carthaginian Peace' assumed that England would remain hostile to Germany, and as England would remain hostile to Germany only if Englishmen thought Germany was unreasonable and France was reasonable, the policy would not work unless France surrendered to England control over her foreign policy. What Keynes did in his book was to convince Englishmen (and Americans) that the Germans of the Weimar Republic were no worse than any other European statesmen—a fair if unexacting standard—and it was irrelevant that he showed this by analysing the reparations settlement which was rapidly corrected, when the provisions which 'laid the foundations of a just and durable war' were concerned with armaments and frontiers. These clauses were not seriously changed until Chamberlain and Hitler got to work in the 1930s.

Wilson devoted most of his energies at Versailles to making sure that England and France joined the League of Nations; and this was a mis-directed effort, for both countries were willing to join. In England the League was seen as something like Gladstone's Concert of Europe, and Gladstonians like Bryce, Ramsay MacDonald, and General Smuts had done a good deal to develop the idea of the League. The Liberal and Labour parties welcomed it, but the Conservatives were more divided on the issue; some of them noticed that Article 16 committed Britain to war to resist aggression in a quarrel that did not concern her directly. In France the League was seen as something much more like an enforcement agency for the Treaty, and it would have been more helpful if Wilson had spent some time establishing just what it was to do. By the end of the negotiations, British interest was declining. Parliament had pushed Lloyd George in a 'Carthaginian' direction early in the negotiations, but towards the end Lloyd George had felt safe in urging a more moderate attitude on Wilson and Clemenceau.

People with a long historical perspective could see after the war that 'America was thus clearly top nation, and History came to a .'[1]—a comment which showed very clearly the British feeling that nothing was worth while if England was not superior to other countries. However, the United States and the Soviet Union kept off the centre of the world's stage for two more decades, and so Europe remained the part of the globe most likely to influence other countries. England emerged as the least devastated European country, with some claims to world dominance by default.

England had an additional claim on the attention of the world because she had been for about two centuries the chief seedbed of new ideas. The world that fought from 1914 to 1918 was the world of Locke, Newton, Adam Smith, Mill, and Darwin. The line had not come to an end: one important intellectual descendant of these men, J. M. Keynes, was just embarking on work that may turn out to be as significant as anything they did. He was a reasonable, logical man, with perhaps a greater gift for intellectual debate than any of them had possessed; Russell, probably the most distinguished English philosopher of the century, said of him:

---

[1] W. C. Sellar and R. J. Yeatman, *1066 and All That* (1930), 115.

'Obviously a nice man, but I did not enjoy his company. He made me feel a fool.'[1] People less concerned about their own intellectual standing found him charming and kind, except in debate. During the twenties he was laying the foundations of his serious work, and incidentally acquiring a fortune on the Stock Exchange; during the thirties he published the books which have convinced most people that it is not enough to run a government's finances like those of a household, making sure that there is a bit left over at the end of the year.

The post-war mood

But men were moving into a world whose main intellectual energy has come from members of the German–Jewish community. The Russian Revolution, and the difficulties of the capitalist system, inspired renewed interest in Marx's writings. Freud's ideas were breaking through to general acceptance; he was of course invoked to justify a somewhat over-due relaxation of the idea that sex, though widespread, was not respect-able,[2] but the more serious implication of his work was that men were dominated by their unconscious minds, over which they had very little control.

An eclipse of the sun (about a month before the Treaty was signed at Versailles) provided the first empirical evidence to support Einstein's Theory of Relativity. The Theory asserted that the speed of light was a limiting factor, because nothing could move faster; that it is not possible to say which of two unrelated events took place first; and that the dif-ference in time between the two events varies when they are seen from different points in space. People on this earth may think that the Battle of Hastings took place 900 years ago and that a new star has just exploded into prominence, but from some point in space the events will appear simultaneous.

The equations linking energy and mass suggested that matter could be disintegrated with explosive effect. Laymen amused themselves with the thought of 'splitting the atom' and blowing up the world. Rutherford, already a dominant figure in the study of radioactivity, made a reassuring statement that this was impossible. Einstein's theory was widely dis-cussed, partly because of a mere play on words: people thought from the name of the theory that it justified a relativist attitude to philosophical and moral questions. This was not a simple matter of ignorance. In the last act of Shaw's play *Too True to be Good* (1928) there is a major

[1] H. Nicolson, *Diaries* (1966–8), iii. 202.
[2] The enormous sales, and considerable scandal, of Marie Stopes's quite harm-less *Married Love* (1918) show how overdue the change was.

speech by an atheist of the Herbert Spencer school expressing the puzzlement such people felt, in moral as well as in scientific questions, as a result of the overthrow of the simple and easily calculable Newtonian laws of motion. The English thinkers of the previous period had assumed that a reasonable man could stand outside the system he was analysing and impose order upon it; Marx, Freud, and Einstein had a common tendency to deny the possibility of taking a detached and unbiased attitude.

The attitude of distaste for Victorianism which had been spreading before the war found expression in Strachey's *Eminent Victorians*, a set of satirical lives of four of the people honoured and respected as great Victorian figures. It was the first public triumph of Bloomsbury and the tendency to frankness and open analysis of motive which the disciples of G. E. Moore had been practising for some years. This attitude was not universal—most of the great political biographies of late Victorian figures were published in the twenties, and they were written with all the adulation and lack of analysis that Strachey had tried to combat—but the fashion of the decade was to look at Victorian prudery with disgust, at Victorian literature with amusement, and at Victorian architecture as little as possible.

Eliot's *The Waste Land*, first published in 1922, finally forced English poets to recognize the work of the French symbolist writers and stop trying to squeeze out a few more drops from the romantic heritage. Almost all the poets already writing were cut off from the people who started writing after *The Waste Land*. Transformations like that of Yeats, who turned himself into a symbolist, were rare, and most of the writers who had emerged in the volumes of *Georgian Poetry*, which began appearing just before the war and continued until 1922, went on writing as they had done previously. Apart from its effect on poetic style *The Waste Land* expressed a feeling, widespread among people who thought about such questions, that the world had suffered a mortal blow during the war. Until 1914 progress could be taken for granted: economic progress was visibly taking place, and everybody felt serenely confident that this implied progress in every other direction as well. There was some justification for this view: England and the whole of Europe were more kind-hearted in 1914 than they had been in 1815. But the war came, and demonstrated that human beings still had a great capacity for causing suffering. Economic progress went on after the war, but it was less easy to be certain that other sorts of progress continued. The war ended in the mood of 'the world's great age begins anew', but the problems of reorganizing society were large enough to make people soon ask 'What are the roots that clutch, what branches grow Out of this stony rubbish?'[1]

Lloyd George once described the House of Commons elected in 1918 as 'the Trade Union Congress on the opposition benches and the Chamber of Commerce on the government side'. Neither this, nor Keynes's more one-sided comment that 'they are a lot of hard-faced men who look as if they had done very well out of the war', was accurate: there were about 20 trade unionists and about 80 business men more than in 1910, and they did not between them make up a majority of the House.[2] But Lloyd George's comment did hit upon the two social changes that followed the war. At the time people talked rather more about the increased political strength of the working class and the possibility of 'Bolshevism', by which they meant anything from Leninist revolution to a reduction of the social and economic gap between the upper and middle classes and the working class. The proportion of the national income that went to the working class did increase between 1914 and 1920, but this did not last long.[3] A certain amount of social legislation was passed, and it became clear that trade unions would continue to be recognized as necessary parts of industrial organization. But none of this altered the relationship of the working class to their 'betters' nearly as much as the war altered relationships within the more comfortable classes.

If the people from the working class were better off by the end of the war than at the beginning, and if manufacturers inevitably became much better off, it might reasonably be asked who paid for the war. First, of course, all those who went off and fought did very badly economically as well as in other ways. Apart from them, the professional classes and the land-owning classes did badly. They were caught by six years of inflation

[1] Lord Curzon quoted the line of Shelley in moving the Address to the Throne to celebrate the end of the war. 18 Nov. 1918, *Lords' Debates*, xxxii. 165; the second quotation is from *The Waste Land*, lines 19 and 20.

[2] J. M. McEwen, 'The Coupon Election of 1918', *Journal of Modern History* (published in Chicago), vol. 34; J. M. Keynes, *Economic Consequences of the Peace* (1919), 133. Keynes attributed to 'a Conservative friend', believed to have been Stanley Baldwin, the remark about the hard-faced men.

[3] From S. Pollard, *Development of the British Economy 1914–1950* (1962), 289–90, it appears that

	Net income per head	Real wages
1920	100	100
1938	118·5	113

Some of the disproportion developed because more of the population was of working age.

and rising taxes, and could do relatively little to raise their incomes to
meet these changes. The most obvious sign of the times was the great
land sales of 1918–21, which produced a transfer of land on a scale
'probably not equalled since the Norman Conquest'.[1] The sales were said
to have been caused by the impact of death duties upon noble and
gallant families in which a number of owners were killed one after another, with duties to pay each time. This interpretation was too romantic:
the Death Duties (Killed in War) Act reduced death duties for the first
owner who was killed and remitted all duties for subsequent deaths in
action. In any case, it was not the owners who were killed; Curzon told
the Lords early in 1917 that six Peers and sixty-two heirs had been
killed,[2] and the death of an heir who had an infant son or a younger
brother would delay the incidence of death duties. The position of the
heirs probably suffered more from the tendency away from leaving the
whole estate to the eldest son. The 1922 Law of Property Act established
a legal preference for equal division of an estate and this weakened the
old system of land-holding. Perhaps because income-tax at 30p in the £
was too much for them, or because they decided that as land would never
again be a source of political power its low economic return was no
longer justified, the old land-owning class gave up the struggle. They
kept their urban land, which with the passing of time restored their
fortunes, they kept up a surprisingly large number of the smaller country-
houses, and they kept their unsaleable shooting-estates in Scotland, but
for the rest they sold out to their tenants or to manufacturers who wanted
a place in the country. There was an upper class in England before 1914,
in the sense that people owned property that gave them a claim on the
personal and political loyalty of their tenants; obviously this class had
been losing its power and equally obviously its power did not disappear
completely during the war. While Lord Derby continued to dominate
Lancashire politics it could not be said that the old upper class had gone,
but Derby's position was exceptional enough to illustrate by contrast
what had happened to the political power of the landowners.

An odd little political issue of the period shows the changes that were
taking place in the ruling class. Lloyd George, as has been noted, brought
business men into the government in 1916; he was in fact very willing to
establish them as members of the ruling class, and they were very willing
to encourage him to do so. The easy way to recognition was through the
granting of honours: the Prime Minister could advise the King to make

[1] F. M. L. Thompson, *English Landed Society in the Nineteenth Century* (1963),
332–3.
[2] 7 Feb. 1917, *Lords Debates*, xxiv. 21.

business men into peers, baronets, knights, or lesser notabilities on account of their contribution to the war effort. This would have been a sensible acceptance of a change in the social structure of the country, though there would probably have been objections from people who already had titles and did not want to be forced to face the changes that were taking place. Lloyd George gave honours lavishly to business men and people who liked neither Lloyd George nor business men could plausibly object to the process because they were being given in return for cash contributions to Lloyd George's political treasure-chest. This was not a complete novelty; honours had been sold previously, and everybody knew about it. But the scale of Lloyd George's operations, and the sort of people to whom he sold them, upset the feelings of the people who thought the existing class structure ought not to be disturbed. Estimates of the amount raised by the sale of honours range from £1m. to £6m.; even the lower figure, at the rates quoted of £10,000 for a knighthood and more for higher honours, disturbed the decent order of things, and also cast a doubt on honours that had been obtained by more conventional means.

The people who had done badly out of the war naturally complained, and were joined by people who had been doing badly in any case and could now blame the war, while those who had done well out of the war remained discreetly quiet. After a very short burst of enthusiasm for reconstruction, strong pressure for getting back to 'before the war' developed. Pre-war levels of government expenditure, pre-war social relationships between manufacturers and their betters, and pre-war patterns of trade were set up as the objectives to be achieved, though this die-hard programme could never be carried out. The manufacturers whom Lloyd George had brought into close relations with the Conservative party tended to settle down there; business men were not unknown in the pre-war Conservative party, but they had been much less important. They were not yet fully convinced of the desirability of Protection, but they were being drawn in that direction.

Tariffs were brought in to provide '"safeguarding duties" in any case in which an industry proved it was suffering from unfair competition. In this way we could build up a chain of cases which proved that protection was right'.[1] This chain of cases was likely to support all the traditional industries of the country, often faced with competition from countries with lower wages, so that they would not be forced to contract. New industries would find it relatively hard to establish a right to be protected while the chain of proof was being built. As traditional industries, like

---

[1] Lord Swinton, *Sixty Years of Power* (1966), 78.

cotton and coal, had to export to keep up to their pre-war levels, a protective policy could not help them, but throughout the 1920s the desire to
get back to 1913 inhibited attempts to get people out of the declining
industries and into those with a future.

This problem had not become visible in 1919. While the boom was on,
immediately after the war, industrial relations deteriorated; supporters
of the Labour party felt that the election had been held in so much of a
hurry that they had not had a fair chance to state their case, and that they
were justified in using strike action to get the political changes they
wanted. 'Direct action', as this approach was called, was used by the
coalminers, who threatened to strike in February 1919 to obtain an
increase in wages and the nationalization of the coalmines. The government did not feel able to resist this pressure, so it appointed a Royal
Commission, six of whom would be sympathetic to the coalminers, six
of whom would be sympathetic to the owners, and an impartial chairman,
Mr. Justice Sankey. Quite possibly the government was ready to accept
a report that favoured nationalization when it set up the Commission;
at just about the same time a Transport Bill which pointed in the direction of nationalization of the railways and an Electricity Bill which gave
much wider powers to the central government were being introduced
into the House of Commons. However, the Conservative backbenchers
who now made up a majority of the House—which they had not
done during the 1917–18 period of Lloyd George's Coalition—forced
the government to promise that it would not use this legislation in any
way that would lead to nationalization. So, when Sankey came down on
the side of nationalizing the coalmines (and the other Commission
members divided as might be expected) the Report was rejected on the
grounds that the government was not pledged to accept a Report which
was so far from being unanimous. The government granted the other
demands of the miners, including legislation for a seven-hour day; the
miners were not ready to have a strike for nationalization when there
were no immediate issues at stake and they accepted the government's
decision.

The seven-hour day for miners was part of a much wider move to a
shorter working week. On the average the working week had been about
54 hours (miners, with heavier work, had a shorter week), and in the
course of 1919 and 1920 it was reduced to about 48 hours. This increase
in leisure was probably the most substantial gain made by the working
classes in the post-war settlement; it narrowed the gap between them and
the middle classes, and made it profitable to provide week-day entertainment all over the country. The cinema, greyhound racing, and dirt-

track (motorbike) racing all depended on working-class audiences with more time, as well as more money, than before 1914.

Legislation and economics

The working classes expected more from Parliament after 1918 than they got. The post-war legislation settled, in a hasty, unidealistic sort of way, most of the burning issues that had kept the Liberal party alive for generations; by the time Lloyd George fell from power in 1922 the party badly needed new ideas because most of its old ones had been passed into law—not always in a very edifying way, but none the less conclusively. For example, the wartime limitations on drinking were made permanent, with the result that the drinking day was cut down to about six hours. Supporters of stricter regulation asked for more, and some people wanted complete Prohibition, but the campaign had lost its fire and never recaptured its nineteenth-century fervour.

The work of legislation had begun before the war ended, with Fisher's 1918 Education Act. The Act raised the school-leaving age to 14 and, while it retained the 1902 division between fee-paying secondary education and free elementary education, increased the number of scholarships. At the same time larger grants were given to local authorities so that teachers' salaries could be substantially increased. The Act also required local authorities to provide part-time education up to the age of 18 for children who left school at 14 but, as a result of the pressure for government economy that soon developed, this provision lapsed. British politics between the wars were marked by considerable hostility to education: there were people who opposed it on the grounds that it made children less willing to work and intensified the servant-problem, and there were people who thought that if the poor were educated they would no longer be content to work hard at boring jobs. When R. A. Butler was introducing the next important Education Bill in 1944 he felt it necessary to say: 'To the question "Who will do the work if everybody is educated?" we reply that education itself will oil the wheels of industry and bring a new efficiency, the fruit of modern knowledge, to aid the ancient skill of field and farm.'[1]

Other people realized that education has very few harmful effects, but believed that the country could not afford it, because it might produce unemployable intellectuals, fit only to teach, and unwilling to undertake more directly productive labour. This was a short-sighted view: it is sometimes said the unemployment of the twenties and thirties made the English working class ill-adapted to change, but as the English economy

[1] 19 Jan. 1944, *Commons Debates*, ccclxxxxvi. 215.

had been inflexible for some time before the period of high unemployment, it would be sensible to look for a more general cause. Undereducation, which was not something that appeared for the first time in the twenties and thirties, was probably responsible for some of this inflexibility.

Lloyd George's government had several pre-war problems to settle. It was pledged to carry out the Home Rule and Welsh Disestablishment Bills left in suspense at the outbreak of war, and to do something about housing. Welsh Disestablishment went through without difficulty: the heart had gone out of the struggle and the Church of England no longer hoped for a position of monopoly. A Ministry of Health was set up under Christopher Addison in June 1919, with a commitment to improve housing. The principle of government responsibility towards which the pre-war Liberals had been moving in Lloyd George's urban land programme, was now accepted. Before 1914, according to Professor Bowley,

builders were free to vary the quality and size of working-class houses according to what they judged to be the demand, that is, according to the willingness and ability of people to pay for them. Since the Great War a different attitude has been taken, rightly or wrongly. A much higher minimum standard for new houses has been established, partly by law and partly by public opinion.

This public opinion required more money to be spent on housing, for the sake of the children or of the neighbourhood, than poor people wanted (or could afford) to pay; and the slums of Glasgow or Whitechapel show clearly enough why public opinion wanted more money to be spent on housing. The Ministry of Health required local authorities to show what they were going to provide for the people who could not afford decent housing and this pushed the local authorities into building in the last and most frantic stages of the sudden and short-lived post-war boom. Naturally the houses that were built were very expensive, and this led to a reaction against government intervention in housing. It would have made much better economic sense if the commitment to government intervention had come after the boom had broken, when it might have had a stimulating effect on the economy. However, people in the 1920s did not believe in stimulating the economy during a slump; before the war the proportion of the national income spent by the government was in any case so small that even a relatively large budget deficit would not have done very much for the economy. Totally ignoring wartime experience, which had shown that a large budget deficit produced a very active and adaptable economy, the men of the twenties were convinced that the way to deal with a slump was to cut government expenditure. If Addison had not committed the government to taking some interest in housing by his instructions to the local authorities, the problem might have been ignored for a good many years to come.[1]

Unemployment Insurance was extended in much the same spirit; while the boom was on it seemed quite safe to extend the 1911 Insurance Act (Part II) to all industrial workers and to promise additional 'uncovenanted benefit' beyond the amount covered by insurance. Only if they remained unemployed for a long time could they lose their (nationally organized) insurance rights and be forced back on the (locally organized) Poor Law system which would keep them from starvation. Unemployed workers preferred the insurance system to the Poor Law system, partly because the Poor Law almost always gave less than the insurance system. Poplar Borough Council, one of the first London boroughs to vote Labour, gave benefits in 1921 at about the same rate as the insurance scheme, but the municipal finances headed towards bankruptcy and the councillors were ordered to pay for their generosity out of their own pockets. When they refused, they were put in prison. People who were free from the fear of unemployment called the whole system 'the dole' and were contemptuous about its organization. The Conservatives and Liberals wanted to run the system of relief as cheaply as possible; the Labour party wanted to bring the level of unemployment benefit as close to a normal wage as possible, which they called 'work or maintenance'—maintenance at a level which bore some relation to a man's trade-union rate of pay.

A little after the extension of the unemployment insurance system, economic expansion came to an end. Prices reached a peak in the summer of 1920; wages continued to rise until the beginning of 1921. Forcing down wages was not easy. Trade unions had become powerful during the war and maintained their position in the two years after the war. In 1919 'direct action' had compelled the government to set up the Sankey Commission. Next year 'direct action' enjoyed something of a triumph. Lloyd George seemed to be drifting towards intervention on Poland's side against Russia; in May the London dockers refused to load arms for Poland on to *The Jolly George*, and the issue then sank out of sight for a few weeks. But during the summer intervention again seemed possible. The trade unions formed councils of action and made it clear that intervention would be followed by strikes. The Prime Minister drew back; presumably he realized that fighting in Poland would be unpopular, and thus allowed the trade unions to push him in the direction he wanted to go, but the episode must have convinced the unions that they did possess political power.

[1] M. Bowley, *Housing and the State 1919–44* (1945), 209. This book has a sympathetic account of the Addison housing programme, pp. 26–8.

As a result they were very unwilling to allow any reductions in wages, and the centre of resistance was the miners. Their wages were high before the war, and they had a tradition of long and inflexible strikes. They wanted to return to 1914, to rebuild the Triple Alliance and join the railwaymen and the transport workers in a struggle against any reduction in wages. Before the war the miners had been looked up to as a very powerful union, and the two other unions had been very glad to combine with them, even though the tactics of a transport strike and a coal strike were quite different—an effective transport strike would probably be a matter of a few days of conflict, or else the government might have to step in, and if it did, the less skilled workers might easily be replaced. Miners were not so easy to replace. Ernest Bevin and Jimmy Thomas, the post-war leaders of the transport and the railway unions, were in any case not men who wanted to strike for the sheer pleasure in combat that sometimes carried the miners away.

When the mines were returned to full private control in March 1921, the owners showed that they wanted to reduce wages and to conduct future wage negotiations on a 'district', not a national basis. The miners preferred a national basis because they wanted the costs of mining 'pooled' so that the good mines would pay for the poor ones and wages would not be driven down to the level that would just keep the worst mines going. A strike over this seemed inevitable, and the Triple Alliance would, perhaps a little unenthusiastically, have supported the miners. But on 15 April the secretary of the Miners' Federation said that negotiations on a district basis might be acceptable; the railwaymen and transport workers were immensely relieved and said the strike was off. But this was not so. The miners went on with their strike, and denounced their allies for deserting them. 'Black Friday' passed into labour legend as the day when the miners were betrayed. It might more reasonably have been seen as the day when the more astute trade unionists saw that the day of the miners' supremacy was over. For thirty or forty years the miners had been the most aggressive union, and miners' wages had risen faster than those of any other large industrial group. But coal-mining was over-extended, there were many more miners than before the war, and for the next two decades they did very badly.[1] In a period in which unemployment was generally high, it was particularly high in mining, and in hours of work and wages earned the miners were less able to hold their position than almost any other industrial group.

[1] 980,000 in 1912; 1,197,000 in 1924. A. J. Youngson, *The British Economy 1920–57* (1960), 40.

The post-war reconstruction had shown little realization of change. After five or six months of transition, during which 70 per cent of the work of demobilization was carried out, the country set off on a frantic boom. The great land sales took place, manufacturers who felt it was time to retire were able to sell their factories at very high prices, and war gratuities, rising wages, easy credit, and the relaxation of government controls over industry all encouraged a brief period of full employment and hope for the future. Until the war England had been able to rely on old and tested branches of industry that were already showing signs of becoming out of date. Investment in prosperous but capital-hungry countries like Canada and Australia provided these industries with some of their export opportunities. During the war all the traditional industries like mining, textiles, and shipbuilding had been vital, and nobody doubted that this would continue to be the case. But so many overseas investments had been sold during the war that England no longer had a large favourable balance of current payments to finance new foreign investment. Former customers for British goods had built up their own industries, and British industry could not rely on old-established markets any longer. The reconstruction boom was only a matter of catching up on depreciation that had been neglected, and there was not much modernization in industry. In any case the policy that the Bank of England and the Conservative backbenchers were determined to follow would have broken even a more soundly-based expansion of trade. By 1921 the economy was in a slump which, measured by the number of people out of work, was as bad as any in the records.

The policy of the Bank of England contributed to a slight extent to the unbalance of the year of boom by allowing the pound sterling to slip from the exchange rate of $4.76 at which it had been held during the war, and the subsequent depreciation encouraged prices to go up. The Bank's policy also provided fairly liberal credit for reconstruction, and for the considerable purchases of land and of businesses that took place in 1919 and early 1920. But the Bank's long-term goal was to restore the pound to its pre-war gold value; as the American Treasury was committed to a policy of buying gold at $20 the ounce, the rate of exchange with the dollar became the vital comparison, and the Bank was determined to get back to the 1914 rate, when a pound had been worth $4.86. The decisive step was taken in April 1920, when Bank Rate was raised to 7 per cent and kept there for almost a year. The boom would not have gone on indefinitely even if Bank Rate had remained at a lower level, but the slump that followed need not have been so severe, nor need the recovery have been so incomplete. Throughout the 1920s Montagu Norman, the

Governor of the Bank of England, was determined to get back to the pre-war world, and to carry out this policy he was prepared to handicap British industry very severely. Successive Chancellors of the Exchequer from 1920 to 1931 seem to have accepted his policy without any dispute. Getting back to 1914 was even harder than the Bank realized; everybody spoke as if it would be enough to reduce the British price-level so that it was in the same relationship to the American price-level as it had been in 1914. Something like this equality of price-levels was reached, at the cost of keeping British interest rates well above American interest rates and keeping British industry much less fully employed than American industry. What could not be restored so easily was London's assured dominance of the short-term money market. Before the war the London money market had not only undertaken large foreign investments but had also been able to make large short-term loans to bankers working in other money markets—the difficulty in August 1914 had been that bankers in other financial centres had found it almost impossible to repay their London debts, and their London creditors had been embarrassed accordingly. But after the war London had no such easy dominance; people with short-term money to lend either were Americans or wanted to send their money to America. This increased the pressure on the Bank of England to keep its interest rates above the American level, which made it all the harder to adapt British industry to new conditions.

The business men elected in 1918 may have been Liberal or they may have been Conservative; they tended to agree on the importance of 'anti-waste' or, in the language of an earlier generation, 'retrenchment'. Austen Chamberlain, the Chancellor of the Exchequer, budgeted for a large surplus at a high level of expenditure, which would have had a deflatory effect. This did not satisfy the opponents of government spending, who wanted a large surplus at a lower level of over-all expenditure, which would be even more deflationary. On the Opposition benches the Asquithian Liberals had to decide what interpretation they would give to the old Liberal slogan of 'Peace, Retrenchment, and Reform' in the post-war world. A peaceful and conciliatory foreign policy naturally appealed to them, and on this point they found themselves in agreement with the Labour party. But 'Reform' in the twentieth century had come to mean heavy government spending on social welfare, and it was not easy to reconcile it with 'Retrenchment'. The Asquithians preferred 'Retrenchment' and called on the government to practise economy. Perhaps this suited the temperament of the older generation of Asquithians, because Lloyd George was bound to do better than Asquith in any contest about who could spend money fastest. But it did mean that, in a period in which willingness to spend money was taken to be one of the signs of a left-wing party, the Liberals were putting themselves firmly on the right. The Labour party was of course in favour of high expenditure, which it expected to see devoted to social services; this was not the most convenient sort of support for ministers to attract when struggling with their backbenchers, and it was made no more helpful by the Labour party's enthusiasm for a capital levy which would take money from all rich men and help the poor. The Liberal party also proposed a capital levy, in the form of a tax on the difference between men's 1914 and their 1918 wealth, i.e. a levy on war gains. This might attract men of established wealths who wanted to penalize the *nouveaux riches*, but men of this type were normally Conservative. People who were enthusiastic about taking money from the rich would probably prefer the Labour party's more sweeping approach, and the *nouveaux riches* themselves, many of whom were pre-war Liberals, felt all the more certain that they were safer if they stuck to the Conservative party which Lloyd George had introduced them to.

Lloyd George's followers in Parliament were not prepared to make the Coalition permanent by joining the Conservatives like the Liberal Unionists. The political leaders among them, Churchill, Addison, Mond, and Montagu were men who had been on the left of the party before the war, and the Liberal manufacturers disliked the enthusiasm their partners in coalition always showed for Protection. Churchill was being drawn towards the Conservatives by his fear of Bolshevism, his belief that the Labour party was riddled with it, and his desire to crush the Communist government in Russia, but his suggestion that Liberals and Conservatives should join to form a Centre party revealed one of the difficulties of the situation. A Centre party meant resistance not only to the Labour party but also to the more right-wing of the Conservative backbenchers. The 'anti-waste' Members, the Members who denounced the sale of honours, and the opponents of negotiations with Ireland were at the time lumped together as Die-hard, though the National Party, whose candidate General Sir Henry Page-Croft was elected on a programme of 'No sale of honours', Horatio Bottomley, who had to leave the Commons for the second time in May 1922, and Lord Carson had very little in common except right-wing opposition to the government. Whether the Conservatives in office were willing to be divided from the Die-hards remained to be seen.

Post-war nationalism: Ireland, India, and Chanak

The sale of honours and even the level of government expenditure caused less trouble than the last phases of the Irish question. In 1918

Lloyd George included Home Rule in his election programme; Sinn Fein asked for national independence for the whole of Ireland, and won almost three-quarters of the Irish seats. It sent representatives to Versailles, although they were not received there, and began to emerge as the effective government in most of Ireland, helped by the fact that Home Rule was coming, which made policemen and other officials unwilling to advertise themselves as pro-English. It owed most of its strength to the fact that Irishmen were tired of waiting for the Westminster parliamentary machine and had been inspired by the enthusiasm for small nationalities which had been part of Britain's war propaganda; Englishmen might have wished this enthusiasm to confine itself to Belgians, Serbs, and subjects of the Austro-Hungarian Empire, but it did not. Irishmen in 1919 were moving towards a system of dual government, with legal rule by Dublin Castle and effective rule by Sinn Fein.

In February 1920 the long-delayed Home Rule Bill was passed. The Coalition had to allow Northern Ireland a Home Rule Bill of her own, so that the 1920 legislation offered Sinn Fein the bare and meagre provisions that Redmond was struggling to avoid accepting in 1914. And in Northern Ireland it remained in force for fifty years; from the battles that raged around Gladstone, Parnell, and Redmond, it might have been thought that Home Rule was a wild and reckless piece of legislation, but in fact it offered Irishmen no more than the limited and revocable powers enjoyed by the parliament of Northern Ireland. Law and order broke down in the twenty-six counties and the British government began trying to restore its authority by force of arms. Fighting began in 1919, went on in 1920, and reached new levels of bitterness and brutality in the first half of 1921. The Sinn Fein forces were not strong enough to fight pitched battles against the British army, but they could ambush patrols, shoot soldiers in the streets of the towns they occupied, and punish Irishmen who obeyed the British government. Warfare in which one side does not wear uniform is bound to be confused and vindictive, and it is made worse when both sides claim to be the legitimate government; if the British took their claims to their logical conclusion, all Irishmen who took up arms could be hanged as traitors, and if Sinn Fein took its claims seriously all Irishmen who co-operated with the foreigner were traitors. To strengthen the police the British government raised special forces, the 'Black-and-Tans' and the 'auxis' (auxiliaries). These irregulars were recruited from demobilized soldiers, like the Freikorps in Germany who beat up political opponents and conducted guerrilla warfare on the Polish frontier; and they behaved rather more like the Freikorps than the government cared to recognize. The practice of 'reprisals', which became official policy in January 1921, meant burning down houses, destroying the farming economy, and shooting prisoners who were always 'trying to escape'; it was likely to be popular in England at first, but it could not be continued for long. By the early months of 1921 Lloyd George was wondering whether he could make peace in Ireland. The Conservative back-benchers did not trust the Prime Minister, and his position became no easier when ill health forced Bonar Law to retire in March 1921. Lloyd George's government would work only if he had a devoted second-in-command as leader of the Conservative party. Law was not only devoted and loyal, but he was also recognized as a man who would look after the interests of Ulster. His successor as Conservative leader, Austen Chamberlain, was no less loyal to the Prime Minister, but had no particular claim to speak for Ulster. If Lloyd George could have negotiated an Irish settlement that Law was ready to support it would have been accepted without too much difficulty.

But there were four months of civil strife in Ireland before Sinn Fein responded to some friendly words (inserted by Smuts) in George V's speech opening the Northern Ireland parliament. The I.R.A. had almost been fought to a standstill by the time the truce began in July, but the British government had decided that if Sinn Fein was not substantially satisfied by the negotiations, no peace except the peace of exhaustion could ever be expected in Ireland. De Valera, the President of the Irish Republic, did not come to London to negotiate; his representatives were slightly less intransigent than he would have been. It was accepted that Ireland would at the very least be placed on a footing of equality with the Dominions. So far as there had been an argument over the question, it had come when Lloyd George had won over Birkenhead and Churchill to support his policy in the spring. But the position of Ulster was not settled, and it was not clear that Ireland was going to stay inside the British Empire.

Lloyd George got his way on both points, on the first by trickery and on the second by a threat of renewing the war. He told the Irish representatives that a Boundary Commission would be set up that would revise the 1920 frontier and reduce Northern Ireland to a small and unviable area; it was unlikely that the boundary revision would ever take place, but the assurance met the needs of the Irish negotiators. They were also required to demand republican status for Ireland, and this meant that she could not be a member of the Empire as it then stood, and so would become a completely independent country with certain treaty obligations to England. Lloyd George reckoned that Dominion status was the most he could offer, and he said the war would begin again if the

Irish negotiators did not immediately accept the offer that their country should become the Irish Free State, with the same status as Canada and a commitment to provide harbour facilities for the Royal Navy at half a dozen ports. The Irish negotiators accepted this without referring it back to de Valera. So, on 6 December 1921, the Treaty was signed. De Valera denounced it, and Ireland disintegrated into a new civil war between pro-Treaty and anti-Treaty parties. As the pro-Treaty party won, the civil war made no real difference to England, but it did provide an opportunity for all the people who thought the Treaty ought never to have been made—they could complain that the fighting in Ireland showed how wrong Lloyd George had been to expect the Irish to be able to run their own affairs.

By 1922 Lloyd George needed a success somewhere. He was wondering whether he could fight another election under the Coalition banner. The boom had been broken altogether too thoroughly, and the supporters of economy forced him to set up a committee, under Sir Eric Geddes, to reduce government expenditure. Its report, presented in February 1922, suggested economies on the army and navy, and economies on education; the government managed to avoid some of the cuts proposed in education, though the idea of compulsory part-time education after 14 disappeared. A low level of spending on arms was accepted, and even welcomed as a gesture to the League of Nations, and no coherent opposition to it could be mounted in Parliament. But, when England suggested disarmament during the inter-war years, the nations of Europe were unimpressed, because they knew that Britain had already disarmed, and had done so for budgetary reasons. In England, the Coalition back-benchers, who would have preferred to see the full range of the Geddes reductions in education expenditure carried out, were not satisfied.

Lloyd George was artful and deceptive in negotiating when dealing with relatively small matters, and was at least as attached to his principles as any normal Prime Minister when dealing with large issues. This meant that the Conservatives in the Coalition got very little that they wanted. Cabinet ministers, who knew that there would have to be changes after the war, trusted Lloyd George to make sure that these changes were not too sweeping, but the Conservative back-benchers simply felt that all they valued was being betrayed. To some extent they blamed the Coalition Liberal ministers: Addison as minister in charge of housing, and Fisher were responsible for increased expenditure on social welfare, and Montagu, the Secretary of State for India, was blamed for giving way to Indian demands for independence.

This was not reasonable; the Indian nationalist movement had been growing for some time, and the British government could not resist all of its demands. Undoubtedly independence for India was not an idea to attract much support in England. Apart from the sentimental appeal of owning a vast empire—whenever people talked about the numbers of people within the British Empire, rather than its geographical extent, they were really talking about the population of India, which made up about two-thirds of the population of the entire Empire—India was of substantial importance to a good many people in England. The Lancashire cotton industry was still a dominant force in the economy of the whole world, but India was its largest single market. There were so many millions of people in India that, though most of them were very poor, they could between them afford to buy a great deal of cloth.

India had once had a cotton industry of its own, and was trying to revive it. The Congress party, the main political instrument of the Indian nationalists, was a curious mixture of saintly leaders like Gandhi, who believed in a revival of handcrafts and village spinning of cotton, and manufacturers who wanted India to be free to impose a tariff on Lancashire cotton. Whatever else might be said, independence for India would do the British cotton trade no good. In the years after 1918, when India was still a long way from independence, the government of India did acquire the right to impose tariffs to promote Indian industry without intervention from London, and it used this right in a way that protected the Indian cotton trade.

The cotton trade was important but it was not the only substantial interest which England had in India. India was ruled by a small number of Englishmen; the Indian Civil Service, recruited by examination and inspired by high and austere ideals, contained only a few thousand men, but these men—the 'heaven-born' or, as Lloyd George put it, 'the steel-frame which holds India together'—were a relatively small part of the English community in India. Engineers and doctors went to India to find work; merchants settled in Bombay and Calcutta and at first formed the majority of the municipal electorates in the big trading cities. The Indian army was as large as all the rest of British military strength before 1914; during the rapid expansion of the Empire in Africa soldiers with Indian experience, like Baring in Egypt and Roberts in the Boer War, played leading roles, and poor but hard-working officers often went to India while officers who joined the army for social reasons stayed in England. Particularly after the Indian Mutiny of 1857 the government of India took care to have regiments of British soldiers available in India, but the Indian forces were a powerful instrument in their own right, guarding imperial interests all round the Indian Ocean, and Indian regiments took part in the First World War; some of them went to France, which was too cold and wet for them, but others fought more successfully in the war in the Middle East against Turkey.

The pre-war Liberal government had considered India's constitutional position, and Morley, the Secretary of State, and Minto, the Viceroy, had worked out proposals for allowing Indians a little more control over provincial and municipal affairs. Morley spoke as if this represented the limit of change, which did not help to satisfy the Indian nationalists. But before the Congress party could fully organize itself to take account of the new situation, the war had begun.

The war-time propaganda of the British government and its allies laid considerable stress on the principle of self-determination. Congress became more militant, and in 1917 the British government announced that in the fullness of time India would have 'responsible government'—a government responsible to an Indian electorate would have control over domestic issues, as in the Dominions. In the event, some issues handled by provincial governors were entrusted to ministers responsible to Indian provincial assemblies and a representative assembly, without much power, was set up at Delhi. These Montagu–Chelmsford reforms took some little time to come into effect, and it was in the months of agitation immediately after the war that Gandhi, the great apostle of non-violent civil disobedience, rose to his position of power in Congress. Under his influence it became more militant; his methods provided a new way to agitate, and his ascetic life convinced thousands of Indian peasants previously not interested in politics, that he was a saint whose political leadership should be followed.

In 1919 General Dyer, in command at Amritsar, found his authority challenged by the mob. Normally the challenge would have been faced and put down by the usual methods of crowd-dispersal, but Dyer used machine-guns. It was officially reported that 379 people were killed. The massacre was unnecessary, for British control over India had not been shaken so much that it had to depend on armed force. Dyer was dismissed, a step which helped to reassure Indian opinion, and the post-war agitation died down. The Indians were divided; some of them were ready to take part in provincial governments, and to serve in the central representative assembly; Congress declared that as the central government was not in any way responsible to the assembly it was all just a sham. The Die-hards at Westminster took a simpler view: they were convinced that Dyer's methods were right, and they felt that Indian nationalism was all Montagu's fault.

They also complained about the Egyptian settlement of 1922. At the beginning of the war Britain had annexed Egypt, which she had been occupying on a temporary basis for the previous 32 years. The Egyptians, who had been independent in practice before 1882, expected to be allowed self-determination after the war, and the British government realized that no formula could fit Egypt into the British Empire. In any case Allenby as High Commissioner realized that no government would be willing to hold down Egypt for long, and he offered his resignation rather than undertake a policy of repression. The government set about trying to recreate the pre-war situation: Turkey's theoretical sovereignty over Egypt which had been ended in 1914 was not to be revived, but Egypt's independence was to be limited. A British officer was to be commander-in-chief of the Egyptian army and he, rather than the Minister for War, was to direct military expenditure. With control of the army thus kept out of Egyptian hands, it could be expected that advice from the British High Commissioner in Cairo would be taken almost as seriously as advice from the British agent-general had been taken before 1914. Even this slight concession to 'Egypt for the Egyptians' increased the back-benchers' dissatisfaction with Lloyd George.

The international scene offered no brighter prospects. At the Genoa conference the government hoped to settle reparations, persuade the European powers to start paying their war debts to Britain at a rate that would cover the British repayments to the United States and at the same time reconcile France and Germany. But it was so complete a failure that it buried the conference system to which the European countries had turned, as they always had done after wars. Russia made an agreement, at Rapallo, with Germany but nobody gained anything at the official Genoa negotiations.

Further east the last part of the post-war settlement had still to be made effective. By the Treaty of Sèvres Turkey had given up not only her Balkan and Arab territories, but also parts of Asia Minor, which were given to Greece. A revolt in Turkey was followed by repudiation of the Treaty, and the Greeks were defeated and driven out of their new acquisitions; the Greeks who failed to get on to the boats leaving Smyrna were massacred. This undoubtedly encouraged Lloyd George in his natural Gladstonian feeling of friendship for the Greeks. He had encouraged them to go into Asia Minor, and he wanted to help them now they had been thrown out. But the Turkish army swept on towards the Dardanelles, where a small British force at Chanak was guarding the area of the Straits, which had been neutralized under the Sèvres Treaty.

The British and the Turks glared at each other, while Lloyd George stirred up his Cabinet to stand ready to go and fight for the Straits. Churchill, as Secretary for the Colonies, went further and summoned the Dominions to send any help that might be needed. This ignored all the changes in Commonwealth relations in the previous half-dozen years. If Britain wanted Dominion help she should have explained what was going on and why. The claim for automatic, unexplained support had never been made before; in 1914 the Dominions had given immediate support without being asked for it and in the Boer War there had been discussion before help was sent. Churchill made matters worse by publishing his message in the press before the Dominion Prime Ministers had received it. Mackenzie King, the Canadian Prime Minister, was not in favour of close co-operation, and he welcomed an opportunity to repudiate the whole system on an occasion when it had not been put into effect properly.

The Turkish government did not insist on its point at Chanak. It knew there would have to be a new treaty, and it could be fairly confident that it would regain the Straits by waiting patiently. The British government assumed that by checking Turkey it had raised its own prestige. But this was not the case. The Conservative back-benchers were on the whole pro-Turkish, and all the natural anti-Turks in English politics were against the idea of going to war at all, even against the Turks. Law, whose health had temporarily improved, appealed to the feelings of both groups when he declared that England could not be the policeman of the world. Nevertheless Lloyd George was now determined to force an election before the Conservative back-benchers could overthrow the Coalition, and Austen Chamberlain agreed to call a meeting of ministers and M.P.s at the Carlton Club at which he would try to win their support for an election under Lloyd George's leadership.

Supporters of the Coalition had only one argument left. The government had not solved the problems of Europe and it had not passed the legislation the Conservatives wanted, but it had steered the country through its post-war difficulties and provided enough social welfare legislation to calm people down. The last argument for continuing the Coalition was that the growing power of the Labour party was so menacing that unless all men of good will stood together, which could only be brought about by a Coalition under Lloyd George, the forces of Bolshevism would sweep over England. Even this argument lost some of its weight when, at a by-election just before the meeting at the Carlton Club, an anti-Coalition Conservative defeated a Coalition and a Labour candidate.

On 19 October the Conservatives met. Partly because of his own desire for a peaceful foreign policy and partly because Beaverbrook had persuaded him that the time was ripe for a tariff policy, Law was there: the back-benchers had an alternative Prime Minister who could replace Lloyd George. His speech, and the even more effective speech of Stanley Baldwin, the President of the Board of Trade, answered the question raised by all discussion of a 'centre party'. They said that the Conservative party should not allow itself to be divided, and should not let Lloyd George drag one section of the party behind him while leaving the Die-hard section isolated and embittered. This argument prevailed. The pro-Lloyd George Cabinet Ministers were rejected by 187 votes to 87; Law, Baldwin, and the back-benchers entered on their inheritance.

5. *From the Carlton Club to the General Strike* 1922–1926

The 1922 Parliament

WHEN Lloyd George had resigned, Law had to form a government without being able to call on the ministers who had supported the Coalition and he had to fight a general election. There had been no purely Conservative government for sixteen years, and the men chosen in 1922 dominated British Cabinets for the next eighteen. Neville Chamberlain, Edward Wood (better known as Lord Halifax), Lloyd Graeme (later Lord Swinton), and Sir Samuel Hoare were first brought into the Cabinet by Law; by the critical period of the later thirties they had already been in office almost continuously for over a dozen years, struggling with problems like unemployment to which none of them knew the answer. Apart from these men of the future the Cabinet contained a number of peers who helped give it strength and respectability among the Die-hards.

On 23 October Law was elected Leader of the Conservative party and then accepted the position of Prime Minister. The electoral prospects for the new government were quite good: the Liberal party was still divided; the Labour party was not considered as an alternative government; Lloyd George depended on his command over the loyalty of his Coalition colleagues and behaved more like a minister pushed out of office by members of his own party than the leader of another party. Law would have to reconstruct his Cabinet to include the Coalitionists unless he won a clear majority, and the new government kept this possibility open by not opposing the Coalitionists. Beaverbrook, who was not included in the government, had no liking for this half-hearted warfare; he encouraged more candidates to stand, in order to keep the breach open.

For perhaps twenty years, ever since Chamberlain raised the issue of Tariff Reform, political life had been in turmoil: Dreadnoughts, the

Budget, the Lords, Ireland, the War, the Peace, Ireland again, and then the risk of war in the Near East had left people exhausted. At the Carlton Club meeting Baldwin had made a considerable impression when he called Lloyd George 'a dynamic force' and had reminded his listeners that a dynamic force could be very dangerous.

Law gained a very favourable response from voters when he said the time had come for 'tranquillity'. No further commitments abroad and rigid economy at home appealed to the feelings of a solid majority of the people. From time to time during the next few years efforts were made to break out of this lethargy, but the mood to which Law was appealing had very deep roots. The clearest example of his unwillingness to disturb things was to be seen in his promise that he would not change the Free Trade system before the next general election, despite his own Tariff Reform views.

Apart from this, he was probably helped by the petulance of the Coalitionists. Birkenhead said the new Cabinet was made up of second-class brains, exposing himself to Lord Robert Cecil's reply that second-class brains were better than second-class characters; and Lloyd George called Law honest to the verge of simplicity, though he was unwise to raise the issue of honesty at all.[1] The new government won its clear majority, free from any dependence on the National Liberals. Many Liberals who had voted for a Conservative for the first time in 1918 seem to have stayed with the Conservatives after the Coalition ended.

	Votes	M.P.s	% of all votes cast
Conservative	5,500,382	345	38·2
National Liberal	1,673,240	62	11·6
Liberal	2,516,287	54	17·5
Labour	4,241,383	142	29·5

Perhaps thirty Coalition Unionists followed Austen Chamberlain, but they were unlikely to vote against Law. The government had the only political organization which was intact and able to fight on a nation-wide scale, and its success was not really surprising.

The other significant result of the election was the advance made by the Labour party. It won 80 seats more than in 1918 and it continued to be the largest party in opposition. The Asquithian Liberals doubled their numbers; the Lloyd George National Liberals were halved, so that even if Asquith and Lloyd George could have patched up their differences the

[1] R. Blake, *The Unknown Prime Minister* (1955), 465; Lord Swinton, *Sixty Years of Power* (1966), 68.

Liberals would have been the smallest party. The two Liberal groups naturally obtained a larger aggregate of voters than the Asquithian Liberals in 1918 but even so they polled fewer votes than the Labour party. Probably the Liberal vote increased because some Coalition voters returned to the party; the increased Labour vote seems to have come from people who had not voted when they were first enfranchised. In 1918 the Labour party had retained its strength in areas where it had been strong before the war, but had not done well in places like Glasgow and East London; in 1922 the total vote cast, and the Labour vote, went up considerably in such places. The Liberal and Conservative vote taken together had not increased; the result could have been caused by elaborate switching of votes, but the simple explanation is that the newly enfranchised were just beginning to use their power.

The consequent increase in Labour strength made the leadership of the party a more important position and Ramsay MacDonald, re-elected to Parliament after his defeat in 1918, challenged the incumbent J. R. Clynes for the post. The new Labour members from Glasgow and the Clydeside wanted a strongly socialist programme at home and abroad. Some of them had been imprisoned for their organizing activities during the war: confronted with a choice between confirming Clynes, who had held office during the war, in his position as leader or turning to MacDonald, who had suffered for his beliefs as they had, it was natural for them to choose the latter and assume that he was strongly socialist in all his views. MacDonald defeated Clynes by a narrow margin; he clearly received support from more moderate men as well as the Clydesiders, and this was perfectly reasonable: he was probably the best man the Labour party could have chosen to get a Labour government elected to office quickly. He seemed born to rule; Emanuel Shinwell said that 'he was a prince among men'; long years later, when MacDonald and the I.L.P. were at daggers drawn, Jimmy Maxton, the sea-green incorruptible leader of the Clydesiders, cried as he listened to MacDonald speaking, though he retained enough self-control to mutter 'the bastard' through his tears; and Beatrice Webb called him 'a magnificent substitute for a leader'. Mrs. Webb regarded her neat, precise, fussy, and omniscient husband Sidney as perfection, and was a little inclined to judge everybody else by the same standards, but there was some substance in her comment. MacDonald's views on foreign policy were the natural product of Gladstonian Liberalism, and did not imply any very determined impatience for socialism. He had joined the Labour party when socialism did not necessarily mean much more than a heartfelt commitment to social reform, with no special implications about the policy to be used.

Throughout his political life he clearly wanted social reform—in a way he knew more about it than any other Prime Minister, for he was the illegitimate son of Scottish peasants, and had at times gone hungry while he was working his way forward. This was no guarantee that he had any policy for reducing poverty, and the sting in Beatrice Webb's remark was that he did not know in what direction he should lead his party.

He possessed the great gift of making his words seem to mean more than they said, which enabled him to arouse the enthusiasm of his followers without committing himself to any very drastic action that might alarm moderate opinion. By the end of his career people had realized that his skill in avoiding a commitment to hasty action was accompanied by some incapacity to take action at all, but this had yet to be seen. He had stood up for his beliefs during the war, and by 1922 people were beginning to feel he had been ill treated for his devotion to his ideals. He was a fine platform speaker, in his prime he was a master of the House of Commons and, until he formed his National Government in 1931, he had no difficulty in dominating the Labour party.

The two Liberal leaders, Asquith and Lloyd George, were too well matched for one to dominate the other and too dissimilar for one to serve the other without reservations. Reunion in the near future seemed unlikely, nor did it look as though Law could easily fit the Conservative Coalitionists into his ministry. They drifted away from Lloyd George, but for a time it seemed that there would simply be two Conservative and two Liberal parties feuding in Parliament.

In accordance with his election pledges Law did very little once he was in power. Baldwin, the Chancellor of the Exchequer, went to Washington in January 1923 to arrange terms for the repayment of the British war debt. The United States wanted the $4,000m. outstanding to be repaid by 61 annual payments of $187m. (interest running at $3\frac{1}{2}$ per cent). Baldwin hoped to reduce the interest payable to $2\frac{1}{2}$ per cent and settle for 50 annual payments of $140m. But his bargaining position was weak: Keynes's comment on the situation, 'It is the debtor who has the last word in these cases', held good only if the debtor was ready to consider repudiation, and Baldwin came much closer to accepting Coolidge's 'Well, they hired the money, didn't they?' He agreed to 10 payments of $161m. and 52 of $184m. and returned to Britain to recommend these terms to the Cabinet.

When he disembarked at Southampton he rashly told reporters that American opinion would not consider a settlement that offered anything less. After this statement the Cabinet could hardly ask for new negotiations and opponents of the terms had to consider the alternative of repudiation. Law was prepared to do so, and the Chancellor of the Exchequer and almost all his colleagues found themselves ranged against the Prime Minister. Law's willingness to stand alone made the Duke of Devonshire think:

It practically meant that there was not a Cabinet but a Dictator, the one thing we had complained about with regard to the last government.[1]

But Law was not Lloyd George; he gave way and relieved his feelings by writing an anonymous letter of protest to *The Times*.

Tranquillity was not enough to please everybody. Three by-election defeats quickly showed that people wanted the government to do something about housing conditions. Neville Chamberlain brought in a Bill to give grants to be administered by the municipalities; for each house built a subsidy of £6 a year would be paid for twenty years. Private building was preferred, but municipalities could make contracts with private firms or employ direct labour on their own account. Only houses with a surface area of no more than 850 sq. ft. qualified for a grant, and this turned out to be the controversial part of the Bill. Chamberlain wanted as many small houses as possible, and did not intend to subsidize houses large enough to satisfy people who could afford to pay a market price. The Labour party objected that his houses would be too small; the issue was made tangible for ordinary people by the question 'Should working-class houses have a parlour?'

Chamberlain argued that one big room (perhaps a combined kitchen and parlour) made good sense and that if there were a parlour it would be left unused. The Labour party replied that courting couples, children doing their homework, and many other people would use the parlour. Chamberlain was probably correct in thinking that people really wanted a parlour to be kept tidy and unused as a sign of respectability but he gave way and allowed houses with a surface area of 950 sq. ft. to qualify for the grant.[2]

Baldwin's reputation continued to rise. His colleagues thought he had taken an honest and straightforward approach to the war debt question, his budget was regarded as sound, and he was widely praised for a speech in which he declared:

Four words, of one syllable each . . . contain salvation for this country and the whole world, and they are Faith, Hope, Love and work.[3]

When Law resigned in the middle of May, a victim of cancer of the throat, Baldwin was available as an alternative to the obvious candidate

---

[1] R. Churchill, *Lord Derby* (1959), 495.
[2] 24 April 1923; *Commons Debates*, clxiii. 303–419.
[3] G. M. Young, *Stanley Baldwin* (1952), 47.

for the succession, Lord Curzon. As ex-Viceroy of India and as Foreign Secretary, Curzon had strong claims, and he had taken the chair when Law had been absent from Cabinet meetings. There were disadvantages, as Balfour told the King, about having a Prime Minister in the Lords when the official Opposition was not represented there. Furthermore, the King was given to understand, in an informal but well-considered memorandum, that Baldwin would be Law's choice.[1] Baldwin had a reputation for amiability and honesty, Curzon a reputation for arrogance combined with great skill, demonstrated in 1916 and in 1922, for deserting sinking ships.

Even so, the choice of Baldwin was a surprise, though one that was quickly accepted. Law in his post-war mood of calm had been surrounded by an air of mild melancholy. Baldwin gave the same impression that he would not undertake any unnecessary activity, but he seemed altogether more cheerful. He could obtain people's respect without standing on his dignity, he was always determined to be conciliatory and nobody believed he would attempt to deceive his followers or even his political opponents: these qualities were the foundations on which a great Prime Minister could have stood.

During the early months of his Premiership attention was fixed on the French government's occupation of the Ruhr in an attempt to extract war reparations from Germany. The British view was that this policy would get nowhere, as indeed proved to be the case. The occupation placed a great strain on Anglo-French relations but a bold British step, of the type Lloyd George's Coalition might have taken, would have attracted very little support. Baldwin would not concentrate on foreign problems when there were questions at home to hold his attention, and by this time the question of unemployment was causing concern in Britain.

Social issues in politics

The sudden increase in unemployment in 1921 had looked like the normal period of crisis familiar to everybody who had lived through a pre-1914 trade cycle. By 1923 unemployment seemed to be taking an altogether different form; the number of men out of work continued to be high, running for most of the twenties at over $1\frac{1}{4}$m. Exact comparisons with the pre-1914 world or, to take another period of depression, with the years of slack trade between 1874 and 1896, are difficult to draw, because the pre-1914 statistics cover principally the relatively prosperous workers who were in trade unions. It seems that in the 1880s unemployment among trade unionists was just over 5 per cent and in the years just

[1] Thomas Jones, *Whitehall Diary* (1969) i, 235–6.

before 1914 it was 4½ per cent which probably meant that 6 or 7 per cent of all workers were unemployed and others were underemployed. These figures contrast very sharply with conditions in the 1920s. On the basis of the monthly figures, Clapham suggests that in an average month 12 per cent of the population who were insured against unemployment (which was by then more or less equivalent to the whole wage-earning labour force) was out of work. And as a result of the 1918 Act, almost all the unemployed had votes.

The conspicuous unemployment was in trades which had belonged to the 'aristocracy of labour' in the nineteenth century. Coalminers and shipbuilders were the most obvious examples of men with a well-established way of life that had been destroyed by changes in the pattern of the economy. Because they were skilled men they would have felt they were stepping down if they took new jobs in other industries, even if new jobs had been available; the sort of shift of work that might have taken place could be seen in transport, where the number of men employed on the railways dropped by over 120,000 in the twenties but the number of people engaged in motor transport rose by 220,000.[1]

A few of the most resilient of the unemployed no doubt found some compensations. The youthful Aneurin Bevan could further his education while out of work but obviously the great majority of the unemployed found their situation incomprehensible in a way that robbed them of the desire to do anything. Because of what Engels once called the 'damned wantlessness' of the proletariat, unemployment never looked like leading to revolution, and the unemployed sank deeper into a passive detachment about what was happening to them. To some extent it was this deadness of the men out of work which D. H. Lawrence was talking about when he suggested that

If only they were educated to *live* instead of earn and spend, they could manage very happily on twenty-five shillings [£1·25 a week]. If the men wore scarlet trousers as I said, they wouldn't think so much of money: if they could dance and hop and skip, and sing and swagger and be handsome, they could do with very little cash.[2].

This path of renunciation was unlikely to win many followers. As Lawrence knew and deplored, young miners wanted motor-bikes and jazz and cinemas, and wanted money to pay for them. Lawrence might be resigned to a two-and-a-half-day week for the mines, but the country

[1] Sir J. Clapham, *Economic History of Modern Britain* (1950–2), iii. 532 and 541 on transport and unemployment.
[2] D. H. Lawrence, *Lady Chatterley's Lover* (1960—first complete British text), 315.

could not run satisfactorily on half-time. In the early twenties three approaches to the problem of unemployment held the field. They were not mutually exclusive: people could believe in all three of them, and certainly several politicians believed in more than one.

The first approach was to revive international trade by acknowledging and paying debts, such as the U.S. war loans, and try to get back to the pre-1914 pattern of trading by steps like returning to the Gold Standard. The next approach, favoured by the Labour party, was the capital levy; nationalization was also a Labour proposal, and speakers did claim that it would reduce unemployment, but the capital levy was the really controversial plank in the Labour platform. Apart from advancing Socialist ideals by reducing inequalities in the possession of wealth, it would lighten the load of debt and make sure that less money went to rentiers who drew interest without taking any risks. The third approach was the Protectionist, designed to defend the home market, and it was to this approach that Baldwin turned when he tried to work out a policy for dealing with unemployment during the later months of 1923. It could be argued that Protectionism was not relevant to the specific areas of unemployment. Coal could not be protected; it was an exporting trade which depended on keeping its costs of production as low as possible. So was shipbuilding; so was cotton. Agriculture might benefit if it was protected by tariffs but the Protectionists of the early twenties felt that stomach taxes—tariffs on food—would take them right back to 1906. Protectionism was by no means certain to be popular. The Conservative party was not united behind it, and the depressed industries were likely to be hostile to it.

Baldwin was undoubtedly convinced that Tariff Reform was the best policy. As an ironmaster he had had experience of one of the branches of British industry in which Protection was most relevant as a way of keeping American and German products out. Nevertheless, it would divide his party and it would force him to consider holding another general election. He felt bound by Law's 1922 pledge not to introduce tariffs before another general election had been held, and this meant that he needed an election to free his hands.

Tariff Reform had some tactical advantages, as well as providing a possible answer to unemployment. Many of the Tories who had followed Austen Chamberlain when he remained loyal to Lloyd George were Protectionists. If Baldwin declared himself in favour of tariffs they would find it relatively easy to accept him as the leader of the party, which might make up for any loss of Free Trade support. Lloyd George was said to be thinking of coming out in favour of tariffs, which would strengthen his

links with the Coalition Conservatives and might attract some of the
Tariff Reformers who had followed Law and Baldwin.

Adopting a new policy is not easy for a party in office: the policy has to
look as if it comes from the Prime Minister rather than being forced
upon him, but he cannot thrust it upon his colleagues without a considerable period of preparation. Baldwin could rely on the support of Neville
Chamberlain and several other Cabinet ministers, but Lord Derby, who
had led the Tories who opposed Tariff Reform before the war, Lord
Curzon, and Lord Salisbury had still to be faced. Baldwin avoided rather
than solved this problem by taking the whole issue at the gallop, and
left Lord Derby complaining (privately) of 'a policy which was only
disclosed in brief to the Cabinet forty-eight hours before it was launched
on the public'.[1] Baldwin first said on 25 October 1923 that he wanted
a free hand to impose tariffs and the general election was held on
6 December. This was not long enough to give the government a reasonable chance of convincing the electorate that it ought to accept a change
of policy.

The failure of the Liberals to appear as the leading party of the left in
this election probably decided their fate for years to come; Free Trade
was their special issue, on which they could hope to attract Free Traders
who normally voted Conservative and to hold a good deal of their
working-class support on the issue of dear bread. Whatever the factors
improving the Liberals' prospects, the Labour party also gained ground
and remained the larger of the two left-wing parties. The Liberal party
had very little to offer that was not in the Labour programme; the Liberal
party might have done well as a rallying-point for people who did not
want to move right to Protection or left to nationalization, but apparently
the electorate contained relatively few middle-of-the-road voters of this
sort. Such a position would have had few attractions for the politically
active people who make up the base of party strength for electoral
organization, and it was certainly true that the Labour party had a very
enthusiastic, if not always efficient, volunteer organization.

The Labour party did not really expect to do well in the election, and
seems not to have thought in terms of becoming a party of government.
MacDonald himself probably looked forward to forming a government at
some time in the future, and one of his services to his party was to think
in these terms. But probably in 1923 he was quite satisfied to hear the
chairman say, at one of his meetings: 'It would be a great loss to public
life if Mr. Ramsay MacDonald did not lead the next Opposition.'[2]

[1] R. Churchill, op. cit. 537.
[2] The speaker was the ex-Liberal Addison. *The Times*, 5 Dec. 1923.

Presumably some of the people who had voted for 'tranquillity' in 1922 were opposed to almost any change; Baldwin's support for Protection made him into an innovator, and the Liberal Free Traders became the defenders of the *status quo*. The issue reunited the Liberals: Lloyd George laid aside any Protectionist leanings he might have had and Churchill buckled on his Free Trade armour once more. The image of the lion lying down with the lamb was brought into several Liberal speeches celebrating reunion; Asquith's daughter, Lady Violet Bonham Carter, tried to put life into the phrase by saying she had 'never seen Mr. Lloyd George look less voracious or my father more uneatable'.[1] Her father may have wondered if it was necessary to cast Lloyd George as the lion of the partnership.

	Votes	Seats	% of all votes cast
Conservative	5,538,824	258	38·1
Liberal	4,311,147	159	29·6
Labour	4,438,508	191	30·5

The first Labour government (1924)

No party had a majority and although the Conservatives had more seats than anyone else the case for a Labour government was quite good: Baldwin had said he could not govern without a tariff and, as he was not going to get a tariff, he had to resign; the Leader of the Opposition had to be sent for, and could probably form a government with some assurances of Liberal support. Many Conservatives feared that the Labour government would take office, present a popular budget including pension benefits and a capital levy, and then dissolve when the budget was defeated. As the election would be fought on the Labour party's proposals it would have a good chance of winning. The Conservative alarmists concluded that the two anti-Socialist parties should immediately form a government of national unity. Mussolini had just come to power in Italy at the head of a Fascist government, set up to keep the Socialists out. His readiness to suspend democracy in the face of an emergency seems to have inspired the proposal that a government of national trustees should be set up to hold power for a fixed period of two years.

The left wing of the Labour party put forward much the same case for forming a minority government and using the ministerial front bench as a platform to state the Socialist programme. MacDonald had no intention of behaving in such a way; he did not believe the electorate knew which way it wanted to go, and he believed that putting forward a programme

[1] R. Jenkins, *Asquith* (1964), 499.

simply to be defeated would convince people that the Labour party was irresponsible. He believed it would suffer if it gave the impression that it was not interested in governing, and that it would benefit if it could show that it possessed the administrative skill to do the job. When he knew that Baldwin was not going to resign until defeated in the Commons, and that some of the Conservatives were thinking of overthrowing their leader to set up a Conservative-Liberal coalition, he denounced attempts to 'wangle the constitution' to keep the Labour party out.[1]

Baldwin's decision to face the Commons placed on the Liberals the responsibility of deciding which of the larger parties should govern. Asquith cut through the confusion by announcing on 17 December that he 'would not lift a finger to keep the Conservative government in office'. He probably wanted to make sure that nobody thought the Labour party was being treated unfairly or conspired against, and he knew that the Liberals who had not been supporters of the Lloyd George government distrusted any idea of a Coalition. A more subtle argument was that if Liberals and Conservatives had to form a single party to keep Labour out, they only made it the more certain that Labour would eventually get in with a clear majority. And, as Asquith reflected, 'if a Labour government is ever to be tried in this country, as it will be sooner or later, it could hardly be tried under safer conditions'.[2]

Apart from this, the decision reflected the problems of the Liberal struggle to survive. The Liberal party was most unlikely to coalesce with the Labour party to the extent of being absorbed into it. The individual Liberal politicians who joined the Labour party attracted more attention than those who joined the Conservative party, though there were several of the latter. Haldane, the only man who had reached the first rank as a Liberal and later joined the Labour party, was balanced by Churchill, who even by 1923 was a Conservative on everything except Free Trade. Men like Hamar Greenwood and Mond could be set against the less important Liberal 'recruits to Labour'. But these individual changes did not affect the roots of the situation; the Liberal party could expect to survive any alliance with the Labour party, but alliance with the Conservative party might easily turn into fusion. If this happened, some Liberals would probably turn into Conservatives, as happened after the Coalition.

The decision to support a Labour government in 1924 and again in 1929 was to some extent an attempt to escape the attractions of fusion and to hold in check the Liberals whose reaction to a move towards the Conservatives would be to join the Labour party. People at the time thought

[1] *The Times*, 24 Dec. 1923.
[2] R. Jenkins, op. cit. 500.

the Liberal party was closer to the Conservatives than to the Labour party; there were complaints that the Liberals were betraying the country by letting the Labour party in, and the Labour party always said that there was no real difference between the capitalist parties.

The eagerness to keep the Labour party out was based on a quite unreasoning fear. Proposals for some nationalization and for a capital levy had been put forward by people outside as well as inside the party, and in any case a minority government could not carry out either policy. The Labour party was prepared to accept the logic of gradualism; MacDonald was applauded at the party's victory celebration when he said 'one step enough for me? Yes, as long as it leads on to the next step', a remark which reflected a realization of the limits of manœuvre.[1] Not all the party thought that the immediate object of holding power was to nationalize the means of production, distribution, and exchange.

The original purpose of the L.R.C. had been to improve the political position of the working class. That spirit can be seen in Clynes's comment on his own moment of apotheosis:

As we stood waiting for His Majesty amid the gold and crimson magnificence of the Palace, I could not help marvelling at the strange turn of Fortune's wheel which had brought MacDonald the starveling clerk, Thomas the engine-driver, Henderson the foundry-labourer, and Clynes the mill-hand, to this pinnacle beside the man whose forebears had been kings for so many splendid generations.[2]

Shortly after the government had been formed, a dispute of some symbolic importance broke out: should ministers wear formal dress for court ceremonies? MacDonald, who wanted to convince another 15 or 20 per cent of the electorate that the Labour party was mild-mannered enough to be trusted with power, was in favour of court dress—his enemies suggested that he thought he looked particularly impressive in it. More implacable fighters of the class war said that court dress was the sign that Labour had sold out to the aristocratic embrace. MacDonald got his way: the Labour government was not going to start with any departures from tradition.

Parliament reassembled, the government was duly defeated, and MacDonald was asked to form a Cabinet. The leading men were those Clynes mentioned, together with Snowden, and they provided a firm working-class foundation. Eleven Cabinet Ministers came from the working class, most of whom—though not MacDonald, Snowden, and Wheatley—had worked in the trade union movement. Three Cabinet

---

[1] *The Times*, 9 Jan. 1924.
[2] J. R. Clynes, *Memoirs* (1937), i. 343.

ministers had been left-wing Liberal Members of Parliament before 1914, Sidney Webb was also an ex-Liberal. The claims of Labour had not been neglected among the fifteen commoners, but MacDonald had a little difficulty finding people to conduct business in the Upper House. His five peers did their work satisfactorily, but except for the veteran Fabian Olivier they had no real connections with the Labour movement.

The whole nine months of the first Labour government's existence was devoted to proving that Labour was fit to govern. Some historians have looked to see what legislation was passed but, apart from the fact that relatively few governments pass important legislation in their first few months, what mattered was simply that the new men showed that administration did not dissolve into chaos in their hands. After that, a large section of the working class would go on voting Labour whatever happened, and as a result the Liberal party could not find any foundation on which to rebuild itself as the party of the left.

The Labour government did a little more than establish its reputation for competence. Snowden as Chancellor of the Exchequer recognized that he could not have a capital levy; instead he had a Free Trade budget which partially reconciled the Liberals to the informal alliance. The McKenna Duties were abolished and the 'free breakfast-table' (i.e. free from tariff charges) was almost established with the reduction of duty on sugar, cocoa, tea, and coffee. These reductions may have encouraged private spending, and the breakfast-table changes certainly helped the poorer classes, but they left little money over for public works to combat unemployment. Public works reduced unemployment primarily by un-balancing the budget, and Snowden at the Exchequer would forbid any deliberate steps to produce an unbalanced budget. The Labour government turned out not to have any proposals in mind which would reduce unemployment, though its supporters continued to believe that it cared more deeply about the problem than the other parties. This was reasonable enough; unemployment benefits were increased, and benefits not covered by insurance payments were declared to be a right, not a grant payable at the discretion of the minister, which in practice had meant that officials at the Labour Exchange interrogated the applicant and decided whether to give him anything. The change made a difference; in the 1924 election Walter Elliot noticed that little boys shouted at him 'Vote Labour—and be treated like a gentleman at the burroo' (= bureau, or Labour Exchange).[1]

Wheatley's Housing Act might in the long run have done something to reduce unemployment. In the short run it brought together the trade

[1] C. Coote, *A Companion of Honour, the Story of Walter Elliot* (1965), 86.

unions and the building contractors, helped by an increase in the subsidy to £9 a year for 40 years, and they guaranteed a higher rate of production without an increase in prices. The emphasis of the Act was placed very heavily on municipal building for renting; the ground area remained the same as in the final version of the Chamberlain Act, which may have shown that the minister realized that larger houses would amount to a subsidy for the middle class.

While the legislative progress of the government was slow and prosaic, its performance in foreign affairs produced swift and impressive results. Diplomacy was made less secret by providing that all treaties must be submitted to the House of Commons for approval. MacDonald took the Foreign Office himself, and was fortunate enough to do so at a time when his Gladstonian principles of peaceful reasonableness made very good sense; they also helped to reassure the Liberals that they had acted wisely in putting him in office.

France was beginning to realize that the occupation of the Ruhr was producing no positive effects; Germany was beginning to realize that inflation and passive resistance would destroy German society before they had much effect elsewhere. This made it easier for MacDonald to act as the pacifier of Europe.

Mr. MacDonald wished to re-establish relations of confidence and co-operation with France and Italy; to break the deadlock over reparations; to secure a French evacuation of the Rhineland; and to reintroduce Germany into the co-unity of nations. He wished to further the cause of general disarmament by strengthening the machinery of international arbitration; and to bridge the gulf that, both politically and financially, sundered Great Britain from Soviet Russia. Within the space of eight months he was able either to attain or promote all these seven objects.[1]

A certain amount of the work was done while Poincaré was still in power in France; his electoral defeat in May and the formation of a left-wing government under Herriot made the restoration of contact easier. Restoration of contact did not restore the *entente cordiale*; from the French occupation of the Ruhr until Hitler's accession to power Britain stood uncommitted between France and Germany, and to some extent this attitude persisted even after 1933. In the twenties it was helpful; neither the Geneva Protocol (the Labour sketch of a return to the Concert of Europe on the basis of League arbitration) nor the Locarno Treaty (the completed Conservative pattern for restoration, running on more traditional lines) would have been possible if Britain had appeared to be committed to France against Germany.

[1] H. Nicolson, *George V* (1952), 393.

Before MacDonald could turn the French withdrawal from the Ruhr and the German acceptance of the Dawes plan for reparations into anything more permanent, his government was in danger of defeat over Russian relations. It had recognized the Soviet government very soon after taking office and had then begun the complicated task of negotiating a trade treaty and of defending the interests of English owners of Tsarist bonds. Eventually two treaties were produced: a trade treaty, which opened up the possibility that new jobs would be created, and a treaty providing among other things that long-term trade credits could be negotiated for Russia once the question of the bondholders had been settled. The treaties could be rejected by the Commons, and soon it was clear that neither consideration for the bondholders, nor memories of their previous complaints about the difficulties of negotiating treaties with the United States which could be repudiated by the Senate, would persuade Liberals or Conservatives to approve of long-term credits which looked like throwing good money after bad.

But before the government was defeated over the treaty, a much more trivial incident had brought it down. The *Workers' Weekly*, a Communist magazine, published an article calling on soldiers not to shoot their working-class comrades during military or industrial warfare. The Director of Public Prosecutions decided to prosecute the editor for sedition; the Attorney-General decided to withdraw the prosecution. Campbell, the editor, had been crippled during the war, and the prosecution looked a little like an interference with the right of free speech; on the other hand, the withdrawal was said to have been forced on the government by Labour backbenchers. The Conservatives accepted the second story and moved a vote of censure; the Liberals offered a way out by suggesting a House of Commons committee of inquiry and, in a last effort to avoid clashing with the government, offered to surrender to the Labour party their places on the committee. MacDonald declined to let the decisions of ministers be referred to committees of the House, and when the Liberal amendment was carried he asked for a dissolution. George V consulted the Liberal and Conservative leaders but found no way to avoid granting it.[1]

The election presented the question 'Should the Labour government go on or not?' In this context the Liberals were irrelevant; Baldwin had been at some pains to lay aside the proposal of Protection and so the tariff issue no longer made it difficult for Liberals to vote Conservative. The election campaign found the electorate returning to a two-party system. In 1923 and in 1924 Selfridges asked every twentieth voter to

[1] H. Nicolson, op. cit. 400.

return a postcard. This poll would not produce an accurate prediction of the result, but it might show how opinion moved between the parties. By the last week of the campaign this poll showed the Liberals doing distinctly less well than in 1923, with every sign that the Conservatives would benefit more than the Labour party from this change.

At this point the Foreign Office published a letter apparently from the Comintern, signed by Zinovieff—whose name was promptly given to the letter—calling on British Communists to take steps to overthrow the bourgeois Labour government. It was not possible properly to test the authenticity of the letter: MacDonald was uncertain about it but, disregarding his instructions, the Foreign Office published it, together with a crisp expression of disapproval, in order to anticipate publication in the *Daily Mail* while he was away campaigning.

It now seems possible that the letter had been forged by Polish anti-Communists, and that because the Conservative party knew about the letter, it was able to alarm the Foreign Office. At the time all that could be seen was that the Foreign Office had published the letter, with disapproving comments, when MacDonald was away campaigning. Publication implied that the letter was genuine, and if the letter was genuine the Labour government had been unwise to negotiate with people who had so low an opinion of it. At a less logical level, the letter may have had the effect of confirming some people in the belief that all Socialists were dangerous and all anti-Socialists should rally round the stronger of the two parties in opposition.

	Votes	Seats	% of all votes cast
Conservative	8,039,598	419	48·3
Liberal	2,928,747	40	17·6
Labour	5,498,077	151	33·0

The shift of votes between the parties was rather larger than the Selfridges' poll had suggested before publication of the Zinovieff letter appeared, so its publication may have made some difference.[1] The Labour

[1] Selfridges' advertisement in *The Times*, 29 Oct. 1924, based on 411,000 replies.

	1923 poll	actual	1924 poll	actual
Conservative	50·74	38·1	55·94	48·1
Liberal	21·26	29·6	15·50	17·6
Labour	27·57	30·5	28·39	33·0

On the Liberal vote, see D. E. Butler, *The Electoral System in Britain Since 1918* (1963), 175–9.

party felt it had been defeated by a trick. The Conservative vote went up by a great deal and, mainly because more candidates come forward but partly also because of increased support in constituencies already contested, the Labour vote went up as well. The Liberal vote fell sharply, with the Conservatives as the chief beneficiaries, and their representation in Parliament fell to a level where they ceased to be taken very seriously.

Baldwin back in office

The period of quick-changing Prime Ministers was over. Evelyn Waugh's *Vile Bodies* (published in 1930) is, politically speaking, set against the background of the twenty-four months in which the Prime Ministership changed hands four times and, like his *Decline and Fall* (1928), it is in other ways a product of the middle twenties. The Bright Young Things, who first achieved public notice in 1924, had begun to fade from the scene before Waugh could chronicle their exploits; and public notice was one of the ways in which they differed from their predecessors. The young men and women of the upper classes who gained notoriety in the middle 1920s probably drank no harder than Lady Diana Manners's 'Corrupt Coterie' had done just before the war, and their sexual morals were probably no more relaxed than had become normal during the war. No doubt there was a little drug-addiction, which horrified Victorians who had brought up their children on laudanum, and certainly there was a great deal of talk about it.[1]

The enthusiasm of the Bright Young Things for being talked about matched the journalistic discovery that they made good copy by their mildly outrageous activities. In an odd and perverse way, they reduced class differences or, more precisely, newspaper publicity reduced inter-class ignorance. To the newspapers could be added the influence of the cinema and the wireless telling people what was going on, and the change in clothes—more particularly, women's clothes—must have helped this development. Before the war women's clothes demonstrated very clearly who worked and who had servants. After the war upper-class clothes were simpler and lower-class clothes were more attractive, which diminished the gap. An industrial advance which encouraged this was the introduction of rayon or artificial silk. Under the latter name it was taxed on the same principles as real silk in the 1925 Budget; although this implied that it was a luxury which would not have a very wide appeal it continued to be sold in increasing quantities and to make life easier, socially and physically, for working-class girls.

[1] R. Graves and A. Hodges, *The Long Week-end* (1940), 125; Lady Diana Cooper, *The Rainbow Comes and Goes* (1958), 82.

Literature no doubt presented life in strong colours, but always took some time to catch it up. As has been noted, *Vile Bodies* came out half a dozen years after the period in which it was set; the book that was advertised extensively in 1924 was E. F. Benson's *David of King's*, which radiated a wholesomeness of moral tone not often associated with the twenties. Galsworthy's second set of three Forsyte novels, *A Modern Comedy*, shows how pre-war values had survived into the twenties. Only in the mid twenties did *Ulysses* and *The Waste Land* begin to be heard of in Britain. Organization followed inspiration; *The Adelphi* and *The Criterion* were rapidly becoming accepted as the leading literary magazines. But of course the country had not become more sensitive artistically than before; hearties and aesthetes continued to grate on one another's nerve-ends at the universities, and Epstein's statues served as red rags to the bull-headed. It was in 1924 that Mary Webb published *Precious Bane*, the novel of the Marches which attracted praise from Baldwin that set her on the road to posthumous and understandably transient fame.

Baldwin had other things to worry about at the time. His new government was designed to reconcile all Conservatives. Austen Chamberlain went to the Foreign Office, which showed that the Coalitionists had returned to the party; other sections of opinion were probably reassured by the appointment of the ex-Liberal Free Trader Churchill to the Exchequer. The inclusiveness of the Cabinet, and the size of the majority, did suggest that Baldwin might have some difficulty in taking positive action in any direction. Perhaps it is unfair to dismiss his government as lightly as this; it demonstrated its competence as effectively as the previous government had done and, with more time at its disposal and a secure majority behind it, dealt with several problems in a way that MacDonald and his followers could not really object to. It also showed the same inability as its predecessor to do anything about unemployment.

In one important way it probably increased unemployment. Conservatives believed that, if Protection was ruled out of court, the best hope of restoring prosperity was to get back to the pre-1914 pattern of world trading conditions, and this meant returning to the Gold Standard. At the time practically everybody took it for granted that this meant returning to a dollar value for the pound of $4.86; the exchange value of the pound was quoted as a discount from $4.86 during the eleven years in which gold exports had been suspended, and it was generally believed that if the Bank of England was allowed once more to sell gold it would be in order to support the rate of exchange at the pre-war level.

In 1924 the pound seemed to be settling at about $4.40. Then it began to climb, without any noticeable changes in the British or American domestic price levels, by about 10 per cent. Churchill's first budget, in 1925, announced that the Bank of England was to be permitted to sell gold or export to maintain an exchange rate of $4.86 to the pound; *The Times* that morning printed a letter by Oswald Mosley denouncing 'an unnaturally high rate of exchange artificially maintained in the chimerical pursuit of the dollar'. The point was expanded, with illustrative details, by Keynes in newspaper articles which were later published as *The Economic Consequences of Mr. Churchill.* The title was neat but perhaps unfair; the ranks of financial orthodoxy insisted that the Gold Standard was the cure for international trade difficulties and Churchill did not really know enough about the subject to contradict them. Snowden moved a Labour motion of disapproval on the grounds that it was not the right time to make the change, but he did not suggest that the Gold Standard had its disadvantages or that the parity accepted was too high. The rest of the budget was unspectacular: it restored the McKenna Duties and imposed duties on silk, but for popular appeal it relied on its forecasts of Neville Chamberlain's proposals for increased welfare benefits.

The increase in the value of sterling meant that British exports cost more unless the price was deliberately cut by the producer. Coal-mining was the trade most deeply affected by revaluation; because labour was so large a part of the costs of production, it was very hard to cut prices except by reducing wages. Neither mine owners nor miners had changed their positions very much since 1921. The miners still wanted a seven-hour day and wage-rates determined by a national settlement, the owners still wanted district settlements and an eight-hour day.

The miners had not digested the lessons of Black Friday sufficiently to set the Triple Alliance on a more effective basis. It still remained an unco-ordinated *entente* in which the miners relied on the transport workers and the railwaymen to take the first shock of a nation-wide dispute. In 1925 this alliance was successful; on 31 July, 'Red Friday', the government gave way before the threat of a general embargo on all transport of coal, appointed a Royal Commission under Sir Herbert Samuel to report on the industry, and granted a subsidy to keep wages unchanged for nine months.

The government also set about improving the emergency scheme for saving the community from the worst inconveniences of a general strike by arranging road transport services, some supply of electricity, and a very limited scheme for dock work. Baldwin certainly wanted to avoid industrial strife. In March 1925 he had resisted proposals by his back-benchers to make trade unions change from 'contracting out' to 'contracting in' when collecting political subscriptions by asking his followers not to use their parliamentary majority to drive their opponents to extremes, and he ended with the petition of the Prayer Book 'Give peace in our time, O Lord'.[1]

In foreign affairs some progress was made towards this objective. The Labour government had been considering the Geneva Protocol, which provided for compulsory arbitration among signatories by the League of Nations. The Conservative government laid it aside, but Austen Chamberlain had to find something to take its place if British opinion was to be satisfied. He set to work to bring France and Germany together. The Locarno Treaty of 1925 confirmed the Versailles frontiers in Western Europe and committed the signatories to defend them against any infractions. The Dominions stayed out of the Treaty system, and its guarantees did not apply to Eastern Europe, though Chamberlain denied that Germany had been given a free hand in the East. The countries of Western Europe were ready to live peacefully together, and Locarno was the formal expression of their readiness. If they returned to their former bellicosity, Locarno could provide the basis of a system of united defence for signatory nations who were prepared to exert themselves.

The major constructive work of the government at home was inspired by Neville Chamberlain, who used the Ministry of Health as the base for an extension of social services that would have gladdened the heart of his father. The biggest change in the early years of Baldwin's government was the establishment in 1925 of pensions for widows and orphans, accompanied by the granting of old-age pensions at 65 instead of 70. These payments were of course the responsibility of the central government, which took another step forward into the welfare problems which had previously been handled by local government. It was logical enough that Chamberlain—despite his family traditions and his own connection with municipal government—should reduce the power of local government authorities. The important part of the work had to wait for a few years, but his Rating and Valuation Act cut down the number of local authorities which could impose rates and showed that the central government felt able to intervene in their affairs; its first intervention was to establish a new and more up-to-date pattern of valuation for rating, but other steps would clearly follow.

The B.B.C.

In July 1925 the government set up the Crawford committee to investigate the position of the British Broadcasting Company, and

---

[1] 6 Mar. 1925, *Commons Debates*, clxxi, 840.

eighteen months later the government took over the company, and called it the British Broadcasting Corporation. The chairman of the company's board of directors wrote in the *Radio Times* just before the change of authority:

The Directors of the British Broadcasting Company have had the steward-ship of a great public service for only four years, during which time broad-casting has emerged from nothing to the position it occupies today—an accepted essential part of the machinery of civilization . . .[1]

The use of wireless had begun partly as a product of military and transport needs, partly as a matter of amateurs putting sets together for the fun of the thing. Broadcasting had not been designed to send out a message or a programme so that a large audience could pick it up; government contracts for communication services seemed to be the only commercial use for the invention, which was why the Marconi Company had been in such close contact with the Cabinet in 1911. Even after the war broadcasting for entertainment was the American rather than the British approach; in Britain technically minded people put together their sets and 'listened-in' to weather reports and other messages not intended for them. They bought wireless parts, and the manufacturers realized that they might widen their market if they put out regular programmes. At the end of 1922 there were about 35,000 licence holders.

Trial programmes, providing 'listeners-in' with something to pick up on their sets, had been running for some months when the manufacturers came together to discuss prospects for a broadcasting company. Partly because the Marconi Company held so many patents concerned with transmitting, partly because the Post Office encouraged them, the large manufacturers of wireless parts formed a single company to put out broadcasts to 'listeners': on its first night it broadcast the results of the general election of 1922.

The broadcasting company was limited to a dividend of 7½ per cent and the manufacturers expected to make their profits by selling sets. The Post Office, which granted the licence to transmit, could not let a company earn large profits from broadcasting. The armed services, which were much more influential in Britain than in the United States in the twenties, opposed almost any expansion of broadcasting, on the ground that they wanted all the wireless-length waves for themselves. The press was alarmed at the thought of competition and was much more likely to be able to get its way than a few decades later, in the early days of television.

[1] The *Radio Times*, 24 Dec. 1926.

Reith, the Managing Director of the Company and later the Director-General of the Corporation, was exactly the man to deal with these pressures. He showed all the best qualities found in the Indian Civil Service: the immense administrative capacity required for taking an entirely novel development and introducing it into the lives of people who had never met it before, the ability to hold together a rapidly growing organization and the determination to use the organization to improve and elevate the people it served were all marks of 'the heaven-born'.

Even if he had wanted to run a system devoted to entertainment, he would have encountered too much suspicion among entertainers to be able to achieve very much. The Company transmitted for only five or six hours a day, of which over half was music. Reith was determined that it should be good music, and between the wars the B.B.C. produced a wide audience that was much more interested in music, and much better educated about it, than had previously been the case. The B.B.C. also made it slightly easier for performing musicians to find work. A good deal of the rest of broadcasting time was devoted to talks, organized at first by the Education Department. Reith had a great respect for education, and also a willingness to extend it into areas which other theories of broadcasting might not have touched.

He was much more willing to allow controversial discussion than his masters on the Board of Directors or in the Post Office. His basic principles of life may have been narrow, but the width of the field in which he thought they should be applied made him into one of the forces opening people's minds in the twenties. 'B.B.C.-English' probably did something to reduce the strain of an accent-divided society, because it meant that everybody who could afford a wireless set—it cost a few weeks' wages—was able to learn what a socially acceptable accent sounded like; the division had of course existed previously and had been made worse by ignorance. The other mass-medium of the day, the popular press, did not treat its audience as responsible people; the B.B.C. never forgot that it was speaking to responsible people.

Reith has sometimes been judged, rather unreasonably, by the standards of later decades and made to look, as in his insistence that announcers should wear dinner-jackets, like a son of the manse out of his depth. But similar criticisms could be made of so many things in the 1920s: witty Mr. Huxley's *Antic Hay* (published in the first full year of Company broadcasting) seems a bit tame forty years later. At the time, handling a mass-medium under public licence, Reith probably did as much as he could. He suggested that political speeches should be broadcast in the 1923 election. The Post Office turned the idea down, but in

1924 one speech by each party leader was allowed. As might have been expected Baldwin did very well on the wireless, partly because he took the trouble to find out what it was all about.

The Crawford committee reported in favour of public ownership of the broadcasting system. Nobody objected; the manufacturers were quite happy to go on selling their sets and the press regarded the wireless as a rival but not as a companion service to be absorbed into the financial structure of the newspaper chains. Reith had shown a blend of caution, rectitude, good taste, and imagination which reassured men in high places and convinced them that he could go on running it perfectly satisfactorily as a Corporation under government ownership. By the end of 1926 there were over two million licence holders.[1]

Baldwin's government had no doctrinaire fears of public enterprise. Electricity had never been taken up and developed in Britain as effectively as in other countries, partly because the generating stations—whether privately or municipally owned—were too small and served too narrow an area. In 1926 a Central Electricity Board was set up to construct a nation-wide power grid. The pylons of the system did not do the county landscape any good, but they enabled efficient power stations, running on the standard frequency, to supply power to the grid which could distribute it to other places. The local producers continued their work, but a considerable step had been taken towards making the central authority the effective controller of the system.

The General Strike of 1926

The strengthening of central authority, which could be seen in the foundation of the B.B.C. and the Central Electricity Board and was a part of Chamberlain's reform of local government, was also a part of the struggle over coal. The miners thought nationalization would make coal cheap and saleable and at the same time keep wages high, if all the coal from good pits and bad was 'pooled' and sold at a rate which meant the good pits would subsidize the bad. Sir Herbert Samuel's Commission reported, in March 1926, along lines which showed some sympathy with this argument. The Report asked for nationalization of the mineral rights and for steps towards amalgamation among the producers. The miners would still have been working for competing private employers, but not for private landlords and not under the system of hundreds of competing collieries. The Commission advised against longer hours and in favour of a national wages agreement; it suggested that the current wage-level, reached when the world supply of coal was dislocated by the French

[1] A. Briggs, *The Birth of Broadcasting* (1961), 18.

occupation of the Ruhr, was too high and should be reduced at least during the period of reorganization. And it advised against continuing the subsidy.

The miners' stand was not flexible: 'not a minute on the day, not a penny off the pay.'[1] Nor were the owners more helpful: district agreements, longer hours, and lower wages was their answer. The government showed no readiness to impose the Samuel recommendations, and yet everybody could see that they would not be accepted voluntarily by the two sides. The owners announced new pay scales for the end of April, when the subsidy ran out; the new scale took the principle of district settlements for granted by imposing much sharper cuts in some areas than in others.

The miners assumed that the Triple Alliance would step forward as effectively and as unquestioningly as in 1925; Bevin of the Transport and General Workers' Union had no desire to see his union placed unsupported in the front line, and asked for the General Council of the T.U.C. to be given powers by its component unions to conduct a general strike on behalf of the miners and to decide when satisfactory terms had been gained for them. The final decision was a little ambiguous; undoubtedly the great majority of unions thought they had committed their power of strike action to the General Council but the miners believed that the other unions had, with an unusual lack of regard for union autonomy, committed themselves to stay on strike until the Miners' Federation was satisfied.

The owners withdrew the demand for district agreements but insisted on a wage cut and an increase in hours from seven to eight; they did not accept the Samuel recommendations for reorganization. The T.U.C. and the Cabinet continued to negotiate; the miners and the owners held aloof with the sulky determination which led Birkenhead to say he could assert the miners' leaders were the stupidest men in the country if he had not had the misfortune to meet the owners. The Cabinet broke off negotiations on the night of 2–3 May, in the belief that a strike at the *Daily Mail* was the beginning of the general strike. In fact the *Daily Mail* dispute was an isolated incident, but the parties in the negotiations were so far apart by this stage that the strike was inevitable.

The organization on both sides proved entirely adequate. The unions had not done much advance planning, but union solidarity was enough to bring about a prompt and almost complete response to the General Council's instructions that transport workers and railwaymen, electrical workers, and some industrial workers should strike. On the government

[1] A. Bullock, *Life of Ernest Bevin* (1960), i. 328.

side food and milk supplies were kept moving and some passenger transport services were provided. No official efforts were made to keep private industry running. The government felt that its duty was simply to prevent the community from being so seriously inconvenienced that a settlement had to be reached.

Obviously the General Strike was designed to put pressure on the government. The government said that this was unconstitutional, and the T.U.C appeared tacitly to have accepted this point, because it denied that it was putting unconstitutional pressure on the government. 'In a challenge to the constitution, God help us unless the government won', as Jimmy Thomas said.[1] At the time many people thought that if the trade unions proposed to force their will upon the government, they must be ready to take the place of the government. The General Strike was certainly not intended by its organizers to be a revolutionary action, and peaceful demonstrations often show a desire to impel the government in one direction or another without any desire to overthrow it. Organizations sometimes try—not always unsuccessfully—to impose their will on the government, as the British Medical Association did in 1911 and 1947, but this is not usually considered to be a revolutionary act.

Once the government had decided that it would not let itself to be compelled to give a subsidy or pass legislation to help the coal miners, a dispute developed within the Cabinet about the right way to handle the strike. Baldwin got his own way, and made sure that there was no brusque policy of repression. But a group of ministers was consistently in favour of stronger action, and of these men Churchill was perhaps the most irresponsible. When he suggested escorting a food convoy through the streets of London with troops carrying loaded rifles, Sir John Anderson asked the Chancellor of the Exchequer to stop talking nonsense. Churchill spent most of his time during the strike editing *The British Gazette*—a newspaper put out by the government during the strike which showed a considerable disregard for the facts by issuing statements like 'The owners have agreed to nearly everything recommended by the Commission. . . . The miners' leaders have not however made the slightest advance towards an acceptance.'[2]

Its attitude was in sharp contrast to the B.B.C. approach. Reith and Baldwin took practically similar views of the strike; they regarded it as an attempt to coerce the government and were determined to prevent this from happening, but they wanted to avoid alienating the strikers from

---

[1] G. Blaxland, *J. H. Thomas* (1964), 194.

[2] J. W. Wheeler-Bennett, *John Anderson* (1961), 106; *British Gazette*, 5 May 1926.

the rest of the community. If the transmitting stations had been 'commandeered', as was legally quite possible, they might have been deployed like the *Gazette*. The B.B.C. gave the strikers no encouragement and it refused to broadcast an appeal for a compromise settlement by the Archbishop of Canterbury, but unlike the *Gazette* it did not put out anti-strike propaganda nor did it compromise its reputation for accuracy by publishing false reports of a return to work.

By telling people what was going on it probably contributed to the general air of calm. With the passage of time this calm has been exaggerated to legendary proportions; there were some struggles between police and strikers, and probably if the strike had begun to inflict hardship on the population at large a greater degree of bitterness would have appeared. Treating the whole thing as a game may have been possible only because nothing very serious seemed to be happening. But when all allowances have been made for this, the observers, British and foreign, who expressed awed admiration at the peaceful way in which the struggle was conducted were still passing a sensible judgement on a civilized conflict.

The T.U.C. leaders did not want the strike to go on indefinitely. A prolonged strike cost money and might direct public opinion to a determined anti-union policy of the Churchill variety. They began to look round for a line of withdrawal, and Sir Herbert Samuel provided one. He presented a memorandum on the settlement of the coal-mining dispute which seemed satisfactory to the T.U.C. But the miners did not agree, for it included acceptance of a wage cut, and the alliance began to break up. The process was accelerated by a speech of Sir John Simon, in which he said that a general strike was illegal and could lead to the forfeiture of union funds. This opinion had no solid foundation and when the government passed an Act the next year, which declared general strikes illegal, it was not considered to be merely a declaratory measure; at the time, however, Simon's view helped to weaken the morale of the T.U.C. leaders.

By 12 May they were convinced the strike should be ended and, after a final attempt to persuade the miners to accept the Samuel Memorandum, they informed the Prime Minister of their decision. The retreat was not well planned; there were a number of struggles over reinstatement, but in general the trade-union movement survived as well as it had any right to expect. The miners stayed out for months, but eventually they obtained neither the recommendations of the Samuel Commission nor those of the Samuel Memorandum.

A whole cycle of working-class militancy, beginning about 1910, had come to an end, though the spectacular closing act had come in an economic situation much less favourable to strike action than the 1910–20 period. The General Strike, for all the reluctance of its leaders, was at least an attempt to make something happen. The forces of change, which had been at work fairly actively during the war and immediately after, had worked themselves out. For the next five years immobility reigned triumphant and almost unchallenged.

6. The years of inaction   1926–1931

The new way of living

THE failure of the General Strike, and the long-drawn-out defeat of the coal strike, ushered in a period of industrial calm.[1] Employers felt that attempts to cut wages drastically might be unwise, and the trade unions took care not to be involved in large and ill-prepared adventures again. The miners, who spent eight times as many days on strike as the average trade unionist, had been the centre of intransigence; their weakness was made obvious when the Act that had reduced their working hours from eight to seven was repealed. Power in the trade union movement passed from the miners' leaders to Bevin and Thomas. The new mood could be seen in the Mond–Turner talks, begun in 1928, between employers and trade unionists: Turner was chairman of the General Council of the T.U.C. and Mond was a progressive Liberal-turned-Conservative who was the major influence in setting up Imperial Chemical Industries. They had no effective proposals for restoring the economy, but at least they could talk to each other more politely than employers and employed had been able to do for the previous fifteen years or more.

This relative harmony in industry was not destroyed by the Trade Disputes Act of 1927. For just over a century, Parliament had preferred trade unions to have as few legal rights and duties as possible, and it had reversed a number of legal decisions in which the courts had tried to treat the unions like companies. No political party wanted to adopt the North American system of giving unions legal claims on employers and legal responsibilities, and as nobody was prepared to eliminate unions alto-

---

[1] Days lost through strikes:

1919–25	194,107,000
1926	162,233,000
1927–32	28,719,000
1933–9	11,918,000

D. E. Butler and J. Freeman, *British Political Facts 1900–1967* (1968), 219.

gether, their industrial position was left untouched. The Act made general strikes illegal, and laid down that civil servants were not to belong to trade unions. These measures guarded against an unreal danger that the trade unions might try to take over the government of the country by syndicalist methods, but they did not affect the normal process of collective bargaining. The only really important change made by the Act was that, when a trade union had voted to contribute to a political party, money could be collected only from individuals who had signed a form specifically permitting the deduction; previously money had usually been collected from everybody who had not signed a form asking to be exempted. This change was inspired partly by a belief that really only a small minority of the working class wanted to support the Labour party, and partly by a belief that the proper way to finance a party was through individual donations. It seems that most of the Conservative party's money came from a relatively few large contributions from wealthy individuals and other ways of raising money were thought improper. But while the attitude of Conservative Members was understandable, it was not the way to establish political peace and harmony. The Act looked as though it was using the General Strike to damage the political prospects of the Labour party, and over the years the proportion of trade unionists subscribing to the unions' political funds fell steadily from 58 per cent in 1928 to 48 per cent in 1945, the last year before the Act was repealed.[1]

The right wing of the Conservative party could also take some satisfaction from the decision to raid the Soviet trade mission in London, Arcos, which was suspected of being a centre for spies. The British government then broke off diplomatic relations though no real proof of spying had been found. On the other hand an attempt to restore the power of the House of Lords to more or less what it had been in 1910 was checked. Baldwin could not convert his backbenchers to his own philosophical acceptance of the post-war world, but he could stop them doing much to put the clock back.

Making positive changes was harder. In 1926 the government was presented with a legacy from its predecessor: the Hadow Committee that had been examining the education of the adolescent submitted its Report. As it laid down the objectives to which Presidents of the Board of Education struggled for the next twenty years, and shaped the pattern of British education for at least twenty years after that, it deserves some attention. It declared that everybody should stay at school until 15, and should receive 'secondary' education for the closing years of school life. Previously 'secondary' education had meant the sort of teaching given to the

[1] M. Harrison, *Trade Unions and the Labour Party since 1945* (1960), 32-3.

7 or 8 per cent of the population that went to grammar schools. The Committee decided to keep the examination, taken at 11 plus, for free places at grammar school, but it did consider whether the schools for everybody else, which it wanted to call 'modern' schools, could be made equal to the grammar schools. On the whole its conclusions pointed in the direction of spending as much money on 'modern' schools as on grammar schools: this did not appeal to the Conservative party, which saw little use in educating the working-classes. Most supporters of the Labour party welcomed the Report because it opened opportunities to talented working-class children, and kept less talented children in school and out of the labour market. However, the Catholic supporters of the Labour party felt uneasy because the Report meant they would have to provide a decidedly larger amount of money, to pay for secondary education, than was needed for Catholic elementary schools. If the government had acted on the Report it might have faced similar protests from supporters of Church of England schools.

The most exciting moments in the 1924–9 Parliament had nothing to do with the government's legislative programme. The Anglo-Catholic section of the Church of England had been gaining ground, and a new Prayer Book had been prepared which moved in a High Church direction. A change in the Prayer Book required an amendment to the Act of Uniformity of 1662, which had defined the position of the Established Church after the Restoration. Eloquent speeches were made in favour of the change when it was proposed in 1927; eloquent and bitter speeches, denouncing the tendency to adopt Roman Catholic practices in ritual, were made against the change. The proposers of the change were defeated and, when they returned to the charge in 1928, they were defeated again. They pointed out how odd it was that M.P.s who might be Nonconformists, Jews, or atheists had a power of veto over the Church of England. But the Established Church, with its special place in the life of the country, was bound to concern everyone in the country; England had always been an anti-clerical country in the sense that there was a strong lay dislike for clerical power, and a good deal of the objection to the inclination to Roman Catholic practices detected in the new Prayer Book came from a fear that clergymen wanted to acquire the power over their parishioners that Roman Catholic priests were supposed to possess.

The fierceness of the debates on the Prayer Book showed that, in the eyes of her rulers, England was still a Christian country. Most of the urban working class had never taken much interest in religion and, at least since 1914, the churches had been losing their influence in other classes. The Church of England made attempts to win urban support but did not gain many new supporters. Previously it had enjoyed a monopoly of high offices such as the Premiership. In the twentieth century several Nonconformists rose to the top in politics, but this was mainly due to a change in the social class of the people who became Prime Minister and did not mean that Nonconformist influence had increased: it had always worked through the Liberal party and the decline of the Liberal party was to some extent caused by the loss of authority of the Nonconformist churches. The Labour party never felt as deep an attachment to any religious group as the Liberals, though many of its leaders were in their rhetoric and imagery children of the chapel.

The influence of the churches was still strong on issues like divorce and birth control, where it reinforced the opposition to change. Before the war divorce was very infrequent; after the war it became more common, though the law on the subject changed very little. People blamed the war and the hasty marriages of wartime, they blamed the influence of the United States, and they blamed the wickedness and depravity of the younger generation. The churches did not condone the change, and George V made it clear that he disapproved. All the same, MacDonald's first Cabinet included Josiah Wedgwood, who had been divorced.

Christian and traditional influences were also ranged against birth control, or at least against the spreading of information about methods of birth control. The birth-rate had been declining since the 1870s, though it is not easy to find out why. The fall appeared first in the middle classes, and in 1905 the Fabian Society took a survey of its membership to discover the reasons. But although Fabians were not the most reticent section of the middle class the survey revealed only that they had chosen deliberately to limit their families and said nothing about the means used for this.[1] During the First World War British troops were issued with contraceptive sheaths to reduce the wastage of troops from venereal disease, and this meant that a section of the male population indirectly learnt something about birth control. After the war it became quite clear that the middle-class families were being restricted, but working class families continued to be large. Efforts were made by reformers to explain to the poor how they could plan their families, but the subject was still regarded as unsuitable for open discussion. A little illogically, some of the opponents of change most enthusiastic about suppressing the spread of knowledge about birth control also deplored the way the working class was breeding faster than the middle class. The Church of England was changing its position, and in 1930 a majority of the bishops declared that birth-control by the use of contraceptives was justified in 'exceptional circumstances'.

[1] E. R. Pease, *History of the Fabian Society* (1918), 161–2.

The decline in the birth-rate did not lead to a decline in population, because people were living longer. The Victorian family, at least in theory, had looked after its members: old-age pensions, and widows' and orphans' pensions, were items in a general recognition that the family would no longer carry out all the welfare responsibilities expected of it. The family unit had never been as effective or as respectable in practice as in theory: during the war the government had had to change the regulations so that Married Women's allowances could be paid to 'unmarried wives' of soldiers. If divorce had been cheaper and easier to obtain, presumably a number of these domestic situations would have sorted themselves out.

Upholders of Victorian attitudes could take some satisfaction from the decline in drinking. Especially when allowance is made for the reduction in the alcohol content of beer, the amount drunk by the average adult went down fairly steadily during the first half of the twentieth century. Smoking, on the other hand, increased steadily. Nicotine and alcohol were accepted and taken for granted as ordinary commodities which were widely consumed, and yielded a gratifyingly large amount of revenue; in the 1920s there was a flurry of excitement about other drugs, such as cocaine and heroin, which frightened or attracted people because they were exotic as well as being more powerful. There was still some mild pressure for Prohibition on the American pattern during the twenties, but there was no force behind it: drunkenness was no longer the menace to home life and to peace and quiet that it had been in the nineteenth century, and not enough people had motor cars to make it a menace on the roads.

Baldwin's Home Secretary, Joynson-Hicks, was determined to restore moral standards to the high level he believed had existed before the war. This involved the police force in a good deal of raiding of night-clubs suspected of serving alcoholic drinks at illegal hours, investigation of parks after dark, and prosecutions for obscenity. The strain of imposing a moral code inappropriate to the period was too much for the police: policemen took bribes from owners of night-clubs who wanted to know when police raids might be expected, and gave perjured evidence against men and women accused of 'undue familiarity' in the parks.

The struggle between writers and the authorities entered a new phase. The Lord Chamberlain continued to uphold traditional standards in the theatre but this was no longer the main area of struggle. *Young Woodley* —not a play of great merit—was banned at first in 1928, but it was put on in a theatrical club, which was free from restriction, and after reconsideration the Lord Chamberlain changed his mind. On the other hand some of the most distinguished novelists of the period were now pressing into new fields. D. H. Lawrence had been recognized shortly before the war as a leading writer in the movement away from the highly rational authors and playwrights who had dominated the scene in the early years of the century. In the twenties he became increasingly committed to approval of untamed nature and the irrational, and he wrote more explicitly about sex than before. *The Rainbow* had been prosecuted in 1915, and *Lady Chatterley's Lover* (1928) could not be published in England without expurgation for over thirty years. James Joyce's *Ulysses* (1922) was kept out of the country for the same reason.

Writers like Eliot and Virginia Woolf did not have trouble with the authorities, but they did suffer in one way from their readiness to explore new stylistic techniques. In the nineteenth century authors like Tennyson and Dickens had been accepted as good writers and had also sold to wide audiences. In the twentieth century it became increasingly unusual for the writers who were admired in literary circles to be popular with the general reading public. The great creative outburst, stretching over about a dozen years, in which modern writers came to grips with symbols, the unconscious mind, and the apparent need to extend the boundaries of language in an attempt to express the complexity of the world, was also a period in which the gap between the writer and the ordinary man widened. It was a period in which the dominant school of writers was not immediately concerned with the problems of man and society; works like Shaw's *St. Joan* and Forster's *Passage to India*, both of which appeared in 1924, were by men of the pre-war generation.

By the end of the 1920s writers were returning to social and political problems. One of the earliest signs of this was the appearance of books about the war; there had been a few, such as A. P. Herbert's *The Secret Battle* (1919) shortly after the war, but they were not popular until about 1928 when Blunden's *Undertones of War*, Graves's *Goodbye to All That*, the immense success of R. C. Sherriff's rather undistinguished play *Journey's End*, and the popularity of Remarque's *All Quiet on the Western Front* (translated from German) showed a revival of concern about political questions. Any honest account of war in the trenches made people feel that this must never be allowed to happen again, and this was reinforced by a belief that the next war would be much worse. Aerial manœuvres in 1927 suggested that, if an enemy country decided to attack London, as much as 200 tons of high explosive might be dropped in an air-raid. This prospect was frightening; nobody realized how little harm 200 tons would do. Great importance was attached to aerial bombing and it dominated most of the thinking about military affairs of the next two decades. Uneasiness about war did not have any immediate effects; the pacifist movement did not really gain strength until the early 1930s, but on the other hand there was no increase in military spending.

Economic attitudes and issues in the late 1920s

Churchill, as Chancellor of the Exchequer, was as enthusiastic about keeping spending low as he had been about high expenditure at the Admiralty before 1914. He induced the service Ministers to accept, as a rule to be changed only by a Cabinet decision, the principle that when preparing their estimates for each year they should assume that there would be no major war for ten years to come. Even with this rule, the purists were never satisfied that his budgets balanced properly. By the late 1920s the budget had settled down at just over £800m. a year: interest on war debt at somewhat over £300m. was much the largest single item, ordinary expenditure was just under £400m. and the surplus for the Sinking Fund to reduce the debt was expected to be £40m. a year. Against this repayment of debt could be set the borrowing by the Unemployment Insurance Fund, at around £5m. a year.

The budget disputes between Churchill and Snowden were among the most entertaining moments of the parliamentary year. On the whole Snowden seems to have been the victor, because he left everybody feeling the purists were right in thinking that the budget did not really balance. This was true only in the sense that the £40m. for the Sinking Fund was not provided every year. The debt was reduced every year, and on this definition the budget showed a surplus. Producing this result required financial expedients too ingenious to be convincing: in 1926 a tax on betting was tried, but it turned out to be administratively impracticable; taxes were collected earlier than usual; money was taken out of the Road Fund, which was supposed to be devoted exclusively to road-building, and was used for the general budget. The direct effect of Churchill's budgets was less deflationary than firmly balanced budgets would have been, though businessmen's confidence may have been reduced by the apparent deficits.

The balance of payments, to which much less attention was given than to the budget, caused more trouble. Imports at £1,100m. were met by visible exports of £700m., and invisible exports (of which interest and dividends were the larger part) of £450m. This left an average annual balance on current transactions of something over £50m. The City of London continued its pre-1914 practice of heavy overseas lending and, because the current surplus was so small, this put the country's international position under some strain. The only defence was to hold interest rates at a relatively high level. Export industries were still doing badly; they were helped by the American boom in 1927 and 1928, but they had not recovered from the problems of the early 1920s.

The government did not have any exciting legislation to take people's minds off the high unemployment figures. The vote was given, almost absent-mindedly and without any agitation, to the women between 21 and 30 who had been left out in 1918. Chamberlain produced a comprehensive reform of local government. In the nineteenth century new organizations had been set up to deal with each new local government problem, such as education or poor relief, when it became serious. Chamberlain's Act, like Balfour's 1902 Education Act, was a step towards handing the responsibilities of the separate organizations over to county councils and borough councils. The Boards of Guardians for poor relief disappeared, as the Minority Report of the Poor Law Commission had suggested in 1909. The parish councils were relieved of their road-making duties, which were growing harder to carry out as motor transport became more important. Local rates on industrial plant were reduced to a quarter of the previous level, and agriculture was freed from rates altogether. To make up the revenue lost by this 'derating', councils were given grants from the Exchequer on the basis of factors like the number of children to be educated.

Derating helped depressed industries to some extent; rates in the depressed areas were higher than average, because their bills for unemployment relief were higher than average. Industries made some attempts to solve their problems by amalgamation. In cases like the launching of Imperial Chemical Industries this was a merger of firms into a single unit which could then expand; some 'rationalization' involved mergers of firms resigned to the fact that industries like cotton textiles were going to contract. Amalgamation did not cause as much unemployment as bankruptcy would have done, but it did not provide many new jobs. A new Unemployment Insurance Act passed in 1927, which gave unlimited cover instead of the previous 26 weeks of payments to anybody employed 15 weeks in a year, was based on the assumption that about 6 per cent of the working population would be unemployed. This was a fairly optimistic assessment of the position in the late 1920s.

Orthodox politicians had accepted the return to the Gold Standard, and its consequences: relatively high interest rates and some degree of deflation. No politician could accept the even higher levels of unemployment that would be needed to secure the exchange value of the pound. Politics became more and more concerned with unemployment as it became clear that there was no other issue to be raised. The Liberal party and the Labour party prepared for what turned out to be the final struggle to decide who was to be the main opponent of the Conservatives. In 1926 the Liberals did not seem to have much chance of making even one more attempt to challenge the Labour party. However, during the General Strike Lloyd George declined to associate himself with the Liberal 'shadow Cabinet's' disapproval of the strike; Asquith rebuked him for this, but it became clear that party opinion was on Lloyd George's side and Asquith had to give up the Liberal leadership. Lloyd George took over the post and began trying to put life into the party.

He showed, as he had done before 1914, some interest in schemes for reviving agriculture, but the main proposal in his programme was the suggestion that the State should issue a large loan which would then be spent on national development, mainly by a great scheme of road-building. The programme, set out in *We Can Conquer Unemployment*, was accepted by his party but more because he was the leader and his followers were tired of quarrels than because they understood it or believed in it. As recently as 1927 Lloyd George had himself been in favour of 'economy', by which he meant lower government spending on armaments. Lloyd George had to take risks to save his party from fading away, but a reputable politician could not campaign on the platform of budgeting for a deficit. Raising a loan might be slightly more acceptable, but it would have been easier to convince people if some pillar of financial respectability had declared that a loan was justified. Lloyd George's reputation did nothing to help him. He had made a number of promises in the past, and was blamed because they had not been fulfilled. In any case, he did not have long enough to explain the economics behind his proposal: his programme appeared only two or three months before the 1929 election.

At the same time as Lloyd George was moving his party to the left, MacDonald and Henderson were moving their party to the right. The Labour programme put forward in 1928, *Labour Faces the Nation*, was concerned with immediate reforms rather than the proclamation of distant visions. The move to a moderate policy must not be overestimated: Snowden, in a later and hostile mood, said that the welfare proposals in *Labour Faces the Nation* would have added £1,000m. a year to the government's spending. The left wing of the party was not satisfied, but it did not feel it was being ignored completely.

It did have suggestions to make. The I.L.P. wanted the government to pass legislation fixing a 'living wage', which would be set at a level that inefficient firms could not meet so they would have to hand the business over to the State, which would then run the firm and continue to employ the workers. This amounted to nationalization, inefficient firm by in-efficient firm, and implied a large budget deficit. Mosley and Strachey issued a proposal, very shortly after the return to gold, that the govern-ment should set up central planning boards and inflate the currency by setting minimum wage levels and making more money available so that firms could pay the new rates. Neither the I.L.P. nor the Mosley–Strachey proposals were accepted by the Labour party; they were too novel and did not fit in with the Gladstonian views of Snowden, the party's financial expert.

Both proposals, like the Lloyd George scheme, would have produced budget deficits that would have reduced the number of unemployed. But this does not mean that the people putting the proposals forward had understood why they would work. The Mosley–Strachey proposals descended from J. A. Hobson's theory that people invest too much and as a result are unable to consume all that is produced. Lloyd George had been advised by Keynes about his plans, but Keynes's position at that time was far from clear. In his *Treatise on Money* (1931) he showed that he was in favour of an increase in prices, but did not lay the responsibility for this on the government. Even in his *General Theory of Employment, Interest and Capital* (1936), the main argument is that a loan to increase public expenditure would have its beneficial effect by providing more investment rather than simply by producing a budget deficit. Chapter ten, 'The Marginal Propensity to Consume', is the basis of the way modern governments run their affairs, but it is really more in the footnotes than the text that Keynes says a budget deficit will cure unemployment no matter how it is produced. This period is not yet far enough in the past for the intellectual limitations of the participants to be taken for granted, and historians are tempted to jump in with good advice and show how much better they could have run things, without looking at the intellectual equipment available for politicians.[1]

In the 1929 election neither the Conservative nor the Labour party were prepared to take any risks. Socialism and Protection, the two electoral bogymen of the twenties, were put out of sight. Baldwin's posi-tion as leader was no easier than MacDonald's. His followers were resigned to the fact that they could not break the trade unions and force down wage-rates; most of them believed that Protection was the only real answer, but they had to admit that it had not in the past been a satis-factory election issue. Instead they went into the election with the new

---

[1] For example: 'The Ministers should have propounded radical schemes for disciplining the economy, for marshalling the unused industrial resources and for increasing purchasing power.' C. Cross, *Philip Snowden* (1966), 257.

road traffic slogan, 'Safety First'. This was less attractive than promises to conquer unemployment, but on the other hand people were far from sure that they wanted a change of government and the results were inconclusive.

	Votes	Seats	% of all votes cast
Conservative	8,656,473	260	38·2
Liberal	5,308,510	59	23·4
Labour	8,389,512	288	37·1

The second Labour government (1929)

Effective changes of government in the twentieth century seem to take an incubation period of about four years: the incubation period may take the form of a steady fall in government popularity leading to electoral disaster, as in 1902–6, or it may involve a period under a government with an uneasy majority like the Labour government of 1950–1. Both of the Labour governments in the years between the wars were of this sort; the electorate flirted with the idea of an effective Labour government, and found the prospect unattractive. The uneasy tenure of the Labour government was shown by the way people, then and later, spoke of 'giving Labour a second chance'. If this meant anything it implied that an unsatisfactory Labour government would be followed by the reinstatement of the Liberals as the major party opposed to the Conservatives. But both Labour governments were followed by elections in which the major transfer of votes was away from the Liberals and towards the Conservatives. The Liberal leaders knew this might happen, because the bulk of their followers were people who felt more at home with the Conservatives' general attitude, but on particular issues agreed with the Labour party. On foreign and imperial policy, and on the great domestic issue of Free Trade, the Liberal party and the Labour party could work together without difficulty. This co-operation did not look like leading to unification; on the other hand, when Liberals and Conservatives came together they formed coalitions, and when the coalitions ended a large number of Liberals stayed with the Conservatives.

The second Labour government was sufficiently like the first not to cause surprise. MacDonald reluctantly allowed Henderson to become Foreign Secretary; Henderson was a little more ready than MacDonald to see that, faced with the choice, Britain would have to support France against Germany in order to prevent Germany from dominating Europe. The French thought MacDonald was pro-German, and they came to think the same about Snowden; he believed that in the long run Reparations should be abolished, and in the short run at The Hague in 1929 he resisted any suggestion that France should be allowed to increase her share of Reparations at Britain's expense. Henderson was needed, to balance this appearance of anti-French feeling. He began preparations for a World Disarmament Conference, to be held in 1932. MacDonald went to the United States to see whether steps could be taken towards naval disarmament, which he kept in his own hands. Not much was done, but MacDonald seems to have been the first British Prime Minister to see that the change of foreign policy that would involve least disturbance was to enter into closer relations with the United States. He was welcomed in America, but he did not imagine that he had done much to end the American desire to stay out of European problems. Henderson resumed diplomatic relations with Russia, though more slowly than the left wing of the party had hoped. In Egypt he dismissed Lord Lloyd, the High Commissioner, for taking altogether too autocratic a view of his position. Lloyd had gone too far for Austen Chamberlain, and much too far for the Egyptians, who were showing signs of irritation.

A Commission under Sir John Simon had been set up in 1927 to investigate the government of India. No Indians were appointed to the Commission, probably to avoid annoying the Anglo-Indian section, though the government said it was meant to avoid upsetting those Indian leaders who had to be left out. The result was that no Indians of importance appeared before the Commission to give evidence, and Indian nationalist feelings were strengthened. After consultations with the new government, which bore the ultimate responsibility, the Viceroy, Lord Irwin, declared in October 1929 that Dominion status was the natural conclusion for India's constitutional development. Baldwin, as leader of the Opposition, did not deny that Dominion status was inevitable but he did say that he wished Irwin had not made the statement. It caused considerable trouble inside his party and it also cut away some of the ground from under the feet of the Simon Commission. The Commission's Report, which appeared in June 1930, recommended responsible government in the provinces. Power over important questions, such as defence and foreign policy, remained in the hands of the Viceroy at Delhi, though an additional conference to discuss these powers was suggested. The proposals were discussed at Round Table conferences at which the Indians who had refused to appear before the Commission were represented. But a wave of civil disobedience had begun in April, when Gandhi led a 200-mile march to the sea and then gathered salt in defiance of the government monopoly. During the year 54,000 people were convicted on civil disobedience charges, and over 23,000 of them were in prison at the end of the year.

In a more peaceful area of imperial relations, the government was preparing the legislation needed to give effect to the Balfour Declaration of 1926. The Statute of Westminster made it clear that Dominions could have as much freedom to legislate as they wanted. This did not worry the British government, which had tended to assume that they already had this freedom. By 1931 Britain was concerned only to try to persuade them to follow a single foreign policy; in 1930 the British government rejected Dominion suggestions, of the sort that had been made for thirty years, that a system of imperial customs preferences should be set up.

All the disagreements in England about these imperial questions were fought out inside the Conservative party. Baldwin's position was weak immediately after the election. He was blamed for defeat, just as in 1923, and for not using the majority gained in 1924 to return to the days before the war. He was also attacked because of his position on Protection and on India. Some Conservatives were attracted by the idea of setting up a tariff system for the whole Empire with all the members, including Britain, taxing imports from outside but accepting each other's products free of tax. The policy of Empire Free Trade was probably never practicable, because the Dominions had no intention of exposing their newly launched industries to competition from Britain. But the scheme had the support of the great newspaper owners, Lord Beaverbrook and Lord Rothermere, and had to be taken seriously by any Conservative leader.

The political influence of their papers was less than people imagined; the *Daily Express* and the *Daily Mail* attracted large readerships but they were readers who did not take politics seriously enough to worry about the details of a particular issue. In his struggle with Beaverbrook and Rothermere, Baldwin said that their newspapers relied on tendentious and selective reporting. To some extent the compressed and emotionally loaded reporting of these newspapers was an attempt to make politics palatable to people who had not previously read a daily newspaper. There were disadvantages about the newspapers with which Baldwin was implicitly comparing the *Express* and the *Mail*; Spender (of the *Westminster Gazette*) in his *Autobiography* and Hammond's *Life of C. P. Scott* (of the *Manchester Guardian*) show how close these respected editors came to running party bulletins. They suppressed news, they wrote editorials designed to influence policy which were deliberately made incomprehensible to anyone who did not know how discussions were going in the Cabinet, and Spender took it for granted that his paper ought to be subsidized by a small group of wealthy Liberals. The mass-circulation papers probably did the job of giving the uninterested a vague outline of what was going on rather better than the 'quality' newspapers succeeded in enabling people interested in politics to find out what they needed to know in order to consider problems properly. But the owners of the mass-circulation papers could not marshal their readers to support a particular policy.

Protection was popular enough in the Conservative party to make their challenge dangerous. Baldwin met the challenge by declaring his support for Imperial Preference, which had from time to time been part of the Conservative programme. This gave him a short breathing-space, but by October of 1930 he had to defend himself again, at a meeting of Conservative M.P.s, peers, and candidates. He won by 462 votes to 116, a majority large enough for survival but not for comfort. The question of India was beginning to make itself felt; Baldwin was pressed not to go beyond the Report of the Simon Commission by expressing sympathy for the idea of Dominion status. In January 1931 Churchill left the 'shadow Cabinet' because he wanted to be free to oppose any move towards it; in the long run this step meant that he was outside the government during the thirties, and for most of the decade was regarded as dangerously right-wing. But in the short-run it made Baldwin's position even weaker. He had placed Neville Chamberlain at the head of the party organization, a risky step because Chamberlain who was much more acceptable to the Protectionists now became his natural successor. In February the Chief Agent suggested that it would help the party if Baldwin retired, and for a few days he thought of doing so. *The Times* had prepared its editorial on the subject, Baldwin had told Chamberlain that he was going, and it is said he had written out his letter of resignation. But he decided to stay and fight. In the Commons he made a successful speech in which he refused to commit his party against Dominion status as the final goal of policy in India.

Beaverbrook and Rothermere had created a larger problem by running Empire Free Trade candidates against official Conservative candidates in a number of by-elections, with some success. A by-election was coming up in the very safe Conservative seat of St. George's, Westminster. At first Baldwin thought he might stand there himself, partly because nobody else seemed to be willing to defend the policy of the party leadership. When Duff Cooper, who had lost his seat in the 1929 election, came forward to resist the Empire Free Traders Baldwin made a speech in his support in which he denounced Beaverbrook and Rothermere for seeking power without responsibility, 'the prerogative of the harlot throughout the ages'. This was hardly fair to the press lords, who had conducted one of the most open attacks on a party leader to be seen in this century. By attacking Baldwin at by-elections, on a genuine issue of economic policy, Beaverbrook and Rothermere were giving him a chance to defend his programme and to test public opinion; other party leaders have been driven out by secret discussions ending in a sudden 'failure of health'. It is a measure of Baldwin's political skill and of his readiness to avoid issues of policy that he could defeat the assault by concentrating on the personal failings of his opponents and retain a reputation as a purifying influence in politics. His success was not decisive; Duff Cooper was elected in St. George's but the Empire Free Trade candidate was not disgraced, and the assault would undoubtedly have been resumed in the autumn.

Baldwin's position survived these attacks better than might have been expected. The other parties had their problems. The Liberals had rallied behind Lloyd George in the two or three years before the election, and had allowed him to write his own policy and control the party machinery. In return for this they expected success. The Liberals may have done less well than they hoped in 1929 because Lloyd George launched his unemployment programme too close to the election to have time to convince people of its merits, or because he committed the party to an economic programme which it did not really believe in, or because no section of society felt the Liberals were whole-heartedly devoted to its interests. In any case they had done badly, and Lloyd George was blamed. As a result he found it hard to make sure that all his followers voted together in the Commons.

Tension was at its highest in the first few months of the new government; the Liberals spoke as if they were going to vote on each measure strictly on its merits and turn the government out as soon as it brought forward any proposal they disliked, and the government was no more conciliatory. But when the Liberals and the government contemplated the disadvantages of having another general election they became less intransigent. The government was taking up the process of rationalization, which had been strictly a matter for private enterprise; as the Commons would reject nationalization of the coal mines it introduced a Mines Bill early in 1930 which reduced working hours to seven and a half and set up a Reorganization Committee with some legal powers to encourage rationalization. The Liberals decided to support the Bill; it was a step away from Free Trade, but Free Trade seemed to have unexpected disadvantages for declining industries. Other industries were rationalizing, or forming themselves into cartels, without government intervention: in 1929 the Millers' Mutual Association was launched; in shipbuilding,

National Shipbuilders Security Ltd. had been set up to buy shipyards and keep them idle so that they would not force prices down still further in an attempt to obtain contracts, and in cotton-spinning Spindles Ltd., was formed for the same purpose. Probably these steps helped the declining industries to contract, but as the new industries were not growing fast enough to take on so many workers the old industries were blamed for reducing their labour force and increasing unemployment.

The slight improvement in British industry in the later years of Baldwin's ministry was coming to an end. It had always depended to a considerable extent on the much more flourishing expansion in the United States, and by the time of the 1929 election the American boom was already slowing down. In the autumn prices fell spectacularly on the New York Stock Exchange, but this only confirmed a decline in production that began some months earlier. The result of the international decline in trade spread to Britain, and unemployment began to rise.

From economic paralysis to economic crisis

Within the government a group under J. H. Thomas had been set up to reduce unemployment. In some ways Thomas was a good choice; he was a genial and ebullient man who could get on well with business men, and he would have been ideally suited for jollying a boom along. But Thomas was not the man to fight rising unemployment. Snowden at the Exchequer insisted on balancing the budget and declined to provide money for public works programmes to relieve unemployment unless they were productive, in the sense that they ought to show a profit and Thomas accepted this point of view. Road-building, the form of public works that came most readily to everybody's mind, had to be strictly limited.

The other members of Thomas's committee, Lansbury, Johnston, and Mosley, could not do much against the resistance of the Treasury. Mosley felt confident that he possessed an answer to the problem of unemployment, along the lines that the Labour party in Birmingham had been considering for some years. What he wanted was an attempt to shut Britain off from the mounting crisis abroad by a tariff wall and run her industries with a managed currency that would if necessary be devalued. This programme was formulated in the Mosley Memorandum and was put to the Cabinet. Thomas felt offended because he appeared to have been ignored, and Snowden refused to have anything to do with the idea.

Mosley resigned, and continued the battle from the backbenches. He explained his programme to a meeting of the Parliamentary Labour party, at which his speech was well received, and then pressed the matter to a vote; loyalty to the leadership triumphed over doubt, and Mosley was heavily defeated. By forcing a vote he had driven MacDonald and Snowden together; MacDonald knew very little about economics, and was not very interested, but left to himself he might have given Mosley some encouragement—he was not a convinced Free Trader and he certainly had no friendship for Snowden. Mosley's open support in the parliamentary party came largely from the left wing of the Independent Labour party. This section of the I.L.P. in effect claimed to be a separate party working in alliance with the Labour party but entitled to vote against it if they chose. The Labour party was not tightly disciplined—over a hundred Members voted against the party Whip on one occasion or another during this Parliament—but the I.L.P. was going too far. The Clydeside group that controlled the I.L.P. drove out all the Members of Parliament who were first and foremost Labour party men and belonged to the I.L.P. much as they might have belonged to the Fabian Society; after this I.L.P. supporters followed I.L.P. policy even when it conflicted with Labour party policy, though for the time being they remained members of the Labour party.

When people were in this mood Mosley could expect a good deal of support. He put forward his policy at the party conference in October 1930; it received 1,046,000 votes against the 1,251,000 votes cast in support of the policy of the official leadership. This was a good enough result to suggest that if he had kept up the pressure, the Prime Minister might have felt it was wise to encourage Snowden to become more flexible. The breadth of his support was too much for Mosley's self-restraint; his combination of planning, tariffs, and national spirit was attractive to Conservatives as well as to Socialists, and this made him think he could set up a party of his own. In February 1931 he launched the New Party to put the case for his economic policy and although it won no seats in the 1931 general election, the Conservatives kept a watchful eye on it for two or three years and wondered whether they wanted Mosley back; he was believed to represent youth in politics and his policy was very like that of the Conservatives after 1931. But his movement drifted towards Fascism, and took up anti-Semitism in October 1934, after which he was politically untouchable.

The government passed very little important legislation apart from its Mines Act, but in the 1930–1 session it submitted three Bills that caused some controversy. Trevelyan introduced his Education Bill again; it had been crowded out in 1930 but was revived and placed high on the list. The most important clause raised the school-leaving age to 15, which would be expensive but was almost essential if children were to go to secondary schools at 11 +, as proposed in the Hadow Report; if they left at 14 they would attend their new schools for only two years. The original Bill provided very little money for Roman Catholic schools, and the Catholic section of the Labour party, made up mainly of Members with a sizeable number of voters who were Irish by descent, moved an amendment to give a grant of the order of £1m. The government opposed the amendment; the Conservatives voted with the Catholic Labour Members, and the amendment was carried. When the government declined to resign and accepted the amendment, the Conservatives, whose support for the amendment was inspired partly by their success in by-elections, said it was being spineless. When the Bill went to the Lords it was thrown out on the grounds that it would cost too much. The government showed no desire to renew a struggle in which they were bound to annoy either their Catholic or their Nonconformist supporters. Trevelyan did not accept this as a good reason for leaving the subject alone, and resigned when it was obvious that nothing more was going to be done.

The Trade Union Bill and the Electoral Reform Bill look like a bargain by which the Liberals would vote for the repeal of the Trade Disputes Act to please the trade unions, and the government would establish the alternative vote to repay the Liberals. The alternative vote would allow people to indicate their second preferences at an election and the Liberals could reasonably hope that both Labour and Conservative voters would pick them as a second choice, while the Labour party had no real reason to expect to benefit more than the Conservatives from Liberal second choices. On the other hand, the Trade Union Bill did not really extend the powers of the unions, and did not allow general strikes for political purposes. By restoring 'contracting out' of the political levy, it would have made Labour party finances somewhat more secure, but the 1929 election results had shown that 'contracting in' was not a complete barrier to success. In February the Liberals turned on the Trade Union Bill and mangled it so much that it was dropped. The government went on with the Electoral Reform Bill, presumably in the belief that co-operation in the Commons might lead on to co-operation in elections, for which the alternative vote might be useful.

By this stage the government had realized that legislation could not solve the three interlinked questions of immediate importance: reducing unemployment, balancing the budget, and maintaining the external value of the pound. In 1929 Snowden had appointed a committee under Lord Macmillan to investigate the working of the financial system and its effect on the economy; the British economy then seemed in some way exceptional, because other countries were enjoying prosperity and full employment. But while the Committee was sitting American production was declining and world trade was contracting. In 1929 unemployment was not a serious problem except in England; by the time the Macmillan Report appeared,[1] in May 1931, America and Germany were in worse difficulties than England.

The collapse in world trade, which fell to about half its 1929 cash value by 1932, affected England differently from most other countries. The world-wide depression was marked by a fall in investment, a fall in the price of raw materials, and a decline in employment. Investment in England had been sluggish in the late 1920s, but maintained this low level without any prolonged drop in the early 1930s. Low prices for raw materials meant that England could buy more in exchange for her exports, and at least in the short run this helped almost everybody in the country. The amount exported dropped rather sharply, but the cash value did not decline so fast.

In its Report the Macmillan Commission asked for international co-operation in raising price levels, as a way of escaping from the great increase in the real burden of debt that resulted from the steady fall in prices in the twenties. It also said that England ought to adopt a managed currency instead of allowing the supply of money to be affected by the working of the international Gold Standard. Its terms of reference did not allow it to ask whether the Bank of England ought to keep the pound at a fixed rate in terms of gold ('remain on the Gold Standard'), but it did consider one question which tended to be ignored: granted that the pound had been overvalued in 1925 and was still overvalued, ought there to be a devaluation? It would have been quite easy for the Bank to retain a fixed gold value for the pound at a lower rate of exchange, such as four dollars to the pound. The Committee rejected the idea of devaluation, on the grounds that it would be a shock to international confidence. But once international confidence was introduced into the discussion, whatever the Report said was bound to be harmful. Saying that the pound was overvalued made people less willing to hold sterling, and the suggestion that prices should be driven upwards was also discouraging; money began to leave London shortly after the Report appeared.

The Report came in a form that was likely to make investors uneasy about leaving their money in London. All the fourteen members of the Committee except the chairman submitted addenda or reservations. The most important reservation was signed by six members including Keynes and McKenna, the Chairman of the Midland Bank—a man radical only

[1] Parl. Papers, Cmd. 3897.

by the standards of other chairmen of banks. They asked for a tariff and a subsidy on exports, which meant a virtual devaluation and they suggested a general agreement to reduce wages and prices simultaneously. They wanted the government to run a managed currency inside the country and at the same time maintain a stable currency unit for international trade; this dual policy was more or less accepted by governments in the 1940s, and was the objective they hoped to achieve through the international financial institutions set up at the end of the Second World War. Two members of this group of six, Ernest Bevin and Sir Thomas Allen of the Co-operative Movement, had further points to make: they went as close as they could to saying there ought to be a devaluation, they said the Bank might be forced off gold if it would not devalue, and they recommended a large loan to be spent on projects that would stimulate the economy. His newspaper and magazine articles at this time suggest that Keynes agreed with this view, but presumably he held back to consolidate support for the Keynes–McKenna reservation.

Arguments along these lines became the orthodoxy of the future. But one of the more important moments in the committee's hearing of evidence came when Keynes questioned Sir Richard Hopkins, who was putting the Treasury's point of view. Keynes argued that investment by the government would stimulate the economy; Hopkins replied that if the government borrowed money for investment, it would force interest rates up, thus making life harder for other borrowers and making marginal borrowers give up projects they had in mind. Thus, government intervention might change the nature of the investment carried out, but could not increase the total amount of investment. Lord Macmillan described the argument between the two men as a drawn battle.[1]

It would be hard for a government to change its policy on the basis of so indecisive an encounter. But even if 'soon or late, it is ideas, not vested interests, that are dangerous for good or evil',[2] politicians could have had ideas of their own without waiting for academic economists to produce them. On the other hand Snowden's reasons for denouncing the deficit-producing schemes were understandable; Keynesian economic policies would at first reduce real wages, in order to provide more employment and a more buoyant economy in which wages would regain their former purchasing power. In 1929 Snowden had claimed that the Labour party would balance the budget as well as conquering unemployment, and this would avoid the initial fall in real wages. Snowden was not

---

[1] R. Harrod, *The Life of John Maynard Keynes* (1951), 422.
[2] J. M. Keynes, *The General Theory of Employment, Interest and Money* (1936), 384.

irrevocably opposed to new ideas: in a Cabinet memorandum in 1930 he denied that he accepted the Treasury point of view on loans in the rigid form in which Hopkins had stated it,[1] and a few years later when the collapse had come and he had lost everything for which he had fought, Gold Standard, Free Trade, and his own honoured position in the Labour party, he came round to the idea of a large loan to stimulate development. He argued that in 1929 there had been unemployed people; in 1934 there were not only unemployed people but also unemployed capital, and it was the business of the government to bring them together. This was just another way of saying that the pound had been overvalued in 1929, though Snowden seems not to have seen the connection. During the half-dozen years from 1925 that England was on the Gold Standard gold was constantly tending to slip out of the country, mainly to France because the franc was distinctly undervalued. Any proposal that would increase the budget deficit would only have encouraged the loss of gold and made it harder to maintain the exchange value of the pound.

Public works provided employment for a few people, but at a cost which was producing a budget deficit. The general financial position of the government was made worse by the steady deficit of the Unemployment Insurance Fund. Insurance contributions to the Fund were supposed to balance benefits paid out, though to listen to some of the complaints of the financial purists it might have been imagined that the Fund was meant to make a profit. The rising unemployment from 1929 onwards forced the Fund to borrow to pay benefits, and this borrowing was seen as one of the causes of financial weakness. Snowden had forced his 1930 budget, which raised income-tax to 22½p in the pound, through the Commons but putting through another budget with a minority seemed almost impossible at a time when a firm policy was thought necessary. In February 1931 he accepted a Liberal suggestion that a committee should be set up to look into ways of carrying out economies. Sir George May, the chairman, had been secretary of the Prudential Insurance and was assumed to be without party allegiance; MacDonald, Lloyd George, and Baldwin each nominated two representatives. The committee was to find out the facts about the government's financial position and if necessary make suggestions about what should be done. Until it presented its report Snowden made no financial changes, perhaps because he thought it would provide all-party support for the policies that he believed to be necessary.

By July 1931 there was definite uneasiness in Paris and New York about the financial soundness of the City of London. The Macmillan

[1] P.R.O., Cab. 24 C.P. 392 (30), 86.

committee made it clear that, despite rumours to the contrary, British investors had not been borrowing money for short periods in order to make long-term loans elsewhere. On the other hand London was less able to attract short-term money than before 1914, and some short-term money had been lent to German firms which either had gone out of business or were not allowed to remit money out of the country, so that the short-term loans became loans of indefinite length. London was not well placed to deal with withdrawals of short-term money. The Bank of England had brought its rate down to $2\frac{1}{2}$ per cent as part of the programme of cheap money which was being undertaken by central banks in an effort to stimulate trade. In July it recognized that this would no longer work, and raised Bank Rate to $4\frac{1}{2}$ per cent. At this level it remained for seven weeks. The Governor of the Bank, Montagu Norman, had been working hard to help deal with the crisis facing the German banks; he possessed the charm and temperament of the artist at a time when physical stamina or deep originality of thought were the qualities required of the Governor, and at this stage he had to take a long holiday.

Just after the second increase in the Bank Rate, the May Committee presented its report.[1] The Liberal and Conservative representatives and May himself declared that the British government was rushing to ruin. They announced that there would be a budget deficit of £120m., and they made their suggestions for dealing with it. Their figures showed a deficit of only £70m., on any normal meaning of the word; they raised it to £120m. by laying down that £50m. of debt should be repaid, apparently reckoning that if only £25m. of debt were repaid, that meant a deficit of £25m. The report examined several government departments in great detail, and made suggestions for cutting expenditure by £9m. Apart from these small sums it suggested more drastic cuts of £13m. from education, £7m. from road-building, and £66m. from the expenditure of the Unemployment Insurance Fund. As the committee itself estimated that the Fund would, at the current rates, need to borrow only £40m., this proposal amounted to saying that in a year of heavy unemployment the Fund should provide a surplus of £26m. Presumably the committee intended that the Fund should produce a steady annual contribution to general revenue. MacDonald may have reflected how wise he had been in 1924 to refuse to have a committee on the Campbell case: the government had intended the May committee to make recommendations on technical issues but it had instead taken a long step into the field of policy, for the report cannot be seen as anything more than a collection of small proposals thrown together around the central assertion that

[1] Parl Papers, Cmd. 3920.

unemployment benefit ought to be cut. Keynes had suggested in January: 'The best guess I can make is that whenever you save five shillings, you put a man out of work for a day.'[1] At this rate a deficit of £120m. would have cured unemployment in England, though it would fairly certainly have forced the government to reduce the value of the pound in terms of gold.

The two Labour members of the committee drew up a minority report. Like the majority they could find very few examples of waste. They did not regard it as their business to propose changes of policy, and in any case they had no desire for cuts in education, road-building, and unemployment benefit. Paragraphs 38–43 of their report are a good statement in non-technical language of the case for high government expenditure in time of depression and paragraph 131 puts what is by now the accepted view of the situation:

> The present financial difficulties of the country and industry do not arise from any pursuit of wasteful public expenditure or lack of responsible control of such but are much more closely related to the policy of deflation followed since the war and confirmed by the return to the gold standard.

The position of the Liberals on the committee was very odd. If they had taken seriously the programme on which Lloyd George had fought the 1929 election, they would have signed the minority report, thus making it into a majority report.

The establishment of the National Government in 1931

From the end of July onward the story grows more fascinating but harder to follow. When the House reassembled politicians re-fought the August struggles, with the result that there are more versions of the events than is usual in Cabinet disagreements. It is hardly possible to indicate all the questions in dispute, but it may be useful to indicate the different levels of disagreement. There are arguments about what was done, and even more about what was said; arguments about the constitutional propriety of the behaviour of the King and the Prime Minister; arguments about the extent to which a politician has a duty to his party and to his election pledges when they conflict with his view of what seems necessary in a particular crisis; arguments about whether the government's economic policy was justified and arguments about whether it could have been expected to have found a better policy. It is hard to say anything about the crisis that will be universally accepted.

The outflow of foreign exchange which had caused the July increases in the Bank Rate became faster after the publication of the May report.

---

[1] *The Listener*, 14 Jan. 1931, later published in J. M. Keynes, *Essays in Persuasion* (1931), 152.

There the figure was in print: a budget deficit of £120m. The bankers in London now declared that it was all the fault of the government, that no financial measures other than a balanced budget would set things right, and that the government should do something to save the City of London. On 12 August the Economy Committee of the Cabinet met to consider the May report. Snowden accepted the May Committee's view that the budget was not balanced until ample provision had been made for paying off the National Debt, and added that the deficit would be £170m. rather than £120m. For reasons that are not quite clear, this figure was accepted for the next four months. Snowden suggested about £70m. or £80m. of new taxation. The Committee then worked out general reductions in expenditure along the lines suggested by the May committee. MacDonald saw Baldwin and Chamberlain, and Samuel who was acting as Liberal leader while Lloyd George was recovering from a prostate gland operation. The government had to have a majority in the Commons to pass economy measures, so the proposals had to satisfy at least one of the parties in opposition, and if measures were to be passed quickly it would be necessary to have the support of both. As a result, MacDonald and Snowden had to have frequent discussions with the Liberal and Conservative leaders.

On the 19th the Economy Committee put its proposals to the Cabinet: £30m. of saving on general expenditure and £48m. of saving on payments to the unemployed. After a long meeting the Cabinet accepted £56m. of the cuts but it rejected the suggestion that 'transitional payments' to unemployed people who had exhausted their rights under the insurance system should be reduced; this was estimated to be a matter of about £20m. These cuts did not include any reduction in the standard rate of unemployment benefit paid to unemployed workers under the insurance scheme. Next day the Cabinet representatives met the opposition leaders again, and appear to have given them the impression that the Cabinet had accepted the full £78m. of cuts proposed in the Economy Committee. Chamberlain said it would be best to make all of the £96m. of cuts suggested by the May Committee, which would involve reducing the standard rate of unemployment benefit. Later in the day the Economy Committee met the National Executive Committee of the Labour party and the General Council of the T.U.C., and Snowden said at this meeting that while various cuts were to be made, the Cabinet had not decided to cut the standard rate of unemployment benefit.

The General Council refused to have anything to do with the government's proposals. In the next few days the Council played an increasingly important role, mainly because some of its members had a coherent idea of what to do. Its proposals—increase direct taxation, especially on unearned income, suspend the Sinking Fund, and perhaps impose a tariff for revenue—come much closer to the proposals made in Keynes's *General Theory* than anything else heard during the crisis. The T.U.C.'s deputation, which included Bevin from the Macmillan Committee and Pugh from the May Committee minority, put these suggestions to the Cabinet, but they were rejected. Sidney Webb said, after hearing the proposals, 'The General Council are pigs'; however, as he said later that nobody told the Cabinet that it could go off the Gold Standard, his opinion was not worth much.

On the 21st the Cabinet discussed the idea of a tariff: fifteen of them were in favour of a 10 per cent duty on manufactured goods, but they did not insist that Snowden and the minority should accept the suggestion. On the other hand the Cabinet refused to impose any cuts beyond the £56m. agreed previously. As a result, when MacDonald and Snowden met Chamberlain and Samuel, the opposition leaders learnt that the cuts would in fact be less than they had been told on the 20th. They protested and asked for more. Snowden and MacDonald told the Cabinet on the 22nd that the Liberals and Conservatives wanted further cuts, including some reduction of unemployment benefits. Snowden spoke of 'reducing the standard of living of the workmen by 50 per cent, which would be the effect of departing from the Gold Standard'.[1] The Cabinet—reasonably enough—was not impressed by this. MacDonald then proposed another scheme to reduce spending by £20m.: £12¼m. would come from a 10 per cent reduction in the standard rate of unemployment benefit, and £7¾m. from economies in other departments. The Cabinet refused to accept MacDonald's scheme; Snowden and Thomas were so annoyed by the refusal that they asked that their dissent should be recorded, which meant that they were considering resignation. Perhaps because of this the Cabinet then allowed MacDonald and Snowden to find out from Baldwin and Samuel whether the new programme, amounting to £76m. including the 10 per cent reduction, would be sufficient for the government to put to Parliament. There would clearly be trouble if Baldwin and Samuel accepted the programme and the Cabinet continued to reject it.

By this time another problem had arisen. The Bank of England was still paying out gold to meet a stream of withdrawals, and was coming to the end of its resources. Additional money, in gold or in foreign exchange, could be found only by a short-term loan arranged by the government, and because the Federal Reserve Bank of New York was

[1] P.R.O., Cab. 23/67 22 Aug. 1931.

not allowed to lend to foreign governments, this short-term loan would have to be raised from the New York commercial banks. So, if the government was to help the Bank of England maintain the exchange value of the pound, it had to find out whether £76m. of cuts would satisfy the New York commercial banks that it was safe to make a loan.

On the 23rd MacDonald saw the King and warned him that the Cabinet might not survive. The King, with MacDonald's permission, then saw Samuel and, later in the day, Baldwin. Samuel put to the King the arguments in favour of a coalition (though of course no Liberal could use this word because it awoke memories of Lloyd George's 1916–22 government) under MacDonald, if the Labour government could not agree on a policy. Baldwin, at his audience, agreed to serve under MacDonald in a coalition if the question arose. That evening the Cabinet met again to find out how the New York banks had responded to the request for a loan. The New York banks passed the question back to London by saying they would provide the loan if the Bank of England considered the programme of cuts was adequate. As the loan was designed to save the Bank of England from disaster, this reliance on its advice was a tribute to its reputation for integrity, though New York could rely on men like Montagu Norman who, at one stage in the German negotiations that led to his breakdown, had noted with some satisfaction that German workers were ashamed to be on the dole. He clearly felt that British workers ought also to be ashamed of it. Norman's economics and his national psychology were wrong: even if German workers had been ashamed of their position it would have done nothing to reduce unemployment, and in any case the German workers seem to have been bitterly angry rather than ashamed. It was in England that the unemployed were corroded by shame at their idleness.

After the request for a loan had been referred back from New York to London, the money would come only if reductions were made of about £76m., including the cut in the standard unemployment benefit. A programme of this sort could never have had an easy passage through the Cabinet. By the 23rd the opponents of reductions were gaining strength, and the idea of accepting a policy on the recommendation of the bankers was in itself distasteful. MacDonald said that the programme could go through only if nobody resigned, but Henderson and seven or eight others said they could not remain in a government which imposed the £76m. programme. MacDonald went to tell the King that the government was about to break up, and returned to tell the Cabinet that he would meet Baldwin, Samuel, and the King next morning, and would then see the Cabinet again. The King asked him to lead a National government and, though he declined that evening, he accepted at the morning meeting with Baldwin, Samuel, and the King. He went to the Cabinet meeting, told the ministers that they were out of office and asked Snowden, Thomas, and Sankey to join his new Cabinet, which they did. Baldwin, Chamberlain, Cunliffe-Lister, and Hoare from the Conservative party, and Samuel and Lord Reading from the Liberals also joined the National Cabinet.

The Labour party claimed that this transformation scene had been brought about by treachery and that the King, the bankers, and MacDonald had plotted to turn the Labour government out. The King's position was quite simple: the duty of a constitutional monarch is to name the head of the strongest government that can be found, so he normally appoints a Prime Minister with a party majority in the Commons, but he has a natural tendency to suggest the advantages of a coalition. The government that MacDonald formed in August 1931 was undeniably strong, and the King behaved reasonably in asking him to form it. On the other hand, if the King meant it at all seriously when he said, a few weeks later, that he would refuse to accept MacDonald's resignation he was behaving a little like George III with Lord North.[1]

The behaviour of the New York banks also seems reasonable; they were being asked to lend money, and wanted to know if it was a sound risk. The Labour complaints that there had been a 'bankers' ramp' presumably meant that the banks had, in order to embarrass the Labour government, departed from normal commercial practice. But lending to London was not a risk-free occupation, because the general fear of devaluation might have led to such rapid withdrawals of gold that the New York loans could not be repaid for some time to come. The New York bankers were entitled to protect themselves against this. The Bank of England's desire to avoid devaluation probably harmed the nation's economy, but this does not mean it was plotting against the government.

MacDonald's behaviour has come under suspicion: it was said he had been plotting to set up a coalition for months previously, but this is hard to pin down because the parliamentary situation had made several people think about a coalition in the previous two years. It was unusual for him to arrange to meet Baldwin and Samuel at Buckingham Palace at the time of his proposed resignation on the 24th; and it is not clear why he did this. The Labour leaders in the new Cabinet were also criticized on less easily tangible grounds: they had been elected on one programme and had now become convinced that a radically different programme was necessary. As MacDonald put it to his Cabinet, 'the proposals as a whole

[1] H. Nicolson, *George V* (1952), 493.

represented the negation of everything the Labour Party stood for, and yet he was absolutely satisfied that it was necessary, in the national interest, to implement them if the country was to be secured'.[1] The harsh rules for statesmen in this predicament have been laid down by two great Conservatives in speeches denouncing their leaders. Churchill in the 1930s argued that, mandate or no mandate, the government had a duty to do what it thought was right and rearm the country. On the other hand Disraeli fought his way to the head of the party by his denunciation of Peel for abandoning the Corn Laws to which his party was pledged.

The National Government

MacDonald was the most convenient leader for a government that included both Baldwin and Samuel. He did not attempt to make his new government all-inclusive by trying to persuade the Labour party to join it. He might have pointed out that only a National government could impose Snowden's programme of taxation on the rich, and only a National government with Labour support could maintain Free Trade. But instead he discouraged Labour junior ministers from joining his government and neither he nor Snowden went to the meeting of the Parliamentary Labour party on 28 August to explain their policy to their ex-followers. Both men seem to have been thinking of retiring from politics very soon. This would explain why they said on 25 August that the new government would exist only for the duration of the crisis. When they disagreed with the main body of the party in the First World War, they had remained in touch with the party, but they made no attempt to remain in touch in 1931. Both of them had been finding the criticism of the Labour back-benchers increasingly irritating.

Snowden's budget of 10 September was deflationary and egalitarian. It imposed £80m. of new taxes, including an increase in the standard rate of income-tax from 22½p to 25p and a ten per cent increase in surtax. Next day MacDonald presented the Economy Bill, which reduced government spending by £70m. This included the ten per cent cut in the standard rate of unemployment benefit, which was defended on the ground that the cost of living had fallen by more than ten per cent. During the debates the Labour leaders in opposition came round to the programme suggested by the T.U.C. and repudiated the cuts. At times they sounded as though they had never agreed to any of them and could not approve of anything like cuts in teachers' salaries.

The formation of the National government did a certain amount to reassure foreign lenders. Although money continued to leave the

[1] P.R.O., Cab. 23/67 23 Aug. 1931.

country, the Economy Bill and the budget might have succeeded in their aims if they had been accepted by all their victims. On the 15th sailors in the Royal Navy at Invergordon went on strike about the reductions in pay. During the week the Bank of England lost £50m. in gold, and by the 19th it was defeated: on the 21st it suspended sales of gold and Britain was off the Gold Standard. The general policy of the Bank was surprising: it had left Bank Rate unchanged throughout the crisis, and the $4\frac{1}{2}$ per cent rate maintained in August and September was in fact lower than the average annual rate for practically every year since Norman became Governor in 1920. Even if it was going to abandon the high interest policy of the 1920s, the Bank was taking a very drastic step when it went off the Gold Standard altogether; a lower rate than $4.86 could have been adopted and defended, and would not have been as unsettling for world trade as a floating rate. Until 1939 the pound was at least nominally free to change in value, and as it started by falling to $3.20 the fluctuations in value were uncomfortably large.

Abandonment of the Gold Standard ignored a major—though completely irrelevant—fear that had been dominating policy for some weeks: about the only economic event that M.P.s recalled in debates was the collapse of the mark in 1923, and retention of the Gold Standard at a different rate of exchange would have helped make sure that the pound would not go the same way. But despite all the expressions of anxiety the Bank did not stick to gold. *The Times* did say 'a suspension of gold payments by a Socialist government would have been one thing. But a suspension by a National government committed to retrenchment and reform is another.'[1] Presumably the Bank shared this feeling that the National government could be trusted.

Certainly the people trusted the National government. The budget was received with enthusiasm. People stinted themselves of old-age pensions, cancelled their War Loan bonds, and paid their income-tax early. It was a great moral vindication of democracy: for years it had been said—and it was soon to be said again—that a democracy would not follow the path of sacrifice. The events of 1931 showed that ordinary people were ready to accept a stern policy applied by a man with faith in himself. Unfortunately this self-denial only made things worse and deepened the depression, but the fine spirit that inspired it should not be forgotten.

The National government held together over the departure from the Gold Standard, and afterwards there was no obvious occasion for it to break up. The Conservatives, who provided most of the votes for the government in the Commons, wanted an election followed by a policy of

[1] *The Times*, 21 Sept. 1931.

Protection. The Labour party was still the largest party in the House, and would be in a strong position if Lloyd George recovered his health and led the left wing of the Liberals away from the National government. Everybody expected that eventually the cuts and the increases in taxation would be unpopular; the Labour party believed that MacDonald and his government would be destroyed by this.

Tariffs were the major difficulty about an election. Snowden and the Liberal ministers were Free Traders. The Conservatives believed tariffs were the only cure for the country's economic problems. After some discussion the government decided to ask for a 'doctor's mandate'; as MacDonald put it in his election manifesto, 'the government must be free to consider every proposal likely to help, such as tariffs . . .'.[1]

The dissolution of Parliament seemed to have settled whether the Liberal party belonged to the left or the right: in the moment of decision it was coming down on the Conservative side. Samuel asked Lloyd George to support the National government in the election, and Lloyd George replied that if he had to die fighting he would prefer to die fighting on the left. But this had no effect; Samuel took over the Liberal leadership with no trouble, because the Liberals reckoned that by joining the National government they could save themselves from dying at all. National government candidates could expect to poll the combined Conservative and Liberal strength, and this by itself would be enough to lead to a great victory.

The Labour party fought as a Free Trade party, saying that a tariff which might have been useful while the country was on the Gold Standard was no longer necessary if the pound was to be on a floating rate. It advocated the other measures of planning and of deficit finance that had been discussed for the previous two or three years. But, just as Lloyd George had done in 1929, it was offering these proposals to the electorate with far too little preparation. Snowdon's broadcast talk of 17 October, in which he said that the policy of the bulk of the Labour party was not socialism but bolshevism run mad, and his encouragement of the idea that people's savings in the Post Office would not be safe if the Labour party was re-elected, were heavy blows to his former party.

	Votes	Seats	% of all votes cast
Conservative and National	13,129,417	521	60·5
Samuel Liberal	1,403,102	33	6·5
Labour	6,649,630	52	30·6

[1] R. Bassett, *1931* (1958), 284.

By-elections before the crisis had shown that the Labour party was losing ground, and its conduct during the crisis could not have encouraged the electorate to think it had a clear policy and knew what to do next. It suffered for being in office at the time of the slump: no government, left or right, had much chance of surviving the slump in any democratic country. In any case, the Labour party revived; it was the ideals of *laissez-faire* and the free play of the market which really suffered a mortal blow in 1931, for there was nobody left to defend them for years to come.

7. The National Government 1931–1939

Domestic record of the National Government

THE election result made it harder than ever to hold an open-minded inquiry into the virtues of tariffs. The overwhelming majority of the Commons were Conservatives who were convinced that tariffs were needed, and they were unlikely to change their views now they were in power. A tariff seemed so certain that a great flood of imports came to England to get in before the barrier fell. The government's first step towards Protection was the Abnormal Importations Act, designed to defend the balance of payments from these imports. More permanent legislation followed; on 4 February 1932 Neville Chamberlain introduced a tariff which, while moderate by the world standards of the period, was a decisive step away from Free Trade. He included an assurance that the tariff could be reduced in favour of countries of the Empire with whom preferential trading agreements could be made, and he ended his speech by reminding his listeners of his father's work for Protection. The Liberal ministers who were committed to Free Trade and Snowden (who had become a peer) wanted to resign over Chamberlain's tariff, but he was able to persuade them to remain on the rather unusual condition that they were at liberty to attack his Bill from the government front bench. Their opposition had no effect, and the tariff was established.

The Tariff Reform movement had always wanted closer links with the Empire. The Commonwealth Prime Ministers had kept up their pressure for Imperial Preference in 1930, and now the National government was ready to co-operate with them. The Ottawa Conference in 1932 went some way to justify the Free Traders who said that setting up a system of Imperial Preference would lead to quarrels. The Conference did produce a network of bilateral agreements among Commonwealth countries, but at the cost of a good deal of irritation during the negotiations; the British representatives had expected a rapturous welcome for the prodigal

Mother Country come home, and were a little taken aback by the sharpness of the bargaining. Nevertheless, agreements were reached, and Commonwealth trade did increase rather more than world trade during the thirties. Acceptance of the agreements, which were to run for five years in the first instance, forced the Free Traders in the Cabinet to recognize that the government was unchangeably Protectionist. In September the orthodox Liberals under Samuel left the government, accompanied by Snowden. Apart from the great central body of Conservatives, MacDonald was left with a tiny group of National Labour supporters, among whom J. H. Thomas was the only person of political importance, and a larger group of National Liberals who accepted Protectionism under the leadership of Sir John Simon.

The difficulties of MacDonald's position ought not to be exaggerated. His relationship with Baldwin was stable and satisfactory and, after the 1931 crisis, Baldwin was in a very strong position to resist the critics inside his own party. MacDonald had become a socialist before it was regarded as synonymous with nationalization; when he thought about economic problems at all, he hoped that there would be a gradual increase of state influence that would reconcile the two sides of industry. The interest in planning shown during the 1930s was in accordance with his ideas. The Import Duties Advisory Committee, which was set up to recommend tariff rates to the Treasury, was bound to carry out some of the tasks of planning the economy. In agriculture there was a Milk Marketing Board and a Bacon Marketing Board, there were import duties for fruit and vegetables, and there were subsidies for farmers growing corn. Co-ordinating agencies tried to lay down a policy for firms inside some industries which had benefited from tariffs. Iron and steel was the most obviously planned industry in the thirties; hostile observers might even say that it had been turned into a cartel with the assistance of a tariff. In reality planning was mainly an attempt at orderly withdrawal from the ageing industries whose position, bad enough in the 1920s, was if anything worse in the 1930s. In the 1920s the government had ignored their position and had not helped their efforts to contract through rationalization, but in the 1930s it did provide some help for them. The industries that flourished and expanded in the 1930s were not planned and did not have much help from the government.

The National government's attitude was not too far from MacDonald's notion of socialism; and its foreign policy and Indian policy were close enough to his own Gladstonian Liberalism for his position not to be embarrassing. The government's Indian policy was more or less acceptable to the Labour party, but caused trouble on the Tory right wing. The

Simon Report had said that a parliamentary government of the British type could not be set up at Delhi to rule India. This judgement was based on the fear that the Hindu majority would not treat the Moslem minority fairly. It did not explicitly rule out the possibility of establishing an Indian government independent of the British Secretary of State for India, which was the essence of Dominion status, but it would, if accepted, have made constitutional development more complicated. The National government, like its predecessor, was in favour of Dominion status but it faced difficulties inside the Conservative party. Not until 1934 did it produce a White Paper on the Indian constitution, in which it suggested that the elected provincial governments should take over all remaining provincial affairs, and that ministerial responsibility for some central government affairs should also be given to elected representatives while the Viceroy retained others (particularly defence and foreign policy) in his own hands. The Indian government would then have reached roughly the position suggested for Canada by Lord Durham in his Report, which had assumed that foreign policy and a few other issues should be retained in the hands of the representatives of the British government while the inhabitants of the country ran their own domestic affairs. The Congress party was determined that India should be as free to run its own foreign policy as the Dominions had been since 1918, and at times asked for independence, and a position outside the Commonwealth. Other Indians opposed the dominance of the Congress party, but did not seriously oppose the idea of independence.

Churchill, Lord Wolmer, and Sir Henry Page-Croft fought the government's policy at debates in the National Union of Conservative Associations and in the Central Council of the Conservative party in 1933 and 1934, and gained substantial support though not enough to make the government change its mind. In late 1934 the Government of India Bill came before Parliament and was again resisted by the Conservative right wing; it was also criticized by the Labour party, for not going far enough. The right wing opposition, though unsuccessful, made life harder for the government, and also convinced the Labour party and the majority of the Conservative party that Churchill was a dangerous reactionary. The Act itself worked as well as could be expected; the Congress party won the Indian elections held under its provisions, and the only organized party that could make any headway against Congress was the Moslem League which stood on an explicitly religious basis.[1] As independence became a possibility, mutual suspicion between Hindus

[1] In the jargon of constitution-makers, 'communal' was used as a euphemism for 'religious', as in 'communal rioting'.

and Moslems increased: the Indians said this was the result of a covert British policy of 'divide and rule', and the British said it was the unfortunate but natural result of the Indian realization that when they had power in their own hands they would have to work out a policy on religious issues. The leaders of Congress were tolerant in religious questions. Gandhi of course had strong religious convictions of his own and the Nehrus, father and son, did not, but all three of them believed that religious differences could be kept out of politics. On the other hand, the effect of their work in turning the Congress party into a mass movement was to bring in many people for whom religion was inextricably linked to politics. Congress used non-violence and civil disobedience to publicize its case, and these methods belonged to the Hindu tradition rather than the Moslem. The great evangelists of the Congress party came from a Hindu background. Inevitably, the mass membership of Congress was overwhelmingly Hindu. The Moslems made it clear that they expected the British to protect them. The British attitude tended to be pro-Moslem, because of a feeling that the Moslems were closer in spirit to the British: non-violence was not a part of the tradition of the Moslems or of the rulers of India. British officials tended to think Moslems deserved support because their demands for independence were less strident, and because the minority's wish for protection was reasonable. Congress regarded this pro-Moslem attitude as the most obvious aspect of the policy of 'divide and rule'.

Congress gained majorities in several states in the 1937 elections and, after some argument decided to form state governments. It did not choose to take any part in running the central government in Delhi in case this should impede its work of continuing the agitation for independence. In most cases the state governments worked well, and this may have shown some pessimists in England that Indians were not as incapable of looking after their own affairs as had been thought. But the creation of Indian state governments at a time when there was continued British rule at the centre did not make it easier for Indians to see their country as a unity in which all interests had to be looked after.

The Government of India Bill made it possible for the National government to present itself as a middle-of-the-road body fighting off wild men to the left and right. The Labour party moved somewhat to the left in the early thirties. It adopted policy statements that committed it to wide measures of nationalization; the Labour government of 1945, which had very deep roots in the 1930s, carried out most of these commitments. The habit of quarrelling with the left wing continued to be noticeable in the party. Most of the argument in the 1920s had been over the issue of keeping the Communist party out but there had also been a good deal of discussion of the position of the I.L.P. In the months just after the fall of the Labour government the I.L.P. had been expelled from the Labour party, and after this step, which involved a considerable amount of emotional anguish, the party was ready to discipline other sections of its non-Communist left wing. Organizations like the Socialist League were discouraged, but the party leaders did not always remember that, if they were going to cut off the flow of ideas from the left, then they would have to do some thinking for themselves. The idea of nationalization was a legacy from the I.L.P. and Lansbury, who became party leader because he was the only Cabinet minister to survive the 1931 election, was a man of the left.

The deep gloom of the economy was bound to cause some movement to the left. Unemployment in the 1920s, running above 1,100,000, had been bad enough; in the 1930s unemployment never fell below 1,400,000, and usually was distinctly higher. Areas which relied on cotton did badly, and areas which relied on coal or shipbuilding did worse: in some towns dependent on these trades the unemployment rate went up to over 60 per cent of the working population.[1] These industries produced for export, and tariffs on imports did nothing to help them. Other countries were increasing their tariffs in order to keep out imports, which reduced the advantages British exporters could gain from the devaluation of the pound, and several countries devalued their currencies in order to remain competitive with British products. The World Economic Conference, held in London in 1933, came to no conclusions, but it did illustrate the diversity of answers offered to the problems of the slump. The co-operation of the United States was essential if world problems were to be solved, and President Roosevelt had told MacDonald beforehand that he believed price-levels ought to be pushed upwards. At the conference people spoke of the need for stability; Roosevelt decided that the United States had to solve her domestic problems first and that she could do this better if she withdrew from any active part in the Conference. The politicians at the Conference were not sorry to be able to blame Roosevelt for their failure, but even if the United States had pledged itself to accept whatever solution was reached by the other countries, they could not have agreed among themselves on a policy apart from repudiating their debts to the United States, which they did in any case. The American departure from a fixed value for gold for some months in 1933, and an eventual stabilization at $35 to the ounce instead

[1] Jarrow 67·8 per cent; Merthyr Tydfil 61·9 per cent. C. L. Mowat, *Britain between the Wars* (1956), 465.

of $20, meant that the dollar returned to roughly the 1925 (or pre-1914) parity with the pound, and the Exchange Equalization Board tried to maintain this level. This did not wipe out all the benefits of the departure from the Gold Standard; the franc remained at its previous level so that France suffered all the disadvantages of an over-valued currency and the British government was free from the obligation to defend an over-valued currency.

In the 1920s England had been almost the only country to suffer from a prolonged depression, and its problems were fairly directly linked to the high exchange rate and high interest rates. In the 1930s British financial policy was much more sensible, but her economy could not prosper when world trade was collapsing. All the Free Trade arguments made much less sense in conditions of high unemployment. The terms of trade moved in England's favour, which would have made it easy to pay for imports if only there had been someone to take her exports. In the event the British balance of payments became less satisfactory, because the foreign interest and dividends on which it had depended for so long were not being paid.

While the export industries did so badly, industries that produced for the home market were more prosperous than in the 1920s. The largest contribution to a revival of investment was made by housebuilding:[1]

£s m.	Housing	Manufacturing, gas, water, and electricity	All other investment (all sectors declined)	Total	Consumption
1930	122	120	195	435	4,206
1934	188	134	145	467	4,482[2]

Low interest rates made it easier for private contractors, building to sell rather than to rent, to finance their operations; low interest rates, combined with the readiness of building societies to lend for longer repayment periods than before, made it easier for people to buy the houses once they had been built. The government withdrew from most of the housing market and concentrated on slum clearance. The houses put up by private builders provoked criticism of the 'ribbon-development' that stuck thin fingers out into the countryside, but in many ways the new houses were a great improvement on anything that had previously been available for anybody below the upper-middle class. They were built in such numbers that by the end of the 1930s there were almost as many

[1] Reasons for the building boom are discussed in M. Bowley, *Housing and the State, 1919–1944* (1945), 81–2.
[2] This table is extracted from a table in H. W. Richardson, *Economic Recovery in Britain, 1932–39* (1967), 126. The non-housing investment did not do much more than cover depreciation.

houses as there were people looking for houses. This did not mean that all housing needs had been met: in areas which people were leaving there were empty houses and in areas of growing population there were short-ages; there were still slums; and possibly economic insecurity made people spend less on housing than in different circumstances. But the supply of houses was more adequate than before or for twenty-five years to come.

At the same time new industries were beginning to flourish, making motor-cars, wireless sets, chemicals, synthetic fabrics, and electrical appliances such as vacuum-cleaners. Most of the new development took place in the south of England. For about two hundred years the country had been sharply divided into a north and west section which was industrialized, except for the hills, and a south and east section which looked like a garden suburb supplied with money from the industrialized area and from foreign investment. In the 1920s and 1930s the south and east section began to develop new industries of its own. Electric power, which became readily available in the years after the setting-up of the national grid, freed industry from its dependence on coalfields, and as the new industries were making comparatively light products they did not have to be near the iron-smelting plants.

This deprived the depressed areas of one way of escape from their plight. The government wanted new industries to establish themselves in the depressed areas and provide jobs for the unemployed there, but it was not willing to offer any large subsidies and obviously could not take the risk of discouraging new factories even in the areas of lower unemploy-ment. The new industrialists could get workers wherever they set up their factories, and they saw no attraction in the depressed north and west. Coventry, Oxford, Slough, and London were closer to the markets in which they hoped to sell their products, and were less encumbered by declining industries. The prosperity of the south and east was very much a relative matter; its unemployment figures of 7 per cent of the working population in 1937 (the best year) may have looked like a boom com-pared with 15 per cent in the rest of the country, but were too high to encourage a really large movement of people out of the depressed areas —there was always the risk that even if they moved to more prosperous areas they might be unable to find work. The expanding trades attracted workers, and could not expand as quickly as the supply of labour accumulated. As a result the unemployment levels in expanding trades were in many cases higher in 1937 than in 1929. Despite a perceptible movement of population from areas of high unemployment to areas of relatively low unemployment, the dominant feature of the industrial scene was still the unemployed army of over a million people in the old and decaying industrial areas. The government produced schemes for helping people to become smallholders, and private organizations tried to provide adult education for some of the unemployed, but activities like this had an effect on only a few thousand of the men out of work. The long-term results of unemployment were over-dramatized; at the time people spoke as though men over forty out of work would never get jobs again and had in any case been corroded by unemployment so that they would not be capable of returning to work if the opportunity arose. But when the war came they fitted back into the economy without noticeable difficulty.

British production recovered fairly quickly from the worst of the slump, and real wages improved. '[The figures for rate of growth of *per capita*] income are not quite so favourable as those of late Victorian times, but they indicate that the slow progress at the beginning of the twentieth century was again being surpassed.'[1] However, a great deal of this improvement must be attributed to changes in the age-structure of the population: 'between 1921 and 1938 the labour force increased from 45·3 per cent to 47·3 per cent of the population, and the number of persons in work from 41·3 per cent to 43·4 per cent'. Over a longer period it could be said:

Between 1891 and 1947 the number of people aged 15–64 per consumer has risen from 0·60 to 0·68. Thus if we still had the 19th century age distribution the national income per head would be . . . about one-eighth lower than it actually is.[2]

Aggregate demand in the economy was so weak that not all of these people could be found work; people did not starve in the 1930s—a family on unemployment benefit in the 1930s was about as well off as a family with a father in normal work before the First World War—but the tragedy was that so much more could have been done. The resources represented by these additional men and women of working age were not used.

The failure of the National government to end unemployment did not reduce its popularity much. The great demonstrations in which unemployed workers marched to London to try to convince Parliament of the sufferings of South Wales or of Jarrow had relatively little effect. The government appeared resigned to high unemployment and to the decline of the traditional industries; its choice of tariffs and easy money as the way to fight the slump helped exporting industries less than the home

---

[1] W. Ashworth, *Economic History of England, 1870–1939* (1960), 415.
[2] W. Ashworth, op. cit. 417; 1949 Royal Commission on Population, quoted in S. Pollard, *Development of the British Economy 1914–50* (1962), 291.

market. Coal-mining and shipbuilding constituencies were likely to vote Labour in any case, and to some extent this was true of all the areas affected by the outburst of feeling over unemployment benefit early in 1935.

Chamberlain as Chancellor of the Exchequer followed a reasonably orthodox policy of administrative reform. Bank Rate, which had been raised to 6 per cent at the time of the departure from the Gold Standard, was brought down to 2 per cent. Apart from the general economic benefits of this step it helped make possible the conversion of £2,000m. of War Loan from an interest rate of 5 per cent to one of $3\frac{1}{2}$ per cent. In 1934 he put through Parliament an Unemployment Insurance Act which accepted the ultimate responsibility of the central government for looking after the unemployed. This was a further and almost a final step in the direction of 'breaking-up' the Poor Law and taking the welfare services out of the hands of the local authorities. The old system could not survive the pressure of unemployment; neighbourhoods already impoverished by high unemployment were pushed down further by the high rates needed for poor relief. The centrally financed Unemployment Assistance Board was to be the financial base for the system. At the same time the insurance provisions of the Act, which rested on the assumption that 15 per cent of the working population would be out of work, show the despair with which the government faced the unemployment figures.

Whatever the long-term administrative implications of the Act, the explosive part lay in its provisions for reassessing the basis of relief. When a man had used up all the unemployment benefit to which the insurance scheme entitled him he had to apply for additional benefit under a means test: his resources were examined to make sure that he did not have savings which he could draw on instead of receiving public assistance. The inquisition into personal property was unpopular in itself; in whatever way it was applied it discouraged thrift and as it was applied to a whole family, by a test of the means of the entire household, it tended to break the family up. The earnings of sons and daughters living at home were included in the total resources and the assistance given was restricted accordingly, which forced young men and women earning wages to move away from home. On the whole the Conservatives were the party most ready to praise the nineteenth-century virtues of thrift and home life; their policies had rather a different effect.

The new Insurance Act altered the basis of the means test and made it uniform for the whole country. In many places the financial position of the unemployed was improved; in many others it became worse. There were demonstrations in Glasgow, Sheffield, South Wales, and elsewhere, and there was an angry debate in the House of Commons at the end of January. The government had believed that a great many Public Assistance Committees were giving unemployment benefit on a more generous scale than it intended. The swift reaction when the new Board tried to apply its uniform nation-wide scale showed that it would be hard to reduce benefits. The unemployed had not agitated in great numbers for the right to work; they did believe they had a right to the existing levels of benefit. The government gave way and withdrew the provisions making benefit uniform for the whole country. Benefit was improved in areas where it had been low, but was not reduced anywhere at this time. The issue died away surprisingly quickly and seems to have had little effect on the general election later in the year.

Two incidental factors helped keep the number of the unemployed high. The failure to raise the school-leaving age, which was constantly under discussion and constantly deferred, meant that employers had a steady stream of cheap workers whom they could take on when they left school at 14 and dismiss when they began to ask for adult wages. The boys and girls were blamed for going into 'dead-end jobs' but, considering the state of the labour market, it was hard to expect them or the employers to act any differently. At the same time one outlet for surplus population was drying up. For over a hundred years people had been flowing out of England to the rest of the English-speaking world. This movement of population was considered normal and even desirable. In the thirties the flow was reversed: emigrants no longer went out, and recent emigrants came back, because employment was even harder to find in other English-speaking countries. Later in the thirties the population increased because of the troubled state of Europe. Many people, mostly though not entirely Jewish, came to England to escape from the spread of Nazism. The drop in emigration meant that more people of working age stayed in the country. Immigration from Europe undoubtedly improved the quality of British scientific and intellectual life, but it also led to some tenseness about the position of Jews in England. A large number of people held a view concisely and honestly stated by Harold Nicolson 'Although I loathe anti-semitism, I do dislike Jews', which seemed to mean that persecuting Jews and depriving them of their rights was detestable, but that Jews were not socially welcome.[1] This feeling in the thirties seemed to follow the general pattern that increased immigration into Britain leads to increased hostility to newcomers.

With a relatively slight amount of help from the recent immigrants, British scientists achieved a great deal in the 1930s. The Cavendish

[1] H. Nicolson, *Diaries* (1967), ii. 469.

laboratory at Cambridge was one of the world's great centres for inquiry into sub-atomic physics, and in 1932, the laboratory's greatest year, Chadwick established some of the properties of the neutron, and Cockroft and Walton succeeded in disintegrating atoms by bombarding them with protons: in this way they reduced lithium to helium. The British discoveries in the 1930s seem, in detached statistical terms measured by the number of Nobel prizes awarded, to have been less impressive than British development in chemistry in the 1950s and 1960s, but they happened to lie in an area which came, rapidly and spectacularly, to be of vital importance. 'Splitting the atom' was a phrase that had been used at least since the public excitement over Einstein's Theory of Relativity. Rutherford decided that his public statement in the early 1920s that it would not be possible to split the atom in a way that could be used for military purposes might have been mistaken; he told Hankey, the Secretary to the Cabinet, that an atomic bomb might be possible. The old ideal of supranational science, in which knowledge was open to all, was dying away and he did not make public his change of mind. By the outbreak of war all the scientific work that underlay the manufacture of the atomic bomb had been carried out. Considering the unresponsive attitude taken to requests for large sums of money for scientific purposes, the technological work needed for further development, peaceful or warlike, probably would not have been paid for if the war had not come.

Foreign policy under MacDonald and Baldwin

The National government was confronted with problems of foreign policy almost immediately it was formed. While it was going off the Gold Standard, Japan was launching her invasion of Manchuria which has often been seen as the first step in the destruction of the League of Nations. In England the most fully committed supporters of the League of Nations were people who believed that foreign policy should rest on principles of morality, and they talked as though conditions in China were as peaceful as in Europe and as though the Japanese invasion was as aggressive and unprovoked as a German invasion of Poland would have been. But Manchuria was not a quiet and settled area; when they invaded it the Japanese were only moving into a troublesome border region like so many imperialists ever since the Romans. The Lytton Commission set up by the League of Nations reported that the Japanese had been badly treated in Manchuria but that they did not have a legal right to take the territory over. The British Foreign Secretary, Sir John Simon, probably leaned too far towards believing that the Japanese were ambassadors of progress, but Britain was not strong enough in the Far

East to oppose Japan, and no other country in the League could do much about it. The United States was willing not to recognize that Japan had acquired Manchuria, and to ignore the puppet government of Manchukuo, but this was not an adequate basis for a policy in the Far East. Throughout the 1930s the British government tried to look after British interests, and protect British traders there, with forces that were too weak. In ports like Shanghai the Japanese had the advantage of possessing a powerful force on the spot, and they were determined to use that advantage to squeeze out British commercial interests.

Britain's inability to intervene over Manchuria might have been taken as a sign that she had disarmed too much; the rule that the armed forces should not budget for a war within the next ten years was relaxed. But as the long-awaited Disarmament conference was beginning, 1932 was no time to rearm. There had not been enough preparation for the conference, but by the normal standards of such meetings it began quite harmoniously. As was to be expected, the countries at the conference began by putting forward schemes that would enable them to keep all their own weapons while their neighbours disarmed—thus Britain, with a strong interest in aerial disarmament because so large a proportion of her population lived in one large city, added to her proposals for aerial disarmament the proviso that she could keep some aeroplanes to bomb rebellious tribesmen on the boundaries of empire. If countries had taken more time to discuss each other's proposals, they might have been able to find some areas of compromise, but because they had not had much experience of disarmament negotiations, they too often took proposals at face value instead of trying to whittle them down to a reasonable form by discussion. In any case the situation inside Germany was deteriorating while the conference sat. Economic disintegration and the breakdown of law and order because of fierce party clashes were leading to a crisis which was resolved early in 1933 when the Nazi leader Adolf Hitler became Chancellor on a nationalist programme that included the destruction of the Versailles treaties. Slow negotiation was now impossible; Hitler was even more determined to gain military equality for Germany than his predecessors, and as France and her East European allies resisted his demands Germany withdrew from the conference in October. By this stage the warnings of the pessimists were beginning to be justified; governments were on the point of rearming if they could not reach an agreement on disarmament, and the breakdown of the conference made rearmament very hard to avoid.

There had been considerable effort in England to arouse support for disarmament; Baldwin, the Lord President of the Council, had said in

November 1932 that if attempts at disarmament failed it would be
because young men were too enthusiastic about retaining aeroplanes, and
that they should not blame the old men if the policy of disarmament was
not successful. The young men at Oxford accepted this view: they were
not certain whether the cause of peace should be defended by pure
pacifism or by adherence to the League of Nations, but supporters of
these two approaches voted together in February 1933 to pass a resolution at the Oxford Union (the university debating society) that 'this House
would not fight for King and Country'. There was probably a considerable amount of pacifist feeling behind this vote, for opposition to all war
was still strong. But in the next few years this feeling turned into support
for the League of Nations.

When the Beaverbrook and Rothermere newspapers began arguing
that public opinion had no use for the League of Nations, a great survey
of opinion was organized by the League of Nations Union, a non-
party group which contained a large number of Liberals, many people
from the right wing and centre of the Labour party, and some pro-League
Conservatives like Lord Robert Cecil. Just over eleven million sets of
answers were collected: responses to the first four questions in the survey
showed that opinion was overwhelmingly in favour of the League and of
disarmament. Question 5 asked 'Do you consider that, if one nation
insists on attacking another, the other nations should combine to compel
it to stop by (*a*) economic and non-military measures (*b*) if necessary,
military measures?' About 10 million people voted in favour of economic
sanctions; 6,784,368 people voted in favour of combined military
measures to restrain an aggressor, and 2,351,981 voted against. Historians
have argued what the answer to question 5b proved; on the whole people
anxious to justify the policy of the British government have written as
though the minority opposed to military sanctions was too large to be
ignored, and people anxious to condemn the policy of the British government have pointed out that over 70 per cent of the people answering were
in favour of military sanctions. The problem is insoluble, because
nobody knows in what spirit the minority voted against sanctions; a
very small group recorded that they were Christian pacifists, but perhaps
most of the minority were people who were ready to fight when Britain's
interests were involved. The Cabinet showed during the Abyssinian crisis,
later in 1935, that they were ready for economic sanctions but would not
fight for the League unless they thought British interests were directly
involved.

In June 1935 MacDonald retired from the Premiership, in which he
was becoming more and more a figurehead, and was succeeded by

Baldwin, and Sir Samuel Hoare replaced Simon at the Foreign Office. The rearranged government seemed to have a choice between two foreign policies: it could work for an alliance between England, France, and Italy (the 'Stresa Front', as it became known) and rely on it to hold German expansionism in check. One argument in favour of this policy was that Mussolini had forced Hitler to draw back from his attempt to absorb Austria into Germany in 1934. The other approach was to rely on the League of Nations and use it as an alliance that would crush any attempt to use force to change the existing political situation. The two policies were not reconcilable, because Mussolini made it clear at Stresa that his price for acting as a stabilizing force in Europe was that he should be allowed to take over Abyssinia. Public opinion, as shown by the survey by the League of Nations Union, supported the League; in September Hoare made a speech at Geneva, which was well received in England, in which he committed the country to support collective action by the League. This did not mean that England would be ready to act as a solitary policeman on behalf of the League, but it did mean that the policy of the Stresa Front had been abandoned.

When Italy did invade Abyssinia the immediate effect on British politics was to disrupt the Labour party. Economic sanctions against the aggressor, in the form of partial restrictions on Italian trade, were imposed by the government, with the support of most of the Labour party. George Lansbury, the leader of the Labour party, felt he could not approve of this policy because it could easily lead to war and he believed all wars to be wrong. He tried, perhaps with insufficient determination, to resign but his followers would not let him go. Lansbury was one of the kindest men in politics and had led his small band of supporters in the House of Commons with considerable skill and great determination; the party's attachment to him was no more than his due. But at the 1935 Labour party conference Bevin set out to make sure that not only was a resolution passed in favour of sanctions but also that it was passed in circumstances which made it clear that Lansbury had got to go. Bevin possessed the talents and the inclination for this work of destruction and humiliation but, stripped of insults, Lansbury had to be told that 'It is placing the movement in an absolutely false position, to be taking your conscience round from body to body asking what you ought to do with it.'[1]

Lansbury was replaced as leader by Attlee, a quiet and modest man who, along with some less obvious talents, possessed the qualification of being the antithesis of MacDonald. He was the first of the men who had

[1] Bevin may have said 'trailing' or 'hawking' your conscience. A. Bullock, *Life of Ernest Bevin* (1960), i. 568.

fought in the First World War—apart from Churchill who had spent a few months in the front line—to achieve a leading position in politics; young men like Eden and Duff Cooper were making their way forward on the Conservative side, but the men who gained power when Lloyd George fell in 1922 still led the party. It was not certain that Attlee would remain leader of his party after the election; his position and Baldwin's unassertive manner meant that party leaders dominated the scene less when Parliament was dissolved in 1935 than in any other post-1832 election. The National government was never in any serious political danger. It still held most of the votes that used to go to the Liberals; as the Labour party's share of the total vote continued to fluctuate between 30 per cent and 37 per cent, only a strong Liberal challenge could draw off enough votes to endanger the Conservative position. But the stability of the Labour vote which was so marked a feature of elections between the wars was not realized at the time. Governments and politicians expected swift reversals of fortune, and the top-heavy 1931 election result made them more apprehensive than usual.

This mood of uneasiness had a considerable effect on foreign policy and rearmament. The Labour party had clearly intended to take advantage of pro-League feeling; the government, by steps like Hoare's speech at Geneva, had made sure that it could not be out-flanked. An election in which both sides concentrated on claiming to be heartily in favour of the League was not likely to clarify policy much. The Labour party put forward its proposals for nationalization in more detail than before, but they did not attract much attention; the government's conduct of the past four years of high unemployment did not arouse much enthusiasm. The Labour party gained a slightly larger proportion of the popular vote than in 1929, its best previous performance, but the Conservatives held on to enough of the Liberal votes they had gained in 1931 to have a large and secure majority. The Liberal party faded further from sight in a world in which everybody professed Gladstonian principles in foreign policy and nobody wanted Free Trade. Lloyd George formed Councils of Action, which urged candidates to support Keynesian economics and the League, but there is no sign that the Councils had more effect than any other pressure group at election-time.

	Votes	Seats	% of all votes cast
Conservative	11,810,158	432	53·7
Liberal	1,422,116	20	6·4
Labour	8,325,491	154	37·9

After the election Hoare went to Switzerland for a holiday. On the way he was ill advised enough to meet Laval, the French Prime Minister (and also Foreign Minister), in Paris and discuss a plan for ending the Abyssinian war by giving Italy a large slice of territory and compensating Abyssinia by giving her a small slice of Somaliland. This plan was hard to reconcile with a pro-League attitude but it made good sense to the French, who wanted to get back to the policy of the Stresa Front. The proposal leaked out in Paris before the details had been completely arranged; the House of Commons and the public were furious when they learned what had been planned. Hoare continued to think that it offered the best way out of the Abyssinian problem, and for a short time the government agreed. But as the storm grew it became clear that Hoare could not be supported, and his resignation was accepted. In the debate on the proposal Attlee, who had retained his position as leader, went so far as to say that Baldwin had been acting dishonourably during the election when he declared his support for the League. The dissident Conservatives decided that this was unjustified, and voted for the government.

Sanctions were maintained for a time, not entirely without hope of success; it is not certain that Italy could have gone on if the Abyssinian war stretched into a second campaign. The League did not prevent oil going through the Suez canal to the Italian armies because the British government was afraid Mussolini would be driven to war by such a step and the Admiralty was not confident that it could hold the Mediterranean against him. As supplies were unimpeded, Italy went quickly forward to a brutal victory, and the British government had to disentangle itself from the policy of sanctions. The failure of collective action had undermined faith in the League, and it was hard to find any other British foreign policy which could command united support in the country. The result of the Peace Ballot suggested that a policy based on the national interest, which would appeal to people on the right who were not ready to fight a League of Nations war, would have to be combined with support for the League to satisfy the large body of opinion that was ready to fight for the League. Abyssinia might have provided an opportunity for uniting the two strands of British opinion behind a firm policy; the next incidents in the deterioration of the international situation divided British opinion so sharply that a firm policy was not likely to be found.

The left had always thought that the Treaty of Versailles was too harsh, and in the thirties the progressive wing of the Conservative party had accepted this view. In 1935 an Anglo-German naval agreement released Germany from some of the restrictions of the Treaty, and in particular allowed her to build as many submarines as England. In March 1936 Hitler removed another of Germany's grievances in the simplest possible way; his armies marched into the Rhineland, which had been demilitarized by the Treaty. France was alarmed but would not do anything without British support. British opinion believed that keeping the Rhineland demilitarized was a futile and unjustified interference with German sovereignty. This may have been a reasonable view, but the fact that he was able to make this unilateral change was bound to encourage Hitler to break other, more defensible parts of the Treaty. The British attitude also reduced French faith in the effectiveness of the *entente*.

In July a revolt broke out in Spain. Most of the army mutinied against the recently elected government. For the sake of propaganda the army was called Fascist and the government was called Communist; but it was less a struggle between Fascists and Communists, and much more a struggle between clericals and anti-clericals, than people outside Spain realized. The Communists were not members of the government, and the Spanish Fascists were only a small part of the coalition gathered together behind General Franco. Both the British and the French governments realized that it would cause them trouble at home if they accepted the rule of international law that it was legal to help the established government and not legal to help the rebels. They proposed a policy of non-intervention, which meant that no country would help either side in the struggle. This was reasonable enough if it meant that Germany and Italy would be restrained from helping the rebels, and the French Socialist Prime Minister, Léon Blum, was able to persuade the Labour party to approve of non-intervention on this ground. Germany and Italy signed the Non-Intervention Agreement but soon showed they were not going to be restrained by it. When they saw that Franco was not going to sweep through all opposition to an easy victory they began to organize volunteers to come to his assistance and sent supplies and weapons to help him. By the time of its annual conference the Labour party was already beginning to regret its acceptance of non-intervention, and it asked the government to increase pressure on Germany and Italy to keep the Agreement.

Life in the late 1930s

The government had problems at home to worry it. Its control over the House of Commons was not secure, because many of its backbenchers distrusted it. The Chief Whip, Captain Margesson, has been blamed for taking an authoritarian approach, but this, after all, is what Whips usually do. The unusual thing was not that Margesson tried to keep the party in order but that the party was so determined not to be kept in order. In April the government lost a division in the Commons and in the summer there were rumours that Baldwin was going to retire. His position became even weaker when he told the House, during a debate on rearmament in November, that the government had been convinced of the need for rearmament ever since 1933 but that since it saw no prospect of winning an election on rearmament at that time it had waited until 1935. This announcement was received with what the *Annual Register* called 'raised eyebrows' and it has continued to be regarded as controversial ever since.[1]

Some people spoke as though Baldwin had said he could not win an election on rearmament in 1935 and as a result had kept the issue out of the campaign. This misunderstanding was reasonable enough, because rearmament had not been discussed much in 1935 and the election had not been used as an opportunity to warn people why it was necessary. But all that Baldwin said to the Commons was that an election on rearmament in 1933 would have led to a Conservative defeat, which he quite reasonably felt would have done nothing to help rearmament. For a man with a mandate—and a mandate that he had acquired two years later than he thought it was needed—Baldwin did not move very quickly in the direction of rearmament, perhaps because he was exhausted by a long term of office, and because he was not certain whether he really had a mandate at all. It has been suggested that one reason for the slowness of rearmament in the 1930s was fear of the Labour and Liberal opposition; this fear would not have weighed heavily with the government if it had really believed that it had put the case for rearmament to the people and convinced them in 1935.

Baldwin redeemed his personal position a few weeks later. George V died early in 1936; he had represented very well one aspect of life in the first third of the century, with his Victorian virtues, his desire to do his best, and his anxiety that everybody should have fair play. His son Edward VIII did not possess the conscientiousness, the stamina, and the willingness to endure boredom that are so necessary for a constitutional monarch. In any case he was in love with Wallis Simpson, who was American and was married. She could get a divorce easily enough, but marriage to a divorced American woman was, for an English sovereign, rather a serious matter. The situation was known all over the United States, and in society in England; the newspapers thought it best that the public should not learn about this distressing problem. So it was for many people a complete surprise to learn that Edward and his ministers were

[1] *The Annual Register of World Events for 1936,* 93.

discussing what should happen to the King. The issue came into the open on 3 December; a little support for the King appeared, but when Members of Parliament went and talked to their constituents they thought better of it. Neither Baldwin nor any other conceivable Prime Minister would serve under Edward if he went ahead and married Mrs. Simpson after she had got her divorce, and Edward had no intention of being parted from her. On 10 December Baldwin presented Edward's abdication to the House of Commons and gave his account of the way he had tried to persuade the King not to follow this course. It was agreed that Baldwin had behaved very well; the Church, the Dominions, and the Opposition all supported him, and the King's few supporters in public life, such as Mosley, Beaverbrook, and Churchill, were regarded as irresponsible. This was unimportant in the case of Mosley and Beaverbrook, but the position of Churchill was more important.

Once the Government of India Act had been passed there was no obvious reason why he should not be taken into the government, but there were still doubts about his reliability. In the course of 1936 he had been rebuilding his position; at one moment it had looked as though he might slip into support for Franco in Spain, but by November he had come to believe that a victory for the allies of Italy and Germany would harm British interests and should be resisted. In the organization 'Arms and the Covenant' in late 1936 he worked with members of the Liberal and Labour parties, putting the argument that the Covenant of the League of Nations must be supported by force. This did not appeal to the government, and it may not have been sorry that Churchill's attitude over Edward VIII's abdication reduced his political authority.

On Abyssinia and on the Rhineland people had at least been able to agree that aggressive unilateral action had been wrong, though they could not agree whether England ought to do anything to stop it. Over the Spanish civil war a division of opinion in England matched the division in Spain: most Conservatives thought Franco was doing a useful job; some Conservatives and almost all the Liberal party and Labour party were convinced that the Spanish Republic had become the first line of defence for democracy. The policy of non-intervention enabled the government to stand between the two opinions, and probably most Englishmen who were not interested in politics would not have been willing to see the country take part on one side or the other. Englishmen who were interested in politics found that the Civil War was the moment of choice for the decade, and also that 'the 1930s saw the last of the idea that the individual, accepting his responsibilities, could alter the history of the time. From now on, the individual could only conform to or protest against events which were outside his control'.[1] Spender may have over-estimated the number of fortunate individuals who could affect the course of history, but there were certainly many people who felt it their duty to go out to Spain and fight. The left, organized in the International Brigade, attracted many more recruits from England than the right. On the whole the people who went to fight on the side of the Spanish government were committed to Marxist point of view, though this did not necessarily mean that they were members of the Communist party. The war reduced the appeal of pacifism; as Fenner Brockway asked: 'How could I regard myself as a pacifist when I desired so passionately that the workers should win the civil war?'[2] Another effect was to provide a well-defined cause for a number of writers of the period who accepted the desirability of political commitment.

Most of the authors who emerged between 1910 and 1930 were not interested in politics and tended either to support traditional values or to be opposed to the zeal for rationality found among writers at the beginning of the century. Most of those who appeared in the 1930s were affected by the slump and the rise of Fascism and Nazism; they were interested in politics and accepted a socialist point of view. A political framework of thought need not have done them any harm, but men like Spender and Auden were temperamentally better suited for an anarchist approach to socialism than for the Marxism that they adopted. Orwell, who spent more time fighting in Spain than most of the writers, decided that he preferred the Spanish anarchists to Communists. His English con-temporaries might have benefited if they had taken a little longer sampling the diversity of left-wing opinions available in Spain; all that they really knew was that the Labour party was not whole-heartedly committed in the way they wanted. Early in 1937 the question arose of a United Front, to combine the Communist party, the Labour party, and the I.L.P. Sir Stafford Cripps and his supporters in the Socialist League were told that if they continued to act as a pressure group for a United Front they would be expelled from the Labour party. This probably made good sense for a party which had to appeal to an electorate which was not very interested in Spain, but it helps to explain why writers who were enthusiastic about politics felt that the Communist party was the genuine party of the left. Writers like this, and their readers, found Victor Gollancz's Left Book Club, with a socialist book to read every month, ideally suited to their intellectual needs.

[1] S. Spender, *World within World* (1951), 290. He went on to mention 'specifically, the cause of Spanish democracy'.
[2] F. Brockway, *Inside the Left* (1942), 338.

By 1937 the pace of rearmament had become fast enough to affect the finances of the country. Chamberlain had been doubtful that England could afford a large armament programme, but as the government had committed itself to a £1,500m. programme, the money had to be found. His proposal for a £400m. defence loan was criticized on the grounds that defence spending in peacetime had always been met out of taxation. He replied that this defence spending was a long-term investment to make up the omissions of the past and to provide for the safety of the next generation. He also imposed a tax on increased profits, arguing that firms had done a good deal better in the last few years because of government spending; he proposed that they should be taxed on the amount that their profits had gone up from the 1933–5 level. Business men argued that this would penalize the active firms which were making a contribution to the economy and would favour firms that were doing less. Chamberlain gave way, and substituted a direct tax on all profits.

The Labour party reconsidered its position on defence, and decided to stop voting against the Estimates. Previously it had thought that because it disapproved of the government's foreign policy it could not vote for the defence expenditure that followed from it. The Labour party was no happier about foreign policy in 1937 but it accepted the argument that a vote against the Estimates would look like opposition to all defence preparations, which would worry the electorate and encourage Germany and Italy.

In May 1937 Baldwin retired. Perhaps of all the politicians of the century, he was the most successful in achieving the objectives he had set himself: the standard of personal integrity in politics had been maintained; the Labour party had been absorbed into the general framework of politics and the danger of class war had been warded off; the possibility that politics would be dominated by men of talent concerned with getting things done rather than men of rigid principle had been averted, so that Churchill, Lloyd George, Beaverbrook, and Birkenhead had been kept out of power. Probably he overestimated the dangers from unprincipled men and from class war—he behaved as if he thought any sudden change must be bad and should be resisted. When he made mistakes it was out of a desire to keep in step with most of the people of the country. Low, the famous left-wing cartoonist of the Beaverbrook *Evening Standard*, drew a picture of Baldwin springing his rearmament policy on an unprepared population and saying 'If I hadn't promised not to lead you here, you wouldn't have come.'[1] But rearmament was not proceeding at unexpected speed when he retired, and subsequent

[1] David Low, *The Years of Wrath* (1949), 40: originally published 14 Nov. 1936.

criticism has always suggested that Baldwin's mistakes were rather the result of too little than too much activity.

Most people had become decidedly better off during the fifteen years since he first took office as Prime Minister, though it would be hard to show that his policies had done much to bring this about, and at the time commentators found it hard to discover that improvements had taken place. Social surveys showed that there was still a good deal of poverty in England in the 1930s. Seebohm Rowntree went back to York and repeated an investigation of living standards and the poverty line that he had first carried out in 1899. By the standards used in the first survey he found that just under 4 per cent of the population fell into the lowest category, which had included just under 10 per cent of the population in 1899. Once it was accepted that standards in general had improved, a new definition of the poverty line was needed and about $17\frac{1}{2}$ per cent of the population fell below the new line. The reasons for falling into poverty were not surprising: unemployment, old age, bad health, and large families brought up on low wages. The results of poverty were studied, about the same time, by Boyd Orr. His *Food, Health and Income* showed that at least half the population was ill fed, and this half included more than half the nation's children. Some of this malnutrition was the result of ignorance, which led to deficiencies in minerals such as calcium. But the poorest 30 per cent of the population were suffering from a great many shortages, and even with the greatest care they would have found it almost impossible to afford a proper diet. These people were better off than the bottom 30 per cent at the beginning of the century; life at the bottom of Edwardian society was grimmer than people realized and it was only in the years between the wars that people began to know enough about the social structure of the country to be able to think about it as one united and interconnected nation.

A fair amount of the increased prosperity took the form of a wider distribution of things that had previously been available only to a small, comfortably prosperous class. The rich had in the past spent their money on quite different things from the rest of the community; there was no substantial diminution of inequality of incomes between the wars, but the rich bought the same things as everybody else, in larger quantities or in better quality. Seen from on top, this meant that some of the best things in life were disappearing. The subsidized and highly literate evening newspapers like the *Westminster Gazette* did not survive the 1920s. In the 1930s the total sales of newspapers increased, as the result of a fierce struggle for circulation between the *Express*, the *Mail*, and the *Herald*. The goal of the contest was to be able to offer advertisers a guaranteed circulation of two million; this did mean that more people saw newspapers than before, and while the quality of news and comment provided by the mass-circulation press was not high, the years of the circulation war were also the years when *The Times*, following the tradition of Scott and Spender, was toning down or suppressing news from Germany in order to avoid embarrassing British foreign policy. The *Express* prophesied peace until the very eve of war, because Lord Beaverbrook believed that people ought to be kept happy, but it did print unedited accounts of what was happening in Germany under Hitler.

The *Express* stood apart from one of the changes in the newspaper business between the wars. Beaverbrook did not try to build up pro-vincial chains of papers in the way that the Rothermere or Berry companies acquired local papers and ran them as parts of a newspaper empire. He dominated his three newspapers in London, though it was unreasonable for people to complain that he gave his editors too little freedom—he was the best editor available for the sort of papers he wanted to produce, and he knew it. He had no printing interests outside his newspapers. The *Herald*, on the other hand, was always being pushed forward by the printing interests of Odhams Press under J. S. Elias, which influenced its activity as much as the control that the T.U.C. had over editorial policy. Pressure from Odhams intensified the circulation war and in particular encouraged the practice of giving premiums such as books by Dickens, travelling clocks, and insurance policies to new readers. This undoubtedly induced people to take newspapers who had not previously done so, though readers of this sort were not the informed students of public affairs who were understood to read the quality papers.

In 1936 an Act was passed to raise the school-leaving age to 15 in September 1939. The change was prevented by the war, but it was a part of the pattern of widened distribution. The same process could be seen in things like holidays and motor cars. Before 1914 and even into the 1920s, motor cars had been treated as though they were just the same as the carriages kept by prosperous people in the nineteenth century. But horse-drawn carriages were practically impossible to mass-produce, and in any case they would have led to traffic chaos much sooner than an equal number of motor cars. In the 1920s lorries replaced most of the horse-drawn vans, and at the same time challenged the place of railways in long-distance transport. The railway workers found that lorry-drivers were rising into the aristocracy of labour; the railway companies found it hard to pay dividends. Private cars became less expensive, and were owned by a wider and wider section of the middle class. At least until the First World War the motor car was a rich man's toy; as the cheapest models cost as much in money terms before 1914 as in the 1960s, they were far beyond the means of the ordinary man, and must have cost as much to keep up as a carriage. In 1915 there were 277,000 car licences current. The new, widely distributed cars made by Morris Motors and by the Ford Motor Company's British subsidiary after the war were fairly cheap; the 'baby Austin' was in no sense meant for the comfortable classes. By 1938 there were 2,400,000 car licences current.

The internal combustion engine provided for a few people the excitements of motor-racing and of air-racing; at the end of the 1920s Britain won the world air-racing championship, the Schneider Trophy, three times running, and there was also a good deal of public attention paid to events like Amy Johnson's flight to Australia—the first solo flight over so long a distance by a woman. But these were special occasions, picked out by the newspapers because they provided headlines, rather than a normal interest of Englishmen concerned with sporting achievement. The division of sporting interest remained much as it had been before 1914: the upper class killed animals, though no longer with Edwardian profusion, the middle class watched and played cricket and rugby football, and the working class watched association football all over the country and rugby football in Wales. Cricket and rugger were for amateurs; soccer had become a game for professionals in the last years of the old century, when the Saturday afternoon holiday had spread enough for a wide demand for entertainment to exist. Somewhat later a professional, speeded-up version of rugger (Rugby League) gained ground in the north of England.

One distinct change took place in the nation's betting habits after the war. Previously the great medium for gambling had been horse-racing; it was a fairly popular sport in its own right, with an aristocratic class owning the horses and a working-class audience to watch the races—though, apart from the Derby, the crowds were not large by comparison with football crowds—but there was a much larger gambling interest, and thousands of men who never watched a race put their money on horses. This was legal for the upper classes, and usually illegal for the working class, because the working class could not bet on credit and according to the law cash betting was allowed only on the racecourse itself. The law was notoriously widely broken, and there was a very large weekly turnover of money through the hands of illegal bookmakers.

In the 1920s the football pools rose quite quickly to become a major outlet for gambling. Because people paid for one week's bet during the course of the next week (when they sent in the forecast for the next matches) it was a form of betting on credit, which was legal, and this made it acceptable to many people who did not bet on horses. The nature of the winnings was different; the pools offered people an admittedly very small chance of winning an amount of money that would transform their whole lives, which was never possible with the relatively short odds offered in horse-racing—the Irish government made use of its freedom to set up a sweepstake with very large prizes, but the football pools offered similar opportunities every week. Another attraction of the pools was that they were honest; horse-racing was no longer nearly as crooked as it had been in the Victorian period, but betting was still a matter of inside information, whispers about what the stable-boy had said, and the possibility that a bookmaker would welsh on his bets. Footballers provided a more straightforward sort of betting; the success of the pools showed that the country was no longer divided as sharply into respectable people and unrespectable people as it had been at the beginning of the century.

Other divisions were narrowing at the same time. Before 1914 the middle class took it for granted that they went away for holidays, and people in the working class who were lucky enough to have holidays never went far from home. In the 1930s holidays by charabanc became popular, and naturally the people who had grown used to substantial holidays before 1914 looked down on them. In the mid-1930s, holidays with pay became much more widespread. In April 1937 4 million manual workers had at least one week of holiday with pay; by June 1939 the number had risen to 11 million. To some extent this was just another type of wage increase, but more people went away, mainly to the seaside, than before.

Before 1914 London had been a great city for public display, but it was display provided mainly by private people. After the war the great houses began to turn into hotels or company offices. The activities of the Bright Young Things were not an adequate substitute for pre-war displays like society weddings, but probably the post-war working class lived less dull lives and did not need the upper class to entertain them. The demolition and rebuilding of the period, which included assaults on the public taste like the destruction of the Quadrant of Regent Street, showed that private artistic taste would not satisfy London's needs any longer.

The enthusiasm for such small steps as Lansbury's Lido at the Serpentine showed how much people wanted something to be done. A great deal of the credit for improvement should go to Herbert Morrison. As Minister of Transport between 1929 and 1931 he introduced a Bill for nationalizing and co-ordinating the bus, tram, and underground electric train system in London; the scheme made such good sense that the National government took it up and passed it into law after August 1931. The London Passenger Transport Board managed to deal with London's traffic problems and at the same time its architecture and furnishing made the capital more attractive than before. Morrison lost his seat in the 1931 election, and devoted his attention to improving the London Labour party; in 1934 it gained control of the London County Council and retained its position until after the L.C.C. was turned into the Greater London Council in 1964. The Labour success owed a good deal to the steady emigration of the middle class to Surrey and to 'Metroland'—the area of Middlesex and Hertfordshire served by the Metropolitan railway. The policy of the new administration was symbolized by the handsome new Waterloo Bridge that it built despite the government's refusal to help pay for anything except a reconstruction of the old bridge.

Compared to the other municipal governments in the country the L.C.C. was a distinguished patron of the arts, though the absence of crippling unemployment in London during the slump and also the pressure concentrating so much of the cultural life of the country in London made its work easier. The B.B.C. had a centralizing effect, and the rapid expansion of cinemas in the 1920s drove theatres out of business in almost all towns outside London. This seemed to the prosperous classes another example of the way that standards were driven down to the level of the lower middle class though, as the English drama was slipping back from the level of Shaw and falling under the dominance of writers of the technical competence and triviality of Noel Coward and Frederick Lonsdale, perhaps the theatre was no longer a centre of intellectual and artistic activity. On the other hand, the films that did well were American; attempts to build a British industry by making cinemas show a quota of British films merely led to the production of cheap and shoddy 'quota quickies'. Well-made and relatively inexpensive documentary films were produced by John Grierson, but this approach did not really come to fruition until the development of television after the war. The magazine *Picture Post*, which flourished in the late 1930s, had a distinguished staff, but they were people who would have done at least as well on television. In 1936 the B.B.C. did begin television broadcasts, though the audience was small and the programmes sometimes makeshift, but when war broke out they were brought to an end. The non-literary arts showed signs of promise for the future during the 1930s. Composers like Vaughan Williams made good use of medieval and folk-music models, and there were the first signs of the emergence of Benjamin Britten. English sculptors like Henry Moore and Barbara Hepworth and painters such as Sutherland were laying the foundations of their fame in the 1930s.

But it was the poets, with their concern about Spain and their fear that another general war was going to break out, who best expressed people's feelings about politics when Neville Chamberlain became Prime Minister. Of the men in politics who wanted to get things done, he was the only one who came up to the standard of integrity set by Baldwin. He was not an amiable man: Halifax, whom he made Foreign Secretary and in 1940 wanted to make Prime Minister, said: 'Chamberlain's great fault was that he sneered at people; he sneered at the Labour Members and they never forgave him.'[1] He did not come to power at a happy time. The recovery from the depression of the early thirties was beginning to taper off. The economy was so sluggish, and had such difficulty dealing with the increase in the working population that, even though demand was helped by rearmament, the proportion of the working population out of work was higher at the top of the 1937 trade cycle than at the unimpressive 1929 peak in the trade cycle. Chamberlain as Chancellor of the Exchequer had not done much to help. He had been the most powerful personality in the Cabinet since 1931; he was devoted to orthodox economics and (except in 1932) had kept his budgets balanced. This had not stimulated demand, but it had kept the confidence of business men relatively high. In the United States large and persistent budget deficits weakened business confidence; government spending by itself was not enough, though Chamberlain may have overestimated the British fear of budget deficits.

He would have preferred to concentrate on domestic problems as Prime Minister. Even in quieter times he would probably not have found any way to deal with the rising unemployment and falling production of 1938 but the legislation of the period shows he was not inhibited by doctrinaire views about the virtues of *laissez-faire*. In 1938 a Coal Mines Act continued the cartelization of the industry begun by the 1930 Act; it gave the Commissioners for the industry the power to compel collieries to amalgamate, and it also nationalized the coal royalties: the government bought out the landlords who owned the coal under the ground, and the colliery owners, who were responsible for the work of digging it up, were freed from all the arguments about who owned a seam at a particular point under ground. The Labour party insisted that nationalizing the entire industry would provide all these benefits, and would make it easier to amalgamate collieries. In 1939 the government bought out the two overseas airlines which it had been subsidizing for some time.

[1] H. Nicolson, op. cit. iii. 260.

Imperial Airways was designed to link the countries of the Empire, and to fulfil this duty, had to fly a set of routes which would have been very hard to run profitably. British Airways flew a more reasonable set of routes to Europe but, despite its subsidy, was not making a profit. Long-distance aeroplanes were intended to compete with ocean liners in comfort and airlines expected that all their passengers would be rich; probably this was a reasonable assumption in the 1930s. After nationalization British Overseas Airways was set up to combine the two lines. Even if the new organization had wanted to change policy it could not have done much because almost all the resources of the aircraft industry were devoted to rearmament.

Reorganization of the army went ahead under the new government. Hore-Belisha, the Secretary of State for War, was a thoroughly modern-minded man. He made life more comfortable for private soldiers, he hastened the leisurely pace of the conversion from cavalry to tanks, and he retired a number of generals: all these steps were necessary preparations for the war, but they were bitterly resisted by army officers. Shortly after the war had begun Hore-Belisha was squeezed out of office partly out of anti-Semitism, partly because he neglected administrative routine but mainly because he and the generals could not work together.

Foreign policy under Chamberlain

Chamberlain was by nature an active and even an interfering Prime Minister; he had said in 1932: 'It amuses me to find a new policy for each of my colleagues in turn.'[1] The circumstances of the late thirties inevitably drew his attention to foreign affairs, and he showed great willingness to find a policy for the Foreign Office. The Foreign Secretary, Anthony Eden, resented this. He distrusted Chamberlain's lack of experience in the field, and in addition disagreed on specific points of policy. Chamberlain accepted the view, which had been widely held in England ever since the Treaty of Versailles, that Germany had some just causes of complaint. He believed that discontent in Europe was a serious matter and should be dealt with, though his ideas were not precise. 'In the absence of any powerful ally, and until our armaments are completed, we must adjust our foreign policy to our circumstances, and even bear with patience and good humour actions which we would like to treat in very different fashion. . . . I am about to enter upon a fresh attempt to reach a reasonable understanding with Germany and Italy, and I am by no means unhopeful of getting results.'[2]

[1] I. Macleod, *Neville Chamberlain* (1961), 164.
[2] K. Feiling, *Neville Chamberlain* (1946), 324.

This ambiguity of approach could be dangerous. If he thought the dictators were prepared for a 'reasonable understanding', then it made sense to satisfy their requests as soon as possible. If he thought that Britain needed to buy time to rearm, it was more prudent to give way slowly, obtaining as much time for each concession as could be managed. Chamberlain showed a tendency to force the pace in negotiation that suggests the process of buying time was not dominant in his mind.

The Spanish Civil War was still the major international problem at the time he became Prime Minister. Eden combined a strong commitment to the policy of non-intervention with a considerable contempt for Italy. The government seemed to have accepted his attitude when it let him take a firm line at the Nyon conference and insist that Germany and Italy should take their commitment to non-intervention seriously, but Chamberlain was not convinced. He felt that Eden's policy showed too little consideration for Italy, and he set out to conciliate Mussolini. This meant accepting Italy's victory in Abyssinia and reducing British involvement in Spanish affairs to nothing. As Chamberlain could not convince Eden of the virtues of this policy, and would not give it up, England moved towards a dual policy. Eden's temper was not improved when Chamberlain waved aside a suggestion by Roosevelt for a conference to discuss tensions in Europe: Eden hoped that, although Roosevelt could not commit his country to anything, the conference might begin the process of bringing the United States into European affairs, but Chamberlain wanted to pursue private discussions with Hitler and Mussolini uninterrupted by the United States or anybody else.

Eventually the dual policy went too far. Chamberlain and Eden had a conversation with Grandi, the Italian ambassador in London, which became in effect an argument between the two English ministers in which Chamberlain put the case that would normally have been put by Grandi. Eden resigned on 20 February at this sign that the Prime Minister had no confidence in him, and was replaced by Lord Halifax who was much more willing to let Chamberlain run foreign affairs. A good deal of influence passed from the Foreign Office to Sir Horace Wilson, a distinguished civil servant who was trusted by Chamberlain but had little experience outside labour and economic issues. The policy of appeasement could now be followed without opposition inside the government.

A settlement with Italy did not mean that it was necessary to appease Germany. The Stresa Front had rested on friendly relations with Italy and firmness to Germany. *The Times* advocated conciliatory measures in each diplomatic conflict with Italy and Germany, but did not put forward a coherent long-term policy. Chamberlain fairly certainly had a single unified policy that he wanted to apply in European affairs. The attitude of the government seems to have been affected by estimates given to it in 1937 that the next war might began with sixty days of German bombing which would cause 600,000 deaths. This assumed that the Germans could drop more than 600 tons every 24 hours, and that every ton of explosive dropped would kill 16 people. The German air force was not designed for flying from Germany to England and even when it had acquired bases in France it was never able to attack in such force; on average a ton of high explosive in the Second World War killed one person. But if Chamberlain believed the figures, which seem to have been put together in the mood that once led Baldwin to prophesy that the bomber would always get through, it was natural for him to think in terms of gaining time.

How much time his policy gained is another question. If Chamberlain intended to make friends with Hitler this objective was not pursued seriously. When Hitler took over Austria in March 1938, the British government might have tried to conciliate him by approving of the seizure, which was not impossible to justify on grounds of ethnic similarity, or on the other hand might have tried to rally opponents of German expansion by denouncing the seizure, but Chamberlain took an attitude of ungracious acceptance that was not likely to do anything except convince Hitler that England disliked his policy but was too weak to resist it.

Once Austria had been absorbed the western end of Czechoslovakia was enclosed in German territory. Hitler could turn his attention to the next of the provisions of Versailles that he wanted to overthrow. The Sudetenland had been given to Czechoslovakia in 1919 partly to give the new country a defensible strategic frontier and partly because of the skill with which the Czech case was presented. A large number of Germans had been placed under Czech rule, which could not be justified on principles of self-determination. The claim that the Sudetenland ought to be given to Germany had some validity and a Sudeten German movement, led by Henlein and secretly financed from Berlin, began agitating in favour of the transfer. In May a flurry of rumours suggested that Germany was about to attack Czechoslovakia: the Czech and the British and French governments took a firm attitude and protested at the idea of changing the frontier settlement by force. Hitler had in fact not intended to attack at that time, and he was not pleased when advocates of resistance to German expansion said that he had been driven back by the firmness of the British and French.

The Sudeten agitation went on, and Chamberlain became convinced that it was a threat to the peace of Europe. In August he sent Runciman to carry out an investigation of the position; the Czech government did not want him to come, because it implied that there was some doubt about their position in the Sudetenland, but Chamberlain said that if the investigation could not be carried out England could not take much interest in Czechoslovakia's problems. Runciman's mission became a form of pressure on the Czech government to make concessions to the German population; this would have been reasonable if the Sudeten Germans had been negotiating in good faith, but as Hitler constantly encouraged them to raise their demands they could not be satisfied. By the time Runciman came back to England at the beginning of September the claims of the Sudeten Germans had risen so high that it was hard to see how they could be met by anything short of a 'transfer of territory' to Germany. When *The Times* said so, on 7 September, it seemed to be only the logical outcome of British policy. Chamberlain had not yet accepted this; he wanted to visit Germany and discuss the issues with Hitler in person.

On 15 September he flew to Berchtesgaden to meet Hitler. He conceded the principle that Czech territory should be transferred to Germany. He returned to London, and then set about convincing the French government that nothing could be done to help the Czechs except persuade them to give up the German areas of the Sudetenland with as little fuss as possible. England had no treaty obligations to Czechoslovakia except a general commitment to the Treaty of Versailles; France had a treaty with Czechoslovakia, but the French government was willing to be argued out of taking it seriously. French diplomacy rested on a series of alliances with the new states in eastern Europe created by the Versailles Treaty, but French strategy depended on adopting a defensive position behind the heavily fortified Maginot line which meant that France made no preparations for helping her allies.

Chamberlain went to Godesberg to meet Hitler on 22 and 23 September. The detailed German proposals showed that Czechoslovakia was to lose parts of the Sudetenland in which the population was mainly Czech, and the inhabitants of the areas to be transferred got no choice of staying or leaving. Chamberlain did not accept these proposals. When he went back to London from Godesberg it seemed possible that the British government would stand firm, would encourage the French government to honour its treaty obligations to Czechoslovakia and would promise to support the Czechs if they resisted. On 28 September the fleet was mobilized, and when Parliament was called together Chamberlain explained the course of the negotiations in a way that seemed to point inexorably to war. But as he reached the last stage of his speech a message was passed to him; he read it; he announced that he would be flying once more to discuss the question with Hitler. His supporters burst into applause.

At Munich on 30 September the British and French were interested only in finding some way of softening the blow that was to be dealt to Czechoslovakia. They made no attempt to resist the German claims, even though the fact that the meeting was being held at all showed that Hitler knew his position was not impregnable. Some of his generals were so convinced that it would not be possible to carry out a successful invasion of Czechoslovakia against opposition that they were apparently ready to overthrow Hitler if he went further on the path to war. Stories like this are always a little hard to evaluate, but it is true that the Czechs had built a powerful defensive system in the hills of Sudetenland which German tanks would have found hard to penetrate. However, the British and French leaders accepted most of the German claims, asking only for plebiscites in the most doubtful cases. They allowed the Germans to take over a wide belt of territory almost immediately, which meant that the Czechs lost their defensive system without being able to remove much of their equipment, and the population had very little time to leave the ceded area. The Czech representatives did not take part in the conference; they were told by the British and French representatives what terms had been arranged, and they received the terms in the spirit of Masaryk's earlier comment: 'If you have sacrificed my nation to preserve the peace of the world, I will be the first to applaud you; but if not, gentleman, God help your souls.'[1] But of course the Czechs gave way only because their allies would not fight. Even so, if the Czechs had resisted a German invasion, England and France might have found it hard to stay out of war.

The Munich settlement has not been regarded kindly by posterity. The name has been applied—even by Germans—to policies thought to err in the direction of softness and compliance, and 'appeasement' has remained a term of abuse. Historians are more ready to see something to be said for Chamberlain. He could reasonably argue that if a war had started in 1938 the English-speaking world would not have been ready to join in; the British Empire would have been divided, because men like Hertzog in South Africa and Mackenzie King in Canada would not have gone to war over the Sudetenland, and the United States would have felt less sympathy for England and France than she did a year later. Against this

[1] J. W. Wheeler Bennett, *Munich, Prologue to Tragedy* (1966), 171.

support from outside Europe must be set the fact that Czechoslovakia had a better-equipped army than any other eastern European country and a strong defensive position; if England and France were to fight for any of the states created at Versailles, Czechoslovakia was the best ally they could have had.

Other supporters of the Munich settlement have pointed out that the Royal Air Force improved its strength so much between 1939 and 1940 that it was eventually able to win the Battle of Britain and retain control of the air over England. This argument seems to assume that, whenever the date at which war broke out, France would have been defeated nine months later, so that if war had begun in 1938 the Battle of Britain would have been fought in the summer of 1939. Opponents of the Munich settlement say this was not bound to happen: if Britain and France had helped Czechoslovakia, Germany might not have been able to fight a war on two fronts and Hitler would have been defeated without bringing the United States and Russia into the middle of European affairs. In any case, Britain did not make full use of the extra time gained at Munich; for instance, the decision to increase the British wartime contribution to the Anglo-French alliance from five divisions to 32 was not taken until March 1939.

Whatever effect the different rates of growth of military strength had on the military situation, it is hard to see what good the British government had done by taking an interest in the Sudeten question. If Czechoslovakia was indefensible, then it had to be abandoned, but in that case the British government only made things worse by taking part in the operation. Chamberlain seems to have thought Hitler was a reasonable man who could be persuaded to accept less than he really wanted. Hitler was not a reasonable man; he wanted his own way and while he did not at this stage want war for its own sake he did not care whether his diplomacy led to war or not. If Chamberlain could do nothing to stop him, it would have been more sensible to keep away and not expose England's weakness. Chamberlain's diplomacy encouraged Hitler to think England would not resist him, and it provoked taunts like the story that Haile Selassie of Abyssinia had written to Benes: 'I hear you are receiving the support of the British government. You have my profound sympathy.'[1]

Munich was the culmination of appeasement. After negotiating the Czechoslovakian agreement, Chamberlain and Hitler signed a separate declaration that their two countries would never go to war with each

---

[1] F. L. Lucas, *Journal under the Terror* (1939), 287. The title is misleading; the author felt shame, as well as terror, at living under a government led by Neville Chamberlain.

other. Chamberlain's policy of pacifying Hitler seemed to have reached a successful conclusion. There were scenes of wild enthusiasm when he got back to London, and he was so overcome by his reception that he said that he had brought back 'peace with honour', just as Disraeli had in 1878. But this reaction from the immediate danger of war did not last long. The First Lord of the Admiralty, Duff Cooper, resigned from the government over the agreement. A number of Tory rebels abstained in the vote expressing approval of the Munich negotiations. Members of the Liberal and Labour parties began to work together. The leaders of the Labour party, who had discouraged the United Front in the mid 1930s, opposed Liberal and Labour co-operation in a Popular Front in late 1938. Despite this, Popular Front and independent candidates did well at by-elections in the last three months of the year.

Chamberlain was not convinced that the settlement had really ensured the peace of Europe and went on with rearmament. Aircraft factories were not stretched to their full capacity but, despite the existence of $1\frac{1}{2}$ million unemployed, the rearmament programme was running into shortages of skilled labour. The unemployed might be a pool of redeployable workers, but one result of the high level of unemployment was that fewer people had been trained for skilled work than would otherwise have been the case. The government wanted to draw up a national service register, so that people in jobs that were vital for a wartime economy would not leave them and join the forces as in 1914. Trade unions were persuaded to co-operate with this scheme, partly by a government promise, repeated as late as March 1939, that there would be no conscription in peacetime.

In the New Year some of the shock of Munich began to wear off. On 10 March Sir Samuel Hoare hoped that a new era of peace and prosperity was about to begin. Hitler, who seems never to have been in the least affected by all the steps taken to appease him, seized what was left of Czechoslovakia five days later. He had applied the Munich agreements in such a way that he had gained almost everything he had asked for at Godesberg; he now went on to sweep up the defenceless remnants. At Munich England and France had promised the Czech representatives that they would defend what was left of Czechoslovakia; after Hitler's coup they said, a little pedantically, that they could not carry out guarantees to a state that no longer existed. Chamberlain seems to have taken a few days to realize how completely he had been hoodwinked, but at Birmingham on the 17th he came forward with a forceful denunciation of what Germany had done, and this led on to a reversal of British policy.

To guard against further German aggression, a guarantee was given to

Poland on 31 March, and Rumania and Greece were given guarantees in April. The question of making the guarantees effective was not considered until too late. The natural way to defend the countries guaranteed was to make an alliance with Russia, but none of them were on good terms with her and the purge trials of 1936–8 suggested that she had her limitations as an ally. France had made an agreement with Russia in 1935, but this did not guarantee the 'little entente' of post-Versailles states that France had built up. Russia and Germany were declared enemies, but this did not mean it was easy to arrange a collective system of alliances in eastern Europe.

To implement the guarantee that had been given to Poland, Chamberlain introduced on 26 April a measure of conscription to provide six months of military training for men aged 20 and 21. Conscription was never likely to be popular with the parties of the left; as it was brought forward without consultation with the Opposition leaders and only a month after the government had said conscription would not be imposed in peacetime, it was bound to be opposed. Chamberlain said in the debate: 'Nobody can pretend that this is peacetime in any sense in which the term could fairly be used', but the situation had not changed since he last gave his assurance against conscription in peacetime. Conscription was probably necessary, but it was introduced in a way that increased the feeling that the government was not concerned about the unity of the country. In foreign policy, and now in defence policy, the government had taken for granted the correctness of its own approach; the parties in opposition remained sceptical; the country was divided.

Negotiations with Russia proceeded slowly. The Soviet Union claimed a very extensive right to resist 'indirect aggression', which probably meant that it would intervene in any country which set up a pro-German government. The British clearly felt that they had a fair amount of time for discussing the issues, but they found the Russians becoming increasingly dilatory. Partly because his army had been weakened by the great purges, partly because after Munich he had become doubtful about the willingness of the western powers to fight, Stalin was turning away from the policy of resisting the other dictators. If he had been offered recognition as the natural dominant power in eastern Europe, he might have completed an agreement with England, but as the British had already made an alliance with Poland, they did not have a free hand. At her most powerful, when she was ready to intervene almost anywhere in the world, England had left eastern Europe to Germany, Russia, and Austria-Hungary. She had now undertaken responsibilities in eastern Europe, and over-estimated her ability to fulfil these obligations without assistance.

Russia was not without diplomatic resources. It was clear, from the German complaints and protests and threats, that Poland was in danger of attack. The inhabitants of Danzig were German; why, Hitler demanded, were they not part of his Reich? East Prussia was cut off from the rest of Germany by the Polish Corridor; was not this a part of the Versailles Diktat that ought to be overthrown? In fact the Polish Corridor was inhabited mainly by Poles, and Danzig had been set up as a free city at Versailles so that Poland could have one port that was not ruled by Germany. But even if Hitler's demands had been in themselves reasonable, they clearly implied that Poland was to become a satellite of Germany. This was a direct threat to Russia, and as the Russian government became increasingly convinced that England and France would not accept its claim to dominance in eastern Europe its thoughts turned to a fourth partition of Poland. So, in the last ten days of August 'the scum of the earth' and 'the bloody assassin of the workers' came together:[1] they announced that they had signed a non-aggression pact, and the treaty contained secret clauses for a partition of Poland. Germany could now intensify the pressure on Poland, and Hitler did so in language that made it clear that the risk of war would not stop his efforts to get his own way. He had not accepted the arguments of the Fascist visionaries who thought war was in itself better than peace; he intended to have Danzig and to turn Poland into his puppet, but probably he thought England and France would not fight on this issue. The Poles certainly would not give way and in the last few days of August German diplomacy concentrated on suggestions for a conference to work out acceptable terms for handing over Danzig and the Corridor. Then, if the Poles refused to put up with the terms, England and France would announce that their guarantees would lapse. This pattern was probably too much like Munich to have worked, and on 1 September Germany invaded Poland. Negotiations went on; Hitler was still ready to get his own way by a Polish Munich rather than war, if England and France would agree.

He had in fact pressed them too far. The revolt inside the Conservative party was on the verge of boiling over. When the House of Commons debated the issue, Chamberlain made a dull and non-committal speech; one Conservative M.P., clearly dissatisfied with the speech, shouted 'speak for England' across the floor to Greenwood, the acting leader of the Labour party, as he began his speech.[2] Greenwood expressed the general discontent when he asked why it was that, thirty-eight hours after

---

[1] David Low, op. cit. 90: originally published 20 Aug. 1939.
[2] Who said 'Speak for England'? Amery, according to L. S. Amery, *My Political Life* (1953–5), iii. 324; Boothby, according to H. Nicolson, op. cit. i. 419.

the attack on Poland, England was still at peace. But the government already felt itself committed to fighting; Chamberlain later explained that he had been making sure that France came into the war at the same time as England, a discreet way of saying that the friends of appeasement had been more powerful at the last in Paris than in London.

8. *The military side of the war* 1939–1945

The first year

EVEN when England and France had made up their minds to enter the war, there was nothing they could do for Poland; the French army had not prepared for a swift forward movement, and so was not able to take advantage of the fact that only about one-third of the German army was in the west. The Polish campaign was soon over, with the Polish cavalry overwhelmed by tanks and aeroplanes. The country was partitioned between Russia and Germany, and the German army moved to the western front. No more fighting was possible before the winter and a period of calm followed. From the point of view of imperial relations, England may have been fortunate that the war came when it did: despite the 1936 Treaty Egypt was not yet in a position to stay effectively neutral, in India Congress had not tried to take up the powers of government and the Viceroy could commit the country to war on his own authority, in South Africa Smuts was able to overthrow the Prime Minister, Hertzog, who wanted to stay out of the war, and in Canada MacKenzie King knew that national sentiment would not allow him to listen to his isolationist advisers in the Department of External Affairs. In a few years' time, the bonds of Empire might have frayed a little more in all these places. In 1939 Ireland was the only Commonwealth country to stay out of the war, and many men from Ireland joined the British army.

The British and French hoped that Hitler was going to fade away under the stress of blockade. A few naval actions took place; the defeat of the pocket-battleship Graf Spee by three British cruisers was a sign that British command of the sea had been established and Winston Churchill, brought back to the position of First Lord of the Admiralty that he had held in 1914, was soon seen to be the active man of the ministry. British confidence rose so much that when Russia attacked Finland in November some people suggested that England should help Finland and fight both dictators at once. The Finns resisted the Russians bravely, but were defeated before anything could come of this idea.

As England and France became more fully mobilized for war, Chamberlain went so far as to say that Hitler had 'missed the bus'. In April a sudden German attack took Denmark over before any resistance could be offered and captured most of the strategic points in Norway. England sent help, but it was hard to find a port to land supplies, hard to fight against the German aerial superiority and hard to resist the power of the German mechanized units. The British had to withdraw and abandon Norway. This defeat led to the replacement of Chamberlain by Churchill, who took up office on the day of the next German piece of aggression.[1] On 10 May an attack by tanks, bombers, and paratroops struck at Holland, Belgium, and Luxembourg. The three countries had been careful about maintaining their neutrality and had declined to have staff talks with Britain and France. Plans for advancing to their assistance had been worked out, because they could not be abandoned if they were invaded. On paper the British, French, Dutch, and Belgians had about the same number of divisions and the same number of tanks as the Germans; in practice they were not co-ordinated, the tanks were dispersed instead of being kept together as a concentrated force, and the morale of the French army was not good. It had become accustomed to the idea of staying in its Maginot line and waiting for German attacks to break against its impregnable defences; in this way the great disparity of numbers would be made up, and eventually the French could go forward to the attack. This was a pessimistic approach: the population of England and France put together was larger than that of Germany, and while the allocation of duties, by which England looked after the sea, air, and industrial production and France provided the army, had left France with the uncomfortable basic tasks of war, the Germans had to do everything alone.

Hitler had no intention of entering a long-drawn-out war. He had been in the trenches, and he was determined that Germany should not suffer as she had done in the First World War. He did his best to save the German civilian population from shortages and hardships, and he tried to win the war by a few decisive victories. The blitzkrieg (lightning-war) was meant to be over before any serious damage was done; it had to be won by tactical skill rather than hard pounding, and the invasion of Holland and Belgium showed exactly what he had in mind.

[1] The replacement of Chamberlain by Churchill, which was one of the turning-points of the war, is covered in detail on pp. 247–8 below.

The British and French forces moved forward into Belgium, and as they did so the real attack burst through the Ardennes and broke the front just above the north end of the Maginot line. Once this blow had been struck there was no recovery; within a fortnight the British and French armies that had gone into Belgium were cut off from the main body of the French army. For England the first concern was to get as many troops back across the Channel as possible. Almost all of the trained soldiers had gone to France, and the danger was that defeat would be followed by annihilation. Hitler held his tanks back from what could have been a decisive blow against the troops on the Dunkirk beaches, probably to avoid blunting their force before the final attack on the French, and on the other side of the Channel the Royal Navy, assisted by an amateur armada of small boats, began the work of evacuation. The beaches were bare of cover, R.A.F. fighters had to fly a long way to give protection, and the German air force was committed to preventing the embarkation and pinning down the troops assembled for departure. The losses among the British and French were heavy, but Operation Dynamo was far more successful than anyone in England had dared to hope; by 2 June about 335,000 men had been brought back and they were the nucleus of an army to continue the war.

Dunkirk was the last stage of a great defeat, but it kept England in the war; the damage had been done long before the men were taken off the beaches, and the relief which Englishmen felt when the troops were saved was justified. Added to relief was an unquenchably optimistic feeling that things could not get any worse, and therefore were bound to improve. This showed little feeling for the position of the French. The blitzkrieg rolled on against them; Churchill flew several times to France to try to inspire the government with some of the hope and determination that he was giving to Englishmen, but the military situation was hopeless. The prolonged German attack was a model of organization, with controlled tactical air support breaking up defensive positions without permanently destroying the lines of communication, tanks forcing their way ahead and arriving long before they were expected by the French, and motorized infantry following up the attack and consolidating the gains.

Churchill's government offered France an Act of Union, to turn the two nations into one. But he had a short time earlier refused—on sensible strategic grounds—to commit the country's last reserves of fighter planes to the air struggle over France; the Act of Union must have looked rather like an attempt to ensure that when France was overrun her fleet, her colonies, and her other assets remained in British hands. The French politicians were already wondering how to make the best peace they could, and for this they needed some bargaining counters. When the Third Republic collapsed, and Marshal Pétain signed an armistice on 22 June, it looked as though the most that could be expected was that the French would be able to arrange for their overseas assets to remain neutral. Hitler agreed to this, probably because he did not expect that England would wait long before following France's example.

1940: Alone

There were some (still ill-documented) peace feelers after the French surrender, but the British government does not appear at any time to have considered asking for an armistice. Its strategic analysis held out little realistic prospect of victory: it hoped that blockade, heavy bombing of Germany, and an eventual rebellion in the countries conquered by Germany would be followed by an invasion of the Continent which would not have to do much more than sweep up the pieces. On the other side of the Channel the Germans hoped that bombing, and the conviction that resistance was hopeless, would undermine British morale and lead to a request for peace. This would save them from the difficult task of mounting an invasion; in the first few weeks after Dunkirk a force might have been rushed across the Channel and established at some port like Dover, but by the time Germany had disentangled her forces from the pursuit of the French and had made peace, the worst of the shock was over and the British had strengthened their positions. A German invasion army was assembled and a fleet of barges collected between mid July and mid August, but by then it was clear that an assault would meet serious opposition, so a large force would be needed with a constant problem of supply. The problem could be solved only if Germany gained and kept naval control of the Channel, which was much better defended than the seas between Germany and Norway. A successful invasion of England was impossible unless Germany gained command of the air and bombed the British Navy out of the Channel before the ships sailed.

German bombing did make life uncomfortable for British shipping in the Channel but it was soon clear that if the German air force was to gain command of the sky it would have to knock out the British air force. The Germans had considerably more aeroplanes, though not as crushing a superiority as was thought at the time. Because the struggle took place over England, R.A.F. planes that had been shot down could be restored to service, and pilots who got safely to the ground could fly again. The pilots were few; the reserves of aeroplanes were limited. Although the odds against them were less overwhelming than was thought at the time, the men of Fighter Command fully deserved Churchill's eulogy: 'Never

in the field of human conflict was so much owed by so many to so few.'
If the fighters had been defeated, the Germans might have been able to
gain command of the Channel, and could then have carried out an
invasion which would almost certainly have been successful. Once
unchallenged in western Europe, Hitler could have turned his full forces
to the east, and Russia's chances of surviving such an assault would have
been slight.

For some weeks in August and September there was a danger that the
R.A.F. might be caught with all its resources committed to the battle, so
that it could not protect its aeroplanes from being bombed while they
were on the ground refuelling. In August the attack shifted from the ships
in the Channel to the aerodromes and communication systems of Fighter
Command. If this attack had been pressed home, Fighter Command
might have been broken; the Germans had a considerable numerical
superiority, and the British system depended on radar warning that an
attack was coming, followed by prompt radio-telephone instructions to
the defending aerodromes. The Germans had a reasonably good chance of
breaking the communication system, after which the weight of numbers
would have told much more than before. Early in September the Germans
threw away their chance of winning the Battle of Britain, by changing to
direct attack on London. This made much less sense; the attacking planes
had to fly further to reach their targets and the defending planes could
operate without any threat to their communication system. The British
fighter pilots, who had been tested almost to the limit, now gained aerial
superiority, and the Germans gave up the idea of invasion. The assumption behind the shift of attack was that bombing would destroy civilian
morale and industrial production, but the German bombers suffered so
heavily in daylight raids that they had to give up the attempt and switch
to night-time bombing. This period became known in England as the
blitz—an inaccurate use of the word because blitzkrieg meant a quick
end to the war, and night-time bombing offered no hope of a quick end.
From October till April German planes attacked towns all over the
country, from Plymouth to Glasgow, but concentrating mainly on
London. It was hard to ward off these attacks; radar provided some help
and as the nights grew shorter, the raids died away.

In the course of the attack the Germans had dropped something like
the 36,000 tons of high explosive anticipated in the pre-war estimates
which had been expected, before the war, to fall in the first two months
of fighting. It had nothing like the destructive effect that had been
expected; in reporting to the people on the attack Churchill said that it
had been demonstrated by statistics that at their current rate of progress

the Germans would take ten years to knock down half of London, after which the rate of destruction would grow less (because they would be bombing areas that had already been devastated) and that one ton of high explosive killed about three-quarters of a person.[1] The German air attack, and its failure, greatly strengthened England's diplomatic position. In July 1940 neutral opinion, which meant primarily United States opinion, was beginning to think Germany would win. The daytime air fighting over England checked this opinion; Hitler had demonstrably fought and lost a battle. Americans who wanted England to win could see some hope of success; Americans such as Joseph Kennedy, the U.S. ambassador, who would not have been disappointed by a British defeat found it less easy to say that her defeat should be accepted as inevitable. The night-time bombing of London reinforced these attitudes. Bombing had been expected to destroy cities and to frighten civilians so much that they would surrender at once. The British people showed no signs of being frightened and went on calmly with their work without being too disturbed by bombs. As everybody had accepted the very exaggerated pre-war opinions of the effectiveness of bombing, it looked as if the English—the Londoners were reported in greatest detail—were doing something that nobody else could have done. Later events have shown that any ordinarily patriotic people will stand up to bombing about equally well, but in late 1940 this was not realized. The effect of the blitz was to convince many Americans that St. Paul's Cathedral was a vital and defensible outpost of their own country.

Around the close of the year a series of British victories helped to show that the war was by no means over. Italy had rushed to the help of the victor in June, and had then overrun British Somaliland and nibbled at the frontiers of Egypt and the Sudan. In December the British struck back in Egypt, and by the end of February the Italians had been driven out of Cyrenaica, the eastern province of their colony of Libya, losing 130,000 prisoners in the course of their flight. In January attacks from Kenya and the Sudan were launched on the Italian position in East Africa, and by May the main Italian armies had surrendered, though a few groups held on until November.[2] The Italians clearly had neither the equipment nor the determination needed for fighting. They had already exposed their weakness to the world when they attacked Greece, from their newly acquired possession of Albania, in October 1940; the Greeks

---

[1] Churchill's broadcast of 8 Oct. 1940. P. Fleming, *Invasion 1940* (1957), 142.

[2] F. S. Playfair, *The Mediterranean and Middle East* (1954), pp. 362 and 447: the Italian army in East Africa numbered 350,000 men but many of them were natives of the region who disappeared without being captured.

had resisted, and then had begun to push the Italians back towards the Adriatic. The prestige of the Axis was reduced by Italy's failures, and this made Churchill's assertion, directed to the American people, 'Give us the tools and we shall finish the job', seem realistic.[1] In this way he assured them that they would not be asked to send men, and by this time Americans were ready to pay for England to fight, though they would not willingly send men to be killed.

The need for imports of food, raw materials, and weapons was forcing England to sell off her foreign investments, and the day when gold and foreign investments would run out was not impossibly distant. In March 1941 the U.S. Congress passed the Lend-Lease Act giving the President the right to supply arms to other countries on any terms he chose. Lend-Lease did not end economic difficulty, but it allowed British production to go ahead without any fear that imports would be cut off by bankruptcy. England could make full use of her access to the world outside Europe, and could realistically hope that Germany would run short of materials before England. One use made of this flood of Lend-Lease material has been questioned: about half the total British production of war material went into making aeroplanes, and a great deal of this aircraft production was devoted to the bombing offensive against Germany. Before the war the Air Ministry had concentrated, just in time, on radar and on producing the newest types of fighter plane; this had been a wise and well-rewarded choice, but the concentration on bombing is hard to justify. The early bombing attacks were useful; when Churchill was asked how he proposed to win the war, he could tell the Americans that he would bomb Germany till she surrendered. On a smaller scale of propaganda, it was useful to bomb Berlin when Molotov, the Russian Foreign Minister, visited his German allies; he was able to fend off Ribbentrop's assertion 'England is finished' by asking 'Then why are we in this air-raid shelter?'[2] But for anything more than propaganda a much larger effort would have to be made. During the air battles of the summer of 1940, Lord Beaverbrook had performed wonders in getting new planes produced and in having planes that had been shot down repaired and returned to service or cannibalized to provide spare parts for planes less badly damaged. After the Battle of Britain his talents turned to producing a mighty fleet of bombers that would destroy Germany without a shot being fired on the ground.

The air force had always believed that an independent aerial offensive could destroy an enemy. In the opening months of the war a few

---

[1] Churchill's broadcast of 9 Feb. 1941. Winston S. Churchill, *The Second World War* (1948–54), iii. 111.
[2] Churchill, op. cit. ii. 518.

important strategic targets had been bombed by daylight, but as Germany was too far away for fighter support to be provided, the losses soon became insupportable. No deliberate attacks on towns and civilians were made, partly because such attacks might lead the Germans to strike back equally devastatingly. So far as morality was concerned the Germans had made the first deliberate attacks on civilians, when attacking Warsaw and Rotterdam in order to help their advancing armies. In the British mood of 1940 it did not matter much that it was the Germans who started it. The object was to hit the enemy, and when France collapsed it looked as if there was no way to hit the enemy except by bombing him. The policy of the air force seemed to be forced on the government because there was no other way to attack Germany. As daylight bombing was not practicable, bombers were obliged to attack at night, just as the Germans had done in the winter of 1940. These attacks were directed against important points inside towns, and the leaders of Bomber Command were sure they could bomb accurately enough at night to hit selected targets, although incidental and unintended harm might be caused to civilians as well.

Before this new approach could be properly tested, a set of defeats was followed by a new cause for hope. The Germans had been establishing their position in the Balkans by the methods of peaceful penetration that they had used before the war. Hungary, Rumania, and Bulgaria passed into their control without much trouble, but an anti-German revolt broke out in Yugoslavia. Hitler had to help Mussolini in any case: he sent troops to Libya, and on 6 April he attacked Yugoslavia and Greece. British forces were moved from the Middle East to help Greece, with the result that the forces left in Libya were in April forced back almost to where they started from, though they retained Tobruk as a stronghold behind the enemy line which could be supplied by sea. Sending troops to Greece was not very wise strategically, though it was probably politically necessary to show that England would support any country that would fight against Germany. The British were soon driven out of Greece and took up new positions on the island of Crete, and here the Germans enjoyed a more spectacular success. The conquest of Greece had after all been no more than an attack by a large force with overland communications on a small army at the end of a long sea route. Crete looked harder. But the Germans established command of the air, and on 20 May launched a paratroop attack, rapidly followed by more troops in transport aircraft. The navy suffered heavy losses from the air—as many sailors were killed in the attempt to hold the sea as soldiers in the land fighting—and within ten days all was over: almost half the British force had to surrender. Hitler had made himself master of the Balkans and seemed to be well on the way to making himself master of north Africa. Wavell, the British commander-in-chief in the Middle East, was dismissed; he may have been worn down by defeat and by Churchill's constant urging to attack, and so have lost his usefulness, but the generals who succeeded him would probably have done no better if they had had to cope with the lack of men and shortages of materials that handicapped him.

The German attack on Russia

Hitler was not concerned about north Africa, and regarded the Balkans as a tiresome diversion from his major enterprise, an attack on Russia. It seems as though war with Russia had always been the final object of his policy, and he may have thought the whole war with Britain and France was only a prelude to the real struggle. The historian of the British blockade of Germany does suggest that fear of future shortages of wheat and oil encouraged Hitler to make his attack,[1] but it had certainly been in his mind since the time of the Hossbach Memorandum in November 1937 and, in vaguer form, since the writing of *Mein Kampf*. The British knew the attack was coming, and tried to warn Stalin. Not entirely unnaturally he regarded this as an attempt to stir up trouble between Germany and Russia. The invasion, on 22 June 1941, came as an almost complete surprise and German forces moved briskly eastwards, capturing large numbers of prisoners and in the Ukraine being welcomed as liberators from the tyranny of Moscow. They disabused the Ukrainians of this idea very quickly, killing them off and confiscating their grain as brutally as Stalin had ever done; a good deal of Hitler's policy was aimed at providing living-space (*lebensraum*) for Germans in the east, and this involved clearing the Slav population out. Partly for this reason the war on the eastern front became much more ferocious than it had been elsewhere. The civilian populations under German rule seem to have suffered the more severely the less Nordic they could claim to be. Norway and Denmark were not too badly treated. France was partitioned; the Pétain government retained most of south-east France, which it ruled from Vichy. The Free French government set up by General de Gaulle after his flight to London in June 1940 acted as a counter-magnet to Vichy. The area of France not left to Vichy was under German rule, and suffered more than Norway and Denmark. The Slav lands were far worse off: no east European intellectual could have written as relatively calmly about the Occupation as de Beauvoir in *The Prime of Life*, and the armies in the east could hardly have adopted an enemy song in the way that the British troops in the North African desert accepted Lili Marlene.

[1] W. N. Medlicott, *The Economic Blockade* (1959), ii, 646.

Quite apart from its ferocity, the scale of the war in the east was larger than that in all the other areas taken together. The Germans never had less than half of their divisions committed to the eastern front, and as these divisions were engaged in combat they had to be above the average in quality. For most of the war (1940–4) the divisions kept in France were a reserve army which included a number of units recovering from the strain of fighting in Russia. The Russians were assisted with equipment; as soon as he heard of the German attack Churchill expressed support for Russia (in accordance with his privately expressed readiness, if Hitler invaded Hell, to make at least a favourable reference to the Devil in the House of Commons) and England began sending material to Russia. In a short time Roosevelt extended Lend-Lease to assistance for Russia as well as England; by this stage the American government was not much concerned about the legal niceties of neutrality, and it provided several opportunities for Hitler to declare war on it if he chose. Measures like the 'shoot on sight' instruction, which allowed American ships to attack German submarines in the Atlantic, were a very broad interpretation of the rights of neutrals to free passage over the seas. Shipping supplies to Russia was even harder than bringing supplies across the Atlantic to England. The northern convoys to Murmansk and Archangel ran throughout the war; they were a drain on shipping resources, and the conditions of cold and bad weather were far worse than the British met anywhere else in the war against Germany. The Russians never expressed as much gratitude for this equipment and its delivery as the British and Americans thought they should have done, nor did they co-operate effectively in running the convoys. They had their own overwhelming problems. The Germans by December 1941 had forced their way almost to the suburbs of Moscow. There they were held up by a desperate defence. As winter settled round them, a Russian counter-attack began and for the first time a German army was compelled to retreat.

A World War

By this time Churchill felt confident that the war, which had suddenly spread to cover the whole world, would be won. Japan in the 1930s had gone on from involvement with Manchuria to open war with China. The United States tried to restrain Japanese expansion in Asia by cutting off supplies of oil, and by 1941 Japan had to consider whether to withdraw from its Chinese involvement or seize territory to the south from which it could get raw materials to go on fighting. It chose the latter, and prepared to do this by striking a paralysing first blow at the American Pacific fleet at Pearl Harbor in Hawaii. On 7 December an air attack on the fleet was almost completely successful, and Japan could move forward on a career of expansion in South-east Asia and the Pacific.

Germany and Japan, and also Italy, were linked in a Tripartite Treaty. Hitler honoured this Treaty by declaring war on the United States when he heard of the attack on Pearl Harbor. This was as crucial as his earlier decision to attack Russia, and as little likely to do him good. He may have thought that once the United States was at war she would soon turn on Germany as well, or he may have felt the strain of the American moves away from neutrality, or he may simply have felt that treaties with allies should be taken seriously—his loyalty to Mussolini in later years shows that in some things he was a man of his word. If he had not declared war on the United States she might easily have concentrated her energies on the war in the Pacific. In 1941 British and American officers meeting for staff decisions on the policy to follow if the United States had found herself at war with both Germany and Japan had decided that the war with Germany should come first; this was probably wise, because the task of landing a force on the shores of Europe would have become much harder if Germany had eliminated Russia, but the American public might have refused to accept this line of reasoning if Germany had not declared war.

While England could feel tolerably sure of success now that she had both Russia and the United States as her allies, it was still hard to find a way to attack Germany. In the summer of 1941 photographic surveys were demonstrating that night-bombing was far less accurate than anyone had thought. Attacking squadrons sometimes bombed the wrong town, and even when they got to the right place their chances of hitting anything important seemed very slight. The British high command did not care to give up the independent air offensive, although it was now becoming something quite different from what had been originally intended. The decision was taken to use aeroplanes for 'area' bombing, which meant that they would try to knock down German cities. This involved some questionable judgements: the air commanders believed that German morale was less good than British, so that an attack like the bombing of London would destroy the German will to fight. The calculations also assumed that the German economy was already under heavy strain, so that it would be likely to crack if extra burdens were placed upon it, whether the additional demand was for consumer goods and houses to replace those destroyed or for fresh supplies of weapons.

A quite separate assumption about bombing was illustrated by Churchill when he heard about the possibility of making an atomic bomb. The decisive step from the study of radioactivity to the making of a bomb came on the British side when it was worked out in February 1940 that if all the atoms of atomic weight 235 (U235 isotopes) were separated from the U238 isotopes in a piece of uranium, the pure U235 uranium would be much more fissile than ordinary uranium.[1] In fact once a lump of U235 uranium had reached a certain size, the number of internal collisions would so far exceed the loss of energy escaping at the surface of the metal, because volume increases more rapidly than surface area, that it would explode. This part of the process was easy enough to work out; it was possible to calculate—though computers, whose development was encouraged by the war, had not yet come into use—that the critical size at which it would explode was so small that it could be carried in an aeroplane. When Churchill was told about these possibilities he said, 'Although personally I am quite content with the existing explosives, I feel that we must not stand in the path of improvement.'[2] The atomic bomb turned out to be far more expensive than had been realized: to purify a piece of uranium and separate the U235 isotopes, of which there were seven or so in every thousand U238 isotopes, the uranium had to be turned into a gas and forced through a series of very fine membranes, sifting away a few U238 isotopes at each membrane. The gas itself, uranium hexafloride, was very hard to handle; the membrane was hard to manufacture; the electricity required for the operation would have serviced a large town. The British had taken the Americans into their confidence, entrusting them with a number of British scientific secrets such as the development of radar, and among other information in the 'black box' delivered in the United States in the autumn of 1940 were notes on the development of an atomic bomb. The Americans were greatly impressed, and it seems that in 1941 the British might have been able to persuade them to establish a consortium which would have done all the work of making a bomb on a basis of equality. But the opportunity was missed and once the Americans were aware that an atomic bomb was a possibility they could devote far more resources to the project; by mid-1942 the British wanted to set up a consortium to handle the entire operation and found the Americans unwilling to consider the suggestion.

Churchill may not have been serious when he said he was satisfied with the existing explosives. But the point was of great importance to the bomber offensive. In the First World War high explosive turned out to be less destructive than expected when it was used to shell enemy trenches. High explosive bombs were never as deadly as strategists expected, and it took a great deal of time and labour to get the bombs to

---

[1] See above, p. 30.
[2] W. S. Churchill, *The Second World War*, iii (1950), 730.

the target. When working out his calculations for area bombing, Churchill's scientific adviser Lord Cherwell reckoned that an aeroplane could on the average drop about 40 tons of bombs in its working life before it was shot down, but in the whole argument about the bomber offensive the considerable cost of building the bombers, manning the aircrews, and providing aviation fuel was not seriously considered, and it seems that Cherwell and a number of other people considerably overestimated the damage that bombing would do to Germany.[1] With the appointment in February 1942 of Sir Arthur Harris to be head of Bomber Command the 'area' offensive became accepted as part of British strategy.

The Japanese plan for expansion in Asia which had begun with Pearl Harbor included a swift attack on British possessions east of India. Hong Kong was captured after a week, but it was known to be indefensible. A far worse shock came when air attacks sank the *Repulse* and the *Prince of Wales*, the two British capital ships sent to guard sea communications in the region. The pattern of the whole naval war with Japan had been set; the heaviest ships were at the mercy of aeroplanes, and the victory would go to the side which could bring up its aircraft-carriers and deploy a crushing aerial attack. On land the Japanese advanced down the Malayan peninsula against troops much less well trained for jungle warfare and much too heavily equipped to keep up with the speed of the Japanese assault. By 31 January the whole of Malaya was conquered, and only Singapore remained. It was primarily a naval base, never intended to resist an attack from the land because no one had imagined that an invading army would be able to sweep through Malaya. Singapore held out for about a week of siege and a week of assault. The garrison then had to surrender because their water supply had been destroyed. This was the blow that did most damage to England's imperial position in the whole war. Her power depended on prestige, on the idea that one Englishman could defeat ten Asians and could rule a province single-handed. British control of India did not give way immediately, but the fall of Singapore showed that an Asian army could defeat the British. The direct consequence in India was that the Congress opposition to British rule, which had been entirely passive, became more visible; the loss of Singapore marked a decisive change for the Empire in India, and also for relations with Australia. In the years between the wars Australia and New Zealand had been readier than Canada or South Africa to think in terms of a closely united Empire, partly because their populations had been almost entirely of British descent but also because they trusted in Singapore as a pledge that the Japanese fleet would never be

---

[1] Lord Birkenhead, *The Prof in two Worlds* (1961), 249.

allowed to endanger them. When Singapore fell the complaints of the Australians sounded a little as though they considered England had betrayed them by allowing the base to be taken. These reproaches were not very reasonable, but it was natural that after this they thought of the United States as their chief defence against Japan. The British found themselves being driven back out of Burma, and by early 1942 the whole of south-east Asia was under Japanese control. Whatever strategic demands might be made for giving priority to the war against Germany, it was not possible to ignore the way that Japan was threatening India and Australia.

Difficulties for Britain and for her allies multiplied in 1942. Auchinleck, who had replaced Wavell in north Africa, was able to advance from his position on the old Libyan-Egyptian frontier and relieve Tobruk, but he was not able to do any better than Wavell. An advance in the western desert merely increased difficulties of supply while the Germans still had a foothold in North Africa. The little island of Malta, which held out against very severe bombing, was vital for restricting German control of the Mediterranean. It was in constant danger of running out of food or munitions and could be restocked only with difficulty. For the vital March convoy to the island there was no stronger escort than a force of light cruisers, which held off a battleship and two heavy cruisers. As the Mediterranean was virtually closed, the army in Egypt could be supplied only by ships that went round the Cape of Good Hope or across the Indian Ocean from the United States and any advance from the Suez Canal area added to the distance that supplies had to travel. Despite an inferiority of numbers Rommel struck back and the British withdrew. This would not have worried people much, but on 21 June Tobruk fell. Because it had held out with such determination after Rommel's earlier counter-attack it had become a place of symbolic significance and its loss depressed people unduly. The British armies withdrew in more or less good order to El Alamein, closer to Cairo than they had ever retired previously. The position was strong and could be regarded as the equivalent of the lines of Torres Vedras, to which Wellington had retired as his final defensive position in the Peninsular War. The British had already, in February, installed a reliable Egyptian government, by threatening to depose King Farouk if he did not accept their nominees. The Germans were now at the end of long supply lines, their control of the Mediterranean was uncertain, their harbour facilities were not good and Hitler was not interested in the North African campaign.

For the Germans the serious fighting was in Russia, and an offensive was launched in south Russia to gain control of the Caucasian oilfields.

This attack thrust into a deep but slender salient which almost reached the Volga at Stalingrad. From July till November the Russian and German armies were locked in a struggle over the ruins of the city. If the Germans could reach the Volga and break this line of communication, the Russians might be cut in two; and while the attack on Stalingrad was kept up, the northern flank of the German armies advancing on the Caucasus would be protected. In November the Russian counter-attack began. As the winter came on, the flanks of the salient were crushed. Hitler had previously had considerable success when he intervened in military affairs, but this time he blundered and ordered his forces not to retreat. Even after they had been surrounded they might have been able to break out, but Hitler refused to let them escape from the Stalingrad area. This turned defeat into catastrophe. About a quarter of a million men were lost. The Russians had proved they could defeat a German army; the German lines fell back, and the hope of reaching the oil of the Caucasus passed away.

The counter-attack begins

While the armies were struggling for the banks of the Volga, a British offensive began in north Africa. The new British commander in the Middle East, Alexander, took his time piling up superiority in material; at last, the British war economy and the immense industrial power of the United States were to be applied to a military situation with no excuse for lack of success. Montgomery, the new commander of the Eighth Army, was one of the most cautious generals of the war; he remembered his days on the western front in the First World War. The battle of El Alamein started on 23 October with an artillery bombardment that would have gladdened the heart of Haig, and this was followed by a steady concentration of armour and eventually a tank battle on the grand scale. This sober approach was justified by its results: the German line was broken at the northern end, and the rest of the line was left stranded in the desert so that very little of it could escape. This time the pursuit into and across Libya was not interrupted: the desert army chased Rommel out of the arena that he had graced for so long and on 23 January Tripoli was captured.

The battle in the desert, 1940–2, was for many Englishmen their happiest memory of the war. The soldiers of the Eighth Army who fought the desert campaigns remembered it as a struggle between professionals, with no civilians getting in the way, gentlemanly behaviour on both sides, and a victory that the British did not have to share with the Americans. Whatever later critics might say about Montgomery his soldiers admired him and knew that he would see that they were better equipped and better prepared than their enemies.

In November British and American troops had landed on the Atlantic and on the Mediterranean coast of French North Africa. This was the first Anglo-American operation of the war, and at the military level the two nationalities worked together harmoniously enough to suggest that they would be able to combine their strength better than had ever before been possible for forces of different nationalities. Despite occasional difficulties, the complicated mechanism of military co-operation worked successfully throughout the war. At the political level there was a little more trouble both in French North Africa and later on. The invading force accepted Admiral Darlan as ruler of the region though he had been anti-British in the past and was regarded as dangerously close to being a Fascist. When he was, to the general relief, assassinated by a somewhat out-of-touch monarchist, the Americans wanted to deal with General Giraud rather than accept the more intransigent General de Gaulle as the French leader. This did Giraud little good, for de Gaulle had too much support and too strong a personality to be displaced, but it was a precursor of other political difficulties.

Churchill and Roosevelt met at Casablanca in Morocco in January, against the background of success in north Africa and even greater Russian success at Stalingrad. They declared that they would accept nothing short of an unconditional surrender. This decision has been criticized on the grounds that it made the Germans more ready to fight to the last when the war was clearly lost. It would have been difficult for anyone to snatch power from Hitler, even to negotiate peace; in any case Churchill and Roosevelt seem to have been concerned more with the need to give the Soviet Union, which was bearing the weight of the struggle, an assurance that Britain and the United States would not make a separate peace. At the same time Churchill and Roosevelt agreed to increase the intensity of the one form of direct attack they could launch upon Germany, the strategic bombing offensive.

The landings in French North Africa and the pursuit across Libya after Alamein had gone so well that the Axis powers almost found themselves shut out of the south side of the Mediterranean. But they got forces across the Mediterranean, rallied the desert army, and by February they were established in Tunisia strongly enough to mean that a long siege operation had to be conducted. When it was all over, in May, a quarter of a million Germans and Italians had to surrender for lack of transport back across the Mediterranean. Their resistance made it impossible for the British and Americans to think of invading France that year. There was a division of opinion, with the Americans pressing for a Channel invasion as soon as possible, and the British saying that it would have to wait until 1944. If north Africa had been cleared without a struggle early in the year, and if a great many landing craft had been available, the choice of invading France might still have remained open, but by May Britain and America had to follow the policy described by Churchill as 'striking at the soft underbelly of the Axis', if they wanted to fight Germans anywhere in 1943.

In July they invaded Sicily, and by August they had conquered it. Under the stress of this attack on Italian soil Mussolini's government turned against him. A new government was formed and it began secret negotiations for an armistice. On 3 September troops landed on the mainland of Italy, and on the same day the Italian government announced that it had arranged an armistice and had changed sides. Neither of these dramatic events led to very much. The Germans promptly disarmed the Italian army, and for the rest of the war treated Italy as an occupied country; the forces landed at the south end of Italy made slow progress because the series of mountain ranges splaying off the central line of the Apennines like ribs were ideally suited to defence and were very inconvenient for attackers. If the planners needed an anatomical analogy Churchill's remark was less apposite than Aneurin Bevan's question 'Is that the soft underbelly of the Axis? We are climbing up the backbone.'

In August Churchill and Roosevelt met again, this time in Quebec. Among other things they settled the arrangements for the use of atomic research. It was decided that British scientists were to be taken into the work of research on a basis of equality wherever they could help, and that atomic weapons would be used only after the British and American governments had agreed about using them. The costs were turning out to be very large. The Maud committee, the body that had decided it would be worth while to go ahead with the attempt to make an atomic bomb, had spoken of costs of the order of £5m.; the Manhattan Project, which finally made the bomb, cost fifty or a hundred times as much. Possibly British scientists, accustomed to making do on less lavish resources, could have done the job for less, but as the American Treasury was paying the whole cost of development it had a strong interest in what was going on—especially as the Manhattan Project expenditure was kept secret till the end of the war—and wanted to secure any financial return there might be. It was agreed that the President of the U.S. should decide how much of the information of commercial value gained while making the bomb should be released to England at the end of the war. When this was settled the Project was ready to employ British scientists, and naturally they learnt about the processes while they were on the job. In terms of mutual aid their services were of considerable use to the United States, and at the end of the war they could return to England with a fund of knowledge about the way atomic installations worked.

The bombing offensive under Harris, which began in earnest with the 'thousand-bomber' raid on Cologne in May 1942, showed the limitations of bombing with conventional high explosive. Changes in Germany at about this time make it particularly difficult to assess the effect of the attack. Until the winter of 1941 Hitler had expected the war against Russia to end as quickly as his other wars, and this calculation was reasonable: Germany did come close to complete success in the first few months. As a quick victory was expected, austerity and a reduction in the civilian standard of living still seemed unnecessary. As a result the German economy was not organized for war in the way that England was running a war economy by 1941. By this time it was too late for the Germans to transform their economy to the same extent by building up new industries, but from 1942 to 1945 Albert Speer, building on the organization left by Dr. Todt, achieved a great deal, mainly by rationalizing production of the existing weapons. Military output rose steadily to a level which showed that in 1941 Germany had not been treating the war seriously. Any material shortages from which the Germans suffered in 1942 were entirely the result of their own over-confidence.

Because of this change the bomber offensive fell on an economy whose military section was growing rapidly. Bombing had no noticeable effect on this development in 1942; partly because the weight of bombs dropped was very small by comparison with the last nine or twelve months of the war. 'Area' bombing involved attacks on women and children which would once have been condemned as 'methods of barbarism', though this moral judgement may be a relic of a bygone age. At a non-moral level the test of the effectiveness of the bomber offensive is to ask what else could have been done with the resources devoted to it. If less industrial capacity had been used for building bombers, other aircraft might have been available for more immediately useful purposes: it was command of the air that enabled the Germans to capture Crete and it was command of the air that enabled the Japanese to sink the *Prince of Wales* and the *Repulse* and subsequently to advance so quickly over Malaya and Burma. In February 1942 the German battleships *Scharnhorst* and *Gneisenau* were able to sail up the Channel from Brest to German waters; 'they were at sea for twelve hours, four of them in daylight, before they were discovered. And it was undoubtedly the failure of [British] air patrols which brought that about'.[1] Command of the air was most immediately useful in a battle zone, and the concentration of the aircraft industry on long-range bombers was accompanied by a failure to ensure tactical superiority on occasions when it was vital.

The Battle of the Atlantic was linked to the bomber offensive. As in the First World War England's ability to keep her industries going depended on a flow of goods from North America. In addition an American army had to be brought across, provided with a base in England and then equipped to invade Europe. Atlantic convoys did not suffer nearly as high a proportion of losses as convoys to Russia, and crews of ships torpedoed in the Atlantic had a better chance of survival than men in the icy waters of the Arctic Ocean, but it was still a desperate battle. In 1942 just over a thousand ships, totalling over five million tons, were sunk; at times in early 1943 things were even worse—in the first twenty days of March 97 ships, totalling over half-a-million tons, were sunk.[2] It was always possible in these months that the link with the world outside Europe would be cut, rations would have to be reduced or the industrial side of the war effort diminished. But in the first half of 1943 as many German submarines were sunk as in the whole of 1942, and they had to slacken the attack; much more powerful submarines were being developed, which would have been a serious threat because of their greater speed and their ability to take in air while under water by means of a schnorkel, but they did not appear in combat until the war was almost over.

In the 1942–3 struggle the air force was not able to help as much as might have been hoped. Bombing raids on the submarine bases were not successful; bombs were dropped off the target, or when they fell in the right place the bases were too well protected to be much damaged. The aircraft of Coastal Command which swept the millions of square miles of the Atlantic were far more useful, spotting and sometimes bombing submarines and intercepting the flights of the German Condors which acted as convoy-spotters for the submarines. But Coastal Command did not really have enough planes for the job, and could have used more if long-range patrol planes had been built instead of bombers. Apart from this, the bomber offensive aggravated some of the shortages; aeroplanes flying deep into Germany consumed enormous quantities of aviation fuel, at a time when bringing oil into England was difficult. The offensive was sometimes in danger of being closed down for lack of fuel; if this had

[1] S. W. Roskill, *The War at Sea* (1960), ii. 159. *Parl. Papers*, Cmd. 6775, makes it clear that Bomber Command was not suited to retaining control of the seas.
[2] Roskill, op. cit. ii. 367 and iii, pt. 2, appendix ZZ.

happened, it would have been caused by concentrating on attacks which could not produce results in the immediate future and neglecting the problems of protecting the supply routes.

Air power had much more effect in the war against Japan. At first it was directed at specific objectives: in the summer of 1942, Japanese expansion was checked decisively in the battles of the Coral Sea and Midway. Carrier-based aeroplanes of the opposing fleets sought out the opposing carriers and endeavoured to sink them by bombing. The Americans were successful, and without air support the Japanese found it hard to advance any further. To some extent their strategy had allowed for this. They had intended to gain a wide screen of captured territory that would take a long time to reconquer, and then wait behind this screen until peace could be negotiated. The American response was to advance by concentrating on a few selected islands, leaving most of them cut off and unable to obtain fresh supplies after the Japanese had lost command of the sea and air. The Americans could choose which island in a group they would pick out, land on it, and establish an airbase from which they could command the skies around. Advances of this sort were not relevant to the situation in Europe, but they did display a sensible use of air power.

The United States had decided at Casablanca to join in the bomber offensive in Europe. Their air force was designed for daytime bombing, and this seemed to offer some hope of hitting the small but important targets which might have a direct effect on the German war effort. The ball-bearing production factories at Schweinfurt were an obvious objective. Daytime raids were made, and some damage was done to the factories. However, too many bombers were lost for the attacks to go on. If daytime bombing was to be carried out, the bombers would have to be escorted by fighters, so a fighter which could fly long distances had to be provided. Fighter production had always been thought of as a matter of producing for home defence; the British Spitfire was an example of a plane superbly designed for attacking bombers which flew over England, and most other countries made fighters along the same lines. The American Mustang (P-51), originally designed for the R.A.F., was adapted to accompany bombers to their targets and then, while they were making their attack, take on the defending fighters.[1] Partly because the R.A.F. was already committed to night-bombing before the Mustang came into production, it never showed much interest in the new aeroplane. It fitted the needs of American daytime bombing very well and after December 1943 German fighters had to penetrate a defensive screen in order to

[1] W. L. Craven and J. F. Gate, *The [U.S.] Army Air Force in World War Two* (Chicago, 1955), 217–19.

intercept the bombers. Once they were opposed in the air the German fighters were steadily driven out of the sky.

This success was not due entirely to American skill. The limiting factor in the German economy was the supply of raw materials. At times people in England compared the British mobilization of labour with that of Germany and concluded that, because British mobilization was even more complete, the British system was superior to that of Germany but this assumed that the two countries had the same problems, which was not the case. Speer might have produced even larger numbers of tanks, guns, and aircraft, but this would have been of little use if the German economy had run out of the petrol needed to move them about or the nitrogen needed to make explosives for them to fight with. As long as the sea routes remained open Britain could import all the raw materials she wanted, and under Lend-Lease she had no trouble about paying for them. On the other hand, though Germany naturally suffered from the shortages of skilled labour that affect all countries fighting modern war, and could not obtain many surplus raw materials or factory capacity from occupied Europe, a constant supply of forced labour could be dragged to German factories from the occupied countries. Hitler had ideological objections to women going out and working in factories and, in a grisly perversion of belief, he insisted that a considerable amount of the resources of the Reich should be devoted to the extermination of the Jews in Europe. This was a monstrous crime; it was also a wasteful blunder, and the whole concentration camp system tended to weaken military production by locking up resources of labour where Speer could not get at them. Even so, it is hard to see that running the Reich on more humane and rational lines would have solved the problems of the actual shortages that arose. The shortage of oil, and more particularly of aviation spirit, as much as the Mustang, crippled the German air force by making it impossible to give adequate training to new pilots and at times forcing the air force to leave the sky open while it accumulated new stocks. The British and Americans could then bomb the synthetic oil refineries on which future supplies depended.

Harris, the head of Bomber Command, spoke of all suggestions that bombing should concentrate on knocking out German oil production as 'panaceas', designed to win the war by a short cut. Later study has shown that the strategic analysis in the original Royal Air Force approach was correct in indicating that oil was the weak point to attack; while England did not at the beginning of the war have the strength needed to carry out the 'oil plan', it would have been a useful guide for future development. Instead bombs fell wholesale on German cities. Many of them fell on or near steel foundries, but as the U.S. Strategic Bombing Survey pointed out after the war, a steel foundry undergoes stresses and strains equal to heavy bombing during the normal processes of manufacture and a blast furnace is built rather like an air-raid shelter. German production went up in 1943 by over 50 per cent.

Towards the end of 1943 Churchill, Roosevelt, and Stalin met at Teheran to discuss the future conduct of the war. When dealing with Roosevelt, Churchill had taken it for granted that England and the United States were equals and that their relationship was closer than that of any of the other nations united against Germany. This was a sensible attitude to take, and the one that held out the best prospect of equality for England. Roosevelt was ready to accept it to some extent, but he did not intend to let himself be put in a position where England and the United States were automatically united against Russia. He shared a widespread American fear that Britain was going to use American help to increase the power of the British Empire; his own opinion was that the British Empire ought to relax its power and perhaps come to an end. In the negotiations for Lend-Lease the United States had listed conditions that were intended to end the system of Imperial Preference. Roosevelt pressed Churchill to grant independence to India, and Churchill's pronouncement that he had not become His Majesty's first minister in order to preside over the dissolution of the British Empire implied some measure of resistance to Roosevelt as well as to Hitler.

At Teheran Roosevelt was anxious to show Stalin that there was no English-speaking alliance against him. As Churchill was eager to create such an alliance, Roosevelt and Stalin found themselves drawn together by a feeling that they did not intend to let themselves be outmanœuvred by perfidious Albion. Neither Roosevelt nor Stalin believed that any country except his own was fit to rule an empire, and both of them spoke the language of anti-imperialism. In any case, 1943 was no time to think of any alignment against Russia; the cardinal fact of the military situation was the Russian army, which was fighting the best part of the German army and driving it back. Stalin's concern at Teheran was to make quite sure that there would be a Second Front, an Anglo-American landing in France which would divert a sizeable portion of the German army away from the east. Russia had only a slight numerical superiority at this stage, and had still to cover a good deal of ground before her own soil was free of the invader.

By the beginning of 1944 the invasion of France was in sight. The operation was difficult, difficult enough to show the sort of obstacles in Hitler's way if he had tried invading England any time after the immediate shock of Dunkirk. An exploratory raid on Dieppe in 1942 had shown that the ports were strongly defended. Capturing a port in working order would be difficult, capturing a devastated port would be useless and landing supplies without a port would be almost impossible. The answer was to build the 'Mulberry harbour', an artificial port made of steel and reinforced concrete, which could be taken across the Channel and set up where it was needed. This gave the invading force great freedom of choice. A crossing from around Dover to Calais seemed the obvious route to take, because the sea journey was shorter than anywhere else. In addition, the Germans were just about to start firing their V-1s, pilotless aeroplanes flown off a ramp and directed to London; the first one was launched about a week after the landing in France. In September the attack was reinforced by the V-2, a rocket fired against London. Both of them carried about a ton of high explosive. The V-1 could be shot down or intercepted by the balloon barrage; the V-2 was harder to stop, though as it arrived without warning it caused less nervous strain. These new weapons were rather an expensive way of delivering high explosive because, unlike an ordinary aeroplane, they could be used only once.[1] But it was disturbing for Londoners, who thought the blitz was over for good. Too few of these weapons were fired to have a serious effect on people's morale, but they destroyed a good deal of housing and reminded people in England that the war was not over yet.

As the V-weapons were launched from near Calais, they looked like an additional reason for landing there and putting them out of action. General Eisenhower, the American commander of the combined invading force, reckoned that the Germans would think along these lines and would concentrate their forces near Calais. A certain amount of mis-information was manufactured to encourage them in this belief, and the attack was prepared for a section of the Normandy beach which, although further from England, did have the advantage of being a little less heavily defended. If attempt at an invasion was made, and was driven back into the sea, it would be hard to launch another attack; the war on land would virtually be left to the Germans and the Russians, with the British and Americans doing what they could in Italy. The preparations for D-Day included sealing England off from almost all communication with the outside world, so that no word of the direction of the attack should leak out, turning most of the south of England into a transit camp, giving up strategic bombing and directing the weight of the aerial attack against railways in France to cut the German lines of communication.

[1] Birkenhead, op. cit. 258–61 and appendix II. The V-2s were particularly expensive.

The whole expedition was nearly put off by gales that blew up at the beginning of June, but in the event they only convinced the Germans that no attack would come at that time. On 5 June Eisenhower took his decision, and the next day the invasion began.

From D-Day to the end of the war

One limiting factor was the supply of landing-craft. The Americans needed landing-craft in the Pacific to fight the Japanese effectively, and in fact had more there than in Europe. A secondary attack on the south of France, which was carried out in August, also required landing-craft. There were only just enough to go round in Normandy; an invasion attempted in 1943, as suggested by the Americans, would have been possible only if resources had been diverted from other forms of production. Despite all that had been done to mislead the Germans and cut their communications, the beaches were still held strongly. Progress was slow, and on the American beaches casualties were heavy, partly through bad luck, partly because they had not provided as many specialized landing devices as the British. D-Day was a splendid opportunity to produce a great range of gadgets. Apart from the artificial harbours there were tanks adapted for going through minefields, tanks adapted for going over soft sand, tanks to act as ramps for other tanks to run up, and an underwater pipeline to pump oil under the Channel to France.

The Germans brought up reinforcements, and established a strong position around Caen at the eastern end of the invasion area. They were not able to block the western end as effectively and the Americans began to advance, slowly at first, towards Avranches and the border between Normandy and Brittany. When, in early August, the Americans broke the last counter-attack and forced their way into open country, there was no second line of defence on which they could be resisted. They swung round to the north-east, so that the powerful force facing the British at the east end of the invasion area was taken in the rear and surrounded at Falaise. The army surrendered in detachments by 21 August, and it seemed for a time as though there was little left to do. German divisions in several parts of France were cut off and stranded with no way of getting home. Paris rose and liberated herself just before the advancing armies could arrive, and the main German force had difficulty finding bridges across the Seine for its retreat; France was freed as rapidly as she had originally been overrun and was cleared of Germans by the end of September. But the pace could not be kept up. Cherbourg was the nearest port that had been captured in reasonable working order and the advance was running ahead of its supplies. A shortage of oil forced the leading formations to go slowly, and eventually brought them to a halt. The Germans had time to reorganize.

On 1 September Eisenhower decided that the forces in France were spread over too wide an area to be treated as a single strategic unit any longer, and he took over field command from Montgomery. At this point Montgomery asked for a single thrust, on a fairly narrow front, by one of the armies, which could be given all the transport it needed. The others would follow up slowly on its flank. His suggestion was that the British army, which held the northern flank, should advance swiftly to try to get to Berlin and if possible strike a decisive blow that would immediately end the war. Eisenhower's American generals were not in favour of a plan which gave the star role to Montgomery, and in addition his talents had never seemed best suited to the war of movement he now proposed to undertake. Although his attempt later in the month to penetrate deep into Holland by landing paratroops at the Arnhem bridges came close enough to success to suggest that he could work out plans for a bold strategy, his victories were won by a judicious massing of force until the enemy was overwhelmed rather than by quick advances into the unknown. The American General Patton had more of the temperament needed for a single bold attack; Eisenhower declined to commit a force to an advance on a narrow front, and ordered his armies to move forward together.

After the wartime alliance with Russia had dissolved, this decision was criticized on the grounds that an advance on a single front would have enabled England and the United States to go a long way east into Germany, and impose a settlement of European frontiers which guarded their interests better than the arrangements finally reached in 1945. This view—the 'how we won the war and lost the peace' theory—rests on a complete misunderstanding of the situation in 1944. In September American anti-German feeling reached its peak with the formulation of the Morgenthau Plan, which would have stripped Germany of her heavy industry and turned her back into an agricultural economy. In October Churchill met Stalin in Moscow and they discussed the post-war settlement of eastern Europe. Russia's position had not changed since the summer of 1939; she wanted to be dominant in eastern Europe, and Churchill accepted this. Greece was placed in the British sphere of influence, Hungary and Yugoslavia were to be treated as areas in which both countries had an interest, and Rumania and Bulgaria were to be assigned to Russia. A couple of months later the first test of the agreement came up; the British suppressed the Greek Communists without a protest from Russia. Eastern Europe could hardly have been partitioned on terms more favourable to England (which was assumed to be acting for the United States); when the agreement was made, Russian armies had already established themselves in much of the area that was being parcelled out. England and the United States would not have claimed they had 'won the war'; they knew how much of the victory had been gained by the Russian army. The plans for dividing Germany into occupation zones were being worked out during 1944, and probably no change in the military situation after September would have affected them.

The bombing offensive against Germany was resumed in the second half of 1944, and rose to its final intensity. Over half the total weight of bombs dropped on Germany fell after D-Day—a little under one megaton had been dropped before D-Day, and a little over one megaton was dropped after. An attack of this magnitude began to show results; German war production began to decline, and fell away steadily, though it never dropped back to the pre-1942 level. Undoubtedly no economy is benefited by suffering a one-megaton attack, but the resources and energy devoted to bombing might have been more usefully spent on defeating the German army in the field.

Inside his besieged Fortress Europa Hitler was coming to the end of his reserves of oil and of military manpower. He decided to gamble on a counter-attack in the west. Just before Christmas the American section of the line near the Ardennes was pushed back some distance. The Germans had so little petrol by this stage that they relied on capturing adequate supplies for a breakthrough. They failed to do so, and had to fall back. Perhaps feeling confident that this attack had made sufficient impression to prevent any further pressure in the west, the Germans now switched more and more forces to the east. When the three leaders met at Yalta to discuss the closing stages of the war, the Russians were facing the sternest opposition and could still claim to be playing the major part in the war.

At Yalta the leaders agreed on the plan for dividing Germany into zones of occupation that had been worked out during the previous year, a scheme for a United Nations Organization was devised which accepted the facts of the situation and did not try to reduce the sovereignty of the great powers, and Russia agreed to join the war against Japan within three months of the end of the war against Germany. After the war it was suggested that Russia had done altogether better at the conference than she deserved, but it is hard to see how the English or the Americans could have taken up a different position at the time. Public opinion in both countries would have been upset and puzzled at the idea of a breach in the alliance, and military opinion would not have encouraged it either.

The east European successor-states created at Versailles could not be entirely free agents except by keeping a balance between Germany and Russia; in 1919 both Germany and Russia had been removed from the effective balance of power, but in 1945 it was only Germany that had been struck down. Yalta recognized this situation. But there were already signs of trouble: the Soviet Union wanted to impose on Poland an exclusively pro-Russian government, England was committed to the government that had been set up in exile immediately after the German and Russian invasions in 1939. The Soviet Union had the stronger position, which it exploited as fully as possible.

By the end it was little more than Hitler's own will that kept the German people fighting; he had spent many years drumming his message of national defiance into his audiences, and the spell was never quite broken. On 12 April Roosevelt died, and Hitler thought for a moment that the alliance might disintegrate. But by the end of the month the Russians were forcing their way into Berlin; there was a last Wagnerian scene of multiple suicide in the Führerbunker, and the driving force of the Third Reich was destroyed. Once Hitler was dead there was a little futile squabbling about the succession, but the doctrine of unconditional surrender did not prevent the German leaders from trying to end the war as soon as possible. The British and American armies had come further east than had been anticipated, and had to withdraw a little to the zones that had been agreed on. The last phases of the war had been relatively simple, with supplies abundant, reinforcements available if ever they were required, and a constant German shortage of everything their armies needed. The attack on Germany failed to find some decisive weakness which could be exploited to destroy the German position, and so resistance went on until the whole war effort collapsed at several points at once, like the wonderful one-hoss-shay.[1] The British took charge of the northern flank throughout the advance and, to some extent because of this, took north-western Germany as the British occupation zone.

Churchill had insisted, during the later stages of planning the war in Europe, that England should play her part in the war against Japan. Fighting was expected to go on for another eighteen months, so the commitment was serious, but one that had to be undertaken to re-establish the British position in the Far East. After the shock of the sudden defeats of the first few months of the war against Japan, British prestige would have suffered if the English position was restored by American victories.

---

[1] The wonderful one-hoss shay 'went to pieces all at once; All at once and nothing first' in O. W. Holmes's *The Deacon's Masterpiece*. Sound strategy tries to find one weak point and make it break down first.

In Burma British forces had been successful in very difficult country; in the summer of 1944 they had eventually won a long-drawn-out battle of Kohima, and they continued to advance slowly against resolute opposition. It took another year, until the fall of Rangoon in May 1945, for Burma to be cleared of Japanese forces: the British had overwhelming superiority in the air, which was vital for transport and for bringing up support when needed, as well as for tactical bombing, and the slow rate of advance shows that reducing the Japanese Empire by seeking out the Japanese armies would have taken a very long time.

In this part of the war the doctrine of strategic bombing came much closer to being justified. Once the Americans had command of the air their bomber attacks on the islands of Japan steadily destroyed its cities and their industrial capacity. The Japanese industrial base was smaller than that of Germany, the area of the country was much smaller and the weight of the attack was comparable to the bomber attack of the last nine months of the war against Germany. The Japanese had begun to consider the possibility of surrender by July but they had not got far towards taking a decision before the situation was changed.

The scientists in the New Mexico desert had exploded the first atomic bomb on 17 July. It seems to have been taken for granted that the bomb would be used; nobody appears to have thought of trying to keep the whole thing secret, though it is true that this might have been constitutionally impossible. But if it was to be used, it would be known to the Russians that such a device existed; the British and the Americans wanted to tell the Russians as little as possible about the atomic bomb—Churchill considered locking up Niels Bohr, one of the world's greatest nuclear physicists, for security purposes[1]—and yet the most important secret was simply that the bomb worked. All the rest was engineering; pro-Communist scientists saved the Russians a little money by revealing the details of processes to the Soviet Union, but the British and American governments behaved as though the processes of making a bomb were some modern abracadabra that could be kept secret. The governments imagined that the Russians would take an indefinitely long time to learn how to make a bomb, though the scientists knew that it would take only about four years.

The decision to drop the atomic bomb was in a sense not made at all. Refraining from dropping the bomb would have involved a deliberate decision and as nobody made this decision, people argued about how to use it. If a demonstration test was announced in advance, but it did not work, the Japanese would be more stubborn than ever. They were not

[1] M. Gowing, op. cit. 358.

people who would give in lightly; their treatment of prisoners of war showed their poor opinion of people who had surrendered rather than dying in battle. It may have been quite certain that Japan had lost, but then Germany had clearly lost the war some months before she surrendered. A decision not to drop the bomb would have been hard to make, and hard to justify. On 6 August the first atomic bomb was released, on Hiroshima; its impact was in the same range as an exceptionally heavy attack with conventional bombs—two thousand planes, each carrying a ten-ton bomb which was the heaviest conventional bomb used in the war, would have had about the same explosive effect, though the incendiary effect would have been rather less. The Russians, who had been acting as negotiators and putting the Anglo-American terms to Japan, promptly entered the war, just three months after the end of the war with Germany. On the ninth another bomb was dropped, on Nagasaki. On the tenth the Japanese peace party prevailed in the Cabinet, and began arranging to bring the war to an end. This part of the war was of relatively little concern to England; the British government had been consulted, as was required by the Quebec agreement, before the bomb was dropped, but it was not at all certain that a refusal to give permission would have been taken seriously.

People in England, except for those directly concerned with the operations against Japan, had lost interest in the fighting. The war had not caused nearly as many casualties as the First War. It was suggested that British soldiers would not have stood up to the long wearing struggle in the trenches, and it was part of British strategy to see that nothing like that happened again. Some sectors of the war were nevertheless extremely dangerous: out of 800 Merchant Navy ships that set out on the Russian run to Archangel, 58 were sunk on the way out and another 27 on the way back; the Atlantic was not as perilous, but many good ships were lost; and Bomber Command used up men quickly—there is a grim note in the Official History about the way the 'Dambusters' were selected for a precision raid from among those reaching the end of their second tour of duty, 'since it was rare to survive two tours of operations'.[1] The airmen of Bomber Command were picked men, like the junior officers who died in the Flanders mud in the First War, and they died as bravely. But very few men in uniform were as exposed to danger as the soldiers of the First War, though civilians were much more involved than civilians in the earlier war. In 1940 and 1941 England might have been defeated and destroyed, and the whole country was involved in a great struggle,

---

[1] Roskill, op. cit. iii, pt. 2, appendix R; C. Webster and N. Frankland, *The Strategic Air Offensive against Germany* (1961), ii. 175.

but there was a much longer period of fighting after the danger of defeat was over than there had been in the First War. In 1918 the issue did not seem to be decided until three or four months before Germany surrendered; the Second World War had ceased to be a matter of doubt by 1943, and all that remained was to finish it off. At just about the same time, England was losing her place as a dominant member of the alliance. Russia and the United States had much larger resources, and could wage war on a vaster scale. In 1940 England had saved Europe by her example, and if Europe had been subjugated Germany might have been able to use it as the base for a wider empire. But England could not save Europe by her exertions; it was not certain that she could save herself without assistance from the United States. With this decline in the country's importance, and the loss of the drama of uncertainty about the result, people in England were naturally more interested in thinking about the country after the war. From 1943 onwards the Army Bureau of Current Affairs had been telling soldiers to prepare for the new post-war world that they were fighting for. In the First War people fought to get back to 1914; in the Second War people were more enthusiastic about the country they saw developing during the war itself than in any idea of getting back to the thirties. War propaganda had been almost entirely in terms of the brave new world to come, and little had been said about what had been happening in Hitler's Europe. Hitler's diplomacy had been a reversion to the morality of Bismarck, but in his treatment of Jews and east Europeans he went back much further, to the habits of Attila and Genghiz Khan. When the concentration camps were discovered, people at first thought of them in terms of Germany's economic collapse at the end of the war, or individual sadism among the camp staff; the idea that it had been government policy to make corpses, much as other governments might make tanks or houses, took a little time to sink in. One aspect of the thirties survived: England was still not very interested in the outside world, and at the end of the war she felt she had done enough for it recently.

9. *The domestic side of*
the war 1939–1945

Gingerly into war

THE outbreak of war did not make much immediate difference inside England. The government had been moving slowly towards a wartime system of organization, and the outbreak of war did not make it move much faster. It had been arranged that children should be evacuated from towns when war broke out; one unforeseen result was that the comfortable classes in the countryside discovered that there were poor and ill-clothed children in England. They could have found this out quite easily by looking at the rural poor, who were very little better off than the children of the unemployed, though they may not have been verminous—one thing that made the comfortable classes realize the plight of the poor was the lice on the 'evacuees'.

The government's domestic policy, launched at the beginning of the war, remained unchanged in principle during the war though it became applied more intensively. The economy was to be controlled, rather than entrusted to the free play of the market as in 1914, and it was run on more egalitarian lines than the German economy, in which there was a complicated system of allocations of priority.

The first instrument for control was the Emergency Powers Act, passed as soon as the war began, which allowed the government to do almost anything it thought was necessary for running the war effectively. The Home Secretary, for instance, could imprison people without trial if he thought they might be a danger to the State; these powers were used to arrest members of pro-Nazi and pro-German societies, and also to arrest refugees who had come to England in the years before the war. A few refugees were German agents and some members of pro-German organizations had transferred their allegiance from England to Germany, but many of the arrests made no sense. They were an early sign of the way that the country was run during the war as a democratic form of totalitarian state. It was accepted that everybody (except for the I.L.P., and the Communists when they had adjusted themselves to the Nazi-Soviet Pact) stood together and the State had unlimited power, just as in an orthodox totalitarian State. But it was also accepted that people had a right to complain and that Parliament had a right to challenge the government; there were regulations against spreading alarm and despondency, but they were amended to 'deliberately' lowing morale, and then fell out of use.

The black-out was something of an example of democratic totalitarianism at work. The exaggerated idea of the effectiveness of bombing that led to the great evacuation at the beginning of the war was accompanied by a belief that the slightest chink of light at night was of immense assistance to German bombers, and so the Air Raid Precautions forces, assisted by crowds of local busybodies, pounced on every flicker of light that they saw. There is remarkably little evidence that careless lighting helped German bombers even at the peak of the night-bombing offensive in the winter of 1940–1, but deaths in road accidents went up by several thousands. The justification for the black-out lay in the field of morale: a great many people felt that by taking care about lighting they were doing something for the war effort, and Chamberlain's government would have done better if it had provided people with more opportunities to feel involved in their country's efforts.

At a more technical level, Chamberlain's government laid down the lines on which the economy was to be organized. It took the decision that money was to be borrowed for the war at 3 per cent. Investors had to be convinced that the rate would never be allowed to slip upwards, and the market had to be controlled to prevent private borrowers from bidding against the government for money. As a result steps had to be taken to prevent people moving their money to other countries, and a formal organization had to be provided for countries whose money was based on sterling. The Sterling Area came into existence at the beginning of the war to make sure that residents in sterling countries (the Commonwealth except Canada, and a number of closely connected states like Iraq) did not rush to buy dollars and deprive the British government of the money it was looking forward to borrowing.

The government realized that rationing would become necessary, though its preparations for this were not as far advanced as its arrangements for controlling the money market. It was not until January 1940 that bacon, butter, and cheese were rationed, and meat was not rationed for another two months. On 3 April Chamberlain, in one of his best appointments, made Lord Woolton Minister of Food. The rationing system ran on the assumption that equal supplies of basic food should be available for everybody, and there was less allocation of special allowances than in the more elaborate German system. When a food was rationed the government felt committed to making sure that enough of it would be in the shops to meet the ration. This objective was attained almost all the time, but unrationed foods were in short enough supply to make housewives spend a great deal of time in queues waiting their turn for whatever they could buy off the ration. The queue became the symbol of wartime Britain, and its implicit values—fair shares, peaceful and patient waiting, and no advantages for the rich—were part of what the country was fighting for. The queues were so long because some people could afford to buy more than before the war. As the unemployed began to be reabsorbed into the economy, they were naturally better off, though this took some time to have an effect; early in 1940 there were still over a million people out of work. As a result of the depression very few skilled workers had been trained in the early 1930s. More people had been trained in the late 1930s, but of course they were men of just the right age to join the army. There was bound to be a shortage of skilled workers, and they could insist that their wages must rise to keep pace with any increase in the cost of living. The government may have been prepared to see a certain amount of inflation as a form of forced saving, but it realized that prices could go up indefinitely if wages were going to rise to keep in step. In November 1939 the government decided to subsidize some food prices on a temporary basis to keep them steady, and for about a dozen years afterwards the government made payments to importers to reduce the shock of rising prices. At the same time it subsidized British farmers to produce as much as possible inside the country. Because prices were held down in this way wages rose less than might have been expected with full employment, and the policy of subsidies also meant that people could afford to buy what was in the shops.

The organization of the domestic side of the war economy was accompanied by a steady increase in war production. The government was planning for a long war, and had no strategic plans for making it into a short war. This meant keeping imports of war materials within bounds, establishing new factories, training workers, and building up machinery that would be producing at full capacity by 1943. In the long run this approach was justified; by 1943 a higher proportion of British resources was committed to war than any other country had ever achieved and

British war production was eight and a half times as large as it had been in the first three months of the war.[1] But for this to be effective it was necessary to survive until production had reached its peak, and the 1939–40 programme certainly had not solved the bulk of its supply problems. Chamberlain's government had set out on the right road, but it was travelling very slowly.

The defeat in Norway was the first sign, since the overrunning of Poland, that anything was happening in the war. It showed a good many solid members of the community—including Conservative backbenchers —that the war was not proceeding as smoothly as they had thought. The difficulties of helping Norway, across the expanse of the North Sea, were perhaps underestimated, but only a very limited amount of comfort could be extracted from the fact that Hitler took care to fight only when he was at an advantage. On 7 May the Commons discussed the question, on the motion to adjourn for the Whitsun recess. There was a good deal of doubt and unhappiness among Conservatives, but no certainty that they would vote against the government. After the first day's debate the Labour party decided to divide against the motion, despite the risk that this would drive the uneasy Conservatives back to supporting Chamberlain; and if the government majority remained unbroken the opposition would be accused of trying to gain a party advantage by dividing the House.

Several Conservatives had clearly been shaken when Amery, who had been a Cabinet Minister under Baldwin, applied to the government the words with which Cromwell dismissed the Rump Parliament: 'You have sat here too long for any good you have been doing . . . in the name of God, go.' Chamberlain made the ill-judged remark 'I appeal to my friends', which left him open to the reply that the crisis was more important than friendship; Lloyd George demanded that Chamberlain should set the example of sacrifice by giving up the seals of office, and added a plea that Churchill should not allow himself to be made into an air-raid shelter to protect his colleagues. When the division came, about 40 Conservatives voted against the government and about 60 others abstained; the government majority, normally over 200, fell to 81.

At first Chamberlain hoped to rearrange his government by bringing in the Liberal and Labour parties, but in case he could not win fresh support he summoned to his office on 9 May his two potential successors, Churchill and Halifax, and asked which of them it should be. Churchill

---

[1] Central Statistical Office, *Statistical Digest of the War* (1951), 139. This aggregate table is made up of the whole wide diversity of things used in modern war, bullets, tanks, radar sets, ships, and so on. But production reached a peak in a sufficient number of items in 1943 to show that this was not just a statistical curiosity.

had previously declared that he would serve under Halifax but—urged by friends beforehand—he remained silent when the question was asked. There was a very long pause, and then Halifax accepted the situation and said Churchill should be Prime Minister. Chamberlain, the King, most Conservatives, and a section of the Labour party would have preferred Halifax, but there was really no choice. Churchill could rule without Halifax; Halifax could be Prime Minister only if Churchill was at the head of a war committee, holding something of the position Lloyd George had asked for at the beginning of the December 1916 struggle for power. Some Conservatives had thought Churchill would not be acceptable to the Labour party because of his attitude in the General Strike and on India, but by 1939 the Labour party had come round to regarding him as an enemy of the dictators and a man who would have liked to save the League. On 10 May the Labour party announced that it was not prepared to serve under Chamberlain, but would serve under his successor. This settled Chamberlain's fate.

Churchill

Churchill's whole life seemed to have been dedicated to preparing him for this moment. Thirty years previously, Sir Edward Grey had said that his activity of mind would disqualify him for any Cabinet post except that of Prime Minister. He had held almost all the important government offices, he knew more about war than any other British Prime Minister, and he possessed the eloquence to summon the people to a task which looked, for some months to come, increasingly difficult and almost hopeless. When he said 'Let us so bear ourselves that, though the British Empire and its Commonwealth last for a thousand years, men shall still say "This was their finest hour"',[1] he had compressed the whole historical situation into a single sentence. England had on other occasions stood decisively against an attempt to bring the whole continent of Europe under the domination of a single power, but never before had the dominant power been as unrelievedly evil as Hitler's Reich, nor perhaps had any other power come so close to success. The strain was immense: the British Empire had been losing its central cohesion under the effect of nationalism, but British dominance within it was accepted until the great efforts of the Second World War sapped her strength. If its strength had to go, it could not have gone in a better cause than resistance in 1940.

During the Second World War there was very little of the vulgar jingoism and petty spitefulness that had appeared at times in the First War. But in the first nine months of the war there was an absence of

---

[1] Winston S. Churchill, *The Second World War* (1948–54), i. 597.

enthusiasm and a feeling that the government was detached from the people and even from the war itself. Churchill changed all this; to use a phrase put in his mouth in another context, he 'put some humanizing ginger' into the conduct of the war.[1] The country now had some idea what it was fighting for, and it knew that the government was whole-heartedly committed to the war and at the same time could understand what the people wanted.

In the debate on Norway a number of speakers had suggested that a small War Cabinet like Lloyd George's would save the situation. Churchill himself had doubts about this, but he set up a Cabinet of five: under his chairmanship Attlee and Greenwood represented the Labour party and Halifax and Chamberlain represented the orthodox Conservatives. The Labour party wanted a much more thorough-going purge of the supporters of Munich, but Churchill knew that he could not unite the country by opening up fresh divisions, and he had no intention of damaging his party in the way Lloyd George had damaged the Liberals. Because Chamberlain resisted the temptation to go away and sulk as Asquith had done, it was fairly easy for Churchill to hold the Conservatives together. Chamberlain had been overthrown in a more open way than Asquith, but he still had a majority of the Commons behind him and if he had appealed to the loyalty of his party he might have caused Churchill some embarrassment. In fact he served with unbroken loyalty until the onset of cancer forced him to retire in October and led to his death a month later. Churchill then took up the leadership of the Conservative party, partly because power would have been inconveniently divided if anybody else had been Conservative leader and partly because it strengthened his position in dealing with his Labour colleagues.

At the time of Chamberlain's retirement the Labour representation in the War Cabinet was strengthened by the promotion of Ernest Bevin. Churchill had brought Bevin, the General Secretary of the Transport and General Workers' Union, into the government as Minister of Labour, and he had quickly seen that Bevin was ideally suited for the job of helping run a war. Until 1940 the job of the Ministry of Labour was to make sure that strikes did not happen; Bevin interpreted his job as one in which he treated the entire population as a reservoir of manpower, some of which should flow into the armed forces, some into war production, and some into replacing workers who had moved from peacetime jobs into the war effort. At first it was suggested that he should use the widespread powers of compulsion given to him and compel people to go to jobs for which

[1] Beerbohm's cartoon, facing p. 306 in Randolph Churchill, *Winston Churchill*, vol. ii.

they were required. Bevin's response was perfectly logical; he pointed out that the factories had not yet been built and there was no difficulty in finding workers for the work to be done. But under this rational reply lay Bevin's determination to avoid industrial conscription if possible and to place labour on the same footing as capital. Eventually he used industrial conscription to sort out a few residual problems, but long before that he had shown that workers and their trade unions were to be taken seriously and had to be regarded as a part of the community. This was something of a new departure: the government had negotiated with trade unions in the First World War, but Lloyd George's tricky habits in negotiation and the unions' conviction that a number of pledges had been broken, combined with the employers' refusal to deal with them as equals, had prevented negotiating habits from changing much. In the Second World War the government was again anxious that work should go ahead without interruption. Striking before using arbitration was declared illegal, and arbitration meant that employers had to accept unions. Bevin insisted that working conditions in factories should be made as tolerable as possible by providing canteens and personnel departments and by enforcing factory legislation; apart from the satisfaction of advancing causes that he had upheld throughout his union career, he knew that making the fullest possible use of manpower demanded a high level of labour mobility, and this could be achieved by making people feel they were being cared for at work.

Bevin's great triumphs were still some way in the future, and in the summer of 1940 Lord Beaverbrook, who joined the War Cabinet at the same time as Bevin, had played the most prominent part in the war effort. The switch from the slow production of bombers to the hurried construction of squadrons of fighters, and his exploits in seizing men and material and diverting them to aircraft production, convinced everybody that here was a Minister who got things done. It was no way to run a long-term war, because it put everybody else's production plans out of order; but in the summer of 1940 the important thing to do was to survive the next few weeks of air fighting.

Churchill had come to power just as disaster began to descend. In his first five weeks of office he made several visits to France to try to encourage the French government to resist, to take its fleet and leave for North Africa, and to merge England and France into one nation. It was no use, and by mid-June the English knew that theirs was the only country left in Europe to resist Hitler. By this time they felt distinctly more cheerful about the war; Churchill made many contributions to the war effort, but his most obvious contribution was that he clearly enjoyed what was going on, and the British people very soon accepted this and they too began to enjoy it. The Germans were supposed to be committed to a philosophy that valued war and struggle but they did not enjoy the war, although they did not allow this to affect their morale. At least until boredom set in during the last year or two of fighting, the English found that the war released them from all sorts of constraints and provided them with challenges—opportunities to change jobs, travel, drop some of the habits of respectability, and to treat everybody else as equal. This exhilaration might not have survived large casualty figures but, as things went, people found the Second War more fun than the First.

Churchill was the man to encourage this mood. He satisfied the need to feel that everybody was doing something worth while, and this was as important as making everybody feel that they were going to win. Very few people seem to have considered the possibility of defeat, and so it was quite easy for Churchill to lay it down, without any real discussion, that the war would go on. People took it for granted that it was entirely reasonable for him to declare that his war aim was 'Victory—victory at all costs'. His behaviour on taking office, when 'he was conscious of a profound sense of relief' because affairs were in safe hands, was reminiscent of Chatham's conviction that he could save the country and nobody else could;[1] in the next few months he seemed more like the younger Pitt with his commitment to war without end and, as Bevan pointed out, with his oratorical triumphs followed by military defeats.[2] But the defeats were—granted the initial collapse in France—more or less inevitable. It was Churchill's task to make them bearable, and in this he was successful.

The 'spirit of Dunkirk' followed logically from what he had to say. The dominant feeling at the time of Dunkirk was that England was a community, in which everybody had to stand or fall together. The English upper class may have believed that fighting would mean the end of its privileged position, but it had no doubt that its duty was to fight—and no other upper class in Europe showed the same simple patriotic readiness to resist Germany.[3] The working class had gone through two very uncomfortable decades after the glowing promises of the First World War, and some of its discomfort had been caused by Churchill himself; it too had no doubt that in 1940 it had to fight for England and the men

[1] Winston Churchill, op. cit. ii. 24 and i. 601. Churchill's speeches were designed for the House of Commons; however, his wireless speeches (sometimes repetitions of what he had said in the House) were what really cheered the public up.

[2] 'If speeches could win a war, then we have as good as won.' M. Foot, *Aneurin Bevan* (1962), 341.

[3] H. Nicolson, *Diaries* (1966–8), ii. 23–4 and references given there.

and women who worked seven days a week in their factories in the summer of' crisis, when it was necessary to turn out arms so that the armies retrieved from Dunkirk could have a fair chance of resisting invaders, were also responding with an enthusiasm not seen elsewhere in Europe. The spirit of Dunkirk has sometimes been invoked to deal with later crises, and people in England have never been very interested, because no later crisis has been as dangerous as Dunkirk and the summer of 1940. But the spirit of community that emerged around the time Churchill became Prime Minister and lasted more or less throughout the war was something valuable. This spirit would have been hard to keep up in peacetime; it rested too much on the democratic totalitarianism mentioned earlier to be an entirely comfortable basis for society. Undoubtedly it helped people put up with the bombing of the winter of 1940–1, though less democratic systems of government turned out to be just as good at nerving Germans and Russians to put up with heavy wartime suffering.

Social demands of the war

The upper class was quite right to think that, at least for the duration of the war, it would have to pay for the British contribution. Real wages remained fairly steady, and there was not much transfer from working-class expenditure to the war effort. But the most spectacular gains were made by using machinery more efficiently and by developing the economy: war production took a steadily rising share of the national income, more because the national income was rising than because civilian expenditure was falling. There were social changes; the mobilization of manpower led to a reduction in the number of servants, which fell from 1·2m. to 0·5m. as girls left for the factories. This decline was sharper than the fall during the First World War, and it was more permanent. Money was extracted from the taxpayer in a more sophisticated way as the Treasury realized that it had to deal in real resources to keep the economy from succumbing to inflation. The 1941 budget was intended to make financial adjustments to meet the demand for real resources, and was entitled to be considered the first budget which really accepted Keynes's general ideas about the effect on the economy produced by the government's financial policy. Previous attempts to explain budget deficits in Keynesian terms had not shown much willingness to consider the economy as a whole. In 1941 Sir Kingsley Wood took the items of government expenditure, showed what would be covered by existing taxes and by borrowing and what would be covered by foreign credits, and treated the difference as the gap that had to be filled up by taxation. Otherwise, as he pointed out, it would be filled up by forced saving accompanied by inflation and rising prices. Once the budget was seen in these terms it was easier for the government to work out what it could really do to expand the war effort and what attempts at expansion would be unrealistic because they would not correspond to any resources that existed. Once it had been established that the United States would give unlimited credit for the purchase of raw materials and food, there were not many limits on resources. Nevertheless, on the financial side the Treasury had to raise taxes as much as possible, in order to keep the inflationary gap under control, and to help with this gave tax credits to be paid after the war.

An earlier innovation in taxation had slightly limited working-class spending: the graduated purchase-tax introduced in 1940 had affected a number of working-class purchases, but they tended to come at the lower levels of the tax. The really heavy incidence of purchase-tax fell on the luxuries of the upper class, just as income-tax combined with surtax raised the marginal rate on the highest incomes to $97\frac{1}{2}$p in the pound. Equality of sacrifice tended to take the form of bringing everyone towards a uniform subsistence level, and as the working class was already quite close to this level, it had much less to lose. Wartime fiscal policy was egalitarian enough for any socialist: Excess Profits Tax, levied on the extent to which profits rose above a peacetime base, went up to 100 per cent, so that people worried much less about war profiteers than in the First World War—some manufacturers could expand their businesses by building factories which would help them prepare for the post-war world, but their activities had none of the socially disruptive effects of the First War profiteers. Wartime economic policy transferred about 10 per cent of the national income from rent and dividends which were usually received by the upper class to wages and salaries, which went mainly to the middle and lower class. The less wealthy also benefited from the Rent Restriction Act, which froze rents at the 1939 level. Changes in income-tax and the increase in money wages brought more wage-earners up to the level at which they had to pay income-tax though, because of the allowances and rebates, it was unusual for a manual worker to pay at the standard rate unless he was married and his wife was also at work. In September 1943 a scheme for Pay As You Earn was introduced, which made tax demands more convenient.

Most of these egalitarian financial measures had been put into effect before it was apparent that political opinion was moving to the left. In the opening stages of the war there were no visible movements of opinion. Between early 1941 and late 1942 there were several parliamentary attacks on Churchill, but they did not come from any particular section of the House of Commons. About a couple of dozen Members were willing to vote against the government's conduct of military affairs, and a rather larger number thought it did no harm for the government to be kept on its toes. The simultaneous defeats in Greece and in the Libyan campaign were bound to lead to criticism; later on the fall of Tobruk caused alarm; and the loss of Singapore, with all its overtones of imperial dissolution, was the worst moment of the war for Churchill. He controlled British war planning so obviously that he was the natural centre of attack. Some of the attackers said that he was trying to do too much, and suggested in particular that he should stop being Minister of Defence so that he had enough time to supervise all the activities of the government. Churchill defended himself by saying that he was in charge and that he would decide the structure of the government for as long as he was Prime Minister. As Minister of Defence he had frequent discussions with the Chiefs of Staff; the three Service Ministers became steadily less important and after Eden became Foreign Secretary when Halifax went to Washington as Ambassador in December 1940, they sank to the powerless position of Kitchener after he had surrendered his control over strategy to Robertson in the First World War. These discussions with the Chiefs of Staff enabled Churchill to keep in touch with strategy; he provided a stream of military suggestions and insisted on being given reasons when they were not accepted, but did not override military decisions except when wider political reasons—which usually meant diplomatic pressure—made it necessary. Lord Alanbrooke's *Diaries* show that Churchill could sometimes be very irritating when pressing his suggestions on the chiefs of staff, but probably it did the chiefs of staff no harm to have an outside force obliging them to think about what they were doing. Churchill was at first a link between the War Cabinet and the Chiefs of Staff, but as the war went on the War Cabinet dropped further and further out of sight. Though it had been a useful shock absorber when the war was going badly, it became less relevant when all was going well. In the second half of the war Churchill spent more and more time in conferences with the American and Russian leaders, and the British chiefs of staff had to discuss questions with the American chiefs of staff. On the military side the American structure followed the British system, but Roosevelt saw no need to consult his Cabinet on strategy and Churchill may have found this political arrangement attractive. His relations with his generals were far better than Lloyd George's, but since he always had much more control over what they did, he had to take the responsibility for it; he could not say, as Lloyd George did in his *War Memoirs*, that he had known better than his generals but they would not listen.

Military relations with the United States were inevitably closer than with Russia, and the social structure may have been affected by having so many American servicemen in England during the two years before D-Day, but people inside England were conscious that the Russian army was bearing more of the strain of the war than anybody else. Churchill, while not underestimating the great military effort of the Russians, never doubted that Communists were dangerous people who wanted to undermine the British Empire, but the movement of public opinion towards the left owed something to the Russian army. The British Communist party denounced the war that broke out in 1939 as an imperialist war, but when Russia was dragged into it the party line promptly switched to approval of the war. Communists devoted their energies to helping the work of war production and are sometimes given a lot of credit for checking strikes, though the increase in production in the previous year shows that their contribution was by no means indispensable. A certain amount of the pressure of the 1942 and 1943 campaign for a Second Front was worked up by the Communist party, but many other amateur strategists, some enlisted under Lord Beaverbrook, also asked for an attack across the Channel as soon as possible.

Japan's attack in the East endangered the British position in India. Although Congress had not been consulted about the declaration of war in 1939, Hitler's Germany was so racialist in its attitudes that Indians were bound to support the British government. But no such considerations applied in the case of Japan: an Asian people was triumphing over European domination, and supporters of Congress became much more ready than before to demand that the British should 'Quit India'. Sir Stafford Cripps who had gained, from the accident of being the British ambassador in Moscow at the time of the German attack, some of the credit for Russia's resistance, was sent to India to negotiate with the leaders of Congress on the basis of promising them independence at the end of the war. Gandhi called the offer 'a post-dated cheque on a crashing bank'[1] and it was rejected; perhaps it was already too late, but this may have been the last moment at which Congress could have negotiated independence for a united India. Civil disobedience began, and the government acted briskly to stop it; by the end of 1942 over 15,000 Indians were under arrest for political reasons. The British government was able to hold its ground after the rejection of the Cripps mission, because the Japanese offensive was checked and the military situation improved. But in 1943 the elements of British control were shaken by a

[1] This is the version given in *Annual Register of World Events for 1942*, 145.

famine in Bengal on a scale not previously seen in this century, during which 1,200,000 people died; it was accompanied by rioting between Hindus and Moslems.

Looking forward to the post-war world

Independence for India followed logically enough from the British war aims of freedom and democracy, though when Churchill and Roosevelt drew up the Atlantic Charter in their first meeting, before the United States entered the war, they used terms which (at least in Churchill's opinion) did not give away any of the British Empire. The people of England had to wait till December 1942 and the publication of the Beveridge Report for a statement of war aims that meant much to them. In 1941 Greenwood, the deputy Leader of the Labour party, had been assigned to planning for the post-war world, a fairly conclusive form of demotion. He asked Sir William Beveridge to produce a plan for social welfare, and Beveridge responded with a scheme that set the pattern for all subsequent British thinking about welfare.

The first principle was the single insurance stamp: people would buy a single government stamp for their government insurance card every week, and this would cover them for all the disasters that cause poverty. Inevitably, after the experience of the thirties, provision for people out of work was Beveridge's first preoccupation; he estimated that on average about $8\frac{1}{2}$ per cent of the working population would be unemployed and he wanted them covered on a permanent basis, with none of the exhaustion of insurance benefits followed by reliance on poor relief that had caused the bitterness of the Means Test. The aspect of the Report that caused most interest after the war was the proposal for a national health service to place everyone in an insurance scheme for medical treatment. The pre-war system had insured wage-earners, but not their wives and families, and had left salary-earners to make their own insurance arrangements. Beveridge's plan also included the old age, widows' and orphans' pension schemes which were already in existence, and proposed a family allowance for children, because large families had been found in the surveys in the 1930s to be one of the causes of poverty. The finances of the Report were hard to work out, because wartime inflation was changing all the wage and price levels, but Beveridge suggested that some benefits should increase by stages, perhaps not reaching their final value until twenty years after the war ended. He also said that an agency would have to be set up to give assistance to people whose pensions had not yet reached the level needed for an adequate standard of living.

The Report was received with immense enthusiasm in England, the United States, and in Commonwealth countries. The German government paid it the compliment of denouncing it as fraudulent. The response to the Report made it clear that one of the things for which the ordinary man was fighting was economic security, and he believed that Beveridge opened the way to freedom from want. Against this background the government might have been expected to welcome the Report, if only because of its value as war propaganda. But the government was not eager to arrange a debate in the Commons, and when one was held Members had to insist very strenuously before they could obtain a third day for discussion. This failure early in 1943 to understand the enthusiasm of the Commons and the people for the Report probably marks the point at which Churchill began to lose touch with the feeling of the country; his parliamentary position was becoming unchallengable as the Germans were obviously beginning to lose the war, but he was thinking only about the war and showed signs of forgetting what people were fighting for. In the debate the Tory knights from Croydon and from Kensington rose to say that their constituents did not think money should be spent on all these welfare schemes, though the debate also showed the truth of the generalization that all Conservatives under 40 approved of the Report and all Conservatives over 40 disapproved of it. The Labour party was whole-heartedly committed to the Report, and most of the Labour Members who did not hold office voted for an amendment pressing the government to act quickly upon the Report. During the debate the government accepted family allowances, and expressed general sympathy for the rest of the Report, but this came as rather a grudging concession.

Beveridge's Report was not the only sign of interest in the post-war world. The Barlow Report in 1940 tried to find some way of enabling the community to get the benefit of increases in land values and the Uthwatt Report in 1941 outlined a scheme for more attractive town planning. The Abercromby proposals for the post-war rebuilding and development of London were welcomed by town planners and by people who believed it would solve traffic problems more or less for ever. The government began to have difficulty in reminding people that the war was still on, and was far from won. In 1943, when the Reports were appearing and were being discussed, the British war effort reached the limit: no more manpower was available to expand the armed forces or the labour force in factories producing for military purposes. Bevin pushed his powers to their furthest point and conscripted women for some jobs, but this did lead to some suggestions that he was going almost too far. One slight weakness in the allocation of manpower was that too many miners had been accepted for military service. Efforts were made to get them back from the army, but this was not enough. Some young men had to be ordered to go into coalmining rather than the armed forces when they reached military age; the 'Bevin boys' did their best, and the immediate crisis was avoided, but it could be seen that the country was stretching all her resources as far as they would go, and after 1943 the overall level of war production declined. Until the summer of 1944 the British military forces in Europe were larger than the American, but it was becoming clear that future weight of numbers was going to determine weight of influence. In 1943 the British government had to face the problem of whether to gamble on the war ending in 1944, in which case the British war effort could go on unchecked, or whether a longer war and a restricted British contribution were to be expected. In these calculations manpower was the limiting factor. People were undoubtedly under heavy strain, which may explain why they thought about the post-war world so much. When the V-1s and V-2s began to fall in 1944, morale was not as good as it had been during the bombing of 1940 and 1941, even though it seemed fairly certain that the V-raids would soon be brought to an end by the military advance through France and Belgium; apart from the shock and disappointment of finding that the Germans still had ways of making life unpleasant, part of this weakness of morale may have been due to the difficulty of life in wartime England.

As has been explained, the general standard of living was brought to something like that of a skilled workman. Food rationing was handled with great understanding by Lord Woolton, who left the mark of his personality on the food policy of the whole war; in fact he was in charge only during the years of military crisis, and in November 1943 he left to become Minister of Reconstruction, but his policy was remembered by his successors. The Ministry of Food had to give housewives advice that would be accepted; the size of the rations went up and went down, but manipulating the ration system was not always practicable, and delicate guidance was needed—for instance people were nudged towards buying carrots, which like other vegetables were never rationed, by being told that carrots would help them see in the dark (which, to a very limited extent, was true). The Ministry composed recipes which looked as though they might be interesting, encouraged people to try stinging-nettles as a substitute for spinach and did its best to get them to put jam on bread and butter straight from the jar without putting it on the plate, where some of it was bound to be wasted. But although there was never a dull moment while Woolton was around, wartime food was not interesting. There is a frequently quoted passage about England in the 1930s, about the way the unemployed wanted 'something a little bit "tasty"' without worrying too much about whether it was properly nutritious.[1] Wartime food was just the opposite: it was carefully balanced to give a healthy diet, but it was not tasty (partly because fat for frying, which was what the unemployed meant by tasty, was in short supply). Agricultural production was increased, as in the First World War. There was much less meat because land was ploughed up for corn which provided more food from the same area. Many people 'dug for victory' by growing vegetables on little allotments of their own. The health of the population improved, perhaps because almost everybody could afford a reasonable basic diet, and perhaps because the Ministry of Food took care that rations provided vitamins and calories that people would not have worried about for themselves. On the other hand, the improvement in the nation's health included a drop in suicide figures, which suggests that people may simply have found life more interesting than in the years before the war. A neat blend of rationing and variety was applied to tinned food, almost all of which was sold on 'points', which meant that people could choose what tinned food they wanted (and could find in the shops) and pay for it with the designated number of 'points'. Clothing was sold in the same way. Chocolate and sweets were sold on another set of 'points', labelled 'personal points' in the ration books to show that this was some sort of treat.

The extension of rationing made British society still more egalitarian, and the 'points' system encouraged this approach in a way; the points operated as an extra currency, issued to everybody on an equal footing. This egalitarian tendency may have encouraged one form of political protest in the last years of the war. The three major parties refrained from fighting by-elections and did not oppose the candidate put forward by the party that had previously held the seat. Just as in the First World War, this led to the appearance of independent candidates and to the emergence of a new minor party. But in the First War the newcomer had been the Page Croft–Bottomley National Party on the right; in the Second War it was the Common Wealth party, led by Sir Richard Acland, an ex-Liberal, which campaigned mainly on the platform that nobody should have an income of over £1,000 a year. Some people voted Common Wealth because it gave them a chance to vote against the government, but its serious political appeal was to the left wing of the Labour party and to voters who thought wartime egalitarianism ought to be maintained in peacetime. It won a number of by-elections, and did well in others, to the fury of the Conservatives who thought it was simply a shadow

[1] G. Orwell, *The Road to Wigan Pier* (1937), 95.

organization representing the Labour party. The Labour leadership was not much happier about the prospect, foreseeing another round of struggle between the right and the left of the party. The political truce, kept up at a time when politics and the shaping of the post-war world were in the air, inevitably transferred the work of shaping opinion about the future to unofficial hands. Beveridge campaigned on behalf of' his Report. Victor Gollancz, the pre-war publisher of the Left Book Club, brought out more books attacking the Conservatives' record. *Guilty Men*, published in the summer of 1940, had blamed the government of Baldwin and MacDonald and Chamberlain for the plight of the men who had to be evacuated from the Dunkirk beaches; *Tory MP* reminded everyone that there had been Conservatives who had been in favour of a policy of friendship with Germany. J. B. Priestley spoke and wrote for a community in which everybody had a fair and equal chance and nobody used this to cut himself off from his fellows. Bevan's magazine *Tribune* asked, in the words of Colonel Rainborough during the Civil War, 'whether the poorest he that is in England has not as great a right to live as the richest he', and clearly did not think the Coalition government—and perhaps not even the official leaders of the Labour party—were concerned with the poorest he.[1]

The government was willing to carry out some social reform. Churchill and Eden, the two leading Conservatives, were primarily concerned with military and foreign affairs. The domestic side of the war effort was co-ordinated by Sir John Anderson, who was at one stage considered by Churchill to be the man to become Prime Minister if he and Eden were to be killed; as Lord President of the Council, Anderson acted as chairman of a committee which had central control of the war effort because it allocated supplies of men, material, shipping space, and finance. Three Labour politicians, Attlee (Deputy Prime Minister), Morrison (Home Secretary), and Bevin (Minister of Labour), were probably the most important ministers concerned with domestic affairs under Anderson's direction, and they were ready to look for opportunities of carrying out changes during the war. But the rule of the Coalition was that no controversial legislation should be passed; the Ministry of Fuel clearly thought that nationalization would improve morale in the mines, but this was not acceptable to the Conservative Party. Bevin had a certain amount of difficulty with his Catering Wages Bill, which set up a wages board for the industry. Working conditions were bad, pay was low or non-existent for some waiters who were expected to live on their tips. About a third of the Conservative party voted against the Bill as an unnecessary

[1] V. Brome, *Aneurin Bevan* (1953), 135.

extension of government activity, but Bevin was able to insist that it was essential for running the industry in wartime and so the government supported it. Nothing on a larger scale could be passed if one party was strongly opposed to it.

The concern for unity appeared on an even wider scale in the 1944 Education Act. This was the only really large-scale piece of legislation passed during the war, apart from legislation concerned with war powers, and it was meant to end all the old struggles. Very few English Acts of Parliament are known by the name of the Minister responsible, but the 1944 Act has been 'the Butler Act' for many years, and the compliment is deserved. The Act took up the school-leaving age problem where it had been left before the war, and gave the Minister powers to raise the age of leaving first to 15 and then to 16, when he thought the expansion could be managed; it was understood that the first step would be taken almost immediately after the war. This extended education was to be secondary education for all. There were to be no more schools which educated children at all ages. All children would change schools at about 11; that was the age at which children who had passed the scholarship examination went on to grammar schools, and it was accepted that probably the examination would still be used to assign each child to a secondary school. Nothing was said about this in the Act or in the debate on the Act because, although the process of selection for secondary education became the leading issue in political discussion about education in the 1950s, it seems to have been taken for granted in the 1940s that things would go on as before, except that more children would take part —that is, nobody had really thought what difference it would make if the country tried to educate every child to the level of a skilled worker.

The debate on the Second Reading showed how important religion still was in educational politics. Butler had made great efforts to bring together the three religious groups—Church of England, Nonconformist, and Roman Catholic—which any policy had to take into account. One step could be taken that would unite all religious bodies in a mood of common approval: the Act laid down for the first time that each day at every school in the state system must start with an act of collective worship, though parents could ask for their children to be excused attendance if they chose. The rest of the religious question was purely a matter of finance, and Butler's grants to the Church of England and the Roman Catholics were generous enough to satisfy their official leaders. When the Bill came up for debate, some Roman Catholic Members were not satisfied, and wanted 100 per cent of the costs paid by the government. They obtained no more than the 50 per cent previously agreed in the Bill, but the argument over religion in education took up almost the entire debate. A few Labour Members did say how glad they were that children were to get more of a chance to be educated, but there was still an air of nineteenth-century idealism over the discussion—a few years later the argument would have moved from religion to the importance of education for maximizing the gross national product. One minor conflict over the Bill disturbed the government for a few days; an amendment laying down that women teachers were entitled to equal pay was added to the Bill. Churchill announced that he would not allow this, and stated that the government would resign if the amendment was not reversed. The government got its way, with only a couple of dozen Labour Members voting against the removal of the amendment.

The Act was not the only sign of interest in education in the closing years of the war. The Fleming committee suggested that the sharp class, division between the public schools and the rest of the country should be reduced by giving at least 25 per cent of public-school places to children selected and paid for by the county councils. The scheme would for some purposes have placed the public schools on the same footing as those grammar schools which had not entered entirely into the scheme of the 1944 Act, but had accepted direct grants from the Ministry of Education and undertaken to admit half their pupils on the basis of the recommendations of their county councils. The Fleming recommendation was not taken up, mainly because paying boarding-school fees for so many children would have cost a lot of money at a time when county councils foresaw much larger general expenditures on education. The ideal that education should be carried on in a gentlemanly way still remained: it was realized that universities would have to show more hospitality to merit, and demand money and social background less than before the war, but when it was suggested that students entering on government scholarships should receive grants which would enable them to live on an equal footing with the average student without any need to work for money in the summer or to repay the grant afterwards, the idea was accepted without much discussion.

The people and their government

Education did interest a lot of people at the time, but probably even more people were interested in the question of unemployment. In 1944 the government published a White Paper on the subject which represented a considerable step forward in official thinking. It is illuminating to compare the approach of the White Paper with Beveridge's book *Full Employment in a Free Society* and to see which was the better guide to post-war policy. The White Paper committed the government to maintaining a high and stable level of employment; this presumably meant a lower level of unemployment than the $8\frac{1}{2}$ per cent assumed for the purposes of the Beveridge Report. But in his book, published just after the White Paper, Beveridge asked for 'full employment', which he defined as 'always having more vacant jobs than unemployed men, not slightly fewer jobs'.[1] He admitted that this would leave a margin of frictional unemployment, but he said that government policy ought to make sure that there was no structural unemployment. The White Paper declared that a budget deficit to avoid unemployment was undesirable, but said national insurance contributions might be varied according to the state of the economy, so that if there was a danger of unemployment the insurance funds could run at a deficit and thus restore the level of demand in the economy. Beveridge said that this would be inadequate, would be administratively inconvenient, and might lead governments to try to cut down on benefits later on. He was wholeheartedly in favour of budget deficits as the way to restore demand, and suggested that the idea of a reserve supply of public works, recommended in the White Paper, amounted to saying that the government should neglect development work, however necessary until it fitted conveniently into the state of the economy. Beveridge stated that the White Paper did no more than pretend to follow Keynes's principles. In this, and in other points, he may have been unfair to the White Paper; public works were recommended in the text of Keynes's *General Theory*, and it was not unreasonable to say that they should wait until the level of demand in the economy justified introducing them. But whatever there may have been to say for the White Paper, post-war practice followed Beveridge. Full employment, in his sense of the term, was regarded as one of the most important objects of economic policy, schedules of public works were not drawn up in times of expansion and then put into effect in time of recession, and a deficit on the current budget was regarded as the most effective way of restoring demand to the economy. Beveridge cannot be said to have shaped employment policy in the same direct way as he shaped social welfare policy for the post-war world, because the influence of his book cannot be estimated as easily as the influence of his Report, but the great majority of the population seems to have shared his view that unemployment was the main economic evil to be resisted.

At the end of 1944 the Labour party moved somewhat to the left. The leaders of the party realized that an election would soon be held, and were preparing to fight on a programme of retaining a good deal of the

[1] W. H. Beveridge, *Full Employment in a Free Society* (1944), 18.

wartime government controls on the economy but not doing much in the way of nationalization. The party conference was not satisfied with this, and asked for a programme of nationalization on the lines of the programmes drawn up in the 1930s, and this the party leaders accepted. The shadow of the end of the First World War still hung over the political scene, and its effect was increased by the first faint suggestions that some people wanted to get back to 'before the war'. Churchill considered that the Coalition government could go on after the war, and at one stage in the negotiations suggested that a referendum could be held to find out whether this was acceptable to the electorate. But the Labour party disliked coalitions, and in any case the coalition would have had more difficulty agreeing about policy if it went on after the war. The Labour half of the coalition had no desire to get back to the days before the war; on the other hand Woolton, one of the greatest practitioners of 'war socialism', was quite certain that conditions in peacetime were so different that the country ought to return as far as possible to the free play of the market.[1] The democratic totalitarianism of the war years was wearing thin by the time Germany surrendered. For good or ill it left relatively little mark on British life.

The government spent a larger proportion of the national income than ever before, just as it had done in the First World War, and although the government's share fell after the war, it never sank to the pre-war level. The lesson that the government could run the economy without unemployment was learnt again, and this time was not forgotten. But the government's relation to the people changed rather less: the spirit of intense national unity, combined with a willingness to allow the government a very free hand, did not survive the war for long.

Just before the war, there had been some early attempts to examine the social habits of Englishmen. Mass-Observation, the organization that carried out these inquiries, was not popular. During the war the government tried similar methods to find out what people were thinking and how their morale was standing up to the war: this again was not popular, and the inquirers were named Cooper's Snoopers, after the Minister of Information. No doubt a government which had to conduct a total war needed such methods, but there was some idea that the government ought not to concern itself so closely with what its subjects were doing. In 1940 the Gallup Poll began to ask people which party they would vote for, but nobody treated their findings seriously for some years. Before the war people had had a highly developed sense of keeping themselves to themselves; this was given up to some extent for the war and when it did

[1] Lord Woolton, *Memoirs* (1959), 295, 304.

return after the war, it was less intense than in the past. Concern with respectability never returned to the height it had reached before the war. Before 1914 neither the upper class, nor the working class below the chapel-going 'aristocracy of labour', were concerned about being respectable; between the wars this habit spread from the middle class to the whole country. It did not survive the war undamaged. Fighting a war is not a respectable activity, and on the underside of society there were people who ran a black market in food or other things in short supply. The black market was never very large, and people did not treat the war as an opportunity for a great display of dishonesty. But it did mark a turning-point for some things: drinking and drunkenness, which were obvious signs of lack of respectability, had been going steadily downwards for over half a century, but after the war they began to rise again.[1] On the whole the largest changes which followed the war were changes in the way that individual Englishmen behaved rather than in the relations between them and the government. With the passage of time, polls and sample surveys were accepted as a reasonable way to find out what people were thinking, but an official government opinion poll would probably not have been well received. Willingness to be polled and surveyed was one small sign of people's willingness not to keep themselves to themselves so much; absence of enthusiasm for government surveys went with a feeling that, except in some moment of emergency, the government and the people were two separate things, and it might be just as well to keep them separate. People expected the government to be helpful, and had more ideas about what the government could do, but they did not propose to be drowned in a flood of gratitude.

One step was taken towards carrying out the Beveridge Report: a Bill setting up Family Allowances, at the rate of 25p per week for each child after the first, was introduced in February 1945. Beveridge had originally suggested that allowances should be at the level of 40p per week, but the government had already said that it intended to give allowances at the lower rate and to provide free meals at school as a

---

[1] D. E. Butler and J. Freeman, *British Political Facts 1900–1960* (1963), 236 lists:

	convictions for drunkenness	mns. of barrels of beer drunk
1910	161,992	35
1920	95,763	35
1930	53,080	24
1940	44,699	27
1950	45,533	26
1960	65,170	27

substitute for the extra money. School meals had been provided on a much larger scale during the war than ever before, partly to enable mothers to go out and work in factories, and the government was quite ready to continue the scheme, particularly because it made sure that children got one cooked meal a day. As judicious planning of the location of industry was believed to be a line of defence against the re-emergence of areas of high unemployment, another piece of social legislation provided assistance for 'special', or depressed, areas to attract new factories.

This Bill passed the Commons in the last days of the coalition. As the war in Germany was clearly coming to an end, Churchill felt it was time to decide what would happen next. He wanted the coalition to go on; his party and the Labour party wanted an election fairly soon. On the one hand, the war against Japan had still to be won; on the other hand it was ten years since the last election, and people had never felt as much interest in the war against Japan as in the war against Germany. Churchill on 18 May asked the Labour party to continue the Coalition government until the war against Japan had been brought to a successful conclusion. He implied that, if it did not agree to this, the coalition would be brought to an end and there would be an election in July. The Labour party said on 20 May that it did not want to remain in the coalition for long, but it asked for the election to be put off until October. Churchill did not accept this suggestion, and on 23 May the great ministry, which had saved the country and had laid solid foundations for social reform, was brought to an end. A 'caretaker' government was formed to run the country for the period until the election result was known. Except for Churchill and Eden, the 'caretaker' ministers were not a very inspiring group, and the contrast between them and the Labour alternative did not help the Conservatives as much as Churchill might have hoped.

The voting in the election took place on 5 July, but to allow time for soldiers' votes from all over the world to be brought back to England for counting, the ballot-boxes were not opened until 26 July. During the curious weeks of suspense in July Churchill led the British delegation to the Potsdam conference, and Attlee came as an observer so that if he were to become Prime Minister he could pick up the threads of policy with as little difficulty as possible. Churchill seems to have been quite confident that the Conservatives would win, though in retrospect it appears that they suffered from a number of crushing handicaps, some of them inflicted by Churchill himself, who was ill advised by Beaverbrook and Brendan Bracken and failed to understand how serious-minded the electorate had become.

To some extent the election was about Conservative pre-war policy. By this time it was taken for granted by everybody that Chamberlain's foreign policy had been ill advised, and some people voted on this basis. The Conservatives were supposed to know about foreign policy, and had failed. Many more people must have voted against the pre-war unemployment; at the time, as had been seen in the 1935 election, it was accepted that nobody could do much about unemployment, but by 1945 people had come to expect full employment, and to associate the Conservatives with the lack of it. To set against these heavy disadvantages the Conservatives had Churchill. He made a great procession around the country, and everywhere he went enormous crowds came out to cheer him. The people felt a debt of gratitude to him, and discharged it by the enthusiasm with which they welcomed him. Churchill thought that their cheering meant that they believed they ought to vote for him, but this did not follow at all—politics cannot be run on a basis of gratitude for what is past, but have to be conducted in the way that will meet the demands of the future.

Churchill did not convince people that he had any clear idea of what to do with the future. The B.B.C. allowed ten broadcast talks by the major parties; Churchill did not have anything positive to say, so his remark that if the Labour party was returned it would set up a Gestapo to run the country was given even more attention than it deserved. The public had never been quite certain how to take his free-flowing denunciations of Hitler and Mussolini during the war, which at times seemed a little undignified, but to suggest that Attlee and Bevin and Morrison were going to set up a Gestapo was silly enough to do him some harm; the Labour leaders were, in their different ways, not men to suffer fools gladly, but they were no more supporters of dictatorship than Churchill himself. They had the advantage, very rarely enjoyed by the opposition at an election, of having been ministers in high repute until a few weeks previously; during the war they had established themselves as men who could be trusted, and presumably Churchill had trusted them. Churchill also did himself no good by getting into an argument about the constitution of the Labour party. The party chairman, who holds the position for one year only, was the effervescent Professor Laski; during the election Laski reminded Attlee of his responsibilities to the party, and Churchill claimed that this proved that the Labour party was dominated by its National Executive Committee, made up of men who had never been elected by the people. Again, nobody believed in this story of Attlee being a helpless puppet—Attlee may well have been, as Churchill said later, a modest little man with a great deal to be modest about, but during the election Churchill seemed fated to pick out the points at which Attlee's armour was invulnerable.

In any case, the election was not to be settled by a popularity contest between the leaders, and Churchill's approach allowed little opportunity for the Conservatives to say what they thought the post-war should be like. In their brief references to the subject the Conservatives said they did accept the Beveridge Report, but from the nature of the two parties, they had to be more explicit than the Labour party if they were to persuade the electorate to believe them on this point. Instead they seemed content to leave the issue as one that all men of good will agreed about, so there was no need to discuss it any more. But it is generally agreed that the electorate was in a serious mood, and would have put up with a great many detailed speeches on the subject. In 1918 people had thought the Germans were going to pay for everything; in 1945 nobody imagined that this would be possible, and it was all the more important to make sure that politicians intended to press ahead with the things they had promised, even if there were some financial obstacles. Because the Conservatives did not stress their determination the electorate may have suspected that the schemes for social welfare might be laid aside if they turned out to be hard to pay for.

As in 1918, the most important single domestic issue was housing. The stock of houses which had been just about adequate in 1939 had suffered losses from German bombing and from the natural passage of time, and new building during the war had sunk almost to nothing. The Labour party could point to the great increases in arms production achieved during the war by government planning of the economy, and could say that a similar approach would solve the housing problem; the Conservatives had nothing distinctive to say in reply.

The only issue on which there was an open difference between the parties was nationalization, and while there is no sign that it aroused enthusiasm for the Labour party among the electorate at large, it did no harm: at least it showed that the Labour party was anxious to get away from the bad old days of the years between the wars, and as the main industries on the nationalization list had been under state control during the war people could see that private owners were not essential for running coal or the railways. Including nationalization in the programme probably raised the enthusiasm of the Labour organization, without provoking any corresponding enthusiasm to resist on the Conservative side.

When the ballot boxes were opened it was soon clear that the Labour party had won.

	Votes	Seats	% of all votes cast
Conservative	9,988,306	213	39·6
Liberal	2,248,226	12	9
Labour	11,995,152	393	47·6
Other	854,294	22	2·8

Conservatives said that it was because Labour men had stayed in England, working in factories, and built up their party organization in the trade unions while Conservatives were away fighting, but they had certainly not thought this before the election or they would presumably have agreed with the Labour party's request that the election should be put off until October. The army was in fact predominantly Labour, which was not surprising because men between 21 and 30 had leaned more to the Labour party than most other age-groups before the war, and organizations like the ABCA had kept soldiers in touch with movements of opinion at home. Although Conservative organization may have suffered, there was really no need for such explanations; from 1942 or 1943 the Conservatives had had a number of warnings that they needed to adapt to a changed world, and the election showed that voters did not believe the warnings had been taken seriously enough.

10. *The post-war world: dream and reality* 1945–1949

England's place in the world

THE Labour government came to office in a world that had changed much more than people in England realized. A good deal of its time was spent on trying to adjust to the new world, and measures which were attributed to its socialist principles were often the result of the external pressures upon it. The most fundamental change was that America and Russia decided to take a full part in international affairs. If they had done this earlier, the affairs of Europe would have run on different lines; their willingness to intervene in 1945 meant that they were the two dominant powers in the world. Compared with the other countries of Europe, which had been invaded, fought over, and defeated, England was in a position that might be envied and admired, and could still be thought of as the equal of America and Russia rather than of France and Germany. People realized that maintaining her wartime position as one of the three dominant powers would be an immense strain, but in 1945 nobody in the country thought it impossible or doubted that it should be undertaken.

The task was all the harder because the bonds of Empire had loosened during the war. The problem of India had to be faced, and other, less obvious tensions had to be dealt with. The commercial aspects of the Commonwealth were bound to be affected by the change in England's position in international trade. Compared with the external difficulties, the situation inside England was relatively easy to understand: the middle class wanted to get back to the pre-war world of low taxes, servants, and an ordered society in which people knew their place, and the working class wanted to keep the full employment, the adequate wages, and the prospect of increased social services that had opened up during the war. There had been a considerable transfer of income from the middle class to the working class during the war, but it had not yet been settled whether this was to become permanent or not.

When the war with Japan came to an end the American government brought the Lend-Lease arrangements to an end, as had been provided in the legislation, and made no alternative provision for England's imports. The British economy could not be adapted for peacetime activity without a longer pause for reconstruction. It had been expected that the war with Japan would go on for some time, which would be a breathing-space for converting the economy back to a peacetime basis because England would not be as fully involved as in the war against Germany. The swift end of the war with Japan meant that there was no breathing-space. So far as the government could see, the only way of dealing with the transition to peace was to negotiate a large loan from the United States. For the negotiations a short statement of the country's financial position was drawn up which gave an outline of the difficulties that the British government faced as a result of the war. Foreign investments worth £1,118m. had been sold off to pay for imports. 15·9m. tons of shipping, worth about £700m., had been sunk. Damage to housing, caused by bombs and rockets, came to about £1,500m. Machinery and equipment had not been repaired adequately during the war, and almost £900m. of depreciation had to be covered by new investment. England still had large foreign investments, yielding a return of about £170m. a year, but on the other hand external liabilities had been run up: British forces in Egypt and India had been financed by loans raised on the spot, and the debts which had arisen in this way amounted to £3,355m. The interest on the debts, at the low rates of the time, was estimated at £73m. a year. Repayment of the debts—or sterling balances, as they were called—would obviously be a long-delayed process.

Before the war, when prices were lower, England had imported about £800m. a year, of which about half was covered by visible exports and the other half by receipts from shipping and by dividends from previous investments. During the thirties the balance of payments had been more or less neutral; the level of foreign investment ceased to rise. It was estimated that England needed to raise her exports to about 175 per cent of the pre-war volume in order to meet the deficit that had been covered by invisible exports, and that this could be achieved in three or four years. To pay for imports during this period about £1,250m. would have to be borrowed.[1]

This sketch of England's position was masterly. Exports did reach 175 per cent of pre-war volume by 1950. The amount received from the

[1] *Parl. Papers*, Cmd. 6707.

United States was slightly more than the estimate of money required, but any difference on this point was due to inflation and the state of the sterling balances rather than to mistaken estimates of the trading position. In 1945 the American negotiators thought the British were being slightly pessimistic about their prospects, and they issued a loan for £1,100m. of which something over £100m. was allocated to paying for Lend-Lease goods which had been on their way to England and had arrived after the ending of Lend-Lease. Repayment did not start until 1951 and the true rate of interest on the loan was 1·6 per cent, which was quite low even at that time. The British negotiators had hoped at first for an interest-free loan, and the government may have concentrated on keeping the interest rate low at the expense of accepting one or two other clauses which had uncomfortable implications for England. They agreed that owners of sterling outside England should be allowed to convert their money into dollars a year after the loan came into effect, and that Britain and America would not discriminate against each other in trade, which meant that the Ottawa system of Imperial Preference would not be expanded, because there were no other areas in which the two countries were likely to discriminate. As part of the terms of the loan England accepted the Bretton Woods Agreement which had been worked out in 1944 in an attempt to avert any return to the trade dislocation of the 1930s, and thus returned to a fixed exchange rate. There was some argument whether this meant a return to the Gold Standard. Nobody wanted to return to gold, which was blamed for the unemployment of the 1930s; defenders of Bretton Woods pointed out that chronic unemployment was specifically laid down as one of the conditions that would justify devaluation, and argued as though exchange rates might be expected to change without much difficulty, but opponents of Bretton Woods (or of the American loan) pointed out that a government did not have the right to change its exchange rate by more than 10 per cent without a great deal of international consultation. They also pointed out that it was hard to tell, in the immediate aftermath of war, what would be a good permanent rate. At the beginning of the war the exchange rate for the pound had floated down to $4.03 to £1, and was held at this level. In 1945 this parity was accepted for post-war purposes, more because nobody could see a basis for another rate than for any positive reason.

The active and distinctive work of the Labour government was conducted with the pound at $4.03. The loan flowed out rather faster than had been expected, mainly because prices rose rapidly all over the world just after the war. Conversion to civilian life, and the work of making up for wartime neglect, as well as the spending of wartime savings, provided a strong demand both for investment and for consumption, and this demand could not be met. The rise in American prices reduced the value in real terms of the loan, and while of course it also reduced the real cost of repayment, this consolation was by its nature distant. The strong post-war demand was entirely familiar to men in government; they had seen it in 1919 and 1920, and there was a distinct feeling that unemployment and depression could easily return. Critics of the Labour government suggested that it should stabilize prices in England with a deflationary policy, and undoubtedly price rises reduced the popularity of the government. But as import prices were going up so rapidly, deflation might not have had much effect. The Conservative opposition at first seemed not to understand the need for exports, and said the government was paying too much attention to exports and not enough to the home market. Because Germany and Japan were too shattered by the war to compete, England had an excellent opportunity to secure new export markets. Pushed on by the government, British exporters made great efforts and were successful at least for a time. It has been suggested that the demand for their goods was so strong in these post-war years that they fell into bad habits and assumed—much as shopkeepers in England did during the years of scarcity—that the customer would put up with anything. As a result, when the Germans and the Japanese returned to world markets, they did not find it too hard to win customers away from the British.

There was another reason why the British export drive began well, and faded later. A great deal of British trade was still with the commodity-producing countries, which were doing well in the late 1940s. People in England grumbled at the rising prices of imports, but the commodity-producing countries could take large quantities of British exports in exchange: when the boom in commodity prices broke, costs fell in England, but export markets weakened at the same time.

As the American loan began to run out the Opposition shifted its ground and complained that too much of the loan was being spent on imports of tobacco, which absorbed 10 per cent of the loan, and films, which took about 4 per cent. The government knew that there were limits to the austerity of life that it could ask of people, but in August 1947 it imposed a prohibitive duty on American films. The consumption of tobacco had gone up considerably during the war and the tax on it was raised sharply, mainly for foreign exchange reasons. But the real drain on the loan was the convertibility clause: by the beginning of 1947 many countries selling to Britain were insisting on payment in convertible currency (money which could be turned into dollars) and in July, when all sterling outside England could be turned into dollars, the loan flowed out faster than ever. The agreement said the loan was not to be used to pay sterling debts from wartime, but the sterling debts were not stationary and easily identifiable. As a trading currency sterling passed freely round the non-dollar world, and when the barrier between the sterling and dollar world came down, a certain amount of sterling debt was turned into dollars. In the loan negotiations it had been assumed, at least on the American side, that England would recover her commercial position as quickly as she had done after the First World War. This had not happened: after five weeks of convertibility the exchange controls had to be restored on 20 August, sterling ceased to be convertible, and the government looked for ways of cutting its expenditure.

Fortunately for England the U.S. Secretary of State, George Marshall, had a few weeks previously suggested that perhaps America should provide financial aid to Europe. Ernest Bevin, as Foreign Secretary, had taken up the suggestion very quickly, and the Marshall Plan was set up to help England and the rest of Europe. England received about £700m. under the Plan, with no obligation to repay. Marshall Aid caused some trouble to the government because it seemed to give every American congressman power over British financial resources. When British politicians suggested that the country was recovering from the war satisfactorily, American politicians would suggest that it was time to save money for the American taxpayer by ending aid to England. By the time Marshall Aid began to arrive, the exchange value of the pound was under some pressure, and this was intensified by a slight recession in the United States. For most of 1949 there was a struggle to avoid devaluation. The balance of payments showed a steady deficit and every business man who could keep out of sterling held his money in some other currency. Sir Stafford Cripps, the Chancellor of the Exchequer, asserted boldly that England would not devalue, and the government seemed to treat the battle to preserve the exchange rate as an affair of national honour rather than a humdrum matter of economic convenience. But by September the pressure was too great, and the pound was devalued to a level of $2.80. Most other currencies were devalued, in terms of dollars, at the same time; the operation was as much a general revision of the exchange rates that had been fixed at the end of the war as an incident in British history, but the British took it much more seriously than anybody else.

Cripps felt guilty because he had said there would be no devaluation; the government had been shown to be unable to control the financial situation; a feeling developed in the country that it was discreditable to devalue and that the existing exchange rate was in some way bound up with national prestige. What devaluation really meant was that there could be no attempt to return to the financial position of the years before the war; the fall was too great, and the dominance of the United States had been too obvious. Devaluation did not affect public opinion much and in fact the government gained ground in the opinion polls in the next few months, but politicians felt that it was bound to lead to electorate disaster. The economic effects were beneficial on the whole, but it was a step that took some of the confidence out of the Labour government and encouraged its opponents.

It might also have been expected to show the government that the world really had changed since 1939 and that England would not be able to regain her pre-war position. When Attlee formed his government he initially thought of making Bevin Chancellor of the Exchequer and Dalton Foreign Secretary. A number of people advised him to change the two appointments round; among them was George VI, and it has been suggested that it was wrong for the King to influence such decisions, or alternatively that he did not in fact have any effect on the choice. Undoubtedly the King was only one among a number of people putting arguments to Attlee, but it was within his right to give advice, and it would be hard to say that the Prime Minister ought never to take the King's advice. One reason for appointing Bevin was that he was thought likely to 'stand up to the Russians'. In the summer of 1945 the Americans were intent on withdrawing from Europe, and the Russians were intent on consolidating the fruits of victory. The diplomacy of the period is not yet disentangled from the archives, but the Russians were clearly determined to establish themselves in all the countries assigned to them in wartime discussions, and in addition to set up a Polish government which would be subservient to them. This post-war acquisition of a sphere of influence was not a morally elevated proceeding, but most of it rested on wartime agreements, and in any case very little could be done about it. The opening months of the peace were embittered by the efforts of England and the United States to persuade the Russians that the three countries ought to decide their foreign policies by voting among themselves. The Russians, who foresaw that England and the United States would always vote together, were not in the least interested and went on building up a defensive belt on Russia's western frontier. The Russians used some very undiplomatic language in this period, but at least they were never unkind enough to call it a *cordon sanitaire*, in memory of the belt of states designed to put Russia in quarantine after the First World War.

If it had been simply a matter of Anglo-American complaints about the way the Russians had annexed territory and established police states, nothing might have happened. The United States would not, and England could not, do anything about what was happening in eastern Europe, so that moralizing and Churchill's references in August to an 'iron curtain' coming down over Europe might not have led to anything more than diplomatic irritation.[1] But behind the complaints about the way the Russians were behaving as conquerors lay a fear that they intended to advance further into Europe and acquire still more territory. This idea seems less convincing in retrospect than it did at the time. Russian aloofness when the Communist party was gaining control of China in the civil war in 1949, and during the Italian general election of 1948, in which the United States government took a keen and active interest, suggest that Stalin was much more concerned to establish a strong defensive position in eastern Europe than to launch a grand assault to carry the revolution to western Europe.

In 1946, the British government found that it had troops in Germany, in Greece, in Persia, in India, in Egypt, in Palestine, and in the Far East, where British rule was re-established. There was some concern in the United States that the war might turn out to have been fought to rebuild the British Empire. But all of this overseas activity had to be paid for in foreign exchange, and the state of the British balance of payments would not allow it to go on for long. Occupying Germany turned out to be expensive; in the winter of 1945–6 the world was moving towards a disastrous wheat shortage, and bread rationing, which had been avoided throughout the war, had to be imposed in order to provide enough wheat to prevent famine in Germany and India. England accepted this, just as she had accepted a good many other things in the past six years, but the strain was growing. Inside the Cabinet Dalton as Chancellor became almost Gladstonian in his enthusiasm for British withdrawal. Bevin resisted this and, as he was politically more powerful, was able to stretch British resources to the limit. Attlee professed not to be directly concerned with foreign affairs, but this amounted to tacit support for Bevin. Attlee was not directly concerned with economic affairs either, and his thoughts (at least as recorded in *A Prime Minister Remembers*) seem to have been directed to foreign policy rather than economic affairs. The economic judgments that he did express showed very little understanding of the problems.

Attlee and Bevin were not militarists or imperialists, but under their rule England, which had spent so little on defence before the war, began spending a distinctly larger proportion of the national income on

---

[1] 16 Aug. 1945; *Commons Debates*, ccccxiii. 84.

armaments than any other country in Europe. England was much more of a world power than any other European country after the war, but nobody explained why she should spend more money on military affairs than other countries of comparable strength and size. The government probably thought England could still play a decisive role in any future war. The Conservatives supported higher military expenditure enthusiastically; they welcomed the National Service Bill in 1947 which imposed 18 months of military service in peacetime and when, under pressure from the left wing of the Labour party, the period was reduced to 12 months, they expressed regret at this sacrifice of military power. Nobody considered the question on economic grounds, for the left wing of the Labour party concentrated on arguing that Russia was not aggressive in her intentions and that conscription in peacetime was an unjustified restriction of liberty.

The government also felt the country had to enter the race for atomic weapons. This was announced as discreetly as possible: the Minister of Defence slipped it in as a subordinate clause when referring to a Defence White Paper which laid heavy stress on research in aviation and avoided any reference to atomic weapons. The remark passed quite unnoticed and while the government frequently referred to peaceful uses of atomic energy it said nothing more about atomic weapons.[1] The decision to enter this very expensive activity was almost inevitable. The announcement that atomic bombs had been dropped on Japan was accompanied by predictions that atomic energy would provide almost unlimited electric power at cheap rates, and England had been so closely concerned with wartime development that she naturally wanted to go into the commercial aspects of atomic energy. In the months after the war the United States exploited the Quebec Agreement at least as fully as it was entitled to. The British government might have been content not to make its own bombs if it had been taken into the confidence of the United States. Instead a policy of exclusion was followed in Washington culminating in the passage of the McMahon Act which prohibited any sharing of American information on atomic matters. Because the British government entered the field of independent atomic research as a reaction against this, British atomic weapons were always in a sense a diplomatic weapon against the United States, which might be used to trigger off a war or to provide other countries with knowledge about nuclear weapons. Attlee and Bevin were convinced that the American alliance was the most important part of the British diplomatic position, and they were supported in this by Churchill, but it was clear that America was not

[1] 12 May 1948; *Commons Debates*, ccccl. 2117; Cmd. 7327, especially p. 7.

going to be a perfect ally from the British point of view. British politicians wanted to be treated as equals by the Americans, and the Americans were by this stage conscious that they were more prosperous and more powerful. At the same time the Americans were often unready to see the difficulties of the British position, and expected complete British agreement with American policy.

Withdrawal from empire

This could be seen in the process of imperial withdrawal. The government made some useful and uncontroversial preparations for withdrawal in the not-too-distant future from West Africa, but the issues that attracted attention were India and Palestine. Over India British and American policy was in agreement: Britain should leave as soon as was practicable. Churchill growled at the way the British Empire was clattering down, but after the war it was impossible to fight a colonial war to hold India. On the whole the Labour party sympathized with the Hindus and the Congress party, and the Conservatives preferred the Moslems. The government did not want to concede Partition to the Moslems, but by the end of the war the Moslem position was so strong, and their determination to obtain Partition so unshakeable, that it seemed unlikely that it could be resisted. In any case Wavell, the Viceroy at the end of the war, was not the man to bring the politicians together in India. He was a taciturn man, well suited to the military requirements of his post, but not able to negotiate with political leaders once the war was over. At the end of 1946 the government decided to replace Wavell and appointed Mountbatten, a naval commander with royal connections, a well-developed political sense, and more sympathy for Congress than anyone of comparable prestige. At the same time the government announced that England would leave on 1 June 1948 whatever the situation might be. This declaration checked American anti-imperialism, and it also confronted politicians in India with a more definite problem than before. Whether people realized it or not, the announcement of a deadline made Partition inevitable. All that the Moslem League had to do was to sit still until the British left; its power among the Moslems was large enough to ensure that a united India could not be created without its consent. Mountbatten saw this quickly enough when he reached India in March 1947, and he also saw that the structure of government was dissolving. Civil servants were worried about their new masters, police forces were beginning to divide themselves into Moslems and Hindus and were showing religious favouritism in the maintenance of law and order, rioting inspired by religious hatred was becoming more frequent, and it was possible that the army would begin to divide on religious lines. Mountbatten decided not only to accept Partition but to advance the date of independence. He hoped to get the Congress leaders to accept Partition by offering independence sooner than previously suggested, and he also foresaw difficulty in maintaining British authority for a whole year. The decision to accelerate the move to independence caused many difficulties, and may have been responsible for a great deal of bloodshed, but it could perfectly well be defended at the time. It was accepted by the British Cabinet and the Indian leaders in May. Early in June Mountbatten announced that independence would come on 15 August, and he then plunged into the work of drawing boundary lines and dividing up the assets of the Indian Empire. Pakistan, two large areas of land separated by an even larger area of India, looked a most improbable country, and it was made even less plausible by ethnic and linguistic differences between the inhabitants of east and west. India was also an assemblage of different people, divided in language and united in religion only in the sense that Nehru's secularist socialism and Gandhi's syncretism—at Gandhi's funeral the hymn 'Abide with Me' was played—had roots in a very sophisticated Hindu faith.

Independence came on 15 August. 'Long years ago', Nehru said at the celebrations, 'we made a tryst with destiny'; now India was going to meet her destiny and the greatest of all the movements for national independence had triumphed. From the British point of view the story had ended happily; England remained on good terms with both of the new countries and Mountbatten stayed on, the last Viceroy turning into the first Governor-General of independent India. Nehru became Prime Minister; Gandhi did not enter the government, but his political influence remained immense. But, while the British withdrew, the Partition lines were crumbling; they had not been established long enough to enable Hindus and Moslems to decide what they were going to do. Possibly British control would have broken down if independence had not been granted so swiftly, but the massacres of the weeks after Partition show that there was a heavy price to pay for this abrupt departure. Moslems fled to Pakistan, Hindus to India; many of them never reached their destination. In the east a fragile peace was established, partly because of Gandhi's presence; on the western frontier fighting went on for weeks. Probably the deaths were under 200,000, but they cannot have been much lower.[1] Nobody can be blamed for this collapse into butchery in the way that Hitler and Stalin can be blamed for taking their bloody decisions, but it was an unhappy way to end the Indian Empire.

[1] E. P. Moon, *Divide and Quit* (1961), 293.

The Palestine Mandate came to an equally unsatisfactory end—in some ways it was worse, because the British government did not emerge on good terms with any of the contestants. This result was perhaps unavoidable. In November 1917 the British government had declared that Palestine should become a national home for the Jewish people. As Palestine was inhabited mainly by Arabs, the Balfour Declaration sowed the seeds of trouble, though the harvest took some years to ripen. England secured Palestine as part of her extensive gains in the Middle East in 1919. As there was no marked Jewish enthusiasm for immigration in the 1920s, no conflicts occurred, but in the early 1930s British policy encouraged a more rapid rate of immigration, and after Hitler came to power in 1933 there was a flood of Jewish refugees. By 1936 the Arabs had become aware of the change in circumstances and began to resist it. In 1922 11 per cent of the population of Palestine was Jewish; by 1939 the figure had risen to 29 per cent. Arab opposition was becoming more desperate and more violent, and in 1939 the British government gave way to it by announcing strict limits on Jewish immigration.

The Labour party had committed itself to the Zionist point of view in its 1945 election programme, and the American government was also Zionist. Once in office Bevin became more and more impressed by the argument that making Palestine into an independent country for Jewish immigrants would mean dispossessing the Arab inhabitants and annoying England's Arab allies all over the Middle East. The oil of the Middle East was not yet established as one of the dominant economic facts of the post-war world, but the Suez Canal and the remains of the Middle East hegemony established after the First World War were powerful reasons why the British should want to avoid offending the Arabs. The United States pressed for permission to be given for 100,000 Jewish immigrants to be admitted; and if this permission had been granted, it would have come close to acceptance of the principle of letting in a practically unrestricted flow of immigrants. The government showed no desire to admit the 100,000 Jewish immigrants, and illegal immigration became an ever-increasing problem. Boats were chartered to smuggle refugees into Palestine, and when they were intercepted by the Royal Navy immigrants tried to swim ashore. Inside Palestine Jewish guerrilla forces took up arms against the British and the country slid towards the condition of Ireland under the Black and Tans. British troops were kept under better control than they had been in Ireland, but Jewish 'terrorist' activity rapidly reduced British sympathy for Zionism. In America, and to some extent in other countries, there was a feeling of guilt for allowing the Jews to be massacred by Hitler; people in England felt quite satisfied that they had done their best to defeat Hitler, and so were less ready to admit that Jewish displaced persons in the refugee camps of Europe had a special claim to be allowed to go to a new country and settle.

During the course of 1946 it became clear that no conceivable settlement would please either side in the struggle. Anti-Jewish feeling was growing in England, as a result of Jewish efforts to establish their position by force. The Arabs were showing no readiness to make concessions to the Jewish desire to set up a state of their own and in fact felt that the British were pursuing an anti-Arab policy by allowing Jews in at all. The government prudently referred the Mandate for Palestine to the United Nations in February 1947 and invited it to settle the issue. In November the United Nations issued its plan for partitioning Palestine and setting up an independent state of Israel and invited the British government to administer the plan. The government refused, and prepared to withdraw all British forces from Palestine. The Mandate came to an end in May 1948 and the newly created state of Israel was immediately attacked by the neighbouring Arab countries, but proved quite capable of defending itself. The Arabs tended to blame England and America for the creation of Israel, and the Israelis had no reason to feel grateful to England. This was one of the least successful disengagements from Empire since Yorktown. The British tended to blame the United States, and in particular attributed an exaggerated influence to the Jewish section of the American electorate.

In other, less inflammable, areas problems were handled quite skilfully. Burma became independent, and left the Commonwealth, but this was more to show that she really was independent than to express a dislike for England. Ireland became a Republic in April 1949, and left the Commonwealth. This was partly out of irritation that the British government did not end Partition by handing Ulster over to Ireland; Parliament passed an Act, at the time of the Irish departure, declaring that Partition would be ended only with the consent of the Parliament of Northern Ireland. Canada abolished the right of appeal to the Privy Council, and acquired the right to amend her own constitution except for the vital clauses defining federal and provincial powers; the French-Canadians felt it might be safer to keep the right to change this section far away in London instead of trusting it anywhere near the English-Canadians. Newfoundland, which had relapsed from its self-governing status and become a Crown Colony during the thirties because of financial difficulties, voted in 1949 to join Canada. In 1950 a conference of Commonwealth foreign ministers at Colombo decided to set up a plan for mutual financial assistance, which provided the framework for aid for the newly independent Asian members.

A more important question for the continuance of the Commonwealth arose when India wanted to become a Republic. In constitutional theory the Commonwealth was a unity because the King was the Head of State of all the member-nations and the Governors-General acted as his representatives. The Indian decision awakened some emotional opposition in England, but the serious question was whether India wanted to remain a member of the Commonwealth. The Commonwealth Prime Ministers at the 1949 conference assured Nehru that remaining a member would not compromise India's independence of action and would provide her with useful diplomatic contacts. India became a Republic and stayed in the Commonwealth; the King gave up his title of Emperor of India but took up the new title of Head of the Commonwealth.

India's presence in the Commonwealth was among other things a source of steady pressure on England not to become too committed in the Cold War. Throughout the period of greatest tension between Russia and America the Commonwealth had to consider the feelings of India as a non-aligned country, and this helped to explain the moderating role which England and Canada tried to play. On the other hand Pakistan was led by her dispute with India over Kashmir to align herself for a time with the West, in the hope of receiving diplomatic support.

The Cold War

But although the Commonwealth had a moderating effect, there was no doubt about England's position between America and Russia. Marshall Aid had no specific political conditions, but the recipients were clearly under some sort of obligation to the United States. In February 1948 the Communist ministers in Czechoslovakia carried out a *coup d'état* and dragged the country into alliance with Russia. The coup demonstrated that it was unwise to give Communists control of the police, but it was not conclusive proof that Russia intended to march west, just as England's intervention in Greece did not mean that she had aggressive intentions in the Balkans. Nevertheless, people were afraid that Russian armies were going to advance to the west. Attlee believed that the United States did not take the Russian threat seriously until free access through East Germany to the American, British, and French sectors of Berlin was blocked in 1948.[1] England and the United States responded by flying in supplies, and after 10 months the Russians gave way and allowed free access again. This conflict was managed skilfully by England and the United States, and it encouraged the western countries to come together. Agreements were made in 1949 which set up the North Atlantic Treaty

[1] Francis Williams, *A Prime Minister Remembers* (1961), 172.

Organization for an initial period of twenty years, which could be renewed; all the signatories gave mutual guarantees of each other's territory, though not of their colonial possessions. The Treaty contained provisions for economic co-operation, but in the event the nations of the alliance worked through the Organization for European Economic Co-operation when they wanted to co-ordinate their economic policies.

The government responded to the military needs of the alliance by starting a programme of rearmament and increasing the period of national service to 18 months. This stretched the British economy even further, but was not beyond the country's powers. The ideal of a united Europe had emerged as an important force on the other side of the Channel, but the government did not believe that Englishmen really wanted to surrender any of their sovereignty to a European Parliament and showed practically no interest in the meetings of the Council of Europe at Strasbourg. The Opposition was more willing to take an interest; Churchill went to Strasbourg and was given the applause due to the greatest living European. He had spoken of England at the centre of three circles, the English-speaking world, the Commonwealth, and Europe, by which he meant that England would mediate between the United States and the countries of Europe and the Commonwealth. The post-war government continued to be America's closest ally, and paid considerable attention to changes in the Commonwealth, but while it took some interest in Europe the interest was that of an outsider.

It seems unlikely that foreign policy could have been any different under a Conservative government. An even more active foreign policy would have strained the economy too far, and it seems unlikely that the Conservatives would have pursued a less active policy. Churchill said fierce things about the granting of independence to India, and possibly he would have involved England in an attempt—almost certainly hopeless —to resist the change. The Conservatives at times suggested that they would get on better than the Socialists with the Americans. It was true that American Congressmen complained from time to time at paying for the excesses of the Welfare State, but if the Conservatives had been in power the Americans would have complained at paying for the British Empire—if anything, relations were less likely to go wrong because the Labour government understood why Americans were suspicious of it; Americans found British imperialists particularly irritating because they never understood what American anti-imperialism was all about. At a more personal level, Churchill was for most people, a more attractive person than Attlee, but whoever was Prime Minister of England in the late 1940s had to establish good relations with Truman and Nehru, and it is at least possible that Churchill would have failed disastrously with both of them. Attlee was ideally suited for getting on with them. Under Bevin the Foreign Office emerged from the obscurity into which it had fallen after Eden's resignation in 1938, but it was greatly helped by the good relations Attlee had with a number of heads of government.

Domestic policy of the Labour government

In domestic affairs the difference between government and Opposition was sharp—perhaps all the sharper because on issues of foreign policy the Labour Front Bench seemed to Conservatives to be such reasonable and moderate people. The Opposition thought of the Parliamentary Labour party as an uneasy alliance of sound men like Bevin and wild men like Bevan. On foreign policy Bevin and Attlee defied the left wing of their party; on domestic affairs, so it seemed, they were dragged at the chariot wheels of the Labour left. This picture was not accurate. The Labour party was, measured by the normal standards of parties of the left, unusually united on domestic affairs. However much the men of the left might feel that Bevin was playing the American or the Arab game, they had no doubt that he was a good Socialist. One of the things that kept the Labour party together was the great mass of legislation placed before the Commons. In the 1940s Labour M.P.s never had as much time for internecine quarrels as in the 1950s.

The mass of legislation passed by the Labour government has been called a social revolution. It seems more useful to call it legislation against a counter-revolution. In the First World War a good many of the developments which became permanent in the 1940s were foreshadowed, but after the war most of this was swept away. Governments in the 1920s wanted to get back to 'before the war' and, if they did not succeed in this impossible aim, at least they reduced the power of the trade unions, made sure that the State would not go very far in providing welfare services and forced the government to retire from the central role in the economy which it had played during the war years. Between 1945 and 1951 the temporary developments of the Second World War were established as normal parts of English life. There was some reaction against this in the 1950s, but by then very few people really thought it was possible or desirable to go back to 'before the war'. In 1945 there was a good deal of enthusiasm for a brave new world, but one of the most clearly defined features of the brave new world was that it should avoid the evils of the 1930s.

The most controversial legislation of the Labour government was the nationalization programme, but even here the political resistance was slight. The Conservatives did not find it easy to understand what had happened in the election, and were desperately afraid that strenuous opposition would only make them more unpopular. The Bank of England was taken over with no trouble at all; most capitalist countries already had state-run central banks, and Churchill fairly clearly thought there were good arguments for nationalization. In fact, there was so little debate that nobody asked what difference nationalization would make. It was hard to see what would be altered by changing the way in which the Governor of the Bank was chosen, if the Governor was always to be a banker with a banker's concern for the soundness and international standing of sterling. A dominant Chancellor of the Exchequer with a policy of his own could impose it on the Bank as Cripps asserted when he said 'The Bank is my creature',[1] but then a Chancellor with a policy might have imposed it on Norman between the wars. Keeping the airlines nationalized was even less controversial: nobody thought a private company could run them without a subsidy, and if the government chose to run them itself nobody would object and the aircraft manufacturers would probably feel safer financially.

The two classic issues of nationalization were coal and the railways. They had been in Labour party programmes for many years, the workers in the two industries were strongly in favour of the step, and the owners were not really in a position to resist. Both industries had done badly between the wars, and had not been able to spend much money on development during the war. The railway lines and the rolling stock were worn down, the mines were running into difficult seams and needed new equipment. Large-scale capital investment was required in both cases, but both industries were declining and offered unattractive prospects to private industry. Really far-sighted men might see that in ten or twenty years' time both industries would be sinking back into their inter-war state of depression. But until that happened coal-mining and rail transport were two of the most vital parts of the economy. There was a good case for nationalizing these industries that owed nothing to the general case for socialism.

Yet it was the performance of these two industries that did more than anything else to reduce enthusiasm for public ownership, and this played its part in weakening the Labour government. Vesting day for the coal industry was 1 January 1947. The flag of the National Coal Board went up

---

[1] A. Shonfield, *British Economic Policy since the War* (1958), 213. But Shonfield went on: 'More to the point is the remark made to me subsequently by a Conservative politician with more exact knowledge of the inner workings of the institution: "Somebody may have to nationalise the Bank of England one of these days; the Socialists don't know how."'

at the pitheads; the miners' long fight against the owners was over. But the first few months of 1947 were the coldest the country had had for over sixty years. The government estimated that only another 2m. tons of coal (in a national production of 200m. tons) were needed to avoid disaster, but the coal did not come; trains could not run, factories had to close down and for a few weeks unemployment returned to the levels of the 1930s and housewives found gas and electricity flowing at such low pressure that a simple meal took hours to cook. Obviously the Coal Board could not have transformed the situation within six weeks of taking office, but equally obviously the public was looking for someone to blame. As a result public opinion was hostile to the nationalized industry ever afterwards. Supporters of the free play of the market must have been amused by the way the Coal Board's attempts to keep down prices added to its troubles. Although coal prices had gone up faster than most during the war, prices could certainly have been raised again after nationalization because there was a large unsatisfied demand. Prices were kept down to check inflation and to provide assistance to British manufacturers so demand continued to be high: there were complaints that the coal-miners were betraying the country, and there were also complaints that the Coal Board was not running at a profit. Small coal was sold at a high price which was used to subsidize the sales of large coal, and people complained that the mines produced too much small and dirty coal and not enough large clean lumps. The miners had enjoyed wage rises during the war which brought them back to something like their pre-1914 position as aristocrats of labour; it was not surprising, particularly when there was so little they could buy with their high wages, that they took more time off than before. The five-day week, with no work on Saturday mornings, was one of the aims of trade unionists at the time and was becoming established in a number of industries. The Coal Board accepted it for the mines. So great was the demand for coal that this concession was withdrawn; union leaders went round their men persuading them that their union and their government depended on them to give up their Saturday mornings. This was a fair enough account of the state of the balance of payments, and the miners went back to a five-and-a-half day week, but there was an understandable increase in absenteeism and in unofficial strikes, and a sharp fall in the miners' initial feeling that the National Coal Board was on their side in a way the owners could never be.

On the railways the story was much the same. There had been complaints before the war about the way they ran, and they had been having difficulty making a profit, mainly because road transport was providing formidable competition in almost every field of operation—the transport of heavy loads of coal was work for the railways, but almost everything else could be done by lorries, by cars, or by buses. The growth of the Transport Workers' Union and the decline of the National Union of Railwaymen reflected this change. During the war the petrol shortage and the need to move great quantities of troops and weapons round the country restored the position of the railways. The Transport Act took over everything that ran on wheels for profit except for short-distance road haulage, lorries used by companies for their own products, and municipal bus companies. This allowed the Transport Commission to think in terms of subsidizing rail traffic from road profits, but passengers noticed that trains ran late, were dirty, and sometimes were cancelled. The railways received no credit for the fact that fares had risen rather less than most other things, and any increase in fares drove customers away. As a result the railways had no financial room for manœuvre.

Both coal and the railways gave the critics of nationalization plenty of opportunity to complain and to blame the principle for the failures of these two industries to provide the quality of service that people wanted. The weaknesses that had made nationalization a necessary step also made it certain that customers would be dissatisfied. Capital was provided for making up arrears of maintenance work, and probably this could not have been done by anyone except the government. Coal production went up, though not as fast as had been hoped. The difficulty was that older miners were retiring and young men felt no great desire to go down the mines. The government assured them that there would be no return to the 1930s and that this time employment in the mines would be secure, but even this did not tempt enough people into mining.

Electricity and gas were taken over with much less trouble in the course of 1948. This did not require any great changes: electricity was already integrated into a single system by the government-operated central grid, and both gas and electricity were in many cases produced by municipal authorities. Gas was at the time a declining industry, and electricity required capital on a very large scale. In industries like this the case for nationalization was admitted to be strong. The Opposition pointed to the failure of nationalization to produce any dramatic improvement in coal or the railways, but did not seem completely confident that private enterprise could run either of the public utility industries.

The only intense struggle in Parliament over the principle of nationalization came over the steel industry. The fight was all the more bitter because there were disputes inside the government about the need for nationalization and about the form it should take. The Bill was not introduced early enough to pass the House of Commons in three successive sessions, but in the 1947–8 session a Bill amending the 1911 Parliament Act was intro-duced instead: this Bill reduced the length of the Lords' veto by a year, and as it was made applicable from the date of its introduction into the Commons, the iron and steel nationalization Bill which was introduced in the 1948–9 session could be passed into law, despite the Lords, before the 1945 Parliament dissolved. The Lords had not previously done much to hinder the Labour legislative programme; Lord Beaverbrook had rallied some opposition against the American loan, but on most issues they had followed the leadership of Lord Salisbury and accepted the Bills sent to them from the Commons without any attempt at drastic amendment. On the iron and steel Bill they did, as had been foreseen, take a more active line, though even on it they were mainly concerned to make sure that the Bill did not come into effect until after the general election which would have to be held in 1950. The steel Bill was not a drastic piece of legislation. It took over the shares of the companies in the steel business, and set up a unifying central board, but this was not accompanied by changes in the organizational structure of the industry. No doubt when new plant had to be installed the board would have taken decisions that reflected some approach to central planning, but it was a form of public ownership which could very easily be reversed.

The nationalization Acts were regarded by many people as the distinctively Socialist part of the government's programme, though of course the way in which it ran the economy might also be included in that category, and the repeal of the 1927 Trade Disputes Act in 1946, one of the first pieces of legislation of the new Parliament, was a symbolic gesture of good will that the trade union leaders valued. But there was in addition a considerable amount of legislation based on wartime reports and recom-mendations. Most of it lay in the areas of reforms to which the pre-1914 Liberal party had been moving before it disintegrated into internecine struggles.

By 1949 it was accepted that Britain was a 'Welfare State'. The phrase was widely used, outside Britain as well as inside, and inside Britain it was always used in tones of approval; Liberals and Conservatives pointed out that their parties had also played a part in building the Welfare State. The contribution of the Labour party was the 1946 National Insurance Act and the accompanying National Health Service Act, which was in fact the enactment of the Beveridge Report. There were one or two small changes; Beveridge's idea that old-age pensions should rise slowly for a period of twenty years was abandoned, and the pensions began at a level intended to enable men over 65 and women over 60 to manage without going to the National Assistance Board unless special circumstances arose. The scheme of a single unified payment for flat-rate benefits assured everybody of a right to a subsistence income without any means test. It also assured people of support in time of unemployment: though unemployment did not return to anything like the level of the 1920s and 1930s the fear of it hung in the air for some years, and everybody was anxious to guard against it.

The distinctive feature of the British Welfare State was the health service. The basic principle was that no money was to be paid for anything to do with medicine. Hospitals were given grants by the government, and this almost eliminated the tiresome practice of flag-days for collecting money from passers-by in the street. Some hospital governors complained that the voluntary principle was being removed, but this aroused very little response. False teeth, spectacles, and medical prescriptions were provided free of charge, and there was an immense immediate demand for them. Critics of the health service suggested that this was wasteful and that people were getting things they did not need. It seems more likely that these patients had not previously been able to afford them: the working-class budgets of the 1930s contain little allowance for medical expenses apart from the cost of insurance for medical consultation.

The serious resistance to the health service came from the doctors. The hospital consultants on the whole felt their interests had been looked after, and they were not sorry to see the fund-raising side of hospital activity become less important. The general practitioners were more unhappy. They were asked, under the scheme, to form practices of 1,000 to 3,000 patients each, for which they received from the Ministry of Health a basic fee and a payment for each patient. Most doctors received a higher income under this arrangement than they had earned previously, but they were afraid that the system might later be converted into a salaried service or that they might lose their right to remain in private practice or that the Minister of Health might use his financial position to dictate on medical issues, such as telling them what drugs to use for particular diseases. The dispute was ludicrously like that of 1911. On the one hand a Welsh minister in charge of the scheme, with a gift for organizing things smoothly and easily but a taste for victory rather than conciliation in debate. On the other hand doctors uneasy about the future, led by medical politicians who were much more intransigent than the men they led. The same votes, in December 1946 and February 1948, to refuse to act inside the service; the same realization that, whatever the votes might say, a doctors' strike was not practicable. Assurances were given on the detailed points in dispute, and doctors were allowed to keep private patients; the patients could arrange to be treated outside the service or be given a private bed in a hospital by paying for it. The health service started work on 5 July 1948.

Critics of the service attacked the great amount of money being spent on it. Some of their points were understandable; the service was free to everybody from all over the world, and this internationalism seemed over-generous. Some of their criticism simply ignored the steady rise in all prices, and judged the health service as though it ought to run on a constant amount in money terms. The politicians tacitly agreed that the health service should year by year receive just under 4 per cent of the national income. More expensive and more effective drugs such as penicillin and the antibiotics were coming into use and in other coun-tries the proportion of national income devoted to medical expenses showed a tendency to go up. The national health service may have provided the same real services at a lower cost than elsewhere, but on the other hand the fear of asking for a larger share of the national income to be spent on the service at a time when medical costs and medical salaries were going up may have had a bad effect on the nation's medical system.

The pre-1939 foundations of the Welfare State were not always easy to trace, but the 1948 Criminal Justice Act was clearly related to earlier discussions, for it was based on the draft Bill that had been prepared before the war but not discussed. The Act moved towards greater leniency for criminals; flogging was virtually abolished, the probation service was extended and an attempt was made to reduce the danger that conviction and imprisonment for young offenders would simply initiate them into the world of crime. The Opposition in Parliament accepted this without too much discussion, but at Conservative party conferences for some years afterwards ferocious women delegates would rise to ask for flogging to be brought back. On a free vote in the Commons an amendment was passed to abolish capital punishment; as was the case throughout the struggle over capital punishment in the next twenty years, the bulk of the abolitionists were Labour M.P.s, the bulk of the retentionists were Conservative. When the Bill came to the House of Lords the capital punishment amendment was defeated, and the original Bill was then accepted. At this stage, the bishops were strongly retentionist; probably the view of the bench of bishops changed more completely during the years of discussion than that of any other parliamentary group. Other changes in the law allowed citizens to sue the government as of right, instead of having to ask the government for permission to sue, and extended the system of legal aid to cover civil cases. This helped increase the divorce rate.[1] Undoubtedly there would have been an increase after the war because wartime marriages were sometimes hasty, and some marriages had broken down under the stress of wartime separation; people's way of looking at life and marriage had been changed, but legal aid made it easier to give recognition to this change.

The old question of the land reappeared, though in a less controversial form than in the 1910s or the 1960s. The Agriculture Act of 1947 put the marketing boards and subsidies for farmers, which had been developing over the past ten or fifteen years and had grown so important during the war, into a permanent form. It allowed eventual dispossession of a farmer for bad husbandry, but in every other way it was designed to make the position gained by the farmers during the war secure; there is an argument whether the working class actually became better off during the war, but farmers undoubtedly had become better off and the 1947 Act stabilized their gains. It was said that only after the Act had been passed did they become rich enough to pay their Conservative party membership fees. Dalton, as Chancellor of the Exchequer, strengthened the National Trust and made it easy to give property of historical or artistic importance to the nation in lieu of death duties. In 1947 the Town and Country Planning Act tried to deal with the old problem of increment in land values that Lloyd George and Snowden had tried to tackle. The Act declared that all future increment in land value caused by development was the property of the State, and set up a fund of £300m. to compensate landowners whose land might go up in price as a result of development, if this potential increase had not yet been realized.

Quite apart from this massive legislative programme, the Labour government had to run the country, and in the circumstances of 1945 the first task was to make the economy work efficiently on a peacetime basis. Dalton was convinced of the virtues of low interest rates. He had praised cheap money in his pre-war book on public finance, and when he took office he was determined to carry his policy into effect. For eighteen months or so he was fairly successful. The war had been financed with loans at 3 per cent; in 1946 Dalton issued irredeemable government stock paying $2\frac{1}{2}$ per cent, the rate offered by Goschen in the

[1] D. E. Butler and A. Sloman, *British Political Facts 1900–1975* (1975) gives figures for divorces on p. 266:

1910	1920	1930	1940	1950	1960	1970
801	3,747	3,944	8,396	32,516	25,672	62,010

1890s. This could be managed only by allowing a larger and larger proportion of the government's debts to take the form of short-term
obligations. Dalton was not particularly worried by this, because it built
up a high level of demand, which was what he wanted. The cold weather
and fuel crisis early in 1947 brought the extreme version of this policy to
an end, but the nationalization compensation was paid in 3 per cent
stock and the combination of a high level of demand and a very liquid
government debt was maintained throughout the Labour government's
period of office. Dalton's budgets began by reducing taxes because military
expenditure was diminishing. But while the general level of income-tax
went down, the level of supertax went up, so that rich people were no
better off. Dalton wanted to restore the death duties to something of their
former importance. They had contributed about 10 per cent of the
national revenue ever since the beginning of the century, but during the
Second World War they had fallen to 3 per cent of national revenue.
Dalton's increase of the rate of duty did for a short time raise its contribution. The improvement did not last for long; mainly because of the
increasing ingenuity of property-owners in handing on their money before
death, the yield of the duties slipped back to the level of 3 per cent of
total revenue.

Dalton's boisterous personality made people think he was deliberately
following an inflationist policy. A remark he made about allotting money
to help depressed areas 'with a song in his heart' was misapplied to
suggest that he was spending money light-heartedly in all directions.[1]
There was a great deal of suppressed demand in the system from war
savings, and he was only concerned that it should push the economy
forward without worrying too much about its effect on prices. His budgets
were much less inflationary than those produced just after 1918, and he
knew that the country's foreign exchange position had to be protected.
Probably he underestimated the dangers of convertibility, though he may
simply have felt that it was a necessary condition of the loan which was
generally recognized to be indispensable. After convertibility had to be
abandoned in the summer of 1947, deflationary measures were prepared,
and Dalton introduced a budget in the autumn. This had been done only
once before in peacetime, in 1931, and the comparison underlined the
fact that a real crisis existed. Dalton genially told a reporter just before
he went into the Commons that the budget increased the profits-tax and
the purchase-tax; this was printed in the evening papers, and Dalton had
to resign on account of his indiscretion.

[1] H. Dalton, *Memoirs, 1945–1960* (1962), 110.

His successor Cripps was more austere in personality, and had a more dominant position in the Cabinet. The contrast in personality led people to overemphasize the differences in policy. Dalton's view that things were going well and the economy could be encouraged to move forward had been shared by the Cabinet, and in 1947 he had been prepared to increase taxes to improve the balance of payments. Cripps came to the Treasury at a time when the need for restraint was generally accepted. He did not remove excess demand from the economy completely, and to some extent he accepted the Daltonian approach of allowing demand to be high and relying on strict control of the supply side of the account. His 1948 budget increased the tax on tobacco to a height that was intended to reduce consumption and thus save foreign exchange. He also imposed a special levy on unearned income that rose at the highest level to £1·40 per pound received, which amounted to a small-scale capital levy. Cripps's puritanism of manner was ideally suited for the task of calling people for self-sacrifice and greater effort, and he obtained a considerable response. Manufacturers felt it was their duty to go out into export markets. For about thirty months from early in 1948 trade union leaders persuaded their followers not to press for wage increases, and real wages fell a little. Nobody enjoyed this period, and the word 'austerity' clung to it and the Labour party for some time to come; Cripps was not a man to make people enjoy things, but it is doubtful whether anyone could have made a struggle to maintain a sound balance-of-payments as exhilarating as 1940. Churchill was often witty at Cripps's expense—'there, but for the grace of God, goes God' caught Cripps's sense of mission rather well. But while people made jokes about Cripps, they were the jokes that schoolboys made about a headmaster behind his back.[1]

Under Dalton the process of planning had not been kept up in all its wartime rigour though individual items in short supply were controlled by allocation and licensing. Under Cripps planning was undertaken in an ambitious mood but it was not successful: the forecasts and targets were not reached, or sometimes were exceeded in a way which disturbed the general pattern of the plan. As the years went by, the forecasts became less sweeping and planning lost its high prestige. Devaluation released the economy from some overstrain but, whether an economy can be fully planned by using more modern techniques or not, the resources available in the late forties were probably not adequate for the problem of planning in peacetime. Planning in war was not so difficult, because the object was to produce a large but finite variety of products for the

[1] M. Sissons and P. French, editors, *The Age of Austerity* (1961), 179.

fighting forces by reducing supplies for civilian consumption. In peace-time the number of different products was much closer to being infinite, and no overriding objective could be set in the way that higher arms production had been the wartime objective. Nevertheless the Crippsian economy did produce more exports, a more controlled increase in prices than had been seen previously in the forties, and a relatively high rate of economic growth.

Opposition to the Labour government

The Labour government, with all this long list of achievements, was increasingly unpopular with some sections of the public. This unpopu-larity was not primarily a matter of grumbling about rationing; un-doubtedly people found rationing a tiresome restriction and queuing an annoying way to spend their time, but this was not the source of the deepest bitterness. Food rationing continued throughout the Labour government's tenure of office. The trivial concessions given by Ministers of Food at Christmastime—an ounce of butter extra, or the right to buy another twopence worth of meat—would have tested the patience of any population by reminding them of the possibility of plenty, and the fact that it was clearly not coming yet. Woolton had a gift for good public relations; his Labour successors had a gift for upsetting their public. Dr. Summerskill may have been perfectly correct when she pointed out that very few people could tell the difference between butter and margarine, but it gave the impression that she was not really interested in making sure that people would be able to indulge their preference for buying butter. Odd food, such as whalemeat, and odd food with odder names, such as snoek, were offered to the public; and were rejected. Such things, it was felt, might be expected of a government dominated by the image of the vegetarian Cripps.

But annoying though all this was, there is little sign that it affected many votes. The strident emotions of the period were felt by the people who had voted Conservative in 1945 and felt, as Evelyn Waugh the novelist put it, that living under a Socialist government was like living under an army of occupation. Insult, it should be remembered, was not a one-sided matter: paladins of the left, like Bevan who said the Tory party which imposed the Means Test was lower than vermin, or Shinwell who said that the rest of the country apart from the working class wasn't worth a tinker's cuss, caused quite understandable alarm, and some people were even more upset when they were told that Sir Hartley Shawcross had said: 'We are the masters now.' Members of the middle class, whose political judgement had perhaps been dulled by the war, mistook Sir

Hartley (who had been slightly misquoted) for the leader of a rebellious working class swarming forward to wipe out civilization in England.[1]

The opposition to the Labour government drew its strength from two rather different sources, which would have had some difficulty in working out a common policy if they had had to go into details. A great many people simply wanted to get back to before the war. At one level this meant having servants again; they had left for other jobs to an even greater extent than in the First World War, and had shown much less sign of coming back. People spoke as if they had all gone off to factories, a comment which suggests that servants were generally underrated; conscientious and tidy girls, who could have got the better jobs (and nobody ever complained about the servant problem without explaining that service in her house was one of the better jobs), went in for typing instead.[2] Members of the middle class who were really determined to get back to 'before the war' emigrated. At first they went to South Africa, and when Smuts's pro-British government was defeated by the Nationalist party in 1948 they went to Kenya or sometimes to Rhodesia instead. In any case Africa seemed to offer the prospect of servants, no income-tax to speak of and no rationing, and they shook the dust of Britain off their feet. This was a drastic answer, though to some extent it was only a re-emergence of the normal British habit of emigration, which had been in decline in the 1930s and during the war. Many people were worse off than they had been before the war, though their position did not deteriorate under the Labour government and their complaints about their financial problems were an assertion that the government ought to be doing something to restore their previous position.

In aggregate terms, the shape of income distribution in the country had not altered much: before the war the top 10 per cent of the population had enjoyed 38 per cent of the national income (post-tax), and after the war the top 10 per cent enjoyed 30 per cent. The next 40 per cent had gained an extra 5 per cent of national income, and the rest had gained an extra 3 per cent. As the actual income to be distributed in the years just after the war was about the same as in 1938, the discontent of the top 10 per cent follows naturally enough from these figures.[3] But discontent was more widespread than this. Aggregate figures do not show how many people were worse off than before the war, because the people filling places in the top 10 or the top 50 per cent were not necessarily the people who had occupied these places before the war. Salaries in old-

---

[1] V. Brome, *Aneurin Bevan* (1953), 189; H. Hopkins, *The New Look* (1963), 154.
[2] Guy Routh, *Occupation and Pay in Great Britain 1906–60* (1965), 25 and 33.
[3] Dudley Seers, *The Levelling of Incomes since 1938* (1951), 39.

established occupations stayed more or less stationary, and did not keep up with the rising cost of living, nor did they increase enough to meet the additional income-tax demands. These people were likely to find they now earned less than skilled manual workers or people in new middle-class jobs, and they resented the change as well as disliking the actual limitation of their resources. The middle class apparently assumed that anybody who worked with his hands should get less than anybody who worked in a bank or an office; the rapid increase in the wages of, for instance, coal-miners during the war contradicted this assumption and led to discontent.

The other main body of opposition to the Labour government supported the free play of the market and untrammelled private enterprise and should have welcomed this development: coal-miners and coal were in short supply, and high wages might be the best way to produce more. In more general terms, the middle class had been overtaken by the laws of supply and demand. For about a century punctuality, literacy, and honesty with money had been in relatively short supply, and clerical salaries had reflected the fact. The demand for people to keep the books for firms and banks after industrialization had created a clerical middle class, but the qualities required were no longer in such short supply. The traditional middle-class occupations lost ground under Conservative as well as Labour governments, but of course just after the war the middle class did not see the problem in that way: it was assumed that the change was all the fault of socialism. *The Economist* put the view of this section of society concisely when it wrote that the middle class should have 'more than its numerical weight in British politics—instead of less, as at present'.[1]

People outside politics could afford to sound the trumpets for class warfare in this way, but the opposition in Parliament had decided not to resist the Labour legislation with any great determination, lest worse befall. As a result, while the rancour among some of the supporters of the Conservative party was as intense as at any time in the century except for the height of the Ulster crisis, resistance in the Commons was not as strenuous as in the 1906 Parliament. Finding out whether the middle class was in fact being neglected by the Labour government is more complicated. A Labour government could not devote itself to reversing the great relative improvement of the position of the working classes that had taken place under the wartime coalition, and to this extent the middle class was bound to feel ill treated. The prices of items for living in a specifically middle-class way went up faster than the working-class cost-

[1] *The Economist*, 14 Feb. 1948, quoted in W. G. Runciman, *Relative Deprivation and Social Justice* (1966), 130.

of-living index during the war and rose slower after the war, and apart from this slight relative gain, the middle classes did unexpectedly well out of the social welfare legislation of the Labour government.[1] A fair amount of this advantage came simply because they knew how to handle the machinery rather better than the working class, so they got all they were entitled to. But in addition the 1911 Insurance Act had been designed to help the manual worker and had assumed that the non-manual worker could look after himself; a good many salaried workers gained by entering the national scheme for health insurance, though this varied according to their previous arrangements. Probably the social changes of the 1940s affected the middle classes most sharply when the 1944 Education Act came into force, and here again people found their circumstances differed from case to case.

The Act carried into effect the proposals of the Hadow Report of 1926, which had laid down that children were divided into academically skilled, technically skilled, and practically minded groups. This happy discovery, which was in accordance both with Plato's theories and the existing organization of schools for education after 11, was accepted without too much argument. The examination by which poor boys had won scholarships to grammar schools was brought up to date by including intelligence tests, and became the universal examination on which everybody was classified. At the same time fees for secondary education were abolished. It might have seemed that this development was bound to help the middle classes, because they had been providing most of the children who went on to secondary education, and had usually been paying fees for this. But one reason why they had been paying fees was to make sure that their children did not go to the same schools as the mass of the population. So the abolition of fees brought very little comfort to them; parents who had been able to guarantee a little social exclusiveness for their children by paying fees and sending them to a grammar school had now to deal with a world in which the grammar school was less exclusive than before and in which their children might be consigned on their examination results to a secondary modern school. And there was never any doubt that this was not a happy fate. People talked about parity of esteem, and the 11+ examination was said to assess children's aptitude, but everybody knew that the examination was just the old examination for grammar school scholarships, and that going to a secondary modern school was a sign of failure. Some of the more thinly populated counties of Wales and some Labour councils with strong views about equality established comprehensive secondary schools to which all the children of the area went

---

[1] Dudley Seers, op. cit. 11–14.

without an examination. The middle class found even the limited egalitarianism of the 11 + examination, combined with abolition of fees, quite distasteful enough. Those who could afford it sent their children to private fee-paying schools, which led to a boom in public-school applications for entrance, and a great many new fee-paying schools were opened. Those who could not afford this way out were not likely to feel in any way reconciled to the Labour government.

There was a second main line of attack on the government, made by people who had no particular desire to get back to the past. Demands for economic liberalism and for a return to the free play of the market were made at both a theoretical and a practical level; at both levels they were sometimes reinforced by appeals to the lessons of the past, though this was not a necessary part of the argument. The theoretical case was that British industry was being tramelled and held back by controls and restrictions, and that if market considerations were allowed greater weight, everything would go much better. There is no evidence to prove this case. The British economy expanded rather faster under the Labour government's system of controls than it had done for any equally long peacetime period since 1873 at least. This does not show conclusively that the government was running the economy in the best possible way; the post-war period was an exceptional one, and rigidly committed supporters of the free market approach might say that the rate of growth fell in the 1950s, after the controls had been removed, because new and subtler problems had appeared that did not have to be faced in the late 1940s.

The relatively rapid expansion of the economy was in one sense the cause of the other, more general discontent with Labour's conduct of the economy. Any business man, contemplating his individual position in the late 1940s, realized that he could sell much more and increase his profits. The obstacle to this was the government: by restrictions on raw materials, by refusals to grant building licences when requested, and by insisting on detailed explanations of why a piece of development was desirable, the government stopped business men from going ahead and doing their job of making and selling things. The government's attitude was presented in its most unattractive light by Douglas Jay, who asked people to believe that the man from Whitehall knew best what should be done. This did not go down well. People had had enough of Whitehall; they wanted to be free to manage, or even to mismanage, their own affairs. Well-meant attempts to help, such as the government's proposal of Industrial Development Councils for each industry, were rejected.

But although any one business man, given a free hand, could have expanded his business very rapidly in the late 1940s, the government had to consider what would happen if all business men were allowed to expand at the same time. In the existing state of more-or-less repressed demand, the natural result would have been a brisk inflation which would have been brought to a speedly end either by shortage of materials or by government action to cause a deflation; the sequence of events of 1919–21 would have been repeated, and the government was determined not to have another slump like the one after the First World War. Imports were restricted, and were allocated by the government, but even if there had not been this limitation on production, there was the question of finding labour. The government, in its attempts to plan the economy, sometimes referred to 'bottlenecks', by which it meant items which were in short supply and were holding up the efforts of other producers. The shortage of steel, which was one of the materials which was in short enough supply to be handled by allocation, was a 'bottleneck' but the term could hardly be used to describe the fact that the whole of the labour force was employed and that in this sense there was a shortage of labour.

The pre-war unemployed had found jobs, though this did not ease the general situation as much as might have been expected. There were about a million fewer unemployed in 1948 than in 1938, but the government was employing about a million more people; about 400,000 more people in the armed forces, which were twice as large as in the year before the war, and about 600,000 more in the civil service, which was about 75 per cent larger than just before the war. The Opposition said the civil service should be cut, and Labour backbenchers said the armed forces should be cut, but until one or other of these steps was taken, employers had to make do with what there was. In the 1930s the labour force (taking employed and unemployed together) rose by about 10 per cent; in the 1940s it increased by about 3 per cent. There was not even the possibility of finding people anxious to leave declining trades, because no trades were declining. Agriculture had been placed on a sounder footing than before, and coal, textiles, and the railways, which contracted and supplied a good deal of additional labour for new industries in the 1950s, were all being encouraged in the late 1940s.

The government possessed some residual powers to direct labour, and could influence the flow through the Labour Exchanges, but this authority could not be used in a sweeping way. The system of controls and licences that limited the activity of business men was negative: it consisted of prohibitions. Positive commands to 'make this' or 'sell that' were harder to use, though some licences (particularly for steel) were given to firms on condition that they increased their exports. Positive commands to workers to go into particular jobs were equally hard to apply. Even so, the overall shortage of labour would have held back some industries. Business men in the 1930s had grown accustomed to a situation in which all the factors of production were readily available, but profits were hard to obtain, and had now been plunged into a different situation, in which profits were easy to obtain but the factors of production were in short supply. They wanted the best of both worlds, and blamed the government because this was not possible.

The business men and the people who wanted to get back to the pre-war world might be united in their detestation of the government, but turning their feelings into coherent political action presented some problems. The Conservative party had been badly shaken by the 1945 result, but applied itself with more resilience than most defeated parties to the work of reorganization. A good deal of its activity was really intended to ease the 'back to pre-war' section out of this frame of mind. Candidates' contributions to constituency funds were strictly limited, to eliminate the practice by which some of the safest Conservative seats had gone to men which could promise a thousand pounds a year to constituency funds. Policy documents like 'The Industrial Charter' were intended to show both the general public and the reactionary party members that industrial workers had rights which must be respected. Lord Woolton launched a public appeal, which was successful, for a million pounds; this freed the party from the fear of being controlled by a few wealthy contributors, or of having to depend on the generosity of people who hoped for honours, and it also showed the general public that the Conservative party was not an immensely wealthy organization. The Central Office now became distinctly richer than Transport House, and acquired a talented staff, quite a number of whom went forward to provide the more promising new recruits for the Conservative parliamentary party in the 1950s. The Conservatives accepted the Welfare State, though they disagreed with some items of the social policy of the Labour party: they would not have taken so firm a line with the doctors over the health service, and at the time of the harsh 1946–7 winter they suggested that the raising of the school-leaving age to 15, in September 1947, ought to be delayed. Nothing came of the suggestion, though the winter of 1947 was probably the moment at which the Conservatives began to feel they might win the next election.

They took more interest in local government elections than in the past. The electorate had become much more stable in its voting habits in parliamentary by-elections than in the past, and as a result the government lost no seats although in the opinion polls, which were beginning to be published regularly but were not yet taken seriously, the Conservatives were ahead from 1947 onwards. The Opposition had to build up its confidence by gaining ground in municipal elections, and had several successes, of which the most conspicuous was in London in 1949, when it won as many seats as the Labour party though the Labour party retained control, because it had a majority among the aldermen.

The press also attacked the government. The *Mail*, the *Express* and the *Telegraph* were strongly committed to the opposition, and the problems of the government were easier to attack in the press than anywhere else. The 'groundnuts' scheme was the best example of this. The government had decided to open up an area of East Africa to cultivation, for planting groundnuts. This would raise the economic level of the region and would provide a supply of vegetable fat for England—the policy of aid to under-developed countries was not yet really accepted, and the government had to show that the scheme would benefit people in England as well as raise the standard of living in East Africa. But while the principle of the scheme might be commendable, the area chosen was quite unsuitable and the undertaking eventually had to be closed down as an almost total loss. People were not yet accustomed to the idea of a peacetime government undertaking large-scale operations on which large-scale losses might be suffered, and it was an issue on which the government could be attacked effectively—the memory of it sank so deep into the minds of enthusiastic Conservatives that almost twenty years later, in the 1964 election, a Conservative heckler shouted 'groundnuts' at the leader of the Labour party.

The Labour government was disturbed by newspaper attacks, and set up a Royal Commission to inquire into the state of the press. It is hard to see what this Commission was intended to do; at the time the press was flourishing, and the papers that attacked the government were really doing no more than their readers and their proprietors wanted. No doubt the government would have preferred newspapers to be run by calm and impartial editors who found that there was always a great deal to be said for what the government was doing, but this was not what readers wanted at the time. They wanted denunciation. The Labour press was weak by comparison with the Labour vote; the Liberal press probably somewhat stronger than the Liberal vote.

The threat of novelty

Some of the feeling of hostility to the innovations of the Labour government may have been part of a general mood of hostility to novelty. There was a sharp fall from the high level of interest in literature and the arts that had developed during the war. Opposition to novelty and resurgent hostility were strikingly demonstrated at the time of the Picasso–Matisse exhibition at the end of 1945. By this time Picasso was the world's leading painter, and it would have been hard to name anyone else who unquestionably stood above Matisse. Nevertheless their exhibition was greeted with tirades of abuse which sounded exactly like the attacks on Roger Fry's exhibition in 1911. British artists were, at just about this time, beginning to emerge from the obscurity, not to say mediocrity, into which they had slipped from the time of Turner. It was only after the war that artists like Graham Sutherland began to win an established position and, in particular, to be accepted on the continent of Europe—the award to Moore of the prize for non-Italian sculptors at the 1948 Venice Biennale was a recognition that there was a British artist whose work was considered important outside the country. The enemies of Picasso and Matisse were not inspired by mere chauvinism: they disapproved of British art as well, and attempts by municipal authorities to beautify their towns by putting up sculpture often provoked objections—it was clear that a large number of people thought statues should be portraits, of a strictly representational type, and the idea of statues as art was still not universally acceptable. When Reg Butler won a competition for *The Unknown Political Prisoner* with an entry in wire, there were complaints from people who clearly thought that marble or bronze were the only materials worthy of a sculptor.

None of this resistance to modern art was new. The enemies of novelty obviously wanted to get back to the days before the war when, they imagined, there was no modern art, and their resistance was the last determined stand against artistic novelty. By the 1950s it was much harder to make public protests about something just because it was new, and enemies of innovation were no longer able to say 'I don't know much about art but I know what I like' without being laughed at. The war did, at least for a time, do something to elevate taste; whether this was through any real change or simply because the better writers and musicians were given facilities for publishing and performing that were not available to everybody is harder to say. It was during the war and particularly with the publication of *Four Quartets* that T. S. Eliot extended his reputation beyond the circle of the specialists and became nationally accepted as a leading poet. He went on to write verse plays and there was a short time, just after the war, when the success of his *Cocktail Party* and plays of Christopher Fry like *The Lady's Not for Burning* led critics to think that the revival of the English theatre might lie in the direction of verse drama with religious overtones. The rest of the theatre certainly needed something to make it more interesting, for it had firmly turned its back on all the changes since Ibsen and was devoting itself to 'well-made' plays in the tradition of Scribe and Sardou. The most talented of these commercial playwrights, Terence Rattigan, who later explicitly acknowledged his debt by writing a modernized version of Dumas's *La Dame aux Camélias*, exposed himself a little too frankly in the preface to his collected plays by announcing that he wrote his plays to appeal to the tastes and habits of Aunt Edna, a lady of great respectability and limited enthusiasm for new ideas. The confession did him no good, perhaps because it explained the situation too honestly for people to like it.

The theatre was firmly fixed as a minority entertainment, and an entertainment in which American musicals like *Oklahoma* and *Annie Get Your Gun* dominated the stage. In the years immediately after the war cinemas were doing wonderful business, and drew upon an almost universal audience. Cinemas primarily meant American films, and when the drain on currency led to the prohibitive duty imposed in 1947, the American companies protested; in March 1948 it was agreed that they could take out $17m. a year of their profits, but that anything more would have to stay in England. The government tried to encourage British film-making by laying down a quota: 45 per cent of films shown were to be British. The quota was too large for the existing Rank companies to fill satisfactorily. They were afraid of controversial and contemporary subjects and were rather too ready to take refuge in expensive historical productions. The film-making success of the late 1940s were the Ealing comedies produced by an independent company, which pleased everybody by showing English people to be kind-hearted, eccentric, and inefficient. The government tried to encourage film production by setting up a National Film Finance Corporation, drawn on mainly by Sir Alexander Korda's British Lion, but even at the height of the post-war cinema boom it was never very successful. Nobody seems to have thought it would change the pattern of entertainment much when the B.B.C. in 1946 resumed the television services which it had begun in a small way before the war.

The all-pervasive use of television was one feature of Orwell's nightmare of the future, *1984*. Orwell was an anarchist with a considerable gift for saying things that dominant intellectual opinion would be saying in two or three years' time; in the 1930s he had fought in the Civil War, and had returned with a dislike for both Communists and Fascists. He said, rather misleadingly, that he was a supporter of the Labour party. In the conditions of the 1940s socialism meant rationing and controls, and Orwell disliked this approach to life. In *Animal Farm* at the end of the war he had attacked the Communist rulers of Russia for betraying the ideals of the Revolution; Orwell was himself deeply attached to the ideals of the Revolution and his dislike for the methods of Stalinism was strengthened by this feeling of betrayal. But his book appealed to people who had no sympathy for the ideals of the Russian or any other Revolution, and was used to show that governments are all the same and there is no point in trying to change things. *1984*, his other really successful book, was also used to teach a lesson rather different from the one Orwell had in mind. The book was written on the assumption, for which Orwell himself had condemned James Burnham a few years earlier, that things would go much as they were at present, only worse. That meant continued rationing, shortages, and a perpetual state of war or preparation for war in which governments insisted on absolute obedience on the grounds that it was demanded by the needs of the struggle. The portrayal of the methods of 'thought-control' was particularly admired. In the diplomatic background of the story there was no sign that Orwell thought the capitalist powers in any way less bad than the Communist; the England in which Winston Smith was brainwashed was Airstrip One of an American Empire. However, the book was treated as an attack on Russia and on the shortages in England at the time, and so it was regarded by most people as an attack upon the left. Orwell's picture of the future turned out to be inaccurate, and Huxley's *Brave New World* (1932), which presented a good account of an affluent society, was a much better prediction of the future. But in terms of his political effect Orwell was much more important; any supporter of the Labour government who heard that Orwell was a Socialist must have asked to be saved from such friends. People were looking for an attack on the way of life into which people seemed to be settling in the 1940s; Orwell satisfied that need, and he also seemed in *Animal Farm* to justify the Cold War, although a good deal of *1984* argues that living in the conditions of the Cold War would be dangerous to freedom.

Orwell did not look at the English middle class, and while he disliked the sort of people who gave *Animal Farm* and *1984* an enthusiastic welcome, he did not write about them. The opposition to the Labour government was at its most intense in the levels of society written about by Angus Wilson; some of the short stories in *The Wrong Set* and his novel *Hemlock and After* give some idea of what life under 'the army of occupation' was like. Neither Wilson nor Orwell could be called innovators in novel-writing, but after the 1930s innovation ceased to be so predominant a concern of writers. It was not necessarily a sign of failure of talent, though it might be asserted that after 1930 or so there were no literary giants of the sort that had been flourishing in the first three decades of the century. Writers seemed relatively content with the techniques at their disposal, and this could perhaps be said in a more general sense. Among artists and writers innovation had been fashionable and not too difficult for most of the period from the turn of the century to the 1940s. Even though the innovations had not always been used to any great extent the artists and writers had been left rather exhausted by the process and now wanted a pause to rest and reconsider their position, at just about the time that their audience was preparing to accept novelty willingly.

11. *The afterglow* 1949–1956

THE first results of devaluation seemed highly satisfactory. British trade figures improved rapidly, and there were suggestions that the rate chosen had been too low and that a revaluation might be appropriate. The 'bonfire of controls' in November 1948 and March 1949 in which Harold Wilson, the President of the Board of Trade, cancelled a large number of economic restrictions, the ending of clothes rationing in 1949, and the steady reduction in the proportion of imports that came in under government bulk-purchasing schemes all showed that the Labour government was prepared to allow the economy to run more freely, while regulating the general level of demand and encouraging specific areas of expansion. Planning was immensely difficult, and in any case there was no real reason why planning had to be part of socialism—it would, after all, be possible to have a society in which all industry had been nationalized and all the rewards of industry were shared out in a socialist manner, and yet the different nationalized industries could compete or use their economic bargaining power against each other.

The Labour party did not look as if it was moving in this direction consciously, but by the end of the 1940s it was hard to see where it did intend to go next. Morrison argued strongly in favour of a policy which would appeal to the middle classes, but did not explain what positive proposals this policy would include. The left wing of the party wanted more nationalization, but apart from making sure that the steel Bill survived the Lords they could not find any industries whose nationalization would arouse any enthusiasm; sugar, water, and cement were on the list to be taken over, and it was hard to think of any of them as 'commanding heights of the economy'. Insurance was considered, but under pressure from the large army of collectors employed by the companies and by the co-operative societies, this was changed to a proposal for making all insurance companies into mutual companies, in which there were no shareholders and the policy-holders kept all the profits. This was not very exciting, but nobody had any better suggestions; Attlee never seems to have been very interested in ideas, and while Bevin was ready to take up new ideas, he was always too autocratic to give other people a chance to discuss proposals that he disapproved of. By 1950 the Labour party was becalmed, though unwillingness to change things may have suited the mood of the electorate very well. Attlee, Bevin, Cripps, and Morrison had been in high office for about ten years and were showing signs of strain.

An election had to be held by July 1950. Cripps thought that any budget produced just before an election would look like an attempt to influence the vote, and he carried Attlee with him. So an election was briskly called and held in February. A slightly later election, held at a pleasanter time of year when people had had a little longer to see that devaluation was working out rather well, would have been tactically wiser for the government. The 1950 election was held in a mood of looking back to the past, back to the immediate past but also back to the 1930s. The Conservatives reminded everyone how unpleasant the post-war years had been, with rationing, drabness, shortages in all directions, and restrictions that left people feeling they were not allowed to do their best to help themselves. Their tactics were to accept the whole of the Welfare State and to suggest that the way forward must now be to set the people free to work out their own salvation. The Labour reply did not place much reliance on new policy proposals; they pointed to the complete and continued disappearance of the grinding unemployment of the 1930s, to the establishment of the Welfare State, and to the reorganization of British industry. To the complaints about rationing they replied with the slogan 'Fair Shares for All'.

This defence was fairly successful; despite the efforts of Woolton and the modernizers, the Conservatives attracted only 4 per cent more of the electorate than in 1945. The Liberals made a great effort, and put up 475 candidates, but so many of them lost their deposits that the chief effect was to make the party look silly. The Labour party held its ground with relatively little loss of votes, and might in normal circumstances have claimed that it had received enough popular support to show that its policy had been accepted. However, the electoral system made the answer more complicated. The 1948 Representation of the People Act had brought plural voting to an end, by abolishing the twelve university seats and the business franchise, which affected about ten seats. This helped the Labour party. On the other hand the redistribution of seats told against it: a large proportion of the Labour votes came from impregnable mining areas where they were in a sense wasted. In 1945 this had been compensated for by the over-representation of slum areas which were safe Labour seats with small electorates. The 1948 Act redistributed these seats out of existence, and so created the situation, which held good throughout the 1950s, that if the Labour party polled 2 per cent more of the total vote than the Conservatives, the two parties would emerge with equal numbers of seats in the Commons. In 1950 the Labour party was 2·6 per cent ahead, but it was also hampered by Communist opposition in marginal seats. The Communist party has never, before or since, had as much effect on the electoral situation; its intervention presented the Conservatives with up to four seats.

	Votes	Seats	% of all votes cast
Conservative	12,502,567	298	43·5
Liberal	2,621,548	9	9·1
Labour	13,266,592	315	46·1
Other	381,964	3	1·3

The government had an effective majority of 6, and it was ill placed for passing contentious legislation, but in fact it was more concerned to build itself a position on which it could fight the next election by steps like ending petrol rationing. These preparations had to be laid aside in June when war broke out in Korea. Because the Soviet Union was at that time boycotting meetings of the U.N. Security Council, the United States and her allies were able to pass a resolution enabling the U.N. to come to the assistance of South Korea when it was invaded by North Korea. Here, it seemed, was the conclusive proof of the aggressive intentions of the Soviet Union, and it was the duty of the United States and her allies to resist. The British government did not hesitate, and committed troops to the U.N. force. Throughout the war the American contribution was much larger than that of any of her allies and although the British was the next largest it was not really comparable; this sometimes led to misunderstandings because the British did not always realize the depth of the American commitment or the extent to which the Americans thought the war was the most important of the world's problems.

Apart from the direct cost of the British military contribution, the war also meant that prices of raw materials went up. Importers were at the time running down stocks as the government was reducing its role in purchasing. Bulk-purchasing had meant that the government always held, or was committed to holding, large stocks of commodities. Private traders were confident they did not need such large stocks, or perhaps could not afford to hold them. For most of the 1940s and 1950s British bulk-purchasing policy fitted the trading conditions very well. Long-term contracts made by a single purchaser on a rising market were the best way to hold back the rise as much as possible, and if individual purchasers had gone into the market they would probably have been played off against each other by the sellers. The Canadian wheat agreement of 1946, by which the British bought on favourable terms on the grounds that the price of wheat might suffer from a post-war slump, was so advantageous that as the market price went up and up the Canadian government became less and less inclined to enter another agreement. When the Korean war was over, prices of food and raw materials slid steadily downwards, and in these new conditions it was probably easier to drive the price down quickly for British consumers when the purchasing for them was being done by individual purchasers buying on a relatively small scale.

The experience of the Korean War suggests that bulk-purchasing was given up a year or two earlier than was wise. The decline in stocks in 1950, because the government was buying less and traders were ready to work with smaller reserves, led to a large surplus in the balance of payments. But stocks had to be built up again in 1951 and by then prices were even higher, so the money ran out even faster than it had come in. The large 1950 surplus seemed to show that the government had been justified in giving up Marshall Aid at the end of the year and saying that the British economy could stand on its own feet. The experience of 1951 was a nasty reminder that the problems had not all been solved. Some commentators added to the gloom by saying the price of raw materials would go on rising, so that the terms of trade would steadily move against exporters of industrial goods, which would be more unpleasant for England than for almost any other country. As it turned out, the Korean war price-rise was the last stage in the advance of the 1940s, and it would not have been nearly so severe if the United States had not begun an immense stockpiling programme at the same time as she was preparing for war. The programme stimulated producers of raw materials but after the war they were left with their new mines that had just come into production when war demand was falling, the market was overshadowed by the U.S. stockpile, and prices fell sharply.

Bulk-purchase or no bulk-purchase, there was not much that the British could do about the increase in commodity prices. Wage stability, which had been maintained by co-operation between trade union leaders and the government since mid-1947, came to an end late in 1950. The balance of payments was bound to come under some pressure as a result. But the government had undertaken in addition a large rearmament programme. About 7 per cent of the national income was already being spent on armaments before the Korean war began, which was by pre-1939 standards a high peacetime level. In the first rearmament discussions, in August, the government agreed to a three-year plan to spend £3,400m. which would raise the proportion to 10 per cent. Quite apart from a general fear of Russian aggression, European countries were afraid that the United States was going to become so interested in the war in Korea and the problems of the Far East that she might lose interest in Europe; American representatives at the negotiations reminded the various European countries about the dangers of a relapse into isolationism which, however unwelcome to the Administration, might be forced on it by the pressure of opinion. If Europe was to be helped, ran the argument, she must show that she was ready to help herself. France, with a large Communist party and a shaky currency, could not take the lead; Germany was still distrusted after the war. If any country was to prove to the American people that Europe was a worthwhile investment, it had to be England. The United States felt able at this stage to pledge additional aid to assist with the rearmament programmes of her European allies.

Willingness to co-operate with the United States carried with it a certain amount of power to influence the policy of the United States. The U.N. force pressed forward into North Korea and advanced towards the Chinese border. When the Chinese moved to help the North Koreans, General MacArthur, the American commander of the U.N. force, suggested widening the scope of the war by bombing China. This alarmed people in England, and in America's other European allies. Attlee flew to Washington early in December 1950, and put to Truman the arguments against widening the war. It is impossible to tell how important this was: Truman implied in his memoirs that he had already decided what to do, and when reminiscing Attlee suggested that his own intervention was decisive. Truman went on to dismiss MacArthur and make it clear that the war was to be limited to the defence of South Korea. When the Chinese army threatened to engulf the U.N. forces, the question of military effort came up for discussion again. The European countries were once more asked to show that they were whole-hearted in their desire to save themselves from Communist expansionism, and once more England was asked to play the leading role. The government agreed, and in February 1951 undertook a three-year plan which would involve military expenditure of £4,700m., which came to 14 per cent of the national income.

The government that faced this new and heavy task looked rather different from the one that had gained so slender a majority in February 1950. Cripps had broken down under the strain, and had resigned in October, to be succeeded by Hugh Gaitskell, a professional economist who was disliked both by the Conservatives and by the left wing of the Labour party for his public school and academic background. By early 1951 Bevin was too ill to run the Foreign Office, and was succeeded by Morrison. The effect of the changes was to make the government slightly more middle class, slightly less imaginative, and slightly more right wing, and to leave Bevan feeling ignored because he had been given neither of these important posts. The Conservative opposition became fiercer, and tried to wear the government out by keeping the House of Commons sitting late at night.

Gaitskell approached the task of drawing up his budget for 1951 with great technical skill. Dalton and Cripps had gone a long way to taking the excess demand out of the economy by running budget surpluses on current account, but it was never completely demonstrated that they understood the relationship between real resources and the money accounts of the budget. Gaitskell did understand and, if the military preparations were to be made, his budget was the best possible way to provide the money without generating inflation inside the country. Prices had already begun to go up, because import prices were going up so quickly, and the Chancellor declined to increase the food subsidies because this would have meant additional taxation; he had raised the standard rate of income-tax by $2\frac{1}{2}$p to $47\frac{1}{2}$p in the pound and felt that this was as much as people would stand. He also limited government expenditure on the health service by imposing charges on prescriptions, on spectacles, and on false teeth. This was too much for Bevan, who resigned at the sight of his creation being put on a cash basis. In his resignation speech he referred not only to the health charges, but also to the possibility that the strain of rearmament was going to make it difficult for western countries to continue to run their affairs democratically. Harold Wilson, who followed him out of the government, gave as his reason for resignation his fear that the new £4,700m. rearmament programme was going to be too much of a strain on the economy.

On the economic point at issue Wilson was right. The budget was a skilful exercise in providing the financial conditions for a transfer of real resources, but in some areas the resources could not be moved quickly and in others—supply of raw materials, supply of skilled engineers, supply of plans to work on—they were simply not available. The American government, with its immensely superior purchasing power, had priced the other countries out of the market. Rearmament primarily affected a single sector of the economy, engineering and metal-working, and doubling the national expenditure on defence meant that this sector was being subjected to a great strain. At the same time the labour market was made less flexible by the extension of national service to a two-year period, which reduced the number of young men available at the time of their lives when they would be readiest to move to new jobs.

The economy creaked and groaned under the pressure of the shift to military production and, as it turned out, away from the export trades. To some extent the balance of payments could be improved by cutting down on imports, but the country was not importing so many luxury goods that this could be done at all easily. A cut in imports meant a cut in food rations. From the summer of 1951 onwards the general balance-of-payments position was made worse by the other countries in the Sterling Area who ran deficits on their trade. They were perfectly entitled to do this, but it made life harder for the British government which, as banker for the whole Sterling Area, had to meet the deficits out of the pool of the Area's assets.

The government had not quite run out of ideas. Wage restraint was urged once more, and after appeals to companies to practice a correspond-ing restraint in dividend increases, legislation to freeze dividends was prepared. Measures were also prepared for abolishing the practice of resale price maintenance by which manufacturers and wholesalers pre-vented retailers from reducing prices. A further difficulty had arisen in the Middle East; at the end of April 1951 the government of Iran nationalized the oil refinery that the Anglo-Iranian Company, most of whose shares were owned by the British government, had built at Abadan. The Iranian Prime Minister, Dr. Mossadeq, was at least by British standards emotional and unstable, and it was suggested that the government was being weak-kneed in not sending troops to recapture the refinery. Morrison, the Foreign Secretary, appears to have been in favour of such a step. The Opposition taunted the government for its weakness. In normal circumstances a government has a clear legal right to nationalize, as long as it pays compensation, but in 1933 the Iranian government had renounced the right to nationalize the refinery. On the other hand, landing a force would be a great military strain and might merely lead to the destruction of the refinery. Action, relying on the 1933 agreement, would have looked like a return to imperialism for undisguised financial motives; inaction was felt to be humiliating, and the loss of the refinery meant that expensive western hemisphere oil had to be imported instead.

By November the government was practically exhausted. There was no sign that things would improve soon, and the majority of six was finding it hard to maintain control of the Commons. An election would clear the air and, if it left the government in office, give an opportunity for repairing divisions in the party. The Conservative party continued to say it would set the people free, a line of approach designed to appeal to Liberals who had given up the struggle or had no candidate to vote for. It declared that a Conservative government would give people 'more red meat' as one of the incentives to work harder, which was undoubtedly attractive at a time when the meat ration was eightpenny worth of meat a week per person. It also promised to build 300,000 houses in a year and to refrain from interfering with the Welfare State; Lord Woolton went so far as to say that the food subsidies would not be cut.[1] The Labour party continued to stand on its record in office, but it could now point to Attlee's flight to Washington, and ask 'Whose finger on the trigger?', to suggest that when a war was going on Churchill might be too impulsive to be really safe.

It is hard to tell how accurate an impression of public opinion was at that time given by the opinion polls. The surveys taken in the ten months before the election suggest that the Conservatives had a lead of about 9 per cent of the popular vote. Whether it was because the Labour party made a great defensive effort, or because people at the last minute felt nervous about changing governments, or simply that the surveys had over-represented the prosperous classes, the Labour party polled slightly more of the total vote than the Conservatives. Not enough to outweigh the geographical advantage enjoyed by the Conservatives, but enough to remind the new government that it could not behave as though it had a strong mandate for its policies.

	Votes	Seats	% of all votes cast
Conservative	13,717,538	321	48
Liberal	730,556	6	2·5
Labour	13,948,605	295	48·8

Overseas policy under Churchill

Churchill as Prime Minister did not intend to try to keep an eye on all departments. At first he tried to run the government by appointing 'overlords', members of the House of Lords each of whom would co-ordinate the work of a number of departments. This was never very

[1] Lord Woolton, *Memoirs* (1959), 367–9.

effective, and power in domestic affairs tended to drift into the hands of Butler, the Chancellor of the Exchequer. Churchill had a poor opinion of Butler, but as he also had a low opinion of the importance of economic affairs, he accepted the situation with a fairly good grace. His main interest was in foreign policy and defence, and even in this field he conserved his flagging energies by leaving to Eden as Foreign Secretary a good deal of freedom of action in the smaller issues which he regarded as specialized questions. Eden could deal with Egypt, Iran, and the Far East without much intervention by the Prime Minister. Of these problems Iran solved itself, or at least was solved without the British government doing much about it. The international oil companies set up a blockade of Iranian oil, and their control of shipping and the sales system enabled them to stop the Iranian government selling any of the oil it had taken. Eventually a coup, encouraged by the U.S. Central Intelligence Agency, overthrew the Iranian Prime Minister, and a new arrangement for the oil was worked out. As the new arrangement transferred a portion of the British concession to American firms, the whole transaction left the British government feeling that it would have to take care not to be extruded from the Middle East by its American ally.

The Labour government had been troubled in its last months of office by the desire of the Egyptian government to revoke the 1936 Treaty which gave the British the right to occupy bases in the Canal Zone. Entangled as it was in Abadan, the government could not afford to look as if it was giving way. The new government had to face the problem, which was complicated by the overthrow of King Farouk and the emergence of a military government, first under General Neguib and then under Colonel Nasser. For a couple of years England resisted the efforts to drive her out, but the government was beginning to realize that this could not go on. In 1954 a withdrawal from the Canal Zone was accepted, the Sudan became an independent country, and the temporary occupation begun under Gladstone in 1882 was at an end. The Canal still remained an international waterway under the Treaty of 1888, and the Suez Canal Company continued to run it under the series of agreements made between 1854 and 1866.

The withdrawal was not popular with Conservatives, many of whom were sensitive when taunted about their bellicosity over Abadan when in opposition in 1951. But in 1954 Eden's reputation rose to new heights because of his handling of Indo-China and European rearmament. France had never fully re-established her position in Indo-China after the war. A Communist-inspired rebellion under Ho Chi Minh challenged the colonial government, and began to gain ground. The United States considered intervening on the French side, but would do so only if England was prepared to help as well. The British government did not think the French had much chance of holding on to Indo-China, and certainly was not willing to join in the war. British influence in Washington was exerted to strengthen the opposition to American intervention.

The situation became easier when Mendés-France became Premier in France on a policy of ending the war. At the Geneva conference in 1954 Eden played a considerable part in persuading the representatives of the Communist powers to be content with slightly less than they might have expected. Negotiations were complicated by the refusal of the United States to take part in the conference; technically it stayed away in order to avoid meeting representatives of the Chinese government, which it had not recognized, but in fact it seems to have thought that the conference was bound to be a disaster for the western powers and wanted to dissociate itself from the débâcle. Eden and Mendés-France emerged with terms which surprised the Americans, who had expected something much worse. The United States had anticipated that the whole of Indo-China would be dominated by the Viet Minh; when it discovered how much had been saved, it began negotiations to set up the South-east Asia Treaty Organization to defend Laos, Cambodia, and South Vietnam against any renewal of the war.

Success at Geneva strengthened Eden's position for his next diplomatic achievement. Almost immediately after NATO had been set up it became clear that the member nations were not providing all the forces they had promised. Pressure from the United States built up in favour of arming West German troops and adding them to the NATO forces in some way. European sentiment was not enthusiastic about this: it was felt that arming Germans would only provoke the Russians to become more hostile, and enough Europeans had lived under German occupation to have some sympathy with the Russians. At first it was suggested that a European Defence Community should be set up to organize a supra-national force; in its army the forces contributed by the member nations would be so completely integrated that they could not be used independently by their own governments. The whole German contribution to NATO defence would be controlled by the E.D.C., and thus the German government would not acquire any forces of its own. The British government thought that this was a good arrangement, for other people. It explained that, whatever Churchill might have said at The Hague and Strasbourg while in opposition, it was not going to join organizations designed to set up federal institutions for western Europe. It declined to join Euratom or the Coal and Steel Community, and it declined to contribute its forces to the E.D.C. This made E.D.C. seem unattractive to France; if England had been willing to make a permanent contribution of troops to the continent of Europe within the E.D.C., that would have acted as a counter-weight to Germany, and German rearmament could be accepted. But, as it stood, E.D.C. looked like another way to create a dominant Germany in Europe. The French government was badly divided, and when the E.D.C. Treaties came up for debate it left the issue to a free vote. The opponents of E.D.C., who were more frightened of Germany than of Russia, prevailed.

American opinion was divided between withdrawal from European affairs and commitment to Germany without regard for France. In the United States France was in any case not regarded as important; in England the Prime Minister and some of his personal friends shared this view. Eden had disliked Churchill's European pronouncements in opposition but his pro-French views made him more eager than other British or American politicians to make sure that German rearmament should be brought about in a way that was not offensive to France. His proposal was that England should soothe French fears by promising to keep four divisions on the continent of Europe for the next fifty years, and by promising that these forces could be withdrawn only with the permission of the W.E.U. countries.[1] This commitment caused a lot of trouble later; when Germany stopped being an occupied territory she ceased paying for the British troops on her soil, and the four divisions became a large and steady drain on foreign exchange which led to uncomfortable pleas that someone should do something to help England pay the cost of the commitment. But at the time the proposal worked. France was reassured by the British promise to stay on the Continent, and German rearmament could go ahead. The British troops were not to be given to a federal authority, and the idea of a supra-national structure for European defence was not revived, but Europe could emerge with a stronger defensive position than before.

Whether because of the increase in European strength or because of the death of Stalin, the attitude of Russia had become more conciliatory. During the 1950 election campaign Churchill had launched the idea of a meeting at the summit, though this had been proposed as a drastic step to escape from a clouded situation which was growing worse, and he remained devoted to the idea of a summit conference. He knew that he had first to convince the United States government that it would be useful, and here he was fortunate; about twelve months after his return to office his old wartime friend General Eisenhower became President of

[1] Belgium, England, France, Germany, Italy, Luxemburg, and the Netherlands.

the United States. In some ways the two men found themselves in curiously similar positions: they used their prestige to bring unprofitable foreign ventures to an end, in the Korean War and in the Suez Canal base, and they persuaded their political supporters to accept the expansion of social welfare carried out in both countries in the previous decade or two. Churchill could reasonably hope to revive the wartime association and ensure that he had a special role of influence at Washington, which he proposed to use to persuade the United States government to agree to a summit conference. On the whole Eisenhower was doubtful about the usefulness of the idea, though he was always ready to listen to arguments in favour of it. In the summer of 1953 Churchill suffered a stroke; this was kept more or less a secret, and very few people realized how seriously ill he was.[1] He might have retired at this point if Anthony Eden, who was universally accepted as his heir-apparent, had not been ill at the same time. Churchill's pressure for a conference revived when he returned to work in the autumn, and Stalin's successors, who were much more eager to visit the world outside Russia than he had been, showed some willingness for a conference. Churchill had retired before it took place but the meeting of Eisenhower, Eden, Faure, and Bulganin at Geneva in the summer of 1955 owed a good deal to his patience and enthusiasm. The meeting did not lead to a permanent relaxation of tension, and relations between Russia and the West deteriorated soon afterwards. Diplomats drew the conclusion that it was wiser to start with preliminary negotiations before a summit conference, instead of leaving all the difficult questions to Foreign Ministers to deal with after the conference, but the idea of a summit conference remained in circulation, and was taken up again when relations between Russia and the West had improved.

The Conservatives had been pleased to find, when they came to office, that the Labour government had made a good deal of progress towards the construction of a British atomic bomb under conditions of strict secrecy. If the new government wanted to continue to claim that England was for some purposes the equal of America and Russia, it had to consider whether to make a British hydrogen bomb. In 1954 Churchill announced that a decision to make the H-bomb had been taken. There were protests from many of the people who would have protested if they had known the atomic bomb was being made in the late 1940s. The reasons for making the hydrogen bomb contradicted too many public attitudes to be discussed completely openly. Anglo-American bombing plans had to be co-ordinated, which implied military consultation between the two countries. The government probably never imagined that the

[1] Lord Moran, *Winston Churchill, the Struggle for Survival* (1968), 431–501.

balance of strength at the H-bomb level between Russia and America was so neatly balanced that the British contribution would be decisive. No doubt some people thought that England could be the equal of Russia and the United States if only she had the bomb—in terms of military technology this did not look so difficult, because the delivery of the bomb was to be entrusted to aeroplanes, and by the end of the Korean rearmament period the British government had enough aeroplanes in its V-bomber force of Valiants, Vulcans, and Victors to be able to deliver the bomb. The successful American and Russian tests had shown that an H-bomb could be made, which had previously been thought unlikely by physicists as respected as Oppenheimer, and once it was known that the device would work it was fairly simple to discover how to make an H-bomb, in which an A-bomb would trigger off a fusion process.

Undoubtedly those who wanted the H-bomb to place England on a footing of equality with America and Russia had failed to understand how the world had changed. In trying to convince the more imperialist of his followers that Suez was no longer useful, Churchill had shown how one H-bomb could devastate the whole Suez area; England was not so much bigger than the Suez area, and was in fact particularly vulnerable to hydrogen bombs. From a strategic point of view the bomb was a weapon that people in England would find very hard to use. But so far as relations with the United States were concerned, the bomb made good sense. Anyone who thought the United States might withdraw from Europe or in some other way ignore British interests would find some consolation in the thought that England could exact a heavy price from anyone who attacked her, and could touch off a general war.

All this depended on taking a slightly unfavourable view of the Americans. Churchill, for whom the Anglo-American alliance was the most important factor in diplomacy, was not the man to suggest such a view. But anti-Americanism in England was more widespread than anyone cared to say openly. Because it occurred in so many different parts of the political spectrum it could not acquire a policy, and the men of the centre could continue to follow a pro-American line. On the Conservative right were people who felt that the United States was always chipping away at the British Empire, at British oil, and at British prestige; these people were often supporters in domestic policy of moves to get back to 'before the war', and they disliked the American way of life which they found vulgar and egalitarian and altogether too ready to think the business man more important than the gentleman. Inside the government there were a good many people who, while possibly sympathetic to some of America's long-term aims, thought the Americans were not very competent at running policy. People who felt like this might adopt Macmillan's philosophical view that they were 'Greeks in the American Empire' and must run it 'as the Greek slaves ran the operations of the Emperor Claudius',[1] or they might share Eden's slightly too obvious feeling that the American Secretary of State, John Foster Dulles, was an international disaster looking for a place to happen. Partly because of the pressures of the situation, partly because Churchill did not propose to lose touch with Eisenhower, these feelings did not affect government policy much. Foreign policy was reasonably successful—in one respect too successful: people were able to slip into the habit of forgetting how much the world had changed in the last dozen years.

This view could survive in colonial as well as in foreign affairs. After the rapid changes of the 1940s, relatively little seemed to happen. In the Gold Coast, elections were held in 1951; as the Convention People's Party won a majority its leader, Dr. Nkrumah, was released from prison, where he had been serving a sentence for political offences, and was made Leader of Government Business in the new legislature. In Nigeria developments were more complicated: the country was divided into three regions, each with a political party of its own, and the British government felt it had to try to reconcile them before independence to make sure that the country did not dissolve on regional lines. The British government also had a direct interest in delay. The leaders of the northern region opposed rapid moves to independence, because their region was short of educated people. They were afraid that, if independence was granted before they had time to organize, the two southern regions might be able to establish themselves in a dominant position. As the northern group was pro-British in sentiment and would form a majority after independence, it was worth supporting. In the Gold Coast the tribes of the north were also backward and in favour of a longer British stay, but as they were a minority there was not much point in supporting them and offending the section that was bound to come to power after independence.

In West Africa independence could be accepted without much difficulty as the objective of policy, because there were no white settlers and the large commercial companies could be expected to look after themselves. In Kenya and Rhodesia there were communities of white settlers. Opinion in England certainly would not have allowed them to be abandoned; a section of British opinion would have opposed steps reducing their political power, and in the early 1950s no such steps were taken. In 1952 a revolt broke out in Kenya, organized by the Mau Mau movement. It blended Kikuyu tribalism and anti-colonialism in a mixture dominated by

[1] Anthony Sampson, *Macmillan* (1967), 61.

the former. Apart from all questions of political control, there was the issue of the Highlands, the best farming land in Kenya, which was monopolized by British settlers. The British government sent troops to protect the settlers, and after a fairly difficult struggle in 1953 and 1954 the revolt was defeated. People in England were prepared to support the use of troops because of the primitive and savage nature of the revolt, but British troops could not be used to stop the majority in Kenya from getting political power in a peaceful way, and Mau Mau had shown that the settlers, outnumbered a hundred to one, could not protect their own position.

In its last months of office the Labour government had shown some interest in the idea of federating the two Rhodesias and Nyasaland as a step towards independence. Such African opinion as could be consulted was hostile to the idea, but when the Conservatives came to power they decided to ignore this. The Central African Federation could bring together the mineral wealth of Northern Rhodesia, the large white population of Southern Rhodesia, and the overcrowded African population of Nyasaland. The Federation would have a large enough financial base to raise development loans, and in particular to finance the building of the Kariba Dam which would provide supplies of electricity and of water for farmers and for miners on the Copperbelt in Northern Rhodesia. The new Federation was presented to the world as an exercise in partnership —a difficult word, which could be presented to people in England as a synonym for equality and could be explained to white inhabitants of the Federation as the partnership between horse and rider. The British government watched to see how it would develop before deciding about progress towards independence.

In Malaya independence in the immediate future seemed much more possible. Communist guerrillas tried to take the country over; the British response to this was among the most intelligent operations in the field of counter-insurgency undertaken by any government in the period, though the task was not as hard as in some other countries. The Communists were almost all Chinese, so that it was not too difficult to enlist the support of the Malayan section of the population by pursuing a sensible policy. The British authorities made it clear that they did not expect to stay in Malaya for ever, and would grant independence as soon as the emergency was over and the Communists had been defeated. With a certain amount of goodwill gained in this way, it was possible to move the population into strategic villages which could be defended against infiltration, and in this way the Communists were cut off from their supporters in the country. The whole operation lasted from 1948 to 1957, but it was successful enough to convince the government that it knew what to do about

Communist revolts; it felt sure that granting independence was a necessary part of resistance to revolt, and this made it more ready to consider
independence for other colonies.

Financial policy under Butler

This success in external policy rested on a fairly sound economic base.
The situation in 1951 had left the government relatively little freedom of
action. Butler had to begin his period of office as Chancellor of the
Exchequer by taking further steps to deal with the balance-of-payments
crisis. To show that the government wanted to use monetary policy as
one way to influence the economy, he raised the Bank Rate to 2½ per
cent from the 2 per cent at which it had been kept, except for a few weeks
in September 1939, ever since 1932. But the main line of defence had to
be physical controls: licences for imports were required, and were given
with a sparing hand. This short-term reaction to a foreign exchange
problem was about the only occasion on which Butler adopted much the
same policy as Gaitskell would have done, but a legendary figure called
Mr. Butskell was invented by *The Economist*, and denounced by the Labour
left as the symbol of a supposed similarity of purpose. Butler accepted
the doctrine of setting the economy free, and followed it in an almost
dogmatic way. The Conservative party was behind him; the modernizers
were convinced by their experience of controls that this was no way to run
an economy, and the people who wanted to get back to the past were
certain that there had been no planning before the war. Those who could
remember that in the 1930s there had been considerable enthusiasm for
planning kept quiet, partly because the Conservative party at the time
felt that its conduct in the 1930s—and more particularly the policy of
appeasement—had not been creditable.

Butler's most extreme venture in setting the economy free did not come
to fruition; the ROBOT scheme, to let the exchange value of the pound
float freely, with no support from the foreign exchange reserves, was
discussed in February and in June 1952. Largely because of Lord
Cherwell's influence with Churchill, the plan was dropped; Gaitskell took
the opportunity later to say how sound he considered Cherwell's stand
to have been.[1] Enemies of the scheme seem to have assumed that, although
the foreign exchange reserves would not be used to support the value of
the pound, the Bank of England would raise interest rates to support it.
This would have taken the economy back to the late 1920s, when high
interest rates checked the development of the economy to defend the
pound. If interest rates had not been used in this way, the pound would

[1] Lord Birkenhead, *The Prof in two Worlds* (1961), 284–9.

have fluctuated in terms of other currencies, which would have been confusing for people conducting trade in terms of sterling, though it would have removed the need for high interest rates.

The Conservative government took a number of steps between 1952 and the end of 1954 which fulfilled its election promise to set the economy free. It reduced the allocating and licensing needed to build anything, it reduced income-tax, it released the sterling balances and encouraged overseas investment, it ended restrictions on hire-purchase sales and restrictions on the right to strike, and it ended rationing. Presumably a Labour government would have ended rationing and brought income-tax down from the Korean War level as soon as it felt safe in doing so, though of course it might have been more timid about these steps than the Conservatives. On the other hand a Labour government would have been much more worried by the slight rise in unemployment in 1952. The steps taken to defend the foreign exchange reserves caused a slight recession. The textile industry suffered most, as foreign competition began to be a serious threat. Manufacturers showed that in general they did not expect the recession to be serious; they had had difficulty obtaining workers in the last dozen years, and in 1952 they kept workers on even though they could have run their factories for a time with fewer men. The economy soon recovered. The increase in import prices caused by the Korean War was short-lived, but England was able to go on exporting at the old prices. This improvement in the terms of trade, which enabled a larger amount of imports to be purchased for the same amount of exports, was a considerable stroke of good fortune, and it helped relax some of the tensions in the economy.

Once the shock of Korea was over, the balance of payments began to show a steady surplus for the first time since before the war. The government laid down the policy that the country needed a surplus of £300–350m. a year for overseas investment and to pay off the sterling debts (or 'sterling balances') left over by the war. The current trade surplus, including invisible exports, ran at something like the £300m. a year that was needed, though military expenditure overseas, from Germany to Hong Kong, reduced it to about half the desired amount. The remainder was invested overseas on a long-term basis; in this sense England had returned to the conditions of the 1920s. But almost all the investment was in the Sterling Area or in Canada, and elsewhere it was restricted as severely as in the 1940s.

This British urge to make long-term investments helped international trade. If the surpluses had simply been accumulated year by year in England, the British reserves of gold would have gone up, but other countries would have found themselves running short of reserves and unable to trade. On the other hand, if the surpluses had been used to pay off the wartime debts with sterling countries, this would also have reduced the amount of money available for international trade, and thus reduced the amount of trading that could be carried on. The Labour government had 'blocked' the debts, which meant the creditors could draw their money only in the quantities and at the times that the British government allowed; naturally it discouraged its creditors from drawing money except to buy British goods. In 1952 the debts were 'unblocked', which meant they could pass from one country to another and be used as money for international trading purposes. India and Egypt could now keep their economies going by transferring their claims on England to other countries, and thus they could survive the economic strain when their exports went down in price in the post-Korea slump in raw materials. The holders of these sterling debts, if they chose, could present them in London and ask for dollars (or gold) in exchange. It would do them no good if they all asked at once, because England's supply of gold and dollars was about a quarter the size of the debts. But if they were patient they could hope for eventual repayment, or if they wanted to import from other countries they could use the sterling balances for payment.

The government allowed Sterling Area countries to borrow money in London, and hoped that in return they would not press for repayment of the wartime debts. When the debts passed into the hands of countries which did not belong to the Sterling Area the British government could not impress them by pointing out the advantages to sterling countries of being allowed to borrow in London. The Chancellor of the Exchequer could harangue Commonwealth Finance Ministers and ask them not to disturb things by running up deficits with the outside world, and this probably had some effect. The independent members of the Commonwealth did habitually run deficits with the outside world, financed to some extent by British investment. The colonies tended to run deficits with England, but to run surpluses with the rest of the world that were larger than their deficits with her, which meant that their sterling balances increased steadily until independence. Almost every colony embarked on a drive for investment at home when it became independent, which meant that it spent its sterling balances, and the balances spent in this way usually passed into the hands of countries outside the Sterling Area.

The government's financial figures depended on obtaining correct returns from importers and exporters, investors and tourists, and everybody else who had anything to do with foreign exchange. This did not always happen; at the foot of the annual balance-of-payments statement a large balancing item always had to be put in to make the sums add up right. Estimating the level of overseas investment was also difficult, and became harder after 1945. In the nineteenth century and the early twentieth century a good deal of foreign investment took the form of sales of bonds by public subscription. The sale, and the later fate of the bonds, could be traced. After the Second World War investment was mainly 'direct', with companies setting up subsidiaries in foreign countries and reinvesting the profits there. These activities were almost impossible to trace accurately.

Undoubtedly the largest single field of foreign investment in the post-war world was oil. Anglo-Iranian (later British Petroleum) and Shell (40 per cent British owned) invested about as large a proportion of the national income as the railway companies in the mid-nineteenth century, but as most of it took the form of ploughing back profits and depreciation reserves, it was hard to tell how much they put into the business. This concentration of investment on oil was matched by the increase in British consumption; it rose at a rate of about 40 per cent a year from 2 million tons a year just after the war to 28 million tons a year nine years later. Consumption all over the world was rising, and was met mainly by a sharp increase in Middle East production. Oil there was much cheaper than in the traditional areas such as the United States, and profits were accordingly high. The oil companies, and the governments that stood behind them, pointed out that one of the reasons for this was the low level of government services provided in the Middle East, which meant that the companies had to spend money on activities that would be undertaken by governments elsewhere.

Emerging from austerity

One result of this foreign investment, which was so much larger than in the 1930s and 1940s, was that England never had large enough reserves to deal with the crises that followed any loss of confidence on the part of the owners of the sterling balances; these crises were all the more likely to find the government unprepared because of the difficulty of finding out the exact state of the balance of payments. Another result of heavy foreign investment was to restrict the amount of resources available for investment inside England. Under the Labour government the level of non-housing investment had been high, but housing was neglected. Bevan, the Minister responsible, was preoccupied with setting up the health service and had to ask for large sums of money from the Exchequer for it. Labour principles indicated that housing should mainly be built by local councils for letting to the less prosperous at subsidized rents, and because

Bevan was not in a strong position to ask the Exchequer to lend money to local councils, all building was held back; this reduced the mobility of labour and forced many people to live in uncomfortable and inadequate homes. The only justification that could be offered was that it was impossible to do everything at once.

In 1950 Churchill argued that the government had got its priorities wrong. He condemned the ambitious school-building programme and asked for 'bedrooms before schoolrooms'.[1] The 1950 Conservative conference asked for 300,000 houses a year, and this aim was accepted by the party leadership. Macmillan was made Minister of Housing in 1951 with the task of increasing production about 50 per cent above the level reached under the Labour government and building the 300,000 houses. By 1953 the target had been reached and the performance was sustained in 1954. The housing problem was nearer to being under control than at any time since 1939.

The pressure of concentration on housing, combined with the relaxation of the system of building licences and the repeal of the 1947 Act giving development rights to the government, launched a property boom; new office blocks were built, houses which could be changed from controlled to uncontrolled tenancies produced large profits, and the price of land went up. The relaxation of controls on the economy produced a good many cases where assets could be bought for less than their market value, and the property boom was only one aspect of this; most of the mergers and takeovers of the 1950s were financial operations by which assets were bought cheaply rather than industrial operations to make firms more efficient. The increase in building was at first matched by a decline in other forms of investment inside England. Until 1955 the amount of non-building investment was lower, after allowing for rising prices, than the 1951 level. A higher rate of overall British investment, at home and abroad, would fairly certainly have led to inflationary pressure or an adverse balance of payments.

Part of the difficulty lay in a certain complacency about what the Labour government had done. This complacency was not restricted to matters of investment, nor confined to one party alone. Life after the war had been so much less comfortable than everybody had expected that it was assumed that investment and the social services had been making tremendous strides. The Welfare State, it was felt, had been built and would stand to be the admiration of the world. To some extent this was true. A good many other countries did feel they should follow England in extending their social services, and they spent money fairly lavishly in

[1] 6 Nov. 1950; *Commons Debates*, cccclxxx. 705. Churchill was taking up a remark made earlier in the debate by a Labour back-bencher.

paying for old-age pensions, family allowances, and other cash benefits. In general they did not venture to fight the doctors to set up health services. One of the possible disadvantages of making health expenditure an item of government spending was illustrated by the Guillebaud Report, which showed that the proportion of the British national income spent on health services was constant in the 1950s, when many other prosperous countries were spending more and more on health. In general terms, the Labour party was quite certain that there was nothing to improve about the Welfare State it had built, and the Conservatives thought that welfare benefits were almost too luxurious. This led to a truce on the welfare front, and nobody suggested improvements. In the same way a great many people were convinced that the level of investment in the late 1940s was so high that nothing more needed to be done.

Defence expenditure, it was conceded, was too high. The £4,700m. programme was abandoned, and expenditure began to fall back from the 12 or 13 per cent of the national income that it had reached at one point. More money was spent on consumer goods, because other things were making smaller demands on the national income: defence and the social services were receiving a declining proportion of it, investment was not increasing very much, and the terms of trade were improving, so that a smaller proportion of the national income went to pay for any given amount of imports. People were better off: the national income, after remaining stable in 1952, went up steadily for the next three years. Although production and average income had reached pre-war levels by 1948 or 1949, the habit of referring to production as 'a post-war peak', with the implication that before the war people had had real peaks, persisted until the mid 1950s.

The aspect of Conservative policy which showed most clearly how completely the supporters of 'setting the people free' had triumphed over the 'back to before the war' group was in trade union affairs. The repeal of the Trade Disputes Act was left undisturbed. The right to strike was accepted and the wartime and post-war system of compulsory arbitration was wound up. Sir Walter Monckton was appointed Minister of Labour and fairly clearly he was told not to disturb good relations between the government and the unions. The trade unions had won during the 1940s the right to be consulted on questions that affected them, and it was accepted that Royal Commissions on most issues had to contain a trade unionist; on committees concerned with economic issues trade unionists and business men usually came in equal numbers, an arrangement that would have surprised business men in most countries outside Scandinavia.

By the time of the Korean War most of the excess demand had been squeezed out of the economy, and as prices of imports rapidly fell back to the 1950 level there was no longer much demand-inflation. On the other hand real wages had not increased since 1947. Pressure built up for wage increases, and the unions' successes were resented by people who felt the government was being too soft with the working classes. A pattern of giving wage-increases, voluntarily or under the threat of a strike, every year seemed to have developed. As the money value of the increases came to rather more than the real increase in production, the result was to encourage a cost-inflation in which prices rose slightly more slowly than money wages. In a world of philosophers this might have been accepted as one of the disadvantages of setting the people free. In the England of the early 1950s it was regarded as shocking that the unions should use their recently recovered freedom.

The discussion was embittered by the belief of the press and many non-specialist commentators that the strikes and the pressure for increases in pay were all the result of Communist infiltration. Communists, it was assumed, had worked their way into positions of influence in trade unions and used these positions to mislead workers into asking for more money. This was not a very useful line of analysis; men of influence in trade unions who supported the Communist party were likely to do so because it approved of a militant policy rather than out of a desire to sabotage the economy, and the idea that only a desire to sabotage the economy could lead people to ask for more money was a very non-materialist way of looking at life. The government avoided taking an anti-Communist line on strikes. The number of days lost owing to strikes in the conditions of full employment in the 1950s was about the same as the loss in the depressed 1930s, and was much less than in the twenties. Strikes caused a much smaller loss of working days than the common cold.

The 1952 budget, which still had to face the Korean War balance-of-payments problems, was inevitably deflationary. The cuts in food subsidies probably made trade unions a little more willing to ask for pay increases, but because of the improvement in the terms of trade prices did not go up. In 1953 the food subsidies were again reduced, and at the same time the standard rate of income-tax was cut by $2\frac{1}{2}$p. This was a step away from the pattern of the 1940s, in which direct taxation had increased sharply and the goverment had acted deliberately to hold down prices, thus benefiting the poor at the expense of the rich. Within the framework of 'setting the people free', which clearly included reducing the process of redistributing income, the end of the subsidies meant that people would pay the full market price for what they wanted, and would not be guided by the government into spending their money on food.

Some people saw the ending of rationing as another great struggle between socialism and capitalism; the more extreme members of the Conservative party spoke as though the Labour party positively enjoyed running the rationing system, and the more extreme members of the Labour party said that ending rationing would lead to economic disaster. The reopening of the commodity markets in London was also seen by some people in these terms of high principle. For a time it seemed as though sterling crises had been a special problem of the years immediately after the war. In 1953, for the first odd-numbered year since the war, there was no sterling crisis—convertibility in 1947, devaluation in 1949, and Korea in 1951 showed how weak sterling had been. The 1953 budget gave investment allowances for firms spending money on new equipment, and this checked the drop in non-housing investment and helped encourage the 'investment boom' of 1954 and 1955. Butler was sufficiently pleased by its success to say in 1954 that if things went ahead as they had been doing, people in Britain could double their standard of living in the next twenty-five years.[1]

At the time this prediction was regarded as bold and daring, and some people even regarded it as wild and impracticable. It amounted to a rate of growth of just under 3 per cent a year, which was distinctly smaller than the rate of growth between 1945 and the Korean War. Nobody had fully appreciated the 4 per cent rate of growth immediately after the war, partly because living conditions were so miserable, and partly because most of the growth went to defence, social services, and the less consumer-oriented forms of investment. Butler's predicted rate of growth was lower than that of the late 1940s for a number of reasons. The Labour government had been able to run a large deficit on its balance of payments because of the American loan and Marshall Aid. In the years just after the war there was a great hunger for goods, and relatively few sellers; the United States had things to sell, but the world shortage of dollars made it hard for customers to buy from her. By 'blocking' sterling the Labour government had created a slightly artificial market in countries which held sterling and could not do anything with it except buy British goods.

Germany and Japan had come back to world export trade early in the 1950s; it was bad luck for British exporters that they returned during the Korean War, when Britain was unusually ill placed for resisting new competitors. As the competition increased, foreign customers who had been ready to take anything in the years just after the war became more selective. They had often been sold goods they would buy only in a sellers' market, and some of them started the 1950s in a mood of suspicion

[1] *The Annual Register of World Events for 1954*, 45, called it 'a daring forecast'.

about British products. The improvement in the terms of trade, although it made the balance-of-payments position easier, was not an unmixed blessing; a good deal of British exports went to countries that produced the raw materials that were going down in price, and as these countries became less prosperous they became less good markets for British exporters.

In the 1940s the Labour government had been running an economy in which no sections were declining. By the time Butler made his prediction it was already clear that cotton textiles were going into a long-term decline. They had done well just after the war, with Japanese competition eliminated for the time being, and countries like India not yet fully organized to export much. By the 1950s this foreign competition, paying lower wages and equipped with newly installed machinery, was driving Lancashire out of the textile business in which she had been supreme for almost two centuries. In 1906 England had been selling cotton goods all over the world, and the cotton industry was devoted to Free Trade. By 1955 England was a net importer of cotton goods, and Lancashire was demanding Protection. The change was inevitable, but it was a nasty shock for the economy. No other industries were in quite the same position, though there were warning signs that coal and the railways might go the same way.

The Conservative government accepted the general principle of nationalization of some industries and never tried to alter the position of coal or the railways—it was most unlikely that any purchasers could have been found if they had tried to sell them back. Denationalization of steel and of road transport had been part of the election programme: steel was sold off successfully, on a basis that gave a preference to the original owners; and only one company, Richard Thomas and Baldwin, could not be disposed of. Road transport was rather harder, and it became clear that a good many of the previous owners had no desire to get back into the business. In the end British Rail was left with a distinctly larger share of the road haulage trade than the government had intended.

By the beginning of 1955 the investment boom, and the accompanying increase in consumption, had gone so far that Butler considered some check would have to be placed on expansion. There were two increases in Bank Rate in quick succession, and restrictions were reimposed on hire-purchase sales by laying down requirements about the size of deposits. Even this slight intervention in the economy was objectionable to the more doctrinaire supporters of the free play of the market, but on the whole they could feel that Conservative freedom had worked, and perhaps had worked all the better because there had been so little attempt to get back to before the war.

There were other examples of the determination of the government not to give any impression that they were putting the clock back. They decided not to restore parliamentary seats to the universities. But the most clear-cut example of unwillingness to listen to the traditionalist wing of the Conservative party came in the struggle over commercial, or independent, television. The television service of the B.B.C. had started again in 1946, but it was a small section of the Corporation's work. Sound broadcasting stood at the peak of its influence; during the war the B.B.C.'s introductory 'This is London calling' had been the voice of truth and of hope to a captive continent, and it owed that position to its refusal to be associated with anything that looked like propaganda. Or, the more sophisticated would say, to its realization that good propaganda rests on a reputation for truthfulness. Its success in the war confirmed all the Reithian principles about setting high and elevating standards. At the time television was returning to action, the Corporation was much more interested in another minority service it was launching—the Third Programme, designed specially for people who wanted modern poetry, classical music, and discussion of scholarly issues. The small audience for television could and did grow; the audience for the Third Programme did not expand, partly because the Programme steadily raised its standard. It did useful things, such as encouraging Dylan Thomas, the last poet to be both popular and taken seriously by other poets, but the Third Programme absorbed too much of the energy of the Corporation and led it to neglect television or think of it as something that should be regarded as subordinate to sound broadcasting.

The combination of the spirit of Reith with this neglect meant that B.B.C. television emerged as a dull and limited service. It may have been suited to the years of austerity, but after that it was remarkably vulnerable. By the time of the 1951 election a group of people with considerable influence inside the Conservative party organization was ready with suggestions for setting up an alternative television system which would run on a profit-making basis. They captured the Cabinet and got their plan accepted. It was of course opposed by the Labour party, who believed in the B.B.C. and had no desire to see another medium of communication in the hands of people who could be assumed to oppose any sort of socialism. The more significant division came inside the Conservative party, where a considerable number of the traditionalists declared their opposition to the scheme. In the House of Lords the government had some difficulty rallying support and defending its television proposals.

It was denounced for being like the American system, and the opponents of the proposal made it clear that they believed 'American' and 'vulgar' meant the same thing. Technically the British and American arrangements differed: in the United States the advertisers supported individual programmes by advertising on them, and could force a change of programme by withdrawing their support if they were not satisfied they were getting a large enough audience. In England the organizing companies were responsible for producing the programmes shown, but all they provided for the advertiser was the right to buy a few moments of time in which he could present his advertising message. The news programmes were produced by a separate company, Independent Television News, and were supplied to all the organizing companies. These provisions did reduce the power of the advertisers over the producing companies, but the difference was not all that important.

The introduction of commercial television was a poor reward for the newspapers' support for the Conservatives when they were in opposition. When it was launched late in 1955 the advertisers hung back until they could see what sort of audience they were being offered, and for about a year the producing companies ran up debts. But when the advertisers found they were being offered a reasonable size of audience they began to buy television time and the troubles of the producing companies were over. Advertisers became more selective about the newspapers in which they bought space, concentrating on the papers with the largest circulations, which provided more customers per pound spent. The other newspapers lost ground financially as a result, and all newspapers lost some of their authority. By the end of the war almost everybody in the country saw a newspaper, a scale of circulation which had never existed before and seems unlikely ever to exist in any other country. The *Express*, the paper for the people who felt they were getting ahead, and the *Mirror*, the paper for the working class, had sales of over 4 million each. The *Express* was probably of some help to the business men against the traditionalists inside the Conservative party, but it did not affect people's political views much. The *Mirror* seems to have increased the Labour vote in 1945 and in 1951. Newspapers tended to have a hint of the pulpit about them and while the *Mirror* and the *Express* were more successful than their rivals at popularizing and secularizing this approach, there was always a note of earnest exhortation, well suited to the serious-minded 1940s. Television had a hint of the university lecture about it, and while I.T.V. was more successful than the B.B.C. at popularizing and de-intellectualizing this approach, the cool, not completely committed and slightly cynical approach of the lecturer suited the mood of the 1950s. No doubt television would have been popular at any time, but it emerged at a time when its characteristic approach suited the spirit of the age particularly well. Newspapers had been something that people talked about; in the 1950s they talked about television programmes instead. And television captured the universal audience that had watched films in the 1940s. The British film industry contracted sharply, as the size of its audience diminished. Television, and in particular commercial television, had a good effect on mass-communication. B.B.C. television became distinctly livelier, and the Corporation realized that it would have to interest an audience if it was to have any effect on it. British films also became more interesting, and began to attract audiences in other countries.

The traditionalists had calculated the situation fairly accurately when they tried to resist commercial television. It promoted a view of society which was much more like a market-place than the orderly system of deference to one's betters which the traditionalists had hoped to see re-established, and it challenged the idea that some affairs of State were too important to be discussed in public which had been one of the strengths of the system of deference. The supporters of the market-place could feel more confident that their view of the world would be accepted. But although opposition to the values of the market-place and opposition to American influence did not affect government policy much, they were still strong in the country, and have to be remembered when considering the political situation at this time.

The 1955 General Election

At the time of the defeat in 1951 the Labour party did not seem at all badly placed. It had polled more votes than the Conservatives, it had a front bench of ex-ministers who were known to the public, and it had a government with a weak majority in front of it. But nothing went as might have been expected. The party had no policy available: it had carried out all the measures about which people felt widespread enthusiasm, and it had no new ideas to unite it. The price of its leaders' intellectual sterility was paid during the 1950s when the party fell to quarrelling over old issues.

Quite early in the new Parliament it was clear that Bevan and his followers had been right about the level of rearmament which was economically tolerable. This might have provided an opportunity for him to return to some high position within the leadership of the party, but a fresh issue had arisen; German rearmament, in one form or another, was accepted by the leadership of the party and was condemned by Bevan. He believed that rearmament would alarm the Russians, and would commit the West to trying to solve issues by military means. He was confident that the only real answer to Communism was to find a social system that was economically and culturally more attractive than it. Militarism, he argued with an echo of Orwell's *1984*, led to McCarthyism —the hunt for anyone with disturbing or subversive ideas which was going on in the United States at the time. And of course a fair amount of the driving-force behind Bevanism came from the belief that the United States was not a satisfactory type of society and England should take care not to develop in the same way. Anti-German feeling entered into it, and Bevan's position was also strengthened by the fact that there was no real hatred of Russia in England. In emotional terms people were balanced between Russia and America: they felt much more positive liking for the United States, but on the other hand they often felt a strong irritation with her, and this irritation found its most overt political expression in the Bevanite struggle.

Bevan was better placed to fight against the party leadership than almost any other party rebel. In 1952 six out of the seven seats on the Labour party's National Executive Committee filled by the votes of the local constituency parties were won by Bevanites, which led the Bevanites to claim that the leadership controlled the party only by careful lobbying among a small group of leaders of large trade unions. In 1954, when the issue of German rearmament came up for discussion, the opponents of rearmament polled about 75 per cent of the votes of the constituency parties. The leadership's majority at the conference was small enough and sufficiently dependent on trade union strength to show that, if the constituency party votes reflected the views of the unpaid party workers, the Labour party machine was going to be disorganized at the next election.

Among Labour Members of Parliament Bevan had too few supporters to threaten Attlee's position, but too many for the party leadership to be able to crush him. Attlee supported the American alliance, and believed in a bi-partisan foreign policy; Bevan thought a bi-partisan policy took control of foreign affairs out of the hands of the people and gave it to the supporters of special interests. Attlee did not support an extreme policy of opposition to Bevan: Morrison, as the exponent of the policy of a Labour party which could appeal to the lower middle class, and Gaitskell, as the victim of Bevan's attacks in 1951, were the chief spokesmen for the party leadership. As Deputy Leader and because of his years of service in organizing the party, Morrison had a good claim to succeed Attlee. On the other hand, Bevan and Gaitskell would be stronger candidates for the post if the cry went up for a young leader.

At the beginning of 1955 Churchill decided to retire, and in April he did at long last hand over power to Eden. The long wait, and the perpetual

subordination to a man with whom he was not on very close terms, had
done Eden no good. But he entered on a satisfactory inheritance: an
election could reasonably be called in a short time, and then he could rule
as his own master. For the election he had splendid prospects, with a
divided Opposition that had produced no new ideas, success in housing,
the end of rationing, his own diplomatic prestige, and Butler's budget.
The Chancellor of the Exchequer, despite his doubts earlier in the year
that the country might be running the risk of balance-of-payments difficulties, felt able to cut income-tax by another 2½p, and the government
asked for a general election. Public interest was lower than it had been
for some time past, and there was a distinct drop in the number of votes
cast.

	Votes	Seats	% of all votes cast
Conservative	13,286,569	344	49·7
Liberal	702,405	6	2·7
Labour	12,404,970	277	46·4

The Conservative majority was now large enough to give the government some freedom of action politically, but it was restricted by economic
circumstances. During the summer the disadvantages of investing abroad
rather than building up the reserves became clear. There was a deficit on
the balance of payments which, although not large, was enough to make
many holders of sterling feel they would be safer if they sold their
holdings. Butler convinced the September meeting of the International
Monetary Fund that England would not adopt a floating exchange rate,
which would have been followed by a sharp fall in the value of sterling,
but foreign confidence in the British economy had to be restored.
Deflationary measures to reduce the pressure on resources caused by the
investment boom were the obvious step. In October a second budget was
introduced in which all rates of purchase-tax were increased by one-fifth,
and in addition purchase-tax was imposed on a number of household
goods such as saucepans which had been exempt. The amount of extra
revenue raised was about the same as the amount remitted by the reductions in income-tax in the spring: taken together, the two budgets
transferred some of the weight of taxation from the rich to the poor and,
whatever the case for an open adjustment of taxation in this direction, the
way in which it was done led to the view that 'The only rational explanation of the reduction in income-tax is that it was an exclusively political
move made with an eye on the forthcoming general election.'[1]

[1] G. D. N. Worswick and P. H. Ady, *The British Economy 1950–1959* (1962), 34.

Butler's prestige fell when the boom had to be stopped. He became Lord Privy Seal and was replaced at the Treasury by Macmillan; in the party the modernizers and business men began to lose ground, and the people who wanted to get back to 'before the war' made their opinions heard more loudly than they had done for some time. They may have felt this was electorally safer once the 1955 election was won, and they were also encouraged by the signs that Butler's power was less than it had been and that modern Conservatism was on the retreat. In a by-election in the normally safe Conservative seat of Tonbridge the government's share of the vote dropped sharply. A campaign in Conservative newspapers suggested that the Prime Minister was not firmly in command of the situation, and within six months of the election Eden thought it necessary to deny that he was thinking of resigning.

The impatience with Eden was not easy to justify; the balance of payments was improving and he could hardly be blamed for the deterioration in relations between Russia and the West. But the more traditionally minded of the Conservatives felt that it was time to reassert old values. Under Churchill they had not ventured to criticize; now they wanted to see policies that would restore the position of the traditional middle classes and revive the strength of Britain's imperial position. The middle class, taken as a whole, had in fact been gaining ground relative to the working class almost all the time in the 1950s, and Butler's two 1955 Budgets had reinforced the tendency of salaries to increase faster than wages. But the middle classes could not be treated as a single unit: the rising level of average salaries reflected the appearance of new and rather well-paid salaried jobs rather than an increase in the incomes of the traditional middle class. The emergence of airline pilots, programme directors for television, and market research consultants meant that there was a prosperous middle class holding jobs that often had not existed before the war, but this was no consolation for solicitors, clergymen, or middle-class gentlefolk living on income from investments—often from gilt-edged stock, on which the income had lost a good deal of its purchasing power in the steady rise in prices since 1939. The assumption that a manual job should not pay as well as a non-manual job was not very reasonable, because there had always been a fair amount of overlapping between skilled workers and clerks or small shopkeepers, but the middle class complained as though the high wages obtained by miners in the late 1940s or by car workers in the 1950s were some infringement of a preordained order of society. The declining section of the middle class blamed the working class, and also blamed the government for not resisting the working class. The government could hardly convince them that really they had lost ground to members of other sections of the middle class, but a government which tried to reinstate all members of the middle class in their pre-war position, as they fondly remembered it, was going to have a difficult job on its hands.

The confused state of the Conservatives was presumably some consolation for Attlee when he retired from the leadership of the Labour party in November 1955. He had been chosen as the man who divided the party least, and had run it on that basis, with an awareness that many members of the party would be suspicious of anything that looked like a return to the personal dominance exercised by MacDonald. Attlee was never a commanding figure in the party at large, though he kept his Cabinet firmly under control when he was Prime Minister. His form of leadership, which in effect left it to other people to put forward ideas, followed the same lines as Asquith's or Baldwin's, and did not involve constant intervention in the manner of Lloyd George or Neville Chamberlain. For his successor the Parliamentary Labour party elected Gaitskell, who polled more votes than Morrison and Bevan put together; Attlee had indicated one of Gaitskell's claims by saying the party needed to be led by someone born in the twentieth century. As a man who was interested in ideas Gaitskell could be expected to give his party something new to talk about, but it was far from certain that the country at that moment wanted—whatever its needs may have been—a leader who had been born in the twentieth century.

Early in 1956 a curious light was thrown on British attitudes by the success of the play *Look Back in Anger*. Artistically and intellectually it was the first of a number of plays that revived the moribund London theatre and was also the first of a series of attacks on the way British life was developing. In 1956 the dominant note in the play which seemed to catch people's political feelings was the hero's complaint 'people of our generation aren't able to die for good causes any more. We had all that done for us, in the thirties and the forties, when we were still kids. There aren't any good brave causes left.' There was also an older man's note of nostalgia.

> The England I remembered was the one I left in 1914, and I was happy to go on remembering it that way. . . . Those long cool evenings in the [Indian] hills, everything purple and golden. Your mother and I were so happy then. It seemed as if we had everything we could ever want. I think the last day the sun shone was when that dirty little train steamed out of that crowded suffocating Indian station, and the battalion band playing for all it was worth.[1]

England had come to a position where it was possible to set up a Welfare

[1] J. Osborne, *Look Back in Anger* (1960), 66 and 84; first performed May 1956.

State running with capitalist efficiency, like West Germany, or a Welfare State running with experimental and socialist overtones, like Sweden; the emotions awakened by Osborne's play did not belong to the real world. But all the signs are that the country turned away from the choice, and decided that the future prospects were too unexciting to be faced willingly. This attitude could do no good in the long run; it was particularly dangerous that it was in the ascendant when the problem of Suez arose.

The Suez crisis of 1956

In July 1956 the American government decided that after all it would not be able to help the Egyptian government to build a dam at Aswan on the Nile for irrigation and hydro-electricity. This may have been because opposition in Congress to foreign aid in general was unexpectedly strong, or it may have been because President Nasser of Egypt was regarded as too ready to negotiate with Russia. As a result the British government also withdrew its offer to help with the costs of the dam. Nasser then determined to acquire money for the dam by nationalizing the Suez Canal Company, paying compensation at the market price of the shares. His right to do so was much clearer than the right of Iran to nationalize the Abadan oil refinery, for Egypt had made no comparable renunciation of the right to nationalize. Nevertheless, British opinion regarded Nasser's action as a blow that had to be parried. The Canal had been the route to India; it was still the route to Australia; it was the route for the growing imports of oil. Besides, the Canal Company had always charged low passage rates, and Nasser might be expected to increase them to help pay for the dam.

When the Commons debated the issue on 2 August, Eden was uncompromising in denying Nasser's right to act as he had. Gaitskell said in his speech that Egypt had done nothing to England that would justify the use of force, but he also compared Nasser to Hitler and to Mussolini. These were dangerous names to use; they encouraged people to think that the nationalization of the Canal was comparable to the occupation of the Rhineland in 1936, and the implication was that it should be resisted. The French government was concerned, for the Canal Company was a French company, and in addition they wanted to see Nasser crushed because they believed he was the main support of the revolt which had broken out in Algeria in 1954 and that it might collapse if he were overthrown. So British and French military planners began putting together forces for the operation known as Musketeer, which involved landing a force in Egypt and occupying the Canal (and presumably overthrowing Nasser, though this was not so clear). The force was mainly

British, the commanders were British, and the bombers needed to knock out the Egyptian air force were almost all British.

A conference of 22 countries with an interest in the Canal was held in August, and 18 of the nations agreed that the Canal ought to be internationalized: the governments whose subjects used the Canal would set up a committee to take the place of the Canal Company and run the Canal, and make sure that it was kept open in accordance with the Treaty of 1888. The Canal Company ordered all its pilots to leave their jobs; it was widely believed in England and France that the Egyptians were not technically capable of running the Canal or finding new pilots, but the Egyptian government proved quite capable of running the Canal, and new pilots were recruited quite easily. Egypt also declined to accept the internationalization proposed by the 18 nations in London and by early September the initial shock of nationalization was dying and the use of force was becoming less acceptable to world opinion; the British and French governments were left feeling that they were not getting anywhere.

Eden did not want to lose touch with the United States at this stage. When Dulles suggested a Suez Canal Users' Association, Eden agreed to discuss it. But he made it clear that he welcomed it only because it meant that the United States would remain in touch with England and France, and he seems to have thought that if Egypt would not recognize the authority of the S.C.U.A., then the United States would co-operate in imposing it upon Nasser by force. Dulles had no intention of allowing this to happen; he stated that the United States did not intend to shoot its way through the Canal, and later on he said that 'there were no teeth in the plan'.[1] But Eden had been interested in it only because he had thought there were teeth in it.

From early August the French government had been supplying military equipment to Israel, with at least a suggestion of co-operation against Nasser. Israel could defend her own frontiers against Egypt, but an advance forward across the Sinai desert was possible only if she had command of the air. France could not provide this, so perhaps late in September and certainly by mid-October the French government suggested to Eden that the Musketeer plan (which had all along been kept at a few weeks' readiness) should be adapted to synchronize with an Israeli advance against Egypt. For Israel the attack on the Egyptian air force was what mattered; the fact that an Anglo-French force would also be attacking Egypt was gratifying but less important. For France, the more people who attacked Nasser the merrier. So far as England was concerned, the outbreak of fighting caused by an Israeli attack provided

---

[1] H. Thomas, *The Suez Affair* (1967), 94.

an opportunity to claim that she was only going into the struggle to separate the combatants. Of course, co-operation with Israel was contrary to the whole line of British policy since at least 1948. England had tried to get on to good terms with the Arab countries, partly because of the growing importance of oil, partly because the Middle East had been a British sphere of influence since the First World War and there was a risk that Russia might begin to take an interest in it. But the sentimental supporters of the Arabs saw them as splendid desert horsemen having nothing in common with the corrupt or downtrodden Egyptians: this view seems to have prevailed in London, though so far as Arabs were concerned Egypt was in many ways the country to which they looked for guidance and leadership.

By mid October the British and Egyptian Foreign Secretaries had worked out six principles on which the Canal could be run. S.C.U.A., teeth or no teeth, was accepted by the Egyptians as a body with a legitimate interest in the level of tolls. France was not in the least eager for the success of these negotiations, but failed to frustrate them. Eden declined to show any interest in the Foreign Secretary's negotiations, and instead took him on a number of more or less well-concealed visits to French ministers in the second half of October. The timing of the plan seems to have been decided by the British belief that the United States would not act in a way that would be hostile to Israel before the American Presidential election in November. This calculation exaggerated the importance of the Jewish vote in New York; the financial support of the Jewish community may have been important to Truman in the months before the 1948 election but no Republican candidate expected to get Jewish money or votes in any great numbers, whatever foreign policy he followed.

On 29 October Israel attacked Egypt. On the 30th England and France called on both sides to withdraw to positions ten miles from the Canal and allow British and French troops to come in and occupy the Canal. Israel could occupy almost the whole Sinai peninsula, Egypt had to give up Sinai and the Canal. Egypt did not accept this ultimatum, and Musketeer was put into operation. At the same time England and France vetoed a resolution in the Security Council asking for all nations to refrain from using force in the Middle East. On the 31st the bombing of Egyptian airfields began, and the invasion fleet set sail. But as it had to come all the way from Malta—Cyprus could be used as an air base, but had no harbours large enough for an expedition on this scale—it could not reach Port Said, at the north end of the Canal, until November 6. Once the Egyptian air force was paralysed there was not much for England and

France to do. Israeli forces advanced through the Sinai peninsula, and arrived at about the ten-mile line. But there was little comfort elsewhere for the government. The Egyptians sank 47 blockships in the Canal.[1] Eisenhower made it clear, in an angry telephone conversation with Eden, that he disapproved of the British action and would do his best to stop it. The Opposition objected so strenuously and violently to government policy that one sitting of the House had to be suspended for tempers to calm down. At the United Nations the General Assembly voted by 64 to 5 (England, France, Israel, Australia, and New Zealand) that there should be a ceasefire; when Israeli forces reached the 10-mile line they were ready to accept the ceasefire, which would have left England and France more stranded than ever. For the invasion fleet was still on its way from Malta, and it could hardly come ashore to keep the peace if both sides had already accepted the U.N. ceasefire. On 5 November paratroops were dropped near Port Said, and on the 6th the fleet arrived. Port Said was taken later in the day, and troops set off on the hundred miles to Suez, at the south end of the Canal.

But before they had got very far they heard that England and France had accepted the ceasefire. To some extent the pressure of the United Nations and of the Opposition in Parliament had weakened the government's position; two resignations by junior ministers, the knowledge that a dozen Conservative Members were about to present a formal protest, and the possibility that dissatisfied Cabinet ministers like Macleod or Monckton might resign meant that the government could no longer be completely sure of its own survival; pressure on the gold reserves, which had had to meet sales of £100m. of sterling, and the knowledge that oil would be in short supply and could only be obtained from the United States all combined to convince the British government that the operation would have to stop. In Paris the franc was steady, the government had no doubts about its parliamentary support, and was not particularly concerned about the United Nations. The British decision to stop came as a most unwelcome surprise, but as the expedition was completely integrated and was under British command the French had to accept the decision. The military operations had been successful—only 21 British soldiers were killed in the whole undertaking—but the political situation made this success useless.

Eden's health was already poor, and it has been suggested that the medical treatment he received may have affected his judgement. At this point he was obliged to go to Jamaica to rest. While he was away the government, temporarily led by Butler, was forced step by step to with-

[1] Thomas, op. cit. 130.

draw from Egypt and to leave the task of peace-keeping to the U.N. Emergency Force, and the work of clearing the Canal to the U.N. and Egypt. Inside England the popularity of the government seems to have been almost unaffected by the whole performance: a fairly vocal section of middle-class opinion which had supported the Conservatives turned to the Labour party, but the opinion polls at the time suggested that a slightly larger section of pro-Labour working-class opinion felt that the operation had been justified. The government's attempts to explain what it had been doing were not impressive: at first of course it said it had intervened to separate the combatants; then it congratulated itself on bringing the U.N.E.F. into existence which, as Healey commented from the Labour side during the debate, was rather as though Al Capone expected to be thanked for bringing about improvements in the Chicago police force; and then it said it had found stacks of Russian arms in Egypt which showed that a Communist plot was afoot. In reality the discovery only showed that Nasser took weapons from both sides in the Cold War, because larger stocks of British arms had been found. The French government admitted straight-forwardly that it had co-operated with Israel, but the British government stuck to its story that it had not even known that Israel was going to attack Egypt. This shows what was really to be condemned about the British government's attitude to Suez: it knew that what it was in fact doing—going back into Egypt to recover control of the Canal—could not be defended in public but nevertheless it went ahead. As nobody outside the country believed its story anyway, it gained the discredit of being dishonest as well as imperialist. England's allies in the Middle East, particularly Nuri es-Said in Iraq, were weakened by the episode, and Nasser was greatly strengthened; he refused to have anything to do with the compromise terms worked out in mid October for the Canal, and kept control of it in Egyptian hands.

While the Suez operations did not affect the feelings of the general public much, they did affect people closer to the centre of politics. Some people on the Conservative side thought the operation might have come off if the Labour party had not protested so loudly; it is most unlikely that the fierceness of Labour's opposition really made much difference, and in any case it is hard to see why the Labour party should have been expected to approve of a policy about which they had never been consulted. A more direct and personal bitterness was felt against Gaitskell, partly because in a broadcast he asked Conservatives to overthrow Eden and, in effect, to set up someone like Butler as a sort of Ramsay MacDonald in reverse, and partly because people thought that in August he had committed himself to the use of force. In addition, he seemed to

be pro-American in his attitude; Bevan was less vehement in his condemnation of the operations and, while it was good tactics for the
Conservatives to play on any division there might be between Gaitskell
and Bevan, it was probably also true that Bevan disliked the way the
United States had come to assert control over British policy. This was
part of the Conservative reaction: the latent anti-Americanism of the
people who felt the United States was working to destroy the British
Empire led to a series of protests. A resolution condemning the attitude
of the United States was put on the Order Paper and was signed by about
120 Conservative back-benchers who were presumably not made any less
hostile to the United States by the Labour party's general willingness to
welcome American anti-imperialism.

Suez also had an embittering effect on the Labour party. In terms of
policy it suggested that the Conservative party had not turned its back
on the past as much as had appeared during the early 1950s. In terms of
the conduct of politics Suez seemed to be a piece of imperialism and
deception which, although it had not succeeded, had been presented to
the public in an untruthful way that concealed the size of the defeat. The
result was that the Opposition remained constantly suspicious of the
government. Consultation between government and Opposition was not
necessary for the conduct of foreign policy, as had been seen at the outbreak of the Boer War and the two World Wars, but some degree of trust
was needed. The general public was not normally told all that was going
on, but from the early 1920s, when Baldwin and MacDonald established fairly friendly relations, down to 1956, Prime Ministers and
Leaders of the Opposition were almost all the time on close enough terms
to discuss things in an amiable way. After 1956 this was no longer the
case; the doubt and bitterness remained at the highest levels in England
long after it had been forgotten by everybody else except the Arabs who
felt that England was still imperialist at heart.

12. *They 'never had it so good'*   1957–1961

Rebuilding after Suez

EDEN'S health never recovered from the strain of Suez. He came back from Jamaica and tried to carry on, but the recurring fever that had attacked him from time to time in the past three years returned, and he had to resign. His career was like that of Neville Chamberlain's in its masterful ascent to the Prime Ministership, followed by excessive activity in office and then a dramatic loss of power. His departure eased the shock of Suez for the country. For some years Butler had been building up his claim to lead the party, and people outside the centre of power expected him to succeed Eden. But he had not given the impression of being totally committed to Suez, and he was blamed for the decision to withdraw taken while he was Deputy Prime Minister. People with long memories remembered that he had been one of the defenders of Munich and appeasement. Macmillan was known to have been one of the keenest supporters of Suez; it has been suggested more recently that he brought the whole operation to a stop by his insistence that he could not any longer defend the exchange value of the pound, but this was not discussed at the time. Opinion in the Conservative party was assessed by private consultations, and not by a vote of the parliamentary party, but there is no reason to doubt that Macmillan was the man the Conservatives wanted.

Between 1924 and 1939 Macmillan had habitually disagreed with the party leadership, first on domestic policy, where he thought much more could be done to reduce unemployment, and then on foreign policy, where he thought Hitler should be resisted. By 1956 both of these views were party orthodoxy, and in any case Macmillan did not look unorthodox; he gave a well-cultivated impression of an Edwardian gentleman of leisure with a great fondness for the past and its customs. The Conservative

back-benchers may easily have thought that Macmillan was less favourable to change than Butler, though on this point they were probably
wrong. Macmillan had one rather traditionalist habit of mind; he had a
low opinion of people who had not served in the armed forces when the
need arose. He had been badly wounded in the First World War; he had
a poor opinion of Gaitskell, who had been a civil servant during the
Second World War. Like Macmillan, Gaitskell was a very intelligent,
rather shy man with no fear of originality or independence of thought.
Apart from the natural party difference that Gaitskell believed in equality
and Macmillan thought people should be able to amass and hold their own
fortunes, there was a personal difference between them: Gaitskell was a
man of rigid principle who thought Macmillan was a crook, and Macmillan was a man of flexible techniques who thought Gaitskell was a
prig.

Probably Macmillan was the best man to lead the Conservatives in the
circumstances of 1957. The Prime Minister had to thread his way through
many difficulties, and he did it very well; he looked more impressive on
other, later occasions, but perhaps he never again solved problems as
skilfully as in the first eighteen months of his term as Prime Minister. One
early and important decision was to treat the alliance with the United
States as England's principal diplomatic concern. Like Churchill he had
known Eisenhower during the war, and he was able to build a close
political relationship upon this personal friendship. In Macmillan's
opinion, England should never embark on positive action in foreign affairs
without the approval of the United States. This meant he had to cut himself off from France, but the position of the French government seemed
unimpressive as it plunged further into the problem of holding Algeria.

The Conservative party was in an anti-American mood, so England had
to be seen to have a position of her own. The British H-bomb was on the
point of completion, and Macmillan ordered it to be tested. Shortly
afterwards the Minister of Defence, Duncan Sandys—the seventh since
1951—announced that National Service would come to an end, on the
grounds that England could reduce her forces equipped with conventional
weapons and rely to a much greater extent on nuclear weapons. In years
to come, this doctrine became less fashionable and people argued that
conventional strength was needed for wars fought at something below the
H-bomb level, but at the time Sandys's line of argument was very attractive for political and financial reasons. After the switch to reliance on
nuclear weapons the government not only ended conscription but also
claimed it was justified in withdrawing troops from Germany despite the
1954 agreements: it was argued that the general strength of Europe would

be increased by the existence of a British nuclear force close at hand. This was a fairly clear statement that the British bomb was built out of a fear that the United States might not be willing to commit its nuclear forces to the defence of Europe in all circumstances, but European opinion was not won over by the thought of a British bomb to back up the American bomb. The troops were withdrawn from Germany because keeping them there cost more foreign exchange than expected. The Sandys strategy looked attractive to anyone who considered how much was spent on defence. In 1953 expenditure reached a peace-time peak of just over £1,500m., over 12 per cent of the national income. Spending was held at this level in cash terms, and as prices went upwards steadily it declined in real terms. Dependence on nuclear bombs, which were relatively cheap to make once the initial plant had been built, helped the government to keep defence spending at the same level in cash terms, and thus bring down the proportion of national income devoted to defence quite considerably. And such was the importance attached to building the H-bomb that only a small minority pointed out that in fact military spending was being cut.

The newly-formed government adopted a more conciliatory attitude over Cyprus than its predecessor had done. The Greek majority in Cyprus wanted Enosis, or union with Greece. Archbishop Makarios, the effective leader of the community, because Greek bishops are elected by their flocks, supported the demand and when its more violent supporters turned to guerrilla activity he did not denounce their attacks on British troops. Eden's government arrested the Archbishop and sent him to the Seychelles; Macmillan's government released him, though he was not at first allowed to return to Cyprus. A change of Governors from Lord Harding to Sir Hugh Foot suggested that negotiations might begin.

Two-ninths of the population of Cyprus was Turkish, and had a natural dislike for Enosis. Most Conservatives valued Turkey's friendship more than that of Greece, and felt that as England had kept the problem under control while her rule was unchallenged she might as well go on ruling the island. Partition was considered but rejected, mainly because there was no region in the island where the Turks were in a comfortable majority. The government fairly certainly wanted to get out of the island, but its back-benchers had no such desire, and Lord Salisbury resigned from the Cabinet when the Archbishop was released. Decolonization in Ghana and Malaya went ahead with less controversy; both countries became independent in 1957, and both of them followed the Indian example and remained members of the Commonwealth. The numerical balance in conferences of Commonwealth Prime Ministers was moving towards the underdeveloped countries, and this in turn encouraged the British government to think harder about providing aid for the underdeveloped members of the Commonwealth.

On his return to Canada from the July 1957 Commonwealth Prime Ministers' conference Diefenbaker, the recently elected Conservative Prime Minister, raised an awkward problem for the British government by saying that Canada should take another 15 per cent of her imports from England and cut imports from the United States accordingly. He seems not to have thought out what it would involve, but the British government could not neglect the suggestion. In September Thorneycroft, who had succeeded Macmillan at the Exchequer, put forward a proposal for a customs union between Canada and England which would eliminate tariff barriers between the two countries and allow British manufacturers to sell more easily in Canada than before, and thus carry out Diefenbaker's suggestion. The 1947 General Agreement on Tariffs and Trade permitted a customs union, though it did not allow preferences based on reductions in duties along the lines of the 1932 Ottawa agreements. But the Canadian government had no appetite for a customs union and the idea was dropped.

The British government had wanted to explore the Canadian suggestion quickly because of its effect on European trade negotiations. In March 1957 France, West Germany, Italy, Holland, Belgium, and Luxemburg had signed the Treaty of Rome and formed a Common Market, a form of customs union in which the members not only have no tariffs between one another but also have a single uniform tariff against all other countries' products. A uniform tariff required, almost inevitably, a unified policy for agriculture and taxation. If England joined, she might find that the Common Market was going to develop into a political union, and under its tariff proposals she would have to end Commonwealth preferences and change the method of giving financial support to British farmers from one of subsidies paid by the taxpayer to one of customs duties that would raise the price of food to the purchaser. As the government did not want to be excluded from the advantages of the wider industrial market that would be opened up by the abolition of tariff barriers, it proposed that the whole of western Europe should form a Free Trade Area, with no customs duties on manufactured products, but with all the members free to set their own tariffs on imports from outside the Area. This would have been in accordance with the GATT, would allow the six-nation Common Market to maintain its unified system and would also allow England to import food cheaply and continue to give preferences to Commonwealth countries. The proposal was discussed for about eighteen months after the signing of the Treaty of Rome, but eventually it was brought to an end by the French government which felt that England had found an ingenious arrangement for getting the best of both worlds, and in particular for preventing French agriculture from getting any benefit from the scheme.

In the first half of 1957 England's international credit seemed to be recovering in both a political and an economic sense from the shock of Suez. The political recovery went on; Macmillan sturdily ignored any coolness there might be, and set himself the task of finding ways to reduce the tension between Russia and the NATO countries. The economic task was harder. The money kept in London on a short-term basis which had left at the time of Suez returned in the spring and, while Thorneycroft's budget maintained the check on investment and domestic spending that had been in effect since the autumn of 1955, he was able by July to speak with some confidence of expansion of the economy. He was then the victim of misfortune; the French franc had been kept steady in international terms since 1949, but prices had been going up so fast that its value had been undermined. In August it was in effect devalued, and people thought that other currencies might change their values. The short-term money that had come in during the spring left London again, and the Chancellor of the Exchequer had to face a crisis of confidence. His immediate reaction was to raise the Bank Rate to 7 per cent, thus making London more attractive for short-term money, which was the orthodox way to deal with this sort of problem.

At the same time he carried to an extreme the efforts to restrain the economy which had begun with Butler's second 1955 budget. In domestic politics this represented the greatest degree of concession to people who wanted to get back to 'before the war' that any government had cared to offer. Price stability was taken as the government's main objective, and linked with this was maintenance of the exchange value of sterling at $2.80. The Opposition agreed that maintaining sterling should be a paramount objective, perhaps out of a fear of being regarded as the party of devaluation; it was coming to believe that devaluation in 1949 had caused the set-back in the 1950 election, and even to imagine that it had led to the increase in prices which had helped cause defeat in 1951. This bi-partisan acceptance of maintaining sterling at the current rate was a sharp reversal of Butler's readiness to think of going on to a floating rate but, once accepted, the new attitude became firmly fixed.

In order to restrain the economy investment was reduced in the nationalized industries, where spending was directly under government control, and lending by banks or hire-purchase firms was again discouraged. The Opposition protested that this would increase unemployment and it argued that, if the economy was planned properly, useful investment could be carried out and the value of the pound could be maintained. This did not suit the mood of the government at all; many of its supporters had felt that Churchill, Butler, and Monckton had been too soft on the trade unions in the early 1950s, and that the time had now come to hold them in check. Thorneycroft's economic theory was that, if the amount of money in circulation was kept strictly limited, wages could not rise faster than production: if a particular group of workers got a wage-increase, there would simply be less money for everybody else unless enough goods had been produced to meet the wage-increase. At a less sophisticated level it was natural enough that Lord Hailsham, who had been one of the leaders of Conservative anti-Americanism just after Suez, should by the end of the year be one of the men most vocal in saying that trade unions were betraying the country: Suez and the worsening of industrial relations were symptoms of a feeling that the post-war world was less pleasant than had been thought. Naturally enough strikes increased, though they did not rise above the relatively low levels of the years immediately after the General Strike.

Keeping the purchasing power of money stable mattered most to people whose incomes were more or less fixed, and this mainly meant people outside industry. But the other industrial countries were also concerned to keep prices steady, and France was always regarded as an awful warning because of the startling rise in prices there in the fifties. The United States and Britain placed more emphasis than France on stable prices, but all three countries spent comparable proportions of their national income on defence. The United States economy in the fifties was if anything even more sluggish than the British was becoming after 1955. Only in Germany, where defence expenditures were low, was price stability reconciled with economic growth.

International comparisons of this sort were becoming more common, not so much out of a greater willingness to look at the outside world as because the figures were available. Macmillan as Chancellor had put the situation quite well when he said that economic forecasting on the figures available was rather like looking up trains in last year's Bradshaw, the very comprehensive railway time-table of the period, but figures for previous years were available and figures issued by the Organization for European Economic Co-operation[1] enabled British politicians to compare their country's performance with others, and select the appropriate items

[1] Several functions of the O.E.E.C., including that of issuing figures, were later taken over by the Organization for Economic Co-operation and Development.

for their speeches. Labour party leaders pointed out that England was devoting less of her national income to new investment than most European countries, that economic growth at least since 1955 was slower, and that it was likely to continue to be slower under the Thorneycroft policy. The economists who advised Thorneycroft, whose views were best expressed by Robbins and Paish, tended not to be interested in problems of growth and to be more concerned with price-stability. They seem also to have been enthusiastic about maintaining a high level of investment overseas. Thus, Paish, after discussing the way that in the years just after the war England had in effect borrowed from the United States to be able to invest in Commonwealth countries, went on: 'It is probably a pity that means could not have been found to continue the process, for the United Kingdom has all the qualifications for a successful exporter of capital—specialized institutions, financial connections, long experience: all the qualifications, that is, except one, the availability of adequate resources to invest.'[1] The City of London went on with its investment operations, adequate resources or not, and this was one reason why the reserves were so low that they were vulnerable to fluctuations like those of August and September 1957. Cutting down foreign investment seemed to be impossible because of the need to remain on good terms with countries in the sterling area.

While the economists advising Thorneycroft were concerned with the problem of checking inflation after Keynesian methods had removed the restraints of large-scale unemployment, the interest of a significant part of the profession was turning to the post-Keynesian question of getting the economy to grow as fast as possible. In 1957 the Labour party conference in effect gave up thinking about further nationalization and began to commit itself to economic growth as an objective. Six years in opposition worrying about nationalization had not convinced people that any industries were as obviously appropriate for nationalization as coal and the railways had been in the past, partly because no other industries could be so easily defined as single units to be taken over. The programme referred to the 500 powerful companies which dominated the economy, and implied that they would be nationalized if they 'failed the nation', but this was really no more than an additional means to control the economy as a whole. Planning, combined with a more expansive economic policy than the Conservatives', would mean that there would be more for everybody.

This change of tack did not go unopposed but it was not the most fiercely contested part of the conference agenda. The Labour party had

[1] F. W. Paish, *Studies in an Inflationary Economy* (1962), 158.

to face the question of the British attitude to the hydrogen bomb, and the result dismayed the left wing of the party. On the whole the people who thought that the country should act according to higher moral standards than other nations were opposed to her possessing hydrogen bombs, and claimed that if, now she had them, the government was to give them up, this would have a great effect on world opinion. The left wing had hoped that Bevan would lead them in the attack on British retention of the bomb; instead he argued on 3 October that Britain needed the bomb to be an important country, and asked the conference 'not to send the British Foreign Secretary naked into the conference chamber'. The supporters of moral force were more surprised than they should have been; their alliance with Bevan from 1951 to 1955 had rested on a common belief that the United States was not behaving as she should, but in 1957 the moralizers wanted to have an effect on the United States by example, while Bevan recognized that the British H-bomb was for most purposes an anti-American bargaining counter, and showed no desire to give it up.

Both sides took it for granted that England was a great power, less important than the United States and the Soviet Union, but still to be compared with them rather than with any other country when forming policy. A few students of strategy pointed out that England was not a great power in this sense, and that her possession of the bomb would have an unsettling effect on the world, by making a lot of countries which considered themselves to be her equal want to have nuclear weapons also— as Crossman put it, 'the right to distrust the Americans cannot remain a British monopoly'.[1] Views of this sort were not popular, especially when accompanied as in Crossman's case by a suggestion that conscription might be needed to keep the army at an adequate level.

If people had fully understood the implications of the success of the Soviet Union and, just a few weeks later, of the United States in launching inter-continental ballistic missiles, they would have seen that the British position was being eroded. While the United States and the Soviet Union depended on aeroplanes to deliver the H-bomb, England was technologically on equal terms with them, though her air force was smaller. But a rocket attack, which could not be fended off, was altogether more dangerous, especially if it was accompanied by an improved rocket defence against aeroplanes. The cost of keeping a nuclear force in being was slight, but building up a rocket delivery system was likely to be much more expensive. Attempts were made to develop British rockets, but they cost too much to be politically practicable. The discussions on conduct of defence became even more difficult because the public

[1] 27 Feb. 1958; *Commons Debates*, dlxxxiii, 634.

found it hard to understand that expenditure on developing new weapons was bound to be high, and that almost equally inevitably many of them had to be scrapped before they came into production. England did not have the resources needed for this expensive form of competition. The cancellation of a weapon in the United States was an inconvenience; in England the cancellation of Blue Streak in 1960 was a step which was likely to change the whole structure of foreign policy.

It could have been argued that England should withdraw from great power politics simply on the grounds that she could no longer afford to take part, but most of the campaign for renunciation of nuclear weapons was based on moral arguments, and assumed that England ought to continue to exercise considerable influence in the world. The moralizers began to organize themselves in the Campaign for Nuclear Disarmament, which asked for unilateral British disarmament. Some of its success in attracting support was due to the absence of any force in politics which could really inspire any enthusiasm; its emergence was one of the first signs that people were beginning to take an interest in political change again after the apathy and tranquillity of the early 1950s. In this way the Campaign had an effect on the world outside England; its marches and the interest taken in civil disobedience by some of its members foreshadowed the methods used by politically active people in several other countries for years to come. The organizing strength of the Campaign came mainly from the left wing of the Labour party, so that it inherited most of the force of Bevanism. Its appeal was distinctly wider than that, because it seemed to be the pressure-group through which people could express a general desire for peace. The Campaign caused problems inside the Labour party, but it was also a strong hint to Macmillan that he should do something about the world situation.

The ascendancy of Macmillan

In 1957 there was little enough that he could do. He had first to make sure that his government held together. He was a more skilful debater than the Leader of the Opposition, and could occasionally play off the Labour left against him. As a result the Conservatives in parliament, many of whom felt that it could not have been right both to go to Suez and to leave so ignominiously, recovered their composure. They survived the strain of passing a Rent Act that, so far as more expensive property was concerned, ended the limitations of rent imposed by the 1939 Act and, in some cases, the 1915 Act. The Labour party said this would lead to evictions and widespread rent increases; the government said it would loosen up the housing market, provide the landlords with a rate of return that would enable them to carry out repairs and might even lead people to resume building houses for rent. Very little came of these predictions: the government amended the Act to restrain evictions; rents did not rise as sharply as had been forecast—in a good deal of the country there was no acute housing shortage, and in London rents had been going up for some time in any case; repairs continued to be neglected and the government was left looking for new ways of persuading landlords to save their houses from turning into slums; and nobody built houses for rent. Small-scale landlords, who in the past had built a house or two for rent, could now invest their money in shares or in building societies, which had not been so easily available previously, and these ways of investing savings were more convenient than owning a house. Before the First World War large-scale developers built for rent because there was not much of a market for selling; they greatly preferred to build and sell, thus turning their money over quickly. By the 1950s many more people could afford to buy a house on a mortgage. On the other hand a new house still could not be built at a price that low-paid workers could rent, so they had to rely on subsidized council building to increase the stock of cheap houses. The Rent Act did not change any of this, and outside London made very little difference. But putting it through the Commons had been a hard battle, in which the Conservatives were afraid they might become unpopular. When it was over they felt much more confident.

By the time of the 1957 Conservative conference party morale was higher than it had been since just after the 1955 election. Lord Hailsham was the hero of the occasion, as the man who had stated most forthrightly the feelings of the party on such issues as the United States and the trade unions. While the party traditionalists were happy, the government was becoming unpopular, because by the winter unemployment was rising to a higher level than at any time since the war, and the rate of production was no higher than in 1955. Macmillan began to shift his ground a little, and to remind people that he had been Member for Stockton between the wars and was determined that unemployment should not return. The Chancellor of the Exchequer was less ready to change; to carry out his policy of limiting the total amount of money in circulation, he said that budget estimates must not exceed those of the previous year. As prices had, despite all the Chancellor's efforts, crept forward during the year, this would reduce the real value of government spending, which would be deflationary. When the issue arose Macmillan decided that estimates could go £50m. over the rate for the previous year. He then accepted the resignations of the Chancellor and the two Secretaries to the Treasury, dismissed this as 'a little local difficulty' and set off on a tour of the Commonwealth to India and Australia. The tour greatly increased his confidence; as he remarked in Australia 'at home you always have to be a politician, but when you are abroad you almost feel yourself a statesman'.[1] The tour may have taken some of the fine edge off his instinct for noticing danger ahead, which had been very strong since he became Prime Minister, but he undoubtedly returned with a public reputation in England that was more impressive than before.

Thorneycroft's resignation made it politically difficult to produce an expansionist budget in 1958. The ex-Chancellor had been regarded as the defender of the stable price-index, and the government could not endanger its reputation in this area. On the other hand a good deal of investment had been carried out since 1955, and there was no extra production to show for it. There was some unemployment and idle industrial plant, so expanding the economy was the obvious thing to do and would not necessarily lead to increased prices. As taxes could not be altered, the government worked on the situation by relaxing credit. Bank Rate was brought down by steps quite quickly from 7 to 4 per cent. Hire-purchase restrictions were made less and less severe. Banks were encouraged to lend, and opened a number of new schemes for encouraging people to borrow. The 1958 budget had ended the tax system by which companies were charged a higher rate on their profits if they paid them to shareholders as dividends, and although to some extent this merely recognized that companies were distributing a larger share of profits than in the early 1950s, it did encourage further distribution of dividends. The Stock Exchange boom that followed helped to put holders of capital into a good mood. The government successfully resisted a strike by London bus drivers, which established its reputation for firmness and discouraged other strikes. At the same time levels of consumption began to rise quite rapidly. Import prices, which had gone up for a short period after Suez, fell once more. Production rose from the low level to which it had fallen by the end of 1957. By the end of the year Macmillan and his new Chancellor, Heathcote Amory, had almost moved back to the position of Butler in the early 1950s when he was setting the economy free and watching prosperity rise.

When Macmillan succeeded Butler at the Exchequer in 1955, his place at the Foreign Office had been given to Selwyn Lloyd. This appointment was generally taken as a sign that Eden proposed to keep a good deal of the responsibility for foreign affairs in his own hands. Macmillan retained Lloyd when he became Prime Minister, partly to avoid suggesting that he felt that the Suez operation had been a mistake and partly to continue

[1] Anthony Sampson, *Macmillan, a Study in Ambiguity* (1967), 138.

to control foreign affairs as Eden had done. Early in 1958 the Russian leaders began asking for another summit conference. Macmillan was immediately certain that this would be useful, but he found a good deal of opposition to this in the United States and in Germany and nothing came of it.

In July there was a revolt in Iraq; the pro-British King Faisal and his chief minister, Nuri es-Said, were killed by the mob and an unstable regime under General Kassem took over. This change was really a delayed result of Suez, but the United States was already worried by the civil war that was imminent in the Lebanon. As a result American troops went to the Lebanon and British troops were flown to Jordan. This elevated what might have been just a normal change of government in the Middle East to the level of a great power struggle. The Russians again suggested a summit meeting, this time associated with the United Nations, and the British agreed. There was no enthusiasm in Washington, and in any case the Russians quickly changed their policy and asked for an emergency session of the General Assembly. The intervention in the Middle East by England and America was accepted rather than approved, but the Russians gained nothing by their change of approach.

By the end of 1958 two lines of discussion seemed to be opening. In Geneva representatives of America, Russia, and England were talking about ways to end the testing of nuclear bombs, a topic which grew more important as evidence accumulated that tests in the atmosphere increased radioactive fall-out to an extent which might become dangerous. At a loftier diplomatic level Macmillan was trying to persuade the western leaders that a summit conference could not do any harm and might have a good effect. One objection to a summit conference was that Eisenhower was not in good health, and in any case was not a man who would shine in dealing with a hostile debater; his talents had always lain in conciliation and in winning over people who wanted to be won over. A more general objection was that, if a conference were held, public opinion in western countries would take it for granted that some progress would be made, and western negotiators might be forced into making bad bargains rather than come home with no bargain at all.

Khrushchev tried to force the western leaders to negotiate by threatening to give East Germany full control over the Berlin situation, so that either there would be a crisis about the position of Berlin or the western powers would have to go back on their refusal to recognize the government of East Germany. In February Macmillan visited Moscow to see if he could persuade Khrushchev not to press this point and, by taking a more conciliatory line, make it easier for the western leaders to meet him.

Khrushchev was unhelpful at first, and on one day of the visit he had a diplomatic toothache to avoid meeting Macmillan. But the discussions became distinctly more friendly as the week went on, and by the time they ended Macmillan felt he had gained enough ground to be able to go on a tour of Paris, Bonn, and Washington, putting the arguments for a summit. Macmillan had thus turned himself into the co-ordinator of the west, and could be seen as the active man of the alliance dragging the other countries behind him to the summit. At the beginning of his Prime Ministership he had been mocked as 'Supermac' and as 'Macwonder'; by the spring of 1959 his supporters were able to feel that these titles were simply an accurate assessment of his position. The shock to British prestige caused by Suez was almost forgotten, and England seemed as dominant a power as she had done at any time in the 1950s.

By 1959 the economy stood on the edge of a great leap forward. Macmillan said in July 1957 that the people 'have never had it so good', a phrase that was to become altogether more closely linked with him than he intended.[1] At the time it was said, it may not have been accurate; production figures in 1958 were no higher than in 1955, and the three years of credit freeze had done more to hold back the economy than to maintain a stable level of prices. But between September 1958, when industrial production was at the 1955 level (105 per cent of the 1954 level) and December 1959, when production was 117 per cent of the 1954 level, there was a sudden explosive expansion, and Macmillan's slogan dominated politics and everyday life. Partly because the expansion was started by making credit easier to come by, and partly because of a change in people's wants, a great deal of the expansion was devoted to buying 'consumer durables': a majority of families had a washing-machine, which was particularly popular in the north; about one family in three had a refrigerator, and in the south the proportion was higher; about one family in three owned a car. Well over half the population had at least one of these consumer durables by the end of the fifties, and in quite a large number of cases they had bought it during Macmillan's years of power. In 1955 40 per cent of homes owned a television set; by 1959 the figure had risen to 70 per cent. Prosperity concentrated on a few specific products, and it was also limited geographically. The metal-working, engineering, car-producing region stretched from London to Birmingham and a little beyond; it changed in the late 1950s as industrial England had changed, over a hundred years earlier, in the transformation from the 'hungry forties' to the peaceful comfort of the skilled craftsmen who came up to London to look at the Great Exhibition of 1851. Older

[1] Sampson, op. cit. 158–9.

industrial regions, particularly Lancashire and Scotland, did not share in the 1958–60 boom. When the Chancellor of the Exchequer came to prepare his 1959 budget there were still relatively large numbers of people unemployed and overall production was not going up very much, despite the gratifying increase in the consumer durable trades. He determined to stimulate the economy by budgeting for a large deficit, and in the mood of the day the deficit had to be produced more by reductions in taxation than by any increase in government spending.

The major item of the budget was a reduction by 3·75p to 38½p of the standard rate of income-tax. There were other reductions in the lower rates of tax, a cut in the tax on beer and faster repayment of post-war credits on income-tax paid during the war, but the budget stood or fell by the cut on income-tax. The economy continued to grow rapidly, though the cut in taxes had more effect in the regions that were already prosperous than in any spreading of the prosperity to the rest of the country. Opposing the budget was not at all easy; Labour Members claimed to have met many drinkers in their constituencies who would have preferred the old-age pensioners to have the benefit of the revenue devoted to reducing the price of beer, but the government was not impressed.

The summer was long and warm and dry. Eisenhower paid a visit to England, and appeared with Macmillan on television. Their conversation was not particularly profound, but it underlined the fact that the Prime Minister was on the best of terms with the President of the United States. By the autumn Macmillan felt the time was ripe for a general election, and in September Parliament was dissolved. The opinion polls showed a fairly comfortable Conservative lead at the beginning of the campaign, but in the first week or two the Labour party appeared to be catching up. The Labour programme paid little attention to nationalization, and not much more to planning and reorganizing the economy, but it did lay considerable emphasis on increasing government spending and improving the social services. In the previous few years the Opposition had been particularly ready to argue for old-age pensioners, and this was repaid by the electorate's willingness to think that the Labour party was the one to turn to for better social welfare programmes.

The Labour rally seems to have died away from the day that Gaitskell said his party's social programme could be paid for without any increase in the income-tax, which raised more doubts than it settled. He was quite correct in saying that, if economic growth went on as it had been doing for the previous twelve months, the increases could be paid for easily. People may not have believed that growth would go on, or they may have wanted to know what Gaitskell would do if he had to choose between social welfare and tax stability; in any case they were not favourably impressed by his statement, and the Labour party began to fall back. In the election the government received only tepid support from some newspapers that were normally Conservative, and other papers went over to the Labour side. They changed mainly out of dissatisfaction with the government's conduct of colonial policy: Suez had lost the government a fair amount of support in intellectual circles, and although a settlement in Cyprus had been reached early in 1959 by which the Turkish minority was given some guarantees inside an independent country, there had been incidents when the troops maintaining law and order had been strained beyond endurance. It had also come to light that Mau Mau prisoners at the Hola camp, who had been reported to have died as a result of drinking contaminated water, had in fact been beaten to death. In Nyasaland the administration had responded to demonstrations in February and March 1959 in favour of independence with a set of measures described as a 'police state' by the commission of inquiry sent out from England. The British government declined to accept the Report, and this was mentioned disapprovingly by the press.

But although this disapproval may have reduced the size of the Conservative victory, it did no more.

	Votes	Seats	% of all votes cast
Conservative	13,749,830	365	49·4
Liberal	1,638,571	6	5·9
Labour	12,215,538	258	43·8

After the election a cartoon appeared, showing the Prime Minister sitting back and saying 'well, gentlemen, I think we all fought a good fight' to the 'colleagues' who had made victory possible—a motor-car, a television set, a vacuum-cleaner, and so on.[1] Some commentators spoke as if the Labour party had gone down for ever. It became fashionable to say that a government in power could now manipulate the economy to produce a boom when it wanted, and could find from the opinion polls when the time was ripe for a dissolution, so that the risk of defeat would be minimized. This ignored the fact that, once people realized the government could improve the economic situation, they would blame it for not producing improvements faster or for not producing the type of improvements that were needed.

[1] D. E. Butler and R. Rose, *The British General Election of 1959* (1960), 201.

Social change in the late 1950s

The theory that people had voted for the government simply because they felt well off was not as sweeping as the suggestion that the country had in some way become more middle-class. The commentators seemed not to realize how difficult it is to explain what is involved in becoming middle-class. Obviously it was not just a matter of voting Conservative: the Conservatives did not get as large a share of the total vote in 1959 as in 1924 or 1935 when, by this hypothesis, the country was less middle-class. It was true undoubtedly more people had acquired possessions, and possibly valuing possessions is a particularly middle-class habit, but the stories of the munition-workers in the First World War hurrying out to spend their high earnings on pianos and fur coats suggest that people in the working classes had always liked buying things when they had the money.

Employees had not become strikingly better off in the twentieth century. In terms of 1958–9 prices, their post-tax incomes were about 80 per cent higher in 1958–9 than in 1911–12—the sharp rise in taxation conceals some of the improvement in people's position, because of course the money taken in taxes is returned in state-provided services.[1] These services are not directly linked to income; social services depend a great deal on size of family, and the benefits of roads and of defence are very hard to allocate.

Levels of income and changes during the twentieth century

	1958–9 post-tax income	per cent of 1911–12
Upper limit of bottom tenth of employees	£205	190
Next	270	165
Next	327	176
Next	405	191
Next (median)	470	194
Next	537	191
Next	601	183
Next	685	173
Next	821	170[2]

One man in a thousand earned £2,632 post-tax.

These changes brought the middle third of the earning population rather closer to the top third, and improved the position of the people right down at the bottom, but the lowest 30 per cent—the poor, according to the definitions of Booth and Rowntree—had fallen behind the central third.

[1] G. Routh, *Occupations and Pay in Great Britain 1906–60* (1965), 88. Note that less than half the working population earn more than the average skilled worker.

[2] Routh, op. cit., especially pp. 4–8 and 43–5.

Probably the state-provided services did something to reduce the gap.

These figures help show that the average worker of the late 1950s was unlikely to get very far in buying consumer durables; when the average skilled worker earned about £800 a year (before tax and national insurance payments), he was not very likely to buy a new car, costing £400 or £500. Workers in exceptional trades, probably working long hours of overtime, or men with families who were just beginning to earn money but had not yet left home might find they could afford such things, but there was a tendency to mistake the exception for the normal case.

From time to time people have noticed that about half the population in England calls itself working-class and half says it is middle-class. On the sort of classifications accepted by sociologists, such as the division into manual and non-manual workers, only about a third of the population can be called middle-class. But neither of these proportions have altered much in the recent past, and they altered very little in the late 1950s. The proportion of non-manual workers in the working population increased from 20 per cent in 1911 to $31\frac{1}{2}$ per cent in 1959, but among men the change was only a rise from 22 per cent to 28 per cent. Among women the change was more marked, with an increase from $16\frac{3}{4}$ per cent to 40 per cent, but it must be remembered that almost all of this change was accounted for by a decline of $1\frac{1}{4}$m. in the number of women in private domestic service (counted as manual work) and an increase of $1\cdot1$m. in the number of typists. Apart from the switch in these categories, which was unlikely to make much difference politically because servants were usually to the right of the rest of the working-class, the change among women was as slight as among men. The tendency of a quarter or a third of the manual working class to describe itself as middle-class when asked has been going on at least as long as sociologists have been asking people what class they think they belong to, and it had no discernible effect on the political situation in 1959.

Some forms of behaviour are supposed to be associated with the working class rather than the middle class. In the economic field, going on strike is a working-class activity. The industrial history of the late 1950s does not suggest that people were becoming more middle-class. The most spectacular single strike was that, in the spring of 1958, of the London busmen, who were trying to maintain a position that was declining relative to other workers. The strike was unsuccessful, and the busmen continued to lose ground. The new aristocracy of labour were the motor-car workers and the electrical workers; the electrical workers pursued an aggressive policy partly because the Communist-dominated union leadership believed in a fighting policy, but there is little evidence that this was the reason why the membership turned against the leadership. The motor-car workers were represented by a variety of different unions, with the result that industrial policy was handled by shop-stewards who took rather a primitive approach to industrial relations. Their attitude looked sophisticated and effete compared with that of some managers; the British Motor Corporation dismissed 6,000 men without notice one morning in June 1956, and for some time afterwards enjoyed the sort of labour relations that ensured that few of their workers were going to think themselves middle-class.

Middle-class respectability had always included a feeling of respect for the police and a feeling that the police were on the side of solid citizens. This friendly relationship was weakened by the problem of motoring offences; middle-class people who had broken the law were fond of asking why the police were not away catching criminals, and showed little sign of realizing that motoring offences were crimes which endangered far more lives than anything done by the criminal classes. As motoring offences increased more rapidly than almost any other sort of crime the opportunities for friction rose quickly. One of the hardest duties of the police has always been that of 'keeping an eye' on some shady activity which cannot be completely suppressed. In the mid-fifties there had been an attempt to enforce more rigorously than in the previous few years the laws against homosexual conduct. The campaign had not really had the support of public opinion and as it used policemen as *agents provocateurs,* it reduced public sympathy for the police force. Two changes in other areas of the law showed that the government felt the police were having to use their discretion to an extent which put them under much strain. Prostitutes in London had always in effect been allowed to solicit in public, subject to occasional arrest and a trivial fine; in 1959 the fine was made much larger by the Street Offences Act and it was made clear that they were not to appear in public, though they could continue their trade in other ways. The Betting and Gaming Act passed by the government shortly after its re-election also relieved the police force from some invidious duties, and illustrated the decline of respectability. Cash bookmakers existed in large numbers, but because cash betting was illegal they were in the same position as prostitutes; sometimes they were arrested and fined, but most of the time the police simply 'kept an eye' on them. The new Act allowed bookmakers to set up licensed betting-shops for taking cash bets, and it also allowed people to set up casinos for gambling. In theory the gambling was restricted by the provision that nobody should have more chance of winning than anybody else, but the gambling provisions of the new law turned out to be much less well drafted than the provisions for betting and there was steady pressure for stricter legislation.

In the late 1950s there was a good deal of earnest social criticism. Osborne followed his play *Look Back in Anger* by *The Entertainer*, which again reflected the attitude that present-day England was in a dreadful mess, that there was something to be said for the old Edwardian stability though it was no longer recoverable, and that nobody had satisfying answers for the future. For a few years plays with a committed attitude were fashionable; they were praised for their realism, and condemned for bringing in the kitchen-sink and the discomforts of lower-class life too often. Translations of most of Brecht's work were put on, and his political attitude of admiration-tempered-by-doubt for the working classes was also to be seen in writers like Wesker. For perhaps five years there was a mood of political commitment combined with willingness to write plays that were meant to shock Rattigan's Aunt Edna; Sheila Delaney wrote *A Taste of Honey* because she saw one of Rattigan's plays and felt sure she could do better than that. By the early 1960s there was a divergence of aim, and writers concerned with social criticism turned to direct political satire while playwrights became less concerned about social criticism though they kept a much wider range of choice of plot, of subject-matter, and of language than they had had before 1956.

In the late 1940s and early 1950s the London stage had been dominated by American plays and musicals; the revival of the theatre after *Look Back in Anger* reduced this dominance and then led to a series of London productions appearing successfully on Broadway. In non-theatrical social criticism American influence became very noticeable in the late 1950s. *The Affluent Society*, *The Organization Man*, and *The Power Elite* were all written about the United States, but they were widely read by people who were afraid that England was going to follow the United States. Galbraith's contrast between 'private affluence and public squalor' was a return to a view that had been neglected in England in the 1950s;[1] the belief that people were being deprived of individuality by commercial and industrial organization aroused some response; the idea that the public was not being allowed to exercise full political freedom because of the insidious influence of an inner ring, denounced by political journalists as 'the Establishment', was held fairly widely. Among social critics the strongest influence was that of people working on the border-land between literary criticism and sociology; Raymond Williams's

[1] Galbraith's famous phrase was simply a translation of Sallust's 'privatim opulentia publicae egestas', which R. H. Tawney quoted in the original in his *Equality* (1931), 116.

Culture and Society and Richard Hoggart's *The Uses of Literacy* argued that once upon a time there had been a rough but wholesome unity about English society but that this had now been broken down and commercialized. Almost all of this school of writing agreed in denouncing the middle class, and in particular the new commercial middle class that had done well in trade; most of these writers took a favourable view of the working class and thought highly of its characteristic virtues of warmth of heart, solidarity with neighbours and workmates, and distrust of the thrusting individual who tramples his way to success. A good example was John Braine's *Room at the Top* (1957), a novel about a Yorkshire accountant who throws over his true love to marry a wool magnate's daughter; its high sales among the London intelligentsia cannot have been due entirely to the hero's exciting sex life.

The writers of the period saw themselves as men of the left, though their enthusiasm for the certainties of the past meant that really they were opposed to the modern world and would probably be against any government that came to terms with contemporary problems. Just after the 1959 election the Labour party presented no encouraging alternative to the government. Gaitskell was generally thought to have done quite well in the election, but as soon as it was over he moved further to the right than was practicable for a man who lacked the prestige of victory. Members of the right wing, who wanted to improve society by relatively small-scale changes directed to strategically chosen points, said that nationalization was no longer an important issue; members of the left wing, who said that only by sweeping change was it possible to carry out reform, insisted that the 1918 commitment to nationalization should be retained in the party constitution.

During the election the party's official defence policy had been to set up a non-nuclear club: England would try to negotiate a treaty under which she would give up her nuclear weapons and potential manufacturers of nuclear weapons, which at that time primarily meant France, would promise not to make them. This formula held the party together during the election, but afterwards the Campaign for Nuclear Disarmament rallied its forces and at the 1960 party conference a majority of the delegates voted in favour of unilateral British renunciation of nuclear weapons. Gaitskell was highly praised for the speech he made at the time, in which he said he would fight and fight and fight again to preserve the Labour party, and he subsequently made it clear that he would remain leader and would not accept the decision of the conference. When Wilson stood against him for the leadership of the parliamentary party, on the platform of working out a compromise between the party leaders and the conference vote, Gaitskell won by 166 votes to 81, an adequate majority but one that would perhaps not have survived another defeat at a party conference. Gaitskell's friends were able to win over enough trade unions to reverse the previous decision in 1961, but the effect of all this was that the Labour party had spent most of the first two years after the election in internal struggle.

Fortunately for the Labour party, the Liberal party had not been able to profit from its divisions as much as might have been expected. The Liberal party in the 1950s had been on the left in foreign policy and on the right in domestic policy; for instance, it had been strongly opposed to Suez, but on the other hand it had voted in favour of the 1957 budget with its remissions of surtax and encouragement to overseas investment. If anything it had been more strongly opposed to planning in the 1950s than the Conservatives, and complained of such vestiges of planning that were still left as the Capital Issues Committee. Between 1955 and 1959 it had done well in some by-elections, but most of its best performances came in Conservative areas of strength, and so far as could be seen many of its votes came from people who wanted the government to be still more active in combating inflation. In the 1959 election it gained slightly more votes from the Conservatives than from the Labour party.[1] The new leader, Jo Grimond, chosen in 1956, was aware that a party in opposition has to oppose the government, and he saw that the Labour party was the most likely source of Liberal votes just after the 1959 election, but he could not find an issue with which to divide the Labour leadership from its electoral support in the trade unions. The Liberal party was committed to nuclear disarmament, and it could hope to win support from intellectual members of the Labour party who were not devoted to Socialism, but this was not really enough to establish it as the party of the left. It had not shown enough interest in left-wing policies to profit from the weak condition of the left in 1960.

Problems after the triumph

Macmillan showed no intention of resting on his laurels in 1959. In the years before the election he had not found a policy which could please all sections of his party simultaneously, but he moved so adroitly from the Thorneycroft policy of restraint to the Heathcote Amory policy of expansion that nobody was worried. Before the election he had pursued a policy of allowing the market to take its course in economic affairs and of standing firm in colonial questions; after the election government grants were used to induce car and steel firms to go to regions that were

[1] Butler and Rose, op. cit. 195.

not prospering, though political considerations led to the plants being located in an uneconomic way, and the appointment of liberal-minded Macleod as Colonial Secretary showed that the accumulating problems of Africa were going to be faced.

Nigeria was proceeding to independence on a basis of universal suffrage that would give power to the pro-British and traditional rulers of the northern region. Tanganyika presented even fewer internal problems, for the Tanganyika African National Union dominated the politics of the country so completely that there was no risk of division on tribal lines. In Uganda there was some difficulty in finding a form of constitution into which Buganda, the largest of the tribal kingdoms, could be fitted. There was a certain amount of pro-Buganda feeling in England, so there was effective political pressure preventing the government from setting up a unitary state in Uganda. But these difficulties were slight compared with those of the countries in which there was a white settler community.

Kenya was the easier white settler problem. The Africans were divided in the accustomed way: the Kenya African National Union, representing the Kikuyu and the Luo, the two largest and best educated tribes, wanted independence quickly under a government with as few restrictions on its powers as possible; and the Kenya African Democratic Union, representing the minority tribes, wanted a federal system with decentralized powers. In Nigeria, in Ghana, and in Cyprus the less powerful group in the community had acted in the same way in Kenya, and in each case the less powerful group adopted a pro-British attitude and asked for independence to be delayed. In Kenya the white minority complicated the situation. Communal electoral rolls, to make sure that all groups were represented, had been used in India many years previously, and were in use in the Central African Federation for the same purpose. In Kenya the communal rolls, in which the Europeans were given more seats than their numbers would have justified, enabled Africans, Europeans, and Asians, who were about as numerous as Europeans, to be represented in the legislative council. The 1960 constitution gave the African members a majority in the assembly, but the Governor still had the powers of the executive in his own hands, and used them among other things to keep the obvious African leader, Jomo Kenyatta, in detention on the grounds that he had been involved in the Mau Mau rebellion and was still politically dangerous. As a result K.A.N.U. refused to form a government in 1961 after the first election under the new constitution. K.A.D.U.— less sympathetic to Kenyatta, a Kikuyu—formed a government but found the pressure of African opinion for the release of Kenyatta so great that they had to join in asking for it. The Governor refused to grant the request, and committed himself firmly against Kenyatta, whom he described as a 'leader to darkness and death'. As soon as there was an African majority in the Assembly white farmers and Conservative back-benchers suggested that the British government should be ready to buy out settlers. The government declined to have anything to do with the suggestion, at least in part because it would encourage Africans to make life difficult for the settlers, who would then move out and leave their land for the Africans. The issue of the land, and the tensions caused by the fact that the small settler community owned so much of the best land, went on making people uneasy, but by the beginning of the 1960s the British government was committed to the very difficult task of setting up an independent multi-racial country in which the African majority would have political power but a great deal of economic power would be retained by a relatively wealthy white minority.

The Central African Federation presented even more complicated problems. The three component parts, Nyasaland and the two Rhodesias, each had about the same number of Africans, but differed sharply in the number of white inhabitants. A government set up in Nyasaland to take over the powers of the Governor could become an African government with as little trouble as in Ghana though it would not be sovereign, because it would still be part of the Federation, which controlled the major financial issues and relations with the outside world. The British government recognized that the police measures of 1959 had not been wise, and Macleod started the process of establishing an African government, which was made easier because there was a satisfactory African leader, Hastings Banda, available to become chief minister at the appropriate moment. In Northern Rhodesia the economic power and superior education of the white population seemed to offset the numerical superiority of the Africans, and Macleod devoted considerable ingenuity to devising an electoral system in which the balance of power in the Assembly would be held by Members who had secured an adequate quota of both African and white votes. In Southern Rhodesia the white population was clearly dominant, and all that could be done for the Africans was to make sure that they had a section of the seats in the Assembly and to establish a Board to review legislation and veto Bills that worsened the position of the Africans.

Apart from all these difficulties, there was the problem of the Federation itself. When it was being set up, the British government had said there should be a review of its progress in the 1960s. The Monckton Commission was set up to carry out the review; its members wanted to have unrestricted terms of reference, including power to recommend the dissolution of the Federation, while the Prime Minister of the Federation, Sir Roy Welensky, was anxious to make sure that they could only work inside the general assumption that the Federation would go on. The British government displayed great tactical skill in persuading Welensky that the Commission could not recommend the break-up of the Federation, while convincing the Commissioners that if they found the Federation had no prospect of success they could say so. The Liberal and Labour parties declined to be represented on the Commission because they felt it had been packed in a way that would lead it to disregard African hostility to the Federation. This probably made the Commission more acceptable to the goverment of the Federation.

While the problems of the Federation were constantly in the mind of the British government in the early 1960s, Macmillan had wider issues before him. In May 1960 the summit conference for which he had worked so hard the previous year finally took place. But the atmosphere of friendship and diminished tension had been wearing thin, and when an American U-2 aeroplane, used for flying over Russia and photographing the country, was shot down, the Russian government began denouncing American espionage in terms which suggested the conference was unlikely to succeed. Khrushchev asked for an apology from Eisenhower when the conference began and, when he did not receive one, declined to take part in any discussions.

British policy for the previous two years had tended to take an uncommitted position which might be described as 'neutral on the western side'. This exactly suited her links with the Commonwealth, because the new members tended to be non-committed between Russia and America. It also suited her commercial partnership with the members of the European Free Trade Association, set up after the failure of the attempt to include all western Europe in a free trade area. The members of EFTA agreed to eliminating their tariff barriers against one another, though maintaining their tariffs against other people unchanged. They regarded the association as provisional, because they wanted to make some sort of agreement with the E.E.C. On the other hand two of them, Sweden and Switzerland, stood outside NATO and were 'neutral on the western side' by choice, Austria was neutral under the treaty of 1955, Norway and Denmark were not enthusiastic members of NATO, and Portugal was a little distant from direct confrontation. If Britain went on standing slightly detached from NATO, EFTA would suit her political position very well. After the failure of the summit conference, the political arguments in favour of the E.E.C. began to look a little stronger.

Macmillan's position may have been a little shaken by the failure of the summit, and a little later he lost ground with the Commonwealth Prime Ministers. On a tour of Africa early in 1960 he had defined the British attitude to apartheid in a speech to the South African Parliament in which he warned his listeners that a 'wind of change' was sweeping over Africa and made it clear that England would not fight against the wind. Later in the year South Africa decided in a plebiscite to become a Republic, and asked to be allowed to come to the Prime Ministers' conferences on the same basis as before. The request had been granted to other members of the Commonwealth when they became republics, but the members who found the apartheid policy objectionable were glad to have an opportunity to make their feelings clear. Only England, Australia, and New Zealand supported South Africa at the Prime Ministers' conference in March 1961; South Africa withdrew before any formal decision was taken. Macmillan's attempts to help South Africa were not universally well received, and his failure suggested that England was now only one among equals.

In international terms his position was at its most glittering in the 1960 session of the U.N. General Assembly. Khrushchev and a number of other heads of governments came to the opening debate, and Khrushchev's opening speech was aggressive enough to dismay the West and to attract newly independent countries. Macmillan's speech the next week was calm, imperturbable, and forceful enough to make him appear as the leader of the West. When Khrushchev interrupted him Macmillan said 'I'll take that in translation'—not a very good joke, but at the time people were so frightened of the Russian leader that anyone who stood up to him was regarded as a heroic figure. As President Eisenhower did not go to the United Nations, Macmillan seemed to be the man to rally countries against Russia.

This aspect of Macmillan's ascendancy inevitably passed away with the election, later in the year, of John Kennedy as President of the United States. Kennedy felt quite capable of handling diplomatic affairs on his own, and showed more enthusiasm for individual meetings with Khrushchev than for summits for four countries. His personal relations with Macmillan were good, and he clearly found the Prime Minister the most attractive of the heads of government he met. But this was not the same as Eisenhower's assumption, based only partly on wartime memories, that the United States should treat England as closer to her than any other friendly country. Although Kennedy's personal tastes, and those of many people in his administration, may have been more anglophile than those of Eisenhower, Dulles, and their followers, United States' policy after 1960 was based to a much smaller extent on the assumption of a 'special relationship' between Britain and America, partly because of the nature of the Democratic party and partly because the 'special relationship' might cause trouble with America's other allies.

Other troubles were beginning to disturb the British government. The 1959 boom began to slow down in 1960; there was not much unused capacity available, and unemployment had been reduced so sharply that it was hard to find extra workers for new development. The increase in production had been so swift, once it began, that there was little time for readjustment. Anything that was in short supply remained in short supply, because nobody had time to look around and analyse what would be needed next. Shortages of capacity meant that imports went up, and exports moved up less quickly. The current balance of payments, which in 1958 had shown a surplus of £455m., well above the annual target laid down at the beginning of the 1950s, dwindled and in 1960 showed a deficit. But as investment overseas went on, the overall balance of payments showed an even larger deficit. Government expenditure went up faster than any other form of overseas spending, as a result of increased spending on aid to underdeveloped countries, the steadily mounting cost of keeping troops in Germany in accordance with the 1954 agreements, and expenditure on keeping troops in tropical areas like Kenya, Borneo, and the Persian Gulf. All of this spending had some justification; aid to underdeveloped countries, quite apart from its humanitarian aspects, made them into better customers for British trade, and most of the troops overseas were in areas where there were British investments. These were long-term considerations, and the question was whether they could be paid for in the short run.

While government expenditure overseas was going up so fast, all government spending was increasing inconveniently quickly. Throughout the 1950s the Conservatives had been proud of the way that the proportion of the national income spent by the government was decreasing. Most of the reduction was the result of restricting spending on defence to the £1,500–1,600m. level; the policy of relying on interest rates to control the economy meant that the proportion spent on interest on the National Debt remained steady, and the ending of food subsidies reduced spending on social welfare.

By the beginning of the 1960s this attitude was becoming harder to maintain. Defence costs began to go up steadily, because soldiers' pay had to be increased to attract volunteers after the end of conscription, weapons were growing more complicated, and the stability of costs in the 1950s had involved cutting down on innovation. The Air Force still used the V-bombers of the 1953–5 period, and replacements never got very far off the drawing-board. The failure of Blue Streak, which had to be abandoned in 1960 because it was costing altogether more than had been intended, had wider implications; the Sandys strategy of relying on a nuclear deterrent made much better sense if the deterrent was a British product, but building a rocket which would hit targets in Russia would cost so much that it could not produce enough diplomatic influence to justify the expense. The government saw that it would be much cheaper to buy an American weapon, and chose the Skybolt missile, which was being designed to be fired from an aeroplane at a target on the ground hundreds of miles away; the Opposition claimed that this complicated device would not work.

Outside the military field also the level of government spending went up. The increase in the number of motor cars in the 1950s, and the preference for road haulage rather than transport by train, meant that the road system had to be improved. The work of building motorways and of tidying and straightening less important roads was just beginning in 1958. At the time of the 1959 election the government could say that the work had begun well. But only the first of the bills had come in; as motorways moved from being exotic things of the future to being normal items of government spending, it turned out that they were very expensive, costing a pound or two per square foot of road surface, and the accompanying bridges over the Forth and the Bristol Avon were also expensive. Roads were a necessary investment but were not counted as a social service, perhaps because they did not particularly benefit the poor. By the early 1960s education was claiming attention as an investment as well as a social service, England had for many years paid less attention than Germany and the United States and the Soviet Union to technological education, but during the 1950s the government had slowly realized something would have to be done about it. When the step forward to school-leaving at 15 had been digested, Colleges of Advanced Technology were set up. Only slowly was it noticed that, perhaps because secondary education was now taken for granted or because the changes carried out just after the war implied that everybody who could benefit from a university education should have one, more and more university candidates were coming forward. To some extent they could be held back by raising the number of 'A' level passes required, but by the end of the 1950s it was clear that this would not work and could only lead to potential talent being rejected by the universities. The government plunged rapidly into setting up eight new universities, and encouraged the older ones to expand. The emphasis on science, which had been encouraged in the 1950s, could not be kept up, because the students who were coming forward in increasing numbers were more interested in the social sciences; sociology, which offered students some hope of finding a good brave cause in curing the problems of society, was particularly popular.

Only a relatively small proportion of the population was likely to go either to colleges of technology or to universities, old or new. High expenditure on this sector was regarded as an investment, as could be seen in the complaints about the 'brain drain', or emigration from England to the richer English-speaking countries of highly educated people, especially scientists and doctors.[1] Emigration had resumed after 1945 and, while it never reached the levels of the 1860s or the decade before 1914, it was higher than it had been between 1918 and 1939. By 1962 the departure of the highly educated was being deplored; in the past they had not been missed but in a more education-conscious world it was realized that their departure might lead to shortages of highly educated people inside England. People did suggest that it was not so much the higher pay abroad as the facilities for research which drew people out of England; this may have been the case, though emigrants from the highly educated section of society had been going abroad, for money or for a change of scene, long before Australia, Canada, and the United States offered better facilities for research than England.

Concern about education as investment was more a Conservative than a Labour attitude. The Labour party was concerned about it as a social service and also as an instrument of social engineering. Pressure for classes of no more than 40 in primary schools and no more than 30 in secondary schools came into the former category, and could be accepted in principle by everybody though the expense was considerable and the government was perhaps rather less willing to spend money on this part of education than on higher education. The clash of principle came over the organization of secondary schools. By 1959 the Labour party was committed to support of comprehensive education in secondary schools. Some people supported the change because they thought that class distinctions would be reduced if children went to the same schools instead of being separated from one another at eleven. Educationists found that the eleven-plus examination was not a good predictor of future achievement; about ten or twenty per cent of children were placed in schools which their subsequent records suggested were unsuitable, and as most of the others could have been placed without much difficulty, the examination did not seem to be doing much, though other ways of placing children in

[1] Between 1900 and 1965 64 Americans, 45 Englishmen, and 43 Germans were awarded Nobel Prizes in physics, chemistry, or medicine. It may be noted that 19 of the Americans and 4 of the Englishmen were naturalized subjects.

secondary schools were even less effective. Assigning children on the basis of teachers' reports on their prospects undoubtedly made sure that primary education was not dominated by preparation for the examination, but teachers' recommendations were not particularly accurate predictions and at times leaned heavily to the side of the better-dressed and better-spoken children. Predicting children's development at the age of eleven seemed too difficult a task.

The idealist and the technical arguments against separation at eleven might not have carried much weight if they had not been supported by the wishes of the parents. At first parents in the middle classes had been gratified to see that their children usually succeeded in the 11-plus examination, and other parents were so pleased that their children were receiving secondary education that they did not worry much about its quality. The 1944 Education Act said nothing about the organization of secondary education, and people accepted secondary modern schools without too much question. Possibly if they had been treated as the equals, in terms of money and staffing, of the grammar schools there would have been less complaint. But slowly people realized that the 11-plus examination was the gateway to a system of education in which a quarter of the children were being educated better than the rest. Using an examination of dubious predictive powers as a prelude to an unequal pattern of education was likely to be heavily criticized once the majority began to be interested in their children's secondary education. During the 1950s parents became more anxious about the examination results, and made their children worried as well. Conservative Ministers of Education had used their power to stop county councils setting up comprehensive systems; in the early 1960s the Ministry was beginning to give up its commitment to the 11-plus examination. This was not easy. A large number of the more devoted Conservatives were supporters of the grammar schools, and in the 1959 election the Conservatives had probably benefited from their support of the grammar schools because it rallied their followers. A switch to comprehensive education after the election would dishearten loyal Conservatives and might not win over parents who had recently discovered the disadvantages of the 11-plus examination and thought of the Labour party as the party committed to abolishing it.

Pressures for a new approach

By 1961 the government had realized that opinion was moving towards a higher level of public expenditure, on education and on other things. Plans began to be made for increasing public expenditure; commissions and committees examined various aspects of education. The

1961 budget had to meet these rising costs, and was designed also to provide some incentives for the more prosperous classes. The surtax allowances were increased so that taxpayers with earned income would not have to pay surtax until a level of about £5,000 a year. A little earlier the Minister of Health had decided that increases in the rate of spending on the health service should be met by raising the charge on prescriptions and the combination of a cut in surtax and an increase in prescription charges infuriated the Labour party, but it seemed still to be in such disarray that the government's position was secure. The budget also gave the Chancellor power to increase or diminish customs and excise duties and purchase-tax by one-tenth of the existing rate.

And this power was very soon needed. The 1960 balance-of-payments deficit worried holders of sterling, and the figures month by month for 1961 did not seem much better. This was not a sudden speculative attack of the 1957 variety; the Chancellor of the Exchequer had plenty of time to announce in advance that he was thinking about ways to restrain the economy. His policy reproduced most of the measures used to check demand between 1955 and 1958: the bank rate was raised to 7 per cent, banks were told to restrict credit, government spending was reduced, and in addition the Chancellor exercised his power to vary indirect taxes. Companies were asked not to increase dividends and a 'pay pause' was proclaimed. The government did not intervene in the economy to the extent of forbidding private employers to give wage increases, but it did announce that people employed by the government would not receive increases.

This transformation scene, from surtax cuts in April to the emergency measures of July, left the Opposition at once hopeful and suspicious. The course of events looked altogether too like 1957: the surtax cuts, the crisis and restrictive measures, and later no doubt the whistling-up of an election boom. These suspicions were not confined to the Opposition; the government's position in the opinion polls dropped sharply, and the reputation of the Prime Minister declined even more abruptly. England's international prestige fell at the same time; there were suggestions that she was becoming 'the sick man of Europe' and had lost all power to control events. All that had happened was that the implications of the events of the 1950s were becoming clear, as they would have done earlier if it had not been for England's relationship with the United States. It could now be seen that she was not a power in the same class as Russia and America although a bit weaker than either; she was a power of the same order of importance as France. People spoke of the change in apocalyptic terms that would have been justified only if a large number of other countries had emerged and had shown themselves more important than England. One of the tests for a great power is the capacity to influence events a long way from its own territory, and by this test England was distinctly less of a great power than she had been twenty or even ten years previously. Some of the decline of the early 1960s was an accurate, though belated, realization of this fact. But part of it was an all too ready acceptance of the antithesis that 'England cannot afford to be little. She must be what she is, or nothing'.[1] She was not a nation of the rank of Russia or America, therefore she was nothing. This readiness to believe the worst was reinforced by people in other English-speaking countries, many of whom had been brought up to think of England as the real centre of the world stage. Men of the generation of Kennedy had a more reasonable picture of the world, but at the time of Suez both Nixon, the American Vice-President, and St. Laurent, the Canadian Prime Minister, had spoken as though it was only at this crisis that they had realized England and France no longer dominated the world. It took other people rather longer to realize the situation, and when they understood what had happened they were more surprised than was justified.

The background of exaggerated feeling that England had collapsed was not the best atmosphere for the government to announce that it had changed its mind and wanted to join the E.E.C. The announcement came within a week of the crisis measures of July, and the government looked as if it had decided that it could not make anything of England's current economic position and wanted to start off in an entirely new direction. The Prime Minister mentioned other considerations in his speech. He referred to de Gaulle's statement that he looked forward to a *Europe des patries* as a sign that the members of the E.E.C. were not committed to setting up a federation in which countries would lose their identity. This remark illustrated one of his problems throughout the negotiations for British entry. In the Conservative party, and in the country as a whole, there was considerable suspicion at the idea of a federation, and no precise commitment to it. A considerable but vague enthusiasm for Europe arose, especially among the intellectual classes. It was fashionable to think of the English-speaking countries as coarse and materialistic, and to dwell on the pleasures of continental holidays and the more relaxed European attitude to wine and irregular hours. This mood may have helped the government win support for its proposal, which was otherwise supported almost entirely on economic grounds; nobody in England was willing to say that it would be desirable to surrender British sovereignty

---

[1] Originally said by Huskisson in 1828, and quoted approvingly in *Cambridge History of the British Empire* (1940), ii. 414.

to a European authority. This was no doubt welcome to de Gaulle, but it made the supporters of European federation among the members of the E.E.C. a little less enthusiastic than they might otherwise have been about British entry.

Before announcing the decision to apply, the government sent ministers round the countries of the Commonwealth and got responses that were at best non-committal and at worst expressed 'grave concern', (the diplomat's phrase for 'violent objection'.) The British negotiators had also to remember their commitments to the EFTA, and they had to bear in mind the fact that unconditional acceptance of the Treaty of Rome meant that agricultural prices would be assisted in a different way. Farmers were afraid they would receive less, and other people were afraid the price of food would go up.

Both major parties were divided on the issue. In the Labour party the divisions were fairly clear cut, because the Labour party was something of a coalition between people who would have been happy with the Liberal party if only it had persevered in the path of social reform that it had seemed to be taking in 1885 and 1909, and people who wanted a more rigorous approach to equality and government intervention in the economy; on the whole the right wing was in favour of British entry and on the whole the left wing was opposed to it, though there were exceptions on both sides. The party's official policy was to wait and see how negotiations went, and Gaitskell held firmly to this position for fifteen months. In the Conservative party the right wing and the left wing were harder to find: a caricature right winger would have opposed the American loan in 1945, voted against leaving Egypt in 1954, and been in favour of Suez, would have supported hanging and flogging, opposed changing the laws on homosexuality, and objected to Britain joining the E.E.C., but individuals who committed themselves to all of these causes were rare. In the Labour party it was fairly easy to find people who had taken the left wing attitude on every issue since 1945 and earlier. Although the Conservative opponents of British entry had no record of organized opposition, they rallied quite quickly, and by the time a group of opponents had been formed the government decided to begin negotiations. For over a year after this, the argument went on at several levels. Most of the press was in favour of British entry, but Lord Beaverbrook's papers were determinedly opposed, and the *Daily Express* in particular was conducted as a campaigning newspaper. General opinion as registered in polls was almost all the time more in favour of the application being made than against, but the margin was never wide, and the number of people answering 'Don't Know' was large enough to be decisive if it came down on one side or the other. Informed opinion was at least at first fairly strongly in favour of British entry, but this feeling came to a peak shortly after the decision to apply, held firm, and then began to dwindle a little.

The negotiations themselves were a matter of extraordinary complexity. Heath, who had been the Conservative Chief Whip, conducted them with great skill; he had to argue with people on the implications of tariff levels, keep in touch with Commonwealth and EFTA opinion so far as they were going to be listened to, and avoid giving anyone in London the impression that England was giving away too much in the negotiations, as well as conducting the discussions in Brussels. Convincing the E.E.C. members that the government was eager to join while not seeming to people in England to be yielding too much was very hard; the critics in the Labour party said that he was 'negotiating on his knees'.[1] The major attraction of entry was that manufacturers would have a much larger market and could obtain economies of scale, because customs barriers would be taken down. The danger was that British manufacturers might not be able to adjust to the new conditions, or might find the E.E.C. common tariff drove up the cost of imports so much that it raised the general level of prices. The rise in cost would be avoided, and the interests of the Commonwealth would be guarded, if a long list of items could be imported free of duty. Canadian aluminium, Indian tea, and New Zealand butter might all be defended in this way, just as former French colonies had been given a special trading position under the Treaty of Rome.

The government badly needed to succeed in the negotiations. The movement of opinion at the beginning of the 1960s suggested that, though the Conservatives had won the election, it was the ideas put forward by the Labour party in 1959 that had become accepted by the public. People wanted a higher level of government spending for public services like roads and universities and for welfare services like old-age pensions. Unless this was to mean higher taxation, which was unlikely to be popular, the economy would have to grow faster, and in this way Gaitskell's attitude on growth in the 1959 election became generally accepted. Between 1959 and 1961 the government had tried to run the economy in the relaxed and uncontrolled way that had been so successful between 1951 and 1955. By 1961 the attempt was clearly not working. A return to planning was becoming fashionable. Macmillan, who had flourished with the slogan 'Conservative freedom works', remembered that in his youth he had been a supporter of planning and began changing

[1] N. Beloff, *The General Says No* (1963), 143.

the emphasis of government activity. The 'pay pause' imposed in 1961 was not the best introduction for this change. Public sympathy for teachers was growing and people began to feel that nurses ought to be paid as much as typists; however, as the pay pause applied only to employees paid for by the government, it was likely to hold back their claims, as was seen when the Minister of Education rejected recommendations by the officially recognized Burnham Committee for a pay increase for teachers.

The government tried to reduce the deficits on the expenditure of the nationalized industries. In the late 1950s more industries were declining as cotton had declined five years earlier. Coal and the railways were sliding back to their pre-1939 condition after a revival of prosperity in the 1940s. By 1955 coal surpluses were beginning to pile up because of the competition from the steadily increasing imports of oil. Suez and the closing of the Canal interrupted the imports of oil, and for a time coal was reprieved. The government reacted to the closing of the Canal by pressing ahead with nuclear power stations which worsened the long-term prospect for coal. When the Canal was reopened the oil flowed again, and coal fell back once more. The pits were bound to run at a loss and were piling up coal for which nobody had any use. Ten years after the government had been trying to persuade people to go into coal-mining because coal was so vital, it was trying to get them out again. Cotton had contracted slowly, with loud protests and with little arrangement for redeployment or for retraining. The coal industry was managed rather better: pits were closed with much less fuss than might have been expected, some miners went from the pits that had closed to the rich coalfields of the east midlands and others were retrained for new jobs. Coal was protected by a duty against oil, but then cotton was protected by tariffs and quotas against the products of underdeveloped countries.

Shrinking the railways was in some ways like shrinking the coal-mines; the organization was large enough to do the job by stages and to make an attempt to fit men into new jobs. But the financial accounts for the railways were far more difficult to work out. It was not too hard to tell whether a pit was paying its way, and to decide that the pits which were losing most were the ones to close. For railways it was necessary to find out what each section of track cost, how much traffic it carried, and how much traffic other lines would lose if it was closed down. This large-scale piece of cost accounting was perhaps more in accordance with the spirit of the 1950s than of the early 1960s. The Beeching Report suggested that about one-third of all railway track in the country should be closed down, but the government realized that closing lines had social costs which had to be considered before taking action; reducing expenditure on the railways might mean that villages were cut off from the world and all the inhabitants moved away to begin new lives, and more money would have to be spent on new houses and schools.

In the early 1960s there was more concern about the 'quality of life' than in the 1950s. Part of this feeling took the form of greater concern about public support for the arts, and of resistance to commercial enterprises which threatened the beauty of the countryside or the amenities of town life. The Commonwealth Immigration Act of 1962 was seen by its supporters as another piece of resistance to change which might have led to rapid economic growth at the expense of quality of life.

Citizens from Commonwealth countries had always been allowed to enter England freely, but they had not made much use of this right before the 1950s. Citizens of the white Commonwealth occasionally came on shorter or longer visits, but nobody took any notice. In the fifties a flow of West Indians, Indians, and Pakistanis began to come to England. From the economist's point of view the country seemed to have found a fund of labour to draw on in the way West Germany drew on East Germany and Italy, or France and Italy drew on their underemployed agricultural labour. This development was not welcomed by the people who found themselves living near the immigrants. Occasionally it was suggested that immigrants took low wages and undercut the market rate, and it was sometimes said that they were violent and noisy. While some of them were bachelors earning more than they had ever earned before, and behaved as might be expected, most of them were quiet people with fairly strict ideas about family life. The hostility to them came largely from a simple feeling that black men were undesirable, just as Irish Catholics had been thought undesirable in the nineteenth century and European aliens had aroused hostility earlier in the twentieth century because they were different. The shortage of housing made matters worse; the immigrants were blamed for it, and then were blamed for living in slums. The Immigration Bill was welcomed by public opinion although it was condemned by a good deal of the Conservative press and by the Labour party. It allowed immigrants to come if they had certain skills, or if they had relations in the country, or if they had jobs waiting for them. The sentiment of liberally minded people was against the Bill partly on grounds of humane feeling and partly to promote economic growth, but most of these humane and tolerant people did not understand that other people who were relatively uneducated and unaccustomed to novelty suffered real problems when immigrants came and lived near them.

13. *The overstrained economy* 1961–1967

Conservatism in a serious mood

THE deflationary measures of July 1961, and the subsequent unemployment, caused more uneasiness and hostility than the 1955–7 deflationary measures. People thought they were entitled to something better than periodic expansion and restraint. In previous clashes between Macmillan and Gaitskell, Macmillan had done well because he was so good at dismissing Gaitskell as a man who took things too seriously. But in 1960 he took nonchalance too far when he wrote 'exporting is fun' in the draft of a speech designed to encourage traders. He thought better of it and left the phrase out when he delivered the speech, but the reporters could see it in the text they had been given in advance and it seemed to fit his approach so exactly that it was printed almost as though he had said it. It did him no good; in the new atmosphere politicians were expected to be serious and to take problems seriously, and Macmillan was suspected of losing touch with reality. Wilson, in the debate on the deflationary measures, gave up almost completely the jokes and quips that had made his economic speeches in the 1950s one of the more entertaining parts of the Commons routine. Instead he was earnest; he referred to the spirit of Dunkirk; he realized that politicians were expected to show a sense of purpose.

The first step towards Conservative planning was the establishment of the National Economic Development Council, which was expected to produce indicative plans by consulting the various industries to see what they could do. In some ways this resembled the French approach, though the French planning authority (*Commisariat du Plan*) had considerably greater powers than N.E.D.C. to control the flow of credit and to direct the large nationalized sector of the economy. The Commisariat was in addition more willing to intervene at selected points in industry; during the arguments about planning in England it was assumed that the government should leave each industry (operating, as the system developed, through an Economic Development Council) to work out its own problems, so the government did not have much opportunity to do anything about a particular industry or a particular part of the economy. The N.E.D.C. launched into serious political discussion the idea that a rate of economic growth of 4 per cent a year ought to be reached, and once this had been said it acted as a magnet on politicians thinking about growth.

The Chancellor of the Exchequer believed that growth would have to wait. His pay pause, in which all wage increases were discouraged, was unlikely to last once discernible increases in production were being made. When the pay pause came to an end, after provoking a great deal of trade union activity among white-collar workers, he proposed a 'guiding light' of $2\frac{1}{2}$ per cent, which presumably represented his estimate of the level future growth was likely to reach. Because people wanted public expenditure to go up, and felt entitled to expect their personal consumption to go up as well, there was mounting hostility to the policy of restraining demand. Government and Opposition seemed even more conscious of the next election as a test of policy than in the past, and studied opinion surveys even more closely than in the 1950s. Polls and by-elections left it uncertain whether the Labour party or the Liberal party was benefiting more from the government's undoubted unpopularity. The Conservatives could hope that the Common Market negotiations might succeed, or that Khrushchev was returning to a more friendly state of mind, or that the economy could be encouraged to expand fairly soon, but meanwhile they could only wait.

The 1962 budget reflected the new serious-mindedness, and a hostility to people who made money easily: it included a short-term gains tax, which taxed a capital gain taken in a six-month period by an owner of shares, or in a three-year period by an owner of land. Deals in land had been attracting so much attention that a tax was only to be expected. The pressure for houses and factories around London was increasing, and owners of land could sell with large profits. In the London area, which was expanding steadily across south-east England, more and more of the price of a house went to pay for the land on which it was built. All sorts of people wanted to come to London, from teenagers who knew that it was the place where things happened to managing directors who wanted a smart company address close to the source of finance. Quite apart from the drift to London, people already in London wanted more space. The dingy, poky little offices of the past were condemned for being ill lit, inconvenient and out-of-date; shiny and conspicuous new office blocks, of varying degrees of ugliness, were put up and attracted a steadily increasing flow of commuters to the centre of London. And while this was happening, the less prosperous parts of the country were falling behind. Even in 1959, when the boom had been running at its fastest, Lancashire and Scotland had not felt the government was doing much for them; the north-east had been less restive, but its economic position was also weak.

Macmillan knew it was desirable to present his government to the world as a group of youthful and modernizing men. He also wanted to encourage economic growth at the earliest possible moment, and felt that Lloyd might be too cautious about this. As the by-elections returned gloomier results, the Prime Minister became bolder in his plans for political changes and in July seven Cabinet ministers out of twenty-one were dismissed. It was clear that he could wield great power, and some commentators who were fascinated by the sweeping exercise of power spoke of the Prime Minister as a Presidential figure, by which they meant that his power was unchecked by his Cabinet, or by his party. But this assumed that the changes were wise and that Macmillan could make them without any damage to himself. The reaction of his party was not favourable; his back-benchers made it fairly clear that they thought he had been too drastic, and Birch, one of the parliamentary secretaries who had resigned with Thorneycroft in 1958, said that Macmillan was altogether too fond of dropping Chancellors of the Exchequer when they tried to restrain demand. Lloyd had his loyal supporters; the taxation of short-term capital gains annoyed some Conservatives but many others felt that he had stuck to difficult jobs for his party, had tried to fight inflation, and deserved better treatment.

Macmillan was much the oldest member of the reshuffled Cabinet, and he looked out of touch both with the seriousness that was becoming more accepted in politics and with the enthusiasm for youth that was growing up in the country at large. He seemed temperamentally unsuited for a period of planning, even though he had supported planning in the 1930s and had been unpopular with his party on account of it.[1] A few days after his Cabinet changes he announced that the government was setting up a National Incomes Commission to try to steer the course of wages and salaries but, because the news came in a speech winding up a Commons debate, the Commission inevitably looked as though it had been produced to extricate him from trouble over the ministerial changes and criticism of the slow growth of the economy. The trade unions declined to have anything to do with the Commission, and while opinion surveys suggest that the public was not favourable to trade unions at the time, there were

[1] His views were best expressed in *The Middle Way* (1938).

not many complaints at the refusal to treat N.I.C. seriously. Planning required either a government which commanded enough prestige to force its will upon people or a system in which people could be confident that they would be treated fairly. Macmillan did not possess either claim to authority after the ministerial changes.

Entry to the Common Market was still one of his hopes for the future. The arguments about planning and rates of growth concentrated on quantitative estimates of effects, and discussion of entry to the Common Market might have been expected to run on similar lines; supporters of entry could have estimated how much extra growth it would lead to, and opponents could have produced rival calculations. But nothing so rational took place. In October the Labour party in effect committed itself against entry, when Gaitskell laid down a set of conditions which, while accepted by everybody in England as desirable, clearly could not be obtained. In his speech, which was directed to the mainly anti-entry left wing of the party, he appealed to 'a thousand years of history' rather than to 'nicely calculated less and more'. And the next month, at the Conservative Conference, Butler replied by leaving to the Labour party the thousand years of history and claiming 'For us, the future'. The Labour left felt a particular sympathy for the anti-American Conservatives who made up a considerable section of the anti-entry minority, but the government was firmly in command of its party; it seemed to have found an issue that would enable it to appear at the next election as the party that got things done and brought England into Europe.

On the whole the Conservatives had had good luck throughout their dozen years of office: declining import prices, friendly people in power in Washington, no need to produce expensive new weapons which would drive up the arms bill, and a fair degree of success in convincing people that the increase in their standard of living was as rapid as it ought to be. The twelve months from the Conservative party conference of October 1962 were a long tale of disaster; some misfortunes followed logically from the way the Conservatives had been governing, but some were sheer bad luck. In November a world crisis broke out because the Soviet Union had been establishing missile bases in Cuba. President Kennedy handled the situation very skilfully, setting up a blockade of the island until the Russian government agreed to withdraw the missiles. It was fortunate for the world that the problem was resolved without any fighting, but the British government's prestige suffered because the issue was settled in a way that visibly owed nothing to British intervention.

In December the American government announced that it was going to scrap the Skybolt missile, on which England rested her hopes of remaining a major nuclear power. The British reaction revealed the extent to which nuclear weapons were regarded as a way of retaining a position of influence over the United States: a large number of Conservative back-benchers signed a motion which read as though they thought the American government had made Skybolt go wrong. The Prime Minister met Kennedy, and said that if the country was to be left without effective nuclear weapons as a result of this decision, the Conservative party would probably decide that the alliance with the United States had been a mistake, sweep away Macmillan himself and replace him with an anti-American government. The President was convinced by this argument, and a new agreement was drawn up: England acquired American Polaris submarines which could be used, without any consultation with other countries, in the event of 'a supreme national emergency'.

An opportunity to obtain Polaris submarines was offered to France on similar terms, without any discussion with de Gaulle. The French President was not interested, and regarded the Anglo-American agree-ment as a final proof that England was in the last resort more concerned about relations with the United States than with Europe. There were already signs of difficulty in the Common Market negotiations, because the European negotiators at Brussels were growing less willing to make concessions and were beginning to insist that if England entered she must change to the E.E.C. method of support for farmers by tariffs without any prolonged transition period, which opened up the prospect of sharp price increases almost immediately after entry. In the middle of January de Gaulle made it clear that he did not think England a suitable member of the Common Market and, since the negotiations went on, he formally declared on 29 January that France would have nothing more to do with her application. Macmillan suggested that the negotiations had been bound to be successful and that only de Gaulle's veto could have stopped them; several difficult points in fact remained to be negotiated, unless Britain was suddenly going to sign the Treaty of Rome without amend-ment, but the immediate reason for the failure of the talks was de Gaulle's concern about the political unity of the 'Anglo-Saxons', as he called the Americans and the British.

The failure of the Skybolt exposed the dangers of the government's desire to have effective nuclear weapons without paying for them, and the failure of the Common Market negotiations showed that it was rash to try to be America's closest ally and a member of the E.E.C. at the same time. But the government was simply unlucky that the winter of 1962–3 was about as severe as that of 1946–7. Unemployment had been rising, because of the steps taken in 1961 to restore the balance of payments, but it would have risen rather less if the bad weather had not held up transport and inter-fered with building. In the worst month 878,000 people were out of work.

The government had claimed the credit for the 1959 boom, and now it was blamed for economic weakness. At the same time it was running into more complex and less rational criticism inside and outside the country. Television programmes satirizing the government became popular; the most celebrated of them, *That Was the Week That Was*, was a B.B.C. show that did a great deal to prove that the Corporation could be more lively than commercial television, but it must have left the government wishing it could control broadcasting as stringently as other governments control their state broadcasting systems. *Private Eye*, the well-informed and sometimes accurate magazine of the satirists, rapidly achieved a circulation about as large as that of other weekly magazines like the *Spectator* and *New Statesman*. Satire was popular in theatres and in night-clubs in the early 1960s; there was a certain amount of general social comment, but one theme of all the satirists was that the government had been in office too long and had lost the respect of the people.

The satirists won general approval but perhaps they did best among the small group of people who take a steady interest in public affairs. At the same time the general popularity of the government, as measured in opinion polls, was low. Its unpopularity among people who were not very interested in politics seems to have been mainly due to the unsatisfactory performance of the economy; the hostility of people who were interested in politics was partly the result of economic weakness, but was also caused by a feeling that the country no longer had a national purpose.

This sentiment also existed outside England. Acheson, an American ex-Secretary of State who was relatively pro-British, felt that he was helping explain the situation when he said 'Britain has lost an Empire and has not yet found a role', and this was greeted with a fury that suggested he had struck a delicate nerve.[1] In the same speech he invited Britain to retire from the nuclear arms race, on the ground that the United States was well equipped to deal with the Soviet Union and the British contribu-tion would be only 2 per cent of the American firepower in a nuclear war, which suggested that he did not recognize that the nuclear force was intended as a diplomatic threat to the United States as well as a military threat to the Soviet Union. But his remark about the country's need for a role seemed to be justified; people were slowly realizing that their country was no longer a great power, but they were having some difficulty deciding what to do about it.

[1] See *The Times*, 6 Dec. 1962 and following days, to find out how much Acheson had upset people.

Her dominance had depended more on the fact that other countries had imitated her than on any physical power that she possessed; it now seemed that other countries regarded her as a lesson in what not to do, and even though part of this was due to the elegance and journalistic skill with which British commentators outlined her weaknesses, her influence was declining to that of an ordinary country of the second rank. People in England who were interested in politics had always taken it for granted that the country was going to be important; on the left they spoke of moral influence and eschewed the emphasis placed on Empire by the right, but there was the same assumption that England was going to influence other people. The discussion over entry to the Common Market had masked these assumptions for a time; the few people who calculated the advantages of entry in economic terms probably did not worry about the effect on England's status, but the people who thought about it as a political question argued whether she could best exert her influence in Europe or in the Commonwealth. The left-wing opponents of entry thought of the Commonwealth in terms of the new members who had become independent since the war, and right-wing opponents thought of the old members from before the war, but the two groups agreed that the Commonwealth was the place to exert influence. Supporters of British entry speculated, often in a tactless way, about the prospect that England would dominate the Common Market politically. Rejection of the application showed that Britain was not in a position to go choosing. At the Commonwealth Prime Ministers' conference a few months before the rejection Macmillan had insisted that England must be as free as any of the other members to decide her own policy. This was reasonable enough, and certainly the suggestions made by people who wanted the Commonwealth to draw closer together were not practical politics; the other members did not want closer unity, and had not done so for a very long time. But because England was the most important member, with considerable influence on the trading prospects of almost all the other members, her decisions had more effect than those of the other members. By choosing to go ahead with the application to join the Common Market, the British government alarmed the other Commonwealth governments. When the application was rejected, the British government could not turn back to the Commonwealth, and the European Free Trade Area felt that she had not paid enough attention to the problems of EFTA during the negotiations.

After the failure at Brussels

The government had the difficult task of restoring its international prestige, its reputation among people who took an interest in politics and its popularity with the electorate. Rapid economic development would probably solve these problems, and the government had begun to un-freeze the economy even before the rejection of the application to join the Common Market. Purchase-tax was reduced, with a particularly large cut in the rate on motor cars, the lower levels of income-tax were rearranged in a way that gave substantial and fairly equal reliefs for all income-tax payers, and Schedule A of the income-tax was abolished, which meant that an owner-occupier no longer paid tax on the notional value of the rent he could obtain by letting his house instead of living in it. Abolition made owning a house and living in it even more attractive than before, and made it correspondingly less likely that anyone would build houses to rent.

These relaxations came only fifteen to eighteen months after the restrictive measures of July 1961, so there was a much shorter period of restraint than there had been in the late 1950s. There had been corre-spondingly less time to build up the foreign exchange reserves, or even to reach a healthy balance on the current account. The gospel of the supporters of growth included recommendations on this point. It was argued that 'the reserves are there to be spent' and Maudling, the Chan-cellor of the Exchequer, accepted this view.[1] It was believed that, as the current balance of payments showed a surplus over the long run, a deficit in the first year or two while growth was being speeded up could be covered from the reserves and could be replaced later when faster growth had been established as a normal feature of the economy. The reserves of gold and dollars had fluctuated around £1,000m. ever since the war and even in 1947, the worst year since the war, the deficit on the current account had been no more than £318m., so, it was said, the reserves could cover the cost on any bad year.

While growth was to be speeded up, the increase in national wealth was not to be devoted entirely to larger private spending. Powell as Minister of Health obtained enough money to carry out more hospital development than for many years past, and he made the spending habits of the National Health Service more efficient. Building roads and putting up bridges across the river estuaries were beginning to cost large sums, but they were also beginning to make travel and transport easier than in the past. The increase in the birth-rate immediately after the war had led to an increase in the number of children of school age and this change—nicknamed the 'bulge'—had been foreseen, but in the 1960s many more children stayed at school after 15. This 'trend' had not been fully foreseen and it meant that schools were still under great pressure.

[1] 3 Apr. 1963; *Commons Debates*, dclxxv. 471.

In January 1963 Hugh Gaitskell died after a very short illness. His political position, and his command of the respect of the electorate, had been becoming steadily stronger during the previous year and had been further improved by the government's troubles over the cancellation of Skybolt and the imminent collapse of the Common Market negotiations. The Parliamentary Labour party wanted above everything else a leader cool enough and ruthless enough to deal with Macmillan and see that the government did not recover as it had done in 1958 and 1959. They chose Harold Wilson as leader, despite his record of opposition to the majority of the parliamentary party and even though they had rejected him in favour of his principal opponent for the leadership, George Brown, when the two men had stood against each other for the deputy leadership a few months previously. Wilson justified the trust placed in him by the Labour party. His first speeches as leader showed that he wanted to restore British prestige by making the country more modern. This line of approach made him look a little like President Kennedy, whose political manner was greatly admired in England. At the same time it set him in sharp contrast to Macmillan; too much of the Prime Minister's reputation had been staked on the Common Market negotiations and after the failure people were less inclined to take him seriously.

The government had been troubled by a number of cases of Russian espionage successes. Unfairly but inevitably it was only when spies were caught that the public realized anything was wrong, but the effect of cases like those of Blake and the Krogers in 1961 was to damage the prestige of the government. Early in 1963 the government struck back at the press, which had assumed altogether too readily that a former Civil Lord of the Admiralty had been closely connected with another spy, Vassall. Two journalists were sent to prison for contempt of court when they refused to reveal the source of their stories.

This probably made the press more willing to attack the government. It was known that there had been some sort of association between the Minister of War, John Profumo, and Christine Keeler, a girl of about half his age. Hints and innuendoes linking them were published; the rumours were obliquely referred to in the House of Commons, and Profumo's position had to be examined. Macmillan delegated this task to a group of ministers and, after discussing the matter with them, Profumo made a statement in the House of Commons. He declared that he had not abused his ministerial position and that there had been 'no impropriety whatsoever in my acquaintanceship with Miss Keeler'. The first point was fairly certainly true, the second was not. When this was revealed a few weeks later and Macmillan's conduct of the case was debated in Parliament on 17 June, Wilson avoided any references to private morals, and stuck to the risk to security raised by the fact that the girl had been having an affair with a Russian diplomat called Ivanov at the time she was associating with Profumo. In the Commons the main point of discussion was whether Macmillan had behaved reasonably; the Prime Minister maintained that he had acted honourably and had been deceived, and his critics argued that he had taken the matter altogether too lightly and had failed in his duty to co-ordinate the security services. This view was not confined to the Opposition benches; 27 Conservatives abstained and one of them, Nigel Birch, quoted Browning's line 'let him never come back to us'. There were rumblings and discussions, but Macmillan said on television that he hoped to lead his party at the next election and his party came round to the view that, although his reputation for good sense had suffered badly, it would look like a confession of something worse if he retired.

Outside Parliament the discussion ranged more widely. It was accepted that as he had made an untruthful statement in the Commons, Profumo had to go. Ten years previously it would have been universally accepted that the mere fact of his associating with Christine Keeler showed that he was unfit for public office. In the 1960s feelings were less clear cut. During his denunciation of the Prime Minister Birch asked 'What are whores about?', but this dividing-line had been becoming blurred. Girls were distinctly less careful of their reputation for chastity than at the beginning of the century, and probably were less careful of their chastity as well. So far as any public event could represent this change, it had been the trial in 1960 for obscene publication in which the jury decided that D. H. Lawrence's *Lady Chatterley's Lover* could be published unexpurgated; conflicting attitudes clashed very explicitly, and not merely in literary terms—it was regarded as anachronistic in more ways than one when the prosecuting counsel asked the jury 'Would you want your servants to read this book?' The verdict that the book was not obscene reflected the advance of a more relaxed attitude.

By the time of the party conference in the autumn Macmillan's control over the Conservatives seemed more or less re-established. But just as the conference was beginning his doctors told him he would have to have an operation on his prostate gland. If he had been high in public and party favour, as Churchill had been at the time of his stroke ten years earlier, he could have retained his position, but in the circumstances he had to resign. At the conference there was a good deal of support for Lord Hailsham as his successor, several Cabinet ministers wanted Butler, and many Conservative M.P.s preferred Maudling. Macmillan arranged a complicated system of consultation to discover a successor acceptable to all sections of the party, and the name produced by this method was that of Lord Home, who had been Foreign Secretary since 1960. Hailsham and Home were candidates only by a curious stroke of fortune. When Lord Stansgate died in 1960 his heir, the Labour M.P. Wedgwood Benn, refused to accept his title, and stood again at the by-election after he had been declared to be a peer. The size of his majority, and the tone of public comment, made it quite clear that the government would have to let people renounce peerages they had inherited. The Act allowed anyone succeeding to a peerage to give it up, and anyone who had already succeeded to one could give it up within the next 12 months. Hailsham announced, at the party conference, that he would renounce his title, and Home agreed to accept the party leadership and give up his title if he were chosen.

The emergence of Home caused considerable surprise. According to Macmillan, who gave Randolph Churchill his account of what had happened, Home had strong support in all sections of the party. The people who had wanted Home kept quiet, but his opponents spoke up and made it clear that they thought the choice was a mistake. Home was condemned for being out of touch with the modern world and for being unable to adapt himself to the work of modernization. This criticism, justified or not, did not fully consider what had to be done inside the Conservative party. Home's supporters thought that he would be able to repeat Macmillan's success in restoring the morale of the party and, after that, winning the support of the electorate. Butler or Maudling might be more effective for winning votes, but if they failed to rally the party behind them they would have no organization to help them convince the electorate. This was not an implausible argument, though Home had no radical background like Macmillan and was unlikely to establish himself by debating successes in the Commons.

The way in which Home had been chosen did the Conservatives no good. Wilson had been elected leader of the Labour party in a straightforward way that everybody could understand; Home had been presented as Prime Minister after consultations that were never intended to be understood by the public. Being elected gives a leader legitimacy in the modern world; emerging as the result of consultations is not a process that commands general respect. Some of the complaints about the selection process simply implied that an Old Etonian conspiracy had gathered together to impose Home on a party and a country that did not want him, but there was also a feeling that Prime Ministers should be seen to be chosen fairly. When Home came to form his Cabinet he had a little difficulty; two of the modernizers, Macleod and Powell, declined to serve under him and it was believed that if Butler had declined to serve, Home would have had to abandon the whole attempt to form a Cabinet.

As Prime Minister he had to follow the policy Macmillan and Maudling had laid down: try to expand the economy as fast as possible and regain popular support by showing that prosperity had returned. This was not very difficult. The rate of growth was showing signs of rapid improvement, and all that had to be done was to avoid disturbing it. The risk of a deficit in the balance of foreign trade seemed to be the only immediately visible threat to foreign expansion, and the doctrine of drawing on the reserves meant that little notice was to be taken of it. The decline in prosperity had been responsible for a good deal of the government's loss of popularity, and as industry began to revive the government's position improved. During his last months in office Macmillan had played, as Kennedy wrote, an 'indispensable role in bringing about the limitation of nuclear testing':[1] Russia, the United States, and England signed a treaty giving up testing nuclear weapons above ground and spreading fall-out of radioactive material. This was a solid sign that the countries which had hydrogen bombs were ready to step back from the expense of an arms race, and it reflected credit on the British government. Countries like China and France, which were working to make hydrogen bombs of their own, regarded the treaty as a step to keep them from challenging the position of the owners of hydrogen bombs, but the world in general regarded it as a victory for sanity.

The government lost some prestige because England's rate of economic growth between 1959 and 1963 rose much less than that of the continental countries and their average domestic product overtook that of people in England. In 1958 the British domestic product per head of £360 a year was smaller than that of the United States, Canada, Sweden, Australia, Switzerland, or New Zealand, but this might be seen as simply the natural result of Britain's involvement in two destructive wars. By 1963 British domestic product had risen to £495 a head, but had been overtaken by France and Germany (with incomes of about £510 a head), even though their rate of growth had slowed down after the formation of the Common Market.[2] Foreigners looking at England, and people inside England who found these international comparisons important, drew the conclusion that England was losing ground, and the more sensational commentators even spoke as though England was growing poorer when all that was happening was that some other nations were growing rich faster.

---

[1] Anthony Sampson, *Macmillan* (1967), appendix.
[2] *U.N. Statistical Yearbook for 1966*, Table 7A. The French figure for 1958 was distorted by inflation, soon to be followed by devaluation.

This was unlikely to mean very much to ordinary Englishmen, who probably felt very dubious about the fine statistical comparisons needed for these judgements. They went in increasing numbers to the continent of Europe for their holidays, and the inhabitants of holiday resorts have never been particularly prosperous, so British visitors were not likely to be impressed by what they saw while abroad. They already knew that it was possible to become somewhat better off by emigrating to Canada or Australia, and people did go and often settled down very happily. But things were not too bad in England; so far as can be measured, after allowing for increases in prices, British incomes per head during the period of Conservative rule since 1951 increased faster than incomes in Canada or the United States. Relatively few complaints about the rate of growth had been heard in those countries until 1960, and there was no reason why people in England should have been much more critical.

The government plunged into modernization and planning with all the fervour of converts anxious to avoid roasting at the stake. The goal of 4 per cent growth suggested by the N.E.D.C. was accepted by both parties; the government published an estimate of future government spending which showed that, on the basis of commitments already undertaken, public spending would grow at the 4 per cent rate. If any additional government spending was to be undertaken in the next four or five years it would be necessary to increase the government's share of the national income, or to reduce some item of spending that was already established, or to drive up the rate of growth beyond 4 per cent. On one occasion during the summer of 1964 Callaghan, the Labour 'shadow' Chancellor of the Exchequer, did say that a 5 or 6 per cent rate of growth would be necessary; Wilson said that he believed the whole Labour programme could be carried out without any permanent increase in taxes but that, if an increase in taxes was needed, it would be imposed.

The preliminary period of waiting for the election was unusually long-drawn-out. After a period of teasing people which did nothing to help his reputation for taking serious things seriously, Home announced that the election would be held in October, the latest time that was legally permissible. This would allow him as long as possible to rally his party and allow reflation to do its work. But reflation was running too fast for comfort; in the budget Maudling increased taxes on tobacco and alcohol in order to reduce the amount of money people could spend. He seems to have wanted the election to be held in June, because he was worried about the balance of payments, and did not want the difficult months of late summer to be disturbed by the excitement of an election. Home reckoned that he needed a little more time to meet the members of his party and build up their enthusiasm. He did not spend much time in the House of Commons, and reckoned that, as he was not likely to out-debate Wilson, he would do better by spending his time touring the constituencies when he was not tied to his desk by administrative duties.

The result of delaying the election to the latest possible moment was that a large number of problems piled up. The government insisted that the state of the balance of payments was not a problem and that the reserves would be enough to ʃ e the country through, but Malaysia, Rhodesia, and the aircraft industry were harder to ignore. The Colonial Office had decided, when it came to dealing with British possessions in Borneo, that as usual federation was the answer; Malaya, the city of Singapore, and the colonies in Borneo were fitted into a federation christened Malaysia, in which it was hoped that Malays and Chinese would be evenly enough balanced to settle down and live together. The government of Indonesia, which had been looking forward to absorbing the Borneo colonies when the British left, protested against this and moved towards a 'confrontation', by a series of guerrilla raids into the British part of Borneo. When Malaysia was launched, in 1963, it had to resist Indonesian pressure and it was uncomfortably aware that when Indonesia had applied pressure on the last Dutch colonies in the East Indies, the United States had supported the Indonesian claim. So far as can be seen, the British government had by early 1964 begun negotiating in Washington on the basis of giving the United States tacit support in Vietnam provided it ceased supporting the Indonesian government.

When the Monckton commission reported on the Central African Federation it said that the constituent states should be allowed to disaffiliate if they wanted to. Nyasaland and Northern Rhodesia chose to become separate states, and the Federation was dismantled. These two sections could progress fairly easily towards independence based on 'one man, one vote'. Southern Rhodesia was a different story; the white minority was numerous enough and sufficiently well organized to be able to assert its strength, and the African leadership was divided and less talented than in most of the other colonies that had moved towards independence. It would have been very hard for the British government to force a large-scale enfranchisement of Africans on the Southern Rhodesian electorate. On the other hand, giving independence to the white Rhodesian minority, which might not have caused too much trouble in 1950, was not possible in 1964 because opinions had changed and so many independent African states had emerged that setting up a white minority government would have caused trouble. At a conference of the Commonwealth Prime Ministers in the summer of 1964 the British government managed to avoid committing itself one way or the other; it could point out the difficulties of making a choice just before the general election, and some of the visiting Prime Ministers may have felt that, as Home would not grant independence to a white minority government, it was safe to wait for the election of a Labour government in Britain which might be more sympathetic to the African position before asking for other decisions.

The difficulties of the aircraft industry were connected with the general problem of maintaining a British nuclear striking force which could be independent in the sense that all its equipment was British-made. The Nassau agreement to acquire Polaris submarines was a step away from independence, but the Royal Air Force still had high hopes for its TSR-2 aeroplane. It could be seen that a surprisingly large part of the country's research budget was going into the aircraft industry, and it was also clear from one or two fairly small-scale incidents that the government did not have effective control over the spending of money by the industry on defence contracts. But the government was trapped by the general failure to understand that large-scale developments under the pressure of modern conditions sometimes lead to failures that have to be written off. The government had already had to write off a number of projects, and it did not feel like cancelling any more just before the election, especially if the cancellations made the idea of a British-built nuclear weapons system seem impossible.

At last the election came, at the end of a warm summer which was believed to have helped the government's chances a little. During the campaign opinion polls showed that the two large parties were running very close together. The Labour party concentrated on domestic issues, stressing the inadequacy of welfare payments, the unsatisfactory effects of selection for secondary education, the rising cost of land and the high untaxed profits made from it, and the general need for modernization by planning the economy. The Conservatives pointed out that the Labour proposals would cost a great deal of money, and reminded people that steps towards modernization had been taken in the last few years and the economy had grown quite quickly since 1962. Home himself dwelt on the nuclear deterrent and the need for England to remain an important country; although the electorate was not very interested in the nuclear deterrent, his approach did remind people that the Conservatives had years of experience of these problems of foreign policy.

When the votes were counted the Labour party had a majority, but it was the smallest majority any party had ever had without being dependent on co-operation with a minor group. Before the election the Liberals had said that if they held the balance in the new Parliament, they would use it to put a Labour government in. So many decisions had been deferred till after the election that a government without a majority would have been in an even more difficult position than the minority governments of 1924 and 1929.

	Votes	Seats	% of all votes cast
Conservative	11,981,047	303	43·3
Liberal	3,101,106	9	11·2
Labour	12,205,812	317	44·1

The new government and the economic position (1964)

The Labour government took one fundamental, if negative, decision in its first days of office: it decided not to devalue the pound. Devaluation would be a drastic cure for a balance-of-payments deficit: it would make imports more expensive and thus reduce the demand for them, and at the same time it would increase the profit margin that manufacturers could expect from goods sold abroad. On the other hand, prices would probably go up, resources would have to shift from domestic consumption towards exports and probably profits would increase at the expense of real wages. In addition there was a clear, even if not very rational, belief that devaluation meant national humiliation. Understandably the government decided to try to cure the deficit by less rigorous methods.

The Treasury reports suggested that the deficit for the year on current and capital account would be about £800m. When the figures were complete, the deficit on the current account was £393m., slightly more than the disastrous 1947 record. The weakness of the theory that 'the reserves are there to be spent' was made more obvious by the impact of investment abroad. The net outflow of capital for investment during the year was about as large as the deficit on the current account; the two together amounted to about £750m., or about three-quarters of the entire reserves. This was not the end of the story. People who held money in London on a short-term basis were naturally alarmed at the size of the total outflow, and decided that the money would be safer somewhere else. As the short-term liabilities amounted to four times the reserves, they could not be met without external help if they were presented for payment.

Taking one year with another, British exports, including dividends and other invisible items, covered the cost of imports. The total outflow was alarmingly high, because of the tendency to invest so much money overseas, and the situation was made even more uncomfortable by the large short-term holdings. But the new government believed that if it devalued it would be allowing the heavy flow of investment to drive the pound to an artificially low level and it rejected this course just as it rejected a policy of deflation which would have imposed an artificially high rate of interest and low rate of economic activity in order to support the outflow of investment.

It was one thing to hold these views, and another to make them effective. As on previous occasions when there had been deficits holders of short-term debts did not become uncomfortable about the British balance of payments immediately, but by November they were showing signs of uneasiness. Though their fears were probably increased by the preview of the budget presented by Callaghan, the newly appointed Chancellor of the Exchequer, the position of the balance of payments was alarming enough in itself. Holders of sterling who had been frightened by the small deficit under Butler and the moderate deficit under Lloyd were most unlikely to remain calm after the enormous Maudling deficit.

The preview of the budget may have precipitated the crisis because Callaghan's changes were believed, probably incorrectly, to have an inflationary effect. Benefits for most of the national insurance schemes were raised, income-tax for the $6\frac{1}{2}$m. people who paid at the standard rate was increased to help cover the cost, and the government cancelled the TSR-2 aeroplane, which meant that the British-built nuclear weapons system would not be retained into the 1970s.

At the same time it was announced that the system of company taxation would be changed. Previously all the profits of companies were taxed at a relatively high rate but dividends were then paid without being taxed a second time; under the new system companies would pay Corporation Tax, at a lower rate than before, but dividends would be treated as untaxed income and be subject to income-tax. All capital gains, and not just short-term gains, were to be taxed. These last two changes were no more than a move towards the American system of taxation, but some people regarded them as a prelude to an attack on property.

The government was in a fairly strong position for raising international loans to meet the strain on the reserves caused by the withdrawal of short-term funds. The United States was suffering from fairly similar balance-of-payments difficulties caused by an outflow of investment money which exceeded her trading surplus; if the pound was devalued the dollar would come under heavier pressure and the American government would in its turn have to choose between deflation and devaluation. The British government hesitated over increasing the Bank Rate, and in the end had to raise it a little higher than might otherwise have been necessary, but with powerful American support the Bank of England borrowed

$3,000m. in short-term loans. The government tried to deal with the balance-of-payments deficit by reducing its own overseas expenditure and by encouraging companies trading abroad to bring their profits back to England instead of keeping them overseas. It also imposed a 15 per cent surcharge on imports except food and raw materials but this step, in addition to annoying many other countries and particularly the other members of the EFTA, was bound to take some time to have an effect. The deficit was too large to be ended quickly, and as long as it persisted the short-term holders of sterling were going to be uneasy. So much world trade was financed in sterling, so many financial institutions had interests in sterling and so many individuals could find opportunities for taking up a position in which they could benefit from a devaluation that it was not possible to think of meeting all the demands for sterling simply by using the reserves. Even if the reserves were supplemented by all the official resources of the western governments, the private resources of the individuals and companies who were convinced that sterling must fall might still be too much for the central bankers, the governments, and the International Monetary Fund.

Inside England it was soon clear that the public blamed the Conservatives for leaving the balance-of-payments deficit. The government appeared at first to be in the happy position of being able to take the credit for pleasant things that happened, and to pass the blame on to the previous government. This could not go on for long; the government was blamed for giving an immediate salary increase to ministers and Members while delaying the payment of increased national insurance benefits for four or five months. The Labour party lost a seat at a by-election and looked as if it might find itself at the mercy of the Liberals after all.

Wilson as Prime Minister rose above all this. He was determined to govern as though he had a majority, and he took it for granted that what the country really wanted was a government which took decisions. He possessed a gift for presenting himself as a man who understood the problems and would work full-time at solving them; the detached and amateur approach sometimes adopted by Macmillan and Home was not in fashion, and Wilson expressed the mood of the times. This did not necessarily mean that his decisions were right; because he had to deal with a short-run crisis in financial affairs, prepare for the next election which was expected from month to month, and solve the problems of Rhodesia and Malaysia, his handling of the situation depended less on the long-term planning which the Labour party had stressed in opposition than on simple ability to adjust policy to circumstances.

Malaysia was in itself relatively easy: reinforcements were sent to patrol the frontier with Indonesia in Borneo, and the government began negotiating to make sure that there was no United States support for Indonesia. President Johnson had just been re-elected on a platform of social reform and opposition to the wild ideas on foreign policy put forward by his opponent, Senator Goldwater. Johnson's Vice-President, Humphrey, had been selected from the left wing of the Democratic party, and all the signs suggested that the American and British governments could get on very well together. They had to co-operate if they were to avoid increasing the strain on their foreign exchange position, and it seemed reasonable for the British government to continue to give Johnson a free hand in Vietnam in exchange for a free hand in Indonesia, and agreement appears to have been worked out along these lines. The Indonesian government could make no headway in its attempts to weaken Malaysia, and eventually began to crumble under the stress of trying to maintain the confrontation. After a period of confusion, in which the Communists tried to gain a monopoly of power in Indonesia and were massacred, a new government was set up which recognized that the policy of confrontation was not doing any good.

Rhodesia was an altogether harder problem. Smith, the Rhodesian Prime Minister, had probably hoped that if re-elected the Conservatives would be more sympathetic to the white Rhodesians than they had been before the election. Some of his followers thought in terms of a unilateral declaration of independence as soon as the Labour government was elected. Wilson spoke briskly and fiercely to warn the Rhodesians against any such step; whether because of this, or because they wanted to make further preparations, the Rhodesians took no immediate action, and negotiations began between the two governments. Inside England the new government could be seen to be acting to deal with a crisis, and the Conservatives were badly divided about the right attitude to take to Rhodesia. The general result was to improve the Labour party's position for the immediate future.

The government's plans for economic change were directed to goals in the relatively distant future. Its two chosen instruments for operation were a 'prices and incomes policy' and a National Plan. The first objective was to persuade industrial management and the trade unions to accept a board to regulate increases in prices and incomes. Because it rested on mutual acceptance, the Board had a better chance of success than bodies like the National Incomes Commission. Within the relative economic tranquillity that the Board was meant to provide, the industrial managers would offer estimates of the probable development of their businesses over the next five years, and when these estimates were brought together and harmonized into a consistent scheme by economists' analysis, a National Plan would emerge. Industrialists would benefit by knowing with more certainty than in the past how much expansion they could expect in other sectors of the economy, and with this knowledge they could plan for a higher rate of growth, which would mean that everybody was better off.

Brown, the Minister of Economic Affairs, was fairly successful in the first stages of this programme. He persuaded the managers and the trade unions to make a declaration of their intention to co-operate in running a policy for prices and incomes, and he could then set up the Prices and Incomes Board and his Department could begin collecting estimates to be worked together into the Plan. The Board began well, and showed signs of becoming an authority which could examine aspects of economic activity that needed investigation. By interpreting rather widely its responsibility to look into price levels, it made recommendations for improvement; for example, it looked into the ways in which banks treated customers, manufacturers of detergents ran their advertising campaigns, and architects fixed their fees. It believed that on issues of wages policy it should act rather like the Swedish central authority, which lays down fairly binding suggestions for pay increases.

The Department of Economic Affairs, like the French *Commisariat du Plan*, was intended not only to collect estimates but also to induce the manufacturers to set their estimates as high as possible. It was not quite clear to what extent the Plan was concerned with recording the present position accurately and to what extent it was concerned with pushing people into making greater efforts in the future than they would otherwise have done. The Plan acquired its own momentum and it did push people forward, and this tendency was increased by the emphasis that had been placed on a rate of growth of 4 per cent a year. When the Plan eventually appeared, it was fairly clear that it was more a matter of aspiration than of practical economics. The point at which the planners had most clearly not accepted the constraints of reality was the supply of labour. They had accepted a target of expanding the national income by 25 per cent by 1970, which meant a rate of growth of a fraction under 4 per cent, but their figures showed that to do this about 200,000 more workers were needed than seemed likely to be available. The prices and incomes policy was intended to check the tendency to inflation that had persisted in the economy ever since Beveridge's definition of full employment—more vacant jobs than workers to fill them—had been tacitly accepted, but no incomes policy could prevent a rise in wages if there was a steady demand for 200,000 more workers than could be found. Employers would naturally bid against each other, by offering higher wages or fringe benefits. If it was carried out, the National Plan would reproduce the very high level of demand that had existed under the 1945–51 Labour government, without the stringent physical controls that had been available just after the war. The government had in 1964 forbidden further office development in London, but in general it was ready to operate the economy with very little compulsion. This may have reassured economists that effort would not be diverted into the wrong channels by government decree, but it did leave open the possibility that a shortage of labour would lead to large wage increases.

More workers could easily have been found: Commonwealth citizens from the West Indies, India, and Pakistan were ready and eager to come. During the election the question of Commonwealth immigration had been lurking below the surface, but the results suggest that the Labour party lost three or four seats on the issue in areas where there had been a certain amount of immigration and where local conditions of life were generally unpleasant enough to make the voters want to blame somebody. The bad housing conditions in Smethwick or Slough were not the fault of the immigrants, but the inhabitants thought differently and were influenced by the slogan 'If you want a nigger neighbour, vote Labour'.

Tension and dissatisfaction over immigration rose after the election, with some Conservatives suggesting that their party ought to take a more determined stand against immigration than it had done in the Commonwealth Immigration Act. The government decided that it could not hold the existing position, and issued a White Paper indicating the way it would interpret the Commonwealth Immigration Act in the future. The policy laid down was decidedly more restrictive than in the past, at least so far as entry to the country was concerned; the White Paper also suggested ways in which the immigrants might be cared for more effectively once they were inside the country, and legislation against discrimination in public places was passed. Some people argued that legislation was not the best way to deal with the problem, though in fact other countries faced with the same situation had, in the end, fallen back on legislation after feeling at first that there must be less formal ways of acting.

The White Paper stated that no more than 8,500 Commonwealth immigrants, of whom 1,000 would be from Malta, were to be allowed work permits every year. All questions about freedom of movement and Commonwealth solidarity apart, this closed one of the ways in which the labour shortage revealed in the National Plan might have been made up.

Rapid economic growth has, more often than not, been associated with rapid increase of the working population; there was no underemployed rural population in England to draw into the economy, as there was in the countries of Europe that had been thriving since the war, but an inflow of people from the underdeveloped parts of the Commonwealth might have enabled the economy to grow as intended. Public opposition to immigration was not inspired by a conscious choice between growth and keeping England white, because most of the people who opposed immigration did not realize that they had such a choice before them, but this was the effect of the policy in the White Paper.

During the first year or two of the Labour government there was in any case no widespread anxiety about the rate of growth. The growth of the economy slowed down in 1964 but it was still going ahead. Profits had already shown a sharp increase; in 1965 trade unions stepped forward to claim their share. Wage increases were well above increases in the national income measured in terms of money, so wages gained a larger share of the national income, mainly at the expense of profits. The Labour government did not resist this process, partly perhaps because it felt that wages ought to receive a larger share of the national income, and partly because it was anxious to conciliate the trade unions in order to get them to accept the authority of the Prices and Incomes Board once it was operating. The government also remembered all the time that it would have to hold an election to avoid being strangled by its narrow majority.

The government stressed its determination to nationalize the steel industry. The decision could be justified by the technical argument that the industry needed to be concentrated into a smaller number of larger units if it was to compete with the vast integrated plants that had recently been set up in other countries, but it did not win the vital Liberal votes over; the government's White Paper, laying down the principles for steel nationalization, was generally regarded as a gesture to convince the left wing of the Labour party that the government was not going to compromise its principles rather than a serious commitment to bring in a Bill before the election. Even so, it nearly led to trouble for the government because a couple of Labour Members could not support the White Paper, and they could cost the government its majority in a division.

The 1965 budget, with its changes in the system of company taxation and capital gains taxation, was complicated but it did not apply new principles to the objectives—as opposed to the technique—of raising revenue. A comparison with the days before the 1909 budget, with its substantial provisions for new spending on battleships and on old-age pensions, shows the changing impact of government activity. In 1908 the national revenue came to about £130m., of which £52m. was raised by taxes on income and capital, such as income-tax, surtax, and death duties, and £75m. was raised by taxes on expenditure, such as the customs and excise duties on alcohol and tobacco. The national revenue came to about 7 per cent of the national income of £1,875m. By 1965 taxes on income and capital had risen to £5,998m. and taxes on expenditure, which had risen less quickly, yielded £3,766m. As the national income had risen to £32,339m., the revenue amounted to 30 per cent of the total. This seventeen-fold increase in national income does not mean that the country was that much better off: allowance must be made for rising prices and for an increase of 25 per cent in the size of the population. The price indexes rose sevenfold, but they combine a lot of different items, some of which (like candles) are used less and less and some of which (like refrigerators) are used more and more. The cheapest motor cars cost less, in cash terms, in 1965 than they did in 1908 and they consumed less petrol to the mile. Food prices had gone up to somewhat more than seven times the 1908 level. House prices, on the average, rose about seven times but this average included sharp rises in the south-east and slower increases elsewhere. Alcohol and tobacco went up, because of high taxation, to far more than seven times the 1908 price. At the beginning of the period there was a tendency to impose high taxes on alcohol to promote temperance; by the end of the period there may have been a feeling that smoking was dangerous and should be discouraged by high duties on tobacco.[1]

The 1965 budget was so complicated that it took up a great deal of the parliamentary year. The Conservatives fought it with considerable technical skill, though this may not have done them any good. Inevitably they emerged looking as if they thought capital gains ought not to be taxed. Furthermore, they took up so much time that the government was under no obligation to bring forward items of its legislative programme such as the nationalization of steel which the Liberals might dislike so much that they would join the Conservatives in a determined attempt to overthrow the government.

By the time it reached the summer recess the government felt exhausted, but no disaster had overtaken it. The Conservatives were less satisfied. After the 1964 election Home had spent some time in arranging a procedure by which future leaders of the Conservative party would be elected by the parliamentary party. He was uneasily aware that he was not a leader to convince people that the Conservative party was modern

---

[1] These figures are taken from various tables in *The Times, The British Economy: Key Statistics, 1900–1966*.

in its attitudes, and that he was not a debater to crush Wilson in the House of Commons. His followers do not really seem to have asked if anybody else could do better; when the opinion polls consistently showed that the public preferred Wilson to Home, Conservative Members became increasingly ready to think that a change of leader would be useful. Home resigned in August, and the parliamentary party chose Heath, the hero of the Common Market negotiations, as his successor. Apparently the Conservatives thought Heath would precisely match Wilson's qualities, would defeat him in debate, would force him into making mistakes, and would deal a swift knock-out blow. Whether the leader of the opposition ought to resemble his opponent or not—perhaps Maudling's unhurried approach would have been a useful contrast to Wilson—Heath did not possess quite the qualities he had been credited with. When he had the better case, he could drive the fact home, but he lacked the debater's gift of making his case look a little better than it was. In some ways his approach to politics was rather like that of Gait-skell; he liked working out policies for himself and applying them to new situations. But this was a long way from the powerful in-fighter, poised to deliver the decisive thrust, that the Conservatives had thought they were choosing.

People spoke as if the choice of Heath as Conservative leader was a great step in the democratization of politics, and it was sometimes pointed out that both party leaders come from grammar schools, as though this was some guarantee that the way to the top was now open to talent with no regard to birth. Their social origins were not really very different from those of Asquith and Law, the two party leaders just before the First World War. Their parents had incomes a little above the national average; it was true that neither man owed anything to inherited wealth or to family connections, but neither of them rose from as low in the social scale as Lloyd George or MacDonald. Wilson and Heath had been at their grammar schools before the 1944 Education Act; they came from an educational background confined to less than 10 per cent of the population.

Social attitudes and external problems

As a result of the 1944 Act, grammar school places were available for about 30 per cent of children going to secondary schools. Comprehensive schools were part of the Labour programme, and could be effectively encouraged without legislation. Conservative Ministers of Education had used their powers to prevent Labour local education authorities setting up comprehensive schools; the Labour minister used his powers to require all local education authorities to submit plans for reorganizing education in a way that would eliminate selection at 11-plus. This was the most complete assertion of central authority in education that had ever taken place, though it was only the logical conclusion of previous changes. A few local authorities tried to resist the process by submitting plans that did not eliminate selection, but they were obliged to yield to ministerial insistence. On the other hand, local authorities that changed almost all of their schools over to a comprehensive system, but retained a few distinguished grammar schools, found that their proposals were acceptable.

Local authorities also undertook an expansion of their housing programmes. Between 1956 and 1963 building barely kept up an average rate of 300,000 houses a year, and this contributed to the increase in prices for houses and for building land in the early 1960s. In 1964 and 1965 about 30 per cent more houses were built, about half of them by municipal councils, who were still the only people building houses to rent.

During the course of 1965 Parliament abolished capital punishment for murder. The issue had become a symbol of the division between people who took a libertarian view of society and people who felt there was a danger that social discipline might break down with disastrous consequences. The Conservative government in the 1950s had tried to produce a compromise by listing murder under certain circumstances as non-capital murder, to be punished by a long term of imprisonment, but the issue was not really one to be ended by any compromise. The opponents of capital punishment regarded it as intolerable that any executions at all should take place; supporters of capital punishment sometimes used arguments that would have justified its use in a great many crimes apart from murder.

The division did not run very precisely along party lines, and the party leaders were quite happy to say that the Whips should not issue instructions to Members on this sort of question. As most Labour Members of Parliament opposed the death penalty, and most Conservatives wanted to keep it, abolition was unlikely to be carried in a House of Commons with a Conservative majority. Most working-class voters opposed the change, but did not seem to be influenced by the issue at general elections. The most determined supporters of the death penalty seem to have been enthusiastic Conservatives, who talked as if it was one way of holding back social revolution. One or two Conservative abolitionist Members had some difficulty with their local party organizations because of their views. Labour party enthusiasts tended to be enthusiastic abolitionists, and in their minds this particular cause was one of a wide spectrum of issues concerned with personal liberty and colonial independence. Sidney

Silverman, the very skilful parliamentarian who was the leader of the abolitionists, was also one of the leaders of the Movement for Colonial Freedom, which agitated for Britain's withdrawal from her colonial possessions.

The nineteenth-century liberal tradition had not disappeared but the political parties continued to be divided primarily on economic issues. The Labour party supported greater equality helped by state action and on the whole it had inherited Mill's belief in giving people a wide range of freedom in issues where their actions did not affect other people; the Conservative party stood for greater individual freedom to prosper in a less controlled economic system, but it was more likely to say that certain moral principles ought to be expressed in legislation on crime even if it did mean restricting people's freedom of action. At the beginning of the century the moral attitudes of the unenfranchised people at the bottom of the social scale were less restrictive than those of the classes concerned about respectability who made up the great bulk of the electorate. By the 1930s the ideal of respectability was accepted throughout society, but by the 1960s it was much less universally accepted and some sections of the middle class, especially around London, were consciously uninhibited and regarded freedom from restraint as a good thing for its own sake.

The greater freedom, or laxer sense of social discipline, showed itself in fashions and styles. In the serious arts, English writers and performers had taken an honourable place from the beginning of the century and earlier. The English style in acting had grown less formal and less exhibitionist as taste turned away from the bravura displays of Irving and Tree, but Olivier and Gielgud were accepted as examples for actors in any country in the world. By the 1940s ballet companies had appeared, where none had existed thirty years before, that could tour all over the world. English composers like Elgar and Vaughan Williams were perhaps too purely British to have much appeal to the world outside, but Britten had won a position of international influence. Interest in music in England had increased, and had become more discriminating; it is possible that the brilliant criticism of Shaw in the 1890s and the complaints of Elgar have given too poor an opinion of British musical performance at the beginning of the century, but it does seem also that, helped by the B.B.C., standards of performance rose considerably and it is certainly true that public interest in classical music increased and became better informed and more wide-ranging. Although it was much easier for people to listen to music at home at the end of the period than at the beginning, because of the developments of wireless and of records, audiences had increased, and the number of orchestras had also gone up.

But while England after the Second World War was no longer an importer of culture, she was still an importer of fashions and styles. English textiles and English tailors made the English gentleman the best-dressed man in the world, but then one of the features of a gentleman's clothes is that they are never quite up to date. English outdoor clothes for the older woman were admired, but they were also in a tradition that took care not to be too exciting. English clothes were the clothes of a ruling class. And so it was all the more surprising that, in an ironic echo of her position of dominance in other fields at the beginning of the century, England in the mid 1960s set the fashions for the young and provided stars for popular entertainment. It was not quite what Macmillan had meant when he said the British must be Greeks in a world in which the Americans were the Romans, but the Greeks had been entertainers for the Roman Empire, and it looked for a moment as though the English were going to take up the same role by providing popular singing groups such as the Beatles and women's fashions for the young such as the mini-skirt. This was not likely to give complete satisfaction to anyone in England; the people who worried about the country's role in the world were serious-minded men and women who wanted the country to be influential in some more dignified way, and the young people who set the new fashions were much less interested in the question. They had grown up in a country which was not in fact a great power, and they probably did not expect it to go round behaving as one. Life would have been easier for political leaders if there had been a more widespread relaxation of the feeling that the world's problems, wherever they might be, were problems for the British government to solve. But even though people realized that British power was less than in the past, there were still pressures for England to take an interest in faraway places.

The Labour government was very proud of its good relations with the American government. Even while Macmillan was Prime Minister the Democratic administration in Washington had been ready to receive potential Labour ministers, and after Macmillan resigned it had been fairly clear that a change of government was expected and would be welcome. Home was not pro-American in the strongly committed way that Churchill and Macmillan had been; the Labour leaders recognized that being received in Washington was good for their prestige inside England. When a doctrine of continued British involvement in Asian affairs began to be suggested, under the slogan 'East of Suez', the Labour leaders did not object; they were quite willing to support the United States to the extent of guaranteeing the former British possessions around the Indian Ocean. The defence of Malaysia went satisfactorily, which suggested that the policy of retaining a post-imperial role might not be unattractive. The United States was glad to have another western power co-operating in the Far East because the expense, and possibly the odium, of operating there might be reduced. From the British point of view the cost was one unpleasant aspect of the case, and as soon as the left wing of the Labour party realized what its government was committing itself to, protests began to be heard. These protests became all the louder when it was realized that the 'East of Suez' policy committed England to some degree of acceptance of the American policy in Vietnam. During 1965 the American involvement there increased. Wilson plunged into attempts to mediate, in order to check the expansion of the war and the embarrassment that it might cause him. A delegation to explore ways of ending the fighting was set up at a conference of Commonwealth Prime Ministers. It did not achieve anything, but it did extricate the British government from an awkward situation. Most of the Prime Ministers at the conference felt that American policy was showing signs of being imperialist and although the British government had never been sorry to show the United States that it was under pressure to move towards the non-aligned position of the majority of the Commonwealth countries, it was committed to allowing the American government a free hand on the issue. A policy of inactivity, punctuated by attempts to mediate, suited the British position better than anything else.

There were also suggestions that England should adopt a more active policy in Rhodesia. The negotiations with Smith and his government made little progress; Smith's supporters were becoming impatient, and on 10 November the government of Rhodesia declared the country independent. The British government, in previous negotiations, had said that it would not use force to subdue a revolt, but that it would employ all possible trade sanctions to cripple the Rhodesian economy. The decision not to use force was probably unavoidable: bringing troops into the middle of Africa would have been a task uncomfortably reminiscent of the Boer War, for the white Rhodesians were about as numerous as the Boers had been, and were well equipped for resistance.[1] There were political considerations; a swift airborne landing immediately after the unilateral declaration of independence might have brought the white Rhodesians back to their allegiance, but on the other hand resistance, followed by the deaths of Rhodesians, would have made it even harder to reach a stable and permanent settlement. People with sensationalized memories of what happened at the Curragh in 1914 even

[1] The technical problems of using force were discussed in *The Economist*, 17 Dec. 1966, 1222.

suggested that the army might have refused to obey orders to subdue the revolt. This was most unlikely, but if fighting between British troops and white Rhodesians had broken out, the British government could not have relied on the support of the Opposition or of the people in general..Wilson did say that, if law and order broke down in Rhodesia, England would intervene, and this might reasonably have been taken as a hint to African resistance movements to attack the rebel government and thus provide a reason for British intervention. But the African political movements were not strong; part of the reason why the position of the white Rhodesians had gone unchallenged was that the Africans had no leader who possessed the power to unite his countrymen behind him in the way that had happened in almost every other African country. Wilson had visited Rhodesia during the negotiations before the declaration of independence and, it is said, had been disturbed to find how limited was the supply of talent among the African leaders.

Other countries were full of enthusiasm for the idea of a British expeditionary force to subdue the rebels, and some Commonwealth leaders suggested that on past occasions, when dealing with rebels who were not white, much more drastic action had been taken. But there were no parallels; no previous British government since 1776 had been faced by a rebel colonial government with an officially organized army of its own. Economic sanctions seemed much less likely to cause trouble than an attempt at armed invasion. The weakest part of the Rhodesian economy was its reliance on imports of oil; the next weakest was its dependence on tobacco exports to cover most of its import bill. For a short time it did look as though restrictions on imports of oil might be effective, but after supplies began to come in through South Africa it was clear that the British government would have to rely on the slow effects of making it impossible for the Rhodesians to sell their tobacco or else come to terms with the rebel government. The best that the British government could hope for was an arrangement that would leave the white Rhodesians in command of the situation for the foreseeable future but guarantee the position of the Africans as a group that could acquire political power with the passage of time, and the white Rhodesians showed no great desire to accept this limitation on their freedom of action.

The British government spent more of its time worrying about economic issues than about these problems of external policy. The deficit on the balance of payments was considerably lower in 1965 than in 1964 and new regulations, which for the first time restricted investment in prosperous Sterling Area countries, reduced the amount of capital sent out of the country and lessened the strain on the reserves. But sterling was still not an attractive currency to hold, and the international authorities found, when there was another run on it in the summer of 1965, that the official resources of the world were put under great strain.[1] England had to contemplate the unpleasant responsibility of repaying these short-term loans which ran up to £1,000m. over the next five years; the loans were mainly banking transactions, in the sense that they would be repaid not out of a British trading surplus but by rebuilding the short-term reserves of the London money market, but this only meant that the British economic position would be as vulnerable to short-term shifts of opinion in the international financial community as it had been for most of the period since the First World War.

Most other governments took an ambivalent attitude to the country's position: on the one hand they believed that she ought to pay her debts, but on the other hand economic advance was slowing down in a number of countries at the same time and deflationary measures in England would do nothing to make life easier elsewhere. As long as the British government was prepared to take the risk that an uncontrollable monetary crisis would force it to devalue at some moment when it did not wish to do so, quite a number of other governments were prepared to support it in avoiding a deflationary policy that would reduce imports.

Reductions in government expenditure were recommended from various directions. The Governor of the Bank of England said in public that they were desirable; it may not have been precisely in accordance with the normal British interpretation of his position for him to criticize the government in public—though central bankers frequently did so in other countries—but Lord Cromer had done so much of the organizing of international short-term credit for the government that he could not be rebuked. On the other hand, he was not reappointed when his term of office came to an end. Some Conservatives led by Enoch Powell turned

---

[1] *The Economist*, 23 July 1966, 364 (just after the deflationary measures) gave figures suggesting that in 1956 the average outcome of the balance of payments was a surplus of £50m. a year, and by 1965 it was a deficit of £50m. a year.

Annual averages for	1954–7	1958–61	1962–5
Current account	97	44	−86
Capital	−152	−138	−209
Total (including balancing item)	24	−9	−258

The heavy weight of the capital account payments is obvious; if the country had given up either foreign investment or government spending on defence and foreign aid, the accounts would have balanced. However, the Bank of International Settlements did say, in 1968, that the pound was overvalued by the 1960s.

against the idea of an 'East of Suez' policy; they said that England was a European country and should not try to revive the ghosts of empire by spending a lot of money on distant defence positions. The government was alarmed by the rate of increase in defence spending in the early sixties, and set up a review of spending which fixed financial limits for defence and then set out to fit the policy into the money available. The navy suffered more than the other services; it was not allowed an expensive aircraft carrier which it had hoped for, and there were resignations as a result. The long-run effect of the refusal to lay out money on the aircraft carrier was to show that the country could not afford the 'East of Suez' policy. Mayhew, the minister who resigned early in 1966 over the aircraft carrier, had adopted the complicated but not illogical position that the 'East of Suez' policy was on general grounds not desirable but that, if the Cabinet insisted on it, enough money should be spent to make it effective. But at the time of his resignation, the government had neither decided to give up the policy nor shown any willingness to pay for it.

Heath, as Leader of the Opposition, had his own suggestions for reducing government expenditure. Some of them were nothing more than the complaints habitually made by parties in opposition, and past experience suggests that these complaints appeal to the electorate only when a government is already believed not to be running things efficiently. There was no sign of this sort of discontent in 1966, and the Conservative attack was not successful. The other aspects of Heath's attack on government spending were more interesting. He turned his back on the movement towards government planning that had been accepted by both major parties for some years previously, and showed some enthusiasm for the free play of the market. He also said that the expense of social welfare was rising too fast, and that payments should be restricted to people who could show, after an examination of their financial position, that they needed help. It was not clear whether he meant that the whole social insurance system which had been built up from the 1911 Act onwards should be replaced or only that items like family allowances which were not financed out of insurance contributions should be put on a means test basis.

Commentators at the time spoke of a struggle for the 'middle ground' in politics, but this seems to have been a misunderstanding of what Heath was doing. In the early 1960s both political parties seemed ready to accept a mixed economy, in which most industry was privately owned, and in which the government acted as a planning agent which influenced individual business decisions but did not impose direct controls on them. There might still be arguments about a wide range of subjects, but the relationship between the organization of the economy and the government did not seem likely to be one of them. Heath stepped away from the 'middle ground', and it is hard to see that this did him any good. When the election came, in March 1966, the Conservatives did not have much chance of success. Wilson looked like a natural ruler; Heath looked like a civil servant, and it was unfortunate for his party that when he wanted to say it would be prepared to take unpopular decisions he always said it would be ruthless, which gave the impression that it might not consider the damage caused to people by its decisions. Wilson spoke of taking tough decisions, which gave a rather more favourable impression of a man who realized that some measures might lead to discomfort.

The government had seemed to know its business; part of its satisfactory reputation was due to relatively small-scale operations, such as the increase in money given to the arts, which remained a small sum even though distinctly larger than before, and the tidying and rationalizing of arrangements for aid to underdeveloped countries. In a preview of the budget shortly before the election the Chancellor of the Exchequer said he would not increase taxes noticeably, but would tax forms of gambling that had previously been exempt. The election was not exciting, and became steadily less exciting as it became clear that the government was going to be re-elected.

	Votes	Seats	% of all votes cast
Conservative	11,418,433	253	41·9
Liberal	2,327,533	12	8·6
Labour	13,064,941	363	47·9

Labour on its own

Ever since the flaws had begun to appear in Macmillan's armour in 1961 or 1962, the country had been living in perpetual expectation of a general election. This had been accompanied, in many people's minds, by a belief that a Labour government would set everything right. To Wilson's left were people who expected a lavish flow of public expenditure unchecked by worries about the balance of payments; to his right were people who thought that the new government would prove more efficient at running the capitalist system than the Conservatives had been. These hopes had survived while Labour had a majority of only three, but they were in the long run likely to be disappointed; at the very least, the government could not satisfy all the people who had supported it.

This should have restrained the people who spoke of the completeness of the Conservative defeat in much the same exaggerated terms as they had used to discuss the Labour defeat in 1959. It is possible that much more serious damage was done to the Liberal party, at least in the form it had assumed in the sixties. Under Grimond the Liberals had moved to the left on domestic issues, and their electoral claim was that the Labour party could not provide an effective challenge to the Conservatives, so people who wanted to end Conservative rule should vote Liberal. In the 1964–6 Parliament the Liberals voted with the government a good deal of the time; this was not a comfortable role for a party in opposition, but at least they could speak as if their support was vital for the survival of the Labour government. After the 1966 election there was no obvious place for them in politics.

The budget contained the promised tax on gambling, and also a tax on employment: in effect employees were divided into three categories, and employers had to pay a tax, receive a bonus, or remain in a neutral position, according to whether their employees were considered to be productive or not. The basis of division was rather old-fashioned, producers of goods being considered productive and producers of services being considered unproductive and being penalized. The differentiation among employees led to confusion, which obscured the fact that the overall effect of the tax was likely to be fairly deflationary, and that it would be sharply deflationary at first because the tax was paid some time before employers received bonuses for the 'productive' workers they employed.

The Department of Economic Affairs brought forward legislation to give it statutory powers to delay wage increases while they were discussed by the Prices and Incomes Board, which would in effect act as guardian of the national interest in deciding what rate of increase was possible in different jobs where wages were fixed by union negotiation. The powers given to the Board were rather too much for the Minister of Technology, Frank Cousins, the leader of the largest of the trade unions, and he resigned rather than remain in a government that deprived his union members of the right to reach settlements on the basis of conditions within the industry.

While Parliament was working over the early stages of this Bill, a new financial crisis was developing. Some people blamed a seamen's strike in the late spring, and some people simply blamed the fact that, although the current balance of payments had improved in 1965, it was still in deficit and showed no signs of getting back in 1966. As the period of summer weakness for sterling came on, people took more and more of their money out of England, and by July the government had to consider, as so many British governments had done previously, what was to be done about the pound. A fair number of members of the Cabinet were in favour of devaluing and running a policy of growth unworried by the value of the pound, in much the way that the French had done in the 1950s. But although the Prime Minister admitted that it might be necessary to consider floating the pound if the economy ran too slowly, he successfully took the lead in opposing devaluation in this crisis.[1]

Granted this decision, there was no alternative to deflation. The international monetary authorities were almost at the end of their resources, and were beginning to question whether England was a sound risk. The main novelty in the deflationary measures was that the Prices and Incomes Bill was amended drastically, to make dividend increases illegal for twelve months, to make wage increases illegal for six months and legal only under special circumstances for the next six and to restrict price increases for a similar period. The cost side of inflation was thus to be stopped by law, while the demand side of inflation was reduced by the traditional measures of reducing government expenditure and restricting investment and credit for business expansion. Four per cent growth lay dead; opinion fell back on the more modest three per cent growth indicated by Butler in 1954. The National Plan was unlikely to recover its prestige and re-emerge as a path to economic growth, at least so long as external pressures might overthrow all its calculations. The Labour government had to show whether it could manage the painful process of deflation and look after the economy at a time of rising unemployment more successfully than the Conservatives had done at times of economic crisis.

The Prime Minister was probably resigned to the fact that the Labour party was not a monolithic party and would never be completely without quarrels, and must have realized that after his return to deflation the left wing of the party would rise again to say that only by a policy of Socialism could Britain escape these periodic bursts of deflation. The Labour leadership faced this problem calmly. A couple of dozen M.P.s on the left of the party regularly abstained or voted against the government on issues concerned with the administration of the Prices and Incomes Act. Wilson at one point was stung into saying that dogs are allowed to bite once but if they bite too often their licences are revoked; most of the time the party leaders ignored the rebels in a more dignified way and did not threaten them with the sanctions of party discipline.

[1] R. H. S. Crossman, *Diaries of a Cabinet Minister*, i (1975), 576–7.

The rebels soon had a larger issue on which to fight. There had been hints, after the election, that the government was thinking again about the E.E.C., but before July there had been no real suggestion that Gaitskell's strict conditions were to be relaxed. The attractions of a larger market appealed to people searching for a way to increase British exports and, although the countries of the Commonwealth did not want England to try to enter the E.E.C., they could not provide an alternative solution for her economic problems. George Brown, who had been a firm supporter of the earlier attempt to enter the E.E.C., became Foreign Secretary a few weeks after the deflationary measures were introduced. He was regarded as the most dynamic man in the Cabinet; his earlier hopes that the Department of Economic Affairs could bring about a rapid economic expansion were likely to be frustrated, which had led him to offer his resignation in July, and an attempt to enter the E.E.C. offered scope to his talents. The government was already convinced of the advantages of consolidating British industry into larger units: the Corporation Tax, the nationalization of the steel industry, and the proposed creation of the Industrial Reorganization Corporation all pointed in the same direction. Entry to the Common Market followed logically from this line of thought. When the government announced in November that it was going to apply again for membership, the left-wing Labour and right-wing Conservative opponents appeared once more, but they commanded less support than in the past.

Because opposition to the policy was weaker the government could commit itself to Europe more fully than its predecessor had done. Wilson and Brown set off on a tour of the capitals of the six Common Market countries. At times the importance of France's position was overstated—Wilson wanted to minimize the obstacles to entry, the other European opponents of British entry wanted de Gaulle to take all the responsibility, and de Gaulle was very willing to be seen as the central figure—but it was true that the most important discussions were those in Paris. The French President gave Wilson and Brown very little comfort; their task became even less hopeful when Dr. Kiesinger, the German Chancellor, made it clear that while he would prefer to see England inside the Common Market he regarded the alliance with France as one of the foundations of German policy, which meant that he would not press the issue of British entry to the point of a quarrel with de Gaulle.

At home the government now had the votes to renationalize the steel industry. Something of the heart had gone out of the struggle; when it had been at its fiercest, around 1950, steel really had been vital to the control of the economy, but by the mid-1960s it had problems of overproduction and surplus capacity; nationalization would come just in time for the government to supervise the contraction of another industry that had passed its prime. Parliament spent rather more time and energy on legislation that recognized people's changed attitudes to government and to private morality. The Conservatives had tended to think the great twentieth-century increase in the power of the government was a consequence of the two world wars and of Socialism which might, given a long period of Conservative rule, fade away. The Labour party thought the problem was more deep-seated and proposed, as one step to deal with it, the creation of a Parliamentary Commissioner (popularly known as an Ombudsman, after the Scandinavian official on whom his role was modelled) who could investigate the confidential files of the civil service when it was suspected that there had been an abuse in the administration of power, and could issue reports on what he found.

The Bill creating the office of Parliamentary Commissioner was brought forward by the government. Private Members introduced two Bills, also inspired by J. S. Mill's type of liberalism, to legalize homosexual acts between consenting adults and to allow abortion when it was justified on medical, psychological, or social grounds. These Bills were handled in the way the Bill abolishing capital punishment had been handled in the previous Parliament: the government did not commit itself officially to supporting them, and issued no party whip, but it allowed enough parliamentary time to make sure that both of them were passed despite attempts to 'talk them out'. Outside Parliament the changes seem to have been welcomed by public opinion; surveys showed majorities in favour of both pieces of legislation, and the opponents of change seemed either to be apologetic about their position or to be unreasonable—the calm, commanding, central position which in the past had been held by the supporters of a restrictive morality was now held by the advocates of a libertarian approach.

The majorities for the two Acts came from the Labour party, and the Acts may have consoled government supporters who were unhappy about other aspects of its policy. Commitment to approval of American intervention in Vietnam, even though it was not accompanied by tangible assistance, annoyed some members of the Labour party; government restriction of wage increases annoyed others. The government hinted that it was going to place the social services on a selective basis; its hints were even more obscure than Heath's had been during the election, but they caused disquiet. When the deflationary measures launched in July 1966 began to take effect, discontent became more widespread; deflation could work only by creating unemployment, and the idea of a Labour government creating unemployment was naturally surprising and unpopular with its supporters. In the 1967 local government elections, which were as usual decided almost entirely by people's feelings about the central government, the Labour party did badly.

A response of perhaps more long-term significance came from Wales and Scotland. The process of curing inflation and balance-of-payments difficulties by a dose of deflation had always worked in a way that hurt stagnant regions more than prosperous regions; deflation in London and the Midlands meant less overtime, but in Scotland, Wales, and the north-east of England it meant that unemployment rose to the level suffered by London in the 1930s. In 1962 the Conservative government had been sufficiently worried by the effect of deflation on the north-east of England to appoint Lord Hailsham as a minister with special responsibility for the region. In 1966 deflation coincided with an increase in nationalist feeling in Wales and Scotland.

There had been Welsh and Scottish nationalist movements in existence for a good many years, but in parliamentary elections, including the 1966 election, they had not done well enough to make anyone take them seriously. But very soon after the 1966 election the Welsh Nationalists won a by-election, which gave them their first seat in the House of Commons. In the months that followed they and the Scottish Nationalists did unexpectedly well. The government seemed uncertain whether to treat them as a transient phenomenon that would pass away when the period of deflation ended, or a real force that should be countered by a devolution of power from Westminster to some regional authority. The success of the Nationalists was accompanied by a complete failure of the Liberals to gain ground. Between elections there had, in the previous dozen years, always been signs of a Liberal revival. In 1967 the conditions seemed particularly favourable: regionalism and devolution of power was a cause the Liberals had championed, and they had always retained some strength in Scotland and Wales. Grimond had shifted the party's emphasis to the left, which might have been expected to attract people who were no longer satisfied with the Labour party. But in England it was the Conservatives, and in Wales and Scotland the Nationalists, who benefited from the government's unpopularity.

Inevitably there were limits to the policy of deflation. The government had no liking for a policy that had to depend on causing unemployment, and its dislike for its own policy made for faulty execution: good trade figures were seen as a sign that British imports and exports were on the right track, and bad figures were waved aside as the result of short-term influences. Private traders were not convinced by this and they became less and less willing to hold sterling. Until some moment in the late summer the existing exchange rate could have been maintained by a steady process of deflation, though it is hard to say whether the government would have had the electoral fortitude to impose such severe deflation or whether it would have been wise to try. But by September or October it was too late. Everybody expected that sterling would be devalued as a result of the Common Market negotiations, either to adjust the British economy to the strains of entry or as a result of the breakdown of negotiations, and nobody wanted to be caught with sterling on his hands.

A dock strike, which distorted the figures of imports and exports, was the final straw. Wilson said, quite accurately, that the monthly balance-of-payments figures for September and October were not typical. But nobody was interested: the best that could be done, as every owner of sterling hurried to buy other currencies from the Bank of England, was to arrange that the devaluation of 18 November should be a modest one of 14 per cent (from £1 = $2.80 to £1 = $2.40), small enough not to touch off a round of competitive devaluations by other major trading countries. The public was understandably enraged: the government had said that it was vital to avoid devaluation, had struggled to avoid devaluation, and had now devalued. De Gaulle within a couple of weeks declared that England was not ready to enter the Common Market and brought the negotiations to an end. When ministers looked at the problems of transferring resources to the task of exporting, they decided that the 'East of Suez' role was too expensive to maintain; troop withdrawals were hastened, and there was a further and almost final contraction of British imperial power, ironically to an accompaniment of requests from Malaysia, Singapore, and Australia that the British should stay. 'East of Suez' had been the basis of the relationship between England and the United States for the previous three or four years; the British withdrawal meant an end to post-imperial discussions of ways to maintain the ghost of an empire in the east.

Devaluation was followed by a ministerial change: Callaghan, the Chancellor of the Exchequer, and Jenkins, the Home Secretary, exchanged posts. By comparison with many of the Cabinet reshuffles that had become a feature of political life in the previous thirty years it was very small but it was fairly significant. Callaghan had carried out a strenuous programme of altering the tax system and had convinced everyone of his determination to defend the sterling exchange rate, but had not been quite so successful at understanding the subtleties of the international monetary system; Jenkins did not impose deflationary taxation quickly enough after devaluation, but seemed more at ease with international problems.

As Home Secretary he had been a convinced supporter of liberal legislation; Callaghan was distinctly less committed to change of this sort and, although a Private Member's Bill to make divorce easier was passed soon after, this seemed to complete the current agenda for libertarian reform. The change should not be seen too much in terms of the personalities of the two ministers. Under Jenkins there had been a change from the traditional requirement of a unanimous verdict of guilty from all twelve jurymen to the acceptance of guilty verdicts given by a majority of ten to two, and this was seen by keen advocates of civil liberties as a blow to an old-established safeguard. On the other hand, it was under Callaghan that the question of the death penalty was taken up a little earlier than had originally been required, and in 1969 the five-year suspension period was made permanent. There was fairly certainly a feeling that libertarian reform had gone as far as the public wanted, at least for a time: this may have been symbolized by the government's unwillingness to take any action upon the report of the Wootton Commission, which had suggested some steps towards the legalization of cannabis, or perhaps by the complete absence of any response to an Arts Council report suggesting the ending of all censorship. The fact that these proposals could be put forward showed that libertarians could see scope for new advances; the fact that nothing was done indicates the general feeling that it was time for reassessment rather than fresh reforms or the reimposition of old standards.

Once Jenkins was fully established at the Exchequer there was no comparable inconclusiveness in financial policy. The government came to realize that if devaluation was to be effective it would have to be accompanied by deflation, or prices would rise by the amount of the currency depreciation and there would be no additional goods to supply to export markets. The housing programme, which had been pushed ahead very rapidly under Crossman in the first years of the Labour government, was cut very substantially. Between 1964 and 1967 1,650,000 homes had been begun; between 1968 and 1971 only 1,400,000 were begun. Much of what was built in the period of rapid growth took the form of flats in tower blocks, which were found far from satisfactory, and in a few cases were not even safe. The need for new housing had been real enough, and had been met, but there was general relief that it was possible to slacken the pace and to transfer resources to other things. But most of the drop in house-building disappeared into the maw of the need for a sound budget and a balance-of-payments surplus rather than into alternative types of expenditure. Apart from the cuts in government spending, the 1968 budget reduced demand by about £900m., and Jenkins warned people that it would be followed by 'two years of hard slog'. At the time, the parliamentary Labour party welcomed the budget, mainly because it included a tax on investment income which ran at above 100 per cent and thus amounted to a form of capital levy. But in a wider context it made more sense to see the budget as the end of one set of attempts to push the economy forward by driving up demand without too much thought about the effect of this financial policy upon real resources.

14. Cracking under the Strain 1968–1976

The Last Years of the Labour Government

FOR three or four years nobody realized how deflationary a policy Jenkins had initiated. Some of its effects were obscured by the way devaluation works: the immediate effect is to increase import prices, which makes the balance of payments even worse for a few months, before those higher prices reduce the demand for imports, and lower export prices improve prospects for overseas sales. So for some months the balance of payments went on showing a deficit, and fears grew that the devaluation had not gone far enough. In much the same way, deflation takes time to work its way through the system, and in 1968 all that people were really feeling was the effects of the earlier deflationary measures taken to try to maintain the old exchange value of the pound. Government spending was kept down fairly effectively, taxes were increased again in November, and the new exchange rate was defended effectively in the turmoil caused by a steady movement of international confidence away from the dollar and towards the Deutschmark.

Those who managed to keep their jobs did not suffer any decline in living standards during the deflation, though the only workers whose real wages went up were those who could claim that their larger-than-average wage increases were compatible with the legislation on pay restraint because they would be matched by future increases in productivity. Much of the cost of deflation was met by a further drop in industrial profits, whose share of the national income had been falling for some time; the process accelerated in the late 1960s and led naturally enough to a decline in investment, which was perhaps made rather worse by the attitude to the return on investment taken by the Prices and Incomes Board. This passed more or less unnoticed; attention was fixed on the other victims of deflation, the unemployed, who had made up just over 1 per cent of the working population in 1965, at the peak of demand generated by Maudling, and made up 2 per cent of the working population at the time Jenkins relaxed his stringent policy in 1970.

This rapid and deliberately planned increase in unemployment was intolerable for supporters of a Labour government; its popularity, shown in opinion polls, or at by-elections or municipal elections, sank very low, and the dissatisfaction of party members with their government threatened to become a deeper-rooted problem. Some of the wide fluctuations in public opinion in the 1960s and 1970s were due to normal discontent with the government, perhaps accentuated because people realized that governments took some notice of what opinion polls said. But some of it went deeper: considerable hostility to authority flourished at the same time as a dangerous overestimation of what a government could achieve. The two attitudes were logically connected: if governments can provide a Golden Age—and earlier in the 1960s governments had been ready to suggest that they could—then a government which failed to provide one was clearly neglecting its duty for corrupt or malevolent reasons. In the late 1960s ordinary members of the public found supporting the Conservative party an adequate way of expressing their dislike of the government. But people working for newspapers and broadcasting, who would have been very ready to describe themselves as a creative minority, were committed enough to change and opposition to conventional ideas to find this alternative unacceptable. They wanted to attack the government for not being left-wing enough. Some of this opposition had roots in the new approach to Marxism that had begun after events in 1956 had shown how far the Stalinist version had gone wrong. This line of thought had some serious intellectual content, and it gained considerable influence in the Labour party in the early 1970s. Another type of left-wing feeling, some of whose features were caught with a rather brutal accuracy in the American phrase 'radical chic', rested much more on a belief that progress ought to shock the bourgeoisie. In the late 1960s the bourgeoisie seems to have been immune to shock, whether because it was too frightened or else too pleased by the new libertarian attitudes—Leonard Woolf mentioned in his autobiography that it was impossible for people in the 1960s to realize how restricted life had been at the beginning of the century, and nobody was very worried by the disappearance of these restrictions. Resistance to this mood came as much from the working class as anywhere else. A number of strands of opinion which went into it came together in opposition to racial discrimination—the desire for equality, the desire for fair treatment, the desire to make moral judgements without qualifications or reservations, and the desire to hit at the sort of patriotism which said that Englishmen were different from everyone else and probably better as well. When Enoch Powell put himself at the head of the opposition to immigration by a speech in April 1968 which hinted at rivers of blood flowing if it was not stopped, his attitude was considered shocking by every public commentator, and was obviously very popular among much of the rest of the population. Powell and Heath parted company over the speech, but neither Heath nor anyone else could resist the mood on which Powell was playing; only about a month before his speech the government had gone back on previous commitments and had announced that Asians of Indian descent who were being expelled from Kenya would not be allowed automatically into Britain even though they held British passports. The relative powerlessness of broadcasting and the press to change people's minds on something they took seriously was shown in successive stages of the argument about immigration: the public was ready to say that immigrants inside the country should be treated fairly, but it had got into its head the idea that immigration had gone too far, and denunciation by those who saw themselves as leaders of opinion did little more than build Powell up to the level of an independent political force in the country.

The 'radicalism of the communicators' was more effective in other directions. Its frequently expressed approval of the young (given added point by the fact that an unusually large proportion of the population was between 15 and 25) had a lot to do with the decision to reduce the voting age from 21 to 18 in 1969. Concern about the rights of women led to legislation requiring employers to move towards equal pay for women. In a slightly more wide-ranging way this attitude carried with it a feeling of contempt for businessmen and for politicians. Some journalists qualified their contempt for businessmen by admiring those who built up fortunes by swift and dramatic *coups* in which they bought or sold companies or selected the right shares to buy, but even these writers clearly regarded building up a firm by saving and reinvesting as dull (or, as they would say, 'fuddy-duddy') and unimportant. Further to the left, opinion was even less tolerant; when Heath in 1973 referred to some exploits of adroit businessmen in avoiding tax as 'the unacceptable face of capitalism', the phrase was taken up and repeated as though he had intended it to apply to the whole of capitalism, which was certainly not what he meant.

Perhaps it was surprising that his remark attracted so much attention, for it was not a period in which politicians received much respect. Allowing for the demands of caricature, a good deal of the public mood was caught by the cartoons of Gerald Scarfe, who drew in a style of brilliant distortion which made it impossible for him to speak well of anyone. The hatred of all men holding authority that was to be seen in his work enabled him to hold up a mirror to his times, and the current of self-hatred that ran so close to the surface also matched an important part of his readers' feelings. Politicians were blamed for not bringing peace, prosperity, and happiness, even though they probably had at this time less power—because of the weakness of the British economy and the relative decline in Britain's international position—to bring peace and prosperity than they had had earlier in the century; blaming them for this did no good, and made people happier only in the shortest of short runs.

A civil war in Nigeria illustrated a good many of these features of British life, including a hostility to the British Empire which might have made sense while the struggle for colonial freedom was going on but, after decolonization had taken place so quickly and so amicably, felt rather as though people needed something to hate. The Ibo tribe waged a hard-fought civil war for a couple of years in an attempt to set up an independent nation of Biafra in the eastern region of the country. The British government, like almost all other governments, supported Nigerian unity, and was the target for a sincere, non-partisan, and ill-informed attack as a result. The supporters of Biafra said that genocide—the extermination of the whole Ibo tribe—was being carried out, and that the British government could and should stop it. The civil war was in fact conducted in a humane way, and the Nigerian government always remembered that it would have to govern the Ibos after it won the war. How much influence the British government could have wielded is not clear; certainly Wilson argued in his memoirs that several members of the Nigerian government wanted to wage war more ruthlessly and that they could have got Russian support for such a policy, so that pressing the Nigerian government too hard would have done the Ibos no good and would only have reduced British influence in West Africa. It was a great relief for the government when the war ended suddenly in January 1970 and peace was restored to a united Nigeria in a calm that stopped the vicarious breast-beating in Britain.

By that time the government was past the worst of its troubles. In the first few months after devaluation it showed signs of breaking up. Lord Longford resigned on the issue of the delay in raising the school-leaving age. In March 1968 Brown resigned and in July Gunter resigned; neither of them mentioned any specific point of disagreement, but both of them said the way Wilson ran his government was intolerable. Less exalted members of the Labour party were troubled by the apparent lack of activity. The 1968 parliamentary session was taken up by a Transport Bill of immense complexity but no great interest except for those concerned with the administrative side of transport. The large simple question of transport could be put into the brief statement that everybody—and especially the railway workers—said that railways were a splendid thing, while steadily declining numbers of people used them and the proportion of traffic that went by road increased year by year. This could not easily be cured by legislation. But the government seemed to have nothing to offer in any other area, and certainly the Prime Minister realized that his position had suffered and could not be restored by any immediate show of activity. Before the 1967 devaluation, about half-way through his tenure of office, he had been eager to hurry off on foreign visits and in particular had tried to help end the war in Vietnam; after devaluation he travelled less, and this withdrawal from doing anything very visible was at its most intense in 1968.

The amount of time spent in early 1969 on an attempt to reform the House of Lords probably encouraged the impression that the government had nothing to suggest for more immediate problems. From time to time the Lords had held up one or two small items of Labour legislation or orders in council, but this aroused very little public excitement. Probably the issue came up mainly because Crossman had made some progress in working out with the Conservatives an agreed measure of reform when he was Leader of the House of Commons. A Bill based on these preliminary discussions was brought forward. It would have changed the House of Lords into an assembly of nominated members chosen by the party leaders in a way that would normally give the government of the day a majority. The Bill was resisted by the Labour left, who did not want to see anything done that might give the Lords more of a claim to a role in politics, and by Conservatives who felt that a nominated majority would destroy all that was valuable in the old House of Lords. The opponents of the Bill could agree in resisting it, if in very little else, and so time-consuming were their speeches and so low the prestige of the government that the Bill had to be abandoned.

This was one of the first signs that the House of Commons was emerging from a quarter of a century of domination by the central organizations of the two major parties. Since 1945 the government could expect, with a degree of confidence which would have surprised earlier generations, to get its legislation passed by the Commons; after 1969 governments could not be quite so sure about it. The House of Commons may have felt some of the loss of respect for authority that was widespread at the time, but in any case it became less predictable and this set the stage for the defeat of an attempt to amend trade union law later in the year.

A Royal Commission on trade union law (usually called after its chairman, Lord Donovan) had reported the previous year, and the majority had concluded that really nothing need be done. It analysed the situation carefully and pointed out that important bargaining took place at plant level rather than in the more widely publicized nationwide negotiations, but its only conclusion was that formal power should follow real power. Its lack of concern about the number of strikes was taken as a sign of complacency, and advocates of reform underlined the fact that three-quarters of the days lost in strikes went in unofficial disputes—which was what the Commission had in mind when it referred to plant bargaining —and suggested that these strikes were more disruptive than official strikes. In the 1950s many of the unofficial strikes had been in the coal mines, and this could be accepted as the result of the long history of bad industrial relations in coalmining. These strikes had no immediate effect on the rest of the economy, but the unofficial strikes of the 1960s in car manufacturing, the docks, and shipbuilding could put a lot of other people out of work because production processes had to be closed through lack of supplies. The number of days lost per thousand workers might be less than in the United States or Japan, but it was argued that the clear-cut and official strikes in those countries disrupted production much less. Despite this, the general tranquillity which had settled on industrial relations in the 1930s had gone on after the Second World War; in the years just after the general strike it was still quite common to lose over 6m. days in strikes in a year, but after 1932 this level had been reached only once, in 1957. If the Donovan Report recommended letting sleeping dogs lie, at least the dogs did seem to be sleeping very soundly.

But sterner counsels prevailed; in April the government announced that it would produce legislation to allow it to impose settlements in some inter-union disputes and to tell workers who had gone on unofficial strike to return to work for twenty-eight days. The accompanying provisions to make it easier to secure union recognition did not reduce the alarm caused among trade unionists by the prospect of fines for going on strike (or, more precisely, for staying on strike after being told to go back to work). British unions had been struggling for a hundred years to stop the courts having any jurisdiction over what was done in strikes; and British firms were not liable to be fined for what they did in strikes. Unofficial strikes might be a real problem in the process of production, but it was not one with which the Labour government could deal at this stage. Too many Labour M.P.s were committed to the trade union movement by belief, by upbringing, and by the nature of their political support. There was no majority for sending the Bill to a committee for detailed discussion, which meant it would have to be debated in sittings of the whole House. Its

Labour opponents would then be able to obstruct it and the Conservatives could put forward their own proposals for much more drastic trade union legislation at a time when the government would be ill placed for defending the unions.

A satisfactory compromise might have been worked out if union leaders had been as powerful as the public imagined. Attempts to work out a prices-and-incomes policy earlier in the 1960s had started from the assumption that the T.U.C. and F.B.I. (later the Confederation of British Industries) really could tell their members what to do. Whatever firms might do, trade unions had very few powers with which to stop their members going on unofficial strike. In June the government gave up the attempt to force its Bill through Parliament in exchange for the T.U.C.'s promise that it would try to stop unofficial strikes. This retreat did the government no good; although Victor Feather, the General Secretary of the T.U.C., hurried round trying to arbitrate disputes, unofficial strikes went on. Partly because the incomes policy was relaxed at the end of 1969, disputes became more common and the number of days lost rose quite sharply— during the 1970 general election the Prime Minister had to help get negotiations started in a newspaper strike when he needed time to campaign. This left open the question whether political leaders were right in thinking that the structure of trade union law should be changed in some way that imposed a greater weight of authority upon the process of collective bargaining, although events were moving in a direction that suggested it was not a time at which imposing new constraints on anyone's freedom of action was going to be easy. Increasing violence and black rioting in the United States, the 1968 riots and general strike which nearly overthrew the Fifth Republic, and the beginnings of political terrorism in Germany were enough to show that the problem of authority was nothing unique to Britain, but it did mean that trying to impose a framework of law upon trade unions which had tried to avoid having any law of collective bargaining was more likely than ever to meet resistance.

The readiness to challenge established authority which had spread so widely in the 1960s produced its most dramatic effects, so far as the United Kingdom was concerned, in Northern Ireland. The Protestant two-thirds of the population of Northern Ireland were so committed to remaining united with Britain, and the Catholic one-third so committed to joining the Irish Free State (after 1949, the Republic) that all politics focused on this single issue in a way that meant the Unionists could never lose and the Nationalists could never win an election. This was not a healthy situation, and to make matters worse the majority reinforced its position by a system of plural voting, of gerrymandered constituencies, and of allocation of jobs in local government and of welfare benefits—especially housing—that made it unlikely that the Catholic minority could play its full part politically or that the system would change into one of class politics in which poor Protestants and poor Catholics could unite to improve their economic position within the United Kingdom.

Late in the 1960s peaceful demonstrations for rights which everyone in Great Britain took for granted, like equal representation and equal chances for applicants for social benefits, did unite fair-minded Protestants with the Catholic minority. The violent response of the unbending Protestants gained for the civil-rights campaign just the sort of sympathy that had been won for blacks by a similar strategy of non-violence in the American South. But history in Ireland was not on the side of non-violence. The difficulty of getting reforms carried out by moderates in the Unionist majority was made clear in February 1969 when Terence O'Neill held an election specifically to strengthen his hand against his own right wing. He and his supporters did not do well, and in April he had to retire in favour of James Chichester-Clark, who was expected to reassure the right. Even so, in the summer, attacks on the Catholic areas by the more violent Unionists reached a point where the British government sent troops to Northern Ireland to protect the minority. The government could now put more pressure on the Unionists at Stormont to end the sort of discrimination that had been exposed in the Cameron Report on conditions in Northern Ireland. A good deal of progress was made in this direction, but, on the other hand, the troops had to work with the Northern Ireland government, and as time passed the army occasionally looked a little like an instrument of the Unionists. The Catholic minority had usually seen its best hope of improvement in the uniting of the thirty-two counties of Ireland in one country, and the violent supporters of this policy, the Irish Republican Army, announced that they would defend the minority against the Protestants and, they claimed, against the British soldiers as defenders of the *status quo*.

This argument could be presented more plausibly after the change of government in June 1970. The Unionist M.P.s at Westminster were members of the Conservative party, and some attention had to be paid to their requests for a slackening of the pace of reform. Suspected troublemakers were arrested and interned without trial. It has been said that Maudling, who as Home Secretary was responsible for Northern Ireland, was a little lazy and felt uninterested and perhaps even repelled by these Irish problems, though it is only fair to say that Northern Ireland probably needed a minister with no other responsibilities. In any case, the situation got worse. Between 1968 and 1970, 39 people had been killed in skirmishes and isolated assaults; in 1971, 173 people were killed. At the same time Catholics in Protestant areas and Protestants in Catholic areas were threatened and attacked often enough to make them move house, so districts became more and more completely homogeneous. The minority moved more completely to the belief that ending partition was the only answer, but, while steps towards equality were too slow to conciliate the Catholics, they came fast enough to disturb and worry the Unionists. In 1971 Chichester-Clark in turn became a victim of the iron law that reforming Unionists offend their own right-wingers, and his place was taken by Brian Faulkner, who had at times objected to the pace of reform, though not so indiscreetly as to make himself unacceptable to the British government.

In 1972 the whole system of government seemed to be breaking down. On 30 January thirteen opponents of the union with Britain were killed in the streets of Londonderry by British troops; there was a long argument over whether they were peaceful demonstrators or a screen for the I.R.A., but clearly such things could happen only when the country was on the edge of civil war. Two months later the British government ended the system of dual control by suspending the Stormont parliament and appointing William Whitelaw as minister responsible solely for Northern Ireland affairs. This brought no immediate improvement; the toll of deaths rose to 467 in 1972, the process of increased separation of the two communities went grimly forward, and there were signs that the I.R.A. proposed to widen the conflict by exploding bombs in Britain.

Although Ireland looked so bleak by 1972, it had in the early months of the crisis done the reputation of the Labour party some good. Sending in troops was seen as a useful and necessary step, and the personal qualities of Callaghan, as Home Secretary, seemed to fit the problem very well; he went to Northern Ireland and showed every sign of feeling at home there, and he applied pressure for change at a rate which produced some effect without breaking up the Unionist government. The spirit of opposition to authority that was so active in Britain inevitably expressed itself in hostility to maintenance of the union; the fact that two-thirds of the Northern Irish population were determined to keep the union intact was ignored on the left and stressed on the right, which led to the comment that a right-winger wanted majority rule in Ulster but not in Rhodesia, while a left-winger wanted precisely the opposite.

The situation had not become so gloomy while the Labour government was in office, and from the middle of 1969 it was able to make up lost ground. Investment in North Sea gas started to show results as—with a little trouble about replacing old appliances—the new supplies began to displace gas made from coal. The shift from coal became precipitate; in the early 1960s the country was still producing a little over 190m. tons a year, or about the same amount as in the late 1940s, but by 1970 the figure had fallen by about a quarter to a little over 140m. tons. New hopes for the country, and fresh problems for the coal industry, arose as it became clear, in 1968 and 1969, that there were significant quantities of oil in the North Sea. Lord Robens, the chairman of the Coal Board, directed the policy of closing coal-pits and finding new jobs for the miners with notable skill, but it was still a difficult operation. Almost inevitably wages in this declining occupation did not keep up with those in more prosperous industries.

The policy of devaluation and deflation, and concentration on the balance of payments at all costs, began to show results. Heath had consistently failed to win people's approval even when Wilson appeared most discredited, and it looked as if the Conservatives had owed their commanding position in 1967 and 1968 simply to the government's unpopularity, accentuated by the fact that much less of the protest vote went to minor parties than in the 1957–8 and 1962–3 periods of comparable Conservative unpopularity. As the balance of payments began to move towards a surplus, the government seemed to have got something right at last, and its position improved. The unemployment figures stopped going up, workers felt they were getting some tangible reward for the long freeze when the prices-and-incomes legislation was for all practical purposes ended late in 1969, and a flood of successful wage claims swept in. The change of mood which followed was natural enough, but it had been so completely taken for granted that the Labour government was doomed that everybody was astonished at the recovery. The Conservative leaders held a private conference at Selsdon Park with mixed results. People were uneasy about their support for the free play of the market, and reduction of government intervention in the economy did suggest that economizing might mean cuts in the social services. On the other hand, they gained support for their proposals to limit the power of trade unions and to defend law and order against the relaxed standards of the 1960s.

Taxes were reduced by about £220m. in the 1970 budget, but the remission looked so slight when the government had all the room for manœuvre provided by a budget surplus of about £¾ billion and a balance-of-payments surplus of £½ billion that it was taken as a sign that there would be no election in the immediate future. But as the opinion polls moved to show a Labour lead, which got some support from the party's reasonably good performance in the municipal elections, it was natural for Wilson to think of an election. Asking for a dissolution, which used to be a formal cabinet decision, is now understood to be the responsibility of the Prime

Minister alone, but sometimes a Prime Minister takes a good deal of advice before acting. Heath consulted a lot of people before dissolving in February 1974; Wilson took quite as many pains to see that the cabinet and as far as possible the parliamentary party agreed with his decision before announcing that there would be an election on 18 June. By the last few days before the announcement the Labour party was so convinced that it would win that Wilson could quite justifiably write in his memoirs, 'Had I decided against a June election I would have been adjudged certifiable.'[1]

In retrospect it seems odd that everybody was so convinced by surveys and municipal elections which showed only that, after lagging behind for years, the government was more popular than the opposition in one particular month. At the time all the politicians except Heath seemed ready to believe Labour would hold most of its seats. What it would do with this majority was far from clear. The election had cut short the parliamentary progress of a Bill to provide workers with pensions linked to their earnings, but this was almost the only piece of legislation to offer. Wilson put his claim for re-election in terms of the balance-of-payments surplus, which was offered as proof of the general assertion that Labour was more fit to govern than the Conservatives. As he was not going to say anything specific he campaigned by visiting committee rooms, saying a few confident sentences for television, and radiating a general conviction that all was well. Like any Leader of the Opposition, Heath had to say things were going badly, and he dwelt on the steady rise in prices, which he claimed a thrifty and efficient Conservative government would hold in check. On election night everybody was just getting ready to say he had again fought a sober and uninspiring campaign when the first results came in and at once showed that the Conservatives would have a modest but perfectly adequate majority.

	Votes cast	Seats won	% of total votes cast
Conservative	13,145,123	330	46·4
Liberal	2,117,033	6	7·5
Labour	12,178,295	287	43·0
All others	906,345	7	3·2

The hints of a nationalist protest in Scotland and Wales faded away. The Scottish and the Welsh nationalists had each gained a seat in by-elections; both were regained by the Labour party, though the Scottish

[1] Harold Wilson, *The Labour Government 1964–1970* (1971), 781.

nationalists won a seat in the Western Islands. The two major parties between them received about eight-ninths of the total votes cast, which meant that as many voters as in the 1960s, though not quite as many as in the 1950s, found one or other major party was politically satisfactory.

Heath in control

The result was regarded very much as Heath's own victory; he had remained confident when everyone round him believed the gloomy tale of the opinion polls, and this probably encouraged him to think he need not pay too much attention to the views of his colleagues in future. His own deepest commitment was to Europe, and here he was able to get off to a quick start because the Labour government had been bringing forward a new application in the months after de Gaulle resigned in 1969. His successor, President Pompidou, might not have inherited all of his prestige, but it was soon clear that he was in a position to veto the application if he chose. It was not until May 1971 that Pompidou made it known, after a long private discussion with Heath, that he was satisfied about Britain's European credentials. This probably meant he had been convinced that Heath believed that entering the E.E.C. was something valuable that should be pursued for its own sake and not just used as part of a plan for repairing the British economy or building up Britain's political standing. Heath may well have been the only British politician who could have persuaded the President that he was in earnest about this, and he probably went on to show that what he wanted was a close association of countries, not a single superstate into which Britain and France and the rest would merge and disappear.

Once Pompidou had given his approval the Brussels negotiations went ahead quickly. The British negotiators realized that they had to accept the Treaty of Rome if their application was to be taken seriously, and that, whatever might have been attempted in 1962, all that they could now hope to do was to obtain transitional arrangements to soften and delay the shock of entry. In particular they accepted the general principle of the Common Agricultural Policy that the six original members had worked out in the mid 1960s. The E.E.C. Commission kept farm incomes up by imposing tariffs on food from outside the Community and buying produce from inside the Community at prices high enough to give farmers a fair standard of living, even when this meant paying considerably more than world prices. This policy almost unavoidably produced surpluses of food which had to be stored or sold at a reduced price with the help of subsidies from E.E.C. taxpayers, because nobody else would buy it at the prices paid by the Commission. When touring Europe to make his application in 1967, Wilson had told the member of the Commission responsible for agriculture that this scheme if applied without modifications would cost the British balance of payments $760m.—then £270m.—a year. This figure, like the implied increase in food prices, may have been overstated, but it indicates one aspect of the struggle over the E.E.C. which was so important a part of British politics between 1971 and 1975.

These questions of food prices helped move the Labour party away from the willingness to negotiate which it had shown when in office, even though Labour supporters of entry said a Labour government would have found the terms Heath negotiated at Brussels entirely satisfactory. This was hard to prove; in any case, when the general principle of entry was debated in the Commons in October 1971, Wilson announced that a Labour government would re-negotiate the terms or leave the Community. While both major parties were divided on the issue, the Labour supporters of entry were more numerous than the Conservative opponents; in a free vote after the October debate, the government's White Paper was welcomed by 356 votes to 244, 39 Conservatives voting against it and 69 Labour M.P.s for it, so that it looked as if it would be easy for the government to carry through the Commons the enabling legislation to give effect to the Treaty. In reality Labour supporters of entry could vote against their party on the general principle but would have difficulty in doing so on a steady succession of small issues, so opponents of entry could hope that, on some issue on which the Labour party was united and the Tory opponents of entry voted with them, the government would be defeated and at the very least would have to return to the negotiating table. This strategy would have been almost certain to succeed if the government had had to put forward the whole Treaty in its Bill. Even the relatively short Bill that it submitted took up the great bulk of the 1972 session. Because the minorities within the two major parties placed the question of Europe on something like the same level of importance as party loyalty, the voting was unpredictable enough to bring a tension into the conflict that had not been known since the great nineteenth-century battles of 1866–7 and 1886. On Second Reading the majority was only eight, on the Common Agricultural Policy it was down to five, and on movements of capital within the Community it fell to four. A more flexible man than Heath would have faltered, or tried to find a compromise where none was to be found. He stuck to his position, the Bill moved into calmer waters, and at last passed Third Reading on 13 July by 301 votes to 284.

Early in 1972 the idea of a referendum came into the discussion. Each of the three other countries negotiating for entry at the same time as Britain was to have a referendum—Denmark and Ireland voted in favour of entry, Norway voted against—and Pompidou held a referendum to find whether the French were in favour of the enlargement of the E.E.C. While a referendum was a thoroughly European device, it could not be dismissed as something unheard-of in the British constitution, because ten days after Pompidou announced the French referendum the British government proposed that referenda should be held periodically in Northern Ireland to reassure Unionists that nobody would try to push them into the Republic against their wishes. From a wider point of view a referendum seemed in accordance with the ideas of greater popular participation in government which had gained ground in the later 1960s. A week after Pompidou announced the French referendum, the national executive committee of the Labour party committed the party to a referendum on membership of the E.E.C.

Britain became a member of the E.E.C., under the transitional arrangements worked out at Brussels, at the beginning of 1973. By that time the pressure of the 1972 session and the desire to get membership off to a good start had combined with the government's concern about its normal mid-term unpopularity to make Heath take drastic action to put more vitality into the economy. The Conservatives never sank as low in public opinion as the Labour government did in the late 1960s, and Heath always received a fair amount of support from intellectual leaders of opinion because of his position on Europe. Among most people who earned their living by handling ideas and concepts—except perhaps economists, who were relatively evenly divided on its merits—the idea of entering the Community was becoming the accepted orthodoxy. The Labour party was blamed for changing its mind after accepting entry from 1966 to 1970, and the general attitude expressed in public was that the Conservatives ought to be supported because of their position on Europe.

While this strengthened their position, it did not mean that the Conservatives could have faced an election in 1971 or 1972 with any confidence. Their economic policy had not been meant to be unpopular, but it was based on so complete a misinterpretation of what was happening in the economy that it threatened to undermine the government; their trade union policy had not been meant to be unpopular, but they might have thought about it more carefully if they had realized how much resistance it was going to encounter. It is a natural political judgement for a Conservative government to feel that its Labour predecessor has been imposing excessively heavy taxes and indulging in over-lavish government spending, and it was probably unavoidable that the Conservatives started with this idea in June 1970. The course of the campaign encouraged them to believe, as a matter of technical analysis, that the main problem in the economy was the high level of inflation and the shaky nature of the balance-of-payments surplus of the last months of the 1960s. Heath's attacks on rising prices had been well received, and an unexpected deficit in the May trade figures encouraged the idea that the economy was being pushed quite fast enough.

Conservative strategy may have suffered because of the death, within a month of taking office, of Iain Macleod, the Chancellor of the Exchequer. His successor, Anthony Barber, was more interested in reorganizing the system of taxation than most Chancellors. The two innovations made by Asquith in 1907 had never been fully fitted into the rest of the income-tax system: Barber wanted to integrate the old standard rate of income tax and the separately administered tax called surtax on higher incomes (it began at £5,000 a year in 1971) into a single income tax rising by steps; and he also wanted to end the calculation of earned income relief, by which taxpayers paid only on a major fraction of income which did not come from interest, rent, or dividends (they paid on only $\frac{7}{9}$ths of their earned incomes in 1971) and replace it with a lower nominal rate of income tax and a special investment surcharge on interest, rent, and dividends. At the same time party policy committed him to getting rid of the existing Selective Employment Tax, and his need for revenue, together with the rules of the E.E.C., led him to set up a value added tax in its place. This tax was designed to be entirely neutral except that it could be remitted in the case of exports; the processor and the manufacturer and the wholesaler and the retailer each paid a tax at the same rate upon the amount by which the article had increased in cost ('value added') between their buying it and their selling it to the next person in the chain. The tax was complicated to set up and to administer, and involved everyone except the final customer in an elaborate relationship with the tax authorities. The net effect on revenue and on demand of these tax changes was not meant to be substantial, but they naturally took up a great deal of Barber's attention.

He seems as a result not to have been able to analyse the economic situation completely, and to have accepted too readily the widespread underestimate of the extent to which the Labour government had reduced the level of demand in the economy, and also not to have noticed the way his colleagues' attitude to government spending was changing as they carried out the policies to which they were committed. His announcement in the autumn of 1970 that there would be a number of cuts in government spending, and that income tax would be reduced by $2\frac{1}{2}$p was clearly in accordance with party principle and the view that the government was spending and taxing too much. The economy was still thought to be running at a high level of demand, and tax cuts were expected to make businessmen more enterprising in their approach. The non-interventionist frame of mind which had led the Conservatives to oppose prices and incomes policies in the late 1960s could be seen in a statement by John Davies, the Minister for Trade and Industry, that it was not the government's intention to help 'lame ducks', as he called industries that needed subsidies if they were to survive.

By the end of 1970 it was clear that all this rested on an incorrect analysis of the economy. The balance-of-payments surplus turned out to be perfectly soundly based, but unemployment, whose growth had been checked in late 1969, was now rising again in an alarming way and was reaching levels that had not been seen in the post-war period. By the time the government realized what was happening it looked as if a million people would soon be out of work, while the 1971 balance-of-payments surplus was so large that it seemed that this habitual constraint on the government's freedom of action could be ignored. Early in 1971 Davies found himself confronted by a very prominent lame duck: the famous car and aero-engine firm of Rolls-Royce had undertaken an ambitious programme to develop a new engine without fully estimating the costs, by 1970 it was having difficulty raising money to continue the programme, and by February 1971 the company realized that it was bankrupt. Losing this old-established firm with its well-deserved reputation for very high-quality production would have been a heavy blow to national pride at any time; to make matters worse, the new engine was intended for aeroplanes produced by the American firm of Lockheed, and if Rolls-Royce stopped work it would drag Lockheed down with it. The American economy was in the same listless condition as the British, and the U.S. government was in no mood to have its unemployment made worse by British opposition to government intervention. Within days of Rolls-Royce's announcement of bankruptcy, the government had been forced by a combination of American pressure and British pride to undertake a rescue operation. The firm was nationalized, the motor-car section was sold back to private ownership, and the aero-engine side went on under government ownership. This was embarrassing, but at least it was over quickly. In June Upper Clyde Shipyards, which had been put together by the Labour government with lavish subsidies as part of the policy of intervention and concentration, went bankrupt. The workers responded by taking over the shipyard and announcing that they would go on working with the materials already available. By occupying the shipyard they prevented any reorganization that depended on selling off the assets; by going on working they made it very hard for anyone to talk about lazy workers going on strike. Partly for these reasons and partly for fear of a revival of Scottish nationalism if unemployment spread on the Clyde, the government found itself once more forced into a policy of intervention to save the shipyard from closing.

Rolls-Royce and Upper Clyde Shipyards were conspicuous departures from the principle of non-intervention, but they did not cost very much money. Much larger increases in government spending took place in health, education, and local government. The 1970 election platform recommended keeping expenditure down and leaving the public with a larger portion of their earnings in the form of disposable income, but in practice these ministries spent money without much restraint, perhaps mainly out of a feeling that the government should be generous in order to raise the level of demand and reduce unemployment: in the last year of Labour government public spending ran at a level equal to 50 per cent of the national income, and by 1972 this figure had risen to 52 per cent.

For centuries local government had been organized rather haphazardly by making towns of sufficient importance into boroughs and leaving the rest of the country organized in counties, which naturally were rural in emphasis. This made a good deal of sense when towns wanted a distinctly higher level of services in paving, lighting, and water-supply than the surrounding countryside did, and when religious differences between the urban nonconformists and the rural Church of England meant that they saw no prospect of agreement on educational questions. But by the second half of the twentieth century these problems mattered much less; the churches' only concern about educational politics was the percentage of the costs of their schools that the government would pay, while questions like overspill housing from cities, the impact of road transport, and the location of places of work for suburban commuters all meant that large towns and their hinterlands needed to work together much more than at the beginning of the century. In 1969 a Royal Commission under Lord Redcliffe-Maud had recommended a very sweeping change of local government, and most of its suggestions were accepted. The most striking proposal was that half a dozen large 'conurbation' authorities should be created which would administer a whole heavily urbanized region like Merseyside or South Yorkshire. Other regional authorities were set up to run the affairs of large cities and the countryside round them; the new county of Avon, for instance, was given boundaries which included Bristol and its rural hinterland. And, by eliminating the smallest authorities, the urban district and the rural district councils, the Report suggested reducing the elected authorities from something over a thousand to something over a hundred.

People may have thought this reduction in the number of authorities would simplify the administration of local government. This was true only in the sense that there would be fewer elected councillors. The amount of work to be done by councils remained unchanged, and in one area it increased significantly. The Seebohm Commission had just proposed increasing the number of social workers and improving their qualifications and pay. This precisely fitted developments in the universities; more students had been graduating, and the expanding profession of social work, like the traditional profession of teaching, fitted the prevailing attitude of repugnance to commercial or industrial careers. But while spending on social work rose sharply in percentage terms, a much larger total increase was caused by following the practice of the most open-handed authority when amalgamating several of them. The financial problems caused by the consolidation of staff after the reduction of the number of authorities was made much worse by the tendency of councillors to imagine that they were skilled land developers who could undertake ambitious, not to say speculative, schemes of new commercial building. Some of these schemes had distinctly corrupt overtones; in the early 1970s the bankruptcy of John Poulson's architectural firm revealed that for some years he had been manipulating the decisions of a number of Scottish and North of England councils through administrative and elected officials who took bribes from him. Other cases of municipal corruption, of which perhaps the most widely ramifying was in South Wales, came to light at about the same time. Enough of them were in old-established Labour strongholds to suggest that the root of the trouble was councillors with entrenched power who welcomed development and could be persuaded to help it along for relatively small amounts of money.

Spending on education also increased, though not for such dubious reasons. Probably the most important development during Margaret Thatcher's three-and-a-half years as minister was the fulfilment of the Labour policy of comprehensive education; in 1970 less than a third of secondary schoolchildren were in comprehensive schools, and by 1974 the figure was over two-thirds. It might seem much less important that her response when Barber demanded economies in his first few months of office was to stop supplying free milk to primary schoolchildren irrespective of parental income, but milk and a means test were emotional matters; putting the two together made her look like some sort of ogre and meant she had difficulty in resisting other pressure for spending. Some of the money went to improve education for the youngest children, and the long-awaited raising of the school-leaving age to 16, which was due to come in 1973, led to growing pressure to provide more teachers. A really powerful minister might have resisted this and shown that a great many children were already staying for an extra year and that the population of school age was about to drop as a result of the decline in the birth-rate in the 1960s; instead, as popular pressure built up, there was a dramatic and unjustified increase in the number of recruits for the teaching profession encouraged to enter the training colleges, though by the time they emerged the need for additional teachers had vanished.

In something of the same spirit of generous government spending, the administration of health and social services was changed. Sir Keith Joseph later came, like Thatcher, to be regarded as an opponent of high expenditure and bureaucratic control, but in his 1972 reorganization of the health service he showed the readiness to spend money and to increase the proportion of civil servants to doctors, nurses, and other health staff which in theory he disliked. This was not because he did not as a minister stick to his principles; it was more that the Conservatives were carrying out the administrative changes, on which reductions in government spending would depend, at a time when the rising tide of unemployment held out alarming prospects for their popularity and their E.E.C. policy. For some years people had been worried by the way that the insurance benefits set up by the legislation of the late 1940s had never been high enough, despite frequent increases, to avoid making a large number of claimants dependent on national assistance or, as it was later called, supplementary benefit. Insurance benefits came as a matter of right; supplementary benefit was means-tested. Joseph tried to reduce the discretionary element, and the attendant bitterness, by setting up a Family Income Supplement scheme to lay down a minimum entitlement for each family, but it could not be kept at a high enough level to avoid the need for supplementary benefit without undermining all the insurance schemes, and rising unemployment naturally pushed more people into needing supplementary benefit.

Unemployment fairly certainly strengthened resistance to Conservative trade union policy. The Industrial Relations Act of 1971 was the first major item of legislation, and it fulfilled their promise in opposition to restrain the power of the unions. It went considerably further towards the North American attitude to trade unions that had been implied in the Labour 1969 Bill. Unions had to register if they were to go on enjoying the special legal status they had acquired over the years; ballots before strikes could be imposed if the government thought it appropriate, and so could delays of up to sixty days before strikes began; as could fines (with the implication of prison if the fines were not paid) for workers who did not obey the law. Unions, whether registered or not, could also be fined, but this was less likely to cause trouble because it did not imply imprisonment. This would put rather more power over their members into the hands of the union leaders, a gift they had no desire to receive. British trade unionists believed American unions accepted this system of registration and control by the courts because in return the law made employers recognize them as legitimate bargainers; British unions were proud that they had won a comparable position without any help from the law. Trade unionists shared the widespread belief that the government could intervene to manipulate the economy in any way it chose, and the fact that unemployment was rising fast while the Industrial Relations Bill was going through Parliament encouraged the belief that the government wanted to weaken the working class by creating a pool of unemployed workers while absorbing the unions into the system as part of the employers' apparatus for obtaining adequate and disciplined labour.

It is most unlikely that the government had such grandiose ideas, but the blend of Marxist and conspiracy theories so widespread at the time did encourage unions to resist more fiercely than they might otherwise have done. The Trades Union Congress resolved that its member unions should formally remove themselves from the register of trade unions, and it suspended from membership of the T.U.C. those which refused to do so. One-day strikes were held to protest against the Act, and the Engineers' Union incurred several large fines because its members were particularly apt to become involved in offences against the Act. In broad terms the Act did nothing to improve industrial relations, and may well have made them worse, in the five years 1970–4 almost as many days were lost in strikes as in the five years of labour unrest before 1914, and one government was discredited and replaced by another which seemed alarmingly dependent on the trade unions. But it is not certain how much of this can be attributed to the Act: 10m. days had already been lost in 1970, and the increase to 13½m. days in 1971 must have been due at least in part to pressure for wage increases; it was unusual for wages to be demanded so aggressively in a period when unemployment was going up, but it was also unusual for prices to keep rising so fast in a recession. Despite a C.B.I. undertaking in July to keep price increases down to 5 per cent, and a government commitment to keep down prices in the nationalized industries by subsidizing their losses, prices went up by about 9 per cent in 1971 and money wages went up by about 10 per cent.

Out of control

In the course of 1971 the government realized that the economy was suffering from severe deflation. Taxes were reduced, in two steps, by about £500m., or about one per cent of the national income. Bank credit was relaxed, and so were the government and Bank of England directives which ever since 1939 had advised banks that certain types of borrowers, such as exporters, or house-builders, were to be given priority and other types of borrowers, such as dealers in property, were to be avoided as far as possible. The clearing banks—reduced by this stage to four large and seven or eight smaller houses—co-operated with one another in observing these rules and in making sure that none of them suffered as a result of doing so. Early in 1971 Barber announced in the White Paper *Competition and Credit Control* that the banks should compete with each other, and should compete simply by lending money to good risks without asking whether they were in priority categories or not. It was only after the money supply (as listed in tables for M3) had increased about 84 per cent in three years that cynics said arrangements had been made for competition but not for credit control.

The change was meant to stimulate development and to allow the businessmen who were taking the risks to decide what were the best opportunities for expansion. But, while new money can be put into circulation at the stroke of a pen, it takes a little while for industrial managers to decide where to invest in new factories or machines. Economic conditions between 1968 and 1971 had not encouraged investment, and it took several months for industrialists to alter course. Meanwhile the banks had to lend the new money coming into their hands, and they had no official restraints on lending policy. They lent to people who wanted to buy existing assets, and as a result the prices of shares on the stock exchange and the price of houses went up very impressively: houses in the London area doubled in price between mid 1971 and mid 1972, and it was noticed that the share index reached a peak just as unemployment touched 1m. early in 1972. If the government had stuck to its free market approach it would have said that this was a necessary preliminary to expansion; and in 1973 and again in 1974 the proportion of the national income devoted to investment did go up. But the government was in no mood to wait for this, and in his 1972 budget the Chancellor reduced taxes by over £1 billion. Unemployment fell so soon after this that it could not have been caused by the monetary effects of the budget, though no doubt the changes were good for confidence. Wages went up very fast, rising in money terms by something like 18 per cent and, as the rise in prices slackened slightly, in real terms by something over 10 per cent.

This was of course too good to last, but the economy was at the happy stage of the economic cycle where real wages and investment can increase at the same time; optimists always attribute this to bringing unused resources and unemployed workers back into the system, and pessimists say that it is always accompanied by a deterioration in the balance of payments, which in 1972 showed neither surplus nor deficit. The expansion of the economy was probably helped by the government's announcement that it would not be tied to defending a fixed rate of exchange, which was really an admission that it had been too co-operative in the currency disturbances of the previous year. Since 1945 the nations of the industrialized West had run in slightly different trade cycles, with the result that they were never all expanding or contracting at the same time. By 1970 these cycles seemed to have moved much closer together, so that nearly all the industrialized nations were in a recession at the same time. In August 1971 President Nixon announced that the United States would no longer be willing to buy gold from central banks at a fixed rate of $35 to an ounce. For some years the United States had been showing signs of strain about maintaining the Bretton Woods system with its fixed link between gold and the dollar, but the announcement caught the world without any immediately acceptable system to replace it. Nixon's step showed what the British government had been concerned about in its long defence of the exchange rate, for after the 1967 devaluation other rates had changed too often for the system to survive. This suggested that the Bretton Woods system could not work unless it was supported by nations that would subject their own economies to some inconvenience for the sake of keeping it going.

When an attempt was made, at the Smithsonian Institution in Washington at the end of 1971, to establish a new range of fixed exchange rates, the British government was persuaded to accept a rate of $2.60 to the pound, or 8 per cent above the 1967–71 level. Other currencies went up more than this in terms of the U.S. dollar, but the trading position of Germany and Japan in the post-war world had been strong enough to justify this. Britain's performance did not justify a higher rate against the dollar, and the government's abandonment of the fixed rate recognized this and also recognized that the Smithsonian system was not likely to last long. This was accepted early in 1973 and the world moved to a system of floating rates very like that of the 1930s, though governments realized that they had to co-operate and could not drive down their exchange rates for trading purposes without bringing back many of the more unpleasant features of the 1930s. After this, although comment in Britain continued to concentrate on the pound–dollar exchange rate, the 'Smithsonian depreciation', showing how the pound had moved in terms of the currencies of other important trading countries, was a better measure of what was happening, and it showed that the pound had gone down by about 10 per cent in 1972.

When Nixon cut the link between gold and the dollar, he also established a prices-and-incomes policy which ran quite satisfactorily for about two years. It was at the peak of its success, and Nixon was on the verge of an enormous victory in the presidential election, in the autumn of 1972. By then Heath seems to have wished that he could do something similar, but at first he felt restrained by his party's opposition to the earlier prices-and-incomes legislation of the Labour government which had sometimes led the Conservatives to vote with the Labour left against it, and several members of his party felt deeply committed to the principle of avoiding the sort of direct intervention needed to run a prices-and-incomes policy. When he held discussions with the T.U.C. and the C.B.I., the T.U.C. came very close to saying that the government must adopt the policy of the Labour party, including repeal of the Industrial Relations Act; and in November Heath switched to a policy very like Nixon's. During a three-month freeze, no increases would be allowed, and then, after a Pay Board and a Prices Commission had been set up, maximum increases of £1 a week plus 4 per cent of existing wages would be permitted.

All the signs were that this was reasonably popular. The Labour party was losing ground, perhaps because of its internal divisions over the E.E.C., perhaps because Labour policy was moving to the left with the adoption of a policy of 'a fundamental and irreversible shift in the balance of power and wealth'. The increasing number and intensity of strikes must have hurt the Labour party as well. In 1972 the number of days lost in strikes rose to 24m. About half of this was lost in a national coal strike early in the year in which the miners reacted against the deterioration in their position in the 1960s. They won a good deal of popular support, and they were able to make their strike effective unusually quickly by picketing power stations. The government had to give way, a great many other unions followed where the miners had led, and they looked like the motive power driving prices up. For whatever reason, the Labour lead in opinion polls became less impressive in 1973 than it had been in 1971 and 1972, though the polls—and some striking by-election results—suggested that voters had gone Liberal rather than Conservative.

The bills for the unsustainably fast expansion of 1972 were beginning to arrive, by no means all from inside Britain. Central banks relaxed their monetary policies in several countries between mid 1971 and early 1973 to an extent that suggested they had taken seriously *The Economist*'s off-hand comment on Nixon's measures that 'Finance ministers . . . should welcome the freedom of not having to look over their shoulders all the time at their balances of payments and to be able [*sic*] to pursue economic goals which should be much more vote-gaining' (28 Aug. 1971). And all over the world people responded by rushing to buy anything that seemed safer than cash. The feature of this international urge to spend that attracted most attention in Britain, or at least in London, was the boom in pictures and other works of art, which enriched London art dealers and later must have left many of the purchasers aware that they had bought things in which they were not really interested at prices which were not maintained for more than a few months. The price of property was a much more real problem; easy bank credit encouraged dealers to buy blocks of flats and sell them to the individual occupiers or to acquire pieces of land which, if they got planning permission, they could develop and sell at a much higher price. Barber did little to restrain this: he called his 1973 budget 'neutral' by which he meant that taxes were not changed and the public sector would again have to borrow about £2 billion. While money remained readily available, the interest rates for borrowing it went up steadily: the rates on long-term government bonds went up to 12 per cent in 1973 and industrial firms had to pay even more, which made fixed investment difficult, though dealers in shares or property expected to make their profit so quickly that the cost of borrowing would not affect them much. The relaxing of credit control had encouraged the development of new 'secondary' banks which borrowed at high rates and lent at even higher, but did not maintain the large reserves or the nationwide branch system of the clearing banks. By their flexibility in handling money, and their optimism about the future, they were the natural source of funds for traders who expected to turn their money over in a short time.

For several years the price asked for British exports had gone up slightly faster than the price of imports. In 1973 this was dramatically reversed; a great many raw materials from wheat to copper and from sugar to gold (now free from its links to any currency and free to move like any other commodity) went up in price. Membership of the E.E.C. insulated Britain from some of these problems of sharply fluctuating food prices, but still the pressure threatened to cut into the standard of living. With this fear the government put forward its plan for the 1973–4 phase of its incomes policy: an ill-defined increase of a little over 7 per cent would be allowed in any case, and if the cost of living went up more than 7 per cent it would be taken to have passed a 'threshold' after which an increase of 40p would be allowed, and each further one per cent increase in prices would allow another 40p in wages. This meant that anyone earning the average wage or less would find that his real pre-tax wages increased with each threshold that was passed. No doubt the authors of this scheme felt quite sure that price increases would be below 7 per cent and just wanted to assure wage-earners that the existing standard of living was a fixed point from which they would not fall. This looked reasonable because living standards had not slipped back, except for workers who became unemployed, at any time since the Second World War, but consumption had never risen as much faster than production as it had in 1972. The consumer boom had come earlier in the cycle than in 1958–60 (the most comparable consumer boom), and people would need quite as much good fortune as in the 1950s if they were to keep what they had just gained.

As in the 1950s, television was the striking novelty in the boom—this time, colour television. The number of licences for colour sets more or less doubled every year from 1970 to 1974, rising from 200,000 in 1969, when it was still regarded as an unreliable toy that ate up television revenue for the sake of a minority interest, to $5\frac{1}{2}$m. in 1974, when it dominated the scene. Although most of the sets in use were still monochrome, no television producer thought in black and white, and nobody objected to the idea of buying colour sets in the way people had objected on intellectual grounds to buying television sets at all in the 1950s. The growth of colour television coincided with a sharp drop in film-making in Britain. Spending on film production dropped to about a third of the level of the late 1960s, and a fair amount of what was made came from firms closely linked to television. American money had financed the boom of the 1960s, and American money was leaving, possibly to concentrate on very expensive productions in the United States, possibly because Britain no longer provided the mixture of glitter and social conflict that had been the basis for films made in Britain in the 1960s. There was certainly no diminution in the number of talented people available; though there were so few opportunities in film-making, the television companies were able to recruit very successful teams for production in serial form of adaptations of books like *The Forsyte Saga* and Trollope's six parliamentary novels, or for long illustrated lecture series like Lord Clark's 'Civilisation'. For actors in these series it was possible to draw on a great range of talent in the theatre, though here a curious and not entirely welcome division was appearing. The government had committed itself to supporting the theatre, and by the early 1970s two successful national companies, the Royal Shakespeare Company and the National Theatre—still based on the Old Vic theatre— were doing well. The trouble was that they were doing so well that the commercial theatres had some difficulty in competing in the realm of serious drama and seemed willing to avoid the challenge by returning to triviality. Undoubtedly this was what a lot of people wanted, and the two-level theatre, of subsidized serious work and commercial triviality, might be the best that anyone could do. Certainly theatres flourished, and, just as the sale of television shows was one sort of export, the British theatre was one of the attractions which by the mid 1970s had gone a long way towards turning tourism into a positive item in the balance of payments.

None of this, pleasant though it was, could meet the drain on the balance

of payments of the flood of imports for the boom. The government said
that it was going all out for growth. Whether this approach could ever
have worked is doubtful, but must for ever remain unknown because the
government's position was destroyed by two problems concerned with
fuel. The miners had at the time been reasonably satisfied by the 1972
settlement, but it had come in the early stages of a period of rising prices
and generous wage settlements, so that eighteen months later they had
lost most of the ground they had gained. The government recognized this,
and offered allowances for shift working in its pay rules for 1973–4 which
would let the miners receive increases well above the average. The Coal
Board offered the whole increase at once; the miners assumed that, as in
normal bargaining, there was more to come. In November they decided,
just after events in the Middle East had improved their bargaining position,
to stop the overtime working on which British mines depended for their
normal level of production.

By 1974 Britain imported about 2m. barrels of oil a day. This immense
increase in consumption, which had cut away the position of coalmining
and had not even been much affected by the development of the natural
gas in the North Sea, owed a great deal to the unchanged or even reduced
prices that had been asked in the 1950s and 1960s. By the beginning of
the 1960s the countries from which the oil came were so annoyed by the
way they got no better prices for their exports while import prices went
up that they formed the Organization of Petroleum Exporting Countries,
and pushed up oil prices like most commodity prices in the early 1970s.
But when war once more broke out between Israel and Egypt in October
1973, the Arab oil-producing countries imposed a partial embargo on oil
for the West, and the members of OPEC found that they could raise oil
prices sharply and successfully. By the end of the year oil cost about $8
a barrel more, which meant that Britain's oil bill might go up by £2½
billion a year. While this strengthened the miners' position, the government was afraid that mining productivity would not go up even if there was
a large wage increase, and it decided to check the growth of the economy
and resist the miners. Their successful strike in 1972 was thought to have
encouraged the great wave of inflation, and the government believed that
other unions would not accept the miners as a special case and would press
forward with claims to match anything the miners were awarded. In
December, when the ban on overtime was beginning to affect stocks of
coal, the government announced reductions in spending calculated to
lower demand by over £1 billion, and special measures to reduce fuel
consumption, of which the most startling was that factories would be
supplied with power for only three days a week, and would have to make

the best working arrangements they could. The three-day week worked better than might have been expected, production fell by only about 20 per cent, and it looked as if the stocks of coal might last through the winter. By mid January the government announced that a four-day week might be practicable. But the miners had not come this far only to lose their pay increase; they took a ballot among their members which produced an 80 per cent vote in favour of a strike. There had been discussions inside the government already about holding a general election; the prospect of a miners' strike, which would probably have meant a two-day week, made an election inevitable.

The Conservatives felt the prospects were good, and the Labour party was decidedly worried: it was true that the miners were probably more respected, because of the unpleasantness and danger of their job, than any other workers, but strikes and trade unions were not popular causes to defend. As unemployment came down to about the 1970 level and was falling fast, and as real wages were still going up, it looked as if the economy was running properly and the miners and the Labour party might be accused of ruining it. On the other hand, the Conservative claim that the election was about who governs Britain did not have much effect. They suffered because of rising prices and also because of a feeling that the government had been so abrasive that it had brought upon itself a number of questions about its authority. The Labour party had its own answer to the problems of rising prices and the place of trade unions in ruling the country; the party leadership and the union leadership said they would agree on a 'social contract' (sometimes referred to as a 'social compact') which meant that the Labour party would carry out certain reforms and the unions would be responsible about wage claims. So little of this had been worked out by the time of the election that people could only have voted for it in a spirit of trust in their leaders. Trust was clearly in short supply, and the major parties were going to suffer for this. In Northern Ireland the intransigent Unionists, or Loyalists, successfully challenged the Unionists who worked with the Conservatives. Scottish Nationalists, who in 1969 had suffered when the Treasury published a hypothetical 'Scottish budget' to show that Scotland could not afford independence, could now say firmly that all their plans for the country were possible because the oil in the North Sea was in the territory that would belong to an independent Scotland. And the Liberals, who in 1959 and in 1964 had seen a substantial bridgehead in public opinion shrivel and fade away as the election came closer, now had a chance to fight while discontent with the major parties was still rising to a peak. The Labour party benefited from one of the few interventions by a private citizen that has changed votes in a recent election; Enoch Powell announced that he would vote Labour because its policy of trying to amend the conditions of British membership of the E.E.C. and then submitting the results to the people held out the prospect of escape from the continental entanglements into which Heath had led the country. Powell's position as a leader of opinion owed so much to his attacks on immigration that the Labour party cannot have been completely happy about his support, but it would have been impossible, and imprudent as well, to repudiate it.

Nevertheless, the opinion polls showed that the Conservatives would get slightly more votes than the Labour party; and this forecast turned out to be correct. What could not be predicted was that the Labour party won four more seats than the Conservatives. It has been argued that this was the result of tactical voting by supporters of the Labour party who voted Liberal or Nationalist in seats that Labour could not win, in order to keep the Conservatives out. The estimate is that this cost Labour 350,000 votes, but cost the Conservatives three seats.[1] This result may not have been caused by such conscious calculation, for one would have thought that such sophisticated supporters of the Labour party would have declared their views to opinion pollsters. Perhaps Labour voters in hopeless seats were a little shaken by the unpopularity of trade unions among their neighbours and took the less controversial course of voting for a third party.

	Votes cast	Seats won	% of total votes cast
Conservative	11,868,906	296	37·8
Liberal	6,063,470	14	19·3
Labour	11,639,243	301	37·1
Scottish Nationalist	632,032	7	2·0
Plaid Cymru	171,364	2	0·5
Ulster Loyalist	366,703	11	1·2
Others	598,444	4	1·9

Heath tried negotiating with the Liberals to put together a coalition but met with no success; the Liberals pointed out that a Liberal–Conservative alliance would still be just short of a majority, and that the Labour party could count on enough votes from Plaid Cymru and the Independents and from the determination of the Ulster Loyalists to vote against what they regarded as the anti-unionist approach of the Conservatives to mean that even a theoretically possible alliance of Conservatives, Liberals, and Scottish Nationalists was most unlikely to be able to survive. The Scottish

[1] M. Steed in appendix to D. E. Butler and D. Kavanagh, *The British General Election of February 1974* (1974), 328.

Nationalists had done well, running far ahead of the Liberals (Conservatives 21 seats with 32·9 per cent of the vote; Liberals 3 with 7·9 per cent; Labour 40 with 36·6 per cent; S.N.P. 7 with 21·9 per cent). The Liberals were understandably disappointed that, because their support was spread thinly but evenly all across the country, they had won so few seats. But the Liberal activists saw themselves as being on the left and would not have wanted to support a Conservative government. The Liberal voters probably had no such commitments, but they may have reflected the general feeling that Heath had had his chance at sharpening issues and putting them aggressively and that it was now time for something more emollient.

One step at a time

And so Harold Wilson became Prime Minister again, somewhat to his surprise. He could have been forgiven for feeling that becoming Prime Minister in 1974 was much less pleasant than it had been in 1970 or even 1964. A settlement had to be found to get the miners back to work as soon as possible and end the industrial paralysis. The balance-of-payments deficit was reaching levels that made previous crises seem petty and trivial; in 1973 it had been about £1½ billion, and the increased price of oil would probably raise it to about £4 billion even if nothing else went wrong. As prices went up, they reached the points at which the thresholds caused a succession of automatic wage increases. A Labour government with the 1966 majority and a Prime Minister with all of Wilson's 1964 prestige would have found the position difficult, but in 1974 there was no majority and it had become fashionable to sneer at Wilson, ostensibly because he had accepted his party's change of front over the E.E.C. and perhaps in reality because so many people were disappointed by what had happened to the dreams of the 1960s.

Many people were also disappointed by what happened to the dreams of the 1970s. Investors on the Stock Exchange became nervous and began selling; prices fell heavily from 1973 onwards until eventually in December 1974 the *Financial Times* index, which started in 1935 at 100, had fallen back to 150, a figure last seen in 1958. As building-society interest rates rose to 11 per cent, house prices stood still; office blocks and land for development, which had been handled in some of the wilder deals financed at higher rates, became almost impossible to sell. Secondary banks which had backed these activities found that such assets, whatever their future prospects, were no use at all as security for short-term loans. Between 1973 and late 1975 the Bank of England and the large clearing banks had to provide money embarrassingly often to keep these energetic and unsound banks from going bankrupt and destroying the London money market; if the secondary banks had tried to realize the security for their loans in one great wave of liquidation, it would have driven prices so low that even the soundest institutions would have been unable to meet their obligations. While the collapse of the secondary banks was handled without catastrophe, it tied up the credit of the clearing banks so that they would have had difficulty providing credit for new investment if anyone had come forward to ask for it. But because so large a budget deficit had to be financed and because money had to be drawn in from overseas to cover the balance-of-payments deficit, the government had to pay up to 17 per cent on long-dated bonds, which drove other interest rates so high that those with any choice in the matter stayed away from banks, borrowed nothing, and repaid old debts.

The budget Healey produced almost immediately after becoming Chancellor of the Exchequer seemed with its increase in income tax from 30p to 33p to be designed to live up to his promise in opposition to bring 'howls of anguish' from the rich. The increase in the price of oil was at first thought to be inflationary, but, because its main effect was to transfer money to the members of OPEC faster than they could spend it or lend it, so that it was withdrawn from circulation, the world quickly entered a recession. The industrialized nations might have been wise to agree on measures to counteract this, but, already heavily in deficit, Britain could not be a very persuasive advocate of such a policy. Healey boldly embarked on reflation in his own country, without being sure that other countries would do the same, and switched from tax increases to tax cuts; in July he lowered value added tax from 10 to 8 per cent and after the October election he reduced corporation tax by over £1 billion. Many companies had been showing large profits simply because the supplies of commodities which they held to use in their work had gone up in price. These profits would do nothing for the companies in the long run, because the supplies would have to be replaced at the new high prices, but in the short run they led to crushing tax bills. Reducing corporation tax looked a paradoxical step in the middle of an inflation which fed on itself as prices went through successive thresholds and wages rose to match. But companies were clearly in trouble; for a few weeks in 1974 it looked as if the Labour left might succeed in nationalizing successive firms as they went bankrupt, but it was quickly realized that the government did not have the administrative talent or structure available to take over the existing companies, and could not offer other jobs to the people working in them. By the autumn it was clear that the government would have to save the private sector, and that unemployment would in any case rise to the level of early 1972.

Although the government could survive without a parliamentary majority for some months, there would have to be another election soon. Public opinion did find the absence of a majority disconcerting, and this was part of the reason why it became fashionable to say Britain was becoming ungovernable. People also found inflation alarming and thought it might be moving towards levels traditionally associated with South America. Although the rate of price increases slowed down in the summer of 1974, so that it was not as pressing a problem as it had been earlier in the year and was to be again in 1975, nobody was convinced when Healey implied that prices were under control. The triumph of the trade unions undoubtedly alarmed some people: Heath might have been making unnecessary trouble over the dispute with the miners, but still it was worrying to think that trade unions might acquire a power of veto over the government.

The Irish situation did nothing to reassure people. In 1972 Heath had tried to meet the fear of being united with the rest of the island that made the Protestant majority into a monolithic block by announcing that there would be periodic referenda on partition. A new assembly was to be created with powers distinctly more limited than those of the old Stormont parliament, and the British government would allow these powers to be exercised only by a Northern Ireland government that represented both communities. The referendum was held in March 1973, and a predictably large proportion of the electorate voted to retain the union with Britain. Opponents of the union advised their supporters to abstain and were able to make this advice effective. The elections for the new assembly in June produced as much support for power-sharing between the two communities as anyone could have expected; three substantial parties emerged, the Social Democratic and Labour party representing the Catholic minority, a set of intransigent Unionist (or Loyalist) groups, and a more flexible Unionist group under Faulkner's leadership. Any two of these parties could command a majority, and a Faulkner–S.D.L.P. coalition would represent both communities. The violence of the fighting was slightly reduced in 1973; 251 people were killed, a little more than half as many as in 1972. Nobody in Britain would have believed that there had been any improvement, because the I.R.A. opened a new offensive by exploding bombs in Birmingham, London, and Aldershot. It may have taken this step because the counter-insurgency methods of the British army were beginning to have some effect, but the new departure certainly made people in Britain both more aware of the problem in Ireland and more pessimistic about it.

Whitelaw's skill and diplomacy in months of negotiation as minister

responsible for Northern Ireland brought the Faulkner Unionists and the
S.D.L.P. together, despite the natural concern of the Faulknerites that
they would be rejected by their supporters for being too conciliatory and
the equally natural concern of the S.D.L.P. that they would be shot by
the I.R.A. for the same offence. By December 1973 the two groups were
ready to work together in a 'power-sharing' executive, and Whitelaw's
success led to his being made Minister of Employment, in the hope that
the skill in conciliation he had shown in Ireland would work as well in
Britain. Politicians in the power-sharing executive were worried by this;
they knew they were starting on a rather artificial basis which needed all
the help it could get. The United Kingdom election in February brought
new pressures to weigh upon the executive before it was able to bear them.
The Loyalists (the United Ulster Unionist Coalition), who had little more
than a third of the seats in the Assembly, polled just over half the votes
cast in the general election, and, partly because the power-sharers were by
no means united enough to put forward a single set of candidates, won
11 of the 12 Northern Ireland seats. This was a harsh warning to the
Faulknerites that their support was disappearing, but they stuck to the
work of the executive, while asking that it should move slowly and in
particular should not lay too much emphasis on proposals for co-operation
with the Republic of Ireland or for the speedy release of prisoners who had
been interned without trial because they were suspected of belonging to
one of the para-military terrorist organizations. The S.D.L.P. thought the
Labour government would be more sympathetic to their point of view
and would apply pressure to the Faulknerites to move faster. The power-
sharing executive might easily have broken up over this, but before that
could happen the Ulster Workers' Committee, a loyalist group with no
visible links with the Loyalists at Westminster, had launched a political
general strike against the executive in May. In its first days this seems to
have been a minority movement which relied on intimidation to keep
people away from work, but when Wilson announced his disapproval of
the strike and was ill advised enough to call the people of Ulster 'spongers'
(on the basis of the financial transfers from Britain to Northern Ireland
that were the natural result of a system of progressive taxation and welfare
measures), the strike won general support among the Protestant majority.
The Faulknerites resigned from the executive because their position had
become impossible, and Northern Ireland seemed likely to be ruled
directly from London for some time to come.

Elections to a proposed Northern Ireland constitutional convention in
1975, in which the Loyalists won about 60 per cent of the seats under a
system of proportional representation, showed that the Faulknerites were

correct in their fears. A good deal of the discrimination of Ulster's first
fifty years had been eliminated; on the other hand, the two communities
were as far apart as ever, and the province's understandable reputation
for instability and violence meant that it was unlikely to get the investment
it needed if it was to reach any modest level of prosperity. As the number
of people killed in 1974 and 1975 ran at about the same rate as in 1973, it
was hard to see any improvement in the situation. Explosions in Britain
in 1974 and 1975 were frequent and deadly enough to show a little of
what Northern Ireland was suffering, though deaths in Britain were only
a tenth of what they were in Ulster. But by 1976 there were signs that the
peace of exhaustion was settling on the problem. Supporters of drastic
change were losing hope, and the army's counter-intelligence system was
penetrating more and more deeply into the I.R.A.

The army had to take an interest in politics in Northern Ireland and this
may have led officers to speculate about their role in a way that led to
rumours in the summer of 1974 that they were discussing, undoubtedly
in a spirit of theoretical inquiry, the question of when they might have to
intervene in British politics. Such ideas were underlined by events elsewhere: a group of army officers was ruling Portugal at the time, there
were hints of an army coup in Italy, and the colonels who had been ruling
Greece for the past half-dozen years were at their least reasonable. But
such ideas would have found no audience in Britain if the notion had not
grown up that the country was out of control.

The 'social contract' announced in June was less reassuring than had
been hoped. The government abandoned the policy of restraining wages
by law, repealed the Industrial Relations Act, increased old-age pensions
and other benefits, subsidized food prices, placed restrictions on rent
increases, and allowed the nationalized industries to run up deficits. In return
the union leaders said they would not ask for wage increases more than
once a year and would keep the increases down to something like the rise
in the cost of living. Even if they had possessed effective control over their
members, it would have been very hard for anyone to keep real wages
undiminished without putting a heavy burden on the economy at a time
when the increase in oil prices was reducing the real national income and
when such large increases were being made in state-financed benefits.
These benefits were referred to as the 'social wage', but most of the 'social
wage' went to people who were old or ill or otherwise outside the main
stream of wage bargaining. People at work paid for it rather than benefiting from it; by the 1970s anyone earning the average industrial wage paid
income tax at the standard rate on two-fifths of his income, and tax increases such as Healey's cut painfully into his take-home pay. Workers set

out to recover the lost ground, and their union leaders were not able to do much to stop them.

Wilson prudently held another election in October before he had to do something about this strain on the economy. Nobody felt comfortable with so fragile a government, though it seemed unlikely that a new election would provide anyone with an overwhelming majority. The Conservatives tried to respond to this by suggesting a government of national unity, but it was never at all clear what substance there was to this phrase. The Labour party could claim that it had taken over at a time of crisis and had made sure that things had not got any worse. It had done enough in its eight months in office to make it clear that this was not the same government as the Labour government of the 1960s, even though there was very little difference of personnel; apart from Michael Foot, who entered the government as a sort of living pledge that the wishes of the trade unions would be remembered, the men at the top in 1974 were much the same as the men who had been at the top in 1970. There was a distinct drop in the number of votes cast, only partly explained by the fact that the electoral register was eight months older than in February. Opinion polls suggested that the Labour party would gain ground and win a clear majority, though not many people were convinced by this. Perhaps inspired by what had happened in February, some supporters of other parties seem to have voted tactically by combining to support the candidate most likely to keep Labour out.[1]

	Votes cast	Seats won	% of total votes cast
Conservative	10,464,817	276	35·8
Liberal	5,346,754	13	18·3
Labour	11,457,079	319	39·2
Scottish Nationalist	839,617	11	2·8
Plaid Cymru	166,321	3	0·6
Ulster Loyalist	407,778	10	1·4
Others	508,040	3	1·7

Unless all the parties in opposition agreed that they wanted an election, Wilson's position was secure; a string of by-election defeats might bring down his government, but it would have this effect more by convincing the opposition parties that all of them would gain by having an election than by making them think some different combination ought to rule the country. The Liberals fell back slightly, and Liberal activists felt unkindly treated by fate and the voters when they won so few seats for so many

[1] M. Steed in appendix to D. E. Butler and D. Kavanagh, *The British General Election of October 1974* (1975), 294.

votes. But people who vote Liberal at one election or another—who are very different from the activists—give the impression that they see voting Liberal as a holding action while they decide what to do next, and they might have been quite unworried by the party's lack of success. No doubt other parties receive some essentially negative votes, but a decidedly larger proportion of their total strength seems to come from people who steadily vote Labour or Conservative election after election.

The two 1974 elections raised in a vital form the question which sort of support the Scottish Nationalists attracted. They continued their upward march, winning a position in Scotland just ahead of the Conservatives in votes (Conservatives 16 seats with 24·7 per cent of the vote; Liberals 3 with 8·3 per cent; Labour 41 with 36·9 per cent; S.N.P. 11 with 30·4 per cent). A three-cornered struggle with Conservatives and Labour might well leave them in a position where they held a majority of the seats in Scotland. It was hard to say how permanent this would be: until about 1972 and the growth of the conviction that 'It's Scottish oil', they had not really been doing better than Plaid Cymru. In 1974 the problems of Plaid Cymru became apparent; it did well in the small Welsh-speaking section of rural western Wales and was clearly to be taken seriously there. In the densely populated industrial areas of Wales it made no progress. Scottish nationalism had no such division to face, partly because it had no linguistic problems. Gaelic was so far gone in decline that saying a few words in it was a pleasant ritual that aroused none of the fears about compulsory bilingualism that alarmed the large group of Welshmen who could speak nothing but English. But while Scottish nationalism could appeal to all regions of Scotland, it was not clear whether it got votes as a protest against the effects of unsatisfactory government policies or because there had been a permanent change of consciousness in Scotland. North Sea oil was likely to accentuate an existing division of Scotland, apart from the picturesque and thinly populated Highlands, roughly into a declining west and a prosperous east. Glasgow and the area round it, now grouped into the region of Strathclyde, in which something like half the population of Scotland lived, had grown to world-wide importance on coal, iron, and shipbuilding during the Industrial Revolution. The Labour party was naturally strong in this region, and went on polling enough of the vote there to mean that the Scottish Nationalists, who drew their strength more evenly across the whole country, stood relatively little chance of winning seats in Strathclyde, though this could change if the people of Strathclyde lost their faith that the Labour party could do something about unemployment. The decline of the basic industries meant that the region faced serious difficulties even if it could attract new types of work, while the east coast had fewer declining industries to impede its progress and had been doing reasonably well before the development of oil began. Although some of the platforms for drilling and pumping the oil came from Clyde shipyards, most of its effect was to be seen on the east coast and in particular in Aberdeen.

The oil lay in areas of the North Sea that, because of the waves and the weather, presented more difficulties than the development of gas had done. In the early years much of the technical skill and the equipment was provided by Americans who had had experience of developments off the Texas and Louisiana shores. But British firms adapted to the needs of this new industry quite quickly, and it could reasonably be argued that if the rest of the British economy had been as bold and as flexible as the oil sector, a good many problems would have been solved. Oil was a very large undertaking: the estimate was that in a dozen years between 1972 and 1985 about £25 billion, or about one-quarter of the national income for a year, would have been invested in it. The costs went up sharply because oil-drilling equipment was in great demand after the OPEC price increases, but North Sea oil was relatively expensive to produce, and might not have been regarded as a satisfactory large-scale investment before the price increases: of the $12 charged for a 35-gallon barrel of oil from the Middle East, about $1 is assigned to capital and production costs and the rest goes to the host government. Capital and production costs in the North Sea amount to about $6, and the British government—after considerable argument and some evidence that in the early 1970s the oil companies got very favourable terms—took the other $6, which indicated an annual revenue of over £3 billion for the British, or alternatively the Scottish, government.

While Scotland's uneasiness had to be taken seriously (and Wales would expect some recognition if Scotland's position changed), it could not receive immediate attention. The government's slender majority forced it to take problems one at a time, and in October 1974 the major problem in sight was the E.E.C. Re-negotiation had begun soon after the February election and it was soon clear that, while the Treaty of Rome would not be re-written, the government could hope for changes that would allow it to honour its pledge that it would win concessions and then submit them to the electorate for approval. With a thin majority and an economy showing signs of slipping out of control, holding yet another general election would be rather like the 1807 election described by Sidney Smith as 'building a brick wall for the express purpose of dashing out their brains against it'. The Labour party would be divided between its E.E.C.-haters and its E.E.C.-enthusiasts, while the Conservatives could present a relatively united front on the issue. So a referendum had obvious advantages for the government. Those who were afraid of endangering Britain's membership talked about the duty of the government to make up its mind on the question, and the sovereignty of parliament. Supporters of a referendum asked for popular participation in the serious, almost irreversible decision to be taken. If they had been very outspoken they might have added that the doctrine of unchallenged parliamentary sovereignty rested on a basis of unquestioned respect in the minds of the people which parliament no longer commanded. However unpopular this might have been at Westminster, it was probably one of the reasons why the referendum—dismissed in the past with relatively little difficulty—became accepted as an addition to the British way of running politics.

A referendum helped the Labour party by reducing to a minimum the discussion about what the re-negotiations had achieved. In a general election the Conservatives would have argued that the negotiations had not produced any substantial improvement on the 1971 terms, and Labour supporters of entry would have had to reply that they had done very well at the expense of the other E.E.C. countries. Food prices and the effect of membership on the balance of payments were the main issues to be discussed in the re-negotiation; no British politician would endanger the whole process by demanding better terms for New Zealand's butter or Mauritius's sugar, though naturally opponents of membership raised such points, and they also asked what would happen to British sovereignty. People who were afraid that the British government would lose control over questions it could previously have settled for itself (which may be taken as a definition of the slightly abstract phrase 'loss of sovereignty') must have been relieved that the idea of European Monetary Union—the most immediately tangible issue that raised the question of sovereignty—with exchange rates fixed immutably, perhaps secured by a common European currency, had receded into the background under the stress of floating exchange rates. The negotiators could hardly take up the undoubted fact that some people simply disliked the idea of close association with foreigners. On food prices they had to accept the initial political agreement of the 1950s that tariffs would be used to support E.E.C. farmers, who were not likely to give up this protection. The British did get fairly generous treatment in successive decisions about the exchange rate at which the pound should be translated into other E.E.C. currencies; because it was habitually valued at a higher rate than its value on the open market, the cost of food from other E.E.C. countries was lower than it would have been if Britain had been buying from them at the current exchange rate. This left the question of the balance of payments: the British income per head was perceptibly below the Community average, but because trade outside the E.E.C. was an important part of the national income there would be a large transfer from tariffs to the Community funds which would be paid to small and subsidized farmers in France and Germany. The re-negotiators were more successful here, and as long as Britain's income per head was no more than 85 per cent of the Community average (which looked like being the case for an indefinite time to come) the British Exchequer would not have to pay the full amount that would have been due under the existing arrangements.

This was not a very exciting concession to bring back, even when accompanied by other gains of similar complexity. The government might have found this mildly embarrassing in an election if Heath had been able to compare it with his own policy. The referendum solved this problem; and in February 1975 Heath lost his position as Leader of the Opposition. He was challenged, under the party's revised rules which obliged leaders to stand for re-election, by Margaret Thatcher. She received eleven more votes in the first round than Heath, who at once withdrew, and in the second round she received a clear majority of the votes cast. Her success in the first round was partly a vote of no confidence in Heath, who was blamed for holding the February election and for losing two elections in a year, but it could also be seen as a vote for the principles Heath had put forward before becoming Prime Minister. Thatcher and Heath came from similar backgrounds: middle- rather than upper-middle-class family with no independent means, and university success as the stepping-stone to wider prospects. In 1970 their views on policy seemed much the same: lower taxes, less activity by government, and more opportunities for businessmen to make money by taking risks. Heath had moved dramatically to an attitude of very great government intervention, and some hostility to businessmen because they did not invest as enthusiastically and patriotic- ally as he had hoped. Some of Thatcher's supporters felt she could revive the principles that the party had accepted in the late 1960s. Sir Keith Joseph, for whose opinions she clearly had great respect, caught public attention if not public approval with a series of speeches in favour of a more disciplined way of life and the ideology of the free market. Unkind commentators did note that Thatcher and Joseph had presided over some of the largest increases in departmental spending during Heath's premier- ship, even if these increases were dwarfed by what happened under the Labour government.

The government apparently felt that, because it had to concentrate on the E.E.C. negotiations, it could not do anything to check the increases in prices, which were rising at about 26 per cent a year by mid 1975, or in

wages, which were going up by about 35 per cent a year. Opponents of
E.E.C. membership might have argued that the Community was to blame
if there was any sharp drop in living standards, and so supporters of membership in the government took the risk of letting the economy run on its
alarming course for the sake of staying in the E.E.C. The referendum
itself passed off with much less damage to the constitution than its
opponents had predicted. Wilson reserved his own judgement until the
spring of 1975, and then declared that, all things considered, he thought
the terms were acceptable. The Labour party announced its opposition
to membership, but it was nothing new for Wilson to find that he and the
party were not quite in step, and there was never the bitterness about the
E.E.C. debate that there had been about the deflation and unemployment
of the 1960s. Ministers who opposed the terms were allowed to 'agree to
differ' (like the Liberals in the 1930s) in speeches outside, but not inside the
Commons. The govefnment devised a simple question for the ballot, sent
a statement of the cases for and against entry to every voter, and provided
£125,000 for each side, though they could raise unlimited amounts from
their supporters as well: the pro-Europeans received lavish support from
a wide range of companies and individuals, and the opponents got much
smaller sums from individuals and trade unions. Despite this imbalance,
the general debate seemed reasonably evenly matched; the supporters of
entry had men like Wilson and Heath and Jenkins to make solid speeches
to reassure the voters, and the opponents had orators like Foot and Powell
and the unexpectedly successful Peter Shore to rouse people to a feeling
of the value of British independence and the possible disadvantages of the
E.E.C. Opinion polls had for some time shown that, while views about
membership were volatile and fairly evenly divided, there was considerably more support for 'membership if recommended by the government'
than simply for 'membership', and the size of the majority for membership
may confirm this. Distinctly fewer votes were cast in the referendum than
in any recent general election, which may show the effect of canvassing
by political parties on elections; and on 5 June the supporters of entry
won by 17,378,581 votes to 8,470,073. The long debate on Europe was
over, and it ended in a way which meant that, even if the details of the
debate had sometimes been hard to follow, the issue had been treated
with all the serious consideration it deserved.

A government which had got through such a struggle, and had managed
to avoid shattering a clearly divided party, might have hoped for a pause
to rest. But instead it had to face those problems of rising prices and rising
unemployment that had been ignored during the E.E.C. debate. During
the period of neglect, public spending had gone up by about 40 per cent

and risen to a level equal to almost 60 per cent of the national income, as a result of increased benefits paid to enable social services to keep up with inflation, wage increases to maintain civil servants' real income, and an increase in the number of civil servants. Nobody, except the civil servants taken on in this period, was in real terms better off as a result of all this, but the economy was wrenched and distorted in an attempt to avoid, or at least delay, the fall in living standards that seemed to be the inevitable result of the overspending of the early 1970s and the worsening in the terms of trade, seen most conspicuously in the rise in oil prices. In 1975 the burden of the decline was being carried by those who lost their jobs, but the unreality of these arrangements came under pressure from two directions. The exchange value of the pound had slipped very little since the summer of 1973, despite the increase in the balance-of-payments deficit, simply because the OPEC countries did not want to put too much money into the United States and found London the only other convenient place to deposit it. Lending it to Britain had the additional advantage of maintaining the level of demand for their oil. By mid 1975 they were beginning to feel uneasy about keeping their money in sterling and, as they moved into other currencies, the pound fell from a 'Smithsonian devaluation' of 24 per cent to a level 30 per cent below where it had been four years earlier.

At the same time inflation inside the country was beginning to alarm everyone, including trade unionists who could see that price increases were eating up all their wage increases. Trade unions agreed to a voluntary policy, with no legal sanctions to back it up, of allowing one increase of no more than £6 a week in the next year to everyone earning less than £8,500 a year. The scheme worked reasonably well; at the end of twelve months prices were rising at about two-thirds the level of mid 1975 and a further year of voluntary pay restraint was then accepted. Even these steps did not noticeably hold back the increase in unemployment, which rose above the 1m. level and seemed likely to stay above it for several years to come. Voluntary wage restraint did not give private industry a rate of return that encouraged investment, and when the government created a National Enterprise Board to carry out public investment in new industries, it soon found itself saving old firms from collapse. The large family-owned electronics firm of Ferranti had to be bought up to avert closure. British Leyland, the largest car firm in the country, was insolvent; the N.E.B. was put in charge, and later almost had to take over the American-owned firm of Rootes, though Chrysler was persuaded to keep its subsidiary in production by a grant of £162m.

The union-based pay policy gave no increase to those earning over

£8,500 a year. They were still a small minority; at just about the time the pay policy was being worked out, a Royal Commission led by Lord Diamond presented a report which had a good deal of information about the prosperous part of society. The 10 per cent of the population with the highest incomes earned £2,857 a year or more, and received 27 per cent of all the income earned by individuals, though after tax this was reduced to $23\frac{1}{2}$ per cent. The highest-paid one per cent received 6 per cent of the total, a decline from 8·4 per cent in 1959 and 11·2 per cent in 1949. Wealth was less evenly distributed; the richest 10 per cent owned £10,500 or more, and held 67 per cent of all personal wealth; the richest one per cent, each of whom owned £44,000 or more, held 28 per cent of all personal wealth; it was noted that in 1913 this group alone had owned 69 per cent of all personal wealth. The report tended to ignore the claims on wealth held by individuals in the form of pension rights, although these rights, whether in the form of an old-age pension or of schemes linked to employment, were a type of wealth that had grown very quickly during the twentieth century. *The Times* commented that owning an unmortgaged house was enough to put one in the wealthiest 10 per cent, and teased the Labour party by pointing out that while this was very pleasant for the half of the population who lived in houses they owned (mortgaged or unmortgaged) the other half could join them in relative prosperity only if they too had a chance to buy their homes.[1]

The point of this was that over 30 per cent of the population lived in houses or flats rented from municipal authorities, most of whom saw themselves as benevolent landlords and had no desire to sell off their housing stock. The government was preparing to increase the activity of the municipalities as landlords by its Community Land Act. Such large speculative profits in land had been made by those who were shrewd enough to get out by mid 1973 that the new Act provided that a piece of land to be developed should be sold to the municipality at its value for its existing use, and might then be bought back at the price appropriate for the proposed new use. This appeared to solve the problem of capturing the unearned increase in the value of land which had puzzled Lloyd George and Snowden and the Labour government of 1945, but it involved laying on municipalities the duty of intervening in a great multitude of transactions, and it remained to be seen whether they could act at the speed required for commercial or industrial or residential development to proceed.

Some of the problems facing Wilson in the 1960s had gone on into the 1970s. Rhodesia was still independent, unreconciled, and unrecognized.

---

[1] *The Times*, 31 July 1975.

Under the Conservatives, Douglas-Home and Smith had worked out a scheme to make Rhodesia legally independent and guarantee the position of the African majority; before the government put it into effect a commission under Lord Pearce was asked to survey African opinion, and the commission was convinced by the mobilization of opinion under the leadership of Bishop Muzorewa that the proposals were not acceptable, so they were laid aside. What seemed likely at long last to change the situation was the withdrawal of Portugal from her African colonies. In 1975 Angola and Mozambique were obviously going to turn into more or less Marxist states which would serve as bases for guerrilla attacks on Rhodesia; so far as could be seen, the problem, which had drifted on for ten years of negotiation in which the British government never had power to make its views effective, was now likely to be settled by force of arms.

As the pay policy worked its way through the winter into the spring of 1976, little enough seemed to be happening. The headlines were devoted to the difficulties of the unlucky Liberal leader Jeremy Thorpe, who appeared to be on the point of being pushed out of his position because of allegations of a homosexual affair over a dozen years previously, when Harold Wilson announced on 16 March that he intended to retire because he had reached the age of sixty. During the uncertainty of choosing a successor, the pound dropped by about 5 per cent against all other currencies; this may have been partly due to the further troubles of British Leyland, but a good deal of it may have been simply that the underlying weakness of the currency was seen at any moment when people wondered what was going to happen next in Britain. The parliamentary party responded rather more calmly, and on 5 April James Callaghan was chosen as Wilson's successor on the third ballot.

It would be unkind to Wilson, or perhaps an underestimate of his virtues, to say that it could be hoped that his departure would mark a change in British attitudes. But his virtues—optimism in adversity, loyalty to his social origins, unwillingness to give pain to his supporters—could not by themselves solve the problems which faced him and the country during his long period of office. His weaknesses were by no means peculiar to him; it was partly the coincidence of name that led to the suggestion that 1957–76 was the period of the two Harolds, Macmillan and Wilson, but what they had in common was not likely to do the country good. Almost unavoidably they overestimated Britain's position in the world; anyone born before the First World War or emerging into politics in the years of Churchill's world-ranging greatness was likely to start with an idea of Britain as a power equal to any other. Both men of course realized that this was no longer the case, but they had not worked out any way to meet the situation, and the degree of reliance that both of them placed on the American alliance in the 1960s was no longer realistic. Both of them were very clever men, and at times behaved as if they thought cleverness would be enough to carry the nation forward, which encouraged other people to think in the same way. An obvious example lay in the area of economic policy. In the years of the two Harolds, no British politician would have called himself anything other than a Keynesian, but what they meant by this was that a budget deficit was an almost magically effective instrument of policy. Keynes may really have been more interested in encouraging investment and in lowering the real wages of those in work so that it would be economically possible to take on new workers.[1] Those who thought Keynesianism meant budget deficits behaved as though they had found an intellectual trick which produced a policy which was both easy and effective. Macmillan once almost committed himself to saying 'exporting is fun'; he and a good many other people seemed to think investing was fun rather than a risky and difficult process. Obviously Britain's problems were not simply an intellectual misunderstanding of what Keynes meant, or even a failure to invest in new machinery. In a very broad sweep, the Britain of 1906 had still been practising a good many of what could be called the Victorian virtues; and its financial strength and political prestige probably owed a good deal to those virtues. As the twentieth century went on, those virtues came increasingly to be regarded as old-fashioned; and no doubt they were dull and constricting.

On the basis of those virtues, Britain had by the beginning of the century established a system of government in which power was used responsibly by a small group of specialized politicians who depended on an electorate that included a steadily widening range of the whole population. This pattern of government had achieved many things, including the acquisition of a vast overseas empire with relatively little difficulty or resistance. In the first half of the new century the system had been changed into one of universal suffrage with a party structure that gave the organized working class at least as large a share of power as it possessed in any other country. The government had set up the framework of a welfare system that endeavoured to recognize the needs of many previously neglected sections of society, and had taken substantial steps towards dissolving the empire peacefully and amicably. In the third quarter of the century things had gone much less well; it would be hard to say how much of the change was due to the fact that Britain had been living on the accumulated reserves, moral and financial, of the nineteenth century, how much to the damage of the

[1] J. M. Keynes, *The General Theory of Employment, Interest and Money* (1936), 14 and 30.

two world wars, and how much to mismanagement in the decades after the Second World War: but it was certainly true that Britain had lost most of its power to make an impact on the minds of people outside the country, and that inside the country decline and decay had come almost to be taken for granted. The decline was perfectly real, and yet seemed to be overstated— Britain could not be ranked with the United States or the Soviet Union, as had been imagined in 1945, but it made equally little sense for people to talk as if it had ceased to rank among the nine or ten most important countries. The immediate question was whether the country should be led in a common-sense sort of way that accepted the decline as irreversible and tried to make the best of it, or whether an attempt to clear away relics of the past that had outlived their usefulness could be carried out in a way that would not divide the country too much for new developments to go ahead.

Labour on a tightrope

JAMES Callaghan's qualities fitted him to fill the post of Prime Minister
entirely adequately. Unlike Wilson and Macmillan, he never appeared
overwhelmed with pleasure at his own cleverness; his capacity for
generating trust enabled him to work with other people in a way that
Wilson and Heath had not always been able to manage; and he conveyed
the impression that common sense was the most important quality in
politics and that he possessed it. He was determined to hang on to power,
without necessarily doing very much with it, which was as much as the
Labour party could hope for. As the party had been led by Oxford
graduates for the past forty years it felt mildly relieved that he had never
been to a university and had stronger links with the trade union movement
than any Labour leader of the first rank since union leaders ceased going
into the House of Commons in the late 1940s. At the time the public felt no
desire for burning conviction in politics, so his inability to project it was no
handicap. The leadership contest showed that the left wing of the party was
growing stronger; in the final round Callaghan defeated Foot by 176 votes
to 137, a large enough vote for the candidate of the left to suggest that he
could defeat anyone who was not skilfully placed in the centre of the party.
Foot had personal qualities that inspired affection and as Secretary of State
for Employment had gained a good deal of support among trade unionists,
so while his political strength reflected the growing importance of the left
he had support elsewhere in the party.

Labour's election manifesto in 1974 had committed the party to close co-
operation with the unions, and also to refraining from imposing an incomes
policy on them by law. The 1975 commitment to a maximum increase in
pay of £6 a week was, at least nominally, a voluntary step on the part of the

unions. They may have reckoned that, election commitment or no election commitment, an incomes policy would be imposed on them by law if prices went on rising by three per cent a month for long, unless they offered a voluntary solution; but this remained unsaid. Prices, wages, and dividends were held down by law, but the only thing restraining wage claims was the union leaders' awareness of the dangers of an economic crisis. They had already, under the social contract, seen welfare benefits increased and legislation passed to protect the job security of the employed, and they went on to press for some of the more controversial items of the 1974 programme, of which the nationalization of shipbuilding and the control of loading and unloading operations in the docks caused the government most trouble in 1976. The government's slender majority in the Commons was fragile enough for the Conservatives to hope that, if they delayed things long enough, death, retirement, or defection might destroy it. A clause in the docks legislation giving dockers some protection from the risk that containerization of ships' cargoes might deprive them of their jobs was defeated by Labour abstentions, and on another occasion the government seemed to have been saved from defeat only by the willingness of a Labour MP to cast his vote when he was supposed to be 'paired'. By the end of the 1975–6 session it was clear that no further legislation could be passed simply by the votes of the Labour party and those Nationalists from Wales and Northern Ireland who habitually voted with it.

In his 1976 budget, Healey had undertaken to reduce income tax if the trade unions extended their voluntary agreement to fix maximum wage increases for another year. This was condemned for surrendering the position of parliament and the control of government policy to the unions, but at the time it seemed to be the only way to run the country. In earlier decades Healey's proposals would have meant little to the unions, for manual workers rarely had to pay income tax before 1939, and up to the 1960s they usually paid only at the lower rates charged on the first few hundred pounds of taxable income. But successive Chancellors had tried to help the less well-off by eliminating all tax at the lower rates rather than widen the band of income that paid at a reduced rate; as incomes rose with inflation and the threshold at which people started paying at the standard rate remained unchanged, more and more trade unionists were paying it by the 1970s, and they were ready to listen to the government's proposals.

These negotiations with the unions, which condemned MPs to voting for budget proposals in principle without knowing what figures would eventually be filled in, led to an agreement that no pay increases should exceed 5 per cent. But discussions had not moved fast enough to reassure overseas creditors about the large balance of payments deficit. The increase in oil

prices and the ill-fated attempt to cope with the deflationary effect of that
increase by expansion, when most countries wanted to combat rising prices
rather than prevent declining production, had left Britain with much larger
debts by 1976 than ever before. The sterling balances of other countries,
which had remained steady around £4bn. for the 25 years after 1945, rose in
the 1970s to about £12bn. The government was in a situation something
like that of the Wilson government in July 1966, though all the figures were
much larger. In June Healey raised a short-term loan of $5bn. in order to
have time to produce deflationary measures in July, but his proposals
turned out to be inadequate. By October the flow of money out of London
had become a torrent. The oil-exporting countries, which had supplied
Britain with oil on credit for a couple of years, began to be afraid that they
would never be paid: in 1975 and 1976 they moved about £2bn. of their
money elsewhere. The pound fell to $1.52 or, taking a wider view to reflect
the increased importance of other currencies, it could be said that in the 12
months up to October 1976 the pound lost 23 per cent of its international
trading value.[1] After brief and brisk negotiations with the International
Monetary Fund a loan of £2.3bn. was arranged on the basis of cuts in the
supply of money by means of reductions in the borrowing requirement so
severe that they would have convinced the bankers of 1931 that here was a
Labour government which knew when it had no room for manœuvre. Tied
down by the I.M.F. agreement and the need to conciliate the unions, with
no reliable majority in the Commons, the government seemed sure to have
a short and far from merry life.

The background to the shift from negotiating with the unions about pay
policy to general restraint was a debate between supporters of two
conflicting interpretations of the views of Keynes. Advocates of budget
deficits to stimulate demand were criticized for neglecting the impact on the
economy of increasing the amount of money in circulation. Concern with
financing the borrowing of the government and other public institutions
such as the nationalized industries—all summed up as the Public Sector
Borrowing Requirement—without putting too much new money in circulation
had a lot in common with the version of Keynesianism to be found in
Kingsley Wood's 1941 budget and Gaitskell's 1951 budget. In 1975 Healey
had taken a step towards accepting the doctrine of monetarism, namely,
that the amount of money in circulation was important, by imposing 'cash
limits' on departmental spending. This reversed the acceptance in 1962 of

---

[1] Trade-weighted indexes of currency values can be worked out. The difficulty is that
when a currency changes value the relative value of the trade of its country also changes,
so that the index loses much of its reliability with the passage of time.

the Plowden Report which had suggested that, once a programme for public spending had been adopted, the level of service should continue unaffected by monetary changes—if prices went up, the spending department should be given money to go ahead as before. 'Cash limits', and the drift of taxpayers into higher ranges of income tax as the result of inflation, looked like a way to bring the economy under the control advocated by the monetarists. In July 1976 the government showed its belief that 'money matters' once more by declaring that the Borrowing Requirement should be held down to £9bn. a year. When this turned out to be insufficient to restore confidence and a further appeal for a loan had to be made, the I.M.F. asked for limits on the amount of money in circulation that took account of the balance of payments as well. The official end of reliance on stimulative deficits was signalled by Callaghan's speech to the 1976 Labour conference in which he condemned the idea that

you could just spend your way out of a recession and increase employment by cutting taxes and boosting spending . . . . that option no longer exists . . . . it worked by injecting inflation into the economy. And each time that happened the average level of unemployment has risen. Higher inflation followed by higher unemployment. That is the history of the past twenty years.

Whether this was an accurate account of the 1950s and 1960s was debatable—Callaghan, like several other Chancellors, spent as much time cutting spending as increasing it—but the shift in policy that he was proclaiming was perhaps as important as the wartime acceptance of Keynesianism, and certainly more important than anything said about growth and planning around 1960. For most of the next decade the Borrowing Requirement was kept at about the £9bn. level reached in 1976 and because Gross National Product increased considerably in money terms as prices went up, the Borrowing Requirement became a smaller and smaller fraction of the national income. This was not the Gladstonian policy of balancing each budget, or the relatively austere Keynesianism of the post-war years when Chancellors matched their budget deficits with budget surpluses, but it was less disturbing than the rapidly increasing deficits of the early 1970s. The performance of the economy suggested that, whatever theory might say, deficits on the scale of the 1970s tended to swamp rather than stimulate it; industrial production was only one or 2 per cent more in 1977 than in 1970, despite the shift from a balanced budget to a £9bn. deficit. Some commentators said that this showed that the long expansion since the war had been caused by cheap oil or was simply the upswing of the long cycle described by Kondratieff, and they usually added that this meant economic progress would be harder in the decades ahead. The change of policy might deal with some of these problems, but it was not going to be popular. Real wages stopped going up in the first year of incomes policy and fell by 7 per cent in the second year, while unemployment rose towards 6 per cent.

When the Conservatives closed in for the kill they found the government was not as defenceless in the House of Commons as it looked. It ignored some defeats in the Commons, and it put together shifting alliances with the smaller parties. For some months it drew support from the Scottish and Welsh nationalists as the issue of devolution came forward. The case for devolution was that the Scots and Welsh had been led to think of independence by London's neglect, and that if they had asemblies of their own to look after questions that concerned them directly they would be satisfied and would stop making demands that would break up the United Kingdom. This involved the risk that local institutions might not solve the problems of these two poor parts of Britain and would then be used by the nationalists as bases for a march towards independence. The more confident among the English, who thought concessions to the nationalists unnecessary, and the less confident among the Scots and Welsh, who thought devolution would open the floodgates to something they considered destructive, were natural allies in opposing it. Home Rule for Ireland and the government of Northern Ireland that flowed directly from it, had been sweeping measures of devolution; though the British government in 1972 had shown that it was nothing more than devolution by taking back the powers given to the government of Northern Ireland in 1920. Late in 1976 the proposals for Scotland and Wales were put forward together in the Devolution Bill, though the two countries were not to be put on an equal footing. The Bill did not give the Edinburgh assembly the powers over police and justice which had given the Northern Ireland government so much freedom of action, but it did offer the Scots legislative powers over education and health, housing, and local government that were wide enough to make the Bill quite attractive to people who simply wanted to look after their own local affairs in the way proponents of devolution had hoped. The power to oversee the devolved powers held by the Secretary of State for Wales had very little to attract anyone; the assembly in Cardiff looked like another sort of county council perched on the top of the municipal pyramid. The nationalists said the Bill gave no recognition to the national aspirations of their countries, and that shortcomings like the denial of revenue-raising powers to the assemblies meant that it provided no stable base for autonomy short of independence.

Even so, they supported the Bill because it was better than anything they could get from the Conservatives, who had lost their previous willingness to grant devolution; and while the nationalists took this attitude the government could hold on. Labour M.P.s, and in particular some Labour M.P.s from Scotland and from the north of England, were not happy about devolution. The dangers of a disunited kingdom, the restraints imposed upon government activity by any dispersal of powers and the risk of competition among sections of the country to attract industrial capital made some of them into determined enemies of devolution and made many others anxious for full discussion of it. As a result the government did not get a majority for imposing a closure on proceedings in February 1977, and the opponents of the Bill settled down for an infinitely protracted debate. The nationalists now had no really solid reason for supporting the government, and so it had to face the fact that it had no reliable majority.

The government saved itself by arranging what became known as 'the Lib–Lab pact'. If an early election meant disaster for the Labour party, the Liberals were quite as badly placed; and the Liberal leader could see more positive reasons for co-operation. The departure of Thorpe in an atmosphere of deepening scandal had been a heavy blow to the Liberals. They had rallied rather successfully by holding a leadership election on the basis of one party member, one vote; the winner, David Steel, a lowland Scot who had made his name by taking the Abortion Bill through Parliament in the 1960s, stood a little to the left of Thorpe. He knew that a proposal to work with another major party would annoy some Liberals who worried about their independence, or would have preferred to work with the other major party, but he reckoned that he could get his M.P.s to co-operate with the Labour party, if only to put off an election. He wanted his party to have the experience of seeing how government worked, and thought it would benefit from being seen in a more serious role than in the recent past. He may also have hoped that closer contacts with Liberals would encourage part of the right wing of the Labour party to think about a party realignment if the pressure from the Labour left grew more intense. The Liberal party could promise steady support to the government for some months because no legislation was coming forward that would cause them any difficulty. They would have found it hard to vote for anything like the nationalization of shipbuilding (though it was becoming clear that the measure had come just in time to save private yards from ruin in the decline of world trade) or for other steps to strengthen the powers of the central government. But after the 1975–6 session very little of this sort remained on the Labour agenda. A Royal Commission had reported in favour of a measure of workers' control in industry, administered through the trade unions, that would have presented the Liberals with a difficult choice; but it was never put forward in Parliament, mainly because employers were fervent in opposing it and the unions were not very interested. So the state of the parliamentary timetable enabled Steel to tell his party that its co-operation with the Labour party involved no concessions to socialism, while Callaghan could tell his supporters that co-operation to avoid electoral disaster had not led to any sacrifice of principle.

The devolution legislation which dominated the Commons during the lifetime of the Lib–Lab pact had attractions for both parties. Nobody could say that it was not important, so the Labour leadership could resist pressure from the left for measures that might alarm the Liberals by pointing to vital legislation already before the House, and the Liberals could reflect that they were helping to pass a measure they had supported long before the Labour party. The Conservatives had to remember that opposition to the Bill might lose them even more votes in Scotland and Wales while merely boring people in England. So, after the 1976–7 Bill had been talked to death, it was revived for the next session in the form of separate Bills for Scotland and Wales, and the referendum in the two countries conceded the previous year was included in the proposals. The opponents of devolution were able to carry amendments requiring the measures to secure not only a simple majority in the referendum but also the support of 40 per cent of the electorate. As no government since 1931 had gained so much support in winning a general election (though the Labour party was supported by 40.01 per cent of the electorate while losing the 1951 election), this was a formidable obstacle to devolution. Apart from this the legislation was changed very little and the two votes were to be held on 1 March 1979, which gave the voters a little longer to forget the drop in real wages and perhaps come back to the Labour party. People in England felt no enthusiasm for what was called 'the break-up of the United Kingdom', but they had accepted so many reverses that another one hardly seemed important: on this issue, then, the government never faced widespread opposition outside Parliament.

The Labour left objected strongly to the general tendency of government policy. Early in the 1970s it thought it had got the party pledged to government action to increase equality, and believed something had been done about this in 1974 and 1975: but it saw the financial crisis forcing Callaghan to change the policy much as Wilson had abandoned growth in 1966 and 1967. Deflation naturally increased unemployment: ever since the end of the war 2 per cent of the labour force out of work had been taken as a danger point, and the left lost its faith in Wilson partly because unemployment rose above this level in the late 1960s. Things had become worse under Heath, but even he had been afraid of letting unemployment reach the one million figure and had undertaken his U-turn in 1972 to end the deflation. But the Labour government, even though it included representatives of the left like Foot and Benn, let unemployment rise above 1m. and reach 1.4m. The left believed that import controls and direction of the use of capital would solve the balance-of-payments problems without the limits on trade union activity needed for an incomes policy or reduction in real wages or deflation; it was distressed by the government's readiness to draw back from the interventionism of the immediate past. Policies seemed to have shifted in a direction no orthodox supporter of the Labour party would want: the civil service shrank in numbers; government spending did little more than keep pace with inflation; municipalities built fewer houses than in the mid-1970s because the central government reduced their grants; and when the government acquired some additional shares in British Petroleum as one result of the financial collapse of 1974, it quickly sold them off at a profit. Under the impact of disappointment, feelings of betrayal grew up not all that different from the hostility to MacDonald of the 1930s. The belief that the party's values were being ignored and abandoned led to an entirely new determination to bring the party leadership under the control of the party enthusiasts by changing the party constitution. Doing this against the wishes of a leadership that had the power and prestige of office was naturally hard, and in 1978 the pressure for change was held back. If the leadership lost the prestige of government before the memory of Callaghan's deflation had faded away, the internal opposition would return to the attack and would be difficult to resist.

After the overthrow of Heath the Conservatives had repudiated the policies he adopted in the second half of his premiership, and had taken up the Selsdon policy of limiting trade union power and withdrawing from intervention in the economy that he had accepted for the first half of his premiership. So the Labour left and the Conservatives could agree in opposing incomes policy, if on nothing else, and the Conservatives hoped to defeat the government by getting the left to vote with them. But while the left voted against the government as often as was safe, it knew it would not be forgiven if it brought about an election in which Labour lost badly.

Rising unemployment and falling real wages made it hard to get an agreed incomes policy for yet another year, but Healey negotiated again with the unions for a wages agreement if income tax was cut, and got an undertaking that wage increases should not exceed 10 per cent. This was interpreted flexibly enough for most of the previous year's drop in real wages to be regained, and the government recovered some of its lost popularity. To defend the 10 per cent limit the government resisted the firemen's demand for a larger increase, taking the risk that if there were a catastrophic fire both government and firemen would be blamed for their obstinacy. Troops were moved to fire duty, to save lives rather than property; no disastrous fire put pressure on the government to settle; and eventually the strike ended on terms that left the pay policy intact and discouraged other unions from attacking it.

The government's hopes for something better than constant negotiations with the unions were based upon North Sea oil, which by 1978 was beginning to flow in quantities large enough to affect the whole economy. Britain moved quickly away from dependence on imported oil, which improved the balance of payments, and, once they had recovered their investment, the oil companies started making large payments to the exchequer. The $12-a-barrel price for oil in the later 1970s would give the government about £3bn. a year, or about 4 per cent of its total revenue.

Britain was at the same time moving away from reliance on imports for food: farmers were the most clear-cut beneficiaries of Britain's entry to the European Community, for the Common Agricultural Policy helped them at least as much as it helped farmers in the rest of the Community and they responded by producing more. At the time of entry Britain grew 49.2 per cent of her food and by the end of the 1970s this figure had risen to 59.3 per cent. (Or allowing for those items, from tea to oranges, that are not grown in Britain, it had risen from 61.2 per cent to 73.9 per cent of temperate-zone foods.) Britain's share of world trade continued to decline; this was in part a sign of a failure to compete in industrial production, but it also represented a shift of resources towards self-sufficiency, based on investment in oil and in agriculture.

By the summer of 1978 the government could hope for some reward for the years of restraint. The Liberals ended the Lib–Lab pact but did it politely enough to show that, while they wanted to fight the next election as a separate party, they hoped the pact could be revived afterwards. As the nationalists would not do anything to forfeit Labour support before the March referendums, the government could hold on; but by August Callaghan was hinting at an election and looked like announcing it at the Trades Union Congress in September. At the same time the government asked the T.U.C., in no very conciliatory way, for a fourth year of incomes policy; no cuts in income tax were offered, and a maximum pay increase of five per cent was suggested. This may have been a sensible recognition that real wages could not go up as fast as they had done in the previous twelve months, but it was hard for the T.U.C. to accept. The day after the proposal was rejected the Prime Minister announced there would be no autumn election. A renewed incomes policy would have been a strong election plank but without it he faced an awkward choice between an election immediately after failing to reach agreement with the T.U.C. and the dangers of unrestricted wage demands. In the event he was blamed for not holding an autumn election, but the real trouble was that he had neither taken care to secure a fourth year of incomes policy nor prepared a plan to deal with unrestricted wage demands.

No previous incomes policy had lasted for a fourth year, and a flood of wage claims like those of 1963–4, 1969–70, and 1975 was only to be expected in 1978–9. The government tried to use its powers over prices and investment to stop private companies giving large wage increases, but by the end of the year the public sector stood out as the main area of discontent. The Ford motor workers, whose strike came just after the end of the incomes policy, started the rush by getting a 17 per cent pay increase, and the strike of the lorry drivers caused more widespread difficulty and dislocation of industrial production than any other dispute, but what caught the public eye was the visible effect of the strike of the dustmen (at a hygienically cold time of winter), the first-ever strike by nurses, and the macabre problems caused by the strike of the Liverpool gravediggers. In the private sector, overtime and allowances for expenses had probably been used to give workers a bit more than the pay policy allowed; Professor Clegg, whose work as director of research for the Donovan Commission had won him the approval of trade union leaders, was appointed as a commissioner to compare public sector pay with that of the private sector to catch up. Later it was said that Clegg had leaned to the side of the workers, but at the time the Conservatives declared that they too would bring his recommendations into effect if they won the election.

At the beginning of what became known as the 'winter of discontent', Callaghan had upset people by suggesting that Britain's troubles were much smaller than those of other countries (soon paraphrased as 'What crisis?'), but there was some feeling that the Conservatives' attitude to trade unions and to the general issue were a bit too extreme. The wave of strikes, which did a great deal to drive the number of days lost up to 29½m. in 1979, and the aggressive picketing with which some of them were conducted, led the public to welcome Conservative proposals to enlarge the police force and reduce the legal immunities of trade unions. The government decided to put the election off until October, the last possible moment, and hope that the summer would restore everyone's good humour, but this strategy was destroyed by the March referendums. In Scotland 33 per cent of the electorate voted for devolution and 31 per cent against it; as devolution had not gained the support of 40 per cent of the electorate only a renewed effort by the government could bring it into operation. The Nationalists asserted that the government ought to make such an effort, but they were losing momentum, as far as could be seen from the shifts in the opinion polls. Undoubtedly the skilful debating of anti-devolutionists like Tam Dalyell had pointed out previously unnoticed difficulties in the proposals, but it also looks as if some people had supported devolution more as a way to signal to London that they wanted attention paid to their problems than as a commitment to the substance of the policy.

On the surface the Welsh referendum was a one-sided rejection of the proposals; 12 per cent of the electorate voted for devolution and 47 per cent against. Part of the difference between the two results was that in Scotland the Labour party campaigned for the proposals while many of the organisations that made up the Labour party in Wales opposed it. The Scottish Nationalists had not concentrated their attacks upon the Labour party; Plaid Cymru on the other hand, had won support by campaigning against Labour governments and against Labour municipal corruption. So it was easy enough for the Labour party to work with the Nationalists in Scotland; while Labour's resistance to Plaid Cymru was a struggle to retain an old-established position. The dominant figure in the debate was Neil Kinnock, descended from a Scottish mining family which had moved to Wales, who took a leading role in a group of half a dozen Labour M.P.s organizing opposition to the proposals. The assembly at Cardiff was an easy target; it looked like another form of the municipal government with all its failings which Plaid Cymru had denounced so effectively. Some Scots were afraid that their assembly might be dominated by Strathclyde, made up of Glasgow and the surrounding region, which might spend too much of the revenue on its local problems of poverty, and relations with Westminster could also cause problems. But the proposals for Scotland won some support from people who valued devolution for its own sake; the proposals for Wales gained very little support except from nationalists who saw them as a step towards what they really wanted. In elections later in 1979 and in 1983 the vote for Plaid Cymru fell much less far from its peak in the early 1970s than the Scottish Nationalist vote, which suggested that for a time Scottish nationalism had attracted the whole country, while Welsh nationalism had a permanent appeal for a cultural and linguistic minority which was strongest in Gwynedd, and had a transient appeal elsewhere for about ten years.

The dispute about Welsh television in 1980 showed that national sentiment could reawaken easily, and illustrated the ambiguity of attitudes to the Welsh language. In the 1979 election all parties promised to set up a Welsh language television channel, but after the election the government considered reinterpreting the pledge in a way that was widely thought to be a betrayal. The protest at this in Wales went far beyond Plaid Cymru and the speakers of Welsh; allowing for those who simply wanted Welsh kept off the three existing channels, quite a number of non-Welsh-speaking Welshmen clearly liked the language as a sign of cultural distinctiveness and would be sorry if it seemed to be badly treated. The government prudently gave way; the Welsh-language channel was set up, but inevitably attracted only a small number of viewers.

By that time a new government was in office, after an election precipitated by the nationalist question but not otherwise affected by it. Because the Scottish Nationalists believed the government should have enacted devolution after the referendum and the Liberals wanted to prove their independence, the government lost a motion of no confidence on 28 March by 311 votes to 310 and for the first time since 1924 an election was held at a time chosen by the Commons rather than the Prime Minister. The Labour party got no time to recover from the damage done by the winter of discontent; Callaghan continued to present himself as the advocate of moderation resisting the Conservatives' proposals for change but, though polls suggested that the voters preferred him to Thatcher, this did not outweigh memories of the 1976 deflation, the steady rise in prices, and the recent strikes. The Conservatives were able to present to the public some converts from Labour—an ex-editor of the *New Statesman*, a couple of Harold Wilson's peers, and so on—and while their collective weight was undoubtedly less than that of Powell's support for Labour in 1974 the display was a reminder that the Labour party was no longer able to recruit members from other parties as it had done in the past. The desire for further cuts in income tax was widespread, and this could only damage the Labour party, which was seen as the party of high taxes. The Labour left had some success in having the tax threshold linked to rises in the cost of living. The Liberals wanted a shift from direct to indirect taxes, which would have surprised their free trade forefathers, and the Conservatives wanted to reduce the standard rate and the higher rates of tax. They promised that government spending would be cut, and talked as if this was just a matter of finding government extravagence and ending it, preferably by dismissing superfluous civil servants. Change on the scale that they implied would have meant deciding what government activities should be ended. In less than twenty years government spending had advanced from 33 per cent of the national income to 41 per cent; if this was to be reversed, the role of the state would have to be reappraised drastically.

For two or three generations the dividing line between manual and non-manual workers (sometimes called the line between the middle class and the working class) had been the most reliable guide to voting habits. Because non-manual workers were becoming a larger proportion of the work-force Labour's original base was being eroded but some non-manual workers were more ready to support Labour than in the past. A good deal of the expansion of government spending went to pay non-manual workers who, though they might go on strike against their central or municipal government employers, had every reason to want the state to raise substantial revenues and were likely to vote Labour as a result. School teachers and social workers were understood to belong to the middle class but by the 1970s they had some interests in common with the traditional unionized working class and no longer paid much attention to ideas about the respectability and social prestige of their jobs. While this group was providing non-manual recruits to Labour, some manual workers were being attracted to the Conservatives by promises of lower taxes, a better chance to work their way forward, and, in particular, the opportunity to buy their own homes. Self-employed manual workers were very likely to respond to this, and by 1979 were voting in very much the same way as the general run of non-manual workers. Owner-occupiers had always tended to vote Conservative; by 1979 this was affecting working-class voting and when the Conservatives proposed to sell council houses to sitting tenants they were not just proposing a further step towards a property-owning democracy: they were proposing to increase the number of electors who leaned towards the Conservatives. If substantial numbers of council tenants wanted to buy their homes, it was still true that the general reputation of council housing was low, and this probably intensified the widespread feeling that governments could not run anything like a nationalized industry efficiently (and it may also be guessed that Labour suffered because some of its supporters poured scorn on owner-occupiers).

The weakening of the fundamental line between manual and non-manual workers and the emergence of new lines of division did not mean that no important issues remained to be settled. The line between collectivist and individualist values remained much the same as it had been most of the century, but workers no longer took quite so clear cut a view about which side of the line they were placed by their jobs.

	Votes	Seats	% of all votes cast
Conservative	13,697,690	339	43.9
Liberal	4,313,811	11	13.8
Labour	11,523,148	269	36.9
Scottish Nationalist	504,259	2	1.6
Plaid Cymru	132,544	2	0.4
Unionists in Ulster	410,419	10	1.3
Others	630,107	2	2.0

The Conservatives gained fewer seats than might have been expected from their substantial lead over the Labour party; since 1974 they had gained votes in about equal numbers from the Liberals and from Labour, but, while the Liberals seemed to be sinking back to the position from which they had risen when the major parties were unpopular in the 1970s, Labour had held on, helped by its underpopulated inner-city seats of which the supply was constantly renewed as the destruction of slums and the desire for more living space thinned out the population of old Labour strongholds.

Labour and Conservatives on a tightrope

Thatcher was a politician of strong and simple opinions. If Callaghan had embodied common sense, Thatcher added conviction to common sense. What she said about reducing the role of government, stopping prices going up, and enabling everybody to become better off by individual effort was very attractive at the end of fifteen or eighteen years of eager government intervention. During those years people felt they had become better off only in short bursts of prosperity when they had escaped from government control; occasionally they shook off restraints like incomes policy but they rather expected restrictions to return after a year or two of growth too rapid to be sustained, accompanied by price increases that became more and more alarming. Intervention seemed to lead to slow growth, rising unemployment, and a steady decline in prosperity relative to other nations. Non-intervention might offer something different.

Thatcher's control of her government was not complete. Supporters of her views, which could be described as the attitudes of the middle class on the way up, were balanced in the cabinet by advocates of a tradition of looking after those lower in the social scale which was upheld mainly by those who already had a well-established position. Her predecessor Edward Heath tried to associate himself with this attitude in his obvious willingness to regain the leadership of the party. So a dispute about Conservative principles might erupt, though the new government had to start by tackling the large amount of unfinished business left by the Labour government.

Labour ministers had tried to resume negotiations with Rhodesia, working with the United States some of the time, though this had served to strain Anglo-American relations rather than to solve the problem. The real force for change was unleashed when Portugal gave up her colonies in Angola and Mozambique in 1975. Once guerilla forces could operate from bases in Mozambique on Rhodesia's north and east borders, they could weaken the Rhodesian economy and make the South African government want to have an African government as moderate as that of Malawi installed in Rhodesia. Smith was able to see the point of the South African approach, and by 1978 he had brought a number of African leaders, of whom Bishop Muzorewa was the most conspicuous, into a delicately balanced coalition of blacks and whites. This government was denounced as a façade for continued white rule, and was said not to be able to control its own territory. In April 1979 it held a general election under universal suffrage, with a variety of guarantees for the position of the whites, though this was not quite like the election going on in Britain at the same time: for the point at issue was whether the government could get a high enough turnout to show that the guerrillas could not make African voters boycott the election. The 64 per cent turn-out showed that the government had quite a strong position: and when Muzorewa went on to become Prime Minister of the awkwardly-named Zimbabwe-Rhodesia, Thatcher's first impulse was to recognize his government.

Recognition would probably have been accepted. The other members of the European Community had never been very worried about the issue and the Muzorewa government had enough support in Congress to make it unlikely that the American government could have opposed the move. But the Foreign Secretary, Lord Carrington, persuaded Thatcher to try to reconcile the guerrillas with Muzorewa's government, to reduce the risk that the guerrillas would fight on and that other African governments would say the whites were still in control. If the guerrillas took part in an election under an impartial authority the war would be over and the winner of the election would hold unquestioned authority. All sides accepted this policy; Lord Soames went to Zimbabwe-Rhodesia as a combination of a proconsul and a returning officer, and in the 1980 election the parties led by the guerrillas won decisively and then presided over the emergence of Zimbabwe as an independent state. The election result was not what Thatcher had wanted, but the British could at least feel that they had ended a problem that had caused them more diplomatic difficulty than anything else in the whole process of decolonization. But the length of the dispute, and the high moral tone in which well-wishers had given advice to Britain, had encouraged a feeling that the Commonwealth had turned into an institution that might deserve 'tepid applause' but was interested mainly in influencing British policy towards Rhodesia and, later on, towards South Africa.[1]

At least it cost very little. The Conservatives came to office just as the high cost of membership of the European Community was becoming inescapable. The transition period in which Britain was shielded from the

---

[1] *The Economist*, 10 Oct 1981 and 3 Dec 1983.

impact of the Common Agricultural Policy ran out in 1978, and it turned out that the concessions gained in the 1974–5 renegotiations would save Britain only about £350m. of the £1 to 1½bn. that would have to be paid out annually. The figures had become known officially only in the weeks before the election, though Labour ministers would at no time have found it easy to return for more renegotiations. Thatcher had no such record of hostility to the Community to live down, nor any perfervid statements in favour of it to disavow. Like most people in Britain, she accepted the Community as a not especially welcome part of the background of political life but saw no reason why it should be a large drain on Britain's financial resources. The other members of the Community agreed it was anomalous that Britain was a large net contributor when she was poorer than six of the nine members, but were less ready to say that Britain should be permanently guaranteed against losses that presumably she had foreseen at the moment of entry. Year-by-year rebates were granted, and the refunds of the early 1980s reduced the net payments to about £500m. Some Community countries argued that Britain's energy resources solved all her problems, which implied that coal and oil were assets more permanent than agriculture or industry. Opponents of Britain's claims could also hope that British agriculture would expand until its C.A.P. benefits balanced Britain's other contributions to Community funds, but the rate of growth of British agriculture slowed in the early 1980s, perhaps because farmers could see that the C.A.P. was being criticized and that other claims on funds would increase as the less prosperous countries of southern Europe (of which Greece in 1981 was the first) joined the Community. Opposition to the C.A.P. could not be taken very far; in 1982 the convention that unanimity was needed for important decisions was ignored and the other nine members increased the farm budget despite Britain's opposition. But Thatcher's strategy of stating a sweetly reasonable case with great determination eventually had its effect, and at Fontainebleau in 1984 an agreement was reached that gave a reasonably permanent guarantee that Britain's payments would only be about half the level they would otherwise have been.

In Northern Ireland the prospect of a settlement lay even further in the future. The assassination of Lord Mountbatten while on holiday in the Republic of Ireland in 1979 could possibly be seen as an indication that the I.R.A. was having difficulty penetrating the defences that had gone up in Northern Ireland, and the fall in the number of deaths in 1980 was a more positive encouraging sign. But towards the end of the year members of Sinn Fein tried a new way to show their refusal to accept British rule: some of them went on hunger strike in prison. As the policy of forcibly feeding hunger strikers had recently been ended they were free to choose for themselves whether to live or die, which gave them an opportunity to emulate the famous Lord Mayor of Cork who starved himself to death in an English prison in 1920. The first attempt was abandoned when one of the prisoners was about to die, but in 1981 an I.R.A. member who had been elected to parliament while in prison did starve himself to death and nine others followed him in the next few weeks. The government stood unmoved and made it clear that unrelenting self-sacrifice by a minority would not be allowed to break up the United Kingdom. In August the hunger strikers gave up; tension had naturally been increased and the number of deaths rose slightly but it never returned to the levels seen in the 1970s. Proposals for political change became no more than the background to a policy of restoring tranquillity by transferring responsibility to the reorganized and more sophisticated Royal Ulster Constabulary and drawing back from military operations, in the hope that this might improve relations with the Republic of Ireland and erode the I.R.A. bases of operation north and south of the border.

While the E.E.C. contributions and the emergence of Zimbabwe were handled at least as successfully as any problems faced by British governments in the preceding ten or fifteen years, the real challenge faced and even welcomed by the new government was that of an economy that had been doing badly for years and now had to meet the results of a round of wage and salary increases far larger than could be matched by the sluggish growth of production. By the time of the election, the winter of discontent was affecting prices: the years of incomes policy had pulled price increases back from a level of 27 per cent between mid-1974 and mid-1975 to only 8 per cent between mid-1977 and mid-1978, but by early 1979 they were going up faster. If the Labour government regretted being forced into an election before people could forget the strikes, at least it did not have to face the bill for them. That fell to the new Chancellor of the Exchequer, Sir Geoffrey Howe, but his budget in June 1979 dealt with questions of taxation and left the problems of prices until later.

His budget brought the standard rate of income tax of 33p in the pound back to the 30p level at which it had stood from 1970 to 1974. The highest rate of tax was reduced from 83p to 60p, with corresponding cuts in other rates of surtax. (The investment surcharge stayed at 15p: those who paid at the top marginal rate of 98p rather than use the methods of tax avoidance, from life insurance to National Savings certificates, provided by the government, would now pay at 75p.) To match these reductions in income tax the rates of value added tax were made uniform at a new, sharply-increased rate of 15 per cent. The long-term effects of these changes upon prices should have been neutral; in theory inflation is driven forward by the total size of the budget deficit, and Howe laid down a medium-term financial strategy which formally committed the government to the approach Healey had taken since 1976: the borrowing requirement would not exceed £8bn. a year, and would decline in the future. Whatever the effects in years to come, the increases in value added tax pushed prices up at once and led everyone to feel that they would go on rising. The government's argument that the changes in income tax and value added tax cancelled each other out was true only at a level of high theory; the small minority who paid the higher rates of income tax were rather better off, and the great majority who paid at the standard rate or did not pay at all were slightly worse off, but the important point was that reductions in income tax were seen as a long-overdue relaxation of the fiscal burden and increases in value added tax were treated as another rise in the cost of living, to be counteracted by pay increases.

The implications of the new government's idea of its role in the economy took some time to sink in. Governments had shifted regularly from expansionist to deflationary policies, but it was taken for granted that what they really enjoyed was spending money; circumstances might make them slow down, but they would spend more when times changed. Thatcher and Howe thought a government should start from the assumption that reducing taxes was better than government spending, so that it should take as little as possible of the national income. The public was probably not surprised to see spending cut once again after enjoying the delights of anarchy when the incomes policy collapsed, but it had not realized that this policy would be maintained and that ministers had few inhibitions about increasing unemployment to cut costs, because they believed that some jobs were of so little use that the workers might as well be turned out to look for something more useful to do.

The new government had, however, some commitments of its own to increase spending. Putting Clegg's proposals for increases in civil service pay into effect would cost at least £300m. a year. In opposition it had vociferously approved of the programme for a three per cent real increase in defence spending that the members of the N.A.T.O. alliance had undertaken in 1977. A smaller item, a promise to spend more money on the police force, was intended to give substance to the claim that the Conservatives cared about law and order, with the implication that their opponents did not.

The phrase 'law and order' linked two issues. After the 1920s indictable criminal offences had risen steadily, unaffected by changes of government or by the increase of the police force that went on throughout the century.

Sometimes it was suggested that a bigger police force just led to better reporting of crime, or that victims had become more sensitive and reported crimes they would have ignored in the past, but most people believed that crime was increasing and that a larger police force would hold it in check. Calls for law and order were also prompted by an increase in what would once have been called 'riotous assembly'. Picketing in strikes, taking part in political demonstrations, and watching football matches do not necessarily have much in common, but by the late 1970s all of them were carried out in a much more violent way than for many years past. The images of strikers fighting the police at Saltley, of political enthusiasts of the extreme left and right fighting each other whenever the police would let them, and of supporters of association football clubs treating matches as an excuse for battles with supporters of the other side (leading up to a riot in 1985 at Brussels in which Liverpool supporters fought with Italian spectators, 38 of whom were killed, which led to an international ban upon all matches with English clubs) left a general impression of violence that made the majority support more rigorous policing, which in turn led a minority to speak as if these changes were laying the foundations of a police state.

Concern about law and order was matched by concern about rising prices; they went up by 12 per cent in 1979 and by 18 per cent in 1980; the government tried to control the effects of pre-election light-heartedness by reducing spending but gave no sign of more direct intervention. The level of unemployment had declined very little during the financial relaxation of the Labour government's last months in office and never fell below 5 per cent, so it was no surprise that unemployment soon went back above 6 per cent when public spending was cut. The opposition protested, but its complaints carried less weight because people could remember that so many jobs had been lost between 1974 and 1977.

Changes in the age distribution of the population and in the shape of the economy made unemployment harder to reduce. Between the 1971 and the 1981 censuses the section of the population aged between 15 and 65 rose by just under a million, moving from 63 per cent to 64½ per cent of the total. The rise in the birth rate had reached a peak in the mid-1960s, so in 1981 2,727,947 people aged from 15 to 17 were about to enter the labour market, compared with 2,239,760 people in this age group in 1971; and it was argued that the wages paid to these young people were too large a fraction of those paid to established workers for it to be easy for them to find jobs. As in the 1920s and 1930s the proportion of the population that was looking for work was rising rapidly, but between the wars the problem was reduced by the convention that married women ought not to bring a second income to their family when other families had no earnings. By the 1970s this attitude was out of date; women demanded greater freedom, and this included freedom to compete for jobs. Even if attitudes had not changed women might well have become a larger part of the labour force: in steel, in coal-mining, in shipbuilding, and in car-making, which had always been more or less closed to women, jobs were disappearing while the posts for typists, clerks, and receptionists offered in the expanding sectors of the economy had come to be seen as jobs for women. So it was hard to say whether women looked for jobs because they felt liberated, or felt liberated because it was easier to find jobs than in the past. Young people entering the labour market might have no preconceptions that some jobs were for men and some were for women, but they still had to contend with the inability of the market to handle a flood of new workers, although clearly this was not going to last long because the birth rate of the early 1980s was only about two-thirds of what it had been at the 1960s peak. Workers looking for a job found their problems intensified by the legislation of the mid-1970s which tried to improve workers' conditions by requiring fairly generous payments linked to years of service for those who lost their jobs (or were 'declared redundant'). This cushioned the pain of losing a job, but it also made employers much more careful about taking on new workers because they had to think about the costs of laying them off if the economy slowed down.

While more workers were looking for jobs and changes in the law discouraged the creation of new jobs, the financial background was transformed in a way that made it harder to expand employment. Sterling sank lower in the mid-1970s and then rose higher at the beginning of the 1980s than the country's economic prospects justified. Oil prices early in 1979 seemed to be moving up gently from $12 a barrel, and the advantages to the economy of North Sea oil were becoming more apparent at just the time when the Shah of Iran was overthrown by a religious revolution in the course of which his country's oil production was sharply reduced. Prompt action by O.P.E.C. then pushed prices up to $33 a barrel by the end of 1980. Any bank or currency dealer trying to put money where it would benefit from increases in the price of oil would naturally think of sterling as the most convenient of the petro-currencies: the readily-tradable national debt provided a vast range of opportunities for investing this money. (Everybody knew that the price of oil could only move upwards, but theoreticians noted that other manœuvres could be carried out in sterling if the oil price fell—facilities for dealing in Arabian ryals or Nigerian cedis were distinctly limited, but there were well-tested facilities for selling sterling short.) As money poured into sterling, its value rose to a peak of just over $2.40 late in 1980. There was another reason for keeping short-term funds in London: because the government could do very little to stop inflation by reducing its borrowing requirement, it resisted price increases by allowing interest rates to go up. By late 1979 the minimum lending rate was 17 per cent and 12 months later it was still at 16 per cent. The effects were much the same as Montagu Norman's policy of holding bank rate at 7 per cent in 1920: employers dismissed workers as fast as they could in order to reduce their overdrafts, and banks received large inflows of money that could not prudently be used for long-term investment in Britain.

The abrupt rise in the value of the pound hampered trade, and the government applied its free-market principles to the problem. The exchange controls imposed at the beginning of the Second World War were dismantled. During those forty years, life insurance had expanded a great deal and pension plans had turned from a rare and ill-understood privilege into a benefit taken for granted in any salaried post, enjoyed by all workers in nationalized industries and coming to be expected by wage-earners elsewhere. Partly because people earned enough to be able to save, and partly because life insurance and retirement pensions were the most tax-efficient way to do so, City of London institutions had built up large investment funds. The system of exchange controls had made it hard for them to invest overseas so, when the controls were removed, they set about balancing their portfolios on a world-wide basis. The beneficiaries of the funds probably got better pensions as a result and some of the impact of short-term money flowing into London was neutralized by the substantial sums that went overseas for investment. The outward flow never took as much of the national income as the outflow in the years before 1914, but funds invested overseas, which came to about £12½bn. when exchange controls were removed, had risen to £70bn. five years later. Money flowed into Britain as well, earning a higher rate of return than the money going out, but on balance about £35–40bn. went out of the country when it might have been possible to use it to finance the expansion of new industries in Britain, although the pound might have risen to heights that impeded exports even more if the money had not gone overseas.

The government seemed unmoved by this, and even gave the impression that it welcomed the process by referring to the need for 'real jobs'. The phrase implied an attack on low levels of productivity and also on the large numbers of people employed by central and local governments. Even when allowance was made for the low level of capital investment per worker, productivity in Britain was lower than in most industrialized countries. Ministers were particularly worried by the nationalized industries, which made losses that had to be met by the exchequer. The Labour government had put the car manufacturer British Leyland in the hands of a clear-headed manager, Michael Edwardes, with instructions that gave him a fairly free hand in cutting losses at the expense of reducing employment. This was a large step away from a policy which, when Labour came to office, looked like a desire to preserve all existing jobs no matter what the cost. The Conservatives embraced the new policy eagerly; an aggressive businessman, Ian MacGregor, was brought back from the United States to cut the steel industry's losses, which he did by paying steel workers generously to give up their jobs, and then closing the more irredeemably unprofitable mills. The new school of managers sharply reduced the long-term drain on the exchequer of the nationalized industries; in the first years of Conservative government the losses were rather higher than before, but most of this money was spent to reduce costs in the future. The policy involved a considerable loss of jobs, but its defenders said that the point of having a steel industry or a motor industry was to provide steel or cars at reasonable prices rather than maintain jobs at great expense in industries that were bound to contract.

Some nationalized industries, such as North Sea oil and gas or the telecommunications section which emerged as a separate organization when the Post Office was divided in two, were likely to be profitable, and ministers became more and more enthusiastic about selling these industries to private investors. The Labour government's sale of British Petroleum shares in 1977 was one example of privatization, but the success of the government's election promise to let council tenants buy their homes was much more important. The opportunity was accepted eagerly, whether because sitting tenants were given large discounts, or because of the attractions of owning property, or because of the irritation of municipal regulations. About three-quarters of a million homes were sold in six years, at an average price of around £8,000. Labour councils denounced this in terms which suggested that council houses were let solely to people on the verge of destitution, and that homes sold to tenants were falling into the hands of incipient members of the exploitative bourgeoisie. The position of councils in the housing market was under pressure from another direction: the blocks of flats put up quickly in the 1960s turned out to be so unsatisfactory that by the 1980s councils faced bills for repairs and restoration considerably larger than all the proceeds of the sale of houses.

Steps towards denationalization, now usually called privatization, fitted government policy in several ways. If privatized industries made losses, that was their own concern: shares in the aircraft firms nationalized in 1976 under the name of British Aerospace were sold to the public and the government could then insist that the firm had to be run simply to make a profit. Proceeds from sales could be counted as a reduction in the borrowing requirement; more British Petroleum shares and a part of the government's North Sea holdings were sold as a way to avoid borrowing more money. The industries nationalized in the 1940s would not be so easy to sell, and the government spent heavily to keep the coal and steel industries going, but it hoped to reduce the activity of the state and to avoid industrial conflict with its own employees in the future. The state employed considerably more people in its non-commercial activities and these activities cost a good deal, not all of it under the direct control of the central government. Ministers hoped that they could be Gladstonian enough to reduce the civil service salary bill; they also disliked the rate support grant system under which the central government paid for about 60 per cent of municipal activity, which cost about £11bn. in 1979–80. The government began by reducing the percentage paid and the activities it had to support, and went on to define what councils should spend and to give the Secretary of State power to fix a maximum rate. Labour councils wanted to keep up a high level of municipal services and some of them seemed intent on setting up 'socialism in one borough'; the central government did not want to see its tax revenues spent on supporting this, but so complex a pattern of dependence on central funds had grown up that the government could not simply tell councils to spend what they liked and pay for all of it out of their own rates. And so the Conservatives imposed limits on municipal autonomy which meant that in the short run they were increasing rather than diminishing the power of the central government.

Early in the 1979 Parliament Labour M.P.s amused themselves by shouting 'U-turn' when the government seemed to be moderating its policies, with the implication that it was about to change course as Heath had done late in 1972. This probably embarrassed the ministers who did want moderation, and it helped Thatcher to rally her supporters behind her slogan 'The lady's not for turning' at the party conference. Government policy was not changed: nationalized industries were trimmed, limits were placed on government spending, interest rates stayed high, and the opposition naturally said that the rising unemployment of the 1980s was a direct result. The phrase 'real jobs' had some validity, in the sense that productivity went up among those who still had jobs, but the immediate effect of the policy was to leave resources of both capital and labour unused. When the rate of inflation began to fall and the level of unemployment went on rising, previous post-war governments had changed course and behaved in the way Callaghan had condemned in 1976. The Conservatives stuck to their policy, and Howe's deflationary budget in 1981 provoked howls of anguish on every side. In the course of 1981 Thatcher dismissed three or four ministers who showed some support for reflation;

and provided new terms for the old debate by calling them 'wet', whereupon the two sides in the struggle in the party came to be called 'wets' and 'drys'. The 'drys' held all the important posts for economic matters; the 'wets' built up a group of ex-ministers and dissatisfied ministers waiting for a chance to overthrow the Prime Minister.

These disputes were almost driven out of the headlines by the more spectacular quarrels in the Labour party. Its members ignored the fact that the margin between percentages of the popular vote gained by the two major parties was wider than that at any election since 1945, and behaved as if waiting for Conservative mistakes would be quite sufficient to recover the lost votes. The left claimed that the defeat was the result of neglect of socialist principle by the leadership, and pressed on with its plans to make the leadership accountable to the party enthusiasts. In 1979 the attack advanced successfully on two fronts: the rules were changed to require all Labour M.P.s to submit themselves to their constituency organizations after each election (with the implication that anyone who had not followed the line preferred by the enthusiasts would be replaced); and pressure mounted to have the party leader chosen not by the parliamentary party but by a conference representing party members. The drive to change the constitution was skilfully organized and was given energy by the sense of betrayal aroused by the defeated government (exacerbated by realizing that some unwelcome Conservative moves could be presented for debating purposes as simply the logical result of steps taken by the Labour government). In the course of 1980 it was agreed that a new method of choosing the leader would soon be adopted and in October Callaghan resigned, allowing the parliamentary party to choose a leader before the new constitution came into effect—this was believed to be meant to give Denis Healey as good a chance of winning as possible. The manoeuvre just failed; Foot was chosen as party leader by a margin of ten votes over Healey. Early in 1981 a special conference created an electoral college for future elections in which the trade unions would have 40 per cent of the votes, the constituency parties 30 per cent, and the parliamentary party 30 per cent. The left expected to have a large majority in the constituency section and support from strong minorities in the other sections, a calculation borne out by the election for the deputy leadership later in the year: Healey beat Benn by the narrowest of margins, and owed his slender majority to the fact that some left-wing M.P.s abstained out of personal distrust of Benn.

Who dares, wins

The Labour party had moved to the left in policy as well as in terms of constitution and leadership. A programme of heavier taxes, of extension of government power by nationalization and planning agreements, and of withdrawal from the European Community, gave the left a chance to fight for the values it thought had been abandoned in the 1960s and betrayed in the 1970s. The right wing was dismayed to see what the party had become. Roy Jenkins, the reforming Home Secretary and hard-hitting Chancellor of the Exchequer of the 1960s had become President of the Commission of the Community; he made it clear that when he came back to England he expected to play a prominent part in realigning the centre and the left. Three members of the last Labour cabinet, who in 1980 had fought to have the choice of party leader placed in the hands of the party members in the same way as in the Liberal party, joined Jenkins after they had been defeated at the 1981 special conference and in March the four of them launched the Social Democratic Party, which quickly attracted a couple of dozen Labour backbenchers. The new party had close links with the Liberals: its creators were deeply committed to the European Community, which the Liberals had supported since the 1950s, while very few Labour M.P.s who worried about the party's shift to the left but were uneasy about membership of the Community joined the new party in the end. The Social Democrats could also find common ground with the Liberals in a desire to 'break the mould' of British politics; the phrase implied that the political dominance of the two major parties should be brought to an end, probably by changing to a system of proportional representation: this would make it unlikely that any single party would win a majority in parliament, so most governments would have to be coalitions of a type entirely familiar in countries of western Europe where parties in the centre of the spectrum can expect to be welcomed as partners in successive governments.

Because the two major parties had been moving away from the centre, people who wanted a policy of moderation and compromise felt that there was no party to represent them. The Alliance, as the less than fully defined joint efforts of the Liberals and Social Democrats soon came to be called, implied that 'breaking the mould' would get people back to the politics of consensus that were attributed to the legendary Mr. Butskell of the 1950s, and in the 1980s this had an obvious appeal: faced with a choice between a government committed to economic theories associated with higher unemployment, and an opposition that seemed to welcome a return to the siege economy, voters naturally welcomed a less brutal approach. While the Conservatives were unpopular for going back to the 1930s and the Labour party for embracing the less enjoyable aspects of the 1940s, the Alliance stood to gain by looking more humane and up-to-date. And gain it did: in a series of by-elections after the Social Democrats' secession from the Labour party the Alliance won a number of seats that had previously been held securely by one or other major party, and did well enough elsewhere to have over 400 seats if an election had been held in 1981.

The success of the Alliance was attributed to the interest that the media were bound to take in anything new, perhaps reinforced by the personal approval felt for it by many journalists and broadcasters. But when politicians in the major parties spoke of the Alliance as the creation of the media and hinted at journalists' bias as an important factor in its rise they revealed that they did not realize how unpopular they had become. Some of this was due to trivial causes, such as the broadcasting of Commons proceedings which showed how raucously the M.P.s behaved, and some of it to a record of 20 years in which politicians had failed to produce effective policies; the Alliance looked like one possible answer to the demand for an effective government.

An entirely different sign of the volatility of public feeling and the inability of politicians to do anything about it (and perhaps of the capacity of the mass media to encourage developments without necessarily understanding them) was provided in the summer of 1981. Discontent might be widespread but drafting new programmes for the Social Democrats was rather a specialized response to it. Tension between the police and young people had been on the increase for some years, encouraged by the development of 'riotous assembly'. Tension between the police and the Indian and West Indian communities had also been growing as these newly created communities tried to work out some sort of relationship with their neighbours and got less help in this from the police than they had hoped for. Youths of West Indian descent in the south London district of Brixton became more and more convinced that the police were discriminating against them on racial grounds; the police and many people around Brixton became sure that it was a less safe place than the rest of the country. In April heavy police patrolling of the district led to riots that looked like a struggle for control of the streets; tranquillity was restored after a week or so, and the subsequent enquiry concluded that the police had a hard job in a difficult area but that heavy patrolling had not been a sensible way to manage things. Well before the report appeared the problem had apparently become much more widespread. At the end of June and in early July riots broke out in a number of cities in England, most notably in Liverpool. Some people said that racial tension had spread to other parts of the country but the riots were much more obviously directed against the police, against whom black and white fought together, than against one race or another. Opponents of the government's economic policy said the riots were the result of unemployment, but outside Brixton the riots took place in the early evening often enough to suggest that the rioters came home from work or school, had tea, changed into thicker boots, and went out to look for excitement. If frustration with the narrowness of life and its prospects helped cause the riots, which would explain why people from the West Indies rioted more than anyone else, it was understandable that the mood of excitement on the streets died away in July as the country prepared to celebrate the wedding of the Prince of Wales and Lady Diana Spencer.

The Royal Family had survived relatively undamaged in the decline of confidence in British institutions in the previous twenty or thirty years. The Queen's Silver Jubilee in 1977 had provided the public with an opportunity to enjoy itself when political and economic affairs gave no reason for feeling happy; the royal wedding in 1981, when politicians seemed to be doing just as little to make people happy, gave everyone something to remember (and greatly helped sales and rentals of the newly developed video cassette recorder in the process). The sophisticated sneered at the fairy tale princess and at the way the ceremony was designed as a spectacle for television, but this minority view showed no understanding of the forces that keep nations together. In the past royal ceremonies had been heavy with symbolism intended to impress the participants, who were the most important people in the country. By the twentieth century these ceremonies had to be designed for the entire country to watch, and the country welcomed the pageantry and the glitter in a more united spirit than could be expected on any other occasion. The outbursts of national feeling provoked by sporting events were unstable and could be destructive. The churches still had a hold on the attention of the faithful, but had almost entirely lost their capacity for making ordinary people feel that they belonged to a community. Foreign visitors undoubtedly still felt that the unarmed police were wonderful, but critics inside the country said they were racist, or unable to catch criminals, or apt to become a political force at the disposal of the government. The police were in any case being issued with firearms more frequently, which led to other problems: the injury and even the death of citizens as a result of police mishandling of their weapons was the immediate cause of a new outbreak of riots in Brixton, in Liverpool, and in other disturbed parts of large cities in the autumn of 1985. The armed services still retained a good deal of public respect, shown in an indirect way by left-wing politicians who sometimes preceded speeches asking for arms spending to be cut by saying that they did not want to criticize the armed forces. The rescue by the Special Air Services of hostages held in the Iranian Embassy in 1980 was a skilful and acrobatic feat, achieved with a level of approval that showed people wanted Britain to have a chance to assert herself. The withdrawal from empire and entry into the European Community looked like steps, however sensible, that had been taken because Britain was not strong enough to do anything else. As a stabilizing force, to show people that changes of this sort need not affect the moral basis of national life, most of the Royal Family served extremely well; and they also gave public recognition to people and institutions accepted as worth attention and approval, though within the limits imposed on constitutional monarchy this approval could be given only to reasonably uncontroversial recipients. The problem of bringing about change was harder than that of maintaining stability and it needed a different source of energy.

People who wanted politicians to provide the energy faced a paradoxical pair of party leaders. Foot's principles were those of an interventionist socialist, ready to let the state sort everything out, but he was never able to convince people that he possessed the competence needed to manage this and his friends said that his instincts leaned towards an anarchist version of socialism. Thatcher clearly possessed the dynamism and probably the efficiency to carry out an interventionist policy but was firmly committed to a non-interventionist role for the state. She was said to be divisive and so, at a deeper level than her opponents understood, she was. For almost a century one of the forces holding British society together was what Beatrice Webb called 'a new consciousness of sin among men of intellect and men of property'. First the dislocation of urbanization and industrialization had caught the attention of the rich in the 1880s; then the troubles of the 1920s and 1930s, not fully understood until the 1940s, had made an important section of the rich accept the case for reform, which in turn had greatly helped the setting up of the welfare state and probably eased the process of decolonization. Most Conservative leaders from Disraeli onwards had allowed this sentiment considerable importance in forming their policies, and several leaders of the Labour party had accepted the same assumptions.

By the 1970s this approach was breaking down. The Labour left repudiated it as paternalist, and Thatcher's supporters in the Conservative party were free from the notion that society owed a debt to the able-bodied among the poor, which had been accepted for a generation or two. The term 'Thatcherism' meant rather more than balancing the budget and cutting government spending; the attraction and also the divisiveness of her approach lay in an appeal to individual effort and a promise that those who made the effort would get what they wanted. This might not be a doctrine for the majority of the country, but no other doctrine seemed likely to win a majority. The dominant wing of the Labour party asked for equality but set out to build up a majority by convincing individuals that each one of them belonged to some disadvantaged minority or other that the Labour party was going to look after. As each minority claim looked like a claim for special treatment, it was impossible to work out a common policy that' convinced them all that they had a common interest. The desire for paternalist reform still survived; but its supporters were divided between the right wing of the Labour party, the Alliance, and the anti-Thatcherite wing of the Conservative party, which clearly placed its hopes in pushing her out. The new guilt-free Conservatives had a considerable appeal to British nationalism, with its own divisive features. Thatcher said in 1978 that she understood why people felt they were being swamped by immigrants. This did little to make immigrants feel welcome, but the small amount of public support gained in the 1970s by the National Front, a fringe political party that depended entirely on its opposition to immigration and immigrants, faded away when the more worried members of the white community felt that the government understood their anxiety.

Fortunately for the government, Zimbabwe was the only problem of decolonization in which common sense required it to withdraw unconditionally. Thus its reputation for an assertion of Britain's position was compromised less than that of almost every post-war government. Problems remained in four colonies in which the population wanted to stay under British rule because the alternative was to be absorbed by a neighbouring state, and the government wanted to defend the position of each of them as far as was possible. Opinion in Gibraltar had been tested in 1967, when the government of the colony held a referendum in which 44 people voted for union with Spain, 580 had not voted, and 12,138 had voted to remain a British colony. General Franco was then ruling Spain, and a vote would probably have been less overwhelming if it had been held 12 or 15 years later when a constitutional monarchy had been set up, but it would obviously be some time before developments in Spain, the reopening of the frontier and the possible effects of common membership of the European Community altered the views of the inhabitants of the Rock. While Gibraltar could hardly become independent, British Honduras could manage well enough as an independent state if it did not feel threatened by Guatemala's claim to a great deal of her territory. British diplomats spent some years persuading other countries that British Honduras had a right to self-determination; and in 1981 it emerged as an independent state under the name of Belize, with about 2,000 British soldiers still stationed there to protect the border.

The 1,800 inhabitants of the Falklands Islands were numerically less significant than the population of Gibraltar, let alone Belize. The islands had been disputed between Britain and Spain in the late eighteenth century, and Argentina stood as the successor to the Spanish claim. The descendants of the people from Britain who had settled the islands in the 1830s showed no interest in relations with Argentina. By 1982 the military government ruling Argentina was so unpopular that it needed a success of some sort; a negotiated transfer of the islands might meet their needs, but the readiness of the Foreign Office to find a formula for a transfer had been blocked on previous occasions by the islanders' friends in the House of Commons. So the government of Argentina decided that seizure by force would show its power more effectively, a decision that led to its own downfall and transformed the political situation in Britain. On 2 April Argentina seized the Falkland Islands, 600 or 700 kilometres east of her coastline, and also South Georgia, another 1,200 kilometres further east. The British government organized a task force which set off to sail 13,000 kilometres to the south, and began negotiating about the islands. With a great deal of goodwill and some concern about the feelings of the islanders, two governments with full freedom of action might have settled the question peacefully; but Argentina had raised the stakes so far and so fast that it was hard to avoid humiliation for one side or the other. The rulers of Argentina were unable to agree among themselves what concessions could be offered to enable the British to concede eventual control over the islands, and the British government clearly needed to win some concessions for the islanders before withdrawing. Popular opinion in Britain thought the campaign was justified and the popular press picked up this sentiment exuberantly and vulgarly. Intellectual opinion was uneasy about fighting for the islanders, and in some cases was rather obviously afraid that victory would be a triumph for Thatcher. Many of those who had never before condemned the principle of fighting against a military dictatorship expressed lurid fears about the feasibility of the operation: on 25 April the *Sunday Times* said that 'a mass invasion could be achieved only at horrendous losses' and spoke of the only courses open to the British being 'as things stand, unthinkable'.

Later on the 25th South Georgia was recaptured without any British casualties, and the expedition turned west to the Falklands. On 2 May an Argentinian heavy cruiser, the *General Belgrano*, was sunk by a British submarine. Later investigation showed that the Defence Minister had not been able to keep fully in touch with the information coming to the naval authorities through the Northwood signals system from the fleet in the South Atlantic; the government asserted that the need for secrecy about intelligence operations (which of course included the question of which countries supplied the information) meant that nothing could be said about it. The sinking of the *Belgrano* became the focus for later criticism of the campaign, but at the time it was simply seen as the next step towards landing troops. To avoid the Argentinian forces in Port Stanley at the easternmost tip of the islands, the British came ashore in the sound between the two large islands of the archipelago, far enough west for the Argentinian air force, at the limit of its flying range, to launch a series of determined attacks on the landing area. Between 21 and 25 May the British lost four ships but the Argentinians lost too many planes to be able to continue the attack and the landing went ahead successfully. After this the British had to move across the difficult terrain of East Falkland until Port Stanley was surrounded. Cut off from help and facing a well-trained, well-equipped force about three-fifths the size of their own, the Argentinian forces surrendered on 14 June. The military government fell, but the elected government that took its place showed no desire for negotiations that might have transferred the islands to Argentina in fifty or sixty years time and the British government was certainly not going to think of moving any faster.

The campaign satisfied everyone in Britain who hoped the country would assert itself, and also pleased those who wanted it to act efficiently and effectively. The popularity of the government and of the Prime Minister rose sharply; she had committed herself totally to the campaign, and its success ended any idea that the Conservatives who wanted the government to concentrate on reducing unemployment would be able to dislodge her. The Alliance approved of the campaign and confined itself to making suggestions for improving the government's policy. Within the Labour party those who opposed the use of force gained ground. Once the expedition had succeeded, the government was bound to benefit, especially as British casualties—255 servicemen and civilians killed—were accepted as a price low enough to be justified by victory, and the attitude that became accepted inside the Labour party could be seen as support in time of war for a government Labour had condemned on moral grounds in time of peace.

In 1983 the government turned in a businesslike way to clarify the position of Hong Kong. Most of the territory of the small, densely-populated and prosperous colony would revert to China under the terms of the 99-year lease by which Britain held it. The Chinese government was eclectic enough in its communism to want to preserve the thriving business community; the British government was much more concerned to provide a long period in which business could go ahead as usual in the whole territory than to hang on to the fragment of territory that had been ceded in freehold in 1842. This provided the basis for an agreement in 1984 that the whole colony would revert to China in 1997, under a form of government that would allow it to keep its own commercial and capitalist way of life for at least the first fifty years after the transfer. The population would undoubtedly have preferred to stay under British rule or at least have the right to emigrate to Britain. The British government felt that, as its legal claim was running down and its military strength in the region was non-existent, it had done the best it could to look after the interests of the people of the colony and stay on good terms with China.

This settlement came after a general election in which the government had won a success that surprised nobody. Unemployment had reached 12 per cent during the Falklands campaign; it went on rising, though much more slowly, in the next couple of years, and passed the 3m. level which (with a smaller working population) was never reached in the 1930s, but even in economic policy the government could claim one substantial success. In 1981 prices had gone up by 12 per cent, which was very close to the average rate of increase in the dozen years after 1970, but in 1982 the increase was only 7 per cent and it soon fell to 5 per cent. This was still much higher than the rate of increase in the 1950s and 1960s, and it could be argued that relative price stability was not worth the cost of unemployment and stagnation of the economy, but people had become frightened of inflation and after the experience of the 1970s they were no longer ready to believe that rising prices would necessarily bring any compensating rise in the standard of living. The government won popular approval by carrying out its election promise; governments had been unsuccessful enough in the recent past for people to be glad to have a leader with a clear policy that was put into effect.

In the exciting days of 1981 the Alliance had attracted not only the people who shared its point of view but also those who simply wanted a government that could get things done properly. Most of this group moved to support the Conservatives in 1982, though the Alliance remained in a much stronger position than that of the Liberals for the past 40 years. The Labour party showed how weak it was by insisting that it was too soon to have an election. In the autumn of 1982 memories of the Falklands might have distorted an election, but even in June 1983 the Labour party was still complaining that the government was holding a 'cut and run' election before the proper time, which suggested that it would have been hard to find a time for an election that really suited the opposition.

Labour's fears were justified. The Alliance improved its position in the weeks before polling day, but probably even the gloomiest Labour organizer did not expect his party's share of the total vote to be lower than at any election since 1918. Foot said the opinion polls must be wrong because large and enthusiastic audiences came to his meetings, but this only suggested he did not understand the strategy to which he was committed. A policy had been adopted to arouse enthusiasm on the left, and the enthusiasts were then meant to win support for it among the rest of the electorate. The opinion polls simply showed that the enthusiasts had failed. Labour supporters cherished the hope that voters would rise up against unemployment, but the issue did not operate this way; the great majority of workers stayed in work and their real wages stayed above the general level reached under the Labour government, while the improvement in 1978 and 1979 was dismissed as something that could not be sustained. Total income fell in the early 1980s and 1½m. people lost their jobs but this produced only one group of discontented people, because the fall in living standards was felt almost exclusively by those who lost their jobs. Maintaining the unemployed absorbed all the money saved by cutting government spending and a good deal of North Sea oil revenue as well, so it was certainly true that all taxpayers were worse off than they would have been if employment had not fallen and production had gone up accordingly. But unemployment caused anxiety only when people were afraid it might spread to them; the government did badly in seats where unemployment was high (which were usually safe Labour seats already), but the issue mattered much less once unemployment had stopped going up.

It could be said, after a brief glance at the percentages of the total vote received by the parties, that between 1979 and 1983 the Alliance had taken about 8 per cent of the total vote from Labour and about 1½ per cent from the Conservatives. It seems fairly certain that many Labour voters went over to the Conservatives, though it is hard to say if they were dissatisfied with their old party or attracted by their new one, and the Alliance won votes from Conservatives, presumably with 'wet' leanings, as well as from Labour.

	Votes	Seats	% of all votes cast
Conservative	13,012,602	397	42.4
Liberal–Social Democratic Alliance	7,780,587	23	25.4
Labour	8,457,124	209	27.6
Scottish Nationalist	331,975	2	1.1
Plaid Cymru	125,309	2	0.4
Unionists in Ulster	436,696	15	1.4
Others	526,612	2	1.7

The seats won bore very little relation to the votes cast: the Alliance polled nearly as many votes as the Labour party but won only a few more seats than the Unionists in Ulster with their tiny fraction of the total vote. Politicians in the Alliance naturally felt that this strengthened their case for ·proportional representation (though their voters showed little sign of sharing their feelings) but could reflect that they had advanced all across the country and had come second in 332 seats, while the Labour party had fallen to what might for some time be an irreducible minimum of about a quarter of the electorate and was in some danger of being confined to South Wales, the less prosperous parts of the industrial north of England, and much of industrial Scotland.

During the election Francis Pym, one of the 'wets' in the cabinet, suggested that too large a majority might have disadvantages. This sounded like encouraging people to vote against the government and he was dismissed immediately after the election, but there was some sense to his remark. The Conservatives had the support of a large section of the nation and no other party had the strength to challenge it, but they had gained more seats than the Labour party in 1945 with a decidedly smaller share of the vote, so perhaps 70 of their seats would be impossible to hold if their opponents reached an agreement to share seats or if a single dominant party re-emerged on the left. So a large group of Conservative M.P.s would find it unusually hard to respond calmly when their government faced the unpopularity that occurs in the normal course of events a couple of years after an election.

Foot resigned as leader of the opposition at once. He had been almost as unsuccessful in leading his party as Arthur Balfour; he had been swept into the leadership by the bitterness aroused by the 1974–9 government and he had watched the right secede and the left impose an unpopular programme on the party without being able to do anything about it and without having any other ideas about what the party could do. His successor, Neil Kinnock, was elected under the 1981 rules which were meant to secure the position of the left, but he soon made it clear that his attachment to the left was qualified by a recognition of its great capacity for annoying people. Some of the effects of recent events were already visible; even before the new leader was chosen it was clear that a Labour Prime Minister·of the late 1980s would be unlikely to find as many as half a dozen cabinet ministers from the 1970s ready to serve in his government. Kinnock had gained part of his support because he had refused office in the government of the 1970s. and most of it because of his power as an orator, but it looked as if he would have to rely on Thatcher's weaknesses and his own capacity to appear reasonable rather than on his party's positive qualities to win back some of the lost supporters.

The government attack on the collectivist state

After the election the Conservatives intensified the attack on public ownership. During the 1979–83 Parliament £1.4bn. of publicly owned enterprises had been sold off; in the first 15 months of the new Parliament £1.7bn. were sold. Well over half of this came from the sale of oil shares and most of the rest from Jaguar Cars, and Cable and Wireless; no other sales produced over £100m. and the industries nationalized by the 1945 Labour government remained untouched. All these sales were dwarfed by the sale of British Telecom in November 1984. It was clearly intended to parallel the sale of council houses in the 1979–83 Parliament: at a sale price of £4bn. it would realize a comparable sum of money and, if the sale of council houses was meant to produce a property-owning democracy, the sale of British Telecom was intended to produce a share-conscious electorate. The issuers used all their skills to get a large number of people to buy and hold the shares, and were very successful: over a million people became owners of shares for the first time in their lives. The shares went to so large a premium that the Labour party said that national assets were being sold for well below their true value. This may have been true, but under public ownership the telephone system had been such a byword for inefficiency and perverse technical ingenuity that very few people questioned the terms that got it out of the hands of the government. The Labour party said it would buy the shares back at the issue price; the sale was so successful that only very brave politicians would have stuck to that pledge. The zeal shown in the early decades of the Labour party for nationalizing inefficient industries, which turned out to be the declining industries, had led the party into a trap: public ownership probably reduced the dislocation that accompanies the decline of an industry, but none of the nationalized industries was successful enough to give public ownership any chance of becoming popular. Earlier in the century public ownership had given the Labour party a distinctive issue with which to win its position on the left, but by the 1980s nationalization was a backward-looking vote loser.

Coal had been one of the first industries considered for public ownership, and was one of the first to be nationalized after 1945. For the next dozen years it had been essential for British fuel supply, and then it had been reduced in a peaceful and harmonious way as oil replaced coal. Between 1970 and 1984 the price of oil rose fifteenfold and Britain became the world's fifth largest oil producer, and these two changes made it hard to plan a future for coal. All fuel became more valuable, but the miners won pay increases to make up for the decline in real wages of the 1960s, so coal never became very profitable. Energy from coal and from oil were sold at about the same price but, as about two-thirds of the oil price went to the

Treasury in tax, only a deep concern that Britain's oil supplies might turn out to be a transient North Sea bubble would lead the government to support coal mines which paid no tax and lost money on their operations.

At first the National Union of Mineworkers and the Conservative government circled each other warily. The government gave up one plan to close uneconomic pits; the miners declined to support their executive when it asked them to vote for a national strike. After the 1983 election the government contemplated the six months supply of unsold coal that had piled up and moved MacGregor from the steel industry, where he had reduced the work force by a half and cut capacity by rather less, to the coal industry in order to make it less unprofitable.

Arthur Scargill, the newly-elected president of the N.U.M., welcomed the opportunity for a fight. He had gained prominence in the union by organizing the 'flying pickets' who went to power stations in the strikes of the 1970s to stop coal being delivered, and by his role in the pickets' fight against the police at the Saltley coke depot in 1972. He firmly believed that the 1973–4 strike deserved all the credit for bringing down the Heath government, though other people thought that the miners' contribution had really been to precipitate an election which Labour won by looking more reasonable than Heath. By 1984 the N.U.M. leadership wanted a strike, but it was not clear if they simply wanted to stop all pit closures or hoped to reverse the result of the 1983 election as well. As they were not sure that they could win a vote for a national strike they called for each region to go on strike: this could be done with no ballot, though inviting prosperous regions to go on strike without a ballot to preserve other men's jobs was asking a lot. In the 1960s miners had been ready to give up their jobs because they could find employment elsewhere; by the 1980s the problem of finding work for young men was so great that one of Scargill's strongest cards was his appeal to preserve jobs for 'your children's children'.

The productive Nottinghamshire region was not willing to go on strike without a national ballot, and the N.U.M. organized its 'flying pickets', bringing miners from Scargill's own Yorkshire region to try to stop the Nottinghamshire miners from working. In 1973 strikers could picket wherever they chose and breaches of the peace by pickets were often ignored, but 'flying pickets' became so unpopular after the 1979 strikes that the law was changed to confine picketing to the strikers' own place of work. The Coal Board and the government were anxious to avoid making the miners look like victims of special legislation, which might have rallied the trade union movement around them, so the authorities avoided using the new law during the coal strike although it turned out to be far more violent than British strikes had been in the past seventy years. The police forces of the country had been becoming more integrated into a national force, and the strike accelerated the process. Police reinforcements were brought from other counties to enable working miners to get through the massed lines of pickets; the pitched battles that followed would have been unthinkable a generation earlier, and may have owed as much to the habit of 'riotous assembly' learnt elsewhere as to the needs of the occasion. The police were able to get working miners through the pickets without using force on a scale that alienated the public, and by the autumn the Energy Minister felt it was safe to say that the supply of electricity would be maintained throughout the winter; imports of fuel, the existing stocks of coal, and the flow of coal from Nottinghamshire had made the strikers' objectives unattainable.

The strike involved over 100,000 men for a year, and had wider ramifications than even the largest purely industrial dispute. Some people welcomed it as an attack on the government, and the 'radicalism of the communicators' may have led the miners to overestimate the pressure of public opinion on the government. The columnist who wrote in the *Guardian* on 7 August 'I hope he [Mr Scargill] will, as he must, make Mrs Thatcher crawl', was expressing the view of an articulate minority; when Thatcher called the miners 'the enemy within', with a hint that they were a bit like the Argentinians, she was probably going further than her supporters really wanted. At a less flamboyant level the government expected that after the N.U.M. was defeated a great many miners would take the rather generous redundancy terms available for anyone who wanted to give up his job, and that other trade unions would then follow a much less militant policy, which would allow employers a freer hand to restructure British industry. At the 1984 Trades Union Congress and Labour party conference the miners and the left were able to push the unions and the party into expressing a degree of support for the miners which it was always clear would not be translated into action, and into a condemnation of the police which would do the party no good. For a moment in October it looked as if the union representing the pit deputies responsible for safety had found a way to a settlement, but the N.U.M. continued to insist that no pit should close simply because it cost too much, and the opportunity passed away. Harold Macmillan (recently created Earl of Stockton as one step towards reviving the practice of creating hereditary peerages) compared the miners with the soldiers at Passchendaele, which expressed the respect many people felt for their determination and endurance, and also conveyed a hint about their leadership and its capacity for choosing sensible objectives. After the negotiations with the pit deputies the strike began to crumble, with about a thousand men returning to work every week; some because their resources were completely exhausted and some because they had lost their faith in their leaders. Certainly their leaders seemed to have forgotten that the hardest task for a trade union leader is to bring a strike to an end when it has been lost. After electricity supplies had flowed uninterrupted throughout a cold winter, the miners were on the verge of abandoning their leaders until the leadership announced at the beginning of March 1985 that, although there was no settlement to the strike, everybody should return to work.

The high standing of the government in the opinion polls began to crumble once the strike was over. Probably some people had been saying they would vote Conservative out of a belief that this best expressed their hostility to a Labour party that seemed subservient to the N.U.M. Once this threat was removed, people could lay aside their support for the government against the unions, and turn to considering the faults of the government and the attractions of its opponents in the way that is normal in the lull between election campaigns. The Conservatives showed signs of alarm, though Pym mishandled an attempt to organize a revolt so badly that it strengthened rather than weakened Thatcher's position. The Alliance insisted that reasonableness and three-party politics were the answer, and was able to show their electoral effectiveness in by-elections and in county council elections. Kinnock demonstrated his independence of his supporters on the left by an attack on them which reminded people of the Gaitskell of 1961 by its eloquence and ferocity. Some familiar problems returned, and helped to reduce the popularity of the government. Partly because of the strain placed on the markets by the issue of British Telecom shares, but mainly because of the immense strength of the American dollar, the pound had sunk on the foreign exchange markets. Ministers had in their non-interventionist way encouraged it to drift lower to help exports, but early in 1985 signs of a crisis could be seen; while the pound was higher in terms of the lira and the French franc, and even a little higher in terms of the mark than it had been when very weak in 1976, the government was forced to raise interest rates sharply for fear that the pound should fall to one dollar. The measures taken to defend the currency were not severe, but they showed that the exchange rate could still cause trouble.

The government faced some difficulties over municipal reorganisation. Conservatives disliked the Greater London Council and the other metropolitan counties created for the conurbations after the 1969 Radcliffe–Maud Report, and in 1983 promised to abolish them. This was an understandable response to their lavish spending, and perhaps a natural way for Conservatives to react against bodies which lay further to the left than the national Labour party, but the government had to create non-elected bodies to undertake some services they performed which could not easily be transferred to the boroughs within the conurbations. A large number of Conservative back-benchers, including some of Thatcher's enemies among the ex-Ministers, voted against the government when the proposals were first put forward, and the House of Lords did its best to provide the successor bodies with enough powers to make it possible to revive them as elected bodies in the future, and Labour councils undertook campaigns of non-co-operation, but the legislation became law more or less as intended.

The episode showed how ready the government was to tackle existing institutions and how much less ready it was to think about constructive measures to replace them. Undoubtedly there was much to attack; twentieth-century Britain had shown very little of the ruthlessness of the Victorians in attacking abuses, so the ground was cluttered with relics that had lived too long. Thatcher's inclination was to sweep them away and take it for granted that a free and unencumbered market would provide any replacements that were really needed. The coal dispute illustrated this approach: because the market and geological good fortune provided a fuel that was cheaper and cleaner than coal, the right thing to do was to close down the unprofitable parts of the coal industry and let the oil industry develop the resources of the North Sea so that taxpayers and consumers of coal could get as much revenue and as cheap a supply of energy as possible. In economic issues a keen eye for questions of profit and loss would reveal plenty of cases where an industry that had been overtaken by change was kept going at a level of activity that penalized everybody else and gave people in the industry a purely temporary respite from change. Some gloomy people said British industry was so accustomed to being directed and supported by the state that it would not respond to opportunities that would have been welcomed elsewhere: in 1981 and 1982 the United States was clearing away obsolete economic interests in much the same way as Britain, but in the United States new jobs were soon created to replace those that had been lost, while Britain simply endured a high level of long-term unemployment. Those who believed in the free market replied that, after a long period of interventionist government, businessmen needed time to become used to creating new lines of work, and all that could be said was that if they took too long a reaction would arise that said unemployment must be ended, no matter what the cost in intervention and possible loss of efficiency.

The wider question was to find how far people could rely on the activity of the market place. The dispute over large municipalities illustrated the problem: it was easy to show their weaknesses, not so easy to show that anything which took their place would be cheaper, and very hard to show that new institutions would be more responsive to public opinion. The structure of payments which lay at the administrative heart of the welfare state was also subjected to analysis, though the course of the debate suggested that the system had grown too large for the politicians to be able to make it comprehensible. The original idea of the 1940s was that all the causes of poverty should be relieved by payments made as a matter of right, usually on the basis of the recipient's contribution to the National Insurance scheme. It was always accepted that some extra payments would have to be made in difficult cases, and as time passed this transformed the whole system. The original plan had paid little attention to the financial problems of large families and the family allowances set up in 1945 had in any case fallen far behind rising prices. In the 1950s and 1960s a number of schemes were developed, some at central and some at local government level, to help large families with low incomes to maintain a decent standard of living; most of them ignored the concentration upon payments as a matter of right laid down in the 1940s and depended on an examination of the family's income to make sure that it really was poor. In 1970 this approach was given more formal expression in the Family Income Supplementation Act, which provided funds for families that applied for help and could show that their income fell below set limits.

Because these schemes for large families were related to income, the assistance provided was bound to diminish or taper off as income increased. By the 1970s income tax was being paid at the standard rate by quite poor families and this, combined with the fact that schemes for income supplementation were based on gross income, meant that it was entirely possible for a worker earning a lower than average wage to find that an increase in pay led not only to increases in income tax and national insurance contributions but also to a decline in the level of various means-tested benefits such that his family was actually worse off. Much more common than these extreme and paradoxical cases was the general problem of the low-paid worker in the band of income where income tax and the tapering of benefits between them meant that 80 to 90 per cent of any increase in gross pay was taken away.[1]

---

[1] *The Economist*, 24 July 1975, p. 60–1, explained the operation of 'the poverty trap' very clearly. At that time people at various points in the income band from £1,500 to £2,400, depending on family circumstances and the grants and rebates that could be claimed, might find that an increase in earnings did them no good.

The Labour government of the late 1970s paid little attention to the growth of the poverty trap, as this band of income became known. Inflation made the problem harder to understand: as prices rose, all the figures involved were changed, so that an income of £30 a week, firmly lodged within the poverty trap in the early 1970s, was far below it in the late 1970s, although in practice a worker earning £40 a week in the early 1970s was probably getting £60 a week by the late 1970s and thus remained inside the trap. Changes of rates of benefit altered the shape of the trap, and this made it look as if the number of people involved ought to diminish. At the same time the government was setting up a State Earnings Related Pension Scheme, to make universal the benefits provided by civil service or company pension plans; the problem was complicated and had been holding the attention of politicians for at least fifteen years, so the difficulties of the poverty trap had to wait until pensions had been settled.

The Conservatives were so concerned to keep government spending down, at a time when the cost of unemployment benefit was rising very sharply, that they did very little about the problem for some years. In 1985 the government explored the possibility of ending the S.E.R.P.S., out of concern that the scheme had underestimated the ratio of pensioners to workers likely to be found in the twenty-first century and place an unrealistic burden on the latter. At the same time it set out to make the payment of benefits outside the National Insurance scheme more rational. The movement towards paying family benefits on the basis of net income, making allowance for the impact of income tax and the tapering of other benefits, would eliminate the paradoxical situations in which pay rises made workers worse off. For the majority of victims in the poverty trap, administrative good sense was not enough: the return to payments linked to income had created a situation in which, unless the government was ready to say that people at the bottom of the scale should become worse off, either people within the poverty trap would continue to find that they lost most of every pay increase gained, or a great deal of revenue would have to be devoted to making the position of people at the top end of the poverty trap distinctly better, so that they would have a substantial differential over people at the bottom end of the trap.

This may have been the most intractable problem of finance to face the government, but defence and the arts also presented difficulties. In both cases it was claimed that their requirements could not be judged on financial standards alone, and in both cases it was claimed that their costs normally rose faster than the general cost of living. The claims of defence had been pressed on politicians throughout the century: the figures had risen two-hundredfold since 1906, although the rise in its share of the national income, which had gone up from 3 per cent in 1906 to 5 per cent by the time war broke out in 1914, had subsequently fluctuated around that figure in times of peace and took no more of national income in the 1980s than in 1914. The demand for very high levels of spending on single weapons had led to changes: the development of the Dreadnought, with its impact on the budget and on diplomacy, indicated the shape of things to come, but no pre-1945 government could have expected to see its successors in the 1980s wondering whether to commit a sum equal to a full year's spending on defence to the purchase from the United States of the Trident submarine-and-nuclear-missile system. Such a purchase, even if the cost was spread over a decade, was likely to lead to awkward reductions in all other defence spending; but the alternative seemed to be to withdraw from the race to maintain a nuclear force under British control that had been accepted by successive governments for forty years.

If questions of defence spending had been annoying governments since before the beginning of the century, spending on the arts was a more recent problem. Apart from a few Civil List pensions, the central government spent practically nothing on the arts before the Second World War. Even after 1945 it spent rather less of its revenue on the arts than most governments of comparable wealth, but it could feel in the 1960s that it was beginning to win acceptance of the principle, and that in the 1970s it was even showing a cash return, in the form of tourist receipts, for its spending. But this expenditure (like so much of the tourist activity that it encouraged) was London-centred: national theatre and opera companies turned out to be a service for Londoners first, with the rest of the country a distant second. It was unfortunate for everyone that the Arts Council became aware of this, and decided to put it right, at just the moment that the government was deciding that spending on the arts would have to suffer along with everything else in the struggle to keep down spending. Lobbyists set out to convince the government that saving a few million pounds in this way would be more trouble than it was worth—it seemed unlikely that Benvenuto Cellini and Sir Peter Hall of the National Theatre had been uniquely ill-treated by their patrons, but the plangency of their protests had a great deal in common. The government also found itself being pressed to help with another revival of the British film industry, based this time in part on the increasingly sophisticated techniques developed in television and in part on a willingness to treat the twentieth century (or at least significant moments in twentieth-century Britain) as history to be interpreted through the camera; and the government responded to this pressure in a way that suggested it did not possess the subtlety and insight needed for encouraging artistic development.

The government's supporters would reply that anyone who wants to scythe through thick undergrowth had to lay subtlety aside or get nothing done, and that the first need was to catch up with the work of clearing the ground that had been neglected for forty years. The Labour party had so many vested interests to defend in the trade unions, among people who worked for local or central government, and in all the other institutions which had passed unexamined for decades, that it seemed simply to ask what changes were going on and then say they ought to be stopped. The Alliance gave the impression that it might be too kind to destroy institutions that ought to be replaced and might be too removed from the practical world to devise anything to take their place. This left Thatcherism in uneasy possession of the field, as a partial acceptance of the idea that the country would run better if it got rid of some self-made obstacles to progress.

The direction indicated for change might not have pleased people from the years before 1914 who saw what was going on, but at least the confidence in progress implicit in Thatcherism would have been more familiar to them than the over-confidence alternating with a gloomy acceptance of decline which had been the hallmark of British attitudes for quarter of a century. The new mood might be philistine, and it might ignore the desire to help the weak at the expense of the strong, but it could not be dismissed or consigned to a backwater. It was better suited for clearing things away than for building them up, but the British had for some time been trying to build things up without clearing away what was useless. Rebuilding after the clearance might be a task for someone else: the removal of rubbish in the early 1980s was a good preparation for a fresh start.

BIBLIOGRAPHY

GENERAL

THERE is no shortage of reading matter for the twentieth century, though of course its accuracy and its readability vary quite a lot. The government is the leading source of primary material: it publishes Blue Books and White Papers in a steady stream that grows wider and wider as the State undertakes responsibility in an increasing number of areas of life. It has also produced official histories of the two world wars, and it has published documents on foreign policy which, while primarily related to the outbreak of the two world wars, will provide a reasonably complete account of British policy from 1898 to 1939 when the work is finished. Government documents, such as Cabinet minutes and departmental papers, are now open for investigation down to 1937 and while this may be of little immediate interest to anybody except the specialist, the fact that the specialists can read these documents will safeguard everybody else and make sure that any gaps in the published government record are filled up.

The parliamentary debates (*Hansard*) are fuller and even more accurate in the twentieth century than they had been previously. In the nineteenth century the reports in *The Times* were often better than in *Hansard*, and were at times the basis for *Hansard*; *The Times* continues to be a useful source, but it is no longer so commanding an authority—it is fashionable to denounce *The Times* for managing the news during the 1930s, but while this criticism is justified we ought to remember that the reason we know so much about it is that *The Times* explained what it had done in its own *History of The Times*. Other newspapers have managed the news, but a confessional history of the *Daily Express* or of the *Daily Mirror* has not yet appeared. Even the *Daily Telegraph* (firmly right wing) and the *Guardian* (moderately left wing) have not opened up their records for investigation, though these are the two daily papers that rank next to *The Times* in usefulness. Garvin's *Observer* was a newspaper of very considerable importance; with the decline in importance of the monthly and quarterly magazines, which played so large a role in the shaping of nineteenth-century opinion, it has become customary to assume that their importance has passed to the serious weekly magazines—*The Economist*, the *Spectator*, and the *New Statesman*—but it seems possible that part of their general influence moved to the heavy Sunday newspapers, the *Observer* and the *Sunday Times*. Finding out what influences the bulk of the population has never been easy; undoubtedly an even larger proportion of the population spends an even larger proportion of its time watching television at the present day than spent its time listening to sermons and reading devotional literature at the beginning of the century, but assessing the effects of this change is very difficult. And finding historical records of this sort of influence is also difficult.

There are some useful general histories which cover the period, or part of the period. C. L. Mowat's *Britain Between the Wars* (1955) is perhaps the best of these; it covers only half of the sixty years under discussion, but within its chosen time-span it is very thorough, very well informed and very good value for money. A. J. P. Taylor's *English History 1914–1945* (1965) covers a somewhat longer period, in a lively and stimulating way; however, it is much less reliable (Henry Pelling's review in *Past and Present*, April 1966, lists an impressive array of errors). The second edition will be a very important contribution to the history of the period. W. N. Medlicott's *Contemporary England 1914–1964* (1967) leans somewhat too heavily to the diplomatic side, and in particular devotes a great deal of space to the diplomacy of the 1930s. A. J. Seaman's *Post-Victorian Britain 1902–1951* (1966) is a good book on a rather less ambitious scale, with a heavy concentration on the Second World War—the account given is enlightening but is out of proportion with the rest of the book. A. F. Havighurst's *Twentieth-Century Britain* (1964) is a good clear account which is well worth reading.

On a much larger scale are the works of reference by private authors. *The Annual Register of World Events* has a long opening section on British affairs—this used to be a sketch of parliamentary events but its scope has broadened, and it is supplemented by an economics section—for some periods, such as the 1950s, the section on British affairs was dominated by the personal eccentricities of the author but the economics section continued to give useful introductory facts about the state of the economy. For economics at a more scholarly level, the *Abstract of British Historical Statistics* (1962) by B. R. Mitchell and Phyllis Deane covers most figures down to 1938, and after that figures can be hunted down in the Annual Abstract of Statistics. Biographical information for people safely dead can be found in the *Dictionary of National Biography*, which now goes down to 1950. For the others, there is *Who's Who* (and also *Who Was Who*, though this does not add very much to the *Dictionary of National Biography*). For political events and personalities, D. E. Butler and Anne Sloman, *British Political Facts 1900–1977* (1978) is much the most convenient single source; it also contains some social statistics and some economics, though for economic reference on a small scale *The Times*'s *The British Economy: Key Statistics 1900–1966*, prepared by the London and Cambridge Economic Service, may be even more useful.

Some long-range interpretations of politics in this century may be mentioned. R. T. McKenzie's *British Political Parties* was very well received when it first appeared in 1955; it argued that the Labour party and the Conservative party were really very similar in their real—as opposed to their formal—structure, an argument which fitted the mood of British politics at the time rather well. More recently Samuel H. Beer's *Modern British Politics* (1965) has tried with some success to show that the formal differences in the two parties correspond to some real differences of attitudes although these differences of attitude are not quite the differences that are made most apparent by the party programmes. W. G. Runciman's *Relative Deprivation and Social Justice* (1966) is a curious mixture of social survey, ethical speculation, and attempt to interpret twentieth-century history; it probably deserves attention.

For the nineteenth century biographies are one of the most useful sources because of the practice of publishing masses of letters and other papers. When completed the *Life of Winston S. Churchill* (two volumes by Randolph Churchill and four volumes by Martin Gilbert bring it to 1941 so far) will be a pre-eminent example of this. Meanwhile Henry Pelling's *Winston Churchill* (1974) is a good one-volume life, at least up to 1951. But since the days of Spender and Asquith's *Asquith* (see below, p. 466), the fashion for full-dress biographies has declined; or perhaps it is simply that not enough time has yet elapsed. Disraeli had been dead for thirty years before the first volume of the Monypenny and Buckle *Life* appeared; it was after an almost precisely similar interval that Robert Blake's distinguished *The Unknown Prime Minister: Andrew Bonar Law* appeared in 1955 and the same gap in time separates the death of Balfour from the appearance of Kenneth Young's rather less distinguished *Arthur James Balfour* in 1963. There is a very good *Ramsay MacDonald* (1977) by David Marquand. Lives of Lloyd George are noted in the comments on chapter 1 and those of Baldwin and Chamberlain in the comments on chapters 6 and 7.

One change since Victorian times is that politicians are much more ready to write and publish their memoirs; to some extent they do it because they are no longer men of independent means and they believe that every man has a book in him that the public will buy, to some extent they do it in self-defence from their colleagues who have told their own story, and to some extent they do it because people are no longer as reticent about their private motives or about the conduct of government as they used to be. Asquith's *Memories and Reflections* (1928) were pretty clearly written for money by a man who did not really want to take the public into his confidence; Churchill and Lloyd George (chapter 3 and chapter 8) were not sorry to have the money but they did also want to vindicate their policies and took some pleasure in denouncing their opponents. Lord Avon wrote to defend his policies (chapters 7 and 10). Macmillan has written his *Memoirs* at great length: six volumes, published 1966 to 1973. It is hard to understand why Attlee wrote *As it Happened* (1954); Dalton wrote three volumes of *Memoirs* (1953–1962) out of an inability to restrain himself, and they are accordingly amusing and informative. L. S. Amery's *My Political Life* (1953) is designed to argue the case for his policies; it is useful but should be handled with care.

There are some impressive biographies of people apart from Prime Ministers. Alan Bullock, *Ernest Bevin*, vol. i (1960) is important for the years 1920–40—the second volume (1966) is too lengthy to maintain the same high standard. Roy Harrod's *Life of John Maynard Keynes* (1951) is an effective eulogy but may be superseded by R. Skidelsky's *Keynes* (vol. i, 1983). Nicholson's *George V* (1952) is informative and pleasant to read; the official lives of Edward VII (P. Magnus, 1964) and George VI (J. Wheeler-Bennett, 1958) are less distinguished, but they contain a good deal of interesting information from the royal archives.

Economic affairs were not really accepted as part of history or politics at the beginning of the century, and analysis tended to be specialized and dull; some life was put into it by the Tariff Reform arguments, and later by the writings of Keynes (*Economic Consequences of the Peace* in 1919; *Economic Consequences of Mr. Churchill* in 1925) but there are not many easy contemporary books about economic events for the pre-1945 period of the type given in the lists for the last four chapters of this book. There are some useful economic histories: Sir John Clapham's *Economic History of Modern Britain* (1952) provides a good solid account of events in the earlier decades of the century, and there is a certain amount in W. Ashworth, *Economic History of England 1870–1939* (1960). There is rather more in S. Pollard's *Development of the British Economy 1914–1950* (1962), and there is a commentary on some developments in A. Y. Youngson's *The British Economy 1920–1957* (1960), though this book assumes a fair grasp of the economic situation in its readers. A. T. Peacock and J. Wiseman, *The Growth of Public Expenditure in the United Kingdom* (1961), is full of useful information about government spending, though there is a point in the text where the authors seem almost to contradict the evidence of one of their charts, which shows that government spending at constant prices per head of population has risen steadily and consistently since well before the beginning of the period. M. Bowley's *Housing and the State 1919–1944* (1945) is a very useful study of one of the most important sectors of the economy. A set of three books by B. S. Rowntree serves to show that things do get better: over the course of half a century he surveyed the condition of the working class and the poor in York on three different occasions, and published *Poverty* (1901), *Poverty and Progress* (1941), and *Poverty and the Welfare State* (1951)—each of them of course appeared a few years after the survey had been carried out. For the sake of completeness Rowntree's *English Life and Leisure* (1951) may be added to the list.

Commonwealth affairs in the twentieth century have not yet benefited from the flow of scholarly study that has been devoted to such aspects as imperial expansion in Africa at the end of the nineteenth century. However there are some very substantial contemporary works: W. K. Hancock, *Survey of British Commonwealth Affairs 1918–1939* (1937, 1942) and N. Mansergh, *Survey of British Commonwealth Affairs; war-time co-operation and post-war change* (1952, 1958). K. C. Wheare's *The Constitutional Structure of the Commonwealth* (1960) almost inevitably is heavily involved in legal forms; A. P. Thornton's *The Imperial Idea and its Enemies* (1959) is a useful corrective to this sort of approach, because it is concerned with power and thoughts about power to the exclusion of forms and precedents. Patrick Gordon Walker's *The Commonwealth* (1960) has the advantages and disadvantages of being written by an ex-Secretary of State for Commonwealth Relations: he knows about the political activities of the Commonwealth but is inevitably a little inclined to overstate their importance. A colleague of his in the Attlee government, John Strachey, accepted the facts of the case rather better in *The End of Empire* (1959), a book which is heavily influenced by the arguments of J. A. Hobson in *Imperialism* (1902), where it is argued that imperial expansion was not only profitable but also of considerable importance to the whole British economy. This view no longer commands much support. There are some interesting biographies: W. K. Hancock's *Smuts* (1962–8) is a well-controlled account of a complicated but well-controlled man; the life of Mackenzie King is appearing in a much more confusing way, under the names of Macgregor Dawson, Blair Neatby, J. W. Pickersgill and D. F. Forster (1959–). M. Brecher's *Nehru* (1962) is written very close to the events it describes, but is still useful.

CHAPTER 1

Two substantial books for general information are R. C. K. Ensor, *England 1870–1914* (1936) and E. Halévy, *The Rule of Democracy*, pt. 1 (1934). More recently P. Rowland, *The Last Liberal Governments*, pt. 1 (1968), covers a wide range of material in a traditional way. C. Cross has a brief sketch, *The Liberals in Power* (1963), but it does not provide very full information. S. Nowell Smith, *Edwardian England 1901–1914* (1964), is a collection of essays by different authors on politics and social life—some of them very useful.

There are biographies of the leading statesmen: J. A. Spender's *Life of Campbell-Bannerman* (1923), and Spender and C. Asquith's life of *Asquith* (1932) are somewhat ponderous and occasionally carry too far the biographer's natural tendency not to exhibit his subject's weaknesses. Spender was a little more relaxed in his autobiography, *Life Literature and Politics* (1927). There is a more modern *Asquith* by R. Jenkins (1964), which is very good for 1906–16; after that it tails off a little. His daughter, Lady Asquith, has reminiscences of the pre-1914 Liberals in *Winston Churchill as I Knew him* (1965). There is a fairly good official life, R. S. Churchill, *Winston S. Churchill, The Young Statesman 1900–1914* (1967) with some very useful companion volumes of documents. The long-awaited last volumes of *Joseph Chamberlain*, by J. Amery, appeared in 1969. There is a rather thin life of *Lloyd George* (1951) by Tom Jones and bigger ones by Frank Owen, *Tempestuous Journey* (1954), and by P. Rowland (1976). Kenneth Young's *Arthur Balfour* (1963) never faces the possibility that some of Balfour's failures were his own fault. W. Stewart's *Keir Hardie* (1921) is probably still the best account. The monarch: P. Magnus, *Edward VII* (1964), suggests that Edward was not really in touch with politics; H. Nicolson's *George V* (1952) is full of useful material on the crises of the reign, is well written and not too courtier-like.

On individual subjects, G. W. Monger, *The End of Isolation* (1963), discusses British foreign policy from 1900 to 1907; B. Semmel's *Imperialism and Social Reform* (1960) is a fairly firmly anti-imperialist account of social reformers like Chamberlain and Milner; A. L. Levine, *Industrial Retardation in Britain 1880–1914* (1967) indicates some economic problems; A. M. Gollin in *'The Observer' and J. L. Garvin* (1958) gets a long way into the mechanics of running a political party; and Austen Chamberlain's *Politics from the Inside* (1936) is also very informative. For a wider perspective, M. Bruce, *The Coming of the Welfare State* (1961), concentrates on the years before 1914 as the central point in his story; and Beatrice Webb gives details of what went on in the Poor Law Commission in *Our Partnership* (1948). O. Sitwell in the earlier volumes of *Left Hand, Right Hand* and V. Sackville West in *The Edwardians* (1936) give accounts of the upper layers of society.

CHAPTER 2

Historians do not agree whether this was a period of repose and tranquillity or one of strife and incipient anarchy. For the first view see R. Jenkins, *Asquith* (1964) or any of a number of memoirs, such as C. Hassall's *Rupert Brooke* (1964); on the other side there is E. Halévy's *The Rule of Democracy*, pt. 2 (1952) or, for a more extreme version, G. Dangerfield's seductively written *Strange Death of Liberal England* (1936). Rowland's *The Last Liberal Governments*, pt. 2 (1971), is more agnostic. There are biographies of the Conservative leaders: R. Blake, *The Unknown Prime Minister* (1952) is a full-length life of Bonar Law; A. M. Gollin, *Proconsul in Politics* (1964), studies Milner in English politics during the Lords' crisis, the Ulster crisis, and the war. The suffragists, in Dame Millicent Fawcett's *Women's Suffrage* (1912) and *The Women's Victory* (1920), and the suffragettes, in Dame Christabel Pankhurst's *Unshackled* (1959), left accounts of the struggle. A. Rosen's *Rise Up, Women* (1974) is a good modern account. M. Hyde, *Carson* (1953), and F. S. L. Lyons, *John Dillon* (1971), present the two men who came closest to greatness in the pre-1914 Irish struggle.

CHAPTER 3

The military side of the war was covered in several dozen volumes of *Official Histories of the War*, published steadily between 1920 and 1948. The work of the government in domestic policy when faced with war-time problems was covered in less overwhelming detail in a series of volumes produced by the Carnegie Endowment. On a more manageable scale, C. R. F. Cruttwell's *History of the Great War* (1936) is a good one-volume account of military operations, told from a standpoint somewhat critical of British commanders and their strategy. The politicians' attitude to strategy is discussed in G. Guinn's *Politics and Strategy* (1966). Liddell Hart's *The Real War* (1930) is more determinedly critical of everybody. Lloyd George's six volumes of *War Memoirs* (1933–6) also denounce the generals, though he was at pains to expose the follies of his civilian colleagues as well, dealing especially brusquely with those of the Asquithian Liberals. It is said that Churchill wrote five volumes of autobiography and the publisher made him disguise it as a history of the World War, *The World Crisis* (1923–9), but it is not much more egocentric than the other memoirs. Haig has been defended by Duff Cooper (1936) and by John Terraine (1963), though without complete success; Robertson by himself (1926) and by Victor Bonham-Carter (1963), again not completely successfully. Arthur Marwick's *The Deluge* (1965) is a very useful account of economic developments and social change inside England while the war was on. David Mitchell's *Women on the Warpath* (1967) is journalistic and sometimes clumsy but it does cover one aspect of change quite interestingly. The political intrigues of the period are covered in Beaverbrook's *Politicians and the War* (1928) and *Men and Power* (1956), in Addison's *Four and a Half Years* (1934), and in A. M. Gollin's study of Milner, *Proconsul in Politics* (1964), as well as in the Churchill and Lloyd George memoirs already noticed. Trevor Wilson's *Downfall of the Liberal Party* (1966) makes more effort than any of these books to see the political struggle in the government from Asquith's point of view.

CHAPTER 4

When Lloyd George wrote *The Truth about the Peace Treaties* in 1938, he knew that if he was to defend his role he had to fight the Keynesian denunciation of 'the Carthaginian Peace' in *The Economic Consequences of the Peace* (1919); Lloyd George did not succeed, and lesser debaters have done no better. Harold Nicolson's *Peacemaking 1919* (1933) gives a good account of Versailles; Harold Nelson's *Land and Power* (1963) gives a good account of British policy before and during the negotiations. R. B. McCallum's *Public Opinion and the Last Peace* (1944) is a helpful reminder of the limits on Lloyd George's freedom of action. A. C. Pigou's *Aspects of British Economic History 1918–25* (1947) shows some signs of the fact that it was written to indicate possible hazards in the economic situation immediately after the Second World War. Blake's *Bonar Law* is again useful; Beaverbrook's *The Decline and Fall of Lloyd George* (1963) concentrates almost exclusively on the quarrels within the Cabinet, without really explaining why the Conservative back-benchers were becoming hostile—S. Salvidge's *Salvidge of Liverpool* (1934) and Gerald Macmillan's *Honours for Sale* (1954) indicate some of the reasons for discontent—nor pointing out that the Labour party was gaining ground; books like G. D. H. Cole's *History of the Labour Party since 1914* (1947) and Catherine Ann Cline's sometimes inaccurate *Recruits to Labour* (1963) present some of this side of the case, and more can be found from M. Cowling's *The Impact of Labour 1920–1924* (1971), concentrating on political leaders, and from R. McKibbin, *The Evolution of the Labour Party 1910–1924* (1974), on the party machine. N. Mansergh's *The Irish Question 1840–1921* (1965) is perhaps a little too much of a commentary without facts; E. Strauss's *Irish Nationalism and British Democracy* (1951) too inclined to stress economic factors. D. Gwynn's *History of Partition* (1950) is a fairly reasonable statement of what went on. Lord Birkenhead's *F.E.* (1965) shows almost too much filial piety, but deals with a man of great influence in the period. Two useful books on foreign policy begin at about the end of the war: F. S. Northedge, *The Troubled Giant* (1966) goes to 1939; W. N. Medlicott's *British Foreign Policy since Versailles* (1968) is mainly about the inter-war years but has some extra chapters tacked on.

CHAPTER 5

This is a period curiously empty of satisfactory biographies or autobiographies —Harold Nicolson's *George V* (1952) is of course an exception, and it is very helpful for the Labour government, but G. M. Young's *Stanley Baldwin* (1952), an official life, contains very little material and attacked the subject of the biography so vehemently that it provoked a defence, A. W. Baldwin's

My Father: the True Story (1955), which makes some good points about the 1930s; Marquand's *MacDonald* (1977) is good; M. A. Hamilton's *Arthur Henderson* (1938) is useful but perhaps makes Henderson a little too good to be true; Snowden's *Autobiography* (1934) is not as informative as its often bitter tone might lead one to expect, and Colin Cross's recent life of him (1967) suffers because Mrs. Snowden destroyed her husband's papers; J. R. Clynes's *Memoirs* (1937) reveal a lot about the attitudes of a Labour leader, but not so much about the events in which he took part. Beatrice Webb's *Diaries 1924–32* (1956) find fault with everyone except Sidney. The issues of the 1920s died with the 1920s—in sharp contrast to those of the 1930s, which lived on and produced a mass of more or less polemical memoirs. R. W. Lyman's *The First Labour Government* (1957) is a neat and thorough study; R. K. Middlemas gives a not-too-sympathetic account of one base of Labour strength in *The Clydesiders* (1965) which is distinctly more coherent than the much more friendly account of the I.L.P. in E. G. Dowse's *Left in the Centre* (1966). The odd events at the end of the Labour government's tenure of office are made rather clearer by *The Zinovieff Letter* (1967) by L. Chester, S. Fay, and H. Young. Almost all of the section on the B.B.C. is drawn from A. Briggs, *The Birth of Broadcasting* (1961). W. H. Crook's *The General Strike* (1931) approaches the topic from the industrial relations point of view; Julian Symons's *The General Strike* (1957) gives more of the social history, though it does not go back as far in time.

CHAPTER 6

The rising importance of Neville Chamberlain makes Keith Feiling's *Life* (1946) very useful for this period—it is one of the better biographies of the century, although sometimes written in a bizarre style. But the years of the Baldwin government have not been well served, which may reflect the fact that not much happened. Sir Charles Petrie's *Austen Chamberlain* (1940) is sometimes useful. The Labour government was a more exciting period, and has been written about more fully: R. Skidelsky's *Politicians and the Slump* (1967) is critical of the government, and leans heavily towards the view that an alternative policy could have been followed without too much difficulty. Sir Oswald Mosley has published his *My Life* (1968), which understandably takes the same approach. R. Bassett's *1931* (1958) is a determined defence of MacDonald and his policies which analyses the various accounts of the weeks of the change from a Labour to a National government, and finds discrepancies in almost everyone's story. On the other hand, his suggestions that MacDonald was really trying to act in the best interests of the Labour party seem a little strained. R. Graves and A. Hodges, *The Long Week-end, 1918–1939* (1940) is one of the best—though not the most serious—accounts of social life. Duff Cooper's *Old Men Forget* (1953), though useful mainly for the 1930s, begins to become informative during this period. On the Labour side Hugh Dalton's *Memoirs*, vol. i to 1931 (1953), is informative and irrepressibly cheerful about the 1929–31 government. The Macmillan report and the May report deserve some attention: they are almost the only reports to have had a direct effect on political and economic events.

CHAPTER 7

The 1930s are one of the most discussed and disputed decades of the century, with supporters of a firm foreign policy, or of Keynesian economics, or enemies of a Conservative government using the events to prove their respective cases, and being resisted in their efforts. The opening chapters of Churchill's *The Second World War* (1948), or J. Wheeler-Bennett's *Munich* (a new edition came out in 1966) or L. B. Namier's *Diplomatic Prelude* (1947) put the case against appeasement in terms which are a little more vehement than a professional historian might be expected to use. The attack is supported by Lord Avon (Anthony Eden) in *Facing the Dictators* (1962) and in Dalton's second volume of *Memoirs* (1957). M. Cowling read every private paper available for *The Impact of Hitler* (1975); Feiling's *Chamberlain* has not been replaced and is still useful; Halifax has been defended by Birkenhead (1967); and Hoare published a good self-justification, *Nine Troubled Years* (1954). Tom Jones's *A Diary with Letters* (1951) was written from an appeaser's point of view, but does not help his side's case. On the other hand, R. Bassett's *Democracy and Foreign Policy* (1952) is a good defence of the National government's policy in Manchuria.

Attitudes to the Spanish Civil War were analysed in a less committed, and less exciting, way by K. W. Watkins in *Britain Divided* (1963). There is an interesting contemporary study of one manifestation of feeling, *The Peace Ballot* (1935) by A. Livingston and M. Johnson. A more deeply committed book about an ugly part of the 1930s, George Orwell's *The Road to Wigan Pier* (1937) is a shout of protest about unemployment without any way out; H. W. Richardson argued, in *Economic Recovery in Britain 1932–1939* (1967), that things were not so bad during the slump, but he did seem to be rather easily satisfied. M. Muggeridge's *The Thirties* (1940) is an impressionistic book by a comedian who would like to write tragedy if only he had a point of view—it is the source-book for some of the jokes in A. J. P. Taylor's *English History*. Colin Cross's *The Fascists in Britain* (1961) probably tells us as much as anyone needs to know about this subject. Harold Nicolson's *Diary*, vol. i (1966), is a great achievement in self-revelation, and is also a useful historical source. Much the same can be said of Sir Henry Channon's diary, *Chips* (1967), and it is even more entertaining.

CHAPTER 8

Writing about military events is dominated by the Official History of the War, military series, edited by Sir James Butler. The series is not yet complete, but only a few volumes remain to be published. A variety of different topics are handled, in one to four volumes; no doubt more will be known when the War Cabinet papers are released, but the series is informative and not uncritical of the British performance. Churchill's *Second World War* (6 vols., 1948–54) is also very helpful, and is much easier to read—Churchill made considerable use of government papers, though his account is naturally Churchill-centred. Chester Wilmot's *The Struggle for Europe* (1959) is a good example of the 'how we won the war and lost the peace' school—the phrase is printed on the cover of this edition. Lord Alanbrooke's diaries were edited by Arthur Bryant into *The Turn of the Tide* (1957) and *Triumph in the West* (1959)—it has been suggested that he wrote his diary late at night, when he was too exhausted to see the difficulties of the day in perspective. C. Barnett's *The Desert Generals* (1960) argues that Churchill and Montgomery, the popular heroes, did less than was believed and that Wavell and Auchinleck were underestimated. J. F. C. Fuller's *The Second World War* (1949) is an attempt to repeat Liddell Hart by arguing that Germany could have been crushed with a lot less effort by the application of strategic principles rather than 'ironmongery', typified by the bombing offensive. The official history of the bombing offensive by C. Webster and N. Frankland (1961) certainly seems to be going rather further than the evidence would allow when it claims that the bombing offensive was 'decisive', which presumably means that Germany would have defeated America and Russia if it had not been for Bomber Command. There are also extensive American military histories, which show that the war against Germany was conducted on fairly amicable terms of equality with England.

CHAPTER 9

The Official History of the War (civil series, edited by Sir Keith Hancock) has volumes on a great variety of topics, but it is a bit harder to see them as a unity than the military series volumes. Churchill was not as interested in domestic developments as in strategy and foreign policy, so his book is not very useful. *John Anderson* (1962) by J. Wheeler-Bennett is quite a useful book about the man who was at the centre of domestic planning, but inevitably it can give only limited space to the war years in a one-volume biography and it does not go into much detail. The *Beveridge Report* (1942) is an important summary of social thought and proposals. N. Longmate, *How We Lived Then* (1971), is a lively account of life at home, Paul Addison, *The Road to 1945* (1975), is useful on political developments, and Angus Calder's *The People's War* (1969) puts a staunch Socialist case well. A. Bullock's *Ernest Bevin*, vol. ii (1966) covers the work of the Minister of Labour in even more detail than the subject will stand. Sentiment around the end of the war can be explored in the novels of J. B. Priestley, though they do lean rather further in an optimistic, egalitarian, and left-wing direction than some people would have liked. Evelyn Waugh's three-volume novel about Guy Crouchback has been praised, but it is written from a much more anti-Russian point of view than was common during the war; once the war was over, of course, sentiment turned against Russia as quickly as it turned against France in 1918. The general election of 1945 was the first to be described in a Nuffield election study, by R. B. McCallum and A. Readman (1946). Studies on similar lines have been written about all subsequent elections, and are useful guides to follow.

CHAPTER 10

Two very good histories of the Labour government, *Labour in Power* by Kenneth Morgan and *The Labour Government* by Henry Pelling, came out in 1984. Biographies of Attlee by Kenneth Harris (1982), of Bevin by Alan Bullock (vol. iii, 1983), of Dalton by Ben Pimlott (1985), and of Morrison by B. Donoughue and G. W. Jones (1973) leave Cripps as the only minister from the inner circle without a biography. The last volume of Dalton's memoirs (1962) and the autobiography of Herbert Morrison are helpful; Attlee's are not. G. D. N. Worswick and P. H. Ady, *The British Economy 1945-50* (1952) is a good account written close to the event; J. C. R. Dow's *The Management of the British Economy 1945-60* (1964) is probably a bit more accurate, but it is also distinctly more technical. M. Sissons and P. French, ed., *The Age of Austerity* (1961) is a collection of essays on various aspects of life under the Labour government; it is very useful for giving the atmosphere of the period, though it is by its nature not directly concerned to give facts. J. Marlowe's *The Seat of Pilate* (1959) explains how the British government found itself in so unpleasant a position in Palestine by the end of the mandate; M. Edwardes, *The Last Years of British India* (1963) provides the background for independence and partition, and P. Moon, *Divide and Quit* (1961) is a good account of the difficulties and disasters of partition at one of the crisis-points. The process of nationalization has been studied by W. A. Robson in *Nationalised Industry and Public Ownership* (1960), which is moderately favourable, and by R. Kelf-Cohen in *Nationalisation in Britain* (1958), which is rather more immoderately unfavourable; both books are naturally concerned with future policy but they do discuss the initial legislation. The historical background for the programme of nationalization can be studied in E. Barry O'Brien, *Nationalisation in British Politics* (1966).

CHAPTER 11

The early 1950s have been reasonably well covered: a few scholarly studies of the period have appeared, such as Joan Mitchell's *Crisis in Britain 1951* (1963), a mildly pro-Bevanite account of the economic problems of the Labour government during its last year of office; and G. D. N. Worswick and P. H. Ady have produced a sequel to their volumes on the 1940s, *The British Economy 1951-1959* (1962)—the authors lean a little to the Labour side, so that the more critical attitude taken to the government in the 1950s may reflect an opinion held on grounds that are not confined to economics. A. Shonfield's *British Economic Policy Since the War* (1958) is really more directly concerned with the early 1950s than with the Labour government. When Leslie Hunter's *The Road to Brighton Pier* was published in 1959 it attracted a considerable amount of attention because it was, by the standards of the time, frank to the point of indiscretion about the internal problems of the Labour party in opposition during the period of conflict over the personality and policy of Aneurin Bevan. Frankness has become more common: Anthony Nutting's *No End of a Lesson* (1967) and Hugh Thomas's *The Suez Affair* (1967) present the facts of the Suez story fully and straightforwardly; Lord Avon's *Full Circle* (1960) is understandably less informative about Suez, but it does contain a good deal that is useful about his work as Churchill's Foreign Secretary. Lord Moran's *Churchill: the Struggle for Survival* (1966) is very interesting about Churchill's personality, and is informative about the period when Churchill was incapacitated by his stroke.

Lord Woolton's *Memoirs* (1959), which may be consulted for chapter 9 as well, is informative about the position of a slightly confused minister, who was more in touch with public opinion than with his colleagues—much the same can be said about Lord Hill's *Both Sides of the Hill* (1964), though Woolton never felt quite as humble as Hill about sitting at the same Cabinet table as all these upper-class ministers of the Churchill government.

CHAPTER 12

It is difficult to find scholarly books dealing with a period as recent as this. As public life becomes slightly more open, well-informed if sometimes journalistic books are published which supplement information from the press, parliamentary debates, and Blue Books. Nora Beloff's *The General Says No* (1963) is a useful study of the Common Market negotiations, marred by a tendency to plunge off the deep end and compare the Labour party with the Nazi party or suggest that de Gaulle is insane. Anthony Sampson's more urbane *Anatomy of Britain* (1962), an amiable eulogy of all the important people he could interview, and his *Macmillan: a Study in Ambiguity* (1967) present rather a bland picture of the world in which almost everything is for the best; Lord Kilmuir's *Memoirs* (1964) show that things were not always as smooth in the Cabinet, F. W. Paish's *Studies in an Inflationary Economy* (1963) remind the reader about the inconveniences that accompanied a policy of full employment (without necessarily proving the author's case for an increase in unemployment), and Sir Roy Welensky's *Welensky's 4000 Days* (1965) is a sharp reminder of just how difficult the problem of the Central African Federation had become and how nearly it slipped over into armed conflict well before the unilateral declaration of independence in 1965. A large number of books urging reforms, such as Michael Shanks's *The Stagnant Society* (1961) and Samuel Brittan's *The Treasury under the Tories* (1964) do contain a fair amount of information which is very useful after it has been disentangled from the surrounding exhortations.

CHAPTER 13

The spreading flood of paperback books made it easier and easier to get some idea of what was going on in England, though whether it was the right idea was harder to tell. Clive Irving's *Scandal '63* (1963), probably the best study of the Profumo affair, was one good example of this; Randolph Churchill's *The Struggle for the Tory Leadership* (1964) was another, with useful chunks of information clearly provided by Harold Macmillan after his retirement—the book was reviewed in a hostile manner by Ian Macleod in *The Spectator* for 17 January 1964. There is a not particularly distinguished life of the winner, John Dickie's *The Reluctant Commoner* (1964). The 1964 election has been covered not only in the normal Nuffield study (D. E. Butler and A. S. King, 1965), but also in A. Howard and R. West, *The Making of the Prime Minister* (1965). One important aspect of the campaign is covered in Paul Foot's *Immigration and Race in British Politics* (1965). The problems of the

Labour government in economic affairs have been described in Henry Brandon's *In the Red* (1966)—an example of the difficulties of publishing instant history, because the book appeared at a time when the problems seemed to have been solved and took an altogether too optimistic attitude— and in William Davis's *Three Years' Hard Labour* (1968), which brings the story up to the 1967 devaluation. There are books about Harold Wilson: the harshest, and perhaps the most informative, is Paul Foot's *The Politics of Harold Wilson* (1968), though there are other lives like that by Leslie Smith (1965) which provide an outline of the events in his career. George Brown writes well enough to make one wish he had said more in his *In My Way* (1971). And a number of books mentioned in the note on chapter 14 also cover the opening years of the Labour government.

CHAPTER 14

Lovers of political history and political gossip have been delighted by H. Wilson's *The Labour Government 1964–1970* (1971) and the memoirs of his secretary, M. Williams, *Inside No. 10* (1972), and by the subsequent opportunity to compare them with R. H. S. Crossman's informative and self-revealing *Diaries of a Cabinet Minister* (3 vols., 1975–7). For his second spell in office these books are paralleled by Wilson's *Final Term: The Labour Government 1974–6* (1979), by Joe Haines, *The Corridors of Power* (1979), and by Barbara Castle, *The Castle Diaries 1974–6* (1980). In a period of so many elections D. E. Butler covered the election of 1970 with M. Pinto-Duchinsky, the two elections of 1974 with D. Kavanagh, and the 1975 referendum with U. Kitzinger, whose *Diplomacy and Persuasion* (1974) covers the E.E.C. struggle of the early 1970s. Economic policy of successive governments since 1964 is studied with fairly impartial disapproval in M. Stewart, *The Jekyll and Hyde Years* (1977), and *The Labour Government's Economic Record 1964–1970* (1972), edited by W. Beckerman, gives a more detailed account of the first half of that period. The Conservative side is not so well documented; among other things, Heath has been too busy producing other books to write his memoirs, but there is an introductory life of him by M. Laing (1972), and a comparable volume about Thatcher by G. Gardiner (1975), and N. Fisher has some interesting things to say in his *Iain Macleod* (1973) and *The Tory Leadership* (1977). The nationalist crises are too recent for books about them to have been assimilated, but the background can be studied in H. J. Hanham, *Scottish Nationalism* (1969), M. Wallace, *Northern Ireland* (1970), and Alan Butt Philip, *The Welsh Question* (1975).

CHAPTER 15

Some of the political developments of the period have attracted the attention of well-informed journalists. *The Pact* (1978) by Alistair Michie and Simon Hoggart gives a sympathetic account of the period of Liberal–Labour co-operation. *The Battle for the Labour Party* (1981) by D. Kogan and M. Kogan acknowledges the skill with which the left pressed forward in the Labour party but is not otherwise sympathetic. Peter Wilsher's *Strike* (1985) is probably as good a narrative of the coal strike as is available yet. Political scientists have analysed samples of opinion in great detail to trace the changes of the 1970s; perhaps B. Sarlvik and I. Crewe, in *Decade of Dealignment* (1983), have their feet planted more solidly on the ground than David Robertson in *Class and the British Electorate* (1984). Tam Dalyell's *Devolution: The End of Britain* (1977) put the case against devolution with a force that may have helped decide the result. Not many of the biographies of the period are polished and deal with completed careers; Susan Crosland's *Tony Crosland* (1982) is a distinguished and melancholy exception, and John Campbell's *Roy Jenkins* (1984) is useful if uncritical. Joel Barnett's *Inside the Treasury* (1982) is the most informative memoir of the period. The zenith of union influence and its subsequent decline are mapped in Keith Middlemas's *Industry, Unions and Government* (1983). Perspectives change with time: Tom Sheriff's *A Deindustrialised Britain?* (1979) gave the impression that things could hardly go worse than they had under Labour, Alan Townsend's *The Impact of Recession* (1983) suggested that they had gone on getting worse, and Martin Holmes's *The Labour Government 1974–1979* (1985) found a certain amount to say in favour of the Labour government. Jock Bruce-Gardyne gives a rather more favourable account of *Mrs Thatcher's First Administration* (1984).

MAPS, CHARTS AND
TABLES

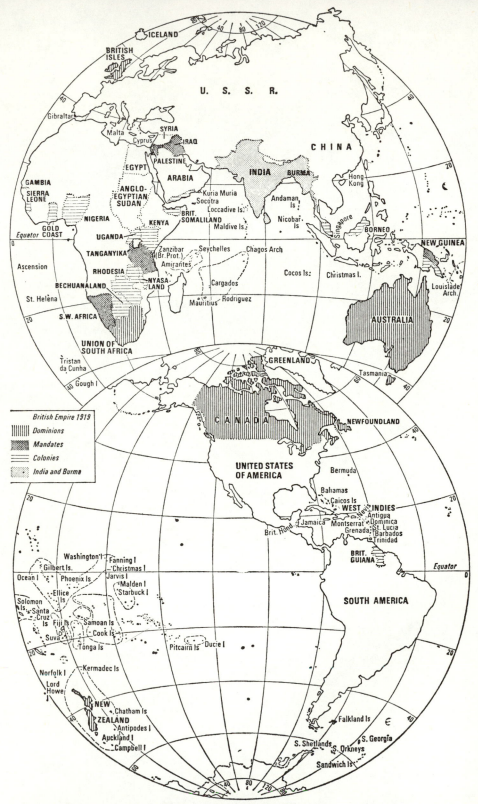

MAP 1. The British Empire 1919

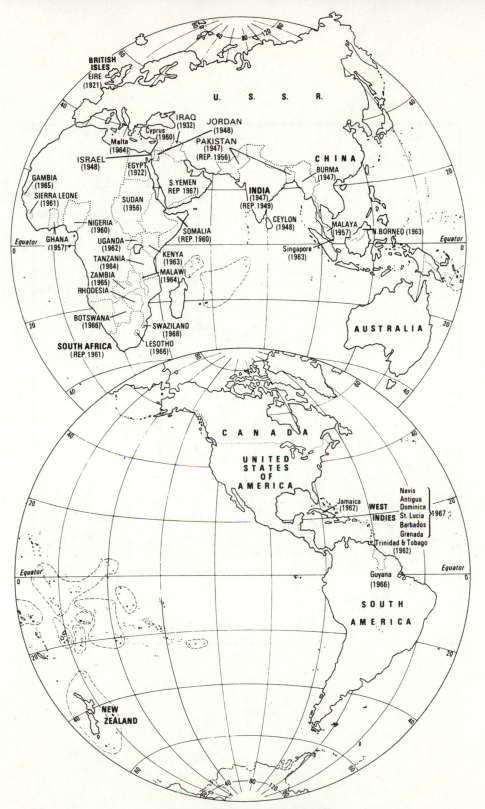

MAP 2. The Commonwealth 1967

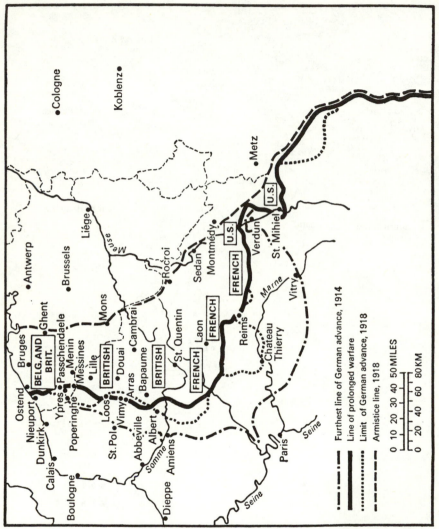

Furthest line of German advance, 1914

Line of prolonged warfare

Limit of German advance, 1918

Armistice line, 1918

0 10 20 30 40 50 MILES
0 20 40 60 80 KM

MAP 3. The War in France and Belgium 1914–1918

Cologne

Koblenz

Metz

Liège

Antwerp

Brussels

Rocroi

Sedan

Montmédy

U.S.

U.S.

FRENCH

Verdun

St. Mihiel

Meuse

Marne

Vitry

Reims

Chateau
Thierry

FRENCH

Laon

St. Quentin

FRENCH

Cambrai

Bapaume

BRITISH

Douai

BRITISH

Arras

Vimy

Loos

St. Pol

Abbeville

Albert

Somme

Amiens

Dieppe

Seine

Seine

Paris

Boulogne

Calais

Dunkirk

Nieuport

Ostend

Bruges

Ghent

BELG. AND
BRIT.

Passchendaele

Menin

Messines

Lille

Ypres

Poperinghe

Mons

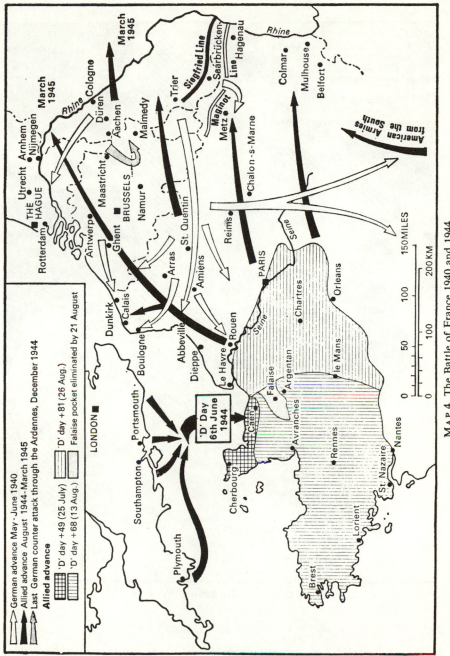

MAP 4. The Battle of France 1940 and 1944

Legend:

Allied advance
⇨ German advance May–June 1940
⬛ Allied advance August 1944–March 1945
⬛ Last German counter attack through the Ardennes, December 1944

▦ 'D' day +49 (25 July)
▤ 'D' day +68 (13 Aug.)
▥ 'D' day +81 (26 Aug.)
▧ Falaise pocket eliminated by 21 August

⬛ LONDON

'D' Day 6th June 1944

American Armies from the South

March 1945

Siegfried Line

Line Hagenau

Maginot Line

150 MILES
200 KM
0   50   100   150
0   100   200

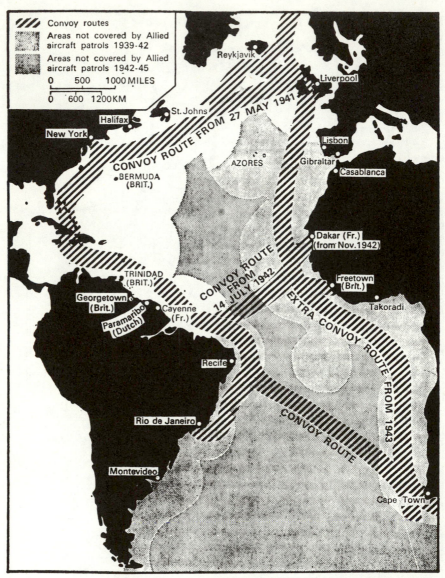

MAP 5. Convoys in the Second World War

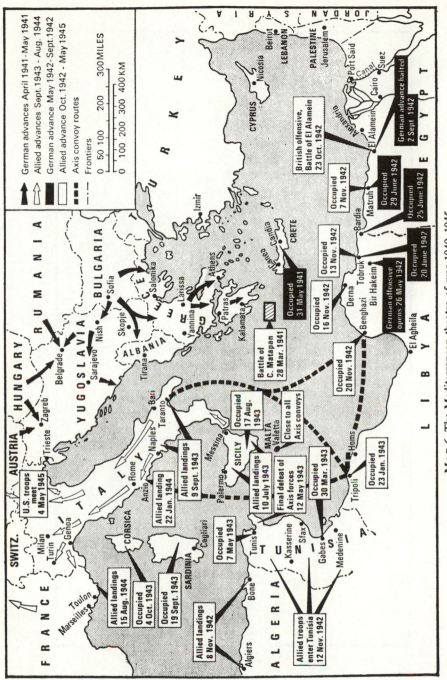

MAP 6. The Mediterranean theatre of war 1940–1945

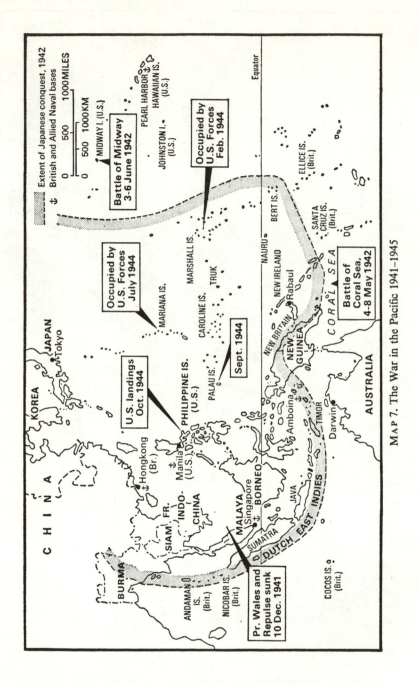

Extent of Japanese conquest, 1942

‡ British and Allied Naval bases

0   500   1000KM
0   500   1000MILES

MIDWAY I. (U.S.)

PEARL HARBOR ‡
HAWAIIAN IS. (U.S.)

JOHNSTON I. (U.S.)

Battle of Midway
3-6 June 1942

Occupied by
U.S. Forces
Feb. 1944

ELLICE IS. (Brit.)

Equator

Occupied by
U.S. Forces
July 1944

MARSHALL IS.

TRUK

CAROLINE IS.

MARIANA IS.

BERT IS.

SANTA CRUZ IS. (Brit.)

NAURU

U.S. landings
Oct. 1944

JAPAN
Tokyo

KOREA

Sept. 1944

PHILIPPINE IS. (U.S.)

PALAU IS.

NEW IRELAND
Rabaul

NEW BRITAIN

Battle of
Coral Sea,
4-8 May 1942

C O R A L   S E A

C H I N A

‡ Hongkong (Br.)

‡ Manila (U.S.)

NEW GUINEA

Amboina

Timor

Darwin

AUSTRALIA

SIAM
FR. INDO-
CHINA

BORNEO

MALAYA
Singapore ‡

JAVA

SUMATRA

D U T C H   E A S T   I N D I E S

BURMA

ANDAMAN IS. (Brit.)

NICOBAR IS. (Brit.)

Pr. Wales and
Repulse sunk
10 Dec. 1941

COCOS IS. (Brit.)

MAP 7. The War in the Pacific 1941–1945

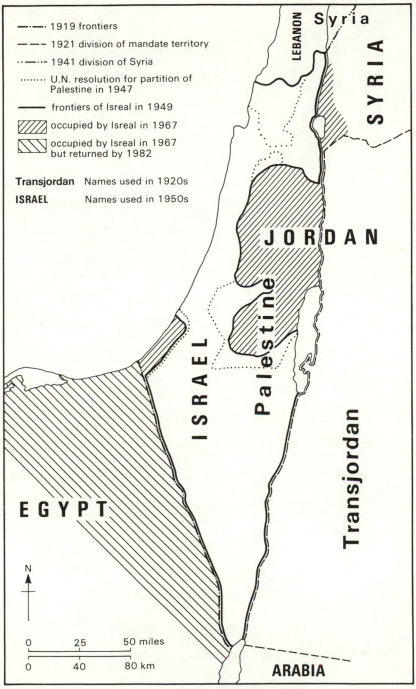

MAP 8. The Palestine Mandate and after

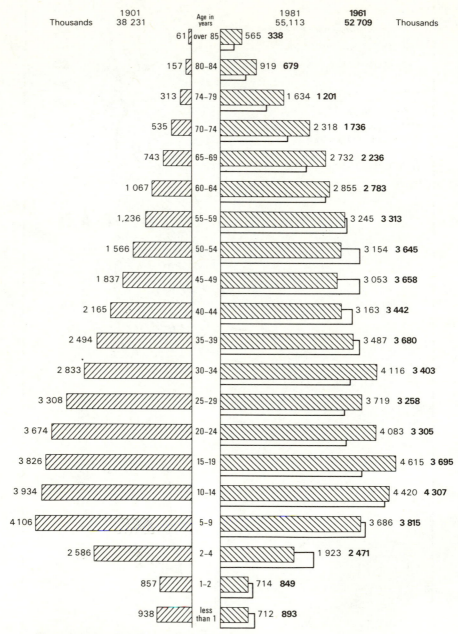

	1901 Thousands 38 231	Age in years	1981 55,113	**1961** **52 709** Thousands
	61	over 85	565	**338**
	157	80–84	919	**679**
	313	74–79	1 634	**1 201**
	535	70–74	2 318	**1 736**
	743	65–69	2 732	**2 236**
	1 067	60–64	2 855	**2 783**
	1,236	55–59	3 245	**3 313**
	1 566	50–54	3 154	**3 645**
	1 837	45–49	3 053	**3 658**
	2 165	40–44	3 163	**3 442**
	2 494	35–39	3 487	**3 680**
	2 833	30–34	4 116	**3 403**
	3 308	25–29	3 719	**3 258**
	3 674	20–24	4 083	**3 305**
	3 826	15–19	4 615	**3 695**
	3 934	10–14	4 420	**4 307**
	4 106	5–9	3 686	**3 815**
	2 586	2–4	1 923	**2 471**
	857	1–2	714	**849**
	938	less than 1	712	**893**

CHART 1. Age distribution of the population

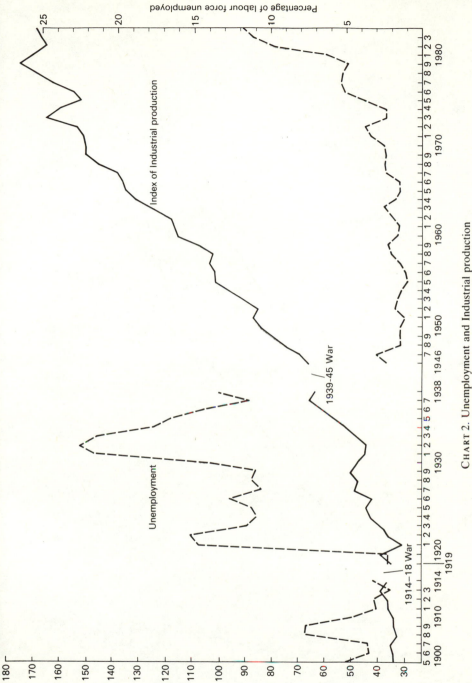

CHART 2. Unemployment and Industrial production

The unemployment series is subject to several sharp breaks; the sharpest is in 1923, when it changes from a record of trade unionists out of work to the government's figures for those seeking work, but from 1927 onwards governments have often modified the way the figures are calculated.

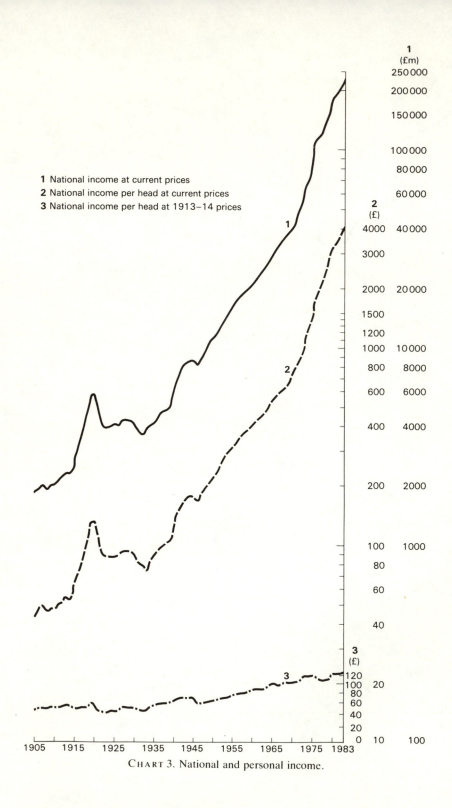

1
(£m)
250 000
200 000
150 000
100 000
80 000
60 000

2
(£)
4000   40 000
3000
2000   20 000
1500
1200
1000   10 000
800   8000
600   6000
400   4000
200   2000
100   1000
80
60
40

3
(£)
120
100
80
60
40
20
0   10   100

1 National income at current prices
2 National income per head at current prices
3 National income per head at 1913–14 prices

1905   1915   1925   1935   1945   1955   1965   1975 1983

CHART 3. National and personal income.

TABLE 1

Cost of living

(This table is used to deflate current prices back to 1913–14 prices in the previous chart. Like any such series it faces obvious difficulties in comparing prices over a seventy-year period in which the things people buy have changed a great deal and prices have changed very sharply. This is made all the harder by the way the figures at the end of the table look very large compared with those at the beginning.)

Year	Value	Year	Value
1906	94	1950	345
1907	97	1951	372
1908	92	1952	395
1909	92	1953	402
1910	96	1954	409
1911	97	1955	422
1912	101	1956	441
1913	101	1957	453
1914	99	1958	466
1915	122	1959	469
1916	145	1960	474
1917	174	1961	490
1918	201	1962	511
1919	213	1963	521
1920	250	1964	538
1921	237	1965	564
1922	203	1966	586
1923	204	1967	600
1924	190	1968	629
1925	190	1969	663
1926	190	1970	705
1927	184	1971	771
1928	184	1972	826
1929	180	1973	902
1930	178	1974	1046
1931	169	1975	1300
1932	169	1976	1560
1933	162	1977	1856
1934	162	1978	1987
1935	162	1979	2227
1936	164	1980	2495
1937	169	1981	2706
1938	172	1982	2940
1939	177	1983	3076
1940	202		
1941	222		
1942	236		
1943	243		
1944	250		
1945	255		
1946	283		
1947	302		
1948	326		
1949	334		

TABLE 2

Government expenditure

(a) *Government expenditure by function, 1900–1967*

(Percentages of G.N.P. and total (i.e. central and local) government expenditure at current prices, £m.)

	1900	1910	1920	1928	1938	1950	1955	1967-8
Administration								
GNP	0·8	1·0	1·2	1·1	1·1	1·5	1·1	1·2
Expenditure	5·9	8·1	4·5	4·5	3·8	3·9	3·0	2·2
National Debt								
GNP	1·0	0·9	5·4	6·7	4·0	4·4	4·2	5·5
Expenditure	7·0	7·4	20·4	27·9	13·4	11·2	11·5	10·0
Law and order								
GNP	0·5	0·6	0·5	0·7	0·7	0·7	0·7	1·6
Expenditure	3·5	4·7	2·1	2·8	2·4	1·7	1·9	2·9
Overseas services								
GNP	0·1	0·1	..	..	0·1	1·5	0·5	0·9
Expenditure	0·4	0·4	0·2	0·1	0·2	3·9	1·3	1·7
Military and defence								
GNP	6·9	3·5	8·6	2·8	8·9	7·2	9·6	7·0
Expenditure	48·0	27·3	32·6	11·4	29·8	18·5	26·1	12·7
Social Services								
GNP	2·6	4·2	6·8	9·6	11·3	18·0	16·3	24·9
Expenditure	18·0	32·8	25·9	39·7	37·6	46·1	44·6	45·2
Economic services								
GNP	1·9	1·8	3·3	2·6	2·9	4·9	3·2	12·9
Expenditure	13·0	13·9	12·8	10·7	9·5	12·6	8·6	21·6
Environmental services								
GNP	0·6	0·7	0·4	0·7	1·0	0·8	1·1	2·0
Expenditure	4·3	5·3	1·6	2·9	3·2	2·1	3·0	3·7
All services								
GNP	14·4	12·7	26·2	24·2	30·0	39·0	36·6	55·2
Expenditure	100	100	100	100	100	100	100	100

SOURCES: (1900–55): Peacock and Wiseman, p. 86; (1967–8): *Public Expenditure: A New Presentation* (Cmnd. 4017).

(b) *Central government spending, 1980 and 1984*

	1980	1984
Social Security (NI benefits)	14,405	21,514
To local authorities (current)	13,201	19,921
Defence	11,327	16,845
Health	11,228	15,413
Grants to personal sector	9,966	17,728
Debt	8,713	14,416
Other final consumption	7,290	9,600
Subsidies	4,299	4,803
Capital transfers	2,305	2,984
Grants abroad	1,823	2,128
Fixed capital	1,758	2,776
Revenue	80,287	119,288
Total spending	86,315	128,902
Spending as % of national income	50.6	54.0

SOURCE: CSO *Financial Statistics*, March 1985. The proportion of national income spent by central government in 1975 was, by this measure, 58%.

TABLE 3

Production and output

(a) *Summary table of output from all census industries,*
1907–1973

	Gross output of production (£ million)	Net output of production (£ million)	Average number of persons employed (Thousands)	Net output per person employed (£)
1907	1,765	712	6,984	102
1924	3,748	1,548	7,979	212
1930	3,371	1,504	7,899	211
1935	3,543	1,640	8,130	225
1948	12,961	5,377	10,149	530
1951	18,733	6,838	10,669	641
1958	25,496	10,441	10,568	988
1961	32,066	14,316	10,639	1,346
1973	70,271	29,865	8,370	3,568
1983	241,903	84,613	7,129	11,869

SOURCE: *Annual Abstract of Statistics.*

TABLE 3

Production and output

(b) *Output of individual industries, 1907–1973*

(£ million)

	1907 Gross output	1907 Net output	1935 Gross output	1935 Net output	1973 Gross output	1973 Net output	1983 Gross output	1983 Net output
Food, drink, and tobacco	283	87	665	203	11,975	3,493	37,425	8,958
Chemicals and allied industries	90	27	206	89	7,673	2,693	18,397	5,456
Metal manufacture	147	45	245	88	5,601	1,823	8,507	3,498
Engineering and allied industries	. .	. .	710	357	22,721	10,572	57,295	23,470
Textiles, leather, and clothing	458	187	656	249	6,143	2,631	10,275	3,852
Other manufactures	. .	. .	413	237	10,884	5,591	73,507	22,994
Mining and quarrying	134	115	167	136	1,439	1,022	4,958	3,326
Construction	. .	. .	295	150	12,531	5,337	29,264	16,284
Gas, electricity, and water	51	32	181	128	3,836	2,043	36,983	13,350

SOURCE: *Annual Abstract of Statistics*. This makes very little mention of oil production, but its value in 1983 was about £14bn.

TABLE 4

Employment in industries, 1871–1983

(millions of persons)

	Agriculture, forestry, fishing	Mining and quarrying	Manufactures	Construction	Trade	Transport	Public and professional service	Domestic service (after 1979 financial services)	Total occupied population
1871	1·8	0·6	3·9	0·8	1·6	0·7	0·7	1·8	12·0
1881	1·7	0·6	4·2	0·9	1·9	0·9	0·8	2·0	13·1
1891	1·6	0·8	4·8	0·9	2·3	1·1	1·0	2·3	14·7
1901	1·5	0·9	5·5	1·3	2·3	1·3	1·3	2·3	16·7
1911	1·6	1·2	6·2	1·2	2·5	1·5	1·5	2·6	18·6
1921	1·4	1·5	6·9	0·8	2·6	1·4	2·1	1·3	19·3
1931	1·3	1·2	7·2	1·1	3·3	1·4	2·3	1·6	21·1
1951	1·1	0·9	8·8	1·4	3·2	1·7	3·3	0·5	22·6
1961	0·9	0·7	8·9	1·6	3·4	1·8	4·0	. .	22·8
1971	0·4	0·4	8·1	1·3	2·6	2·0	5·7	. .	24·4
1979	0·4	0·3	7·3	1·3	4·3	1·5	6·2	1·7	23·2
1983	0·4	0·3	5·6	1·0	4·2	1·3	6·2	1·8	21·1

SOURCES: Deane and Cole. p. 143; *Key Statistics*. p. 9.

TABLE 5

Trade unions and strikes

	Total no. of members of trade unions (000s)	Working days lost (000s)		Total no. of members of trade unions (000s)	Working days lost (000s)
1906	1,997	3,019	1945	8,087	2,835
1907	2,210	2,148	1946	8,775	2,158
1908	2,513	10,785	1947	8,803	2,433
1909	2,485	2,687	1948	9,145	1,944
1910	2,477	9,867	1949	9,319	1,807
1911	2,565	10,155	1950	9,274	1,389
1912	3,139	40,890	1951	9,289	1,694
1913	3,416	9,804	1952	9,535	1,792
1914	4,135	9,878	1953	9,583	2,184
1915	4,145	2,953	1954	9,523	2,457
1916	4,359	2,446	1955	9,556	3,781
1917	4,644	5,647	1956	9,726	2,083
1918	5,499	5,875	1957	9,762	8,412
1919	6,533	34,969	1958	9,813	3,462
1920	7,926	26,568	1959	9,626	5,270
1921	8,348	85,872	1960	9,610	3,024
1922	6,633	19,850	1961	9,821	3,046
1923	5,625	10,672	1962	9,883	5,795
1924	5,429	8,424	1963	9,872	1,755
1925	5,544	7,952	1964	9,917	2,524
1926	5,506	162,233	1965	10,068	2,925
1927	5,219	1,174	1966	10,180	2,398
1928	4,919	1,388	1967	10,034	2,783
1929	4,866	8,287	1968	10,036	4,719
1930	4,858	4,399	1969	10,307	6,925
1931	4,842	6,983	1970	11,000	10,908
1932	4,642	6,488	1971	11,128	13,551
1933	4,444	1,072	1972	11,353	23,909
1934	4,392	959	1973	11,449	7,197
1935	4,590	1,955	1974	11,756	14,750
1936	4,867	1,829	1975	11,950	5,957
1937	5,295	3,413	1976	12,286	3,284
1938	5,842	1,334	1977	12,846	9,985
1939	6,053	1,356	1978	13,112	9,306
1940	6,298	940	1979	13,289	29,474
1941	6,613	1,079	1980	12,952	11,964
1942	7,165	1,303	1981	12,162	4,266
1943	7,867	1,785	1982	11,694	5,313
1944	8,174	2,194			

These figures are taken from D. E. Butler and J. Freeman *British Political Facts, 1900–1966* (London, 1967); I am grateful to David Butler for giving me permission to reprint them and for supplying me with more recent figures.

TABLE 6

The volume and direction of trade

(£ million and percentages)

	1910		1930		1950		1975		1983		
Total imports	678·3	100	919·5	100	2,602·9	100	24,037	100	65,963	100	
Commonwealth	144·8	21·3	292·8	31·8	937·0	36·0	8,686	36·1	30,098	45·6	E.E.C.
Western Europe	299·7	33·9	223·9	24·3	630·6	24·2	3,518	14·6	10,444	15·9	Other Western Europe
Eastern Europe	3·3	0·5	25·7	2·8	40·3	1·5	3,203	13·3	9,027	13·7	North America
Russia	43·6	6·4	29·2	3·2	34·2	1·3	1,784	7·4	5,159	9·8	Other developed countries
Middle East	21·5	3·2	25·4	2·8	112·3	4·3	3,324	13·8	2,824	4·3	OPEC members
Far East	15·0	2·2	23·5	2·6	38·5	1·5	741	3·0	1,533	2·3	Communist countries
North and Central America	151·7	22·4	196·9	21·4	450·9	17·3	2,665	11·1	6,786	10·3	Rest of world
South America	59·7	8·8	66·2	7·2	190·5	7·3					
Other areas		1·3	..	3·9	..	6·6					
Total exports and re-exports	522·0	100	523·3	100	2,255·0	100	19,761	100	60,534	100	
Commonwealth	136·8	26·2	226·6	41·8	935·7	41·5	6,349	32·1	26,513	43·8	E.E.C.
Western Europe	185·2	35·5	146·8	27·6	595·1	26·4	3,268	16·5	7,517	12·4	Other Western Europe
Eastern Europe	2·6	0·5	14·1	2·6	23·7	1·1	2,319	11·7	9,342	15·4	North America
Russia	21·2	4·1	22·6	4·2	14·2	0·6	1,890	9·6	3,133	5·2	Other developed countries
Middle East	9·6	1·8	17·7	3·3	115·3	5·1	2,280	11·5	6,122	10·1	OPEC members
Far East	24·6	4·7	12·0	2·3	32·6	1·4	680	3·4	1,112	1·8	Communist countries
North and Central America	93·0	17·8	57·3	10·8	279·6	12·4	2,934	14·8	6,661	11·0	Rest of world
South America	48·2	9·2	31·9	6·0	130·2	5·8					
Other areas		0·2	..	8·6	..	5·7					

Commonwealth = all except Canada (i.e. all in Sterling Area).
Western Europe = Finland, Sweden, Norway, Iceland, Denmark, Germany, Netherlands, Belgium, Luxembourg, France, Switzerland, Portugal, Spain, Italy, Greece, Austria, Turkey.
Eastern Europe = Poland, Hungary, Czechoslovakia, Albania, Bulgaria, Rumania.
Middle East = Egypt, Syria, Lebanon, Arabia, Muscat and Oman, Iraq, Iran, Afghanistan, Israel, Jordan.
Far East = Siam, China, Korea, Taiwan, Japan, Portuguese India, Sumatra, Java, Dutch Borneo and other Dutch possessions, Burma.

SOURCE: *Statistical Abstracts*; E.C.A. Mission.

TABLE 7

The balance of payments

(£ million)

	Imports	Domestic exports	Re-exports	Net overseas investment earning[1]	Net invisible trade	Overall balance on current account
1900	523·1	291·2	63·2	103·6	109·1	37·9
1910	678·3	430·4	103·8	170·0	146·7	167·3
1920	1,932·6	1,334·5	222·8	200·0	395·0	252·0
1930	1,044·0	570·8	86·8	220·0	194·0	25·0
1937	1,027·8	521·4	75·1	210·0	176·0	−144·0
1950	2,608·2	2,171·3	84·8	237·0	357·0	221·0
1965	5,071	4,848		435	215	−110·0
1975	21,972	18,768		949	1,695	−1,673·0
1983	61,341	60,625		1,948	3,632	2,916

SOURCE: Mitchell and Deane; *Annual Abstract*; *Key Statistics*.

[1] This figure is taken after allowing for investment income paid to foreign corporations and individuals.

TABLE 8

Overseas investment

	Accumulated balance (£m)[1]	Investment income (£m)
1906	2,745	134
1910	3,351	170
1930	3,725	209
1937	3,754	198
1946	2,329	110
1956	6–7,000	660
1964	10,000	800
1979	12,500	1,100
1984	70,000	5,000

SOURCES: Imlah, *Economic Elements in the 'Pax Britannica'*; E.C.A. Mission; Schonfield, *British Economic Policy since the War*; 1965 Budget speech; *Economic Trends*, October 1984.

[1] There are of course debts and foreign investments in England to be set against these assets. In 1964 foreign investment in England was about £4,000m., the sterling balances amounted to £3,100m., and the government had other debts of £1,300m. and assets (not counted above) of about £1,000m.

INDEX